BITTER TASTES

DONNA M. CAMPBELL

BITTER TASTES

LITERARY NATURALISM
AND EARLY CINEMA
IN AMERICAN
WOMEN'S WRITING

THE UNIVERSITY OF
GEORGIA PRESS
ATHENS

Paperback edition, 2018
© 2016 by the University of Georgia Press
Athens, Georgia 30602
www.ugapress.org
All rights reserved
Designed by Kaelin Chappell Broaddus
Set in 10.7/13 Arno Pro Regular by Kaelin Chappell Broaddus

Most University of Georgia Press titles are
available from popular e-book vendors.

Printed digitally

Library of Congress has cataloged the hardcover
edition of this book as follows:

Names: Campbell, Donna M., author.
Title: Bitter Tastes : Literary naturalism and early cinema in
American women's writing / Donna M. Campbell.
Description: Athens : The University of Georgia Press, 2016. |
Includes bibliographical references and index.
Identifiers: LCCN 2015043954 | ISBN 9780820341729 (hardcover : alk. paper) |
ISBN 9780820349442 (ebook)
Subjects: LCSH: American fiction—Women authors—History and criticism. |
Women and literature—United States—History—20th century. |
Motion pictures and women—United States. | Naturalism in literature. |
Naturalism in motion pictures.
Classification: LCC PS374.W6 C36 2016 | DDC 813.009/9287—dc23
LC record available at http://lccn.loc.gov/2015043954

Paperback ISBN 978-0-8203-5468-2

For Chris, Elizabeth, and Madeline

It must not be regarded as diminishing Mr. Lewis's achievement to remind his readers that he was not the first discoverer of Main Street. Over thirty years ago, Robert Grant situated "Unleavened Bread" in the same thoroughfare; and so, a little later, did Frank Norris his "McTeague," and Graham Phillips his "Susan Lenox"—and they were all, as it happens, not only "great American novels," but great novels. But they came before their time, their bitter taste frightened a public long nurtured on ice-cream soda and marshmallows, and a quick growth of oblivion was trained over the dreary nakedness of the scene they had exposed.

—EDITH WHARTON, "The Great American Novel" (1927)

CONTENTS

ACKNOWLEDGMENTS • xi

INTRODUCTION • 1

CHAPTER 1
Grim Realism and the Culture of Feeling:
Rebecca Harding Davis, Elizabeth Stuart Phelps,
and Lillie Chace Wyman

22

CHAPTER 2
The Darwinists:
Borderlands, Evolution, and Trauma

64

CHAPTER 3
Bohemian Time:
Glasgow, Austin, and Cather

112

CHAPTER 4
Red Kimonos and White Slavery:
The Fallen Woman in Film and Print

150

CHAPTER 5
Where Are My Children?
Race, Citizenship, and the Stolen Child

199

CHAPTER 6
"Manure Widows" and Middlebrow Fiction:
Rural Naturalism in the 1920s
237

CHAPTER 7
Waste, Hoarding, and Secrets:
Modernist Naturalism and the Servant's Body
275

CONCLUSION • 325

NOTES • 329

WORKS CITED • 351

INDEX • 375

ACKNOWLEDGMENTS

I am deeply grateful to all those whose help and encouragement enabled me to write this book. Thanks are due first of all to Donald Pizer, who first encouraged me to think broadly about the implications of considering women writers as naturalists and to write this book. I owe a great debt also to the many scholars of realism and naturalism who provided support and invaluable suggestions throughout the process of writing the book, including the editors who gave me not only an opportunity to work through the ideas about women and naturalism that inform this book but also supportive and incisive comments about them. Gary Scharnhorst and Jeanne Campbell Reesman provided early inspiration and continuing support, as did Mary E. Papke. The fine insights of Keith Newlin and Stephen Brennan challenged my thinking about women writers and naturalism during the preparation of an early article about the subject; also vitally important were the insights of Leonard Cassuto and Clare Virginia Eby, John Matthews, and Carol Singley on later essays on naturalism, as well as Janet Beer and Laura Rattray for their responses to my ideas on Kate Chopin and Edith Wharton. Their comments helped to shape and refine the ideas that underlie this book in ways that immeasurably improved them.

Equally important are the conversations with colleagues who generously shared their expertise on the authors and subjects that comprise this book, both individually and as participants in various conferences where portions of this book were presented: the Modern Language Association, the American Studies Association, the American Literature Association (ALA), the Society for the Study of American Women Writers (SSAWW), the Edith Wharton Society, the Western Literature Association, the International Association for the Study of Zola and Naturalism (AIZEN), the Jack London Biennial Symposium, Multi-Ethnic Literatures of the United States (MELUS), the Modernist Studies Association (MSA), and the 2007 ALA Symposium on Naturalism. At these and other venues, Charles Crow, Clare Virginia Eby, Monika Elbert, June Howard, Gerald Kennedy, Eric Carl Link, John Lowe, and Mary E. Papke contributed nuance and depth to my understanding of naturalism, realism, and the Gothic.

Edith Wharton constitutes a touchstone of sorts for this book, and discussions of her work benefited from the insights of many in the Edith Wharton Society, among them Janet Beer, Melanie Dawson, Hildegard Hoeller, Katherine Joslin, Jennie Kassanoff, Emily Orlando, Alan Price, Irene Goldman-Price, Laura Saltz, Carol Shaffer-Koros, Gary Totten, and especially my colleagues on another project, Carol Singley and Frederick Wegener, whose knowledge of all things Wharton appears to be infinite. Lively discussions with Meredith Goldsmith, Deborah Lindsay Williams, Jaime Harker, and Susan Tomlinson informed the discussion in later chapters on modernism and the middlebrow. For the inclusion of the authors Kate Cleary and Elia Peattie, I have Susanne George Bloomfield and Nicolas Witschi to thank for calling my attention to their work; Paul Sorrentino and Stanley Wertheim provided helpful information about Stephen Crane; Owen Davis and Katherine Fusco shared their insights on naturalism and film; and long conversations with Lawrence Berkove, Kenneth Brandt, Andrew Furer, Earle Labor, Jeanne Campbell Reesman, I. Milo Shepard, and James Williams deepened my understanding of Jack London.

Organizations supporting this project include the Lilly Library at Indiana University, for a 2011 Everett Helm Visiting Fellowship; the Edith Wharton Society, for a 2009 Beinecke Research Award; and the College of Arts and Sciences at Washington State University, for the Lewis and Stella Buchanan Distinguished Associate Professor of English Fellowship (2007–10), a travel-to-collections grant, and two Buchanan Summer Fellowships. This project could not have been completed without their generous support, and they have my most profound thanks. Thanks are also due to the librarians at the Beinecke Library at Yale University, the Lilly Library at Indiana University, the Library of Congress, the Bancroft Library at the University of California at Berkeley, and Sara S. Hodson at the Huntington Library for research assistance and encouragement. Despite the limited time frame of my 2013 visit, Nancy Kauffman and Jared Case at the George Eastman House Film Archive arranged for showings of several rare films. At Washington State University, Trevor Bond of Manuscripts, Archives, and Special Collections has been and continues to be a valuable resource for information about Pacific Northwest writers and archival materials more generally.

None of this work could have been completed without the generous assistance of Washington State University, especially the College of Arts and Sciences and its associate dean for research, Paul Whitney, who provided helpful advice about grant applications. Todd Butler, chair of the Department of English, and before him George Kennedy have been unfailingly supportive of my efforts to complete this book by supporting applications for travel grants and release time. Colleagues Todd Butler, Debbie Lee, Donna Potts, Will Hamlin, Carol Siegel, Anne Stiles, and Joan Burbick have offered unstinting support and encouragement for this project, and former students from my regionalism and naturalism seminars, especially Jessica McCarthy, Amber LaPiana, James Trout, Becky Wagenblast, and Nora Wiechert, offered stimulating comments on the works that informed my own thinking about them.

At the University of Georgia Press, Nancy Grayson, who first approached me about this project, and Walter Biggins have been unfailingly helpful and gracious, despite many unanticipated delays. I deeply appreciate their assistance and that of the press in bringing this project to fruition.

For their generous reading of the manuscript, special thanks are due to Katherine Joslin and the unnamed second reader for the University of Georgia Press, whose enthusiasm for the manuscript and astute suggestions for revisions made it a better book. Although they were not directly involved with this project, I also wish to acknowledge two scholars whose work has had a lasting influence: Alfred Habegger, under whose direction I first studied naturalism and regionalism and whose continuing presence as a scholar serves as an inspiration; and Arthur Lennig, who in my undergraduate days introduced me to the complex language of silent film in a class on D. W. Griffith and Erich von Stroheim, sparking a lifetime of interest and study that has reached at least partial fruition in this book.

For their support of the project and discussions about academia more generally, Nicole Tonkovich and Patricia Terry deserve—and have—all my gratitude and special thanks. Finally, I want to thank my family: my mother and my late father; my husband, Christopher Blodgett, for his unfailing support and for expert advice on all matters psychological, including trauma theory; and my daughters, Elizabeth and Madeline, for their hours of listening, their fresh perspectives, and, not least, for their admirable tact in not asking when the book would be done.

I am grateful to the estate of Edith Wharton and the Watkins/Loomis Agency for permission to publish excerpts from Edith Wharton's unpublished fragment "One Day," which appears courtesy of the Beinecke Library, Yale University.

Some of the material from *Bitter Tastes* appeared elsewhere in earlier form. Grateful acknowledgement is made to the journals and presses for permission to excerpt sections from the following:

"*At Fault*: Kate Chopin's Other Novel." *Cambridge Companion to Kate Chopin*. Ed. Janet Beer. Cambridge: Cambridge University Press, 2008. 27–43.© 2008 and reprinted with permission of Cambridge University Press.

"Edith Wharton and Naturalism." *Edith Wharton in Context*. Ed. Laura Rattray. Cambridge: Cambridge University Press, 2012. 353–63. © 2012 and reprinted with permission of Cambridge University Press.

Introduction. *The Fruit of the Tree*. By Edith Wharton. Boston: Northeastern University Press, 2000. v–l. © 2000 by Donna Campbell.

"The Rise of Naturalism." *The Cambridge History of the American Novel*. Ed. Leonard Cassuto and Clare Eby. Cambridge: Cambridge University Press, 2011. 499–514. © 2011 and reprinted with permission of Cambridge University Press.

"'Where are the ladies?' Edith Wharton, Ellen Glasgow, and American Women Naturalists." *Studies in American Naturalism* 1, nos. 1 & 2 (2006): 152–69. © 2006 and reprinted by permission of the University of Nebraska Press.

"Women Writers and Naturalism." *The Oxford Handbook of American Literary Naturalism*. Ed. Keith Newlin. Oxford: Oxford University Press, 2011. 223–41. © 2011 and reprinted by permission of Oxford University Press.

INTRODUCTION

In the archives at Yale University's Beinecke Library, an unpublished fragment of a story called "One Day" features as its protagonist "Mamie Saffrell of Hester Street—born Maria Addolerata Zaffarelli." With a few words, the author signals the limited geographical coordinates of Mamie/Maria's universe: "Hester Street" places her in the immigrant neighborhoods of New York's Lower East Side, and Mamie's glance out the window at "a discoloured brick wall a few feet distant, & a languid dance of ragged underclothing" defines her physical space. Turning from the window, she looks around a bare, neat room and at the "haggard face" of Oscar, her lover, a tubercular young artist lying asleep on a cot. Of a higher class than Mamie, Oscar has taught her "the rites of cleanliness" and has made her promise not to solicit men for the sake of a few dollars, but now, as he lies dying, Mamie knows that he must have better food and a doctor's care, both requirements that she cannot afford.

The threats to Mamie's precarious situation are ones that she understands well, and all involve the intrusions of power and wealth into a situation in which she has known happiness. If Oscar's estranged wife returns, Mamie imagines, she will kill them both, for "[a]ccording to her inherited code"—that is, her Italian heritage—"such questions could be settled only by the knife." If she requests aid from the settlement worker who calls on her, the forces of those who impose their will on the poor "with intentions of mistaken benevolence" will steal Oscar from her. Like the "lean cat who patrolled the roof in a life-long hunt for sparrows," Mamie is trapped in a hand-to-mouth struggle for survival, with no prospects beyond the brick-encased prison of the Lower East Side. She prays for Oscar with "the incantations of her ancient faith," but the distant strains of an inherited Catholicism provide no assurance of Oscar's recovery or of Mamie's escape from her environment. Recognizing that her work in the "clothes-factory" will not pay the doctor's bill and the rent, Mamie realizes that her only option is to leave the confines of her room "for the street."[1]

The fragment breaks off shortly after this point, but the opening of "One Day" recalls other slum sketches, such as Edward Townsend's *A Daughter of the Tenements* (1893) or Brander Matthews's *Vignettes of Manhattan* (1894). Unlike these, "One Day" does not soften its sharply etched details but shows its naturalistic roots in Mamie's status as an immigrant and her resigned acceptance of violence and prostitution as inevitable solutions to her problems. The setting contributes to the naturalism of the scene, with its environmental determinism of Bartleby-like brick walls and blocked views and its Darwinian animal imagery of a hungry cat stalking sparrows. With its slum setting and young woman on the verge of prostitution, "One Day" reads like a city sketch by Stephen Crane, Frank Norris, or Theodore Dreiser. But "One Day" was written by Edith Wharton, an author whose reputation for portraying New York life rests on her portrayal of a wealthy social world, not the narratives of young Italian immigrant women living in poverty. Written in all likelihood before Henry James famously advised Wharton to "do New York,"[2] "One Day" shows a portion of the city that Wharton was to revisit in fiction several times before taking up permanent residence in the more familiar environs of "Old New York." The slum setting for "One Day," like that of "Mrs. Manstey's View" and "Bunner Sisters," suggests a level of interest in classically defined naturalistic subject matter that Wharton would never entirely abandon.

Wharton was part of a new generation of Americans born in the 1860s and 1870s who, armed with the biological theories of Herbert Spencer, Charles Darwin, and Ernst Haeckel, questioned Victorian orthodoxies and challenged the genteel realism of the day. In the critical assessments of twentieth-century literary history, however, the writers of this generation were divided into two groups. Writers in the first group, consisting primarily of Stephen Crane, Theodore Dreiser, Frank Norris, and Jack London, were called "naturalists." Their work set the conventional limits of American naturalism: the period in which it was written; its practitioners, who were by and large white, male, and young; its settings, typically urban jungles or an unforgiving wilderness; its characters, often poor and ill educated, victims of primal forces that they could neither control nor understand; and its deterministic philosophy. Writers in the second group, among them Edith Wharton, Kate Chopin, Willa Cather, and Ellen Glasgow, were called, variously, regionalists, novelists of manners, or local colorists, all labels that signified the same thing: "women writers." *Bitter Tastes* questions this division and investigates the ways in which late nineteenth- and early twentieth-century American women writers wrote naturalistic fiction. Taking its title from Edith Wharton's comment that Americans preferred the "ice-cream soda" of popular fiction to the "bitter taste" of writing that told the truth, *Bitter Tastes* places women writers at the center rather than at the periphery of American literature of the period.[3] This book explores an alternative literary genealogy of naturalism rooted in the culture of print and of early film, which, like classic naturalism, claimed the ability to represent elemental social truths through a documentary method.

Classic naturalism is grounded in an evolutionary and environmental determinism that challenges the idea of individual free will. Its emphasis on scientific objectivity in the study of elemental human nature meant that naturalist writers saw characters through the lens of gender-, race-, and class-based traits that combined to shape and often overshadow their status as individuals. What drives the characters of classic naturalism is desire in all its forms: for food, shelter, sex, and addictive substances, and, more abstractly, for objects, revenge, power, and dominance. What drives its plots are the ways in which these desires are checked and thwarted by internal and external forces of heredity and environment. These tensions drive the classic naturalistic plotlines of struggle, violence, addiction, and degeneration, all played out in a landscape of extremes. The characters' struggles constitute the narrative trajectories of classic naturalism.

Unlike French naturalism, which Émile Zola defined through a number of essays and the Rougon-Macquart series of novels, American naturalism had no manifesto or affiliated school of authors. With the exception of Norris, who claimed a literary kinship with Zola, its practitioners described their work as writing about what was true or real. Even in reviews, according to Nancy Glazener, "naturalism barely surfaced in influential journals except with reference to Émile Zola, and ... the authors we associate with naturalism were not grouped together by contemporary reviewers."[4] "Naturalism" is a term more often applied after the fact to a type of fiction that shares a particular set of features than a category used by the novelists themselves, the best-known description being George Becker's phrase "pessimistic materialistic determinism." Indeed, June Howard notes that after Becker's definition, which she cites, "the next most frequently made observation about naturalism must surely be that it is *not* pessimistic determinism."[5] As Eric Carl Link suggests, if Becker's criterion of "pessimistic materialistic determinism" were strictly applied, naturalism would have to exclude Norris and Harold Frederic "for their mystic strains," Crane for the spiritual content of his poetry, and London for his "improbable and fantastic narratives," leaving "a school of one: Dreiser."[6]

Yet definitions such as Becker's continue to limit the canon of naturalism. Less a consistent philosophical and literary school than a series of contradictory narrative practices, naturalism incorporates theories of evolution, psychology, race, and Social Darwinism. It is also the literature of excess, in terms of its detailed style and lengthy descriptions, its violent and sensational events, its characters driven to extremes by obsessive emotions or inherited traits, its grim and sordid subjects, and what Donald Pizer has called the "naturalistic aesthetic of length."[7]

Because naturalism is an excessive form by definition, I argue that placing women's naturalism at the center rather than the periphery of the movement reveals an "unruly" counterpart to the rules of classic naturalism.

"Unruly" naturalism transgresses the rules by its unevenness or excess. It departs from the tenets of classic naturalism by concluding novels with unlikely happy endings instead of the plot of decline, for example. It exceeds even naturalism's capacious definition of relevant details in its pursuit of truths as yet unrevealed. It expresses an interest less in philosophical consistency in its treatment of determinism than in the complex, sometimes uneven workings of social forces that operate on female characters constrained with the extra complications of women's biological and social functioning. It includes novels not regarded as classically naturalistic because they have too much social protest, like David Graham Phillips's *Susan Lenox* or Paul Laurence Dunbar's *The Sport of the Gods*; or too much mysticism or sentiment, like Mary E. Wilkins Freeman's *By the Light of the Soul* or Fannie Hurst's *Lummox*; or characters too elevated in social class, like Frank Norris's *The Pit*; or too many themes or story lines, like Wharton's *The Fruit of the Tree*, Chopin's *At Fault*, or Nella Larsen's *Quicksand*. As is evident from these examples, pairing novels of classic naturalism like *The House of Mirth*, *McTeague*, or *The Awakening* with their "unruly" counterparts—*The Fruit of the Tree*, *The Pit*, or *At Fault*—reveals new facets to naturalism unavailable to those judging them against a checklist of classically naturalistic categories. Treated as a logical extension of the spirit of excess inherent in naturalism, "unruly" naturalism brings with it with a restless energy that pushes the boundaries of naturalism past conventional limits. Neither solely the province of women writers nor a substitute for classic naturalism, unruly naturalism provides a different way of looking at pervasive strains existing in the background rather than the foreground of classic naturalism, including the issues of waste and abjection, disability and age, structural unevenness or excess, sentimentalism and melodrama, social reform, and women's use of technology.

Like their male counterparts, women wrote classic naturalism with themes of determinism, Darwinism, and death, but they transgress its boundaries with "unruly" features, often present but unremarked in the work of classic male naturalists, such as sentimentalism, disability, and overt concerns with social justice. Women writers of naturalism challenge naturalism's celebration of physical and evolutionary strength by including sympathetic female characters whose disabilities, age, or unattractive appearance make them unsuitable subjects for the novel of classic naturalism, which more commonly features young, sexually attractive women like Dreiser's Carrie Meeber or Crane's Maggie Johnson. They critique its fascination with sexual violence by staging tableaux of women victimized by that violence. Women writers show women's bodies traded as commodities, as in the white slave narrative and the autobiographies of prostitutes and madams. They depict women laboring in the fields and women laboring in childbirth, as in Edith Summers Kelley and Evelyn Scott; women disfigured or discarded by commercial culture, as in Ann Petry and Edith Wharton; and elderly women living on the edge of poverty and starvation, as in Mary Wilkins Freeman and Edith Wharton.

Moreover, women writers of naturalism intensify their male counterparts' fascination with the universe of material objects. They complicate classic naturalism's interest in an economy of consumption by focusing on an economy of waste, in a patriarchal culture that socially as well as economically has many ways of discarding women as abject or unclean. The catalogs of refuse and discarded objects that form the backdrop of urban naturalist novels support Georges Bataille's point that "one best understands a society through its waste, its by-products, its unproductive accessories."[8] Women writers add to this list the waste products of desire: the abandoned children, abused wives and mistresses, and women disabled by addiction, disease, or age whose presence constitutes an affront to the male gaze. In addition, women writers contrast biological time in women's lives with the artificial speed of urban life or the irregular rhythms of time measured in Bohemian spaces. Into the cityscapes of naturalism they place the figure of the mute, unmoving, and often unconscious body of a woman on display before an uncomprehending man, and they chronicle the ways in which women's bodies transform urban spaces by the threat of victimization and violence. They reveal the mingled violence and desire that exist in familiar domestic spaces, including the cramped rooms that naturalistic heroines experience as sites of imprisonment through forced prostitution or the experience of childbirth. Women writers add the issue of gender to debates over race and citizenship by examining women's efforts to control their surroundings or their bodies and by critiquing the state apparatuses that render these efforts futile. Finally, they use both mechanical and visual technologies, especially in scenes of moviegoing, to represent a broader cultural context of modernity and to sharpen the contrast between essentialized portraits of women in popular media and the visions that these authors present through their writing.

Recent criticism extends naturalism in ways that facilitate the exploration of these ideas.[9] Mary E. Papke's *Twisted from the Ordinary: Essays on American Literary Naturalism* (2003) includes women writers and extends naturalism's areas of inquiry to gift theory, sentimentalism, imperialism, and chaos theory as well as detective fiction and social justice fiction. The essays in Papke's collection expand the diversity of authors who could be considered naturalists, including women writers Elizabeth Stuart Phelps and Evelyn Scott and writers of color Paul Laurence Dunbar and Ann Petry. Eric Carl Link, in *The Vast and Terrible Drama* (2004), contends that many of the problems in defining naturalism arise from the confusion of the three separate, if related, concepts of scientific naturalism, philosophical naturalism, and literary naturalism. Instead, argues Link, "the artistic integration of naturalist theory as theme" defines naturalistic works.[10] Both books, Papke's through its greater inclusion of authors and Link's through its thematic approach, extend the definition of naturalism, as does *The Oxford Handbook of American Literary Naturalism*, edited by Keith Newlin. June Howard's "Sand in Your Mouth" in that volume contends that naturalism remains a productive category when "novels concerned with causality and haunted by the problems of agency also mobilize the topos of the brute" and suggests that "naturalism and other genres" might include "non-literary forms," the approach I adopt in this book.[11] Other essays in the collection discuss women writers as naturalists, including Stephen C. Brennan's psychoanalytic reading of Glasgow's *Barren Ground*, Jeff P. Turpin's essay on Wharton and evolutionary psychology, and Linda Kornasky's discussion of Chopin and Edith Summers Kelley in her essay on naturalism and sexuality.

Recent studies of naturalism include features associated with women's writing, such as its supposed sentimentalism, interest in household rituals, and advocacy of social justice. In writing of naturalist sentimentalism, Francesca Sawaya and Jennifer Fleissner contend that sentimentalism is not antithetical but integral to naturalism. Fleissner reads the "begging man," such as Hurstwood in *Sister Carrie*, as a central figure in naturalism that exemplifies its rewriting of the sentimental novel's seduction plot.[12] Sawaya contends that "naturalist sentimentalism" in Norris's *The Octopus* allows the reader to sympathize with the feminized artist, Presley.[13] To take Sawaya's insight a step further, any reading of the supernatural and mystical return of Norris's Angèle, who "was realised in the wheat," must recognize her as the figure of the organic, eternal feminine called forth by men's sentimental fantasies, just as the force of the railroad signifies the manufactured product of men's visions. The wheat itself, in Presley's mind, is equally romanticized as "untouched, unassailable, undefiled, that mighty world-force" that "moved onward in its appointed grooves" as smoothly and inexorably as the railroad engine of the novel's opening chapter.[14] Women writers of naturalism dismantle this dichotomy between female embodiment and male production with characters such as Cather's Alexandra Bergson of *O Pioneers!*, Glasgow's Dorinda Oakley of *Barren Ground*, and Edith Summers Kelley's Judith Blackford of *Weeds*. They are neither earth mothers nor the land's symbolic representatives but stark evidence that the "resistless" wheat cannot "move on" or in fact be produced at all, without the presence of women who know how to farm.

Similarly, the domestic rituals and spaces traditional to women's writing share naturalism's interest in objects and obsessive movement. Bill Brown, in *A Sense of Things*, proposes that habit, rendered in *McTeague* as compulsion or pathological repetition, becomes "a symptomatic effort to stabilize and possess the physical world ... to achieve stability or stasis." Naturalism transforms the loving attention to objects in domestic fiction into, for example, *McTeague*'s "aberrant modes of possessing physical objects."[15] Fleissner too finds repetition fundamental to naturalism, seeing the characteristic movement of naturalism not as a classic plot of a man's decline but as a proliferation of details and gestures that constitute the modern woman's "stuckness in place."[16] Monika Elbert locates a similar dynamic in the short fiction of Mary E. Wilkins Freeman, whose heroines' incessant shopping and cleaning, and with those activities the fetishizing of objects, place her in the ranks of naturalist writers since the fetish is "the overriding symbol of the Naturalist text." If fetishism and the "sexual impulses" that drive its expression are the province of women as well as men, according to Elbert, "[i]t is time that Freeman be seen as a sexual writer, as sexual and sexy as any Naturalist writer of her age."[17]

An "unruly" naturalism paves the way to consider forms other than fiction as naturalism, including journalism, prostitution memoirs, and early films. Claiming that the traditional naturalistic ideal of authorial objectivity has been overemphasized, Katherine Joslin contends that Zola's concept of the "experimental moralist" has been neglected, for "[t]he moral task of the writer, in Zola's paradigm, is to expose the conditions that cause human misery." Joslin argues that Jane Addams's writing, a type of naturalism, "turns Émile Zola's theory inside out." Instead of investing fiction with clinical objectivity, as Zola does, Addams uses the techniques of fiction to dramatize the clinical facts of writing social science.[18] Most pertinent to this issue of reclaiming the journalistic dimensions of naturalism is Donald Pizer's call for a renewed recognition of "the powerful radical center of naturalistic expression." Discussing Crane's and Garland's "investigative journalism" for *McClure's* in 1893–94 and Hurstwood's rejection of class solidarity during the strike in *Sister Carrie*, Pizer emphasizes "the deep roots of late nineteenth-century American naturalistic writing in the failings of the nation's industrial system" and reminds readers that naturalism was a "threat to the established order because it boldly and vividly depicted the inadequacies of the industrial system which was the foundation of that order."[19] Like Joslin's analysis of Addams's insistence on the affective as well as the clinical dimension of writing about urban life, Pizer's reinstatement of naturalism's radical past opens the door to a broader consideration of writers who treat urban and industrial conditions with an eye toward reform rather than clinical objectivity.

Placing women's naturalism at the center also responds to the need for a more inclusive canon of American literature. Elizabeth Ammons has called for a more comprehensive view of realism through a "comparative model," for "if American realism means anything, it means attention to the multiple realities figured in the work of the broadest possible range of authors writing in the late nineteenth and early twentieth centuries."[20] As exemplified in her *Conflicting Stories: American Women Writers at the Turn into the Twentieth Century*, Ammons's model provides a more broad-ranging examination of realism by juxtaposing a variety of works and writers from the period rather than those conventionally described as "realist." The comparative model that Ammons proposes avoids the pitfalls of the "parallel tracks" model that Anne Boyd describes in *Writing for Immortality*, which treats the trajectory of women's writing "from sentimentalism to domestic literature to local color to modernism" as parallel to but distinct from "the romanticism-realism-naturalism model that has governed our understanding of mainstream (men's) literary history."[21] As Wai Chee Dimock suggests by calling genre a "self-obsoleting system," "a broad spectrum of affinities" discovered through "a phenomenal field of contextually induced parallels" rather than "linear descent" or literary genealogy yields a more multilayered portrait of the ways in which varieties of literary forms intersect with one another.[22] Recent work on African American naturalism by John Dudley and Kenneth Warren extends Lisa Long's provocative question about whether "'African American' practices [would] remain outside the purview of traditional (read: white) literary genealogies" if works like Paul Laurence Dunbar's *The Sport of the Gods* (1902) were considered integral, rather than peripheral, to the strategies of naturalism.[23]

These strategies of inclusion extend to the varieties of publication contexts within which the work of women writers appeared. Although Willa Cather, Edith Wharton, Ellen Glasgow, and Kate Chopin are the women writers typically associated with naturalism, they are often read in the context of their high-status literary peers rather than their popular competitors. To understand their cultural context requires a broader scope of investigation, however, one that also includes the visual and print media environments of their original readers: popular fiction, early film, journalism, prostitution confessionals and testimony, social justice novels, and the fiction of writers better known in their own time than they might be today. Accordingly, in addition to film, it is important to consider women writers at all levels of critical reputation: the critically admired, like Mary Austin, Nella Larsen, Mary E. Wilkins Freeman, Sui Sin Far, Alice Dunbar-Nelson, Gertrude Stein, Evelyn Scott, and Ann Petry; the popular and middlebrow, such as Edna Ferber, Ruth Suckow, Fannie Hurst, and Bess Streeter Aldrich; and the currently obscure, such as Emanuel and Marcet Haldeman-Julius, Cornelia James Cannon, Kate Cleary, Elia Peattie, Dorothy Scarborough, Batterman Lindsay, and Lillie Chace Wyman.

Women's Naturalism and the Body

Bitter Tastes reads the common naturalistic trope of the woman's body as spectacle not from the vantage point of a man's game of desire and consumption but from the point of view of the woman figure herself and that of the woman author who creates her, typically for very different reasons than those that drive a male author of a naturalist text.[24] Women's writing critiques private surveillance and public spectacle as sources of violence and destructive power over women's bodies. For example, the sexualized woman of Crane's and Dreiser's fiction becomes in women's fiction a character whose presence raises questions of agency and citizenship as well as sexuality: who owns the woman's body and speaks for it, and who determines its staging as a spectacle of desire or of aversion? In the work of women writers, women are not merely the consumable subject matter of male fantasies but the producers of spectacle and merchandisers of their bodies. The emphasis on women's bodies is central to this book, for the true subject of the naturalistic text is the human body, the battleground for the clash of external and internal forces. Dissociated from its connotations of transcendent humanity, the body becomes one more machine in a mechanistic universe or one more organism within a hostile ecosystem. Whether machine or organism, the human body is governed by the laws of nature, but it is endowed with consciousness and the ability to suffer.[25] Naturalistic characters have a dual existence: their bodies live and die within the relentlessly material realm of the present, but their souls or spirits are caught between a primitive past inscribed in their genes and a future signified by urban modernity. The body is central in naturalism because it appears so frequently as a damaged or compromised instrument for the carrying out of the instructions of the will. Naturalistic bodies are frozen, starved, or otherwise abused by violent acts, to which women's bodies add the tally of assaults resulting from sexual violation and death in childbirth.

Many naturalist novels are driven by a fear of and fascination with women's bodies, including the fallen girl and the monstrous mother of the slums.[26] For example, in *Maggie: A Girl of the Streets*, Crane presents the twinned bodies of the fallen woman and the monstrous mother, untouchable outcasts at opposite ends of a social spectrum that punishes them for violating its idealistic images of female purity and maternal self-sacrifice. The pale and "painted" body of Maggie contrasts with the "red, writhing body" of her mother, Mary Johnson, the monstrous mother of the slums whose body suggests the violence of childbirth as well as the fecundity that populates the streets of New York.[27] Fear and fascination with the body also inform Darwin's theory of sexual selection, which is central to naturalism. Since Darwin's *Descent of Man* had established sexual selection as the province of the female of the species, novelists influenced by Darwin, including Harold Frederic, Hamlin Garland, Kate Chopin, Ellen Glasgow, and Edith Wharton, rewrote the courtship plot common to realism into novels about sexual choice. As Bert Bender demonstrates, Frederic, Norris, Chopin, and Dreiser followed closely Darwin's observations about animal courtship behavior, including the role of such secondary sexual characteristics as prehensile hands, body adornment, and the power of music to influence the selection of a mate.[28] But when social and economic realities rather than these biological preferences dictate the heroine's choices, the result is predictably disastrous. In *The House of Mirth* (1905), Lily Bart must choose between Lawrence Selden, the man to whom she is attracted, and a series of more powerful potential mates whom she rejects until it is too late. In evolutionary terms, Lily is an anomaly because unlike most of the women around her, she fails to adapt and does not select powerful men. In contrast, Undine Spragg of Wharton's *The Custom of the Country* (1913) is an evolutionary success story, her entire absence of scruples enabling her rise in the world through successive divorces, each time adapting so perfectly that her triumph is inevitable.

As courtship, not marriage, is the focus of realist novels, so the process of sexual selection, not its results, is the focus of naturalist ones. Despite the illusion of choice that the doctrine of sexual selection implies, classic naturalistic novels rarely feature successful and procreative unions, in large measure because social forces interfere with the process. For all the sexual relationships in naturalistic novels written by men, there is a surprising lack of children: Norris's Trina and McTeague have no children, nor do Dreiser's Hurstwood and Carrie Meeber, nor Lester Kane and Jennie Gerhardt, the latter being explained in a mild reference to birth control when Lester says that he can arrange things so that Jennie will not have a child unless she wants to. Crane's Maggie has no children although having a child out of wedlock, the public emblem of a private shame, is traditional in the seduction plot. In contrast, women's naturalism presents children but frequently casts them as punishment or waste, the unwanted by-product of biological drives and a lack of agency, as in Nella Larsen's *Quicksand*, Edith Summers Kelley's *Weeds*, and Evelyn Scott's *The Narrow House*. Unwanted children are part of the pattern of the woman's body betraying itself either in minor ways, through autonomic nervous system responses like blushing or fainting, or in major ones, like becoming pregnant. The human body is always troublesome in naturalism, and because of its ability to bear children, the woman's body is doubly ungovernable.

Ubiquitous in naturalism, the grotesque body often signifies a threat to the social order, typically less because of its actual power to harm than because of its uncanny and disturbing nature. For example, Stephen Crane's "fat man" in *Maggie*, Maggie's mother (Mary Johnson), and Henry Johnson, the African American hostler disfigured by fire in *The Monster* (1898), all exemplify the grotesque body, rendered doubly grotesque by attitudes about race and gender. These include the body of unusual size, such as those marked by obesity or dwarfism; the disabled body, often additionally marked as a character disadvantaged by class, race, or gender; and the body laboring in and transformed by childbirth. Obese characters such as Glasgow's Edmonia Breadalbane of *The Romantic Comedians* (1926), Marie Louise in Chopin's *At Fault*, and Mrs. Manson Mingott of Wharton's *Age of Innocence* gain power by maintaining a body weight that exceeds the norm and places them beyond the reach of social criticism. In a repressive culture, they become its truth-tellers, the only figures as unconstrained by social conventions as they are by corsets. Ann Petry's *The Street* (1946) includes both figures: Lutie Johnson as a spectacle of desire, and Mrs. Hedges, the scarred and hairless madam, as its truth-telling figure of repulsion. The fear of the grotesque naturalistic woman informs the naturalistic aesthetic of disgust, which in turn capitalizes on the uneasy tension between naturalism's professed objectivity and its heavy reliance on the affective dimensions of sentimentalism, the Gothic, and melodrama.

Technologies of the Real: Naturalism and Film

Early film, which rose to prominence in the same 1895–1905 period as American naturalism, rendered visually the sort of authenticity promised by naturalism. The technology of the kinetoscope transformed the ordinary into the extraordinary, creating a presentation of the real that, as critic George Parsons Lathrop reported in 1891, "reproduces the movement and appearance of life with such truth of action that if colors could only be given at the same time, the illusion that one was looking at something really alive would be absolute."[29] Struck by the fidelity of the images to real life, other realist and naturalist authors recognized the parallels between visual properties of naturalistic literature and film. Harold Frederic praised Crane's descriptive passages in *The Red Badge of Courage* as a "photographic revelation" as of an "instantaneous camera" like Eadweard Muybridge's famous studies of horses in motion, a professional judgment that drew on Frederic's years spent working in a photography studio as well as his astuteness as a literary critic.[30] Joseph Conrad, another friend and mentor of Crane's, remarked that he and Crane "must have been unconsciously penetrated by a prophetic sense of the technique and of the very spirit of the film-plays of which even the name was unknown to the world."[31]

William Dean Howells likewise saw the aims of realism and cinema as similar. His September 1912 "Editor's Easy Chair" column for *Harper's Monthly* praises cinema's depiction of "a veritable incident," saying that images of poor children working in factories while the directors sit at ease in "their oriental-rugged and mahogany arm-chaired parlors" and "the spectacle of policemen clubbing mothers from a train in which they are trying to send their little ones out of town beyond the struggling and starving, would impart an idea of our civilization which no amount of study could without it."[32] The visual crosscutting to convey a social justice message that Howells describes actually occurs in D. W. Griffith's *A Corner in Wheat* (1909), based on Frank Norris's "A Deal in Wheat," with bits borrowed from *The Octopus*.[33] By 1919, Howells had given up hope that film, as "an enterprise frankly commercial," could be instructive but continued to plead that "the pictures should represent the evil as well as the good of our life."[34] Even though the movies disappointed Howells by not living up to their promise as an instrument of social justice, they remained the closest analog in another medium to what naturalism attempted to do in print.

Film technologies challenged the boundaries of identity by both embodying and challenging what spectators knew to be "real," much as naturalism did with its readers. Film as a medium promised to surpass photographic representation because of its immediacy and its duration, the ability to capture subjects moving in time and space. Tales of spectators mistaking the fictive for the real abounded in the early years of film, with what Tom Gunning describes as a "myth of origin" consisting of reports of front-row spectators diving out of the way when watching scenes featuring an onrushing train.[35] Indeed, early films sought to enhance this confusion between representation and reality: Hale's Tours presented its films as though viewers were looking out from a train, even supplying train-style seating and the sounds of brakes and escaping steam to enhance the illusion.

In contrast, movies such *Uncle Josh at the Moving Picture Show* (1902) called attention to the boundary between reality and illusion by commenting on it. From a theater box on the stage, unsophisticated Uncle Josh views a sequence of three short films: when a woman does a modest can-can in "Parisian Danger," he leaps from the theater box and does a jig; when the train called the "The Black Diamond Express" lumbers into view, he dives into the box in fear; and when he sees a man embrace a country maid in "The Country Couple," he tears down the screen to fight with the man. There he sees the Oz behind the curtain: the Edison Projecting Kinetoscope and its operator. *Uncle Josh at the Moving Picture Show* functions as entertainment in itself and as a preview of typical film attractions—a woman showing her legs, a train, a love story. It is framed by the kinetoscope represented on the title card at the beginning and, in an extra shot, as a mechanical wonder at the end, a revelation of the technology behind the marvelous illusion that functions as an advertisement as well. *Uncle Josh* invited spectators to reflect on the boundary between film and reality and to congratulate themselves on being able to distinguish between the two by virtue of their positioning as experienced moviegoers. As Judith Mayne suggests, such films function "as both surface and threshold" of the boundary, and they provide a visual commentary on the confusion of identities rendered possible by the new technology."[36]

As a medium concerned with truth, film shared with naturalism not only issues of realistic representation but also a fascination with machines and transcription technologies. What the phonograph delivered in terms of accurate vocal transcription, film promised in reproducing a visual record of movement and gestures. In *The Material Unconscious*, Bill Brown explains that "the train and the cinema have become privileged as the 'two great machines of vision' for historicizing the modern sensorium—machines that reproduced the world in framed, panoramic, and narrative form."[37] The effect of film's framing of reality through panoramic and narrative forms, like the broader use of shorthand in the workplace, represented not only a leap in accuracy in reporting events but also a paradigm shift in the understanding of what accuracy meant. As Lisa Gitelman demonstrates in *Scripts, Grooves, and Writing Machines*, when systems of stenography became the norm, the standard of accuracy became a literal, rather than approximate, record of past speech, a process hastened by advances in recording technologies. Edison's invention of the phonograph, which he saw primarily as a means of stenographic recording for business purposes, "converted aural experiences into authoritative, inscribed evidence."[38] Neither stenographers nor mere transcribers of truth, women writers of naturalism participated in a cultural atmosphere where machine transcription, including film, was beginning to shape audience expectations about the possibilities and limits of representing the real.

From the very beginning, women workers were part of this shift to transcription technologies, with middle-class women joining a newly professionalized managerial class as information mediators between managers and machines. They became secretaries, stenographers, switchboard operators, and telegraphers, mastering mechanical technologies such as typewriters and dictographs as well as new systems of communication, such as stenography and filing systems that displaced the old letter books of previous generations. The term "typewriter" for a few years did not differentiate between the worker and the machine she operated. In keeping with this shift, films and fiction showed women using technology to equalize the gendered balance of power. For every man figuratively crushed under the wheel in the movies, a woman escaped a threatening situation through the clever use of technology. Scenes of women using technology to save themselves appear in several films, from the telegraph in *The Lonedale Operator* (1911) to the use of telephones and even fabricated fanciful inventions for distant writing in white slave novels and films such as *My Little Sister* (1913) and *Traffic in Souls* (1913).

Just as they had infiltrated the previously all-male sanctuary of the business office and learned its technologies, women writers in the early twentieth century were a significant presence in the motion picture industry. They worked not only as actresses but also as scenario writers, directors, and producers, with some, including Nell Shipman, Lois Weber, and Alice Guy-Blaché, heading their own production companies. Indeed, film historian Cari Beauchamp estimates that women wrote half of all the films produced through 1925.[39] In this particular era of visual culture, women writers of naturalism and women filmmakers addressed the same sorts of social problems, such as poverty, birth control and abortion, and prostitution. In addition, naturalistic novels such as Wharton's *Summer* and Hurst's *Lummox* feature key scenes in which characters go to the movies, a self-reflexive activity that allows the distanced perspective of the narrator to render ironic commentary. Scenes of female moviegoers reflect the reality of movie audiences at the time, for as Shelley Stamp and Miriam Hansen have shown, female audiences comprised a majority of those filling theaters—as much as 75 percent of seats by the early 1920s, according to Hillary A. Hallett.[40] The context for women's naturalism included rural and "hillbilly" films, conventional melodramas, and "social problem" films on prostitution (*Traffic in Souls*, 1913), child labor (*The Cry of the Children*, 1912), drug abuse (*The Devil's Needle*, 1916; *Human Wreckage*, 1923), poverty (*What Shall We Do with Our Old?*, 1911), and abortion (*Where Are My Children?*, 1916).

In style, method, subject matter, and the visual positioning of the spectator, naturalism and film pursued similar modes of representation. Officially committed to shaping the reader's response through indirect means rather than authorial intrusions, naturalist narration paralleled the narrative invisibility developing in early film. The earliest films followed past practices of lantern shows by employing a lecturer to help the audience follow the plot. In *Realism and the Birth of the Modern United States*, Stanley Corkin draws a parallel between this practice and the narrative voice in naturalist novels: "Both the lecturer and the naturalist narrator intrude on their text to draw out the implications of their documentary presentation of the world. Both function as knowing experts who instruct their audiences while asserting that their presentations are simply the facts as they exist."[41] The implicit contract of authenticity guaranteed to the audience by the medium and its producers was held so strongly that, after complaining about the "jerky, spasmodic movements, more characteristic of automatons than of human beings" caused by the sixteen frames-per-second projection speed of films of the time, C. H. Claudy, in the October 1908 *Photo-Era*, called for censorship of "those artistically simulated [moving pictures] which are so near real life that they can be distinguished only by the expert."[42]

But with the audience's trust in film's authenticity comes the potential for sensationalizing the truth. Jonathan Auerbach reports that Edison's film crews even toyed with the idea of stretching authenticity by restaging McKinley's assassination. They decided against it, but the next news film, which featured crowds, described the mass of people as a "mob," thus inflaming the audience's response.[43]

From the first, the audiences for early film were as drawn to sex and violence as audiences today, and they had a similar need to disguise their motives as educational, morally improving, or otherwise worthwhile. As Lisa Cartwright explains, filmed violence in spectacles such as *Electrocuting an Elephant* (1903) "demonstrates that the motion picture functioned as a means for lay-audience participation in the 'scientific' pleasure of conducting visual analysis and thereby vicariously exerting control over a living being's life and death."[44]

When films shifted from the "cinema of attractions" model to the "story films" that became common after 1907, audiences became accustomed to invisible narration by acclimating to features that are now so commonplace as to be invisible: cutting between locations, close-ups, insets of a character's thoughts, and the interruption of dialogue titles rather than simply the cards establishing place and time common to earlier films.[45] In commenting on early film technique, Paula Marantz Cohen identifies its resistance to European formalism and its insistence on what she calls the Emersonian "nouns" of nature: its insistence on the primacy of the visual "elements of body, landscape, and face" as exemplified in the cut, the long shot, and the close-up, respectively. Cohen suggests that these elements contributed to the production of American myth by virtue of their "particular representational history" and "distinct meanings."[46] Even without accessing the same representational history, naturalism too focuses on body, landscape, and face as its primary visual tools, if for "face" one reads the visual cues that substitute for the limited grammar of primitive emotions that comprise the vocabulary of the typical naturalistic character. Film audiences and readers of naturalism had to fill in the gaps left open for interpretation: in film these resulted from the novelty of the medium, and in naturalism they resulted from the incomprehension or inarticulate nature of the characters treated with an objective form of narration. The communal nature of the film viewing experience aided in this process, when early audiences developed the practice of reading intertitles aloud for those who could not read English.

Moreover, scenes of spectatorship at the movies function as learning experiences for characters' engagement with other narrative conventions. Scenes of lower-class characters attending the movies occur frequently enough in naturalism to bear comparison with realism's scenes of middle- and upper-class characters visiting art galleries or discussing literature at dinner parties, as in the novels of Henry James (*Daisy Miller*, *The Portrait of a Lady*) and William Dean Howells (*The Rise of Silas Lapham*). In naturalistic novels like Wharton's *Summer* or Norris's *McTeague*, lower- or middle-class characters' disparate responses to what they witness at the theater reveal their aesthetic principles and feelings, just as the discussion of novels, paintings, and opera does in the middle- and upper-class milieu of Wharton's, James's, and Howells's fiction. For instance, Norris's

McTeague features a scene in which McTeague treats his fiancée, Trina Sieppe, and her mother and younger brother to a variety show at the Orpheum. McTeague roars and shouts at the slapstick comedians and admires the "musical marvels, two men extravagantly made up as negro minstrels," who can "wrestle a tune out of anything."[47] The "sentimental songs" of "The Society Contralto" captivate the upwardly mobile and culturally aspiring Trina, and Mrs. Sieppe declares the yodelers in Tyrolese costume to be "joost like der old country" (62). The scene functions as a realistic representation of turn-of-the-century vaudeville and as an index of class that distances reader from character. The "lightning artist" at the Orpheum who draws "caricatures and portraits" is a self-reflexive figure for the novelist, and as such the scene invites parallels between reader and character, lower-class spectatorship and middle-class reading, and vaudeville spectacle and the text-based representation of the novel (61).

In addition to their parallels with reading naturalism, the audience's responses to moving pictures mirror naturalism's affective physical responses. The experience of the spectators in *McTeague* demonstrates this principle when, as the penultimate act of the vaudeville show, the curtain parts to reveal "the crowning scientific achievement of the nineteenth century, the kinetoscope" (58). The film "fairly took their breaths away" (62) with its mundane pictures of a horse tossing its head, a cable car approaching, and a man crossing the street. One response appears through the comic counterpoint provided by Trina's brother, Owgooste, whose whining, twisting, and leg-swinging provide a reality-based performance that contrasts with the spectacle onstage. Mrs. Sieppe, enraptured by the show, ignores Owgooste until reality intrudes when he wets his pants, a comic embarrassment that demonstrates the power of the screen. As Brigitte Peucker observes in her discussion of Siegfried Kracauer, "moving images provoke visceral responses in the deep bodily layers" beyond those evoked by photography, and Owgooste's visceral response humorously confirms the theory.[48] Mrs. Sieppe's wet eyes and Owgooste's wet pants testify to the characters' emotional excitement and loss of bodily control, confirming cinema's affective power.

A final image links naturalism with early film: the scene of a woman looking through a window, often the plate glass window of a department store. In naturalistic novels, female characters are not so much questing as desiring: they search for meaning and identity through the world of things, which in the case of urban settings means consumer culture and gazing through a department store window. Unlike the mirrors of realist texts, which prompt self-assessment on the part of the character, the plate glass window of the department store transports the character through the screen rather than reflecting meaning back, suggesting her transformation into a better consumer and a better self. In another form, the ordinary window of a house functions variously as the aperture through which Mrs.

Mallard projects her desiring self in Kate Chopin's "The Story of an Hour," the barred window overlooking the garden peopled by creeping women in Charlotte Perkins Gilman's "The Yellow Wallpaper," and the window view of encroaching progress in Wharton's "Mrs. Manstey's View." In the department store scenes of Dreiser and Zola, the window represents a world of aspiration, but windows also suggest the illusion of space and the reality of imprisonment, as in the white slave narratives where the window offers an illusory means of escape.

The window propels the observer into another realm just as the movie screen does, and the idea of the window as lens or screen is central to naturalism. Zola argued in *Le roman expérimental* that a "transparent screen" constitutes the "naturalist's view of the world,"[49] and the screen or window is by analogy another form of camera lens, subject to the same distortions of emphasis, perspective, and depth of field. In film and in text, naturalism literalizes Zola's "transparent screen" through its use of apertures—doors, windows—that signify the visual frame. Anne Friedberg explains the shift from window to screen in "Les Flâneurs du Mal(l): Cinema and the Postmodern Condition": "The window frames a tableau, placing it behind glass and making it inaccessible, and arouses desire. Cinematic spectation, a further instrumentalization of this consumer gaze, produced paradoxical effects on the newfound social mobility of the *flâneuse*.... [T]he shop window succeeded the mirror as a site of identity construction, and then—gradually—the shop window was displaced by the cinema screen."[50] In tracing naturalism across two forms of media, film and print, the substitution of screen for narration, glass for screen, and mirror for reality marks the construction of the modern self. In their evocation of distortions of time, of desire, of visuality, of technology, and of dirt and waste, and in their frequent focus on women's lives and bodies, early films provide a useful medium for understanding the context of women's naturalism.

In addressing multiple texts and authors through these consistent themes, the individual chapters of *Bitter Tastes* unfold different dimensions in the evolution of women's naturalism from the 1870s through the 1920s. I am not claiming that women writers consciously wrote within a particular tradition of naturalistic practice or that these dimensions do not occur in the work of male naturalists. Rather, naturalism and its supposed quarrels with sentimentalism, with narrative objectivity, with social justice, and with middle-class life and middlebrow tastes provide a distinctive means for women writers to represent the conditions of women's lives and the limitations that they faced. Expanding the boundaries of naturalism temporally and thematically, and extending the cultural context to include the medium of early film, allows a different vision of those boundaries. Recognizing unruly naturalism provides a more flexible and expansive vision of naturalism that is not strictly gendered as classic or formulaic naturalism tends to be, thus yielding a richer, more inclusive, and more diverse canon of works and authors. Each chapter discusses naturalistic texts through a different lens, bringing into focus the background elements of naturalism in the work of women writers: issues of sexuality, work, and disability; interior landscapes of violence; gendered narratives of waste and filth; representations of childbirth and its terrors; women's use of visual and recording technologies; and images of film and photography.

The affective and visual elements of late nineteenth-century "grim realism" are the subject of the first chapter, "Grim Realism and the Culture of Feeling: Rebecca Harding Davis, Elizabeth Stuart Phelps, and Lillie Chace Wyman." The idea of a culture of feeling may seem entirely alien to naturalism, given naturalist writers' professed objectivity, yet both naturalism and social justice fiction operate within an aesthetics of revulsion or disgust. As Jane Thrailkill explains in *Affective Feelings*, the biological theories underlying late nineteenth-century texts require readings "focused on sensory perception, emotional receptivity, and the embodied mind."[51] The transmission of affect, and the early development of an aesthetics of disgust that complemented when it did not supplant the sentiments of benevolence fiction, inform Rebecca Harding Davis's "Life in the Iron Mills" and *Margret Howth* in ways that anticipate naturalism. Tracing three separate portraits of the fallen women in Elizabeth Stuart Phelps's fiction reveals Phelps's development of the character from the sentimental vision of the fallen woman needing to die for redemption in "One of the Elect," to a vision of the heroine's intellectual redemption in *Hedged In*, to the tough-minded and courageous figure who rescues the hero of *A Singular Life*. Deeply invested in abolitionism and prison reform, Lillie Buffum Chace Wyman fused regionalist fiction with the aesthetics of disgust in creating the "grim realism" of the stories in *Poverty Grass*, which, like Phelps's and Davis's work, features a prototype of naturalism's fallen woman.

The second chapter, "The Darwinists: Borderlands, Trauma, and Evolution," examines the range of women writers' debts to the evolutionary theories of Charles Darwin, Herbert Spencer, and their popularizers, and it explores the common naturalistic theme of dissolving bodily boundaries between human and animal, health and disability, and madness and sanity. In the first part of the chapter, harsh regional landscapes provide a brutal testing ground for human nature of the sort familiar from the work of Jack London. The short stories of writers such as Batterman Lindsay, Mary Hallock Foote, Elia Peattie, Kate Cleary, and Mary E. Wilkins Freeman examine the violence and trauma that attend women's experiences in these borderland spaces. The deadly consequences of biological drives and naturalistic desires pervade these works, in which the supposed security of domestic life or tribal rituals reveals itself as a position fraught with as much danger from family members within the group as from natural and human dangers without. Exploitation, starvation, and loss for their characters signal a Darwinian reality as, in some cases, characters begin to shed their humanity and devolve toward animality. Equally Darwinian in their approach are Kate Chopin's *At Fault* and Edith Wharton's *The Fruit of the Tree*, novels of unruly naturalism that address a host of social issues: the plight of workers, including people of color, under industrial capitalism; divorce, desire, and sexual selection; and violence, poverty, disability, and addiction.

Chapter 3, "Bohemian Time: Glasgow, Austin, and Cather," analyzes the ways in which Glasgow, Austin, and Cather pit women's biological time against the artificial temporal modernity of Bohemian spaces. Despite the woman artist at the center of Howells's *The Coast of Bohemia* (1893), the Trilby-inflected naturalistic novels of Bohemia written by Norris (*Vandover and the Brute*, written 1895 and published in 1914) and Crane (*The Third Violet*, 1897) confine women to roles as sexualized muses. In contrast, Glasgow, Austin, and Cather dismantle the pretensions of Bohemia by contrasting real time—women's time, biological time—with the irregular definition of it that existed in Bohemia. Glasgow's *The Descendant* and *Phases of an Inferior Planet*, Austin's *No. 26 Jayne Street*, and Cather's "Coming, Aphrodite!" disrupt the earlier novels' segregation of virginal middle-class women and sexualized artists' models by administering a bracing dose of biological reality. Their heroines recognize that while Bohemian spaces may be congenial for modern women seeking the freedom to live their own lives, Bohemian time is not.

Chapter 4, "Red Kimonos and White Slavery: The Fallen Woman in Film and Print," explores prostitution narratives as variants of women's naturalism.[52] As critics have long noted, the fallen woman was a primary subject for naturalistic writers such as Norris, Dreiser, and Crane. During the Progressive Era, the white slave panic sensationalized the problem of prostitution by organizing the discourse surrounding it into a narrative in which "foreign" men captured, drugged, and sold innocent American girls from the countryside into sexual slavery in the cities. The white slave plot expressed not only fears of urbanization and dehumanization but also of the era's increase in immigration, which, according to the popular press of the day, threatened the national character. During their short-lived popularity, white slave narratives proliferated in several forms of media almost simultaneously: sociological reports such as Jane Addams's *A New Conscience and an Ancient Evil* (1912) vied for attention with white slave novels such as Elizabeth Robins's *My Little Sister* (1913), Virginia Brooks's *Little Lost Sister* (1914) (American counterpart of *My Little Sister*), and Estelle Baker's *Behind the Rose Door* (1913).

At the same time, with the development of feature-length story films, the white slave panic gave rise to films like *Traffic in Souls* (1913) and *The Inside of the White*

Slave Traffic (1913), which promised the same combination of sensational content and educational purpose that audiences had earlier learned to expect. Not to be outdone, reformed prostitutes such as Louise Wooster and Josie Washburn as well as unrepentant madams such as Nell Kimball and Madeleine Blair published memoirs that debunked much of the white slavery hysteria while exposing the political corruption that made the smooth operation of their trades possible. The white slave panic took on additional xenophobic and racial overtones in San Francisco, where Frank Norris set the mysterious disappearance of a white woman in Chinatown in "The Third Circle," and Miriam Michelson parodied his concerns through her portrait of an intrepid female reporter in *A Yellow Journalist*.

Chapter 5, "Where Are My Children? Race, Citizenship, and the Stolen Child," raises issues of voice, agency, and control of the woman's body in the context of debates over birth control, abortion, and the production of citizenship. Increasingly stringent criteria for immigration, struggles over woman suffrage, and court battles over African American rights rendered citizenship an unstable category in the Progressive Era, the subject matter of movies such as Alice Guy-Blaché's *Making an American Citizen* (1912) and the pioneering African American filmmaker Oscar Micheaux's *Within Our Gates* (1919). Featuring unmarried American girls who consult foreign abortionists, Lois Weber's film *Where Are My Children?* (1916) and Edith Wharton's *Summer* (1917) address eugenics-inspired explorations of "blood" or ancestry, class, and degenerate "hill folk" populations, themes reinforced in citizenship films and "hillbilly films," a trend in film during 1913–15. In *Summer*, Charity Royall, born in the lawless colony of the Mountain in western Massachusetts but raised in the village of North Dormer, exhibits the defiance and bloodlines of the unruly colonial subject but the "civilized" quality of the assimilated immigrant.

Another form of citizenship regulation exists in the theme of the stolen child. In contrast to the fortunate adoptions of orphans in sentimental slum tales, the child in women's naturalistic stories is stolen from its parents by governmental forces, a plotline that critiqued Progressive Era models of social uplift. The figure of the stolen child rewrites one of the key questions of naturalism. Instead of asking "who controls the body of the woman?" it asks, "who controls the body of the child and with it the transmission of cultural heritage?" Appearing in stories by Sui Sin Far, Alice Dunbar-Nelson, Mary E. Wilkins Freeman, and Ann Petry, child stealing by supposedly benevolent white institutions such as wealthy philanthropists and government-sponsored social workers express the mother's, and by extension the oppressed culture's, anxieties about abuses of governmental power that put the lie to the nation's celebration of democracy.

Chapter 6, "'Manure Widows' and Middlebrow Fiction: Rural Naturalism in the 1920s," examines naturalistic responses to the 1920s publishing boom in farm novels, pioneer narratives, and rural films. In the 1920s and 1930s, middlebrow writers such as Edna Ferber and Bess Streeter Aldrich wrote pioneer novels and multigenerational sagas of triumph and endurance that integrated immigrants into a shared project of nation building, yet women's naturalistic farm novels refuted the optimism of these popular middlebrow writers. Using Darwinian narratives, Emanuel and Marcet Haldeman-Julius, Ruth Suckow, and Cornelia James Cannon focus on the transformation of human beings into what Jack London called "work beasts," with human qualities diminishing due to the grueling work of the farm.[53] Willa Cather's *O Pioneers!* (1913) and Edith Summers Kelley's *Weeds* (1923) depict a production-model relationship between women and the land. Rather than employing traditionally naturalistic landscapes, spaces in which the primitive beast within emerges under the stress of extreme poverty or confrontation with the wild, these novels demonstrate the harsh reality beneath the nation's cherished myths of Jeffersonian yeoman farmers, rosy-cheeked farm wives, and comfortable small towns. Drawing on the two central images of naturalism, animals and machines, Kelley, Cannon, and Cather remind readers that humans differ little from the animals they manage and the machines that regulate their waking hours. Their protagonists search for beauty but find themselves trapped by deterministic forces of poverty, sexuality, and maternity. Dorothy Scarborough's *The Wind* and its film adaptation present a visual portrait of a harsh, isolated environment and conflicting desires that send a woman into despair and madness.

Chapter 7, "Waste, Hoarding, and Secrets: Modernist Naturalism and the Servant's Body," shows how Wharton, Stein, Larsen, Scott, Hurst, and Gale use the figure of the servant or household drudge to transform a nineteenth-century naturalistic subject matter using modernist techniques, thereby critiquing modernism's obsession with cleanliness and speed. Surrounded by and associated with the dirt, secrets, and other detritus of civilization, the servant woman is an evolutionary throwback, an embarrassing reminder of bodies and the waste that even a technologically advanced, streamlined modernity cannot banish. With excesses of emotion expressed through melodrama and treated as waste, both elements abhorrent to modernism, the figure of the servant woman counters modernism with the naturalistic staples of dirt and women who are treated as waste. Burdened with secrets and potential sentiment, sometimes primitive or violent in her desires and actions, and covered in the messy detritus of a culture that refuses to include her grotesque, sometimes lumbering female body as part of its aesthetic of a fast-paced technological modernity, the servant woman of these novels reminds modernism of what it leaves behind and the naturalistic elements that it can never entirely erase.

CHAPTER 1

Grim Realism and the Culture of Feeling
Rebecca Harding Davis, Elizabeth Stuart Phelps, and Lillie Chace Wyman

In November 1910, the month before human nature forever changed, according to Virginia Woolf, a writer from another era, Elizabeth Stuart Phelps (1844–1911), wrote "Stories that Stay" for the fortieth-anniversary issue of the *Century*. In it, she recalled the "crystallization" of stories' power that remained long after some of their titles and authors had vanished from her memory.[1] Factors that caused stories to stay in the memory included "originality, humanity, force, and finish . . . some surprise or shock of novelty; some hell or heaven of human feeling; or some grip of absolute strength" (123). Phelps praises the "incisive impression" of Harriet Prescott Spofford's "The Amber Gods" for its "invention of expression after death" (119) and admires Kipling's "The Brushwood Boy" for its "beautiful prose" (120), but she devotes much more space to stories by Rebecca Harding Davis—and, more unexpectedly, Jack London. Davis's "Life in the Iron Mills" derives its power, according to Phelps, from its description of "the iron world—its tragic action, its denied aspirations, and . . . a certain grim picturesqueness which partook of the nature of the metal" (120). The idea of "grim picturesqueness" underlies her choice of two stories by Jack London: one a "horror story" from his autobiographical novel *Martin Eden* and the second a tale of a starving man and a starving wolf, which Phelps recalls as not being by London but is in fact his story "Love of Life."

Phelps's judgment rests not on the genre or literary tradition of the story, its place in realism or naturalism or women's writing, for she is, she insists, "little concerned with the canons" (119). What Phelps focuses on is the story's effect, its ability to carve a place in the reader's memory that persists after the title, or, in the case of London, the author of the story has been forgotten. She does not separate Davis's story from London's, nor does she characterize his approach as different from Davis's. Her fundamental criterion is the author's ability to make the reader respond to the work: the power of affect. Second, Phelps uses science and the visual properties of photographs to characterize her impressions, calling them "these films of the fiction of my day" and suggesting that they share "some optical or chemical laws for their election from the mass of short stories" (123). The memory and imagination of the author, in other words, impress themselves upon the reader's memory as a photographic image impresses itself upon a receptive plate through a chemical process of exposure and time. In *A Familiar Strangeness*, Stuart Burrows proposes that "in a world governed by photographic reproduction—in which everyone and everything is typical of everyone and everything else—nothing *can* happen—since every experience is as reproducible as a photograph."[2] The affective power of the grim picturesque is the chemical that etches the unique feeling into a receptive, reproducible memory.

A quarter of a century earlier, W. D. Howells anticipated Phelps's grim picturesque by describing the stories of Davis, Phelps, and Lillie Buffum Chace Wyman in *Harper's New Monthly Magazine* as "simple, grim, [and] true to misery," terms that he reserved for realism rather than regionalism.[3] By 1905, in *London Films*, Howells, like Phelps, had adopted the language of visual media, of photography and film, in analogizing the transmission of his memories and impressions through writing. With his "mental Kodak," Howells makes himself a human camera, albeit one that improves on the promise of realism's photographic representation by his selectivity and judgment as a writer.[4] His "trivial Kodak could not bear to dwell" on the "fashionable quarters" in the middle of September when the London season was "dead" (181). But reproducing some scenes required technologies beyond those of simple photography. During a visit to Hampton Court, Catherine Howard appears as if in an "instantaneous photograph escaping from her prison chamber" (141), with screams as vivid as if "a phonograph were reporting them"—a vision that, as Owen Clayton notes, recalls Edison's experiments in marrying film and sound.[5] Howells's mental Kodak, his "I am a camera" conceit, allows for selective vision and recollection as well as for photographic impressions. As a camera with a memory and the power of selection, he realizes the dual sense of potential inherent in realism and photography. Both represent a moment in time through the process of applying a chemical fixative to the moment through pen—or chemicals—and paper, and both rely on the visual techniques of composition and selection. Seen from a speeding automobile, villagers, to Howells, appear in "a sort of cinematographic shimmer" (153), with Howells-as-Kodak in rapid motion rather than the film within the movie camera.

But Howells does not find in London what he had found decades earlier: the grim picturesque. Although Jack London gathered ample evidence of poverty for his documentary report in *The People of the Abyss* during the same period when Howells visited the city of London, Howells, seeing "nothing slumlike," speculates that poverty is at least "shyer than it used to be in the days before slumming (now itself of the past) began to exploit it" (107). What Howells recalls from earlier visits is another form of enhanced snapshot, this one with the smells of the slums attached: "My memory is still haunted by the vision of certain hapless creatures who fled blinking from one hole in the wall to another, with little or nothing on, and of other creatures much in liquor and loudly scolding and quarrelling, with squalid bits of childhood scattered about underfoot, and vague shapes of sickness and mutilation and all the time a buying and selling of loathsome second-hand rags" (107). Howells's picture of what he expected to see, but did not, is a veritable postcard of grim realism and naturalism. Visually, Howells's memory blends human beings into the waste that surrounds them until a flash of light or insight reveals the distinction between human and waste, the discovery-of-squalor sequence common to grim realist and naturalist texts. Materially, it encompasses the poverty, rags, and depiction of children as "hapless creatures" or fragmented waste ("squalid bits of childhood"). Thematically, it resounds with the pervasive verbal or physical violence ("loudly scolding and quarreling") and figures of disability ("vague shapes of sickness and mutilation") comprising the catalog of refuse and misery characteristic of naturalism.

The "grim picturesque" suggests what may be called "grim realism," a precursor to naturalism that uses similar tropes of waste but lacks naturalism's commitment to determinism and violence. Often used to describe the work of Tolstoy, Zola, and Jack London, the term "grim realism" in reviews concentrates on the affective dimensions of the work, as in Elizabeth Stuart Phelps's memory of the "grim picturesqueness" of Rebecca Harding Davis and Jack London.[6] Grim realism engages readers by repelling them, and use of the term "grim realism" is not necessarily an endorsement. For example, a review in the *Bookman* of Robert W. Chambers's "fantastic collection of short stories" *The King in Yellow* praises its "fine facility" in style but warns that "the grim realism, ghastly sometimes, and a something undefinable but disagreeable about his stories repel us."[7] The "disagreeable" nature of grim realism differentiates it in approach and effect from the "benevolence literature" described by Jill Bergman and Debra Bernardi and from the strain of "realist humanitarianism" that William Morgan identifies in *Questionable Charity*. In their introduction to *Our Sisters' Keepers: Nineteenth-Century Benevolence Literature by American Women*, Bergman and Bernardi locate benevolence literature at the intersection of gender and social reform, a "literature of philanthropy" that incorporates nebulous social reforms but really "becomes a means of rescue for the middle-class heroine."[8] Passages describing squalor, for example, yield purposeful signposts registering the heroine's growing moral consciousness. Morgan views realism as "engag[ing] in an unresolved debate about the problems of modern subjectivity, humane agency, and individual complicity in an inhumane social order," a perspective that focuses on the purposes of realism rather than, as in grim realism, on its effects.[9] Describing with considerable relish the slime and muck of slum spaces, the grim realists forced a direct, immediate apperception of and revulsion from the poverty they described, a process prefiguring the aesthetics of disgust of classic naturalism and the interest in bodies as waste common to other women writers. A generation earlier than classic naturalism, "grim realism" is in fact a form of unruly naturalism.

Grim realists such as Davis, Phelps, and Wyman test the definitional boundaries of naturalism because they exist at the crossroads of classic naturalism's traditional sticking points: sentimentality, narrative subjectivity, and the moral imperative to reform. In addition, they provide an important correlative to the thematics of vision in naturalism, for the documentary purposes of photographic description in grim realism provide important parallels with naturalistic description and film technique. Further, the use of direct address, which breaks the fourth wall of naturalistic objectivity, insists that the reader look *at* rather than past social ills. Novels of grim realism expose social problems, but unlike the benevolence novel they fail to outline a tidy solution or Christian resolution within the text, instead proffering obviously inadequate solutions that undercut the redemptive promise of benevolence fiction. The grim realism of Davis's, Phelps's, and Wyman's fiction bridges naturalism's problematic relationship with sentimentalism by combining the aesthetics of disgust, lower-class subject matter, and attention to visual style found in naturalism while providing solutions that implicitly critique rather than reinforce the text's inadequate remedies.

Untouchable Objects:
Grim Realism, Affect, and the Aesthetics of Disgust

Sentimentality is the primary sticking point for considering the early grim realists as naturalists. Beginning in the eighteenth century with the language of sensibility, the term "sentimental" described a literature of feeling leading to an understanding of correct moral reasoning. Its actions were expressed not solely through a character's language but through descriptions of biological responses that could not be simulated or at least could not seem to be so. As characters' bodies expressed emotions through tears, a flushed face, dilated or contracted pupils, fainting, trembling, a rapidly beating heart, or other physical phenomena, readers became adept not only at reading the moral sentiments behind these involuntary behaviors but also at replicating the tears in their reading process.[10] In canonizing tears and sympathy as visible signs of readerly engagement, sentimentalism in the form of domestic fiction linked visible bodily expressions of sympathy with the elevation of moral consciousness. For writers of domestic fiction, the language of sentimentalism provided a means of expressing moral solidarity, a social contract between author and reader. When the sentimental novel as novel of sensibility gave way to the sentimental domestic novel, the emphasis on individual lessons in virtue became instead lessons in community virtue through an increasing emphasis on social reform, as evidenced in novels ranging from Susan Warner's *The Wide, Wide World* to Harriet Beecher Stowe's *Uncle Tom's Cabin*.

The idea of affect recovers sentimentalism as a valid category for the analysis of naturalism because it provides a language to discuss its embodied dimensions, such as the blood, bruises, tears, and wounds absent from the realism of W. D. Howells and Henry James. In naturalism, the transmission of affect as a visceral response of disgust and revulsion rather than sympathy overcomes the ironic distance that modern readers experience at sentimentalism's more artificial gestures. The performance of sentimentalism is determinedly artificial, according to Faye Halpern, for, like François Delsarte's vocabulary of artificial gestures, it must be "read as if there is not any artifice at all."[11] In contrast, grim realism relies on immediate rather than ritualized responses to a stimulus. The term "affect" refers to the physiological state of arousal through emotion and has a bodily dimension that aligns its processes with those of grim realism and naturalism. According to Teresa Brennan, it differs from the concept of "feelings" in that although feelings have a sensory dimension, unlike affect "they suppose a unified interpretation of that information" and find "the right match in words." A feeling that can be articulated, such as envy, "may appear relatively bloodless," Brennan continues, but affect has "an energetic dimension" that transmits that state to others.[12] For Brennan, the term "affect" imputes qualities of excess to affect, since it cannot be contained or organized within language and is located in the body and its sensory organs. As Fredric Jameson points out in *The Antinomies of Realism*, Brennan's concept of affect includes the idea that "the contagion of affect—its interpersonal transmission—is historically the result of smell."[13] Smell, as an integral component of naturalism, is central not only to its well-recognized treatment of desire—think, for example, of McTeague's rapturous plunge into Trina's closet and his response to the smell of her blue-black hair—but also to the aesthetics of disgust.

The qualities of excess that Brennan ascribes to affect, chief among them its inability to be organized and contained within words, provide a correlative to understanding the inarticulate or self-deceiving characters of naturalism and help to cement its relationship to sentimentalism. In her work on sentimentalism, June Howard approaches the concept of affect from a philosophical and literary perspective, suggesting that sentimentalism needs to be separated from its uses in domestic fiction in order to recover its roots in "[e]nlightenment notions of moral sentiments and sympathy." Stripped of its pejorative meanings and its links to domestic fiction, according to Howard, sentimentalism becomes a more free-ranging convention that signifies "emotion, embodied thought that animates cognition with the recognition of the body's engagement; [and] sympathy, firmly based in the observer's body and imaginatively linking it to another's."[14] Howard's formulation is important for locating feeling in the observer or reader's body, and, as in Brennan's concept of affect, emphasizing the transmission of feeling from text to reader. Taken together, Howard's and Brennan's perspectives define the primary characteristics of a sentimentalism that informs grim realism and naturalism: an affect ("feeling," in Howard's words) that (1) is expressed primarily through the body's involuntary responses, (2) outstrips the language available for its expression, (3) is spread to others through a process of emotional rather than intellectual transmission, and (4) leads to enhanced consciousness of external forces and thus to individual reform or collective action.

Grim realism and naturalism share with sentimentalism a working vocabulary of affect, but their purposes differ from those of sentimental or domestic fiction. A key distinction is that whereas sentimentalism operates within an aesthetics of sympathy and shared feeling, naturalism operates within an aesthetics of revulsion. The bruises and blood of characters, and the misery of the cramped spaces that reflect their tortured lives, create a sensory reaction within the reader. This evokes emotions in a two-stage process: readerly disgust at the vivid depiction followed by pity for the character who must become part of it. The uneasy oscillation between disgust and pity varies with the intensity of the affect evoked by the text, for as Jameson writes, "[a]ffects are singularities and intensities, existences rather than essences, which usefully unsettle the more established psychological and physiological categories."[15] The fitful nature of affect destabilizes the reader and the comfortable narrative perch from which she views the characters, contributing an unsettled feeling that recalls the anxiety about proletarianization that Howard associates with naturalism: "That couldn't happen to me (could it?)."[16] The narrative transaction between reader and subject engendered by this aesthetics of disgust is central to naturalism and to grim realism as well, thus providing a crucial link between the two. Unlike sentimentalist sympathy, however, which encourages a connection between reader and the environment of the text, disgust and pity are nonreciprocal emotions. They are felt *by* the observer or onlooker and visited *upon* the object of spectacle or of charity. They confirm the class differences of the characters toward whom the disgust or pity is directed and thus register a visceral, legible difference between viewer and subject.

Contributing to this effect is the rhetoric of waste and the accompanying aesthetic of revulsion that animates both grim realism and naturalism. Its signature trope is the catalog of refuse: the set-piece description common to naturalistic novels in which a heap of waste products is described in scrupulous, almost loving, detail by the narrator. The filthy bin of garbage under the sink in Norris's *Van-*

dover and the Brute is one such catalog, and the heap of rusted dishes that the dead Zerkow clutches to his chest in *McTeague* is another. The "chuckling and leering" fat man with the dripping mustache and blotched features in Crane's *Maggie* provides a human analog: "On going forward she perceived it to be a huge fat man in torn and greasy garments. His grey hair straggled down over his forehead. His small, bleared eyes, sparkling from amidst great rolls of red fat, swept eagerly over the girl's upturned face. He laughed, his brown, disordered teeth gleaming under a grey, grizzled moustache from which beer-drops dripped. His whole body gently quivered and shook like that of a dead jelly fish. Chuckling and leering, he followed the girl of the crimson legions" (72). This passage, which was deleted in the 1896 edition of *Maggie*, evokes several categories of repulsion and waste. Most immediately, the excess of flesh and straggly hair suggest disorder and the disintegration of the body, thus prefiguring Maggie's imminent death. This figure, the prototypical "fat man" that James R. Giles identifies as a "metaphor for the uncensored reality of the inner city," embodies the exotic terrain that fascinated and frightened middle-class readers.[17] Crane's fat man is a "great figure" and is referred to as "it," and his body moves spontaneously, initially not under his own volition.

The waste that Maggie's customer barely contains on and within his person—his greasy garments, brown teeth, and "beer-drops"—reinforces the fat man as embodying Julia Kristeva's concept of the abject. Kristeva defines the abject as the repugnance that exists for the waste from the borderland of being alive and from which the body "extricates itself" through excretion. The abject is not simply that which "lack[s] cleanliness or health" but that which "disturbs identity, system, order . . . . [t]he in-between, the ambiguous, the composite." The corpse, for Kristeva, is "the utmost of abjection . . . death infecting life."[18] Crane's use of "dead jelly fish" evokes not only death but also the devolutionary formlessness that "disturbs identity" and suggests the dissolution of human boundaries. In touching the indeterminately bounded body that the man represents, and in intimately touching him, as her calling demands, Maggie defiles herself and participates in her own dissolution, rendering moot the question of whether she commits suicide or is murdered.[19] The catalog of refuse indexes the character's degeneration by symbolically indicating that the character associated with it becomes part of the refuse being discarded even when less intimately associated with it. Above all, it threatens the position of the spectator because, in the scenes where such instances of touching filth appear, the narrative proximity promised by the catalog of refuse matches the physical proximity of unequal classes within naturalism's urban, public spaces.

Both naturalism and grim realism rely on olfactory as well as visual imagery to convey the affective charge of the catalog of refuse and the risk of contamination that surrounds it. As Peter Stallybrass and Allon White explain, in the city's "promiscuous" spaces of "the tram, the railway station, the ice rink, above all the streets themselves... the fear of that promiscuity was encoded above all in terms of the fear of being touched. 'Contagion' and 'contamination' became the tropes through which city life was apprehended." Smell is part of this aesthetics of disgust and contagion because smell, unlike touch, "had a pervasive and invisible presence difficult to regulate."[20] For example, the repeated imagery of smoke and smell found in Davis's "Life in the Iron Mills," of copperas in *Margret Howth*, and of the generalized "filth" as opposed to "pure air" of Phelps's *Hedged In* matches the pervasive smell of creosote, ether, and finally blood, as in a butcher's shop, in Norris's *McTeague*.[21] The famous description of the "careening" tenement in Crane's *Maggie* illustrates this point about the promiscuity of touch as well as of smell. A structural metaphor for the teeming fecundity of the women who inhabit it, the building figuratively expels "loads of babies to the street and the gutter" and contributes the smell of "a thousand odors of cooking food" that permeates the street. The smell may be of food, but since the building "quiver[s] and creak[s] from the weight of humanity stamping about in its bowels" (11), the true correlation is that of digestive processes. In its depiction of a building indiscriminately excreting babies and the smells of waste, the novel reinforces the idea of human beings as waste common to naturalism.

Narrative subjectivity is a second sticking point between classic naturalism and grim realism. Classic naturalism proposes a dispassionate attitude toward its subject matter, one that strives for Zola's ideal of the objective scientist elevated above the organisms being studied. The class distinctions of observer and observed, the relative elevation of the observer and the abject position of the observed, reinforce naturalism's characteristic tendency toward irony rather than sympathy. The logic of sentimentalism dictates the opposite stance: a melding of reader and narrator within the shared language of sympathy rather than a distancing of the two. The power of readerly sympathy, which constitutes a transmission of affect from fiction to reader, confirms a social contract between reader and author. For Philip Fisher, sentimental discourse creates an "extension of feeling" whereby an unfamiliar situation involving a marginalized subject—the enslavement and abduction of one's children, in *Uncle Tom's Cabin*—is rendered familiar through an "experiential equation" that bridges unfamiliar situation with familiar subject matter, as in the reader's tears at the death of Little Eva.[22] In addition to these general properties of sentimental discourse, Robyn R. Warhol describes two characteristic patterns of the sentimental mode that parallel the transmission of affect in grim realism and naturalism: the inadequacy of words to transmit emotions, and the "earnest, direct address to a narratee."[23] The inexpressible nature of transmitting overwhelming emotion, in sentimental narratives often a sense of loss or grief that renders characters senseless as they fall into a faint or into tears, recalls Brennan's criteria for affect: that it cannot be transmitted in words and that it will involve a physical response. Warhol's second pattern, and the one most closely associated with sentimental discourse, is the direct address to the reader. Direct address drags the reader into the narrative space, demanding engagement and threatening an excess of feeling despite the reader's involuntary revulsion from the subject matter. Excess feeling in grim realism and naturalism pervades the atmosphere of the text, undercutting its surface objectivity and setting up a tension between narrative surface and the excesses of its subject.

Both sentimentalism and naturalism achieve their effects, an aesthetics of sympathy or of revulsion, through language that positions readers within the text and aligns them with the narrator's perspective. Words that perform this function are, in Ragnar Rommetveit's terms, deictic words; they are "the set of pronouns, adverbs, and demonstratives that shift their meaning according to context" through specific references to person, place, and time.[24] The immersive quality of deixis and its shifting contexts invites, or occasionally forces, the reader to assume a position beside the narrator within the text. Davis's "Life in the Iron Mills," for example, begins by placing "you" and "I" in the same narrative space: "A cloudy day: do you know what that is in a town of iron works? ... It stifles me."[25] The narrator continues in the same pattern of pronominal gestures throughout the early pages of the story, revealing her thoughts while challenging or taunting the reader to participate fully in the emotional framework that the story establishes. Thus the educated reader, perhaps proud of his or her understanding, is castigated as "you ... who study psychology in a lazy, *dilettante* way," the allusion to the academically abstract idea of "psychology" and the French phrase mocking the listener even as they signal class solidarity with him or her. Switching to plainer English, the narrator challenges the reader to "come right down with me" (4) to the scene of the narrative. What appears as a simple authorial intrusion is instead a means of engaging the well-meaning but resisting reader by placing him or her in the same frame as the narrator.

The deictic function of Davis's statements prefigures a similar feature in naturalism: the ironic observational phrase or authorial intrusion that joins reader and narrator in a conspiracy of understanding. Bill Brown suggests that a distinguishing feature of Norris's *McTeague* is its use of iterative narration, which "substitutes, for an account of discrete events, the account of events that recur in an iterative series," a usage that facilitates the plot's "serial alternation between custom and its violation, routine and event, monotony and novelty."[26] In *McTeague*, the narrative performs a similar iterative function of accumulated meaning through repetition of the word "true." "It was true" and "it wasn't true" alternately point to the sensational and the petty alike with references that call attention to the truth quotient of the narrative; they position the reader as complicit with, and occupying the same narrative space as, the narrator. The narrator's protest "It was true" occurs in *McTeague* even when the assertion seems in no danger of being doubted by the reader. When Miss Baker, already described as a "little old lady," protests that she never has any junk "lying around like that," the narrator needlessly cuts in to reinforce the message: "It was true. The retired dressmaker's tiny room was a marvel of neatness" (24).

Perhaps because of her later penchant for lying, Trina's earlier statements are especially prone to narrative reinforcement. When she explains that she cannot make the "manikins" that she paints, the narrator explains "[i]t was true" that Trina could not compete with mass production methods (78), and her deduction that Marcus was going away is interrupted with "[b]ut it was true" (140). McTeague hesitates before drinking, because "[i]t was lamentably true" that drinking hard liquor did not agree with him (163), the narrator's adverbial reinforcement adding a moral weight to a supposedly objective confirmation of fact. The most striking example of the phrase is one that Norris struck from the text before publication: as McTeague begins to administer his final and fatal beating, Trina protests, "Mac, you're *killing* me"—and before describing the brutal details, the narrator adds, "It was true" (206n4). As if to balance and counter the use of "it was true," characters repeatedly deny the truth by saying "it wasn't true": in denial over the theft of her gold, Trina repeats the phrase four times before declaring "It *is* true" (191). By calling attention to the truth quotient of the characters' assertions, Norris seems to be reinforcing their claims. Yet the net effect is to undermine the text, to draw attention to the narrator as a fictional device, and to emphasize the text's fictionality and the reader's positioning within it. In a metacognitive sense, Norris introduces a dissonance or disruption in the narrative surface, and this aligns his interruptions with the deictic gestures of the grim realists, both of which destabilize the safe objectivity of the middle-class reader by opening the possibility of readerly engagement.

Other naturalist authors employ similar narrative tactics to question the ironic distance between perception and reality. Dreiser's *Sister Carrie* exhibits this quality in its numerous philosophical digressions, including its famous judgment in the first chapter that "[w]hen a girl leaves her home at eighteen, she does one of two things. Either she falls into saving hands and becomes better, or she rapidly assumes the cosmopolitan standard of virtue and becomes worse."[27] The worldly wise, sententious tone has the same effect as Norris's statement: it undercuts the objectivity of the narrative voice by calling attention to the narrator's superior judging consciousness in issuing such statements. Crane's elaborate similes and aphoristic tendencies perform the same function. His frequent use of third person—"one" and "a man"—for philosophical musings in clauses such as "when it occurs to a man" that the universe would not mind disposing of him in "The

Open Boat" complements the multiple physical perspectives from which a scene is narrated. When the narrator reports, "Viewed from a balcony, the whole thing would doubtlessly have been weirdly picturesque," the reader appears above and removed from the danger that the men in the boat face.[28] The narrative voice in naturalism avoids the impassioned second-person direct address of sentimental fiction, but its alternative interruptions serve the same purpose: to call attention to the fictionality of the self-affirming objectivity of the language.

In addition to the catalog of refuse and the use of deictic language to position a reader uneasily within a scene, scenes containing a clutter of material objects occur in grim realism and naturalism but operate differently from their counterparts in domestic and regionalist fiction. In domestic fiction, the clutter of homely everyday objects signals the owner's state of mind and the position of the woman associated with it, as in Dinah's kitchen in *Uncle Tom's Cabin*. In regionalist fiction, scenes of disorder signify a healthy individualism and dissent from the threat of a repressive domestic reform agenda. For example, in Mary E. Wilkins Freeman's stories, cluttered corners or disordered gardens become the only means of resisting the level of surveillance endured by powerless women. In "A Mistaken Charity," two elderly sisters gleefully abandon their institutional white caps from the poor farm and flee to their crumbling cabin. Their ramshackle home stands in defiance of the laws of gravity and signifies their rebellion against the forces of organized charity. In "A Church Mouse," Hetty Fifield resists the attempts of the churchgoers to oust her from the only space in which she can live independently. Despite the spotless order of the church building under Hetty's stewardship, her tenancy features as a form of disorder a universal signifier of poverty and its disagreeably sulfurous odors: the smell of cooked cabbage, a form of contamination that even the "legitimate savor of the sanctuary, the fragrance of pepper-mint lozenges and wintergreen," cannot quite vanquish.[29] The poorhouse confers neither individuality nor dignity upon its inmates. In Alice Brown's "Joint Owners in Spain," for example, two elderly women bicker constantly over the space in their shared room until they agree to an imaginary division that grants each a space of her own. According to Karen Tracey, the poorhouse's "panoptic and sentimental paradigms" signify the "contradictory impulses to sympathize and to discipline" that exist in the functions of the poorhouse itself, chief among them separating "worthy" from "unworthy" poor.[30] The clutter of things resists the disciplinary impulse, in domestic fiction by creating a sense of familiarity and narrative coziness, and in regionalist fiction by rendering legible women's resistance to an oppressive reform agenda.

The profusion of things operates differently in grim realism and naturalism. As Peter Brooks maintains, the discourse of things—"heavy in referential material, in names of places, people, things, in sociohistorical explanation—constitutes a type of babble typical of the realist text," and this "descriptive imperative points to the primacy of the visual in realism."[31] The "babble... of the realist text" is already apparent in domestic fiction, in contrast to heavily symbolic references in the romances of Hawthorne and Melville, where each "thing" has layers of resonance and none appears solely for "sociohistorical explanation." The clutter of things, in Bill Brown's terms, requires the reader to ask "two rather simple questions— How are objects represented in this text? And how are they made to mean?"[32] To ask Brown's questions, however, requires examination of the way things are signposted and "made to mean" in realist modes such as grim realism and naturalism.

The babble of things exists in naturalism to make the reader uncomfortable rather than comfortable, by challenging the boundaries between things and the human subject. Two settings characteristic of grim realism and naturalism, the urban street and the cramped room, provide mechanisms for challenging those boundaries. In grim realism and in naturalism, the street becomes a visual threshold for spectacle and display, as seemingly random encounters like the collisions of atoms operate to disguise the deterministic structure of the world that the characters inhabit. The other slum setting is what might be called the cramped and disordered room, something that is carried over from the slum fiction of grim realism and naturalism into the films of the day such as D. W. Griffith's *The Musketeers of Pig Alley*.[33]

Scenes of naturalism and grim realism shift between domestic confrontations engendered by inadequate space in the cramped room and the spectacle rendered by the teeming street crowds. In *Bodies and Machines* Mark Seltzer describes what he terms the "realist and room-size genre of the still life" operant in naturalism, which expresses the plenitude of the market and its foods while excluding "the human subject and the human body since it is precisely the human subject and the human body to which the still life... makes reference and pays homage" (139). Appearing in the grim realism of Phelps and Davis and referenced extensively in naturalistic texts, the cramped room is the obverse of this still life of plenitude. It replaces order with disorder and the plenitude of the market with the plenitude of waste. Broken furniture, garbage, and spoiled food transform the tableaus of social encounters into the aftermath of objects of bodily need, once whole but now used, digested, discarded, or otherwise destroyed by human agency. At points the bodies themselves appear within these tableaus of waste, often scarcely distinguishable from the broken objects and waste upon which they rest. In *Hedged In* Nixy blends in with the straw pallet upon which she lies, and the "fatally poor and dingy" Gerty Farish in *The House of Mirth* blends into the décor of her "small flat" within which Lily Bart can barely move without knocking over a teacup.[34] After one pitched battle between Maggie's parents in Crane's *Maggie: A Girl of the Streets*, Maggie's brother Jimmy sees "a glow from the fire [that] threw red hues over the bare floor, the cracked and soiled plastering and the overturned and broken furniture. In the middle of the room lay his mother asleep. In one corner of the room his father's limp body hung across the seat of a chair" (18). Broken furniture and broken bodies mingle in this tableau of waste in which a man's body lies "limp" while Mrs. Johnson's body, the center of the quintessentially naturalistic tableau of the woman's body lying motionless in a room where violence has occurred or is about to occur, is quiet and unmoving only temporarily before resurrecting itself as an instrument of terror.

Grim realism, like naturalism, uses the cluttered foreground or disordered background to establish the characters as at once of their environment, an outgrowth of its squalor, and not of their environment, as individuals with the humanistic ability to change themselves if not their surroundings. Nowhere is this more evident than in a common scene in grim realism and naturalism: the discovery-of-squalor sequence. In slum stories, initial scenes of contact between the well-meaning visitor and the tenement dwellers follow a specific pattern. The observer/narrator descends to the depths of the slum, as in "Life in the Iron Mills" and *Margret Howth*, or enters a cramped room darkened by the absence of windows and the presence of squalor. At first she literally cannot see the individual as distinct from his or her surroundings. She distinguishes individuals from the waste that surrounds them only after the flash of the initial perception, which is usually described as overwhelming the senses with visual clutter and noisome smells. Grim realist writers metaphorically throw open the tenement door and snap a picture, distinguishing human beings from the squalor that surrounds them.

The same process of visually differentiating foreground from background occurs in photographic documentary slum literature such as Jacob Riis's *How the Other Half Lives* or Jack London's *The People of the Abyss*, which feature documentary photography as an intensification of their realist texts. In Brander Matthews's "In Search of Local Color," for example, De Ruyter, a novelist, asks Suydam, a settlement worker, to introduce him to the worst of Mulberry Bend, a neighborhood made infamous in *How the Other Half Lives*. Descending to the cellar, they are stunned by the foul air and gradually see that "[i]n the damp heat of this room ten or a dozen men and boys [are] seated on old chairs and on broken boxes, smoking, playing cards by the light of a single foul and flaring kerosene-lamp, and drinking the dregs of beer-kegs collected in old cans."[35] The initial impression is physical and olfactory, later resolving itself into vision by means of the "flaring kerosene lamp." In a variation of this scene, the visitors' intrusion introduces sunlight into a dank cellar or crowded tenement, the light catching individuals unawares as they blink at the unaccustomed intrusion or pose on the trash heap that identifies their home.

"A Child of the Dump," from Jacob Riis's *The Children of the Poor* (1907), illustrates the "children treated as waste" theme.

The discovery-of-squalor sequence affords a double vision of the spectacle, first through the eyes of the spectators in the story and then through the readers who assimilate it into their own vision of the slum. Yet even reconceived as documentary photography, realism includes the promise of entertainment. As Nancy Armstrong suggests in *Fiction in the Age of Photography*, even what seemed to be a "purely documentary project," a photographic record of "the most abject pockets of urban decay" transformed "misery into popular entertainment" for the middle classes, a relishing of the details of misery already familiar from the work of Charles Dickens, Elizabeth Gaskell, and Benjamin Disraeli. Armstrong calls it "urban Gothic, a genre to which photography came late but nevertheless made a unique contribution."[36] Phelps's, Davis's, and Wyman's works, with their discovery-of-squalor sequences, suggest the same sense of photographic discovery but diminish the Gothic qualities to emphasize redemption rather than entertainment.

In addition to photography, grim realism borrows from the subgenres of realism that Fredric Jameson recognizes in *The Antinomies of Realism*. After melodrama, these include the bildungsroman, the historical novel, the novel of adultery, and naturalism, which he distinguishes from sentimentalism by the "late-nineteenth-century panic as it confronts a sinister and radically different space." In grim realism and naturalism, Jameson's "sinister and radically different space" is the slum space, with Howellsian realism's hopeful answers to Tolstoy's question "What is to be done?" devolving in naturalism to the fear that nothing can be done. The grim realism narrative expands on the character types associated with each of Jameson's subgenres, respectively "the young man, the political 'world-historical individual,' and the woman."[37] It focuses on the worker-figure associated with naturalism and the grim realist heroine who requires an education in social responsibility.

In Davis, Phelps, and Wyman, the grim realist novel is often a bildungsroman in which the protagonist constructs self-identity through service to others in her society rather than through individuation from it. Its basic outline includes a heroine, intelligent yet heedless of the misery that surrounds her, who comes into abrupt social contact with a personification of the misery of the industrial system, often in the form of a poverty-stricken child or disabled character. The poorer member of this reform pair, often a young girl burdened by a family member whose disability or drunkenness causes her to assume responsibility beyond her years, serves as a touchstone for the heroine and a symbol for the reader of all the misery that surrounds her. According to Rosemarie Garland Thomson, this "mutually defining dyad of vulnerable Other and maternal benefactress generates a feminine self with many of the valued qualities of liberal individualism."[38] As the heroine progresses in her quest to find a solution, she discovers that none is entirely satisfactory, and her dissatisfaction leads her to a novel solution, one more radical than existing institutions allow but never as radical as supporting a strike for better working conditions. Rebecca Harding Davis's *Margret Howth*, Elizabeth Stuart Phelps's "The Tenth of January," "One of the Elect," *Hedged In*, and *A Singular Life*, and Lillie Chace Wyman's *Poverty Grass* follow the familiar pattern of developing the reader's social consciousness through affective and intellectual means, but the lack of satisfactory solutions to social problems undercuts the affirmative message at the surface of the story.

Rebecca Harding Davis, *Margret Howth*, and the Waste Economy

"LIFE IN THE IRON MILLS"

Rebecca Harding Davis presents the best-known example of grim realism approaching early naturalism. Sharon Harris has called Davis's "Life in the Iron Mills" "one of the earliest renderings of naturalism in American literature," noting that it uses naturalistic tropes such as the caged bird, the drifting lives of characters, the indifference of nature to human troubles, the plot of decline, and capitalists' control of workers' voices.[39] As Harris suggests, the "dirty canary" suggests a naturalistic universe, as does the narrator's clinical detachment in classifying the millworkers by ethnicity and their possession or lack of "pure, unmixed blood."[40] Despite the story's religious conclusion, Harris places it at the heart of a more general reassessment "of realism and naturalism as literary movements."[41] Following Harris, Sara Britton Goodling identifies *Margret Howth* and Phelps's *The Silent Partner* as naturalistic texts, stating that "sentimentalism... anticipates naturalism" in its "subject matter, its thematics, and its marriage of reformism and determinism."[42] Jean Pfaelzer disagrees, declaring that because Deb and Wolfe in "Life in the Iron Mills" aspire to more and come to understand their moral rights, they lack the mute acceptance of their fate that naturalistic characters share. The presence of a "moral referent" lacking in Norris or Crane disqualifies the story, Pfaelzer continues, because it is shaped by "the sympathy of sentimentalism rather than the inevitability of naturalism."[43]

Instead of classic naturalism, "Life in the Iron Mills" suggests grim realism through its industrial surroundings and doomed characters, its "fog and mud and foul effluvia" (41), and its tale of Wolfe, a talented artist trapped in "the vast machinery of system by which the bodies of workmen are governed" (45). Wolfe and his father live with the devoted care of their cousin Deborah, who is "deformed, almost a hunchback" (43). Deborah (or "Deb") is a familiar figure in women's grim realism and naturalism: the disabled character who provides an identifiable face for the abuses of the industrial system. Despite the hopeless grind of his working life, Hugh Wolfe has managed to carve the figure of a nude woman in industrial waste called "korl," a statue so filled with a hunger for something of the spirit that it catches the attention of three educated men visiting the mill. One of several such groups of male judges of morality in women's grim realism, they debate the sculpture and the impossibility of reform as Deb steals money from one of the men to give to Hugh, for which he is caught and imprisoned. Facing an imprisonment filled with hard labor and despair, Hugh cuts his own living flesh now rather than the korl, and his last creation is his own death. Deb is rescued by a kindly Quaker woman, but the frustrated genius that Hugh represents has no place in an industrial culture that values its "hands" only as part of the larger machinery of the mill.

Striking instances of grim realism in "Life in the Iron Mills" occur in its deictic references, as discussed previously; the treatment of human beings as waste through the catalog of refuse; and the discovery-of-squalor sequence. In "Life in the Iron Mills," the discovery-of-squalor features Deb as the subject of the figure-ground confusion common to grim realist and naturalist texts: "Miserable enough she looked, lying there on the ashes like a limp, dirty rag,—yet not an unfitting figure to crown the scene of hopeless discomfort and veiled crime: more fitting, if one looked deeper into the heart of things,—at her thwarted woman's form, her colorless life, her waking stupor that smothered pain and hunger" (9). Boundaries between animate and inanimate objects, sleep and waking, and the human and nonhuman are elided in this scene. Deb, a "limp, dirty rag" barely distinguishable from her ash heap, is powerless ("limp") and disabled, a naturalistically grotesque figure in whom Davis forces the reader to see humanity. As first introduced she is scarcely more alive than the flesh-colored statue of the korl woman whose hunger she shares. In this system, Deb is waste, a Cinderella lying in the ashes whose fairy godmother, the Quaker woman, appears only at the end of the story. The figure of the korl woman, representing the starvation of the spirit—as Hugh says, "Her be hungry"—exists as a counterpoint to Deb's grotesque figure, indistinguishable from its background of rags. Both represent naturalism's unmoving figure of the still woman, appraised by the gaze of uncomprehending men. Although Hugh is the artist-protagonist of the story, the twinned female figures in tableau, both of whom are shaped by and considered industrial waste, represent two sides of the portraiture of women in grim realist and naturalist texts. Portraying a living woman as waste and a woman made of waste (korl) as a work of art, "Life in the Iron Mills" highlights the woman's body in its blurring of the boundaries between the living woman, waste, and art.

MARGRET HOWTH

Margret Howth was Davis's first novel, and, like "Life in the Iron Mills," it appeared in the *Atlantic Monthly*. *Margret Howth* is the story of a woman who finds her salvation in service to others, ultimately marrying Stephen Holmes, the man she loves, after serving an apprenticeship in working with poor people. Living near a mill town in the countryside of Indiana, Margret, as the novel opens, celebrates her twentieth birthday amid the catalog of refuse that defines her world: "There were the walls with their broken plaster, showing the laths underneath, with here and there, over them, sketches with burnt coal, showing that her predecessor had been an artist in his way,—his name, P. Teagarden, emblazoned on the ceiling with the smoke of a candle; heaps of hanks of yarn in the dusty corners; a half-used broom; other heaps of yarn on the old toppling desk covered with dust; a raisin-box, with P. Teagarden done on the lid in bas-relief, half full of ends of cigars, a pack of cards, and a rotten apple."[44] The detailed description shows what happens to artists in such a world: they are left with the rest of the broken waste and debris and consigned to marking their names on ceilings and raisin-box lids simply to record the fact of their existence. In a window scene familiar from other grim realist and naturalist works, Margret then "look[s] out of the window. In it, as if set in a square black frame, was the dead brick wall, and the opposite roof, with a cat sitting on the scuttle. Going closer, two or three feet of sky appeared. It looked as if it smelt of copperas, and she drew suddenly back" (11). The frame of the window enclosing a Bartleby-like "dead brick wall," the cat, usually a figure of predatory hunger in naturalism, and the intimation that even the sky smells of copperas recall Wharton's fragment "One Day." In grim realism, windows are apertures that should provide an exterior view of possible freedom but instead confirm the character's entrapment.

Margret is not alone, since a caged "miserable pecking chicken" (11) shares the space. Leaving work for the day, she tries to free the chicken, only to be sharply reprimanded by Dr. Knowles, the factory owner: "You take it for a type of yourself, eh? It has another work to do than to grow fat and sleep about in the barnyard" (14). In a deterministic universe, all animals, of which Margret is one, have their place, and all must serve a master, as Dr. Knowles reminds her. Moreover, her place is to work for social betterment in the here and now rather than to use her talents and inscribe her identity where they will never be seen, as did the unfortunate P. Teagarden. As she walks home through the town, she might be "a slave putting on a mask, fearing to meet her master" (17). The grimy surroundings, the specter of industrial enslavement, and the chicken, which Dr. Knowles, in a Puritan turn of phrase suggests is Margret's "type" or emblem, all signify a suppressed, imprisoned soul in much the same manner as McTeague's canary, Louisa Ellis's canary, and other caged birds in naturalism define the limits of their owners' lives. The appearance of Dr. Knowles, with a face "that repelled most men: dominant, restless, flushing into red gusts of passion, a small intolerant eye, half hidden in folds of yellow fat" (13), suggests naturalism's grotesque "fat man." Yet Dr. Knowles embodies James R. Giles's "fat man" not by representing the menace of the inner city but by serving as its ambassador, awakening Margret to the needs of the poor and to her own hidden desire to help them.

The tension in *Margret Howth* derives from Margret's sense that she must choose which of three masters to follow and the reader's understanding that she has a fourth possibility that she does not see, that of following Lois Yare's Christlike path of love and forgiveness. Margret sees as choices the man she loves, Stephen Holmes, whom she gives up in a gesture of self-sacrifice; Dr. Knowles, who claims her for his philanthropic enterprises; and her nearly blind father, whose ideas of philosophy and the intellectual life keep Margret in harness supporting him. Confronted by three selfish men, each blinded by his own idealism and desire to use her as a tool to improve a deeply flawed society, Margret initially believes that she cannot be free of them but can only choose which she will serve. As in Henry James's *The Portrait of a Lady* and George Eliot's *Middlemarch*, the great question is, as Henry James poses it, "Well, what will she *do*?"[45] Like James's

Isabel Archer and Eliot's Dorothea Brooke, Margret has the capacity to choose, the great motivating force for nineteenth-century heroines, but her choice, like theirs, may ironically lead to a closer confinement than her illusions of freedom had promised. Holmes and Knowles offer two conventional paths to Margret: marriage and the love plot, which Holmes embodies, and the social justice plot, which Knowles represents.

Despite their pretensions to power and self-reliance, both Holmes and Knowles act as their heredity demands, an irony that the novel exploits by endowing each character with hereditary traits based in race and gender and manifested in physiognomy. Besotted by what Jean Fagan Yellin calls "the debasement of the Emersonian doctrine of self-reliance,"[46] Stephen Holmes embraces wholeheartedly "the great idea of American sociology—that the object of life is *to grow*" (121). But extensive time devoted to self-analysis requires ample money, and he allows Margret to break off their engagement so that he can marry the wealthy Miss Herne. Like Hollingsworth in Hawthorne's *The Blithedale Romance*, who also combines ideological rigidity and a readiness to marry for money rather than love, Holmes never sees the irony in becoming an Emersonian individualist by relying on his wife's money.[47] Holmes's contradictions are manifested in his physiognomy, for, as Polston, a worker, tells him, he has his "father's eyes... [h]ungry, pitiful, like women's" but his "heavy iron jaws" are like his mother's, and "[s]he never—let go" (133). With his "massive head... overhanging brow, square development... and lowered crown" (111), Holmes reflects his mother's stubborn "Yorkshire blood." In Holmes, conventional gender traits are reversed: his father is gentle, and his mother is rigid and grasping. Yet Holmes, committed to Emersonian individualism, refuses to acknowledge any deterministic constraints. "Never mind; outside of this life, blood or circumstance matters nothing," Holmes explains to Dr. Knowles, not recognizing the irony that for the immediate future, there is nothing "outside of this life" and that environment and heredity ("blood or circumstance") still matter.

In contrast to the rigidity and moral failings displayed by those with unmixed English blood, characters of mixed race or those who, like Margret, have been transplanted from another environment demonstrate evolutionary flexibility and a generosity of spirit. The mixed-race Lois Yare is mutable and giving, a "born colourist" and an artist, destined by the shape of her head and the quality of her brains for "worship" (111), according to Dr. Knowles. Knowles himself is part Native American, "his veins thick with the blood of a despised race" (50) that the narrator hints influences his concern for the poor. But environment matters as much as race in Davis's deterministic calculus. Disapproving of Dr. Knowles's social agenda, a racist southern doctor "spitefully lisp[s]" that Knowles's affinity for prisoners comes from inherited criminality: "His mother was a half-breed

Creek, with all the propensities of the redskins to fire-water and 'itching palms.' Blood will out" (85). In the novel's taxonomy of environments and their influences, the doctor's southern blood defines him as soft, and his "spite" and his lisp confirm his effeminacy. Margret has southern blood too, but hers is "Virginian blood [that] was cool, high-bred." Although "life in the West had not yet quickened her pulse" (71), the "yet" suggests that the western environment will temper Margret's weakness.

In addition to the hereditary and environmental traits that shape his judgments, Holmes experiences a visceral reaction that affects his intellectual processes when he ponders his marriage to Miss Herne: the contaminating smell of the mills and her perfume. Pacing in his room and deciding whether to sign the deed to the mills that will guarantee his marriage, Holmes recalls Miss Herne's "light blue eyes and yellow hair and the unclean sweetness of jasmine-flowers mixed with the hot sunshine and smells of the mill" (126). As he continues to think about Miss Herne, the smell of "unclean" flowers shifts to something more sinister and artificial: "The woman luxuriated in perfume; some heavy odour always hung about her. Holmes, thinking of her now, fancied he felt it stifling the air, and opened the window for breath. Patchouli or copperas,—what was the difference?" (126). Patchouli signifies bodies for sale, for its heavy scent was a proverbial favorite among prostitutes.[48] Holmes experiences the heavy artificial scent of imagined patchouli and the copperas smell of the mills as indistinguishably oppressive scents that stifle his breathing and signify Miss Herne's ownership of him. As Jean Pfaelzer writes, "Miss Herne's decadent sexuality ... has ... evolved into a female metaphor for the seductive power of industrial capitalism itself," and, through the patchouli allusion, directly with prostitution.[49] Invoking an aesthetics of disgust, the novel links repellant smells with repellant ideas that will, Holmes realizes, become part of himself once he sells his body to Miss Herne. His response is a feeling of suffocation that no open windows can obliterate, since the impurity of motives that the mingled smells represent signify a visceral sense of contamination.

At this point favoring intellectual reasoning over the evidence of his senses, Holmes signs the deed and commits himself to Miss Herne. His mistake is driven home a short while later, when, riding in a carriage with Miss Herne, he passes Margret on the road. Miss Herne mocks his relationship as "a second romaunt of 'King Cophetua and the Beggar Maid'" (137), an allusion to the African king Cophetua and his instant love for a beggar maid, Penelophon, whom he marries and elevates to his own status. By committing himself to Miss Herne and rejecting Margret, Holmes has failed as both an Emersonian individualist and as a romantic hero; indeed, in Davis's original plan, he was to die in the fire that destroys the mill.[50] But the King Cophetua story offers him a chance at redemption. If, as

Yellin suggests, Joe Yare is "a Black Destroyer, an African American responding to Old Testament justice with Old Testament vengeance" (286), the King Cophetua allusion links Holmes with African courage and New Testament mercy, overlooking class, as Cophetua did, in the name of love. Holmes is the white man who holds dominion not only over white women like Margret but also over the mixed-race and working-class poor like Lois and Joe Yare, and in this capacity his stiff-necked righteousness has harmed them. To redeem himself, he must model himself on the African and African American ways of merciful conduct modeled by King Cophetua and Lois Yare.

The alternative to Holmes for Margret is Dr. Knowles and his work among the poor. Both Holmes and Knowles value Margret for her ability to further their ambitious plans, but Knowles offers a wider scope beyond the domestic sphere. Echoing Davis's narrator in "Life in the Iron Mills" and its invitation to "[c]ome right down with me," Knowles tells Margret, "I want to show you a bit of hell: outskirt" (149). "It's time you knew your work, and forgot your weakness," he continues, her weakness being the "curse of pampered generations, her 'High Norman blood'" (150). In grim realism's classic discovery-of-squalor sequence, Dr. Knowles leads her to a room "where a flaring tallow-dip threw a saffron glare into the darkness. A putrid odour met them at the door" (150). As Margret adjusts to the "putrid odour" and the flare of light, she sees a place "swarming with human life" (150) of all ethnicities, with "drunken Irishmen," Italians, and runaway slaves completing the vision of an industrial hell promised by the catalog of waste that Margret experiences in the first chapter. Unlike Holmes, who fears contamination from the patchouli-scented charms of Miss Herne, Margret does not flinch from the test of touch. She exceeds Knowles's expectations by picking up a "child, kissing its brown face" (151). Knowles attributes this comfort with touching a member of another race to her southern heritage, drawing on the stereotype, perpetuated in *Uncle Tom's Cabin*, that although northerners preached liberation from slavery, they drew the line at touching African Americans, a reversal of the southerners' attitude.

In a scene that anticipates one in Wharton's *Summer*, Knowles leads her to another room, where she witnesses a scene of death: a "girl of fifteen, almost a child," lying dead in "a dirty plaid skirt, and stained velvet bodice, her neck and arms bare" (153), "neck" being a nineteenth-century euphemism for the body between the chin and the waist. The girl, Hetty, has drunk "herself to death—a most unpicturesque suicide" (153) after a life of shame. The naturalistic tableau of the body of an unmoving woman, often incompletely clad, who is either unconscious or dead, tests the spectator's powers of interpretation here as in Davis's "Life in the Iron Mills" and in Wharton's *Summer* and *The House of Mirth*. As in her willingness to pick up the African American child, Margret passes this test with flying colors. Instead of simply staring at the girl's body or being repelled by it, she pins her own "handkerchief about the child's young neck" (153). The scenes of enslaved childhood and brutalized womanhood she has witnessed have cracked Margret's habitual reserve. In touching the social abject (the little girl) and touching death without fearing the contamination that might result, Margret recognizes their bodies' current of humanity as one with her own. She agrees to help Dr. Knowles as the "dark and windy" storm outside subsides in "warm summer rain" (156), another symbolic analog for the cleansing release of her emotional turmoil.

Lois Yare presents an alternative to the embodied male rectitude of Stephen Holmes and Dr. Knowles. Her disorderly cart, "a home-made affair, patched up with wicker-work and bits of board" (53) contrasts with the orderly quality of the men's professions, evoking the domestic clutter and ramshackle structures that signify rebellion in regional stories. Lois's impulsive honesty and open, "child's face, quick, eager" contrasts with their rigid features and ideological bookkeeping, much as the "deformity of her legs" (55) that makes her walk with a "curious rolling jerk" (55) and "the taint in her veins of black blood" (56) renders her as doubly distinct from the two men. She is peripatetic where they are stationary, flexible where they are rigid, as poor as they are wealthy, and a disabled woman of color in a culture of empowered white masculinity. Unlike the Creek heritage of Dr. Knowles, which seems to influence only his concern for the poor, the linking of Lois's disability and her African American heritage evokes what Stephen Knadler has described as the debates over citizenship in a post-Reconstruction era, in which race and disability were linked and "disability was recruited as a medicalized biopolitical sign of the legal child-like dependent status of African Americans."[51]

The description of Lois as having a "child's face" would seem to confirm Knadler's point, yet the combination of her face and her "old and stunted" body (55) suggests a character that, despite having "that pitiable beauty you always see in deformed people" (55), is both contradictory and unreadable in ordinary terms. Davis's recourse to direct address—"you always see"—underscores the disparaging and stereotypical categorization of "deformed people" that the narrator seems to place on Lois. Framed by an elaborate description of the incongruous, grafted-on quality of Lois's cart, her unusual gait, and her young face that does not match her old body, however, the catchall term "deformed people" is rendered as inaccurate as well as insulting. At first drawing the reader into agreeing with this casual stereotyping by "you" and "always," the narrator undercuts the label and exchanges it for a more accurate one, calling Lois a "queer little body" (57). Lois is "queer" in that she refuses to conform to the stereotypes of disability with which the narrator has just forced the reader to agree. Much as her prosthetic cart grants her mobility despite her disability, Lois's Christlike love queers the grandiose definitions of virtue under which Holmes and Knowles labor.

The conclusion of the novel confines Margret within the domestic sphere once more, albeit with a broader sense of the world beyond. In his final scene with Margret, Holmes emerges from Emersonian egotism to admit his neglect of Margret's love and of his own better self, yet there is more than a hint of mastery and patriarchy in these actions. Dr. Knowles has transformed Margret into a worker rather than a woman. Holmes, his near-homophonic twin, reverses the process. As the two stand in the "red fire-light" near the end of the book, Holmes drapes her with a "crimson shawl" and loosens her hair, no longer a drab brown but "a mist of tawny gold," bringing color to her life at last. His words show the price that Margret must pay for this renewed vision of life: "I need warmth and freshness and light: my wife shall bring them to me. She shall be no strong-willed reformer, standing alone" (242) but a wife who "keeps her heart and its secrets for me alone" (249). The public work that Margret had devoted to the poor becomes a private charity for one: Stephen Holmes.

Davis's conclusion can be read in at least two ways. Seen as a redemption narrative and as a love story, both Holmes and Margret get what they want, each other and redemption through trauma. Both combine the traits of the other gender with their own initially rigid conceptions of themselves and, in so doing, reveal a more complete human being. Throughout the novel Holmes has been dominated by women: his mother's Calvinism dictates his judgmental views, and Miss Herne's money has so emasculated him that he cannot behave honorably toward Margret. In practicing womanly forgiveness and tenderness, however, Holmes's masculinity is restored rather than threatened. He looks down on Lois from his position as "a powerful figure, with a face supreme, masterful, but tender; you will find no higher type of manhood" (212). Margret is transformed because "[s]omething of Lois's live, universal sympathy has come into [Margret's] narrow, intenser nature" (266). But in a pattern repeated in other works, for the white heroine, Margret, to live, the disabled African American character, Lois, must die.[52] The happy ending of the novel strikes another jarring note, for by the penultimate chapter Margret and Stephen have been reunited and the Howths have struck oil. Davis has already signaled her impatience with the necessity for this happy conclusion, first by dispensing with the good fortune at the beginning of chapter 11 in order to linger on Lois Yare's saintly death, and then by opening it with the simple declaration "I am going to end my story now" (247), thus breaking the spell of the text through direct address. She snaps the story closed with an authorial decisiveness that calls attention to the fictionality of her enterprise, shutting readers out where she had once drawn them in and abruptly cutting off the current of affect that she had created.

Elizabeth Stuart Phelps's Redemptive Recycling

Like that of Rebecca Harding Davis, the fiction of Elizabeth Stuart Phelps (1844–1911) combines grim realism with social justice, and like Davis, Phelps invests her fiction with an affective charge that situates the reader in the text. Based on the famous Pemberton Mill collapse on January 10, 1860, her story "The Tenth of January" combines a standard mill-girl romance plot with an unusually gruesome level of detail in its grimly realistic denouement. Three other pieces of fiction, "One of the Elect" (1865), *Hedged In* (1870), and *A Singular Life* (1894), reveal the evolution of her treatment of the fallen woman. Called "Magdalene," the conventionalized, almost typological sinning heroine Maggie in "One of the Elect," she emerges as the more complex survivor "Magdalena" or Lena of *A Singular Life*.

"THE TENTH OF JANUARY"

"The Tenth of January," first appearing in the *Atlantic Monthly* in March 1868 and later collected in *Men, Women, and Ghosts* (1869), blends traditional romance with what Davis had called "A Story of To-Day," undercutting the traditional romance with grim realism. In establishing this pattern, Phelps invites a visceral response to the horrors that she describes in vivid detail. The affective charge of the story relies on the contrast between the reader's anticipation of the conventions of the mill-girl romance that begin the story and the shocking violence that concludes it. For readers familiar with the real-life Pemberton Mill tragedy, the title brings a "ripped from the headlines" immediacy as well as the grim picturesqueness that gives the story its power.

The story seems at first a piece of mill-girl fiction like other stories by Phelps. Asenath Martyn, called "Sene" by her pretty friend Del Ivory and "Senath" by her father, lives in the midst of waste, a "damp, unwholesome place" with a broken fence. Disfigured by her drunken mother, Asenath conceals her scarred face and shoulders beneath a cape, but hers is not the typical story of the mill girl as starved and exploited victim. Her home is neatly mended, and her father, a shoemaker, is still valued for the craft that industrialization has wiped out elsewhere. In addition, "her employers dealt honorably by her ... [and] she was fairly paid."[53] Despite her disability, she has a suitor, Richard Cross, who promises that Asenath will "have me always" (55). After hearing her pretty rival Del Ivory's confession of love for Richard, however, and after seeing the two together, Asenath realizes that her duty is to give Richard up, in what would conventionally be the moral point of the self-sacrificing romance plot (59).

But Phelps has already signaled her departure from the conventions of romance, first through her choice of the disabled character as romantic heroine, which breaks up the pairing of conventional heroine and disabled friend, and then through authorial commentary. When Asenath realizes that Richard and the conventionally pretty Del love one another, she struggles with her conscience about giving him up and recalls "Floracita, in the novel" as a moral guide to the correct action (66). A common feature in the work of Louisa May Alcott and other nineteenth-century women writers, the unattributed quotation or allusion to "the story" or "the fable" compliments the reader's cultural literacy and makes her supply the allusion for herself, making her complicit with the text.[54] Here, "Floracita, in the novel" refers to a mixed-race character in Lydia M. Child's *A Romance of the Republic*, who according to Phelps's narrator "never so far forgets the whole duty of a heroine as to struggle, waver, doubt, delay" (66). As in Davis's *Margret Howth*, an African American literary character demonstrates for a conflicted white character what the correct moral path should be. Yet Asenath "was no heroine" (67), the narrator reminds us, and this is "no novel" but a biography, with all the darkness and longing of real life. Unlike a conventional heroine, Asenath is depressed enough to flirt with suicide, first in her reckless swinging out over the river on a young aspen tree after a conversation with Del, and later on a walk with Richard to a "dreadful place" (73) of frozen isolation, when she fantasizes about her death and Richard's in the icy waters of the dark river.

This variation on a duty-versus-love romance plot descends in the second part of the story into the violence and tragedy associated with grim realism and naturalism. Asenath, miserable in her indecision after talking with Del and with Richard, awakens on the tenth of January to a red sky, a traditional portent of danger ahead. At work in the mill, she looks up just in time to see "iron pillars reel, and vast machinery throw up its helpless, giant arms, and a tangle of human faces blanch and writhe" (79). In the classic naturalistic exchange of machinery becoming human and vice versa, the mill and its machinery become human, and human beings become disaggregated into a "tangle" like that of vines or wires. As part of the disaggregation, Asenath, trapped in the inferno of wreckage, sees that "one of her fingers ... was gone; it was the finger which held Dick's little engagement ring" (81). The physical severing of her relationship with Richard through the gruesome loss of her engagement finger symbolizes to her the correctness of the choice she has struggled to make about releasing Richard from their engagement: "This, then, was the way. It was better so. God had provided himself a lamb for the burnt-offering" (86). Having flirted twice with death by ice and water, as Phelps has heavily foreshadowed in the episodes of swinging in the tree and of her suicidal wishes during the last walk with Richard, Asenath instead dies by fire, accepting death so that Del might be rescued in her place.

Phelps uses a real tragedy, the Pemberton Mill Fire in Lawrence, Massachusetts, not only to ground but also to undercut the romance plot that she has set in motion. Although the realism plot seems a sharp departure from the romance plot, the story's original *Atlantic Monthly* readers would have immediately recognized the foreboding in the unusually specific time and place of its opening paragraphs—"Lawrence, Massachusetts, in the last of November, 1859" (45). Much of what appears in "The Tenth of January" is confirmed in newspaper accounts and *An Authentic History of the Lawrence Calamity*, which was published in the year of the tragedy and includes first-person testimonials from those who survived. Asenath's experience combines several of these "touching stories." The "Scotch girl" with her arm torn off in Phelps's story, for example, recalls the "poor girl, alive and fully conscious, [who] was dragged from the east end of the fallen mass, with her left arm torn from its socket,"[55] and the highly symbolic loss of Asenath's engagement finger borrows from an episode in which a young woman trapped by machinery "had two fingers caught in the machinery. In an agony of despair she literally tore them off and escaped" (*Authentic History* 20). As Asenath sinks "dreamily" (85) into a trance of observation after the collapse, she hears that an overseer "had cut his throat, and before the flames touched him he was taken out" (85), echoing a report that the overseer, Maurice Thomas, had cut his own throat before being rescued (*Authentic History* 15). Asenath's choice that Del be rescued instead of herself has its genesis in two incidents: in one, a child, "knowing she was pinned and would not be rescued" (*Authentic History* 19), gave her pay packet to another girl to give to her father, and in the other, Lizzie Flint, a young woman, bore the weight of a beam without complaint and helped her male companion to survive. She fainted after he was rescued and was left behind to die in the flames as the cries of others were answered.

Integrating real events into the romance plot helps to impose order on a senseless event. Despite Phelps's positioning of Asenath's death as Christian consolation, the story, its use of journalistic details, and its overt rejection of the mill-girl romance plot cannot but remind the reader that indifferent machines and indifferent fate destroy the human beings helplessly trapped within their power. Having drawn readers in through the familiar outlines of the romance plot, Phelps turns their engagement with the text and with Asenath as a character into a brutally naturalistic tragedy, complete with dismemberment, suicides, and horrifying deaths by fire, in which the worthy characters are left to die while those unfit are rescued, a reflection of indifferent nature.

"ONE OF THE ELECT"

Appearing in *Men, Women, and Ghosts* with "The Tenth of January," "One of the Elect" was first published as "Magdalene" in the September 1865 issue of *Hours at*

Home: A Popular Magazine of Religious and Useful Literature. As its title suggests, the story chronicles a family's forgiveness of its erring daughter when she returns from the city to die in their rural home. On a cold, windy night, Amos Ryck and his wife Martha recall that this is the seventh anniversary of their daughter Maggie's disappearance. Martha, on her way up to bed, builds up the fire and unlocks the door, but as a deacon in the church, "one of the elect," Amos cannot countenance her action. The door at home provides a transition to the next scene, in the city, where Maggie, now called Meg, stands outside the door of the Temple, the name recalling Jesus's action in throwing the moneychangers out of the temple. Hearing a hymn whose words recall Handel's *Messiah*, she repeats them to herself: "Wounded—for our transgressions," she murmurs, wondering "he was bruised for her,—for *her*?"[56] But like Crane's Maggie Johnson, she is physically shunned by all when she seeks help. A child approaches and is told "Don't touch that woman," and a lady "clad in velvet, brushed against her, then gathered her costly garments with a hand ringed and dazzling with diamonds, shrinking as if she had touched some accursed thing" (186). Even the pastor offers nothing more than a referral to the institutional charity of the "Penitents' Retreat" (189).

Driven away, Maggie heads toward her childhood home, "tired of being Meg" and recalling her childhood name, Maggie, and the "mournful, unconscious prophecy of the name . . . Magdalene" (191). As the snowstorm swirls around her, she looks "from the city to the drifted path" and walks "where the snow lay pure and untrodden" (192), reflecting her "drift" from the "pure and untrodden" path. Nearly frozen, she "crawl[s] up the path on her hands and knees," an unconscious gesture of penitence, before "kissing the very dumb, unanswering wood" of her parents' door that had been shut against her (195). Phelps returns to the device of the door, which now swings open at a touch, and the acceptance of Muff, the dog, to foreshadow the welcome that Maggie will receive. The next morning, Maggie's mother finds her on the floor, her arms about the dog. "The door was unlocked," she tells her mother, to which Martha replies, "It has been unlocked every night for seven years, my child" (198). As if her presence in her mother's arms can erase time and corruption, Maggie gradually transforms into a child once more, "her features in the firelight softening and melting, with the old child-look coming into them" (198). The scene of forgiveness is complete when Amos comes in and says he will not send her away. Recognizing that she is dying—"I think I shall be your little girl again"—(200) she assumes her final name, "Magdalene, chosen from all eternity" (199) and dies smiling, her innocence restored.

"One of the Elect" is a parable of the fallen woman, with its four stages of return, repentance, acceptance, and redemption through death. Maggie's journey takes her from the city and moral death to her home and physical death, because for the fallen woman, death is the only possible redemptive act. The double meaning of the story's later title only becomes apparent at the end of the story, for in traveling back to Christ, who "was bruised for her," Maggie truly becomes "one of the elect" as "the light flashed broader and brighter about the room," signifying her transfiguration and acceptance into heaven. The transformation of Maggie into a child, with a child's death, the tears in the eyes of all three, the dog's innocent acceptance, and Maggie's "transfigured" (200) face recall the deaths of innocents in other works, including that of Lois Yare. But the parable structure leaves Maggie and her fallen cohort with no possibilities for a life after leaving prostitution, a problem that Phelps addresses in Hedged In and A Singular Life.

HEDGED IN

Hedged In provides a different perspective on the fallen woman. As in "Life in the Iron Mills," its first-person narrator, Jane Briggs, reports on and indicts a particular social evil: the stigma of unwed motherhood. As the novel opens, in a typically naturalistic conflation of waste material and wasted human potential, the narrator picks her way along an alley, where nature is represented by "a little cold chickweed" (3), and "heaps of babies and garbage became distinct" only with the narrator's careful vision (3). In a classic discovery-of-squalor sequence, the narrator asks a ragpicker to see the occupant of one of the rooms, and the ragpicker "nodded sullenly, flinging open the door without knock or warning" as is customary in such scenes (5). In the "full and foul" tenement room, drunken women and babies crowd the space, and, looking through the window, the narrator sees "a muddy line of harbor, wharves, and a muddy sky" (5), a dead-end visual panorama like that which greeted Davis's Margret Howth.

Peering through the "unclean steam" from a woman washing clothes in the corner, the steam embodying the smell of slum contamination made visible, Jane Briggs sees "a certain dull stain, which bore a rude resemblance to a spider" (5). As "a hospitable lady in a red frock" informs the narrator with relish, it marks the spot where an earlier unwed mother had dashed out the brains of her infant. Closing "the sunken door with suddenly blinded eyes" and stumbling over neglected babies as she exits "back through the filth into pure air and sunshine," Jane imagines the scene a few years earlier as if seeing a fifteen-year-old girl, Nixy Trent, on "the mass of rags and straw upon which she lay with her two-days baby" (13). Like Deb in "Life in the Iron Mills," who is scarcely distinguishable from the rags she lies upon, Nixy and her child represent the culture's waste as they lie before the observer, their reclining positions suggesting the abject position that they occupy. There is no instinct of maternal love where poverty is concerned, the novel suggests, for Nixy's baby is an irritation to her, and she spends time idly wondering how difficult it would be to strangle him or to dash his brains out as the previous occupant of her room had done with her child.

Nixy's choices are limited. Dr. Dyke Burtis, a sympathetic physician, offers her a spot in a Magdalene home, but Nixy refuses, citing her knowledge of orphan asylums as proof of just how punitive a so-called "charitable" organization could be: "I know all about your 'sylums.... I ain't going from one prison to another so easy" (27). The presence of the baby bars her from employment when she tries to find "honest work" rather than work in a dance-hall, the novel's metaphor for a potential descent into prostitution. She feels no love for the baby although she "tried to like him" (58), and so, as she would with any other burden, she leaves him on a doorstep and moves on after being turned away on every side by so-called "good" women. As in "One of the Elect" and *A Singular Life*, Phelps indicates that Nixy, through her love of the affective medium of music, is spiritually wayward but not emotionally hardened. Hearing Monsieur Jacques, the guitar-maker, singing and playing, "Can there be?—can there be? / Mercy still—At the bottom of the hill" (35), Nixy is moved to declare that "There's honest things to do, and I'll hunt till I find em!" (42). "Honest things" include work as a servant for the hypocritically righteous Mrs. Zerviah Myrtle, who turns Nixy out when she learns of Nixy's past. Sick and dazed, Nixy falls against the window of Jane Briggs's friend Mrs. Margaret Purcell and is rescued.

At this point, Nixy has followed the same path as Phelps's Maggie in her wanderings and in seeking only death rather than redemption. But *Hedged In* goes further by asking the question too neatly elided by having the fallen woman die: what happens next? Helping Nixy to reenter society will be neither pleasant nor easy. As Mrs. Purcell explains in a letter to Jane Briggs, "If I had gone into the business of daguerreotyping for the rest of my life, the paper would have smelled of ether, and the pen would have told of silver-baths. As I have chosen the business of saving one wicked little girl from Thicket Street, are you prepared for the details of 'the trade'?" (124). As the photography metaphor suggests, grim realism, like photography, represents an unflinching version of the truth, signified by Phelps's metaphor of the strong and viscerally unpleasant smells of the photographic chemicals. To prepare her correspondent Jane Briggs, and by extension the reader, for the expression of these truths, Mrs. Purcell inserts this warning in epistolary form, setting possible reactions to it apart from the main narrative. Her strategy replicates the well-worn practice of the author's apology for her book, a tradition from Anne Bradstreet and John Bunyan to Stephen Crane, who wrote in Hamlin Garland's copy of *Maggie: A Girl of the Streets* a sentiment similar to Mrs. Purcell's: "It is inevitable that you will be greatly shocked by this book.... For it tries to show that environment is a tremendous thing in the world and frequently shapes lives regardless."[57] By anticipating Jane Briggs's disapproval, Mrs. Purcell indemnifies herself (and Phelps) from charges of indecency or sensationalism.

Nor, as Phelps suggests in all her works, is repentance solely the task of the rescued fallen woman, for rescuers have as much learning to do as those whom they save. Mrs. Purcell and her daughter Christina, despite her Christlike name, have their own prejudices to overcome. Christina is shocked at Nixy's coarse friends, and Mrs. Purcell initially denies Nixy the right to wear pink ribbons or a white jacket like Christina's, an act that differentiates the two girls' levels of innocence through the colors of their clothing (135, 136).[58] Specifying the colors and their prohibition is important, for because of her class and her status as a fallen woman, Nixy not only cannot wear white, with its connotations of purity, but is also not quite white herself. When she falls dangerously ill, she plucks at "the counterpane with her little brown fingers" (125). Christina, in contrast, dresses in white and has "eyes like a white star" (89); when Nixy first sees her, she exclaims, "She's so white!" (130). In keeping with their mutual progress toward redemption, Mrs. Purcell faces down school board members who want to fire "Eunice Trent" (Nixy's proper name) because of her past. Nixy, in turn, demonstrates her redemption by rejecting her old friends; by finding and reclaiming her child, Kent, from the orphanage where he has been placed; and by refusing to marry Dick, her child's father, because their mutual wrong demands suffering as expiation. Nixy has excelled at mathematics as first a student and then a teacher, and in the novel's Christian calculus, she reasons that his reappearance was "mathematics, not affliction" (252), a just retribution for her relationship with him.

Nixy has learned the mental calculations necessary for her redemption, but she has not yet mastered the emotional ones. In her treatment of the novel as benevolence fiction, Jill Bergman suggests that "as long as Nixy needs mothering herself, she will never be able to 'reform'" or to "mother her own child."[59] Nixy has failed to achieve this with Kent, her son, for although she tries, she does not love him and is sorry for having so little feeling when he dies. Despite her response to Kent, mothering is the key to Nixy's regeneration, for it is something that she can extend outward to help others like herself. Committing herself to a life of service, Nixy looks to her future as a helper to the increasingly ailing Mrs. Purcell and as a social worker among the inhabitants of Thicket Street. She has long been treated with respect by Mrs. Purcell and Christina, despite her despair that "[s]ociety had hedged her in on every side" (210). Her life of service renders her not only a Christian but also a white woman, for although she has never, since she had been rebuffed over the white jacket, sought to wear any color but black, she wears all white at Christina's wedding at Christina's request. Having grown from a young girl with "brown fingers" to pure whiteness, Nixy's transformation into the white Eunice is complete, something the text renders by calling her Eunice from this point forward.

As Nixy sits apart from the rest of the wedding party, her "dress changed from white to gold, to pallid pink, to rose, to red" as "all the world lay bathed in redness," a natural apotheosis in which, as she interprets it, nature mimics "the blood of Jesus Christ, which cleanseth all from sin" (290). It brings Nixy's journey full circle, from the blood of the murdered infant under which she spent the days after giving birth to her son, to the blood of Christ above her. Nixy's redemption is confirmed in the book's final scene when she climbs the stairs in her "heavy white dress" (293). Shortly thereafter, a giant tempest, an echo of the one that had occurred during the night of her son's death, strikes the house. Mrs. Purcell and Jane Briggs find Eunice's body, still clad in the white dress and clinging to a giant wooden cross, an enactment of the line "Simply to the cross I cling" from the hymn "Rock of Ages."[60] Although Eunice cannot marry, Phelps grants her not only Christian redemption before her death but also a pattern for a successful life of service, one that requires change and forgiveness on the part of benefactors as well as contrition on the part of the fallen woman.

A SINGULAR LIFE

Phelps's turn-of-the-century *A Singular Life* rests uneasily on the cusp of modernity, with its intimations of urban reform, its nineteenth-century treatment of the perfect Christian hero, and its portrayal of two different types of the New Woman: the upper-class Helen Carruth and working-class Magdalena. Writing at the end of the century, when the masculinity crisis was in full force, Phelps adapted her typical narrative to emphasize Bayard's masculinity as well as his Christianity. Beginning with the moment in which, in an echo and reversal of Perley's encounter with Sip in *The Silent Partner*, Bayard rescues the drunkard Job Slip by pulling him into a carriage, Bayard uses his brawn as well as his brains in the service of the Christian message. According to Roxanne Harde, Bayard combines "the feminization of the Christian church, Muscular Christianity, and the Social Gospel." Yet Phelps promotes a church that prizes strong women as well as strong men, with Helen Carruth and Lena representing a New Woman's strength and vigor that makes them fit comrades for Bayard.[61]

Emanuel Bayard is a poor young theological student who takes reform to be his life's work. He is neither buried in abstruse theological doctrine, like his teacher, Professor Carruth, nor is he a milquetoast who trims his opinions to fit the expectations of his audience, like his hypocritical schoolmate, the Reverend Fenton. Christian acts rather than Christian theology become Bayard's hallmark as a preacher, and he chooses a ministry among backsliding drunkards and prostitutes.[62] He establishes his mission in the notorious Angel's Alley in the port town of Windover, Phelps's Gloucester under another name, and uses his Harvard-honed muscular training as well as his theological knowledge to minister to his flock. He swims out to rescue those on the wreck of the *Clara Em*, refuses to back down when the saloonkeeper Ben Trawl threatens him with physical violence, and redeems Job Slip after Job has fallen off the temperance wagon again. Additional proof of his masculinity lies in his reading of Darwin and Huxley, for masculinity in this novel is coded as modern, and modernity is marked by readings in evolutionary theory.

Bayard's Muscular Christianity parallels the physical and emotional strength of the two women whose lives are entwined with Bayard's until his early death: Helen Carruth, who, in an inversion of the usual plot of women reforming men, converts to a social justice message through Bayard's love, and Magdalena, or "Lena," a young, working-class woman whom Bayard converts through his respectful treatment of her. Helen Carruth is a New Woman who takes pride in being intellectually and physically fit, reading Herbert Spencer's *Law of Rhythm*, hiking, and literally as well as figuratively rowing her own boat. But in keeping with Phelps's theme of rescuers needing rescue, Helen is searching for a sense of purpose: she is "no more use in the world—in this *awful* world—than the artificial pansies in my hat."[63] Susan V. Donaldson has argued that Phelps typically reverses the gender roles of hero and heroine, as in *Doctor Zay*, by creating heroes who cling to or otherwise behave hesitantly in contrast to the briskly decisive heroines they encounter.[64] Bayard's tentative courtship of Helen fits this pattern, for she meets him more than halfway when they confess their love to each other, and she brushes aside his reticence and mortification over the imagined insult of confessing his love before he can propose to her. In Donaldson's terms, Bayard acts as the overscrupulous heroine and Helen as the voice of reason, reversing their roles of hero and heroine.

The tertiary story of Lena reveals the fallen woman as a New Woman, one whose redemption does not end in death. Lena shares a version of her full first name, "Magdalena," with her predecessor Maggie of "One of the Elect," and, like Nixy of *Hedged In*, she had a child out of wedlock when she was fifteen years old (303). But Lena is a more fully realized character than the others. She backslides and redeems herself, keeps her vigorous ways, and never becomes unrealistically malleable and saintly like her predecessors. Her "coarse fur shoulder cape" and "rude face" blooming with healthy color (118) indicate her working-class origins, but as in "One of the Elect" and *Hedged In*, her susceptibility to music and her beautiful singing voice demonstrate her essential goodness. As she walks down Angel's Alley, Bayard asks her to come into his church because "they might like the help of your voice" (181), and she does so. Later, however, as Bayard prepares to preach to a crowd, he hears the other side of Lena's voice, "a rude sound ... a girl's coarse laugh" (262). As in its use as a descriptor of Lena's face, "rude" connotes primitive vigor rather than a simple lack of propriety. The difference between Lena and earlier heroines lies in this distinction between coarseness and refinement, for although Lena grows in refinement when she gives up her life of prostitution, she retains a level of cheerfully coarse but refreshingly natural behavior throughout the book. In equating coarseness with vigor rather than with sexual waywardness, Phelps creates a character that never entirely abandons her original personality but instead learns figuratively to modulate her natural voice to fit the aims of church rather than saloon.

In Lena's story, *A Singular Life* develops beyond the allegorical pattern of return, repentance, acceptance, and redemption through death. Instead Phelps recycles the fallen woman into a useful member of society as Lena confesses the wrongs done to others, makes amends for them, and returns to useful work despite occasional backsliding. When Bayard confronts Lena after one episode, she declares herself ready to die. Again using the instrument of Lena's voice, Bayard gives her a sense of another path, telling her, "You might have been a singer, Lena, and sung noble things" (301). He commands her to "look into my face" as if in a mirror, and she sees "[a]ll the loathing, all the horror, all the repulsion" that he feels for the sin (301). Lena begins her redemptive process by telling Bayard the story of her baby born out of wedlock and the difficulties she has had in earning a respectable living. A nonplussed but earnest Bayard offers "the groping masculine idea that a domestic career was the only one open to a girl like Lena." But as Lena herself recognizes, the employment available for fallen women has not kept pace with the theoretical fact of their rehabilitation. As she explains, "There ain't a lady in Christendom would put up with me" (304), the unconscious irony in her term "Christendom" resonating in the reader's mind. Although reformed street girls were retrained as servants, it was nearly impossible for them to be hired, since an unblemished moral character was necessary to be employed as a domestic servant. Knowing this, and understanding that her free-spirited nature would not be acceptable in service, Lena insists that she will work at the gunpowder factory instead, a more fitting place for her personality.

Just as Bayard has saved Lena's life, so she is able to save his for a time, another of Phelps's gestures of reciprocal salvation. Hearing that Bayard's temperance fight to close the rum shops has succeeded too well, and that Ben Trawl plans to kill Bayard for it, Lena attempts to save Bayard by warning him to leave town. Bayard declares that he will stay, however, to keep his promise to treat Lena as a decent woman by "lift[ing] his hat" to her as he enters the church. Hearing this, Lena drops her "dark face" but then lifts it again "with the touching pride of lost self-respect regained" (402). Although she watches Bayard to protect him, she cannot keep Ben Trawl from throwing a rock that strikes Bayard in the chest. With no thought to her own safety, Lena races into the bay and catches Ben Trawl by the throat, strangling him with her strong hands even as he tries to drown her. After Ben is taken into custody, she explains, "I thought I'd be able to stop him. I'm pretty strong.... I see [*sic*] him fling that rock!" (413). Instead of sliding gracefully into death, like the twice-named Maggie-Magdalene, or finding death as an apotheosis to a reformed life, like the redeemed Nixy-Eunice, Lena, shedding the "Magdalena" portion of her identity, uses physical strength and fierce determination to protect the man who had protected her. Bayard, called the "Christman" (426), has died for her, but Lena has redeemed herself through her actions. Lacking Helen Carruth's educated perspective and middle-class ways, Lena is a working-class New Woman whose vigor and physical strength match her commitment to acting on moral principles, especially if they involve the protection of a man who is important to her.

To emphasize how much *A Singular Life* looks to the future, Phelps expands her repertoire of symbolic effects to include not only storms, shipwrecks, and red-tinged sunsets but also an unusual number of references to technology for 1894. The metaphoric use of communications and transportation technologies, including electric cars, electric signs, and phonographs, blend the modernity of the framing message with the antiquity of the subject matter. When the *Clara Em* is wrecked and men on the shore hold hands to their ears, they hear "shouts from the vessel" against the wind: "The whirling blast, like the cone of a mighty phonograph, bore a faint articulation from the wreck" (119), nature acting as technology rather than the other way around. In this image, Phelps intensifies the tragedy of the doomed *Clara Em*, for as Jonathan Sterne explains in *The Audible Past*, early sound recording was a medium associated with death, since "*death somehow explained and shaped the cultural power of sound recording*" (italics in original) as another "product of a culture that had learned to can and to embalm."[65] The haunted voices from the wreck and the distanced, quavering voices of early sound technology such as Edison's wax cylinders, which for the first time in history reproduced voices of those not present, not only resembled each other but also required technological magnification through the "cone of a mighty phonograph."

Electricity and illumination play an equally important role in *A Singular Life*. Early in his mission, Bayard had enticed parishioners into his Angel's Alley church with a prominent sign, a "beautiful new transparency" that "flashed out in strong white and scarlet lights the strange words, now grown familiar to Angel Alley:—'THE CHURCH OF THE LOVE OF CHRIST'" (180). When antitemperance forces set fire to the church in Angel's Alley and it burns to ashes, miraculously "the electric wire which fed the illuminated sign in front of the mission had not been disconnected by the fire" (322). Although the first part of the illuminated sign has been destroyed, the "little colored glass globes" that remain project "four white and scarlet words ... THE LOVE OF CHRIST" (322). Given its never-failing light, the sign is a visible reminder of the omniscience and omnipresence of Christ, conveying the message technologically even if the human messenger has faltered. Phelps confirms this use of technology unambiguously after Bayard is struck by the rock. Throughout the novel the electric railway car has played a role. Now the townspeople volunteer to carry him to the electric car, the "people's carriage" (415), so that he can return home before his death. He is transported physically by their bodies and then by the carriage that represents them. As he is carried from the car to his home, the fishermen see a "red flash ran over earth and sea and sky," a red flash that dyes Helen's "bridal white" dress, confirming Bayard's apotheosis and mirroring the similar moment in *Hedged In*. After Bayard's death, the fishermen put on an "extraordinary display of the signs of public mourning ... the flags of Windover floated at half-mast" (426), as if a beloved public official had died.

Bayard, whom Phelps described in her autobiography *Chapters from a Life* as her "dearest hero," signifies the public man as well as the religious man, as the historical context for the novel makes clear.[66] Bayard is a public man, much beloved by those who rely on his leadership, and in the midst of a crowd he is wounded—assassinated—by Ben Trawl, a disgruntled figure representing opposing interests. Carried home by the electric car, Bayard lingers seven days before dying. For Phelps's original audience, the image of a wounded man carried to a place of rest on a specially cleared train track would inevitably have recalled the assassination of President James A. Garfield on July 2, 1881, by Charles Guiteau, a disappointed office seeker. Garfield survived the shooting but grew increasingly worse through the ministrations of the physicians surrounding him. As he declined in the Washington heat, a specially built railroad spur and train conveyed Garfield to the home of Charles Francklyn in Long Branch, New Jersey, on September 6, 1881. Although doctors felt that the cool sea air might contribute more to his recovery than the miasmas of Washington, Garfield died on September 19.[67]

By 1894–95 when Phelps published *A Singular Life*, reflections on the Garfield presidency were appearing in public media in preparation for the fifteenth anniversary of his death in 1896. Augustus Saint-Gaudens's statue of Garfield, commissioned in 1889, was completed in 1895 and dedicated in 1896, and the February 1896 serialization of *Chapters from a Life* ran concurrently with lengthy features about Garfield, including Murat Halstead's "The Tragedy of the Garfield Administration." Although Bayard lingers only seven days instead of several weeks before his death, the brutal assassination by a disgruntled enemy, the details of the train, the days that elapse before the man's death, and the massive outpouring of grief with flags at half-mast at his passing mirror those surrounding Garfield's assassination. The Garfield parallels confirm Phelps's point that a "Christman" may be more man than Christ, and that engaging with rather than simply preaching about social problems can regenerate lives. Adding depth and historic resonance to the reform plot that Phelps had used earlier in *The Silent Partner* and *Hedged In*, the assassination parallels in *A Singular Life* suggest civic as well as religious reform on a national scale. In this and in its use of technology and historical parallels, it models a reform text for a modern era, one that infuses not only strong men but also strong women into reform discourse.

Wyman's *Poverty Grass* and the Failure of the Industrial Home

For Lillie Buffum Chace Wyman (1847–1929), social activism was a family legacy as well as an individual passion. Part of a family of prominent Quaker mill owners in Rhode Island, Wyman grew up in the abolitionist movement and counted Frederick Douglass, Sojourner Truth, and William Wells Brown among her family's friends. Her mother, the abolitionist Elizabeth Chace, had advocated for prison reform after the Civil War, testifying before government commissions and writing nonfiction pieces such as "The Prevention of Pauperism and Crime" (1877). After the war, Wyman focused on industrial reform in studies of factory life such as "The Village System" (1888) and "Girls in a Factory Valley" (1896) and on the history of the abolition movement as she saw it. She wrote of celebrated cases of slaves captured and returned under the Fugitive Slave Law, most notably those of Anthony Burns and of Margaret Garner, whose story of killing her children rather than returning them to slavery Wyman retold for the *New England Magazine* in 1891, nearly a hundred years before Toni Morrison made Garner's case the basis of *Beloved*.[68] In 1924, Angelina Weld Grimké (1880–1958) prefaced her review of Wyman's *Gertrude of Denmark*, a feminist retelling of *Hamlet*, by praising not only Wyman's "true literary gift" but also her promotion of abolitionism and "an equality of opportunity with the white man, politically, educationally, and socially. She is one of the very few fearless enough to push their reasoning to its logical conclusion, for social equality with her means intermarriage."[69]

In her 1886 story collection *Poverty Grass* as well as in her nonfiction, Wyman focuses on the bodies of women workers as prisoners of the system and on the bodies of children as the system's innocent victims. In particular, she concentrates on what may be termed a failure of mothering in the industrial home. The term "industrial home" has meaning at several levels: the literal space of the reform school or "industrial home" that is the setting for Wyman's best-known story, "The Child of the State"; the tenements owned, policed, and neglected by the factory owners; and the metaphor of the vanished industrial home that existed within what Wyman terms the "manorial system" of factory work. Anticipating the monstrous mother tales common to naturalism, Wyman's stories of failed mothering indict the failed stewardship and callous abuse of indifferent factory owners. Ostensibly stepping in to replace the neglectful, abusive parent, the factory system itself becomes the abusive parent, and its products are the broken bodies and spirits of children. Just as the factory cares only about the profits to be made from each child's body, so too is the parent within the manufacturing system concerned primarily with the child's wages. Neither the state, in "The Child of the State," nor the educated, upper-middle-class families of "And Joe" in Wyman's *Poverty Grass* (1886) are powerful enough to interrupt the cycle of industrial abuse that renders disability and social dysfunction a normal condition in the mill town. The best hope for the mill town and the nation are the cross-class and interethnic marriages modeled by couples in "Luke Gardiner's Love" and "Valentine's Chance."

Considered by W. D. Howells and Jane Atteridge Rose as one of Wyman's best stories, "The Child of the State" demonstrates the failure of mothering on an institutional level.[70] In it, Josie Welch, an intelligent, impulsive girl, becomes "a child of the state" and ends up in the reformatory system that ultimately destroys her, the fate that Nixy Trent avoided in *Hedged In*. Wyman takes care to show that Josie is not doomed by heredity. On the contrary, Josie "had the instincts that in higher ranks of our society are called Bohemian," but in her station she looks for excitement in the wrong places, running away frequently until her aunt has her arrested and sent to reform school at age ten.[71] In the superintendent's mistaken nod to nineteenth-century views on gender, the school promotes inequality of treatment: boys are given a play yard for their rough-and-tumble exercise, but girls have only the corners of the laundry yard and cannot run about, a detail especially significant for Wyman and her mother, who, like Louisa May Alcott, promoted physical activity, dress reform, and a healthful, Grahamite diet. Worse, although boys are taught a trade, girls are taught only housework, a useless gesture since no one will hire the morally suspect girls.

One day a well-dressed woman, Mrs. Keyes, and her daughter visit the school. Echoing Wyman's views, Mrs. Keyes castigates the superintendent: "[Y]ou take the children who are the worst born and bred in the world," she tells him, "and put them under circumstances which would render desperate, and consequently depraved, the best natures you could find. Your system is a failure, and you know it is" (127). In response to the superintendent's bland assurance that "there's a peculiar devil in women" that makes them naturally bad, Mrs. Keyes protests that the boys succeed because they are treated with respect, whereas the girls, "chained down to this life of hopeless monotony" will assuredly find an outlet for their "feverish feelings" in "some wrong way" (129). Providing rewards for good behavior, such as outings away from the institution, would be more effective. But a few indignant words from a well-meaning philanthropist have no effect if not followed up by action, especially in an environment that grinds strength into weakness and individuality into conformity.

In depriving children of every trace of individuality, the industrial home misses the chance to instill a sense of beauty and a feeling of maternity in its residents. Josie repeatedly attempts to seize a possession that she can call her own. She even cherishes as her own a hole in the fence through which she can see a different world, an echo of other window scenes in grim realism. When Mrs. Keyes persuades her daughter to give Josie her doll, Josie, starved for affection, lavishes attention on it and dresses it in a piece of cloth torn from her own scanty petticoat. Such evidence of maternal feeling would be encouraged in a middle-class girl, but in the industrial home the behavior is considered evidence of individuality, and Josie is punished for it. This reverberates in a later incident when, after intermittent healthful interludes working on a farm, Josie is once again dumped back into the industrial home. Her crime is that her budding beauty has attracted a young man, Charley Manton, and consequently the jealousy of the farmer's daughter who wants him for herself. Returned to reform school, Josie cherishes both the memory of Charley and a scraggly geranium that he has given her. This possession too is taken from her. Finding the plant, a matron throws it into the fire before Josie's eyes, much as Gertie's kitten is thrown into a pot of boiling water in Maria Cummins's *The Lamplighter* (1854).

Hemmed in on all sides, Josie rebels, striking the superintendent as he tries to punish her and then stealing boys' clothes to escape from the home that has never really been one. The "girl in boys' clothing" motif is a central premise of E. D. E. N. Southworth's wildly popular novel *The Hidden Hand* (1859), but unlike Capitola, Southworth's heroine, Josie fools no one. When she accidentally meets Charley and he convinces her she has no other options, Josie, without education or prospects, has no choice but to go to his home and take the path she did not want to take. Seven years, a name change, and a few children later, Josie is once again a child of the state, this time in a house of correction, where she is incarcerated for prostitution and attempted suicide. Wyman saves her strongest indictment of the industrial home for this final scene. When Mrs. Faber, a different farmer's wife with whom Josie had stayed for a time, visits the reformatory and recognizes her, Josie looks at her with "hopeless eyes" and comments, "It would have been better for me if I could have stayed with you always" (158). "I wish you had," Mrs. Faber sobs, yet it was her casual action in turning Josie back to reform school because a relative had taken her place as a servant that sealed Josie's fate. The words of well-meaning visitors are scarcely enough, Wyman implies, for Josie's failure is really the failure of the two mother figures—Mrs. Keyes and Mrs. Faber—who turned aside from their moral responsibility to this child of the state.

"And Joe" adds misguided philanthropy to the problems of institutional mothering, echoing the themes of novels of philanthropy such as Elizabeth Stuart Phelps's *The Silent Partner* (1871) and W. D. Howells's *Annie Kilburn* (1888). The story opens as bored socialite Theodora Justice sits with her friend, the physician Margaret Denton, and reflects on her abandoned plans to build a Gothic library for her father's millworkers. Going on a house call with Dr. Denton, Theodora nearly stumbles over Joe, a young French boy whose seizures make him unemployable and the subject of persecution by the Irish boys. Joe is not the first of Wyman's disabled characters, which include "lame Lucy" and Flit in "Luke Gardiner's Love," but his character broadens the issues of just treatment for disabled people in a utilitarian society where worth depends on the ability to work. Amid a complex plot that involves Joe's sister (Annie), Annie's child, and her bigamous husband, Andrew (who cajoles his first wife, Ellen, to run away with him), Wyman makes some of her strongest and most overt pleas for social justice. She challenges the idea that the Irish or other ethnic groups are inherently troublesome by proposing that environment and training play the greater part, noting the "notorious fact that the children of Irish parents are a turbulent, disturbing growth in that social condition which we in besotted contentment persist in naming our civilization, notwithstanding the fact that it is very inadequate to produce the best results in all its component parts."[72] For Wyman, the solution lies not with the workers but with the owners, whose "fear" of violent action "may supplement" their "tardy conscience" if simple benevolence does not spur them on to behave justly to their workers.

In a later scene, Mr. Justice, Margaret, and Theodora debate methods of addressing poverty. Taking a Social Darwinist stance, the ironically named Mr. Justice argues that progress relies on the brutal disposal of unfortunates—"the weak man goes to the wall [and] ... the strong man steps forward, with his foot on his feeble brother's corpse" (227). In keeping with the era's attempts to erase Native identity, he applies Social Darwinism to the plight of the Indian: "Our nation ... is built on the Indian's grave; ... we are a people better worth having in the world than the Indian" (228), he declares, as if one nation must perish so that the other might thrive. But Margaret immediately protests, "[W]e should have been still better worth having in the world if we had been noble enough to live with the Indian, and civilize instead of butchering him." "I think we are the savages," Theodora adds. Although Wyman cannot see beyond assimilation as a useful strategy for Indian settlement, her frank statement directly links social justice for the millworkers with that for Native Americans and, indirectly, with other people of color. In short, the story argues that the test of civilization is not industrial progress but that the nation's wealthy should truly aid its unfortunates—disabled individuals, like Joe, among them—by integrating them into the life of the nation rather than indulging in the false philanthropy of erecting Gothic libraries as monuments to their own importance. The story ends when, in nursing Annie through her last illness, Theodora meets Ellen, who has come to adopt Annie's baby. Their mutual sense of responsibility for the helpless in their midst, Ellen for the baby and Theodora for Joe, ends with intercultural friendship and a vision of feminist cross-class solidarity. Gestures of maternal concern that depend on social rather than biological ties succeed where institutional philanthropies and industrial systems fail—at the level of the individual.

Wyman promotes cross-class and interethnic solidarity in "Luke Gardiner's Love" and "Valentine's Chance," which share the plot of an American man of English descent falling in love with an immigrant girl, Irish in the former story and French-Canadian in the latter. Ethnicity here connotes a lack of whiteness for both the Irish and the French Canadians, and thus, by extension, serves as a displaced marker for racial difference as well. Both stories are tales of rescue, as Wyman's stories tend to be, but "Valentine's Chance" reverses "Luke Gardiner's Love" by suggesting that the immigrant rather than the Anglo male is the rescuer. "Luke Gardiner's Love" is the story of a character tellingly named Eden, an innocent girl who loves the foreman Luke until her abusive Irish stepfather, Johnny Ronian, breaks off the connection. As with many of Wyman's stories, the plot includes a disabled character, Flit, Eden's mentally challenged sister, who begs for pennies in the street and, like *Hamlet*'s Ophelia, speaks a garbled version of truths that others are afraid to articulate. After tribulations including a drunken stepfather, a threatened sexual assault, and the death of Flit, Eden and Luke are reunited.

Wyman connects the abuses of industrialism with those of slavery, using the familiar scenes of Stowe's fiction and various slave narratives to deepen her social critique. The main plot centers on Eden's attempts to evade the advances of the lecherous overseer Joe Glancy, who presses on her a pair of cheap earrings as part of his campaign to seduce her. Eden's plight resonates as both a real occurrence in the mills of the time and a deliberate echo of the sexual abuse suffered by female slaves, a parallel that an allusion to *Uncle Tom's Cabin* underscores. In a notable subplot, Flit bursts into the home of the Quaker mill owners, Mr. and Mrs. Comstock, to beg for rent money, and their failure to help her recalls *Uncle Tom's Cabin*. Wyman establishes that externally, at least, the Comstocks are proper Quakers with impeccable abolitionist credentials. Their possessions include the Book of Discipline of the Society of Friends, copies of *Uncle Tom's Cabin* and *The Wide, Wide World*, and portraits of William Lloyd Garrison, Theodore Parker, and Wendell Phillips on the walls. As Flit enters, Mr. Comstock is even reading the *Liberator*, and the governess, Miss Firth, is reading Thoreau's *Walden*. The sharply realized details are no surprise, for Wyman draws on her own family experiences to describe the Comstocks. Their reading material was hers as she was growing up, and the "Miss Firth" of the story is clearly based on Sophia Ford (or Foord) of Concord, Massachusetts, who believed herself a "twin soul" to Thoreau and was Wyman's much-disliked governess.[73] The Comstocks' impulse toward charity begins and ends with words, however. They give Flit a penny in response to her request for rent money and, after she is dragged away by her stepfather, observe only that "the introduction of foreigners among the operatives had quite changed the conditions of life in New England."[74] They take refuge in nativist rationalizations, never connecting the plight of the slaves for whom they work tirelessly and the plight of the millworkers whose situation they refuse to address.

Wyman also draws from temperance literature in constructing the story. When their stepfather, Johnny Ronian, finally throws Flit and Eden out of the house, they have nowhere to go until they are taken in by a trio of rough but goodhearted Irish girls, Kate, Rosa, and "lame Lucy" McCannah, a rescue that has its own dangers. The girls take Eden to a grog shop, where she must show her class solidarity with them by drinking and dancing lest she be thought part of the "Yankee temp'rance folks" (100). By now tipsy with the unaccustomed drink, Eden is in danger of losing her virtue to Joe Glancy until Luke steps in and fights him. Although Luke fails to rescue the unfortunate Flit from drowning in the millstream, he and Eden are reunited over Flit's grave at the end of the story. Read symbolically, the ending suggests that if the prayers and begging of the powerless, such as Flit, have no effect on the mill owners, those smugly blind heirs of the abolitionists, the power to rectify such abuses may lie in a coalition of working-class Irish and other Americans. Despite the redemptive ending, the story includes elements of naturalism and grim realism, including sexual abuse, industrial dehumanization, drunkenness, ethnic tensions, and death.

The cross-cultural romance "Valentine's Chance" anticipates stories such as Kate Chopin's "At the 'Cadian Ball" and "The Storm" in its pairing of a reserved Anglo male with an earthy, sensual French girl, the darkly beautiful French-Canadian Rose Beauvais. Lazing in a hammock all summer and reading the letters of Fanny Burney, Dr. John Valentine is subject to a worrisome "self-analyzing tendency ... which endangered his growth in sunny and vigorous manhood" (280) until he meets Rose. At a mill hands' picnic where "[e]verybody had a foreign color and air" (289), he contrasts her with his friend Miss Jeffreys, a pallid blond woman of his own class. Wyman renders Valentine's increasingly uncontrollable feelings for Rose through the symbolic use of water as a sign of fluid sexuality and the loss of boundaries. At first afraid to ask Rose to row in the boat with him, Valentine crosses the river several times to go to her, and when she wears a dress that Miss Jeffreys had given her, a cross-class disguise that obscures the class differences between them, the two go for a long boat ride together. Rose's borrowed dress suggests not only the possibility of class assimilation but also that class is a garment to be worn or discarded rather than a component of the essential self.

In keeping with the familiar theme of the highly educated and repressed Anglo learning about real life through contact with a dark Other, Valentine recognizes civilization as a "constraining power."[75] He wants to learn about "the elemental tie which binds the race together," an idea that arises from his glimpse of the tenements where there was "life enough,—laughter and speech, whispers and cries" (292). Valentine's epiphany is that dividing ethnicity into multiple "races" leads to enervation, whereas recognizing "race" as the human race, with its "ties" of common humanity, leads to a vigorous and healthy life. Rose rescues him from an arid, ineffectual life, but her appeal for him is not merely that of the senses. Rather, he sees her as able to confront life as he cannot, as when he admires Rose's calm in the face of an industrial accident that sends the American mill superintendent into hysterics. Wyman skillfully interweaves late nineteenth-century concerns about overcivilized, neurasthenic men with those about immigration to propose a startling conclusion. As suggested in Grimké's assessment of Wyman's commitment to racial equality, which is treated through coded ethnicity in *Poverty Grass*, the solution to the dark, unassimilated ethnic Other is not only to promote assimilation, as suggested by Rose's borrowed dress, but also to join the two of what Wyman in her preface calls "people of different races . . . Yankee, English, Irish, and French" in marriage (v, vii). Marriage to a partner of another race not only benefits the immigrant whose acculturation is thus hastened but also revives an enervated, effete American culture with fresh contributions of vigorous foreign blood, an argument counter to emerging nativist fears about dilution of old New England Yankee stock.

The grim realism of Rebecca Harding Davis, Elizabeth Stuart Phelps, and Lillie Chace Wyman anticipates the concerns of naturalism in its use of the aesthetics of disgust, the discovery-of-squalor sequence, and the transformation of sentiment through the transmission of affect. Their work requires not only the immediate and visceral response to the violent or squalid circumstances that their work describes—the vividness of the smell of burning copperas in *Margret Howth*, the bloodstained wall in *Hedged In*, or the violent death and extended mourning at the end of *A Singular Life*, for example—but also an intellectual willingness to divine the bittersweet conclusions to so many of their works. They provide an ongoing critique of a social system that can conceive no place for a woman who has been in prison, like Josie in "The Child of the State," the fallen woman, or an independent woman like Margret Howth, who bows to her husband's insistence that his wife's talents must be used entirely for his benefit. All three writers deliver some highly charged political truths to an audience that may be reluctant to hear them. All three criticize the indifference and neglect of workers by profit-hungry mill owners and suggest that the owners bear some responsibility for subsequent industrial violence. Through direct address and deixis, they facilitate a form of readerly détente and narrative coziness that draws readers into the text, yet they do so to hold readers accountable for the abuses that they witness in the world beyond the text. Their excesses pave the way for naturalism.

CHAPTER 2

The Darwinists

Borderlands, Evolution, and Trauma

In 1896 the *Atlantic Monthly* published a short story in which an elderly Native American man is abandoned by his tribe in harsh conditions. As he listens to the tribe packing up its belongings to move to better camping grounds, he reflects that his abandonment was the law of his clan and remembers seeing the same process played out with other old men when he was young. Now it is his turn, and he accepts the coming of his death philosophically. The story recalls Jack London's "The Law of Life," in which old Koskoosh waits for death after being left behind by his tribe. But the story described was published five years before Jack London's "The Law of Life" appeared in *McClure's Magazine* in 1901. It is Batterman Lindsay's "Abandoned: A Tale of the Plains," and it is as stark in its naturalism as London's story. Yet Lindsay's story has a difference: the old man has a disabled wife who, being blind and unable to survive after his death, commits suicide after she has sung the proper death songs for him.

The harsh, isolated geography of "Abandoned: A Tale of the Plains" recalls similar deadly environments in London's Yukon stories or the western landscapes of Frank Norris, but instead of a man braving the unforgiving nature of the physical landscape, "Abandoned" features a man and a woman, the latter with a disability. To naturalism and grim realism's familiar theme of unforgiving human nature, "Abandoned" adds the initial tolerance but ultimately the indifference of a white ranch family, who feed the couple through the summer but turn them loose with just enough provisions to travel to the reservation where the couple have already said they will not go. To the "death in the wilderness" theme of Norris's *McTeague* and London's "To Build a Fire," it adds the death of a woman who, having assessed her own position in relation to nature and society, chooses to die as Chopin's Edna Pontellier does, by drowning. No one survives to sing the songs for her, for she is doubly discarded, a remnant of the man who is himself the remnant of the tribe.

Lindsay's story suggests the overlap between classically defined naturalism written by men and women's naturalism, not only in its themes but also in its settings. Themes of survival of the fittest, competition for scarce resources such as food and sexual partners, atavism, racial inheritance, and the courtship behavior described in Darwin's *The Descent of Man* pervade the short stories of women writers as they pervade the stories of their male counterparts. Yet the implicit perception that women write regionalism and men write naturalism can overshadow the naturalistic elements in women's short fiction. A quick scan of women's late nineteenth-century stories reveals that stories of women in rural or wild borderlands are classed as regionalist but similar characters in stories written by men are classed as naturalistic. The classification schemes signal a category crisis (Marjorie Pryse's term) that provides a provocative and creative space for reconsidering genre boundaries.[1]

In addition to calling attention to the possibility of violence and the resulting trauma in domestic spaces and seemingly peaceful rural landscapes, women writers emphasize the ways in which social perceptions of people of color and women charge the landscape with the possibility of violence, with themselves as victims rather than perpetrators. Reading the wilderness in light of the characters within it renders interpretation of the landscape contingent and partial, suggesting the ways in which other spaces in naturalism depend for their effect on the gender and race of the characters within them. In Paul Laurence Dunbar's *The Sport of the Gods*, for example, the superficially peaceful spaces of a plantation reveal themselves to be dangerous for the African American Barry family when an employer unjustly accuses the father of theft. The serenity of the space, in other words, is contingent and volatile rather than stable, dependent on a racist consensus about boundaries that cannot be crossed.

This transformation of spaces depending on the person traversing them exists in London's and Crane's stories as the theme of "the man who knows," the man who understands the terrain, climate, and inhabitants of what white men claim as a wilderness. "The man who knows" believes that the wilderness is a closed book that most Native Americans but few white men other than himself can read, although ironically his pretense of knowledge often leads to his undoing. In London's "To Build a Fire," for example, the main character believes he is the "man who knows" and is caught out in his arrogant rationalizing by refusing advice and freezing to death. The genuine "man who knows" is the old sourdough at Sulphur Creek, who had warned the protagonist not to travel alone. Crane's Swede in "The Blue Hotel" believes he is the "man who knows" the West, only to cause his own death through assailing the other men at the Palace Hotel in Nebraska with his wrongheaded interpretations of their actions.

On a global scale, these spaces transformed by the "man who knows" extend to narratives of empire in which wilderness is reclassified as territory ripe for expansion. In such spaces, the "beast within" trope of naturalism is mapped onto entire "primitive" populations suddenly deemed incapable of self-government and put in the charge of the "man who knows natives."[2] In contrast, in women's naturalism, wilderness is often positioned as a borderland or contact zone, a place whose meaning is contingent upon those who pass through its space rather than a place ripe for ownership. Mary Austin's *The Land of Little Rain*, for example, resists the exploitation of the desert by reversing this "man who knows" idea into the "woman who learns." Austin rejects the idea that wilderness failing to serve the needs of majority populations is useless. Instead she reveals that the seemingly empty desert contains intricate ecosystems and useful plants and animals for the tribes that live there.

In fiction by Elia Peattie, Kate Cleary, Mary Hallock Foote, Annie Batterman Lindsay, Mary E. Wilkins Freeman, Kate Chopin, and Edith Wharton, borderlands settings reveal anxieties about the dissolving of spatial and psychological boundaries, anxieties sharpened by Darwinian theories implying that a continuum rather than a sharp delineation exists between human beings and other animals. Peattie, Cleary, Foote, Lindsay, and Freeman explore actual borderlands, with characters living on the intersection of settlements and wilderness where relapses into animality or human savagery, distortions of time and space, and clashes between modernity and tradition occur. In setting the stories within literal borderlands, these authors explore boundaries existing between genders and between races. More abstractly, they probe the fine lines between humanity and animality, wilderness and civilization, madness and sanity, health and disability, human and machine, and sobriety and addiction along with the violence and trauma that the blurring of these boundaries engenders. Peattie's "After the Storm" and "The Man at the Edge of Things" and Cleary's "Feet of Clay" show isolated spaces as fostering a devolutionary slide into madness. Foote's "The Trumpeter" and Lindsay's "The Old Law," "My Great-Aunt's Wedding," and "Kwelth-Elite, the Proud Slave" address the cultural implications of racial descent in contact zones, while Freeman's "Old Woman Magoun" uses landscapes to signify the human cost of distorting biological time for social ends. Sharing a common subject matter in their treatment of courtship, divorce, and addiction, Kate Chopin's *At Fault* and Edith Wharton's *The Fruit of the Tree* examine Darwinian themes of courtship behavior and racial inheritance in the borderlands between rural and industrialized spaces, focusing on the position of women in regional spaces that intersect with a national or global economy.

Darwinism in the Borderlands:
Peattie, Cleary, and Foote

ELIA PEATTIE

Elia Wilkinson Peattie (1862–1935) worked as a writer for most of her life, publishing crusading journalism for the *Omaha World-Herald*, short stories in the *Atlantic Monthly*, *Harper's Weekly*, and *Cosmopolitan*, travel narratives such as *A Journey through Wonderland; or, The Pacific Northwest and Alaska*, young adult fiction, murder mysteries, histories, and novels.[3] She represents rural life in the borderlands of the Midwest and West as a location where boundaries between human and animal, and between rationality and madness, erode in the presence of isolation and the crumbling of civilized customs. Peattie's "After the Storm: A Story of the Prairie" and "The Man at the Edge of Things" depict a decline of intellectual and social powers that threatens descent into madness and then mindlessness as human beings elide the distinction between human and nonhuman.

One of her best stories, "After the Storm" (published in the *Atlantic Monthly* in 1897), presents a horrifying version of prairie life and what may be called the farm-wife plot. The farm-wife plot features a woman living on a hardscrabble farm, often isolated or on a frontier, whose ceaseless toil is essential to the life of the farm. She loses something of herself in the process, often the ideals or trappings of gentility that her former life in the East or in a city (or both) had afforded her. Because of her belief in her husband or the promise of rural life, she continues to work while dogged by poverty, endless work and isolation, her husband's indifference or cruelty, and the arrival of children for whom she has few resources to spare. Feeling increasingly trapped, the farm wife dreams of some form of escape, either a temporary retreat from the demands of life on the farm or a permanent flight to a better life. The position of the farm wife is a double servitude, for just as mortgages and railroad rates enslave the farmers, so too are their wives tied to the farm by poverty, children, and their husbands' neglect.

In "After the Storm," an outsider, Ralph Tennant, watches as an abused farm wife, Mrs. Maria Sharpneck, lies dying. Sharpneck's Nebraska cattle ranch is a savagely Darwinian place where the strong prey on the weak much as Sharpneck has bullied and driven his wife to her death. In a naturalistic evocation of predatory animals, "voracious" cats whose eyes shine with "evil phosphorescence" fill the farmhouse as they circle the dead body in "grim carnivorous atavism."[4] Peattie's choice of the term "atavism" suggests not only Darwinian theories of descent but also the degeneration of tame cats into predators and scavengers, a descent from civilization into savagery that Sharpneck's lack of all decency has caused. As the cats scratch and hiss, Tennant calls for order and demands that Sharpneck send for a physician, a Dr. Bender, in a seeming return to decency. But in this borderland space, institutions of civilization such as professional medicine mask rather than curb the savagery within. Bender has red hair, a "sensual mouth," and "avaricious eyes" like those of the cats, and he does nothing but look at the dying woman with "a peculiar gleam" (394) in his eye. In naming the doctor "Bender," Peattie provides a clue to his unsavory nature, for the infamous real-life Bender family of serial killers had murdered at least a dozen people in their inn near Cherryvale, Kansas during the early 1870s before their deeds were discovered. The Benders were never found and brought to trial, leading to contradictory legends of a lynching, alluded to in Laura Ingalls Wilder's *Pioneer Girl* manuscript, and of a long and punishment-free later career. Bender's enjoyment of the dying woman's pain hints at the sadistic pleasure that the Benders were said to take in their victims' deaths and foreshadows his part in the story.

Only the daughter, Kitty, and the outsider Ralph Tennant, whose punning surname signifies his temporary status, stand outside this savage universe. Like the easterner Steavens in Cather's equally naturalistic "The Sculptor's Funeral" (1895), Tennant, the outsider, watches in horror as the reality behind the pastoral dream of American prairie myth unfolds before him. As her name suggests, Kitty is a domesticated version of the voracious cats, civilized enough to understand the savage home she inhabits but spirited enough to resist her father's attempts to force her to live there. Although she has her mother's dark hair, Kitty lacks the conventional pale face of gentility, for her "little brown" (393) face hardens and flushes with "a bright red spot" (396) when she thinks of her mother's life. When the women from surrounding farms prepare a funeral feast, Kitty refuses to eat, as though, like Persephone, she will remain trapped if she eats or participates in the rituals of this hellish place. The town shares in the corruption of the farm: as Kitty explains to Tennant, she apprenticed herself to a milliner to learn the trade but "I did not like her, nor the other girls, nor things that happened" (397). She does not specify the "things," but one possibility is suggested by the dubious sexual reputation of milliners. As Nell Kimball, a retired madam, explains in her memoir, when on vacation with a female friend "[w]e said we were milliners: usually at that time a kind of amateur whore or at least considered fast."[5] Caught between the corruption of the town and of the farm, Kitty is trapped by her environment in the classic predicament of naturalism, for the more expertly she repeats her mother's actions in preparing food and keeping house, the more certain it is that she will be trapped in her mother's place.

While Kitty and Tennant watch over the body and Sharpneck is off drinking with friends, she shows Tennant a portrait of her mother, Maria, as a young and beautiful bride. A common feature of the farm-wife tale is an object that represents the wife's former life, either a portrait or an object associated with gentility, such as Annie's silver thimble in Kate Cleary's "Jim Lancy's Waterloo" or the china shepherdess that Caroline (Ma) Ingalls carries from place to place in Laura Ingalls Wilder's "Little House" series of juvenile novels. Kitty notes how different the printed image is from her gaunt, silent mother with the "parchment-like face," a face now kept cool with damp cloths to preserve the body long enough for the funeral (393). This naturalistic detail, like the voracious cats with eyes of "evil phosphorescence" (393), provides a visceral and tactile picture of death. The "phosphorescence" of their eyes suggests a glowing, unnatural decay, and the details of dirt and smells intensify in a naturalistic description of Maria as having "toil-stained clothes" and "garments smelling of smoke" (393), positioning her even in life as waste (399).

As Sharpneck's wife and appendage, Maria is named only once in the story, and as subsequent events prove, she exists for Sharpneck only in the amount of money that her body can make for him. With great fanfare, Sharpneck orders a fine coffin from his brother, the undertaker, and rebukes the driver for allowing the coffin to bump into the sides of the wagon, not because of the disrespect for his wife but because "[t]here's reasons why I don't want that there coffin scratched up" (400). A suspicious Tennant returns to the grave and discovers, as he tells Kitty, that her father had only pretended to bury his wife. He had instead returned the coffin to his brother for cash and sold his wife's body to Dr. Bender for dissection. The minister at the funeral, the money-grubbing undertaker, and her father all collude in keeping the facts from Kitty, who as a woman has no say and by custom cannot go to the gravesite. Even Tennant, a stranger and an Englishman, has more access to the language of power than she does, despite her position as a rancher's daughter and a nominal citizen of the town. Faced with such savagery, and filled with "horror and disgust" (402) at the corruption of a town that would countenance such an action, Kitty refuses either to return to the farm or to live in the town.

After they hide in a coal shed while a furious Sharpneck hunts for Kitty to drag her back to the farm, Tennant and Kitty take the train to Council Bluffs, Iowa, a "charming place" with "green ledges" and rambling vineyards (403). "Coming as they did from the treeless region, the place was enchanting to them," the narrator explains. Kitty's escape from her former enslavement across the Missouri River into this promised land alludes to similar scenes of deliverance in slave narratives as the escapee literally crosses a border into a green and fertile land. Once out of the lawless plains of Nebraska and its devolution into savagery, the two marry, live in a "little green cottage," and evolve into model citizens (405). From being an observer, Tennant becomes a participant in the American Dream, rising to the top of his profession. From being a wary survivor of domestic abuse, Kitty acquires mentors who teach her "all manner of things that could not be learned in books" about genteel living and home décor, such as "to keep a potted fern on her table" (405). "It was quite wonderful how quickly they became an orderly part of the community—these two from the wilderness," the narrator concludes. Given the proper environment, away from the Darwinian struggle on the borderlands represented by the rapacious cats and brutish Sharpneck, Kitty can become civilized in ways not possible in the savage wilderness of her father's ranch.

Writing to Dorothy Canfield on October 10, 1899, after reporting a "delightful day" spent with the Peatties, Willa Cather declared that "Mrs. Peattie has at last arrived, so to speak, for her story 'The Man at the Edge of Things' in the September Atlantic is literature, as good as most modern French things and as elusive and artistic."[6] Cather's characterization of Peattie's story as "modern" and "French" is high praise, for Cather had a few years earlier described herself as "Maupassant mad."[7] Peattie's "The Man at the Edge of Things" (*Atlantic Monthly*, September 1899) examines borderlands and their isolation from the man's instead of the woman's perspective. In addition, with its plot of a young eastern college graduate who moves to a remote sheep ranch and nearly goes mad with isolation, "The Man at the Edge of Things" responds satirically to Theodore Roosevelt's call for Americans to adopt the "strenuous life." Speaking in Chicago on April 10, 1899, Roosevelt had called for military preparedness by arguing that the health of the nation rested with individual Americans leading "clean, vigorous, healthy lives," with women who did not shrink from childbirth and men who have "those virile qualities necessary to win in the stern strife of actual life" rather than "to seek ease." Peattie's story, published a mere six months later, explores what happens when young men take up Roosevelt's challenge to "dare mighty things" rather than to "live in the gray twilight that knows not victory or defeat."[8] As in "After the Storm," Peattie explores the thin naturalistic line that separates human from animal, but unlike Roosevelt she concludes that civilization rather than the strenuous life is the making of a man.

The protagonist, Dilling Brown, is a perfect specimen for the Rooseveltian experiment. Following the commencement at his eastern university, "Dil" talks with his guardian, Aunt Betty, and his friend Tommy Letlow about his future. His abundant hair of "a perfect hay color" signals both his vitality and his Anglo-Saxon heritage, a heritage that according to Roosevelt and to Frank Norris signals an innate desire for adventure.[9] An afternoon spent with two pallid, lemonade-drinking eastern girls seals his desire to leave the East, presumably lest he become effete, a Rooseveltian "molly-coddle" rather than "red-blood."[10] Dil's desire to go west in quest of rugged masculinity echoes the themes of Owen Wister's *The Virginian* (1902), which was in turn satirized in later films such as Alice Guy-Blaché's *Algie, the Miner* (1912), in which a simpering, effeminate easterner moves west and learns to handle a gun.[11] Encouraged by Aunt Betty, who in an echo of Roosevelt's speech encourages him to "go out and make discoveries" (324) as she never did, he heads for the Esmerelda Ranch at "the Edge of Things where the free grass grew" (325). With the help of Louis Papin, the Esmerelda's overseer, and a Chinese servant, Li Lung, Dil moves to a remote sheep ranch, abandoned when its previous owner, Fred Cusack, had "lost his health" (328). Once at the sheep ranch, he is ready to live in solitude amid the beauty of the "pale gold dustiness" of the days (332), and, like Thoreau, he names the animals as his neighbors. But the Thoreauvian idyll and isolation that might have been possible in a small eastern space such as Walden Pond fails in the vast landscape of the West. Dil learns from Big Hank Brown, one of his shepherds, that Fred Cusack's loss of health had actually been a loss of sanity during which he stopped talking to outsiders and began to "drop down . . . an' take t' eatin' grass" beside the sheep (334).

The conflation of human beings with objects and animals with human beings occupies center stage in many naturalist texts. Here it signals the blurring of boundaries between humans and animals and a consequent loss of humanity and agency. This is in large measure a story about things, in Bill Brown's sense of the term: "We begin to confront the thingness of objects when they stop working for us," Brown writes, adding, "The story of objects asserting themselves as things, then, is the story of a changed relation to the human subject and thus the story of how the thing really names less an object than a particular subject-object relation."[12] Peattie suggests this idea in the uneasy categorization of the animals that Dil sets out to watch and the "changed relation" he has with them: the sheep. They are single organisms and a mass organism at once, a "writhing, restless, half-alive, wholly unintelligent body," Papin tells him (326–27), as if they are cells organizing themselves into a more sentient and intelligent whole than they can be in single units. Even as a uniform body, however, the sheep are incapable of true thought, and the two shepherds who work for Dill likewise lack individuality and conversation.

To compensate for his loneliness, Dil imagines animals as women and carries on oddly erotic conversations with them, which challenges the homoerotic charge of the all-male Esmerelda Ranch cohort but scarcely marks a psychologically healthy adaptation to the isolation of the ranch. He names his female dog "Bet" after his aunt and addresses her affectionately by saying, "You flirt, I believe you're trying to make up to me" (329), a courtship conversation that contrasts with his earlier stilted conversation with the eastern girls. He tames a "pretty wether," or castrated male sheep, and names him "Dickie Bird," feeding and pampering him until "the little creature became offensive to him, and he resented its intimacy" (334). After making the sheep develop affection for him, he grows angry when it rubs its head against his leg (334). The eroticized language describing the relationship, almost a courtship in which Dil spurns the affectionate advances of the creature that he had once cherished, segues into the hallucinatory language of seduction: "In the grotesque twilight, when the cacti looked like hobgoblins, and Bet's eyes grew phosphorescent... it seemed as if Dickie Bird—the little wether—were inviting him to drop down on all fours with him and say 'baa'" (334). Bet's eyes recall the phosphorescent eyes of the savage cats and their animal atavism in "After the Storm," and here they signal a similar threat. The invitation that Dil hallucinates is doubly transgressive, both in the sexually charged language that he imagines as inviting him to cross the human-animal boundary and in the possibility that he might cross the boundary of madness to join his predecessor, Fred Cusack. Reflecting on this scene the next morning, Dil "came near laughing too long" (334), adding a touch of hysteria to the madness that he only barely skirts through his isolation.

In short, the man determined to go it alone to live Roosevelt's "strenuous life" risks turning himself into a beast and erasing the boundary between human and animal. He transforms himself not into Norris's inner Viking or from a "mollycoddle" into a "red-blood," as Roosevelt would later advocate, but into a docile, feminized sheep with no sense of thought or volition. Dil has answered Roosevelt's call in "The Strenuous Life" to be "the man who does not shrink from danger, from hardship, or from bitter toil" (1), and he even echoes Roosevelt's language when reflecting that "[h]e could have enjoyed adventure... even when accompanied by great hardship and danger, but this endless stretch of nothingness was as wearing as life in a mephitic dungeon" (337). Just as Jack London's Malemute Kid will later experience "The White Silence," Dil is unprepared for the "endless stretch of nothingness" that the silence of the wilderness brings.

The efforts of nonwhite men and of women, the very figures whom the white man is not supposed to need, save Dil from merging with the nonhuman. The nonwhite man essential to Dil is Li Lung, his servant. Hearing Dil cursing "a miserable gum tree" (331), Li Lung recognizes Dil's homesickness and mixes him "a cool drink with water and claret... to coax the gentleman out of the sun" (331). Later, when Dil invents imaginary conversations among his absent friends, Li Lung advises him to visit Papin, and Dil takes the advice. But Dil classes Li Lung with Dickie Bird and Bet, seeing him as less human than himself and describing his singing, unlike that of the shepherds, as the "croon[ing of] an awful song in a heathen tongue" (334). Dil reports to Letlow that "a sore-eyed wether" (339) is his only confidant, ignoring Li Lung and further relegating him to the realm of the nonhuman. Dil's failure to recognize Li Lung as fully human and as a possible companion reflects the failure of Roosevelt's imperialist and colonialist mentality. The fear of "going native," of Americans falling to the level of those whom they govern, pervades "The Strenuous Life," in which Roosevelt contends that many of the "half-caste and native Christians, warlike Moslems, and wild pagans" (17–18) of the Philippines are "utterly unfit for self-government, and show no signs of becoming fit" (18). Read as a commentary on the white man's place in colonized lands, Dil's temptation to get down on the ground and munch grass beside Dickie Bird satirizes the dangers of considering the ethnic Other as nonhuman and the madness that lies in such a perspective.

The second agent of Dil's regeneration and reintegration into society is an absent woman, Katherine Cusack, who left objects behind at the ranch when she accompanied her brother, Frank, to the asylum. The glove, thimble, and hand-lettered sign through which Dil constructs his imaginary Katherine Cusack become fetish items for him. All are associated with the hand of a woman and consequently the promise of a woman's touch both physically and aesthetically. From them he cobbles together a vision of Katherine, to whom he writes long letters every day even as his letter writing to his friends decreases. The creation of an imagined person through letters occurs in other regional fictions and vacation romances, which are by definition set far from the centers of contemporary life. In Sarah Orne Jewett's *Deephaven*, for example, Helen and Kate Lancaster read the proud Miss Brandon's letters from friends but leave untouched her lover's letters "tied with a very pale and tired-looking blue ribbon."[13] And in Thomas Bailey Aldrich's vacation romance "Marjorie Daw," one friend writes letters to another describing an imaginary young woman, with whom the recipient of the letters falls in love. Rather than an amusing imaginative exercise in identity construction, however, Katherine's artifacts become the talismans of civilization to which Dil clings, since he has little ability to construct his own art. When he lives alone, his sole attempt at décor hints at his state of mind, a gunnysack tacked up in place of a door that he then paints with some dull, red "conventionalized lizards" (331). As in Glasgow's *Phases of an Inferior Planet* when Mariana wears a gown with patterns of lizards, reptiles signal Darwinian evolution, or, in Dil's case, devolution. With no companions, Dil clings to these artifacts even after a letter informs him that Aunt Betty has died and he is her heir.

The imagined presence of Katherine by itself cannot save Dil from the prolonged consequences of isolation, for when Dil finally goes to Papin's house, he lurks outside, "a creature with haggard eyes and a drawn face" (338), until Tom Letlow, Papin, and the others force him into the light. Only the worldly Papin can endure the loneliness of the sheep ranch because he is "wedded to...solitude," to his volume of Shakespeare, and to a naturalistic philosophy in which "he was, personally, an immaterial accident" (338). Relieved that Dil is all right, his friend Letlow proposes that both travel to the Klondike for "the experience, merely" after which he "may go to Hawaii. Things are looking up for us over there, you know" (340). In contrast to Dil, Letlow is the untested Rooseveltian imperial adventurer, thrilled at the prospect of "mak[ing] a fortune" in the Klondike gold rush or Hawaii, where "[t]hings are looking up" because U.S. corporate interests had overthrown the existing monarchy in 1898 and annexed the islands as a U.S. protectorate. But Dil has seen enough to recognize the consequences of imperial adventures. Although he does not want to return to the East, "The Klondike did not appeal to him. He had a vision of a solitude as complete as that of the sun-baked desert, and more unkind" (340), a vision of Klondike solitude that Jack London was beginning to describe in "To the Man on Trail" (*Overland Monthly*, 1899) and "An Odyssey of the North" (*Atlantic Monthly*, January 1900). Instead Dil recognizes what has saved him in the solitude of the ranch, the "prehistoric traces" of the imagined woman Katherine Cusack, the study of which has "kept [his] soul alive" (341). "I haven't found a woman out there, Mr. Papin, but—but I have found the soul of a woman" (341), he explains, as the men stare at him in uncomfortable amazement.

As in "After the Storm," events end fortuitously, with Dil getting both the adventure and the woman that he wants. After he reveals that the woman's name is Katherine Cusack, Letlow tells Dil, "That's the girl who is going to Alaska on the same boat with us" now that her "bleating wretch" of a brother is dead (341). But Dil has learned something about himself after all. After questioning Letlow about his route to the Klondike—"the Dyea, the Chilcat?"—he reveals that he intends "to go into business in—in Juneau" (342). Rather than simply being a capitulation to his fears of isolation, Dil's decision heralds his wish to take the next step toward conventional manhood instead of imperial boyhood by presumably settling down with Katherine—and, incidentally, given the economic fallout of the gold rush, making more money as a businessman and supplier than as a gold-seeker. His choice looks past the turn-of-the-century U.S. imperial moment toward the twentieth century, when, to paraphrase another president, Calvin Coolidge, in 1925, the business of America became business. In the final analysis, "The Man at the Edge of Things" questions Rooseveltian individualism, imperialism, and the ability of men to survive intact without women. Ultimately, as in most of Peattie's work, the resolution to the character's problems is the prospect of heterosexual romance through the cherishing of women, just as the rejection of heterosexual romance through the neglect of women leads to desolation.

KATE CLEARY

Like her friend Elia Peattie, Kate Cleary (1863–1905) was a prolific midwestern writer, but her short life included poverty, the deaths of some of her children, a five-year struggle with morphine addiction, and surviving the attempt of her husband to have her committed to an insane asylum. Drawing on her life in Hubbell, Nebraska, Cleary protested the hard lot of the farm wife under a patriarchal economic system that viewed women as work beasts to be used up in the service of a husband's money and status. Unlike stories of her contemporary Hamlin Garland, who likewise protested the farm wife's plight, Cleary's tales show no compensating sense of the beauty of the landscape as a consolation for women trapped on the land. Two of her stories, "The Rebellion of Mrs. McLelland" and "Feet of Clay," illustrate the primary approaches to the farm-wife story: the first, in comic mode, a story of revolt and escape, and the second, in tragic mode, the tale of madness and death. Cleary uses the prairie women's spoken language to signify the isolation and repressive social structures that they endure and its absence to show their resistance.

The comic side of isolation in "The Rebellion of Mrs. McLelland" (published in the *Chicago Tribune* in 1899) recalls Hamlin Garland's "Mrs. Ripley's Trip" and especially Mary E. Wilkins Freeman's "The Revolt of 'Mother,'" whose title Cleary seems to have consciously echoed. Mrs. McLelland has given all she has to the farm and to her stepchildren, but when she receives a telegram from her own adult daughter, whom she has not seen in fifteen years, telling her that her granddaughter is ill, she decides to leave the farm. A friend offers to lend her the money, and she plans to borrow it, only to be challenged by the parsimonious Mr. McLelland, who accuses her of taking the twenty dollars he has hidden in the barn. Now aware of where she can get the money, she takes it from the barn and travels to see her daughter. A week later, stricken by conscience, she returns home to confess. Like Sarah Penn of Freeman's story, her rebellion emboldens her to speak plainly to her husband. Seeing that he had "$20 layin' ubiquitous," she says, she took it to be compensated for all she has done for "your other wife's prodigy," noting that "I never stood up again you before."[14]

The comic malapropisms that characterize Mrs. McLelland's speech ("prodigy" for "progeny") throughout the story give it a lighter tone than Freeman's story, but the seriousness of Mrs. McLelland's message is the same. When Mr. McLelland, astonished at her revolt, begins to gulp his tea in disbelief, she has the same solution to restore peace, a hearty "chicking potpie" for dinner, that, like Adoniram Penn's favorite pie in "The Revolt of 'Mother,'" reconciles the husband to his rebellious wife tangibly, without the use of words or apologies. Women have no money or official power in the farm-wife plot, but in its comic versions they can mend relationships and restore their place in the farm partnership by what they literally bring to the table. Husbands control the money and houses in Freeman and Cleary, but wives control the pie.

The tragic side of the farm-wife plot and a different form of significant language appears in Cleary's "Feet of Clay." An easterner, Margaret Dare, marries Barret Landroth and goes to live on his farm, where his domineering mother, Rebecca, aids Barret in working Margaret past all endurance. Rebecca is the monstrous mother of naturalism, with a face like "one of those grotesque images the Chinese cut from ivory. It was thin, of a pale yellow, and covered from brow to chin with a spider web of minute wrinkles."[15] With the reference to "Chinese" ivory figures and her "yellow" skin, Rebecca evokes the stereotypical nineteenth-century figure of the cruel Asian villainess, an idea reinforced through her "black and piercing" eyes and insistence on the respect to be paid to her as a venerated elder.

In stories of the farm wife, the farm itself becomes the wife's rival for the affections of her husband, an expensive mistress upon which he lavishes every cent, including the pittance that his wife has saved or inherited. All beauty and tenderness vanishes from Margaret's life as Barret ignores and Rebecca bullies her. When she asks to go home for a visit, Barret tells her that his mother "hasn't been off this farm for twenty years" (148), a fact that he considers a point of pride. In a classic instance of redirecting the woman's money, which she wishes to spend on the intangibles of beauty or art, to suit the man's practical needs, Barret takes Margaret's small inheritance, with which she wanted to buy a piano, and spends it on a "thrasher" (150), all while continuing to upbraid her for not saving up enough money so that he can run for the legislature. Running for the legislature as a badge of citizenship recurs frequently in Cleary's fiction. It signals the doubled nature of the husband's privilege, as a farmer and as a voting citizen, and it emphasizes the farm wife's lack of a voice in the affairs of the farm and of full citizenship in the nation.

Cleary signals this dual disenfranchisement through Margaret's diminishing ability to speak. As Margaret begins to break under the relentless labor of the farm, she begins "repeating some senseless words" and her mouth starts to twitch, a sign of the inner dissonance between what she wishes to express and the language she is allowed to use. The breaking point occurs during the portrait scene common to the farm-wife plot. When Barret, seeing a picture of Margaret as a bride, says she was "a good-looking girl," her daughter Lilian refuses to believe that the "pitty lady" in the photograph is Margaret (150). Faced with this crisis of identity, Margaret loses her grip on reality. Just as the narrator in Gilman's "The Yellow Wallpaper" experiences synesthesia, smelling the color of the yellow wallpaper as it drives her mad, so too does Margaret begin to hear as well as see the "frightful, relentless yellow waves" of corn closing in on her. As in naturalistic novels such as Norris's *McTeague* or *Vandover and the Brute*, the repetition of a phrase or echolalia signifies madness, and when Margaret wakes at night, with eyes "quite vacant," she begins dully repeating, in broken phrases, all the chores she must do (151). For a farm wife, the spoken response to the grinding work of the farm can take only two forms: to internalize the patriarchal language of its ceaseless work and to become brutal to others, as Rebecca does, or to repeat the meaningless language as a form of helpless acceptance, as Margaret does. Now quite insane, Margaret is taken away by her family, and all the sympathy goes to Barret and his dreams of being a legislator, since, as the narrative voice notes with irony, "there had been nothing in her life to cause insanity" (151).

MARY HALLOCK FOOTE

The author of twelve novels and numerous short stories, Mary Hallock Foote (1847–1938) published fiction and illustrations widely in commercial and literary magazines, including the *Century* and the *Atlantic Monthly*. As Janet Floyd contends, Foote does not create "a feminized regional world . . . her interest was in the social and psychological space that [men and women] *shared*," a judgment particularly apt for "The Trumpeter," which focuses on the western borderlands of nations and races.[16] Published in two parts in the *Atlantic Monthly* (November and December 1894), Foote's "The Trumpeter" takes place between the "Bisuka barracks" of the U.S. Army outpost and the Bannock Reservation.[17] It incorporates Darwinian courtship rituals, racial inheritance theories, and shifting identities in its romance plot, all factors that intersect in a plot contrasting timeless borderland rituals and a time-defined national event, the movement of Coxey's Army in 1894.

As Henniker, the trumpeter and acknowledged flirt of K troop, plays his trumpet, two girls stop to listen: Callie Meadows, the fair-haired daughter of the base commander, and Meta, the dark-haired daughter of a Scottish father and a Bannock mother. Meta accepts her share of the Bannock tribe's money from selling horses, but in her consciousness and profile she was "all white," and the two girls consider themselves sisters (I: 579). Henniker's music is heard before he is seen, when his "trumpet blare, most masculine of all musical utterances, goes straight from his big blue-clad chest to the heart of his girl" (I: 577). The physical implications of musical transmission from Henniker's chest to theirs confirm his sexual attraction for them both. Exercising Darwinian female sexual selection based on Henniker's courtship display of a "fine gait and figure" as well as his music, Callie boldly tells him of her interest, leading to their engagement after a single week of courtship.

Less bold than Callie, Meta meets Henniker in person at a dance and minstrel show, appropriately a place where racial identities and stereotypical representations are displayed openly for the amusement of the crowd. She wears a long white dress, yet, dissatisfied with her appearance, wishes for a necklace and makes one from the "gold-colored pompons with silver-gray stems that spangle the dry hills in June" (I: 580). The natural gold of the necklace of flowers complements her black hair, which is worn loose and "crisped like a war-steed's encolure" that makes "her face and throat look pale against its blackness" (I: 580). Foote contrasts the natural and primitive elements with those of civilization, for both have their part in creating the woman that Meta has become. The fashionable dress with sleeves that "were puffed and stood out like wings" (I: 580) is set off by the necklace of natural gold plants. Compared to a horse's mane, her dark hair links her with animals and with the sophisticated quotation about the "war-steed's encolure" from Robert Browning's "The Statue and the Bust." Meta's white skin, set off by her dark hair, is intensified by the "spot of white electric light" that touches her chest, a virtual spotlight that emphasizes her skin and her sexual charms. Natural and manufactured artifacts combine to reveal Meta as blending two worlds.

But white and Native names for Meta distinguish her solely through what her body represents for each race. The soldiers call her "the little broncho" because of her "great mane of hair," connecting her with the horse, physicality, and sexuality, an objectification of Meta as a sexual object that Henniker, to his credit, resents (I: 582). In contrast, the Bannocks call Meta a mariposa lily, white when closed but "with a dark purplish stain" when it opens (I: 579), suggesting both purity and the white of Meta's blood. After Meta marries Henniker and experiences her sexual initiation, the narrator comments, "[t]he wild white lily had opened, and behold the stain!" (I: 588). The "dark stain" has racial as well as sexual implications, for the narrator declares that in "the beauty of their women lurks the venom of the dark races which the white man has put beneath his feet" (I: 581), an allusion to a line in Psalm 91 ("Thou shalt tread upon the lion and adder: the young lion and the dragon shalt thou trample under feet"). Portraying the "dark races" as snakes crushed by the white man's subjugation, the image suggests that the beauty of Native women conveys the "venom" by which the tribes strike back at their oppressors. To cast Native women's sexuality as "venom," however, blames the innocent Meta, and by extension other Native women, for the white man's actions of seduction, rape, and abandonment, as though, like other violent actions of empire, seduction and rape are the fault of the victimized rather than the oppressors.

Meta and Henniker share a common bond in their outsider ethnicity: the Irish Henniker and the Scottish-Bannock Meta are not "white" but in disguise as white, something that narrative attention to their elaborately described costumes makes clear. As his multiple performances in disguise suggest, Henniker is the trickster who entertains and disrupts the community but fails to bring it together as a trickster should. He is a transient in the borderlands, in contrast to the established cyclical returns of the Bannocks, whose rights of domicile and horse-trading grant them an accepted place in the economy of the place. Fittingly, at the minstrel show, he plays the part of the wandering minstrel "Mr. Piper Hide-and-Seek," a name that hints at his later travels and his fondness for drink, Piper Heidsieck being a brand of champagne. Later he disguises himself as "a stage peasant" who plays upon the willow pipes, and then as a colorful Zouave. Unaccustomed to the conventions of the minstrel show, Meta takes all of his performances at face value, including his showy riding in formation during a military exercise.

The two women respond to his music differently as well. When Henniker courted Meta's white sister, Callie, his flirtatious language had made her declare him to be "magnificent fun" (I: 578), but his courtship of Meta through music rather than English words suggests their deeper emotional bond. Henniker finds a way "to talk to Meta with his trumpet" (I: 589), as a jealous Callie tells her parents, unaware of the phallic overtones of her remark. Sometimes playing "When my mother comes to know / That I love the soldiers so / She will lock me up all day" and sometimes Robert Burns's "Oh, whistle, and I'll come to you, my lad" (I: 589), he signals Meta to stay away with one song and to come to him with another. Henniker subverts the official use of the trumpet, issued to him to maintain order through a set series of tunes, to seduce Callie and Meta rather than to preserve the order of the post. Callie interprets the words, identifying the message through the lyrics associated with the tune, but Meta interprets the music, evoking Darwin's theory of female sexual selection in courtship, when the female chooses her mate based on the song of the male bird. For the half-Bannock Meta and the Irish Henniker, "[I]t was fit that a trumpet's reckless summons, or its brief inarticulate call, like the note of a wild bird to its mate, should be the language of his love" (I: 589). The spaces in which they meet position them as beyond social laws, since instead of "vine-shaded porches," the lovers meet in the hilly borderlands, a wild space belonging to neither Bannocks nor whites (I: 588). Meta tells Mrs. Meadows that "a judge, or a justice, in the town" (I: 590) has married her to Henniker, but the overtones of seduction and betrayal are strong since Henniker leaves her behind when his troop is posted to Fort Custer.

Meta too adopts a disguise, shifting her appearance from the white to the Native American half of her ancestry. After her son is born, Meta finds herself displaced from both cultures: she is isolated from members of the Meadows family, who are disappointed in her, and from the Bannock men, who "turned away their eyes in silence from her shame" (I: 592). Throughout the story Meta is most herself when she mixes parts of her biracial heritage. The white dress she wore to the minstrel show and dance signified her white self, yet it also made her skin seem darker, revealing both portions of her identity. Now, however, she must suppress her white heritage so that she can travel on the railroad, something she can afford only by dressing as a full-blooded member of the Bannock tribe. When she walks along the road to meet Henniker, he sees her as he is riding in a wagon going the other way. She recognizes Henniker and holds up their son to him as the wagon speeds past. With his cultural prejudices intact, Henniker sees only "a little squaw facing the wind" who does not fit the profile of a Bannock woman, for she carries her child in her arms rather than on her back. He then recognizes that "this creature was his wife... and that the animal-like thing she held up, that wrung its face and squeaked like a blind kitten, was his son" (I: 596). Henniker refuses to recognize the "creature" and her "animal-like thing" as his wife and child. The trauma of his denial ultimately kills Meta.

Seven years after abandoning Meta, the alcoholic Henniker returns to the region. He has been reduced from his former splendor as a trumpeter in the U.S. Army to traveling with Coxey's Army, which in the spring of 1894 marched toward Washington, D.C., to protest unemployment. As Darlis A. Miller explains, Foote, whose "political conservatism infuses this story" had no use for Coxey's Army, which she portrays unsympathetically as ragged, lazy, down-and-outers, unlike the disciplined soldiers of the local camp.[18] Coxey's men, "calling themselves American citizens, were parading their idleness throughout the land" (II: 723), the narrator reports in disgust, and only thorough training and good character prevents the regular army from firing on such sorry specimens. As a member of this sham army, Henniker reveals the cowardly self he had earlier hidden behind his U.S. Army uniform.

At the Bisuka outpost, Henniker revisits his past. He sees Callie, happily engaged at last after his jilting of her. He encounters Mrs. Meadow, who tells him that his son believes him dead. Henniker is crushed to see pity and disdain in the eyes of the fine son that he can never acknowledge. His son, Ross Henniker, is a Darwinian "case of 'throwing back'... [with] none of the Bannock here" (II: 723). Fully assimilated into the white world of the Meadows family, Ross is proud and accustomed to command, including, as the narrator reports with seeming approval, the white child's cruelties of breaking a stick over his pony's back and kicking him in his eagerness to see the Coxeyites on the move, a far cry from the horse-handling skills of his Bannock forefathers. Not recognizing his father, Ross tells him to "Go back where you belong, you dirty man," a "sentence" harsher to Henniker's ears than the one handed down by the judge who commits the Coxeyites to jail (II: 727). Henniker's well-fitting uniform had constituted his identity as a soldier, all external showiness but with a hollow man inside. His rags now define him as a soldier of Coxey's Army, and he despises himself. Wanting to be a "clean man" again, he sheds his rags and slips into the river to drown (II: 726).

In addition to Darwinian echoes of music, racial inheritance, and female sexual selection in courtship, Foote injects a national and global dimension into her story by refuting the terms of the transracial romance. As Mary Louise Pratt explains, the transracial romance or love plot appears in its characteristic form in narratives of colonial encounter: "It is easy to see transracial love plots as imaginings in which European supremacy is guaranteed by affective and social bonding... in which romantic love rather than filial servitude or force guarantee the willful submission of the colonized." As in Pratt's description of the colonial love story in which "the lovers are separated, the European is reabsorbed by Europe, and the non-European dies an early death," Henniker abandons Meta and returns to his troop, after which she dies.[19] But Foote challenges the terms of the transracial romance, for when Henniker returns to his own people, as the transracial romance requires, he is despised rather than commended by all for treating Meta badly. The Bannocks are portrayed sympathetically for the era, as trading partners who carefully preserve Meta's horses and help her to follow Henniker when he leaves her. The only disorderly group requiring military action is Coxey's Army, white men, whom Foote represents as preferring idleness to work. Transients in a borderland where white and Native American populations exist in some degree of reciprocity, the Coxeyites represent the white man at his devolutionary worst.

Batterman Lindsay's Trickster Language

Like Elia Peattie, Kate Cleary, and Mary Hallock Foote, (Annie) Batterman Lindsay (1853–1924) incorporates Darwinist and naturalistic elements in her serious fiction. Lindsay was a popular and prolific writer who wrote of the West and the Northwest, focusing on its mining camps, its wilderness, and its dangers. Born Annie Batterman to General C. C. Batterman and his wife on May 18, 1853, Lindsay grew up in the West, living in Virginia City when her father was the Nevada state treasurer, and later moving to Seattle, Washington with her husband, Robert H. Lindsay.[20] Lindsay began publishing short stories in 1895, with many appearing through syndication in newspapers across the country. In addition to western short stories, she wrote essays on mysticism and a quasi ghost story called "The Reapers," which was so popular that, after its publication in the *Black Cat* in 1897, it was reprinted there in 1910 by popular request. Her work appeared in many of the same periodicals as Jack London's stories: the *Atlantic Monthly*, the *Overland Monthly* (where one of her stories appeared in the same number as his "To the Man On Trail" in 1899), and the *Black Cat*. A note appended to "The Lone Star's Bonanza," published in *Land of Sunshine* in April 1899, states that Lindsay is on the *Land of Sunshine* editorial staff and is "one of the very few California writers who were born in California—perhaps the only one in her class."[21] Lindsay died on February 9, 1924, but her work remained popular and was reprinted even after her death.

Lindsay's best stories are those that chronicle the lives of Pacific Northwest and California tribes. The biographical note in the *Land of Sunshine* asserts that her "most important" work is "Extracts from Mrs. Lofty's Diary," the fictitious observations of a wealthy woman, which appeared in the *Overland Monthly*, and "Under the Headin' of Truth," the latter considered to be "the best Irish dialect ever written by an American."²² Yet most reviewers in her own time praised her western and Native stories for their "strength" and "virility," terms more commonly applied in Lindsay's time to the rising literary star Jack London. In 1899, Herbert Bashford, in "The Literary Development of the Far Northwest," praised her "admirable studies of Western character."²³ The *San Francisco Call*, in its 1896 essay "California Talent Finds a Gratifying Reception among Eastern Literati," praised the "virile force" of "Abandoned on the Plains" [*sic*] in the *Atlantic Monthly*, noting that "it has already been highly praised in some of the Boston papers."²⁴

Collected into the single volume of her work published in her lifetime, *Derelicts of Destiny* (1899), several of these stories gathered critical praise. A review of *Derelicts of Destiny* in the *San Francisco Call* on February 24, 1901, declared that the "tales represent some very clever work." Apparently missing the *Call*'s 1896 description of Lindsay as "a daughter of General C. C. Batterman, an old-time Californian," the review singles out "Mr. Lindsay's" story "Kwelth-Elite—The Proud Slave" as "the most virile," although it devotes half the review to disparaging the "nondescript garb" of the volume's cover and presentation, saying that "with a few Remington pictures to illuminate the text ... [the stories] would receive much more courteous treatment."²⁵ A review in the *Critic* repeats the gender error, saying "Mr." Lindsay's stories were "done with an unpracticed hand" yet "have a touch of genius in them," adding for good measure that "the proofreading is deplorable." Quoting this review, Ella Higginson in the *Seattle Times* sets the record straight about "Mrs." Batterman Lindsay but adds, "[S]eldom, indeed, does a woman write with such strength and independence. These grim, fearless, powerful stories cannot be too highly recommended."²⁶ In short, for her contemporaries, Lindsay was that desirable rara avis, the woman who wrote like a man, as evidenced by the repeated term "virile" applied to her work.

Many of Lindsay's Native American stories focus on tribal customs and feature a twist wherein a woman either evades a punishment for breaking a law or physically resists punishment by resorting to violence. In these stories, Lindsay inverts the stereotypes current in popular literature of the day, which depicted Native men ruled by codes of violence and Native women who are wretched in their submissiveness. One such story of a defiant woman, "The Old Law," features a tribal council of patriarchs condemning a woman to be stoned to death for the crime of adultery with a white man, as evidenced in her child with "pink skin and gray eyes."²⁷ As she waits for her execution, she pictures at length the gruesome details of their deaths, imagining the men crushing her baby's skull with a stone and wagering over how long she and the child will take to die. But her husband, Komo, who guards her, briefly recalls the image of the Crucifixion, picturing the blood on her head instead of Christ's. He frees her despite her taunts that he should kill her: "What shame to you! No wonder the young men laugh at you"

(38). Komo, feminized by Christianity, receives no credit from his unconverted wife for saving her life. The theme of male shame and feminization occurs again in "Squaw Charley," in which a male "Pi-Ute" is punished for his cowardice by being sentenced to wear a "discarded hoop-skirt, garnered from some ash-heap."[28] Like Dave in Charles W. Chesnutt's "Dave's Neckliss," who is forced to wear a chained ham around his neck for a theft that he did not commit and then believes himself to be the ham, Charley wears the hoopskirt as a form of identity even after he is isolated from the tribe, and it is found imprisoning his skeleton after death.

"My Great-Aunt's Wedding" and "Kwelth-Elite, the Proud Slave" likewise focus on women who outwit or defy tribal customs. "My Great-Aunt's Wedding" was originally published in *Land of Sunshine* as "The Half-Breed's Story," its title a tongue-in-cheek trick or misdirection of what readers would have assumed about the subject matter. Instead of a white and Native pairing, as in some of Lindsay's other stories, the title refers to the narrator's mother of the Duwamish tribe, a "fair people with grey eyes," and her darker father, whom the narrator resembles.[29] The main story is the mother's account of T'saquinza, her great-aunt, the daughter of Quo-doultz, the Hyas Tyee (important ruler) of the Duwamish.[30] At her father's insistence, T'saquinza marries a chief's son, Yoot-skut, "a young chief of the Snoqualmies" (248). After an elaborate wedding, in which the bride walks "on a road of swan's down a foot deep" (248), T'saquinza runs away with the young and handsome Skootsa. When Yoot-skut finally tracks them down, T'saquinza threatens to jump from a precipice with her child in her arms unless Yoot-skut lets her remain with Skootsa. As in "The Old Law," a man suffers shame because of his love for a woman: despite the jeers of his friends, Yoot-skut lets her live and returns to camp, recognizing that he has seen true love even if he has not received it from T'saquinza. Speaking to the narrator's mother as a child, T'saquinza admits that Yoot-skut was doubtless the better man, adding, a little mischievously, "But we do not love men for their goodness" (250).

Lindsay authenticates this story both through the manner of its telling and its use of specific details. The frame story uses a first-person storytelling mode—"I have often heard my mother tell about her aunt's wedding"—with the daughter as an imagined listener who questions the mother, the narrator of the inner story. At one point, the mother interrupts herself to say "Princesses? Yes they *were* princesses, real ones" (248). The listener has obviously asked a question about whether her ancestors were Indian princesses, a cliché of stories featuring Native Americans even in 1897 when the story was published, and the mother distinguishes between authentic and inauthentic rank by emphasizing the "real" nature of her family's heritage. As in the writings of Zitkala-Ša, the narrator emphasizes the superior qualities of Indian parenting: her grandfather was "strict with his daughters" but Indians "never strike their children ... more than to give them a push or a little box on the ear" (248). Like the original title, this detail undercuts readers' expectations, since a "little box on the ear" could negate the "never strike their children" part of the sentence. The contradiction highlights the issue of how words and facts differ depending on the context, since for a nineteenth-century white audience accustomed to sterner chastisement of children, a box on the ear might indeed have seemed an action too minor to qualify as corporal punishment.

The specificity of Lindsay's use of Native language also undercuts readers' expectations. In their regionalist fiction, writers such as María Cristina Mena, Kate Chopin, Sui Sin Far, and Alice Dunbar-Nelson sprinkle phrases in Chinese, Spanish, or French to authenticate their stories and to give the reader a sense of immersion in the culture, yet the untranslated words are either insignificant exclamations or easily understood from the context. Lindsay liberally interweaves Native terms in her text, which positions her narrator as an insider and a Native, and translates only a few of them: "'o-quack-a-cull' (my wife)", "'tl'kope kowmux' (beaten dogs)" (250). Yet the terms that Lindsay employs, though unfamiliar to easterners and possibly to most of the *Land of Sunshine*'s western readers, are a form of language called "Chinook Jargon," used widely in the Pacific Northwest by white settlers as well as tribal members. Rather than requiring knowledge of the actual Duwamish language, all the words that Lindsay uses can be found in the 1887 edition of *Dictionary of Chinook Jargon with Examples of Use in Conversation*.[31] Using a language that outside readers would assume is tribal in origin, the narrator validates the authenticity of the subject matter while fooling only outsiders, not those who know Chinook Jargon.

"Kwelth-Elite, the Proud Slave" explores the position of women in spaces defined as regional but intersecting with a national or global economy. It deploys the same authenticating techniques, including dialect, as her other work, but it addresses the issue of slavery and sexual abuse from the perspective of the slave herself. In addition, it mingles past and present by juxtaposing legends and fairy tales with accounts of regional and transnational commerce. Though a slave and a member of a hop-picking group at the Snoqualmie Hop Ranch, Kwelth-Elite (with "Kwelth" meaning "proud" in Chinook dialect and "Elite" translating the name for general readers) is distinctive not only for her attitude but also for her body and bearing. Lindsay's narrators usually offer only a brief description of characters, but several paragraphs are devoted to Kwelth-Elite: her isolation as a captive, her exceptional height, and her features, which the narrator claims resemble neither those of the inland Northwest tribes nor those of the coastal tribes. Instead Kwelth-Elite, purchased from "a wandering band of Shoshones" (534), may be from a southwestern tribe, for the narrator speculates that a dying Pueblo mother's blood had "crimsoned the acequia's [irrigation stream's] crystal" as she watched her baby being carried away by Apaches.[32]

The narrator's romanticized vision of Kwelth-Elite's origins, combined with her philosophical comments about "a Prehistoric World and a Vanished Race" (534), obscure Kwelth-Elite's modernity and that of her region. Kwelth-Elite picks hops as part of a large contingent of itinerant labor, all because her owner, a "dreadful old woman... must have the Boston Man's money to buy the Boston Man's goods; so she brought her slave to earn it in the Boston Man's hop-fields" (535). By working on the Snoqualmie Hop Ranch, called "the largest single field in the world," Kwelth-Elite participates in an agribusiness within a modern global economy, run by eastern capital, as signified by the repetition of "Boston Man." She picks crops and loads them onto the train, always a symbol of modernity at the turn of the century, for shipment and distribution all over the world. Yet her enslavement also renders Kwelth-Elite herself a commodity in the ancient culture of slavery that trades her from owner to owner throughout the Pacific Northwest, on lands already the site of Native displacement and trauma following earlier generations of "the Boston Man's" appropriations of territory.

By emphasizing the contradictions between the woman's pride and her status as slave, "Kwelth-Elite, the Proud Slave" follows the fairy-tale convention of the foundling princess whose hidden nobility is disguised by her lowly status. In true fairy-tale fashion, Kwelth-Elite's nemesis is a little person ("dwarf," in the story's terminology), her mistress's grandson, Okinakeine, who is "scarce more than three feet high," with a face "abnormally large" (535). Continually harassed by his face, "grinning and grimacing at her" (535), she consults a "magic doctor," the Keelally Tamanahwis, for a means to rid herself of Okinakeine. Like Kwelth-Elite's owner and the white men collectively known as the Boston Man, however, the Keelally is more interested in profit in this world than a mystical contemplation of the next, for his purpose in going to the hop harvest was "to gather in the shekels of the credulous" (535). By using the Hebrew word "shekels," which became American slang in the 1880s, Lindsay again links Kwelth-Elite with global modernity and the circulation of capital.

Another link to economic modernity is Kwelth-Elite's payment to the Keelally, "a silver dollar given her the week before by a kodak fiend to induce her to pose for him" (536). Despite believing that the "kodak fiend" or photographer can "bring evil at his pleasure on each separate member of her body" (536), she allows him to take her picture. The technology of photography is another intrusion into Kwelth-Elite's world, transforming her person into a fetish for the white man's viewing pleasure and bringing her further into the modern economy of the Boston Man. The belief that Native peoples fear that the photograph will steal one's soul appears in Kwelth-Elite's fantasies of torture and dismemberment if the photographer "brings evil at his pleasure" to each limb of her body. But her labor under the oppression of two exploitative economic systems, the ancient slavery of the tribe and the modern slavery of laboring in the hop fields, confirms that her body is not her own in either system.

Kwelth-Elite reclaims her bodily autonomy dramatically in the story's climax, a prolonged and bruising struggle on a precipice, often the symbolic site of significant action in Lindsay's stories. Kwelth-Elite and Okinakeine fight "with set teeth and straining sinews" like animals. Theirs is an unusually physical, hand-to-hand fight between a man and a woman, as Okinakeine, "snarling like a beast" (538), proves no match for Kwelth-Elite. The "black ichor of hatred and revenge," the godlike blood that years of slavery have produced in her, gives her superhuman strength. She bends back Okinakeine's head until he falls into the river below and drowns—an outcome, as Paige Sylvia Raibmon notes, that mimics what "Chief Seattle was said to have done to a Yakima war party."[33] Okinakeine's dying grandmother accuses Kwelth-Elite of turning him into an owl and demands that Kwelth-Elite be buried alive with her. Facing certain death, Kwelth-Elite stares up out of the grave, astonished to see the narrator and other "white faces" who happen to be passing by and rescue her. Like her midnight quest for a magic that would free her, the last-minute rescue by whites seems borrowed from a fairy tale, as the romantic imagination of the narrator might wish. Yet Kwelth-Elite's life after rescue is decidedly prosaic. She serves the family of one of her rescuers for a time, an echo of her former slavery, later "marr[ying] a prosperous half-breed rancher on the Puyallup reservation" (539). Dispelling any sense of the "vanishing race" trope that the narrator had invoked early in the story, the ending successfully integrates Kwelth-Elite into capitalist modernity, reservation life, and a traditional marriage.

The Native American stories of Batterman Lindsay occasionally stray into the era's tendency to invoke the Vanishing American theme, especially in the title of *Derelicts of Destiny*, which combines the then-current ideology of the degeneration of Native Americans and the hypothetically deterministic destiny that awaits a "vanishing" race, "derelict" in the sense of being left behind. Yet the voice of the narrator renders ironic the possible clichés that she may be invoking. Lindsay's use of Chinook Jargon caters to but also mocks the turn-of-the-century passion for authenticity and getting the inside story, just as her use of a romanticizing narrator with dubious judgment challenges the preposterous events she describes. In stories such as "Abandoned: A Tale of the Plains" or "Kwelth-Elite, the Proud Slave," with its description of a capitalist economy in which bodies are circulated as migrant workers and sold in the marketplace as slaves, its physical fight to the death between a woman and the man who tries to sexually abuse her, and its comparison of human beings to animals, Lindsay suggests grim realism and naturalism.

Arresting Biological Time in Mary E. Wilkins Freeman's "Old Woman Magoun"

Mary E. Wilkins Freeman's "Old Woman Magoun" is naturalistic not only in its "murderous mother" plot, as Linda Grasso has called it, but also in its emphasis on Darwinian inheritance and degeneration, its setting of rural squalor, its conversion of human beings into things in a marketplace of exchange, its focus on female sexuality, and the futility of its characters' attempts to retard the biological processes associated with time.[34] It incorporates naturalistic themes of repetition, obsession, and the fetishization of objects. The desire for possession of a dream that results in the destruction of the object possessed is a naturalistic staple, as when *McTeague*'s Zerkow, the junk man, kills his wife Maria Macapa when she can no longer furnish him with a story of gold. "Old Woman Magoun" demonstrates that women can be fetishists, for Mrs. Magoun is obsessed with making time stand still and with preserving the innocence of her granddaughter Lily's body, an obsession so profound that she kills Lily in order to save her body from violation, never recognizing the irony of her greater transgression. In addition, "Old Woman Magoun" challenges the favored tropes of women's regional fiction with its decisive catalog of rural degeneration, its use of the woman herbalist character as destroyer rather than healer, and its annihilation of natural processes in favor of a fetishization of the past. Like Wharton's *Ethan Frome*, "Ethan Brand," and "Bunner Sisters," it models a women's naturalism that incorporates but refutes regionalism. The story operates on three levels of discourse: a biblical level of the struggle between good and evil that parallels the white slave narrative, a fairy-tale level that relies on repetition and ritualized language for its effect, and a naturalistic and evolutionary level, using animal imagery and Darwinian themes.

"Old Woman Magoun" takes place in a location doubly identified by name and by region. Set in a traditionally remote locale, a high valley with hills lying "in moveless curves like a petrified ocean ... in green-cresting waves which never break," the "hamlet of Barry's Ford" is positioned in terms of the familiar spatial conflicts and reader expectations of the regional story, those of a village that time forgot and the incursions of modernity that threaten its existence.[35] But the "petrified" quality of the waves that should signify movement and life suggests unhealthy stasis rather than preservation. Adopting the tone of a historian or anthropologist, the narrator carefully explains that "it is *Barry's* Ford" because of the family's importance and "*Ford* because just at the beginning of the hamlet the little turbulent Barry River is fordable" (361). In this objective third-person perspective, the etymology of a place name becomes as important as its location on a river that despite its turbulence is "little," like the diminished prominence of a degenerate aristocratic family. In another departure from regionalist conventions, an older woman, the title character, is an agent of change, for it is she who causes a "rude bridge across the river" (361) to be built. Spreading her "strong arms like wings" (361), as if she is an avenging angel, "Old Woman" Magoun scatters the weak "masculine element" at the country store, her title presumably voicing the perspective of the men who do not dare to stand up to her.

The story presents a series of struggles for mastery between biological time and deathly stasis, although neither presents a good alternative for Lily, Mrs. Magoun's granddaughter. Mrs. Magoun, whose evolutionary inheritance makes her the "best of the strain" (363), tries to retard biological time, and Lily's father, Nelson Barry, the "fairly dangerous degenerate of a good old family" represented only by himself and a "sister of feeble intellect" (362), seeks to advance it. Seen clasping a doll, a "poor old rag thing," Lily appears to be "only a child" at "nearly fourteen," although "her mother had been married at sixteen" (362). Lily's maturity, or lack of it, forms the subject of Mrs. Magoun's conversations with her friend Sally Jinks, with Sally asserting Lily's maturity and Mrs. Magoun denying it. The white clothing that Lily wears, her absence of education and worldly speech, and the rag doll she carries signify her childishness and innocence yet also her potential for motherhood. Lily's ambiguous status as a symbol of contradictory chronology intensifies when Mrs. Magoun asks her to go to the store to buy salt. Lily carries her rag doll over her shoulder, and "the absurd travesty of a face peeped forth from Lily's yellow curls" (363). The "travesty" makes Lily Janus-faced, with one face looking toward her future by visiting the store and the other face looking backward toward her grandmother.

The fairy-tale element emerges in Lily's trip to the store, an excursion into the world of men and experience that takes her across a bridge from innocence into experience and from her grandmother's protection to the world of men, alcohol, and sexual violence. The built environment of the hamlet, the bridge, and the store all contribute to Lily's loss of innocence, for by building the bridge and assenting to Lily's trip to the grocery store, Mrs. Magoun is the means of Lily's awakening and her downfall. Lily meets a "handsome, well-dressed man," Jim Willis, on the way to the store. He asks Lily, "Where are you bound, you and your dolly?" (364), a question that anticipates "Where Are You Going to, My Pretty Maid?"— the song used in Elizabeth Robins's white slave novel *My Little Sister*.[36] Lily feels "complete trust" when he takes her "little childish" hand in his (364) and takes her to meet Nelson Barry. Nelson, also a "handsome man" (367), offers her candy in exchange for her doll, the first of a series of exchanges in which Lily's body is offered for sale and of instances when she is offered or denied food. When Lily refuses to make the trade, with "the reproach of a woman" (366) as if understanding that the doll represents herself, Nelson, undeterred, sends the candy home with her. At the dinner celebrating the completion of the bridge, Mrs. Magoun separates Lily from the drunken men at the table and, refusing Nelson's candy, gives Lily her usual dinner instead. She has slowed but not stopped the outside world from feeding Lily with unfamiliar food and experiences.

Mrs. Magoun's other interventions into Lily's life are less successful. The bridge that Mrs. Magoun has had the men build is a "primitive structure built of logs in a slovenly fashion," with a gap that shows "the way men work" (371), she remarks disapprovingly to Lily. In contrast to the men's slovenly construction of the bridge, Mrs. Magoun's construction of Lily as a spectacle fit for town illustrates the way women work to create a work of art: she curls Lily's hair "punctiliously" until it is "two rows of golden spirals" framing her face, and Lily's new clothing makes her a "little pink fluttering figure" (371). Both bridge and outfit have been constructed to change the course of nature, the bridge to offer access across the river and the dress to conceal Lily's age and present her as a fit object for adoption by Lawyer Mason and his wife. But the bridge can fulfill its function regardless of its imperfections, because its greater aim is to permit what the frozen and petrified waves of the valley cannot: the flow of life and the perpetuation of the species through reproduction.

Biblical echoes of the knowledge of good and evil emerge when Nelson Barry knocks at Mrs. Magoun's door after Lily's meeting with Jim Willis. Although she tries to shut Nelson out, he appears as "a rebellious animal which she was trying to tame" (371), the animal imagery aligning him with nature and its Darwinian imperative to reproduce. "You know me of old. No human being can turn me from my way when I am once started in it," he declares. Nelson's handsome but dissolute face, his position as a degenerate specimen of a once-noble family, his claim of extraordinary powers, and his statement that "you know me of old" hint not merely at his seduction of Lily's mother but of Satanic powers. He strengthens the impression by announcing, "[A] knowledge of evil is a useful thing. How are you going to avoid evil if you don't know what it is like?" (370). The question of knowledge of good and evil evokes the Garden of Eden and also the white slave literature of the period, a subset of which pleaded for educating girls about sexuality. In contrast to ideals of purity that relied on girls' total ignorance, *The Great War on White Slavery* and novels such as Elizabeth Robins's *My Little Sister* and Cosmo Brooks's *The Blindness of Virtue* (1904) proclaim that far from preserving innocence, ignorance of sexual matters renders a young girl subject to misunderstanding the intentions of the men she meets. Mrs. Magoun can keep a physical barrier, the door, between Nelson and his daughter, but by keeping Lily ignorant of the facts of life, she permits Lily's exposure to greater danger.

Lily's ignorance of the danger that Jim Willis and her father pose is one harmful extreme, but Mrs. Magoun's deep suspicion of men and her unwillingness to allow Lily to mature is another one. After Nelson demands that Lily be turned over to him in a week, Mrs. Magoun intuits that she is to be used as the payment of his gambling debt to Jim Willis. That Nelson would sell Lily, his own flesh, and that he would sell her to Willis, his twin in good looks and dissipation, in an act of symbolic incest confirms his Satanic persona. Against his power, Mrs. Magoun can say only "Oh, my God!" (370) as if in prayer, but she is no longer the powerful angel figure who can spread her "strong arms like wings" and vanquish Nelson and the other loafers. Sexual drive and control over commerce give men a power on earth that no appeal to heaven can banish, and, emphasizing her connection to earth and time, "the old, heavily stepping" Mrs. Magoun must now rely on earthly men rather than heavenly fathers to save Lily from corruption.

The equation of food with physical experience structures a series of events in which Lily's fate unfolds. Her initiation begins when she is sent to the store to buy salt for her grandmother, a staple of life essential to the food that Mrs. Magoun is preparing to serve to the bridge builders as part of the banquet. When she meets Nelson Barry at the store, he kisses her and strokes her cheek. She shrinks from him when she smells the whiskey on his breath, a naturalistic detail that evokes her visceral rather than reasoned repugnance, but Nelson's touching her cheek causes "[h]ereditary instincts and nature" to emerge in "the child's innocent, receptive breast" (366). Lily's comment that Willis is "a real handsome man" (367) demonstrates that her awakening to the world of men is imminent, as signified by her acceptance of Nelson's candy. On their walk to Lawyer Mason's house, Lily says of the deadly nightshade berries, "Those berries look good to eat, grandma" but her grandmother says that she "can't have any now" (372), the qualifier "now" leaving room for Mrs. Magoun to change her mind later.

Despite her careful attempts to prepare Lily for the visit to Lawyer Mason and his wife, Mrs. Magoun cannot control Lily's eating or the outcome of the visit any more than she can control her sexual maturity. Lily's "new muslin dress with a pink sash" (371) echoes the "lavender muslin" (373) that Mrs. Mason wears. In appearance, she should be acceptable to the Masons, who have lost a daughter of their own. At Lawyer Mason's house, Mrs. Mason offers and Lily accepts "a plate of cake, a glass of milk, and an early apple" (372), an action that should seal their relationship, yet the combination of sweets, nourishment, and the too-early apple commonly associated with sexual knowledge in the Bible indicates otherwise. Lawyer Mason refuses to adopt Lily, seeing beneath the socially coded surface the

"Barry blood in her veins" (373). Misapplying Darwinian principles, he declares that "[t]he stock has run out; it is vitiated physically and morally" (373), an interpretation of degeneracy theory that equates physical descent and literal blood with innate moral traits. Defeated in her attempts to rescue Lily from Nelson, Mrs. Magoun on the return trip does not prevent Lily from eating the nightshade berries, which Lily accurately describes as "real sweet" (375). This action parallels that of Nelson's gift of candy, for in each case, Lily uses her own uninformed judgment to accept a food dangerous to her, something that Mrs. Magoun refuses to prevent by giving Lily the necessary knowledge about relations between the sexes. Mrs. Magoun may have poisoned her daughter as well, for Nelson recalls that Lily's "mother was very sick once from eating [apples]" before her early death (377). Substituting the sweet poison of the deadly nightshade for what she considers the poison of sexual experience, Mrs. Magoun classes both as leading to death.

Eating the nightshade berries leads to a fully naturalistic death scene. Lily's symptoms are described in visceral detail, beginning with her "difficulty in swallowing" (374), burning feeling in her stomach, vertigo, and nausea before her pupils grew "so dilated that they looked black" (375–76), a well-known effect of belladonna, the drug made from deadly nightshade.[37] Spinning stories of a material heaven with a rainbow-colored gate and streets of gold, Mrs. Magoun watches Lily but makes no move to save her by administering an antidote. As Mrs. Magoun had caused to be built the bridge to the town where commerce and sexual knowledge awaited Lily, now she guides Lily to a land with white rooms and gold streets where she "will never be sick any more" (376). Significantly, the only specific response Lily makes to Mrs. Magoun's description is to connect gold with "the ring grandpa gave you" (376), the wedding ring that she will never have. About to be sold for gold to pay a gambling debt, now Lily will be in a place where the gold is so ubiquitous as to be meaningless. After Lily's death, Mrs. Magoun carries Lily's doll with her "as one might have carried an infant" (377). Yet for the monstrous mother who kills her grandchild lest she grow into sexual maturity, the doll is less a memento of Lily than an emblem of the sort of daughter and granddaughter she wished to have, a doll that can "love you back" (376) without ever growing up.

Darwinism, Desire, and Addiction

Kate Chopin's *At Fault* (1890) and Edith Wharton's *The Fruit of the Tree* (1907) are less familiar in their authors' canons than *The Awakening* and *The House of Mirth*. Unlike *The Awakening* and *The House of Mirth*, they do not follow the classic naturalistic formula of following a single individual, trapped by hereditary and environmental forces, who spirals downward toward an inevitable death. Instead each includes the characteristic excesses of unruly naturalism, with a focus on social problems, hints of a reform agenda, numerous subplots and themes, evidences of sentiment or melodrama, and a more expansive, less structurally symmetrical plot and sequence of action than in classic naturalism. The novels share some striking similarities. They center on unhappy marriages and the potential social consequences of divorce, with each male character tied to a mismatched partner and separated from the woman he loves, the character from whose perspective the novel is largely told. The marriage and divorce plots are set against an industrial background, which echoes the divorce plot not in structure but in the theme of social turmoil and the conflict between preindustrial and modern ways of life. The industrial plots represent Chopin's and Wharton's most sustained attention to the plight of workers and the consequences of industrialization. In keeping with its exploration of old and new worlds, each novel includes conflicts between an old order aristocracy and a newly professionalized class as well as portraits of the New Woman and of addicted individuals.

At Fault and *The Fruit of the Tree* demonstrate a commitment to Darwinian principles, from hereditary weaknesses, rules of attraction, female sexual selection in courtship, and sexual desire to failures of adaptation. As Bert Bender describes them in *The Descent of Love* and *Evolution and the Sex Problem*, indicators of Darwin's theories include male courtship display through performance, secondary sexual characteristics such as facial hair, the grasping hands of the male, using music to woo a mate, "natural settings that are wild and entangled," primitive culture and evolutionary progress, and female sexual selection, the ability of women to choose mates based on evolutionary principles.[38] Combined with their use of naturalistic features such as the grotesque bodies of women, women's social courtship choices at odds with their evolutionary preferences, and the persistent image in naturalism of a woman's unmoving body on display before those who try to interpret her but cannot, Chopin in *At Fault* and Wharton in *The Fruit of the Tree* reveal a Darwinian logic in their unruly naturalism.

AT FAULT

Kate Chopin credited her reading in Darwin, Spencer, and Huxley, her "daily companions" in "the study of the human species," as central to her work, although she "quarreled" with Darwin's theory of female passivity in the matter of sexual selection.[39] In the stories of Guy de Maupassant, which she translated for publication, she found "life, not fiction," and she studied his techniques closely.[40] Yet although Chopin kept a notebook and took notes until she felt as though she were "wearing Zola's coat," Zola's methodically detailed naturalism was antithetical to her own.[41] In fact, she attacked Zola's *Lourdes* because the reader can never "lose sight of the author and his note-book," and she criticized Zola's clumsy editorializing through characters whose words express "what the author himself thinks of those things."[42] Despite Chopin's ambivalence about Zola, *At Fault* includes naturalistic themes of violence, sexual desire, environmental destruction, waste, addiction, and disability that identify it, like *The Awakening*, as a form of naturalism.[43] Like Wharton's *The Fruit of the Tree* and some novels of grim realism, *At Fault* is, as Winfried Fluck contends, a novel caught between genres, but, seen in the context of women's unruly naturalism, *At Fault*'s many plots are characteristic rather than anomalous.[44] The language and plot of the book affirm the power of naturalistic determinants, including environment, addiction, and race, to trump the best-laid schemes of social regulation.

At Fault centers on the life of Thérèse Lafirme, the beautiful young widow of a wealthy older man, Jérôme Lafirme, who has left her his plantation, Place-du-Bois, in the Cane River country of northwestern Louisiana. Against her neighbors' expectations, Thérèse decides to manage the plantation herself and sells the timber rights to an outsider from St. Louis, David Hosmer. In what seems at first a conventional double love plot, Hosmer, a serious-minded businessman who manages the sawmill, falls in love with Thérèse, while at the same time her nephew Grégoire, an irresponsible but charming Creole, falls in love with David's sister, Melicent. After learning that Hosmer has been divorced from his alcoholic wife, Fanny, the Roman Catholic Thérèse breaks off her relationship with him and urges him to return to Fanny. By the end of part 1, Thérèse has restored order to her property but has placed her emotional life in turmoil by sending Hosmer back to his ex-wife. In part 2, as Bernard Koloski observes, "Thérèse's world begins to crumble" from order into chaos as her plans to organize others' lives go awry.[45] Those who had acquiesced to her wishes in part 1 chafe at her control in part 2. Marie Louise, Thérèse's old nurse, refuses to have her cabin moved back from the crumbling banks of the river. Joçint, the mixed-blood Native American and African American son of old Morico, rebels against factory work and burns the factory to the ground. Grégoire impulsively kills Joçint, and old Morico dies in rescuing Joçint's body from the flames of the burning factory. Thérèse has learned that the high ideal of indissoluble marriage she forced on Hosmer has led to a miserable existence for him, and she recognizes that she is "at fault" for having caused unhappiness in the lives of her immediate circle and, as an agent of modernization, those of her workers.

At Fault anticipates Wharton's *The Fruit of the Tree* in its dual plot of an unhappy marriage in the foreground of the narrative and the industrialization of a region in the background. The novel focuses on change and resistance to change, as an idea worked out on the regional level and on the individual level with the passing of Jérôme Lafirme and the old order, and the coming of David Hosmer, representative of the new. According to Donald Ringe, the novel begins in 1881, "the year the Texas and Pacific Railroad was built in Natchitoches parish," bringing with it access to markets that make Hosmer's sawmill possible and signaling "the intrusion of modern industry into the agricultural world of the plantation."[46] Although the lush descriptions suggest that Place-du-Bois is a "latter-day Arcadia," the intrusions of technology—the classic "machine in the garden" described by Leo Marx—and not the pastoral landscape surround the plantation.[47] Despite her opposition to divorce and her Creole heritage, which position her as a figure of the old order, Thérèse has already accepted the encroachment of industry, simply bidding her forest a "tearful farewell" once she has made the deal.[48] She literally has a dual perspective: she is first seen surveying her land through an instrument of technology, a field glass, through which she can see the railroad station, "a brown and ugly intruder within her fair domain" (742). Yet her unaided and more sentimental vision of the place as she sits in the wide hallway presents a pastoral picture of "a section of the perfect lawn" (743), emblematic of the false vision of serenity attained only by resolutely ignoring the world beyond its boundaries and the African Americans who labor to create the perfect lawn that Thérèse takes for granted.

As in other naturalistic novels, the material world abruptly disillusions Thérèse when she tries to resolve social disunity in the divorce plot, by reuniting Hosmer and Fanny, and in the industrial plot, by integrating Joçint and Grégoire, representatives of the agrarian South, into the industrial culture that Hosmer brings to the region. Chopin reinforces this idea through the clash of ideals with reality early in part 1 during a scene in which Grégoire and Melicent, the secondary set of lovers and foils for Thérèse and Hosmer, glide down the "dim leafy tunnel" of the bayou. Melicent, restless and emotionally detached where Thérèse is calm and emotionally engaged, is an example of the New Woman who seeks social and intellectual parity with men. She lives by her ideas of freedom as Thérèse lives by her ideas of duty. Grégoire tells Melicent, "You got to set mighty still in this pirogue" (748), but since it is not Melicent's "fashion to obey at word of command" (749), she ignores him until she sees the reason for the order: an alligator that Grégoire promptly shoots. A few minutes later, Grégoire issues a similar directive: "You betta put down yo' veil" (749). Declining for the second time to obey without questioning, Melicent is bitten by mosquitoes and, symbolically, by a reality that she refuses to accept. In contrast to Melicent, who, Grégoire says, seems to know everything, Grégoire, with "eyes black and brilliant as the eyes of an alert and intelligent animal" (749) does know everything, at least about the bayou and his culture. His knowledge is instinctual and experiential, for, as he tells her, he "ain't 'fraid o' any thing I can see an on'erstan.' I can han'le mos' any thing thet's got a body" (750).

The distinction between realities that have a body and those that exist only in the mind cuts to a central conflict in the book between naturalism and idealism. If Melicent treats love as an intellectual game, or Thérèse tries to paper over the realities of human emotions with idealism, as when she pressures Hosmer to remarry Fanny, their ideas necessarily fail when confronted by "any thing thet's got a body"—in short, anything tangible or real. Bodies constitute a means of measuring the character's grounding in reality: the more substantial the character's body, the better she understands real life. Through repeated descriptions of bodies and body types, Chopin explores the correlation between physical and emotional attributes, a Darwinian typology of gesture, self-adornment, and sexual attraction. Thérèse's blonde "roundness" signals that despite her prejudice against divorce she is more grounded in reality and more able to change than her thin, dark counterpart, Hosmer's sister Melicent. Melicent's thinness, like that of Hosmer, his never-seen friend Homeyer, and the intellectual but ineffectual Mr. Worthington, signifies a masculine level of idealism at odds with the realism of many of the novel's women. Melicent's slight build and ceaseless motion place her on one end of the scale whose point of balance is Thérèse.

The other end of the spectrum is Thérèse's former nurse Marie Louise, who is "so enormously fat that she move[s] about with evident difficulty" (806) yet possesses equanimity so vast that she alone can calm the troubled Thérèse. Like Edith Wharton's Mrs. Manson Mingott of *The Age of Innocence*, her size, an example of the grotesque body of naturalism, grants her an inordinate power in her culture based in part on her literal and figurative immobility. Unable or unwilling to move, Marie Louise and other characters of similar size grant themselves the authority to rule over their respective kingdoms, since supplicants and advice seekers must come to them rather than the other way around. Fanny's figure is indeterminate—"[t]here was no guessing at what her figure might be" (778)—but those of her friends Belle Worthington and Lou Dawson are comic exaggerations of the figures of Marie Louise and Melicent. A bottle blonde with a false hairpiece of blonde curls, Mrs. Worthington is "one hundred and seventy-five pounds of solid avoirdupois" (780) dressed in flashy clothes, a woman with so little use for books and ideas that she uses her husband's volumes of Schopenhauer and Emerson as bricks to weight down the washing she has put on the roof to dry. By contrast, Fanny's friend Lou Dawson is as thin, dark, and attractive to men as Melicent Hosmer.

As she was later to do in *The Awakening*, Chopin uses naturalistic imagery of ungovernable forces, repetitive movement, and animals to represent the characters. Grégoire and Joçint, men at ease in the bayous and woods, are described in terms of animal imagery, whereas Melicent, the restless New Woman, is perpetually in motion, although her movements are usually aimless and rarely propel her anywhere, as when she swings in a hammock. Her repetitive motions align her with what Jennifer Fleissner identifies as the typical naturalistic heroine, who, like Dreiser's Carrie Meeber, engages in repetitive actions that never move her forward.[49] Similarly, the opening chapters link Hosmer, water, and Thérèse's desire, a pattern that also foreshadows the cataclysmic deaths by drowning that conclude the novel and allow the two lovers to be together.[50] For example, as Thérèse leaves the mill one day, she climbs the stairs to a precarious platform and "watche[s] with fascinated delight the great logs hauled dripping from the water" an act that leaves her "giddy" (747). Barbara Ewell attributes this delight to Thérèse's love of industry and a "new orderliness," but Chopin's language bears out Pamela Menke's contention that the dripping logs constitute an "almost phallic vision."[51]

Through his relationship with Thérèse, Hosmer learns to regard the natural world as something more than goods to be measured and harvested. His clinical detachment and Thérèse's awareness of the physical reveals itself when she and Hosmer let their horses drink spring water from a hollowed-out cypress log, seeing them "[plunge] their heads deep in the clear water; the proud Beauregard [Thérèse's horse] quivering with satisfaction as . . . he waited for his more deliberate companion" (758). "Doesn't it give one a sympathetic pleasure," Thérèse asks Hosmer, "to see the relish with which they drink?" (758). The horses' plunging their heads into the water and "quivering with satisfaction" does not give Hosmer a "sympathetic pleasure," however. "I never thought of it," he says, using thinking rather than feeling to describe his initial response. His frame of reference is intellectual and technological, so his growing attraction to Thérèse is couched in those terms as well. When Thérèse's "warm, moist palm met his, it acted like a charged electric battery turning its subtle force upon his sensitive nerves" (762). Water and electricity, both currents of considerable force if not controlled, lead Hosmer to confess his love a moment later.

The emergence of Hosmer's atavistic self in this scene intensifies later in his dealings with Fanny, his ex-wife, as he moves from the rational man to the brute of naturalism. Brought to Place-du-Bois at Thérèse's urging, Fanny soon realizes Hosmer's feeling for Thérèse. She confronts him, for she, like Joçint and Gregoire, has volatile and primitive emotions to which she gives vent. "I won't stay here and have you making love under my very eyes to a woman that's no better than she ought to be," she tells Hosmer. Driven to fury, Hosmer "grasp[s] her arm with such a grasp, that had it been her throat she would never have spoken more" and swears, "By heaven—I'll—kill you!" as his "usually calm face [is] distorted by a passion of which she had not dreamed" (860, 861). Having roused both of them to animalistic fury, Fanny is momentarily satisfied, since she did not have "the fine nature that would stay cruelly stunned after such a scene" (861). Later, when Hosmer finds Fanny drunk at Marie Louise's cabin, he watches the rain and "want[s] to feel that rain and wind beating upon him" to escape the "atmosphere of hate that was possessing him and beginning to course through his veins as it had never done before" (865). The conventional symbolism of the storm without and the storm within signifies the coursing of violent passion throughout the body, and Hosmer understands that to submit to the wild rain coursing "in little swift rivulets" down the bank (864) would be less harmful than yielding to the hatred coursing through his veins.

Fanny Hosmer is neither savage nor morally bankrupt but simply a victim of circumstance who happened to marry the wrong man. Chopin's portrait of Fanny as an addict defies the customary stereotypes, for Fanny becomes more pleasant rather than less so when she drinks, and her drinking is portrayed as physical craving rather than a moral failing. What the novel shows, presciently, is the physical side of Fanny's addictive personality. Deprived of Hosmer's love, she takes to drink. Deprived of drink, when she comes to Place-du-Bois at Thérèse's request, she finds a soothing substitute in long talks with and the sympathetic touch of Thérèse, "so un-American as to be not ashamed to show tenderness and sympathy, with eye and lip," who touches Fanny "caressingly" or "gently stroke[s] her limp hand" (801). At Place-du-Bois, Fanny rallies for a time, due to "[o]utside influences meeting halfway the workings of unconscious inward forces" (801). She returns to alcoholism, however, and to Marie Louise's cabin, where she can drink. Despite Hosmer's efforts to save her, she is washed away in the flood that undercuts the embankment beneath Marie Louise's cabin.

After Fanny's death in the flood frees Hosmer and Thérèse to marry, the two meet again a year later on the train returning to Place-du-Bois, thus reuniting them on the instrument of progress—the railroad—that brought Hosmer and his business to the region in the first place. In accepting the railroad and the mill in the opening chapters, Thérèse made her peace with new technology and industrialism, but her inflexible idealism about divorce kept her moored in the old world. Now that a more realistic view has tempered that idealism, she marries Hosmer, who insists that he does not want to take over the plantation and, as he tells her, "rob you of your occupation" (874). In having an occupation, unlike any other white woman in the novel, and in keeping her home as well, something few other female characters in the novel can claim, Thérèse has the best of both worlds.

The industrial plot, by contrast, concludes less neatly and raises questions that it does not answer about racism in southern industrial culture. Although Joçint's action in burning down the mill has been criticized as lacking sufficient motivation, it is actually a key to the novel's ambivalent treatment of racial politics in the context of industrialism. Chopin buries the historical fact of racial violence within the novel's obsession with African American loyalty and willingness to work for whites. Like those of plantation fiction, the hierarchies of the southern industrial plot are reinforced through what Janet Beer has called the "post-colonial relationship of Louisiana to the United States" in which the "domesticated racism" of Louisiana "obtains complicity from the black population in order to sustain alterity from the rest of the American nation."[52] Complicity—or, in the novel's terms, loyalty—is measured in what are meant to be humorous discussions among white characters and authorial asides about African American characters.

Measured in terms of complicity or loyalty, African American characters in the book are judged in relation to the labor that they perform: industriously and independently, in the case of Marie Louise and Morico; grudgingly, as when Nathan tells Hosmer that "dis job's wuf mo' 'an I gets fu' it" (866) or Joçint sabotages the work at the mill by knocking logs off the carriage (757); or not at all, as when no one will stay after dark on Halloween or clean house at any price for Melicent. But the surface humor, which itself rests on racist stereotypes about the work ethic of African Americans, is undercut by the recent history of violence during slavery and Reconstruction. Chopin pointedly evokes this history by having Grégoire and Melicent visit the grave of Mr. McFarlane, rumored to be the prototype for Harriet Beecher Stowe's Simon Legree in *Uncle Tom's Cabin*.[53] The choice of when and how to work, like the unionized strikes that pervade the industrial novel, may be called ingratitude or disloyalty, but it is in fact a legitimate expression of resistance to assumptions about the ownership of one's labor.

A more subtle reference to this legacy of labor, ownership, and racial abuse is the seemingly minor detail of the reason why no one at Place-du-Bois will work for Melicent: the issue of white surveillance of black bodies and power over them. As Ann Laura Stoler observes in "Intimidations of Empire," "matters of the intimate are critical sites for the consolidation of colonial power."[54] A deft use of the politics of touch in *At Fault* helps Thérèse to manage her domain of Place-du-Bois, whether preventing Hosmer from continuing his work by laying "her hand and arm—bare to the elbow—across his work" (745), "gently stroking" the "limp hand" of Fanny in "mildly sensuous exchanges" (801) that soothe Fanny's fretfulness, or permitting Marie Louise to massage away her headaches through the magic of her "smooth hands" on Thérèse's forehead and unbound hair (808). The unacknowledged racial divide that separates servant from master makes the touch of black hands on white skin acceptable if a service is being rendered. Ignorant of the delicate power negotiations implicit in these exchanges, however, Melicent impulsively threatens to cut off Mandy's pigtail one day, which results in a boycott of her household. The African American community recognizes, as Melicent does not, that her gesture proclaims that the white body may do with the black body whatever it wishes, a colonizing gesture that carries with it a remembered legacy of trauma and violence.

Another episode in the novel's continuing economy of touch also makes this point: Thérèse proposes to visit "that dear old Morico" and "comb out that exquisite white hair of his" before taking his picture (805). Thérèse's nonchalant assumption that Morico will stand for these "monkeyshines," as Grégoire calls the double appropriation of assuming the right to comb Morico's hair and to take his picture, is different in degree from Melicent's action but not in kind, for both take for granted their right to control the body of another. Thérèse is more aware of the "alien hands" of the African Americans that serve her than Edna Pontellier of *The Awakening* is, and *At Fault* allows them more of a voice, albeit a stereotypical one. But for all her Lady Bountiful gestures within what she sees as the harmonious community of black and white on Place-du-Bois, Thérèse still participates in what Michele A. Birnbaum has called "the collective amnesia regarding the abuses and uses of the color line in the postwar south."[55] Birnbaum argues that Edna Pontellier's pursuit of autonomy participates in a colonial enterprise that erases and dispossesses the characters of color in *The Awakening*. Although Thérèse is more socially aware and less self-absorbed than Edna, her treatment of Joçint means that she shares responsibility in this colonial enterprise through her industrial-agricultural fiefdom.

Given this context, the "unmotivated" gesture of Joçint burning down the mill makes better sense. First of all, Joçint has been multiply displaced: as a figure half African American and half Native American, he belongs nowhere and rejects being "civilized" by either of the two racial cultures whose blood he bears, by Creole culture, or by the industrial ethos that the mill represents. Neither an independent craftsman like his father Morico nor a socially mobile up-and-coming worker in an increasingly racialized and racist South, Joçint, like Grégoire, has been turned out from the natural world of the piney woods, the only place in which his work has meaning. When his clumsy Luddite actions of spilling logs for the sawmill fail, he takes the next step, and, "creeping along with the tread of a stealthy beast" (820), sets the mill on fire. Chopin takes pains to make Joçint a villain as well as a victim: before he sets the fire, he softly calls his faithful dog to him and, as it licks his hand, strangles it to death and hangs it from a tree, deflecting the sympathy the reader might otherwise feel for him but also demonstrating that he, like the dog, has no place any longer.

Yet in rebelling against the power of the industrial world that Hosmer and the sawmill represent, Joçint rejects complicity in the postcolonial fiction of racial harmony in Louisiana and reveals its submerged violence with his violent act. After he is shot dead by Grégoire, Joçint lies "across a huge beam, with arms outstretched ... staring up into the red sky" (822) in a Christlike pose. His father,

Morico, brushes aside those who are trying to remove his body from the flames and accuses the crowd of being murderers, but he dies of exertion in the process. The violence that Joçint initiates leads to a chain of other destructive events, from Melicent's rejection of Grégoire because of the murder to Grégoire's recklessness and subsequent death at the hands of a stranger. Neither the community imposed by the industrial system nor the community of Place-du-Bois is sufficient to contain the inherent violence in the system, once the fabric of its surface civility has been ruptured.

Thérèse's story ends happily, with marriage and a less rigid worldview, but her path is littered with the bodies of those who died during the course of this journey of discovery: Joçint, Morico, Fanny, Grégoire, and Marie Louise, who dies in the flood with Fanny but is ignored (as the *Natchitoches Enterprise* reviewer remarked, "the authoress forgot to drop a tear over Marie Louise's watery grave").[56] As Mary Papke notes, "One of the most disturbing elements of the novel is that Black characters must die, in essence be sacrificed, so that she [Thérèse] may relinquish her sense of totality to the new ideology embodied in David."[57] Joçint's and Morico's stories stand out from the stereotyped humor with which the novel's other African American characters are treated, such as Aunt Belindy failing to grasp the idea of purgatory when Belle Worthington's daughter explains it to her. Their deaths are dramatic and disturbing, and Morico's cry of "Murderers!" lingers over the text (823). It remains unanswered or stoutly denied, both in the white community's acceptance of Grégoire's deed and by those who believe that the life of a man of color is a fair exchange for the destruction of property.

THE FRUIT OF THE TREE

Like Kate Chopin, Edith Wharton incorporated evolutionary principles into her work while disdaining what she saw as the formulaic application of naturalistic doctrines. Wharton read Zola, as she read all of her French contemporaries. Her references to his work suggest this, and among the surviving volumes from her library are copies of his *Le naturalisme au théâtre* (1881) and two novels of the Rougon-Macquart series, *La Conquête de Plassans* (1874) and *Germinal* (1885). More central to her practice of naturalism was her avid reading in evolutionary theory. Wharton devoured not only volumes of Darwin and Spencer but also T. H. Huxley's *Discourses Biological and Geological* (1897), Ernst Haeckel's *The History of Creation* (1893), Vernon L. Kellogg's *Darwinism Today* (1906), and Robert Lock's *Recent Progress in the Study of Variation, Heredity, and Evolution* (1906).[58] Equally important in her self-education were evolutionary accounts of social and literary forms, such as William Lecky's *History of European Morals from Augustus to Charlemagne* (1869) and Hippolyte Taine's scientific account of literary history as an expression of the author's race, milieu, and moment rather than the exclusive product of individual genius. In writing to her friend Sarah Norton in 1908 about a "very interesting but rather painful book" that challenged Taine's work, Wharton explains, "As Taine was one of the formative influences of my youth—the greatest after Darwin, Spencer & Lecky—I feel as if things were falling in ruins."[59] Yet despite such challenges to theories that had served as scientific touchstones for her, Wharton continued to integrate their insights into her writing. As Tricia M. Farwell, Linda Kornasky, and Bert Bender have shown, she incorporated Darwin's theories of sexual selection into her novels, and studies by Jennie Kassanoff, Judith Saunders, Paul Ohler, and Laura Saltz demonstrate that Wharton applied Darwinian concepts of survival, competition, inheritance, evolutionary development, and extinction to the system of social mores in her novels.[60]

Yet Wharton did not hesitate to criticize what she saw as the limitations of naturalistic subject matter. She wrote to her editor William Crary Brownell in 1902 to express irritation about reviewers' "assumption that the people I write about are not 'real' because they are not navvies & char-women."[61] A quarter of a century later, years of being pigeonholed as a writer of upper-class subjects caused her to renew her complaint: "The idea that genuineness is to be found only in the rudimentary, and that whatever is complex is unauthentic, is a favorite axiom of the modern American critics.... [T]he modern American novelist is told ... that only the man with the dinner-pail is human, and hence available for his purpose."[62] Like the other naturalists, Wharton did not question the idea that lower-class subjects—"the man with the dinner-pail"—were "rudimentary" or further from civilized behavior in managing their emotions, but she disagreed with their assessment that this quality made lower-class characters the best subjects for fiction. In addition to the limitations that critics placed on naturalistic subject matter, Wharton also objected to the limitations of its method, at least as practiced by the imitators of Zola. In a late essay, "Tendencies in Modern Fiction," she notes that the "feebler [realists] beat their brains out against the blank wall of 'Naturalism,'" drawing "helpless puppets on a sluggish stream of fatality," a cutting indictment of naturalistic determinism. Her solution to such formulas is the application of what she sees as the true foundation of literary art, the selection and transformation of the raw materials: "Transmutation is the first principle of art, and copying can never be a substitute for creative vision."[63]

In her naturalistic fiction, Edith Wharton concentrates less on the physical laws of a deterministic universe than the unwritten laws of a rigid, multilayered society in which each positive action toward change ironically leads to disproportionately negative consequences. As Nancy Bentley explains, Wharton did not focus on "the extinction of the social" being in favor of the physical, animal self, as Norris did. Rather, she made the "social self" the focus of her scientific and anthropological investigations.[64] Wharton pursued this idea in her fiction from her early stories through *The House of Mirth* (1905), *Ethan Frome* (1911), and *The Age of Innocence* (1920). Indeed, all her novels convey a sense of desperation as circumstances tighten around the protagonists largely as a result of their attempts to free themselves from an intolerable future. In *The House of Mirth*, Lily Bart meets her death when she refuses to align her inner self with her social self. A gambler at the bridge table and in the marriage market, Lily accepts at one level that she is a beautiful object, "a moment's ornament" with a variable value in a culture of acquisition and speculation exemplified by Percy Gryce's collecting of Americana and Gus Trenor's speculation in stocks.[65] Yet Lily protests and disrupts this ethics of exchange by refusing to accept its valuation of her and by paying her debts "within a system in which nonpayment is the norm."[66] At odds with her culture, Lily sees herself in Darwinian terms as "rootless and ephemeral, [a] mere spindrift of the whirling surface of existence, without anything to which the poor little tentacles of self could cling before the awful flood submerged them" when in fact she is not simply an individual but a type, an icon of racial perfection at the moment of "Anglo-Saxon extinction."[67] She becomes a naturalistic heroine not only by reason of her entrapment but also because she embodies the fetishization of the Anglo-Saxon "race" common to Norris's and London's fiction.

A similarly naturalistic tightening of the rings of the plot occurs when Ethan, of *Ethan Frome*, and Newland Archer, of *The Age of Innocence*, find that their choices diminish with each action that they take. Ethan's most decisive action is his sled ride with Mattie, which he imagines will kill them both and free them from the tortures of living without one another. But at the last moment, "his wife's face, with twisted monstrous lineaments, thrust itself between him and his goal" (150), causing him to miss the tree and consign Mattie to a life of invalidism from her injuries.[68] On a symbolic level, Zeena has blocked him in his quest for death as in his quest for life, but her grotesque woman's face with its "twisted lineaments," a consistent trope in naturalistic fiction, suggests both the face of the Medusa-like Mrs. Johnson that turns the children's "blood to salt" (18) in Stephen Crane's *Maggie: A Girl of the Streets* and the Furies, the monstrous forces of fate and retribution, that haunt Lily Bart in *The House of Mirth*.

In addition to her Lecky-inspired treatment of the evolution of social mores and the naturalistic figure of the monstrous mother, Wharton uses the language of anthropology and science to explain psychological phenomena. *The Age of Innocence* hinges on the interplay among three language registers: the language of society, which conceals truth and stifles any attempt at conveying information; the absence of language in the characters' silent pauses, which reveal truths that they can never speak; and the language of anthropology adopted by the impersonal narrator, who interprets the events in terms of tribal norms but neither judges nor affects the characters' actions. Newland Archer repeats Ethan Frome's pattern of inevitable entrapment because he cannot admit the truth of his feelings for Ellen Olenska to himself, to his fiancée May Welland, or to the New York social world that he simultaneously criticizes for its hypocritical morality and takes care not to offend. Each instance of attraction to Ellen leads Archer to take steps that actually make their relationship impossible, such as urging May to hasten the date of the wedding or advising Ellen not to divorce her husband.

Archer orders the latest books, thinks of himself as a modern man, and laments the metaphorical "bandage" that blinds innocent young women like May to life's realities, yet he is himself one of the least-informed members of a primitive culture, as Wharton's use of anthropological language implies.[69] This language also emphasizes the beauty and the uselessness of the sacrifice demanded by old New York, as when, in meeting at the Metropolitan Museum, Ellen and Archer ponder the "small broken objects" of dead civilizations, now labeled "Use unknown" (186). Only when the guests at the final dinner for Ellen expertly deflect Archer's attempts to announce his departure for Europe can Archer interpret all three levels of meaning. In a flash of illumination, he understands that in anthropological terms, "the whole tribe" "by means as yet unknown to him" had conveyed without speaking their support of May and their belief that he was Ellen's lover (201). The naturalistic "veneer of civilization" may seem to be an unusually thick layer in Wharton's fiction, but the primitive emotions that lie underneath it erupt as easily as they do in more traditionally naturalistic settings.

Earlier and later novels by Wharton criticize Society defined as a proper noun, but *The Fruit of the Tree* is her most significant work of social criticism as generic noun, one that challenges the conditions of the economic order. In its depiction of workers cast aside and destroyed by an uncaring industrial system, its advocacy of professions for women through the strong and original portrait of its heroine, Justine Brent, its frank portrayal of drug addiction, and its complex portrait of marriage, divorce, and desire, the novel is at once inescapably bound to its Progressive Era setting and startlingly modern in its themes. Wharton's handling of these issues and of the novel's central event, Justine's mercy killing of her childhood friend, make this not only one of Wharton's novels "with a purpose," but also one that introduces readers to a forgotten Wharton, the writer of unruly as well as classic naturalism.[70]

The Fruit of the Tree anticipates *Ethan Frome* and *The Age of Innocence* in its use of Wharton conventions: the plot of the double heroines who compete for the hero's attention, for example, and the characteristic Wharton dilemma of one character being tied to an inferior partner.[71] As the novel opens, John Amherst, the reform-minded assistant manager at the Hanaford textile mills, meets trained nurse Justine Brent at the hospital bedside of Dillon, an injured mill worker. Both agree that deprived of occupation, Dillon would be better off dead, a conversation that unites them in their approval of euthanasia and sets in motion the novel's major incident.[72] In the course of pleading Dillon's case, Amherst meets and later marries Bessy Langhope Westmore, the wealthy young widow who owns the mills at Hanaford. But like Ralph Marvell in *The Custom of the Country* (1913) and other love-blinded husbands in Wharton's works, he realizes too late that the frivolous Bessy does not share his interests. Neglected by the work-absorbed Amherst, Bessy retreats into her own realm, that of the senses. During one of his absences, she defies Amherst's wishes by riding her spirited mare, significantly named Impulse, and suffers a near-fatal spinal injury when she falls during the ride. Called to Bessy's side in her capacity of nurse as well as friend, Justine helplessly watches Bessy suffer at the hands of Dr. Wyant, the ambitious young doctor determined to keep his patient alive at all costs. When Wyant leaves the house one afternoon, Justine, moved by Bessy's plight, administers an overdose of morphine.

The final third of the novel brings Justine and Amherst together in marriage after Bessy's death, but, as is often the case in Wharton's novels, their happiness is short-lived. Dr. Wyant, now addicted to morphine and in need of money, threatens to reveal Justine's action to Amherst. Pressed into confessing, Justine tells Amherst the truth and shortly thereafter leaves him so that his relationships with his former father-in-law and stepdaughter, Bessy's daughter Cicely, can continue undisturbed. When Cicely falls ill and pines for Justine, Amherst seeks Justine out and they renew their relationship. Like many of Wharton's lovers, Amherst and Justine survive their ordeal but scarcely do so unscathed. A final ironic twist has Justine lying to preserve Amherst's memory of Bessy. Finding a set of plans for a luxurious gymnasium and pleasure house that Bessy had planned for herself, Amherst erroneously concludes that Bessy had learned to care about the workers at last. When he asks Justine about Bessy's motivation, Justine, who knows the truth, lies to preserve his image of Bessy. In an unmistakable echo of Milton's *Paradise Lost*, the narrative suggests that "the world lay all before them" as they look over the wooded slopes of the symbolically named Hopewood to the "smoke of Westmore" (633).[73] But like others who have eaten of the fruit of "that forbidden tree," the tree of knowledge of good and evil described in the Book of Genesis, Justine and Amherst can never again inhabit the innocent paradise of their first few months together.[74]

Although contemporary reviewers praised this heavily plotted book, some, like Henry James, even calling it superior to *The House of Mirth*, more recent critics have deplored the work's multiplicity of genres and themes. Typical is James W. Tuttleton's characterization of it as a "broken-backed novel," although Ann

Juricec, Ellen Dupree, Katherine Joslin, and Jennie Kassanoff have found an internal coherence.[75] Indeed, many commentators follow R. W. B. Lewis in stating that "there are too many 'subjects' in the book," although, as Gary Totten suggests, "Justine's... assertion of intellectual and moral autonomy and her use of technology" and "Wharton's difficulties in portraying this particular experience of women... are perhaps the reason why some critics have characterized the novel as thematically disjointed."[76] Cynthia Griffin Wolff enumerates the novel's themes in *A Feast of Words*: "Euthanasia, the need for industrial reform, the old problem of idealized expectations coming up against the harsh realities of real-world existence, marriage, the role of women, the devastating results of failures in communication between the sexes, men's unrealistic expectations of women, the insufficiency of women's education and of the roles they are given to enact—the list could go on and on."[77] As a novel of unruly naturalism, however, and one that more than any of Wharton's other novels attends to the social currents of the day, *The Fruit of the Tree* necessarily engages a multiplicity of issues. It explores the central tension between the personal and the political—specifically the ways in which the scientific discourses of professional medicine, industrial management, urban planning, architecture, and even psychology sought to regulate the personal, the lives and bodies of Americans, for the benefit of the political, the body politic.

Justine Brent and John Amherst transcend social class as a category through an insistence on professionalism. Both Amherst and Justine are, in effect, hybrid aristocrats, members of a professional-managerial class that Wharton positions as a replacement for the effete, idle, Jamesian figures of Mr. Langhope, Bessy's father, and his companion, Mrs. Ansell, who resembles Henry James's Madame Merle in *The Portrait of a Lady* and other such well-bred managers of people and customs. Further, each profession rejects the model of the Veblenian body at leisure—the useless body, the body that does no work—as a mechanism for defining class. Instead it provides a model in which intellect must express itself continually through the useful body in a kind of unending service to the helpless at both ends of the social spectrum, from the mill hands to the idle rich. Like other works of naturalism, *The Fruit of the Tree* is a novel about physical bodies: mechanized bodies, workers' bodies, women's bodies, bodies broken into fragments ("hands"), and bodies existing as symbolic sites of power struggle or spectacles of display. It literalizes the theme of the mind at the mercy of the body, the classic naturalistic trope of desire, by providing at its center the body of an immobilized woman, the motionless woman as spectacle common to the naturalist text, whose mind is imprisoned within her body.

The context of reading indicated by the characters' books provides Wharton with the means for exploring one of the several levels of signification in her courtship plot: the disjuncture between the ideals that her characters profess and the biological drives that cause them to act. The spirit of the book pits Bessy's decorative but untouched library sets and her father's sophisticated, superficial taste for a "volume of Loti" against Amherst's well-marked books: "some text-books of biology and kindred subjects, and a few stray well-worn volumes: Lecky's European Morals . . . Seneca, Epictetus . . . a pocket Bacon" (398–99).[78] The allusion to biology recalls the list of evolutionary theorists that Wharton studied, among them "'The Origin of Species,' . . . Huxley, Herbert Spencer, Romanes, Haeckel, and Westermark."[79] The title of her 1904 story collection *The Descent of Man* shows that she had also read Darwin's work by the same title. By interweaving these texts with Justine's and Amherst's responses to one another, Wharton demonstrates the ways in which the characters' bodies speak with a biological eloquence that equals and opposes their idealistic rhetoric.

As befits a "scientific" heroine, Justine sees herself in biological terms, and, as an evolving specimen, she is changeable in her appearance. Her complexion is first "dusky" and then "pale" (9) with sometimes a "bright pallour" (302), and her luxuriant coif of "dense black hair which clasped her face like the noble metal of some antique bust" (144), like that of Frank Norris's Trina McTeague, is later a repository of energy and individuality (614). Justine's spiritual aspirations link her throughout the story with birds: she is at various points compared to a kingfisher and a thrush; she wishes to be a house-swallow (303); and she sees herself as "a phoenix risen from [the] ashes" (146). Indeed, she tells her friend Mrs. Dressel that she has begun to sprout "wings under the skin" now that she has met a kindred spirit, and she fears the strictures of an evening gown, a symbol of Hanaford conventionality, will symbolically stop this evolution (148). Justine even believes that she sees herself scientifically, musing at one point that she is "a little fleeting particle of the power that moves the sun and other stars" (222).

In part because her profession has given her a lifetime of training in scientific observation, Justine has also evolved as the novel's most consistently self-aware character. Although she seeks connectedness and service to others, telling Bessy "self isn't a thing one can keep in a box" (229), Justine has no illusions about the origins of her own philanthropy. She admits that her impulsive need to slip into other people's skins and a penchant for meddling had much to do with her career choice. Because of her commitment to scientific observation, Justine prides herself on understanding her own motivations, yet, as Rebecca Garden demonstrates in analyzing *The Fruit of the Tree* through theories of disability studies, Justine's commitment to sympathy renders Bessy's death inevitable: "[Justine] acts rather to relieve *herself* of Bessy's suffering and of the troubling issue of incurable paralysis. . . . Justine's role as an angel of death is bound up with her identity as an angel of mercy, just as the logic of sympathy enables euthanasia when it cannot account for the incurable."[80]

Although most critics discuss Wharton's depiction of Justine's sexual presence, Bessy most overtly embodies sexual desire. As in *The House of Mirth* and *The Age of Innocence*, Wharton reverses the conventional dark/evil and fair/innocent signification of the fair and dark heroine motif. It is the fair-haired Bessy whose interest in Amherst is primarily physical, especially after a sled run that prefigures the later, more tragic one in *Ethan Frome*: "Bessy had put out a hand to steady herself, and as she leaned forward, gripping his arm, a flying end of her furs swept his face," furs that she loosens, "panting a little," shortly before Amherst proposes to her (134). If Justine is seen as a bird flying above the town and observing its people, Bessy is an earthbound animal, dressed always in "rich depths of fur" (49) and displaying the luxuriant hair that Darwin identified as an important marker of sexual attraction. In contrast to Justine's restrained hairstyle of "some antique bust," Bessy's hair, and her sexuality, is unchecked, demonstrating a lack of control that will later cost her her life. In one of several such descriptions, the narrative figures Bessy's hair as almost a force of nature in itself: "[I]t did not seem to grow in the usual orderly way, but bubbled up all over her head in independent clusters of brightness, breaking, about the brow, the temples, the nape, into little irrelevant waves and eddies of light, with dusky hollows of softness where the hand might plunge" (42). The fantasies of touch and immersion here recall that, as Kassanoff, Joslin, and others have shown, hands are an important signifier in this novel. An upper-class hand seeking pleasure may plunge into the golden skeins of Bessy's hair and become entrapped, as Amherst fantasizes being dragged into the machinery of Bessy's household (340), but a working-class hand must plunge into the treacherous threads of the machine's heart and risk dismemberment.

Amherst, the third member of the triangle, exemplifies a similar lack of self-awareness despite his scientific objectivity, an ironic state of affairs given his professed concern for others. He sees the mill and its machinery as a monster, but he believes himself to be the hero who can tame it rather than one of the workers whose bodies must feed it: "He felt a beauty in the ordered activity of the whole intricate organism ... the dark side of monotonous human toil, of the banquet of flesh and blood and brain perpetually served up to the monster whose insatiable jaws the looms so grimly typified" (57). Seeing himself as a hero in his own mind as well—a modern St. George taming the industrial dragon—Amherst is overly confident in his ability to regulate the conduct of the body in its confrontation with technology. With strength, however, comes the obligation to regulate oneself physically, and in this arena Amherst is less successful than his idealistic rhetoric might suggest. Early in the novel, Amherst immerses himself in the corporation not as a shareholder, but as a representative of the soul that it should but, as an intangible corporate body, cannot have. In an unusual move and a wry twist on Victorian notions of sexual spending, he contracts himself sexually to Bessy to stave off her attempts to drain the body of the mills dry with her insatiable need for more money. Amherst substitutes his own sexual energy and vitality for the money that the mill produces, for as long as Bessy has his full attention she is willing to cut back on her purchases. Only after he turns away from her for long periods does Bessy turn to spending more money, and his threatened absences and promise of renewed sexual attentions regulate her behavior. For example, when Bessy rejects his plan to increase funds for the mills and announces her decision to travel to Europe, Amherst walks away from her toward his separate bedroom, turning back only after she tearfully embraces him and announces, "I'll do anything" as he holds her to him and "hate[s] his victory" (206).

Bessy's accident, the turning point of the novel, causes all the characters' sophisticated defenses and self-delusions to unravel, returning them to the primal naturalistic selves that the accident unmasks. Already depicted as an animal in her physical appeal and impulsive behavior, Bessy becomes a "helpless body" in which "throes of neuralgia . . . were reducing their victim to a mere instrument on which pain played its incessant deadly variations" (423). Her last utterance is "I want to die" (424), after which she lapses into "the monotonous whimper of an animal—the kind of sound that a compassionate hand would instinctively crush into silence" (431). Reduced to whimpers and eventually silence, Bessy, like Lily Bart in the *tableau vivant* scene in *The House of Mirth*, becomes the naturalistic image of the unmoving woman who remains an enigma despite being the object of scrutiny and attempted interpretation, the still figure in a turning text.

Justine too is reduced to primitive emotion rather than reason. After Justine injects Bessy with the overdose of morphine, Dr. Wyant, who had hoped to polish his tarnished professional reputation by keeping Bessy alive despite her pain, enters the room, and, finding Bessy dead, "hang[s] over the bed like some angry animal balked of its prey" (434). After he descends into drug addiction, he demands payment for his silence. Justin's payment of Wyant's blackmail leads her to a burst of self-deluding, fear-driven rhetoric through which she tries to assume an objectivity that she does not feel: "She had not told him *because she was not afraid*. . . . [She] was actually under a kind of obligation not to force on him the knowledge of a fact that he could not alter and could not completely judge. . . . Was there any flaw in this line of reasoning?" (483). The ironic emphasis on rationality in this rhetorical question foreshadows its reversal a few pages later when the unsuspecting Amherst gives her a check for what she has told him is a charity case: "She felt the touch of a narcotic in her veins. How calm and peaceful the room was—and how delicious to think that her life would go on in it, safely and peacefully, in the old familiar way!" (489). In rationalizing her motives as Wyant has done, she too becomes an addict. The fact that her narcotic is metaphoric rather than material negates neither the impact of the image nor its thematic value.

After learning that Justine had believed his theoretical statements about euthanasia as a justification for her actions in Bessy's case, Amherst recoils. When he learns of Wyant's blackmail, in a moment of atavistic rage he follows Wyant into the streets and beats him: "'I've given that cur a lesson he won't forget,' he exclaimed, breathing hard, the redness deepening in his face.... [Justine] felt its heat in her veins—the primitive woman in her glowed at contact with the primitive man" (530–31). Like Chopin's Hosmer in *At Fault*, Amherst discovers a primitive self at odds with his cool rationality, and Justine responds to it in kind. In exposing the biological nature of Justine's and Amherst's attraction to each other, this incident, like the euthanasia episode, illustrates human behavior under the pressure of "those searching questions which call into play emotions rooted far below reason and judgment, in the dark primal depths of inherited feeling" (526). The "primal depths," however, are just what Amherst refuses to recognize. Without Bessy's money, Amherst cannot regulate the bodies of workers, but even with Bessy's money he cannot regulate himself, as the beating of Wyant indicates. Nor does he ever acknowledge that he relies on physical traits including his handsome features to advance his cause, preferring to believe that Bessy loves his ideas rather than his beautiful eyes. In preferring idealism to the lessons taught by his own body and emotions, Amherst remains a man whose reading shields him from life rather than forcing him to confront it.

In the context of naturalism and its central preoccupation with the body, Justine's mercy killing of her friend Bessy defines the novel in terms of euthanasia and reproduction, for the question of who lives and who reproduces pervades the novel from beginning to end. As noted earlier, courtship and sexual relationships, not children, are the focus of the naturalistic novel, and the extinction of one family after another confirms this theme in *The Fruit of the Tree*. Amherst and Bessy's infant son dies, and Amherst and Justine have no children and seemingly plan to have none. The specter of Dillon's family living on and reproducing while the Westmores, Langhopes, and Amhersts die out evokes the era's eugenics-inspired fears of "race suicide." When Justine applies the same logic of euthanasia to the pain-wracked and paralyzed body of Bessy Westmore, however, she unwittingly exposes the class-based eugenics with which euthanasia is allied. Defined as a rich woman whom Amherst had never been able to wean from the position of social parasite, Bessy is already, according to the laws of class and consumption, a useless body. Thus her accident intensifies but does not transform her status, a status that according to the laws of class validates the right of the rich to be useless.

Through the contrasting euthanasia sequences, Wharton exposes the unwritten rule that science or its representative may kill the useless body of the poor but not of the rich.

Despite their differing approaches and subject matter, Peattie, Cleary, Foote, Lindsay, Freeman, Chopin, and Wharton reveal in their fiction the Darwinian premises and evolutionary underpinnings of life on the borderlands, where the minor prospect of class slippage is replaced by the possibility of transgressing more significant boundaries. For Peattie, the transgression manifests itself as an anxiety about the trauma women endure in borderland spaces and the possibility of slipping from human to nonhuman. Kitty Sharpneck and the atavistic cats of "After the Storm" exemplify this blurred boundary, and Dil's gradual confusion about the boundaries between human and animal exposes an unspoken danger posed by the Rooseveltian experience designed to equip him for American imperial masculinity. For Cleary, questioning the boundaries between sanity and madness common to the farm-wife plot reveal themselves in echolalia and the hopelessness of an escape through madness. Foote's "The Trumpeter" uses the borderland spaces of the West and its army camps as an intersection of races and a site for challenging contemporary ideas of civilization based on race and whiteness, with Henniker, who acts as white men in the West have often done in seducing or marrying and abandoning a Native woman, receiving condemnation from the community. In denying his wife and child due to their race, he renders himself an outcast in what Foote tries to portray as a spurious occupying force, Coxey's Army, and as a result has no square foot of earth that he can claim for his own.

Lindsay's tales feature the clash of cultures between Native traditions and the modern global economy that encroaches on Native territory and lives. The Christianity that informs Komo's gesture to release his errant wife in "The Old Law" disrupts the traditional rituals of justice for the tribe, just as the incursions of the "Boston Man's" money and goods, like the implicit appropriation of Snoqualmie land to establish the world's largest hop ranch, place Kwelth-Elite under a double servitude until she can escape the ancient bonds of slavery and in essence marry into modernity. The use of Chinook Jargon, seemingly initiating readers into a timeless tribal culture, actually positions them in the contemporary language of trade used in the Pacific Northwest. Using different measures for time, Freeman's "Old Woman Magoun" confirms Lindsay's point that encroaching economic modernity cannot be resisted in borderland spaces any more than the Darwinian imperatives of desire and reproduction can be suppressed in the human body. The bridge that links a borderland with urban modernity may be imperfectly built, but its effects of leading rural life into modernity are as inevitable as the process of biological maturation and sexual desire.

Chopin's and Wharton's industrial novels incorporate the many subplots and occasional thematic tangles that occur in unruly naturalism. Although secondary to the love plot, *At Fault*'s story of Joçint and Morico, rendered obsolete by the transition to industrialism, and Grégoire, destroyed by the loss of his traditional Creole culture, represent some of Chopin's most overt concern for the racially or culturally dispossessed. *At Fault* presents an unusual counterweight to its happy ending between Thérèse and Hosmer in its tally of lives spent in addiction (Fanny) or in the deaths that must occur to enable their happiness. *The Fruit of the Tree* asks difficult questions about divorce and the responsibilities of mill owners under industrial capitalism, but Wharton reserves as the most salient questions ones that challenge the boundaries of the body, questions of euthanasia and desire among them. The novel asks who has the right to act and speak for those who cannot do so for themselves, not only Bessy and, through his books, Amherst in the decision to end Bessy's suffering, but also the workers whose lives can be altered irrevocably by the decisions of mill owners. Despite the industrial settings to which neither Chopin nor Wharton returned, their attempts to challenge the boundaries of the body in the shadow of the machine age, as much as their use of Darwinian concepts, brings their work into congruence with the other writers exploring the shifting states of human beings on geographic or temporal borderlands.

CHAPTER 3

Bohemian Time
Glasgow, Austin, and Cather

In October 1859, trying to explain the idea of Bohemia to the readers of *Harper's New Monthly Magazine*, the writer of the "Editor's Easy Chair" column captured in his definition both the freedom that Bohemia embodied and middle-class anxiety about the threat that it posed to bourgeois life: "Bohemia is the realm of vagabondage.... a fairy land upon the hard earth...[I]ts denizens are clad loosely—seedily, in the vulgate—and they are shaggy as to the head, with abounding hair. Whatever is not 'respectable' they are."¹ Bohemians saw themselves as architects of modernity but rejected its most common associations, the technologically enhanced industrial capitalism and obsession with speed that spelled progress at the end of the nineteenth century. Beginning with Henri Murger's *La Vie de Bohème* (1851), the term "Bohemia" became shorthand for an alternative to bourgeois life. As Joanna Levin explains, "[I]n plots and tableaux derived from Murger, scenes of Bohemian life routinely involve overlapping tensions between artists and 'Philistines,' art and commerce, wealth and poverty, women and men, propriety and license, work and play, youth and age ... the regional and the national, the national and the cosmopolitan."² Yet as Mary Gluck points out, this "sentimental Bohemia" "affirmed but also neutralized" its radical potential by reducing the idea of a colorful life in Bohemia to "a form of apprenticeship in the artist's life."³ Bohemia as a place became Bohemia as an imagined space for artists mapped onto an actual urban terrain of lower-class neighborhoods in a cosmopolitan city, with an evanescent temporality linked to the artist's apprenticeship rather than to the rhythms of commercial life.

The *Künstlerroman* set in Bohemia chronicles a young artist's struggles to develop artistically and intellectually, culminating in the artist's creation of a masterpiece—or, in Émile Zola's *L'Oeuvre* or Frank Norris's *Vandover and the Brute*, his failure to create a masterpiece. The love and work plot pits the idealistic struggling artist against his culture, sometimes as represented by his conventional fiancée but often as a clash of ideologies staged in gallery openings, *bal masques*, and society dinners. At the end of the nineteenth century, the most popular version of artistic Bohemia appeared in George du Maurier's *Trilby*, first serialized in *Harper's Magazine* in 1894 and a runaway best seller when it appeared in book form later that year. The story of three British art students studying in Paris and a statuesque model, Trilby O'Ferrall, *Trilby* captured the public imagination with its portrait of the impresario Svengali, who mesmerizes Trilby into singing beautifully but drains her soul in the process. The combination of romance, Gothic excess in the characterization of the villainous Svengali, unconventional freedom in Trilby's relationships with the art students, and du Maurier's light comic tone made *Trilby* a publishing phenomenon and set the pattern for a post-Murger generation of Bohemian novels.

In American novels, the charming seediness of du Maurier's Paris was translated into the imagined foreignness of an artistic Bohemia existing in the immigrant communities of U.S. cities. Like urban slum fiction and regionalist stories, Bohemian fiction provided a mirror for testing the national self and encouraged writers of ethnically and racially diverse backgrounds such as Paul Laurence Dunbar and James Weldon Johnson to set scenes within Bohemian spaces. As Susan L. Mizruchi writes in *Multicultural America*, writers of the time "confirmed widespread perceptions of America as a nation of many cultures that were increasingly set against one another," as authors participated in magazine cultures that served as "multicultural laboratories" for experiencing other cultures as picturesque rather than threatening.[4] In Frank Norris's *Blix*, for example, Condy Rivers and Travis "Blix" Bessemer are jolted out of conventionality by "consuming ethnic and racial Otherness," according to Joanna Levin, and their experience provides the foundation for a relationship free from the artificiality of conventional society.[5]

Like the prostitution and working-girl narratives of the 1890s, the Bohemian artists' novel was a powerful draw for naturalist writers, in part because, as in narratives of prostitution, its objectification of the female figure provided an ideal mode for examining spectatorship and sexuality. The application of naturalism to the Bohemian novel is not as much of a stretch as it might seem: both forms allow voyeuristic descent into the realm of the picturesque and the squalid, and Bohemian spaces evoke the presence of sexual danger for women. In *The Coast of Bohemia*, *The Third Violet*, and *Vandover and the Brute*, for example, W. D. Howells, Stephen Crane, and Frank Norris inflect the basic Bohemian setting with naturalistic elements that resonate with their other work. Just as he promoted serious realism in his "Editor's Study" columns for *Harper's New Monthly Magazine*, Howells traced the quarrel between sentimental art and realism in the person of his serious-minded independent heroine in *The Coast of Bohemia*. Crane undercut romantic ideas of Bohemia in *The Third Violet*. In *Vandover and the Brute*, Norris traced the degeneration of a sensitive upper-class aesthete instead of a brutish lower-class dentist as in *McTeague*. Bohemia also appears in naturalistic novels that focus their attention elsewhere, as in the Celia Madden subplot of Harold Frederic's *The Damnation of Theron Ware*, the Banner Club episode in Paul Laurence Dunbar's *The Sport of the Gods*, and the gambling club sequences in James Weldon Johnson's *The Autobiography of an Ex-Colored Man*.

Bohemia as a naturalistic subject owes its popularity to its ability to reconfigure urban space, rendering the poverty-stricken slums of naturalism as safely picturesque rather than threatening and disreputable. In contrast to naturalism's threat of proletarianization, Bohemian spaces protect cultural tourists through the same bourgeois attitudes and perspectives that middle-class observers come to Bohemia to escape. As Daniel Borus writes in "The Strange Career of American Bohemia," each successive wave of Bohemianism is a "fun-house mirror of bourgeois life" that reverses its values, and each in turn ceases to be an active site of resistance since its very success at arousing interest causes its attitudes to become mainstream and "irrelevant."[6] Yet whereas bourgeois attitudes and perspectives protect the cultural tourists of Bohemian romances, naturalistic novels of Bohemia expose the dangers of class slippage and poverty that result from too long a residence in Bohemia.

Women writers added gender to the reconfiguration of Bohemian space, turning the tables on the *Trilby* pattern of Bohemian fiction as their female characters became agents rather than subjects, artists rather than models, and Darwinian models of sexual aggression rather than avatars of Victorian reticence. Set in spaces already defined as indeterminate and foreign, women's Bohemian novels reflect the themes of naturalism: Darwinist courtship and sexual behavior, an emphasis on the visual, a focus on the woman's body, and a plot of decline set in an urban environment. They examine the divide between idealism—usually gendered male and rendered as obstructionist, oppressive, or both—and realism, gendered female and struggling against the material and social consequences of male idealism. In negotiating this divide, the Bohemian artists' novels of Ellen Glasgow, Mary Austin, and Willa Cather differ from those of their male counterparts and from earlier novels of women artists such as Phelps's *The Story of Avis* or Louisa May Alcott's *Diana and Persis*. In earlier novels by women, characters are torn between the pursuit of an artist's career and the demands of domesticity. In the naturalistic Bohemian artists' novel written by women, Darwinian desire for sexual expression vies with a socially imposed desire for respectability.

The tension between the ideals of modest domestic femininity, which constituted marriageability, and the requirements of artistic training equal to that of men, which required exposure to the nude human form and tested the limits of that modesty, made Bohemia a particularly fraught place for women artists. As Christine Stansell has argued, Bohemian tales "invite young men of sophistication to believe that enlightened solutions—a shared urbanity rather than separate spheres, mixed company at cheap restaurants rather than same-sex jollity at gentlemen's clubs—might reconcile men's customary dominance over women with a belief in women's right to a wider sphere of action." But "the belief in women's right to a wider sphere of action" could not overcome the insuperable barrier of the double standard. Living in boardinghouses, young women were subject to "two competing discourses" about their activities: the nineteenth-century reformers' perspective of helpless women "always threatened by unscrupulous men" and the twentieth-century view of, among others, "moviemakers" who depicted women as "active, pleasure-seeking, and opportunistic."[7] The time women artists spend in Bohemia may be temporary, but the threat to their sexual reputations renders its effects permanent, since the physical coordinates of artistic Bohemia—boardinghouses and artists' studios—offered freedom but also unchaperoned proximity to what society saw as its free-living sexual mores.

Like the reconfiguration of space, Bohemian time, which includes extended stays in poverty and a refusal to participate in the constant busyness of the bourgeois world, exists as a counterpoint to the success timetable of an increasingly regimented modernity. Its milestones are not pinned to maturational processes but are marked by paintings completed, exhibitions attended, and works sold. When the artist achieves success, Bohemia reaches its temporal end point as the artist moves on into a world of standard economic commitments and rewards. Existing outside both sequential or linear time and Julia Kristeva's idea of women's cyclical time, Bohemian time resembles Elizabeth Freeman's conception of "queer time," which exists "in counterpoint to modern time" with its standard biological markers of heterosexual courtship and births.[8] Another model for Bohemian time and its temporal distortions appears in Wai Chee Dimock's *Through Other Continents*. Citing Homi Bhabha's conception of "postcolonial time" as breaking the "single, enforceable chronology" of the nation state, Dimock proposes "an alternate conception of time: at odds with the number, and working most immediately against the chronology of the nation."[9] Existing in a shared, irregular space bound by a system of values and memory, Bohemian time resists the chronology of the nation and its restrictive vision of the future. When social or biological life events impinge on Bohemian time, they destroy the fabric of continuing work, forcing artists prematurely into the temporality existing in the world beyond.

Within the larger context of evolutionary time, to which Bohemian novels allude through references to Darwinian courtship behavior, Glasgow, Austin, and Cather challenge the indeterminate construction of Bohemian time by juxtaposing real time—women's time, biological time—with the irregular definition of it that existed in Bohemia. Ellen Glasgow's *The Descendant* and *Phases of an Inferior Planet*, Mary Austin's *No. 26 Jayne Street*, and Willa Cather's "Coming, Aphrodite!" place women in Bohemian spaces to mock Bohemian pretensions and challenge categorization of women as sexualized muses and helpmeets. In doing so, they disrupt the paradigm of Bohemia as a male-defined space of indefinite temporality. Their novels of unruly naturalism, which focus on women's desires thwarted by evolutionary, biological, and social restraints, demonstrate that while Bohemian spaces may be congenial for modern women seeking the freedom to live their own lives, Bohemian time is not.

Bohemia in Early Film

The social context for women's Bohemian fiction includes not only novels and magazine fiction but also early film, with a wave of films featuring Bohemia and Bohemians appearing in the 1910s. In the 1880s, serious articles such as Mellie A. Hopkins's "Female Bohemian Life in Boston" dominated public debate over the propriety of women in Bohemia, including same-sex couples,[10] but by the 1910s Bohemia and its character types had become so popular as to be a subject for satire in film, as reviews from *Variety* and *Moving Picture World* suggest. Then as now, the movies mirrored an era's cultural preoccupations, and films set in Bohemia revealed the tension between the modern woman's desire for autonomy, signified by her residence in Bohemia, and the claims of the domestic sphere. With Bohemian character types providing comic relief, films set in Bohemian Greenwich Village dissected the conflict that the New Woman experienced but tended to confirm domesticity as a desirable status quo. As in O. Henry's stories of Bohemian New York, the primary message of Bohemian films mirrors that of novels like Gertrude Christian Fosdick's *Out of Bohemia* or Howells's *The Coast of Bohemia*: that Bohemia for a young woman is a detour into mildly unconventional living before she returns home to a suitable marriage.

One such film, Howard M. Mitchell's *A Girl in Bohemia* (1919), based on a popular play by H. B. Daniel, brings the small-town girl to Greenwich Village. Winifred Bryce, a would-be novelist, is stung when her fiancé declares her portrait of Village life unrealistic. She travels to Bohemia to experience the atmosphere, but, while there, according to *Motion Picture News*, she is "cheated by the members of the Bohemian set and finally taken to jail" for stabbing a woman.[11] The Bohemian nightmare ends in the fifth reel: "Fade-in on the authoress pounding her Remington, appearance of publisher, acceptance, the conventional fade-out clinch and the onlookers leave pleased with the happy ending," according to the

Variety reviewer.¹² Among the "catch lines" that *Motion Picture News* suggested for exhibitors were "Where one conventional girl becomes unconventional and then scurries back chastened to the convention" and "She wanted to obtain Bohemian atmosphere first hand to provide material for her forthcoming novel and secured enough 'atmosphere' for six books."¹³ A reversal of this plot, Lawrence B. McGill's *The Girl from Bohemia* (1918), starred the famously sophisticated dancer Irene Castle as Alice, who moves from Greenwich Village to a small town in order to take up an inheritance, only to shock its residents by smoking, redecorating the house "in the futuristic manner," and wearing "a gown that looks like a hula costume."¹⁴ But Alice is a good American girl at heart, and she reclaims her womanhood and citizenship respectively by rescuing a child from drowning and by stopping a threatened strike by brandishing a U.S. flag.

Just how widely dispersed the image of Bohemia had become in a few short years is evident in Edgar Keller's 1916 one-reel film *The Yellow Girl*, the Vitagraph production of O. Henry's *A Philistine in Bohemia* (1920), and the addiction drama *The Devil's Needle* (1916). *The Yellow Girl* is set in a Bohemia only as far as it ostensibly occurs in an artist's studio flat, but its subtitle—"A Decorative Playlet"— indicates that the visual design trumps any sense of plot. In *The Yellow Girl*, the color yellow in itself resonates with associations of 1890s Bohemia. In addition to Chambers's *The King in Yellow*, the color alludes to *The Yellow Book* (1894–97), a favored publication outlet for Decadent writers and artists such as Aubrey Beardsley and Max Beerbohm, and the poisonous yellow book, Joris-Karl Huysman's never-named *À Rebours*, in Oscar Wilde's *The Picture of Dorian Gray* (1891). All three films emphasize the artificiality of Bohemian time and spaces, *The Yellow Girl* through its visual design, *A Philistine in Bohemia* through its rejection of cherished Greenwich Village clichés in favor of interethnic marriage and domesticity, and *The Devil's Needle* through its sudden descent into melodrama.

The Yellow Girl presents a highly artificial and proto-expressionistic Bohemia: characters are dressed in vivid stripes, checks, and plaids, and the geometric patterns of their clothing compete with the striped and patterned walls for the viewer's attention. Flat panels with stylized vegetation such as painted weeping willow trees constitute the external sets, and the names are as self-consciously artistic as the sets and as those in Thomas Janvier's *Color Studies*.¹⁵ "W. Allston Black," named after the American painter Washington Allston, and his friend Harry White, meet Flora the Florist and Corinne the milliner, each named after the actress who portrays her (Florence Vidor and Corinne Griffith). The slight plot involves jealousy and false identity: White courts Flora and Black courts Corinne, but both men are entranced by Mlle. de Jaune (the Yellow Girl) and her Eastern dance. When Mlle. de Jaune poses for Black in his studio, Corinne spies on him and becomes jealous, one of the many references to visual misprision and mis-

Corinne and Flora walk by a park bench in *The Yellow Girl* (1916). Note the deliberate artifice of the painted backdrop and the geometric patterns of their clothing. Courtesy George Eastman House, International Museum of Photography and Film.

interpretation in a two-dimensional world. All ends well when the Yellow Girl, whom Corinne fears as a rival, instead commissions Black to paint her portrait and White confesses his love for Flora. "This is my futuristic bride," he says in introducing Flora, and the film ends happily.[16]

In *The Yellow Girl*'s version of Bohemia, artificial settings in which three dimensions are flattened into two reflect the artificial courtship conventions—misunderstandings, jealousy, overheard conversations—that the flat setting helps to define as trite. The temporary and artificial nature of Bohemia extends to live animals painted in solid colors, human beings disguising themselves through excessive makeup, and the geometric flatness engendered by costumes and scenery. The relentless emphasis on the visual includes not only the stylized painted sets and the geometric shapes of the costumes but also the doubling of pictures in the mistaken identity plot. Conflict arises when the main characters look at one portrait but mistake it for another, Corinne's sketch of Mlle. de Jaune, a photograph of Corinne, and Black's painting of Mlle. de Jaune all playing their role in sowing confusion. Contributing to the art references are the peacock backdrop used as a hiding place and a stylized shop sign featuring a blank face with a monocle, the peacock and the monocle both well-known emblems for the artist James McNeill Whistler. Only two segments of the film intentionally break its artifice. In the first, Mlle. de Jaune, enveloped in white veils and then in an all-enveloping cape, concludes her "Oriental" dance by moving toward the camera for a medium close-up and gazing toward the audience, breaking the fourth wall. The second instance occurs in a process shot when Flora and White look into a pond and see themselves reflected as a married couple in traditional rather than stylized garb. *The Yellow Girl* bills itself as a farce, but it envisions Bohemia as an artificial time and space, with marriage as the moment that couples move into three-dimensionality and biological time.

A Philistine in Bohemia (Vitagraph, 1920), a two-reel comedy, satirizes the conventions of Bohemia through a plot of mistaken expectations hinging on popular stereotypes. Like the O. Henry story of the same name from which it is adapted, the film contrasts key features of ethnicity, including the Irish brogue and Italian dialect of the main characters, with audience expectations of Bohemian life. Its true theme, however, is the contrast between false and true identities integrated with issues of class, among them sham European aristocrats versus authentic lower-class immigrants and a tourist-infected Bohemia versus the real thing. The plot is slight: Katy Dempsey and her mother, the keeper of a boardinghouse, worry that Mr. Antonio Brunelli might be an Italian nobleman who will skip out on the rent, since sad experience has taught Mrs. Dempsey and the other Irish landladies that a titled nobleman is certainly a deadbeat, especially if his claims of nobility are true. Brunelli falls in love with Katy, which in a melodrama would trigger suspicions of a seduction plot with an upper-class man seducing a working-class young woman.

But Brunelli has courtship rather than seduction in mind: he takes Katy to a restaurant, which, as a series of intertitles suggests, is cannily designed to attract Bohemian artists. The restaurant has no sign, in order to appeal to Bohemians' preferences for discovering authentic haunts unknown to tourists, an inexpensive menu of ethnic food to confirm their rejection of bland and bourgeois restaurants, and clotheslines full of laundry to complete the effect of picturesque poverty. This false "Bohemian resort" attracts a variety of patrons, including "a sprinkling of real Bohemians present who came for a change because they were tired of the real Bohemia." Dazzled by the spectacle that the Bohemians present and by the unfamiliar and exotic food—spaghetti—that a waiter brings, Katie worries about how Antonio will pay for such splendor. In the concluding moments of the film, he reveals that he is the owner, a cook, which in her eyes and her mother's is a more satisfactory profession than being an impecunious count or duke. Like many of O. Henry's New York stories, *A Philistine in Bohemia* satirizes both classes, the snobbery of upper-class Americans who blindly worship poseurs with European titles and the innocence of lower-class Irish immigrants who, ignorant of social distinctions, judge others by their actions rather than their lineage.

Despite retaining O. Henry's original quotations in many of the intertitles, the film version extends the story's satire of Bohemians by expanding the shots devoted to them with characters never mentioned in the story. In one early shot,

A tambourine-playing Bohemian New Woman annoys a Trotsky lookalike in *A Philistine in Bohemia* (1920). Courtesy George Eastman House, International Museum of Photography and Film.

a wild-haired man wearing glasses, who looks vaguely like Leon Trotsky, ignores a woman in a tunic and beads brandishing a tambourine next to him as he intently reads a book. Prominent among the characters is a table of women with short hair who wear loose tunics. Their appearance confirms the common description of Bohemians as "long-haired men and short-haired women," a pejorative phrase current since the 1890s that took direct aim at a reversal of gender norms and a host of other offenses against middle-class propriety. As George Chauncey explains, the two categories signaled "accusations of perversity" as well as gender reversal, in a constellation of opprobrium that included being "regarded as unmanly as well as un-American, and in some contexts calling men 'artistic' became code for calling them homosexual."[17] Sinclair Lewis's *Main Street*, published in the year that *A Philistine in Bohemia* was released, confirms Chauncey's observation when the solid midwesterner Will Kennicott accuses his artistic wife, Carol, of preferring "long-haired men and short-haired women," and he threatens to "take these [artists] . . . and make them be patriotic" since they are obviously un-American.[18]

In *A Philistine in Bohemia*, the short-haired women reject standard gender expectations not only through their shapeless garb, sandals, short hair, and utter lack of interest in the men at other tables but also by smoking, singing, arguing loudly, and dancing wildly around the room with a tambourine after one of them commandeers the piano to accompany them. The Bohemian women compete for screen time with Katie, who sits demurely on the sidelines observing but not sharing in their antics. Their behavior brands them as embracing Bohemian womanhood, and, by the logic of the time, rejecting American womanhood and conventional femininity. In contrast, Katie is a paragon of American womanhood despite being a lower-class Irish immigrant, just as Brunelli is an American by virtue of his capitalist's grasp of marketing false Bohemian authenticity as the real thing. His Italian ethnicity and hence longer residence in the district paradoxically confirms his American identity, since the "Ninth Ward, dominated by working-class Italian immigrants" began "to be called 'the Village' again" only after Bohemians colonized it, according to Chauncey, a demographic shift that Andrew Jewell confirms by noting Willa Cather's familiarity with the "Italian Quarter" that adjoined her residence on Bank Street.[19] As in other O. Henry stories such as "Extradited from Bohemia," *A Philistine in Bohemia* proposes that gender, when accompanied by appropriately feminine behavior, trumps ethnicity in classifying lower-class women, just as honest toil makes Antonio an American man rather than a deadbeat European nobleman. When Antonio proposes to Katy, two ethnicities unite as Americans and as longer-term residents than the un-American Bohemian interlopers.

The Devil's Needle (Fine Arts Film Company, 1916; rereleased with different character names in 1923) approaches the problem of Bohemia and artistic creativity more directly. The free-spirited New Woman in it, the artist's model Renée Duprez (Norma Talmadge), is unconventional not only in her living arrangements but also in being "an ardent worshipper at the shrine of Morpheus," as an intertitle puts it.[20] The plot concerns a painter, John Minturn (Tully Marshall), who wrestles with artistic inspiration until Renée advises him that morphine is "inspiration ready made." He falls in love with a society woman, Patricia Devon (Marguerite Marsh), whom he sees as an ideal model. But when Patricia's father forbids her to see Minturn, preferring instead her upper-class fiancé, Sir Gordon Galloway (Howard Gay), Minturn despairs. Recalling Renée's words, he injects himself with morphine and finishes the picture.

After a year of addiction, however, Minturn has become "an almost hopeless addict" and tries to inject Patricia so that she can share his experience. He hallucinates visions of nymphs dancing in a forest glade as if he is watching a movie, an effect of film-within-film that looks almost as if he is watching television. When he overhears Patricia talking to Gordon about his addiction, Minturn, at Renée's recommendation, goes to the country for a cure, not telling Patricia where he has gone. The film has thus far represented a realistic situation: the artist's fears of reduced creativity, his turning to drugs, and his shame at exposure. The remainder of the film descends to melodrama when the drug dealers kidnap Patricia because they fear she will damage their business. Renée, who has by this time "fought the good fight and won" against her addiction, joins forces with the newly sober Minturn to rescue Patricia, who has been rendered unconscious by a leaking gas

Minturn and his drug-induced hallucination of wood nymphs, from *The Devil's Needle* (1916). Note the needle held close to his cheek.

pipe at the drug dealers' lair. The police arrive, Patricia is revived, and Renée, in her final act of "atonement . . . convinces Minturn his wife still loves him."[21]

The Devil's Needle was initially released with great fanfare, since Tully Marshall, who portrayed the main character, had in an earlier play "given one of the greatest performances of a 'dope' [addict] that the American boards had seen."[22] *Variety*'s reviewer was less impressed, calling *The Devil's Needle* "a very commonplace story and picture in these modern days" that "ended in the same old way" as most of the drug films put out during the "vice frenzy" of a few years earlier.[23] As Kevin Brownlow describes them in *Behind the Mask of Innocence*, these films included D. W. Griffith's *For His Son* (1912), in which a physician "creates a soft drink containing cocaine" to make his son rich, only to see the son become addicted, a twist on the origin story of Coca-Cola.[24] Other drug-themed films were released after the 1909 Opium Exclusion act, including *The Cocaine Traffic*, also known as *The Drug Terror* (1914); *The Drug Traffic* (1914); *The Derelict* (1914); *The Dividend* (1916); and a comic "parody of Sherlock Holmes," *The Mystery of the Leaping Fish* (1916), which features Douglas Fairbanks as "Coke Ennyday."[25]

Women scenario writers were responsible for several of these, including *The Secret Sin* (1915), written by Margaret Turnbull and featuring D. W. Griffith star Blanche Sweet in a dual role as twin sisters, one of whom is addicted to opium, and *The Rise of Susan* (1916), written by Frances Marion, in which the female addict keeps her hypodermic needles in "a beautifully bound book."[26] A major production starring Bessie Love as a female addict, *Human Wreckage* (1923) appeared in the same year as the reissue of *The Devil's Needle* and was produced by Mrs.

Wallace Reid, who would later produce and appear in *The Red Kimona* (1925). Her husband, the major film star Wallace Reid, was known for his handsome, all-American image but had died earlier that year of morphine addiction in one of the first well-publicized Hollywood deaths from this cause. *The Devil's Needle* may have resembled the "vice frenzy" films, but its star-filled cast, with stars like Norma Talmadge and Tully Marshall, reveals that the film is a serious attempt to present the problem of addiction, despite what some critics saw as its optimistic presentation of hard work and country air as a cure.

The Devil's Needle anticipates *Human Wreckage* in its treatment of drug addiction as a physical malady rather than as a criminal act or failure of will, and its intertitles promote sympathy for the Bohemian woman Renée, whose addiction has a sympathetic origin in the 1923 reissue. After the first time she injects herself, an intertitle explains that she has "An [*sic*] heritage of shattered nerves from wartime service as a nurse" and, when Patricia, her rival for Minturn's affections, appears on the scene, Renée returns to the drug because "[t]aken first to stimulate a tired body the drug becomes the prop of a sorrowing mind." The audience is spared the visual evidence of her addiction, for when Renée injects herself, the film cuts away quickly to another scene. Only Minturn, peering through a screen, sees the actual act of Renée injecting herself, a scene that links him both to the early cinema's self-referential tradition of scenes showing men peeping through an opening to see a forbidden sight and to what Susan Zieger has called the "new kind of erotic spectacle" of "imagined private moments in which women perform their addictions."[27] When the camera cuts back to her, Renée shows no ill effects, no slumping loss of consciousness. Rather, she smiles and teases Minturn playfully as he tries to work. Although Norma Talmadge, who plays Renée, would later become known as a dramatic actress, in 1916 she was also known for her humor and charm in comedies such as *The Social Secretary*, and her performance as Renée draws on this persona, making the character even more sympathetic.[28]

Renée has an artist's eye as well as a model's figure, and she plays an unacknowledged role as Minturn's critic as well as his muse. Although she encouraged Minturn to turn to morphine, she is quick to see that the picture he paints after he uses the drug does not measure up to his previous work. Despite her sadness at Minturn's marriage, she joins the chase to rescue Patricia, at one point physically fighting with the drug pushers, a vigorous action usually reserved in the movies of this era for women fighting to avoid rape. Renée does not suffer death, the traditional fate of the fallen woman and the addict. Instead, she sacrifices her feelings in order to atone by bringing Minturn and Patricia back together. Witnessing their happiness, she stands apart and alone, weeping and holding the artist's smock that represents her outsider status. For Renée, the period of time spent

Renée prepares to inject herself with morphine
in *The Devil's Needle* (1916).

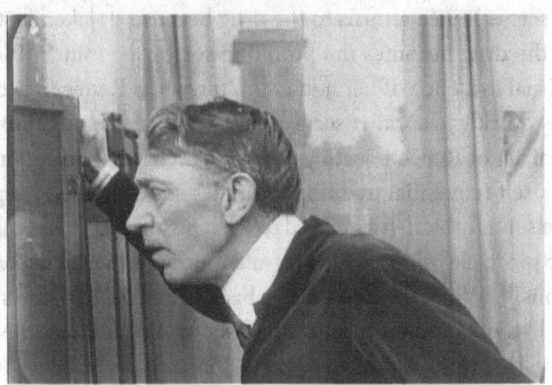

Minturn spies on Renée as she injects herself with morphine,
from *The Devil's Needle* (1916).

in Bohemia, and the complications of addiction and sexual freedom that she encountered there, results in her being trapped within it. Unlike Minturn's wife Patricia, she cannot move out of Bohemia and escape Bohemian time.

Bohemia through a Darwinist Lens

Ellen Glasgow's (1873–1945) literary reputation rests primarily on her novels set in Virginia, including *Barren Ground* (1925) and *In This Our Life* (1941), for which she won the Pulitzer Prize. But Glasgow began her career with two novels set in Bohemian New York, *The Descendant* (1897) and *Phases of an Inferior*

Planet (1898). As Julius Rowan Raper writes in *Without Shelter*, his account of her early career, Glasgow's knowledge of New York was limited to a two-week visit, but her knowledge of Darwin, Spencer, "William Graham Sumner, Walter Bagehot, Thomas Huxley, and August Weismann" was extensive.[29] As she writes in her autobiography, *The Woman Within*, Glasgow read Henry James and "immersed [herself] in Flaubert and Maupassant," Tolstoy, and Chekhov in her search for a flexible style. Determined to follow her "revolt from the philosophy of evasive idealism" and the "little vessels of experience," she resolved to "take as [her] theme those ugly aspects of life the sentimentalists had passed over."[30] The result is *The Descendant*, the study of a poor southern white boy who becomes a radical journalist, and *Phases of an Inferior Planet*, which follows a writer through engagements with evolutionary thought and religious idealism. Both novels combine two turn-of-the-century plots into one novel: a Darwinian novel of development with a male protagonist, a naturalistic bildungsroman in the vein of Jack London's *The Sea Wolf* (1904) or Frank Norris's *Vandover and the Brute* (1914), and a Bohemian art novel that pits love against art, with a New Woman protagonist caught between realism and romance, as in W. D. Howells's *The Coast of Bohemia* (1893) and Gertrude Christian Fosdick's *Out of Bohemia* (1894).[31] Through the secondary plots of women artists making their way in relationships with male idealists, Glasgow emphasizes the effects of ephemeral male Bohemian time on women's biological clocks, creating women's unruly naturalism through a Darwinist lens.

THE DESCENDANT

The New Woman artist story in *The Descendant* features Rachel Gavin, who becomes the lover of the protagonist, Michael Akershem, a country boy born out of wedlock who fights his way to the pinnacle of journalistic success. Born in poverty, Akershem scorns the world as a result of his environment, for as the narrator explains, in a metaphor from the Book of Jeremiah that Theodore Dreiser would later adopt for his play *The Hand of the Potter* (1918), "Circumstances are mighty and man is weak. The wheel of the potter grinds on and the clay is moulded into symmetry or distorted by mishap. If it is misshapen by the mishap and regains not its rounded form, is it the fault of the potter or of the clay?"[32] Akershem shares Glasgow's naturalistic perspective on urban spaces and on the place of human beings within them. Just before purchasing laudanum for a projected suicide attempt, he reflects that "he was but one atom moving in its given line amidst many thousands. Then the denseness of population oppressed him, humanity jammed into a writhing mass, like maggots in a cheese. The tenements, with their smoke-stained windows—their air of dignified squalor—seemed to cut off all means of ventilation" (28). Granted a degree of self-awareness rarely accessible to characters in early naturalism, Akershem uses the language of naturalism to describe his plight: human beings are for him both infinitely small atoms in an indifferent universe and a "writhing mass" of swarming maggots fighting for sustenance amid the suffocating smells and lack of air common to squalid urban environments. Rachel undergoes a process of artistic development that parallels Akershem's, but like many women in Bohemian fiction, she struggles with a commitment to her art at odds with the domesticity that her love for Akershem demands. She sacrifices her reputation by becoming Akershem's lover rather than his wife so that he need not compromise his rigid opposition to marriage. Rachel's narrative melds the New Woman conflict between love and work with the Darwinian courtship novel of biological desire.

Rachel first meets Akershem in the Chat Noir, a Bohemian cafe, and begins sketching his head for a study of "John the Baptist—as he left the wilderness, of course," as she tells him shortly thereafter (47). Her boldness challenges Akershem and piques his interest. Accustomed to controlling everyone around him, Akershem accuses her of not asking permission to sketch him. Her answer is to tear the sketch in half and declare, "St. John was hardly worth it" (48). Intrigued despite his disdain for women, Akershem seeks her out at her lodgings and offers to sit for the St. John portrait, and she invites him to her studio. As in other Bohemian novels, the studio signifies liberation and female sexuality because it is an unchaperoned interior space whose work function makes it neither parlor nor chamber. In W. D. Howells's *The Coast of Bohemia*, for example, the frivolous Charmian Maybough cross-dresses and wears dramatic garb in her artistically cluttered studio, and in Harold Frederic's *The Damnation of Theron Ware*, Celia Madden invites Theron up to her studio and slips into a sleeveless dressing gown before playing Chopin on the piano for him far into the night. When Akershem visits the studio, Rachel, like Frederic's Celia, greets him wearing a revealing gown "that was loose and full and of some dim, nondescript shade. When she lifted her arms the sleeves fell in soft folds back upon the shoulders" (77). The classical lines of the loose gown and the erotic promise of Rachel's bare arms confirms the blend of art and sexuality that imbues the studio setting with a dual meaning.

As they begin their courtship, Rachel and Michael unconsciously enact the principles of female sexual selection from Charles Darwin's *The Descent of Man*. Their gestures underscore their unspoken mutual attraction, including grimaces, clasped hands, narrowed eyes, and significant movements involving secondary sexual characteristics such as hair. As Bert Bender explains in *The Descent of Love*, hands and hand clasps suggest the courtship gestures that Darwin had identified in *The Descent of Man* as the male's prehensile grasping of the female with claw or hand as a part of the mating ritual. In Michael and Rachel's scenes together, the narrator carefully specifies each character's gestures, with Rachel alternating gestures of self-exposure and self-enclosure that determine the pattern of their courtship. In the midst of their intellectual sparring, for example, Rachel "lean[s] back against the cushions of the divan and [throws] her arms above her head with a quick, impulsive movement.... She was alive to her fingertips, and warm with the flow of her rich, red blood" (78). Her gesture, with arms above her head and "rich, red blood" flowing beneath the skin, opens her upper body to him, and Michael "lean[s] towards her, his eyes narrowing," an unconscious predatory advance, with his narrow eyes revealing his attraction to her. Shortly thereafter, Rachel leans forward and feels his "scintillating magnetism" (78, 79). When she holds out her hand at parting, he takes it and "[feels] a swift desire to lean down and touch the white nape of her neck upon which the dark hair was coiled" (82), the "coil" of her hair, like that of Trina Sieppe in Norris's *McTeague*, suggesting Darwin's famous "tangled bank" image from *The Origin of Species*.

After Michael leaves, however, Rachel rests her chin upon her "clasped hands," a gesture of self-enclosure that suggests her independence. Although she knows her "half-finished Magdalen" is "work that shows the hand of genius, a hand whose strokes are powerful and falter not," she drops the cloth over the painting and thinks instead, "How strong he is" (82). Instead of admiring her own power, she shrouds her work and turns her attention to Michael's strength. With the gesture of Rachel's clasping her hands under her chin, Glasgow emphasizes the self-contained and solitary nature of her desire at this point. Rachel's spirit is untroubled by the flesh: although Michael takes her "cool, frank hand" and feels "an electric current" that "dart[s] through his veins to his heart" (91), she feels no corresponding transmission of feeling, and "no electric thrills had broken the calm serenity of her pulse" (91). Instead she substitutes strokes of the hairbrush for those of the paintbrush, "soothed into drowsiness" through the "long, firm stroke of the brush" as she brushes her hair after he has left (92). Despite her efforts to ignore it, her painting of the Magdalen "seemed to quicken and come to life, to look back at the living woman with a great forewarning in her awful eyes" (92). The Magdalen has a dual warning, not only against Rachel's sexual fall from grace but also against her abandoning her art. Rachel sees only "the work of her own strong hands—her great work" (92) and prays for the ambition to finish her painting. The possessive pronouns—her hands, her work—signal her wish to shape her destiny, but her involuntary physical responses to Akershem suggest that her life is not in her control.

Glasgow reinforces the evolutionary nature of Rachel's choices by setting a key scene in a spot rife with anthropological and evolutionary associations: the Metropolitan Museum, which Wharton would later use for a similarly coded meeting between Newland Archer and Ellen Olenska in *The Age of Innocence*. Continuing the balance between exposure and self-enclosure, when Rachel and Michael meet, Rachel's hand "wander[s] to the violets upon her breast" (98), a recurring gesture of reassurance that Michael notes. He focuses upon her hands, which he sees as having "the power of a man and the lightness of a woman" (98). Rachel sits with her back against "the mummy of an Egyptian lady," which as in *The Age of Innocence* suggests the temporary nature of the flesh and desire, and she announces her devotion to "Joan of Arc" as her "gospel" (100), the reference to Joan of Arc confirming Rachel's commitment to self-determination and virginal purity. But Rachel's high ideals and religious devotion to her art contrast sharply with the Darwinian echoes of her gestures. When her eyes tear up because of the cold, Rachel "burie[s] her face in her muff," a merging of human and animal that arouses Michael. He gazes at her with a "devouring earnestness," noting the Darwinian touches of the "dark curves" of her hair blending into the "soft fur" of her collar. His attraction to her is primitive, animalistic, and instinctive, a desire for possession and dominance that anticipates the combination of sexual invitation, verbal independence, and a woman enveloped in furs that attracts another ideologically fixated man, Amherst in Wharton's *The Fruit of the Tree*.

References to evolution repeatedly redirect Rachel and Michael's discourse from idealism to physical reality. Their discussions of evolution reveal a sexual awareness that neither can otherwise express, with ideology consistently crumbling before the physical presence of the desired other. After their first meeting, for example, Michael takes refuge in viewing men and women from a Nietzschean height as "but moving atoms" (50), and he fends off his attraction to Rachel by quoting Huxley and declaring that marriage begins "as an experiment" but degenerates into "a fetich" (75). However, Rachel's presence clouds his judgment about his thoughts, leaving his brain "in a muddle" that he attributes to "too many cigars" (76). In a later meeting, Rachel tells Michael that she has read *The Evolution of the Horse* and accepts its ideas wholeheartedly, reading it in her bath and immersing herself in the book as in the water. Immediately after telling Michael of this, her hair falls from its place into "a heavy wave upon her shoulders" and her lips "curved and quivered in their sensitive, bewitching way" (107), a Darwinian loosening of hair and curling of lip that Michael reads as a signal to kiss her.

Rachel tells him that she "always did hate to kiss men" (107), but, as predicted by the model of female responses to courtship outlined in *The Descent of Man*, her resistance is only temporary. A few days later, waiting for Michael, she hears the "little silver clock upon the mantel," signifying the biological time that she cannot ignore. When he kisses her this time, she gives up "the struggle" as the blood surges to her pulses: "She had sold them all for this, and she did not regret her bargain" (119). Reversing the course of Louisa Ellis in Mary E. Wilkins Freeman's "A New England Nun," who sells her birthright of marriage for a symbolic mess of pottage, her life as a single woman, Rachel sells her artistic dream for a different ideal—not marriage, which Michael abhors on ideological grounds, but being a "blessed comrade" to him, forgetting that, as the narrator comments, "it is less easy to mould life than it is to wound one's hands in the attempt" (122).

Despite Rachel and Michael's professed commitment to shared ideals, Michael destroys their relationship with his primitive attachment to conventionality and the double standard. Their life becomes a one-sided tale of understanding and constancy on Rachel's part and infidelity and condescension on Michael's, culminating in Rachel's acquiescence when he hypocritically deserts her for a "good woman," Anna (189). A social reformer, Anna cares for her disabled niece and courts Michael by taking him on the same kind of slum tour that appears in Davis's *Margret Howth* and Phelps's *Hedged In*. Although he had "hurl[ed] editorial thunderbolts" at the exploiters of poor people, Michael shrinks from actual contact with them, but Anna does not hesitate to pick up an "unwashed baby," which in Michael's besotted gaze frames her as "a young Madonna" in contrast to Rachel's Magdalene (187). The difference between the women appears in the books they read. Rachel had attracted Michael with her reading of *The Evolution of the Horse*, but Anna piques his interest by reading Weismann's *Heredity*. As Julius Rowan Raper notes, Weismann was "the first Darwinian evolutionist to contend that not acquired characteristics, but only those new structures which first arise in the reproductive material, called 'germ-plasm,' are hereditary." With this allusion, Raper contends, Anna frees Akershem from "the worry that 'blood tells' everything" and that he will repeat the mistakes of his ancestors.[33] But destiny for Michael is gendered. He sees his own character as flexible but Rachel's sexual transgression in becoming his lover as an immutable blot on her character: "Would a good woman have loved him as Rachel loved him?" (189). Like other idealistic men in women's naturalism, he requires a woman to conform to his exacting standards and then punishes her for doing so.

Once Akershem and sexuality depart from her life, Rachel becomes the artist she had wanted to be. After a "cabbage" existence in which all her "animal vitality has become exhausted" by painting illustrations for fashion magazines in order to survive, she emerges, as from a chrysalis, as a talented realist painter (260). Rachel cannot truly paint Mary Magdalene until she becomes a Magdalene in Akershem's eyes, because only her experience of suffering and sexual humiliation allows her to understand her subject's plight. Her old teacher, Dupont, urges her to go to Paris to study, and she is on the cusp of greater achievement when Michael appears, haggard and suffering from the last stages of tuberculosis after a stay in prison. Instead of leaving for Paris and the artist's life, Rachel chooses to take him in, exulting, "He is mine, mine for all time!" (275), an echo of Jane Eyre's rescue of Edward Rochester in *Jane Eyre*. In a domestic novel, Rachel's choice would be redemptive, but in naturalistic terms she has chosen poorly. As the narrator editorializes, "Hers the scattered crumbs from the bread of life, hers the stagnant slime left of an all-powerful passion" (275). Already an afterthought in Michael's renewed desire for revenge upon the world, Rachel settles for the waste, the "stagnant slime" of a relationship. Her action puts an end to her artistic career and is not worth the sacrifice, for it renders Rachel, as Akershem's discarded mistress, as waste.

Glasgow foreshadows the death of Rachel's career when, late in the novel, Akershem picks up Robert W. Chambers's *The King in Yellow* on a train and reads an extended passage from it. Although William J. Scheick posits the "looming triumph of the supernatural" as Glasgow's reason for including the allusion, the section that Akershem reads is "The Studio," taken from "The Prophets' Paradise," a later story in the book.[34] The passage recalls to Akershem a vision of Rachel's studio as a reflection of her interior self: "the plaster casts above the door, the marble statue of 'Hope' upon a little table . . . all the objects upon which she had impressed her vivid personality" (233). Throughout *The Descendant* Rachel has been associated with red flowers. In *The King in Yellow*, the segment that Akershem reads concludes with a woman who pours blood on flowers, declaring that she has "killed him who I loved."[35] Another story in *The King in Yellow*, "The Street of the Four Winds," is a Poe-like tale of the body of a beautiful woman, Sylvia Elven. When her cat, with a silver garter about its neck, wanders into the studio of Severn, an artist, he makes inquiries about its owner and learns Sylvia's address. Arriving at her door, he hears movement inside, but when he enters, he discovers her lying dead, with "eyes, wide open, smiling." He muses about her death and kisses her mouth—a violation, since she cannot assent to it—cast as a tribute to her beauty.[36] Sylvia's body evokes the naturalistic scene of the woman's still body lying in a tableau before a man who fails to comprehend her. The Bohemian spaces invoked in *The King in Yellow* reveal charming studios as death-haunted chambers that harbor grotesque, necrophilic impulses. The extended allusion to Akershem reading *The King in Yellow* evokes the darker side of romantic Bohemia and, with Rachel's decision to sacrifice her art for Akershem's life, the pitfalls for women who, like Chambers's Sylvia Elven, extend their stay in those regions.

PHASES OF AN INFERIOR PLANET

Glasgow's *Phases of an Inferior Planet* retains *The Descendant*'s dynamic of a relationship between a male idealist and a woman artist, but it shifts the issues of aesthetics from writing and painting to posing and performance. Its principal characters represent evolutionary and Aesthetic theories. Anthony Algarcife, the aggressive intellectual with a telling "bulging brow," proposes to revolutionize evolutionary science through a "theory of heredity which will reconcile Darwin's gemmules, Weismann's germ-plasm, and Galton's stirp." Mariana Musin, an aspiring singer, associates herself with the Pre-Raphaelites in look and actions.[37] Algarcife and Mariana are different varieties of a similar character, the idealist undone by biological imperatives. The two meet, marry, have a child that dies, and finally leave one another, she to pursue a career on the stage as a singer and he to pursue his career as a writer until, crushed by poverty, he turns to a successful career as a preacher of religious doctrines that he no longer believes. Although it is formally divided into two books or "Phases," *Phases of an Inferior Planet* encompasses three stages of Mariana and Algarcife's lives as artists: their courtship, their descent into a hellish naturalistic Bohemia, and their professional success and personal disillusionment after their divorce.

Like Michael Akershem in *The Descendant*, Anthony Algarcife is an intellectual whose idealism wreaks havoc on his own life and the lives around him. As Edith Wharton would later demonstrate in *The Age of Innocence*, a character's intellectual awareness of scientific theories does not guarantee his making rational choices, and Algarcife, like Wharton's Newland Archer, believes he operates as a free agent when he is in fact driven by biological forces. Algarcife forms a close homosocial bond with Father Speares, an Episcopal priest who mentors his intellectual development and advises him not to marry (107), but he is equally attractive to women, drawing adoring female students to his lectures at the Bodley College for Women.[38] Mariana shares Algarcife's magnetism but not his intellectual approach to art, for she has a physical, instinctive response to music. Her "scantily made gown of green, with strange reptiles sprawling over it, relieved against the ardor of a purple sunset" (25) aligns her in coloring with the Pre-Raphaelite and Aesthetic movements and in subject matter—the reptiles—with evolution. In addition to her "heavy hair" (15) and friendship with a group of women artists, one of whom, Juliet Hill, resembles "Rossetti's 'Beata Beatrix'" (57), Mariana, the name she gives herself, alludes to the 1851 painting of John Everett Millais and to Tennyson's poem of the same name. As an artist and a southern woman, Mariana exaggerates her sensitivity and emotional lability. Attending a performance of *Tannhauser* with Algarcife, who is untouched by the music, she weeps hysterically because it makes her feel that she "want[s] something," as Darwin's section on "Vocal Music" in *The Descent of Man* predicts for the female of the species (119). Their responses are consistent with Darwinian evolutionary theory, which holds that the female animal responds to music as a courtship gesture. Her emotionalism, as extreme as Algarcife's intellectualism, leads not to the reconciliation of opposites typical of a romance plot but to a confirmation that their temperaments will never find common ground.

The last five chapters of the first book, "Phase One," comprise a naturalistic novella featuring the marriage of Algarcife and Mariana, the birth and death of their daughter, the couple's descent into poverty and separation, and Algarcife's mental breakdown. All four of these stages confirm Mariana's failure to adapt, which she proudly accepts as a mark of her gentility. Declaring that her delicate southern heritage makes her sensitive to quality, Mariana refuses to eat with a "pewter fork" (10) or drink smoked tea (119). Mariana had earlier told Algarcife that she would "almost as soon starve as live on cabbage" because her stepmother, "a very coarse woman," cooked "cabbage one day and onions the next" (92). Now unable to escape the smell of frying cabbage from the downstairs apartment, she must confront the reality of poverty that no posturing about sensitivity will alleviate. After Algarcife loses his teaching job for publishing "a series of articles upon the origin of sex" (147), the two cannot escape the material consequences of poverty, including its smells. As is consistent with women's naturalism, the realities of the body challenge the characters' illusions.

Maternity brings to Mariana neither consolation for her plight nor automatic love for the child. During her pregnancy, Mariana tries to bear in mind the words of her singing teacher, Signor Morani, that she will succeed because she is "an artist first, and a wife and mother afterwards" (123). Yet after reading John Stuart Mill, she feels "as if I had committed a sin" by "forcing something into the world to fight with poverty and discomforts" (128). Immediately after the birth, Mariana, in a haze of chloroform and digitalis, feels herself on "some ice-crowned summit" and, irritated with her newborn daughter, Isolde, asks the nurse to take her away (130). She muses that women who "had once known the agony of maternity" were "ridiculous" to go through it a second time (131). Gazing at Isolde, Mariana confesses, "I don't care for it in the least" and calls it her "dear, poor, ugly little baby" (132) a refutation of the sentimental ideal of maternal instinct.

Childbirth strips Mariana of pretenses and forces her to confront some disturbing realities beneath her posturing. After Isolde's birth, Mariana asks for brandy and recalls her southern childhood, claiming that because her grandmother, who "owned a great many slaves," had sensitive skin and "couldn't bear to be touched by anything but silk," her daughter must have linen sheets, since "[i]t is in the blood" (136). By reclaiming the sensitive body of a southern aristocrat and artist, Mariana rejects the maternal body that ties her to biological time and to poverty. But her memories fail to rescue her, for in drinking the brandy, Mariana recalls a repressed memory of threatened sexual abuse. As a child lost in the city, she wandered into a barroom. There, in her memory, a strange "gentleman with a very red face" pulls her behind a screen and offers her a "taste of toddy" (133), which she refuses, saying that she has "plenty of that at home" (133). Mariana falls asleep after relating this incident, but veiled beneath the recollection of plentiful mint juleps and silk garments are menacing realities. The vaunted sensitivity to fabrics that white southern women like her grandmother enjoyed rested squarely on the abuses of slavery, and the child Mariana's memory obscures the sexual dangers that she and other children might suffer at the hands of red-faced male strangers who pull them behind screens and offer them drinks.

Mariana's calling for brandy introduces the idea of substance abuse in their world, for, in a daring move for its era, *Phases of an Interior Planet* conflates religion, sex, and drugs as interchangeable methods of augmenting or numbing consciousness. Faced with extreme poverty, Algarcife begins taking regular doses of caffeine so that he can write fifteen hours a day and support Mariana and their child (150). When Isolde dies, overcome by the extreme heat of the tenement on Fourth Street to which they have moved, Mariana leaves Algarcife, saying that she cannot bear the "stale odor of cooking, which rose from the apartment below, the dustiness of the floor, the blackened ceiling, the hard and unyielding bed," all signposts of the catalog of waste associated with naturalistic fiction (165). Recognizing that his "use of stimulants, in exciting his nervous system, had made sleep impossible," Algarcife begins to take "morphia pellets" (177, 179). At his lowest point, having lost everything and tempted to commit suicide with a bottle of "Hydrocyanic Acid" (184), he sits on a park bench with a woman who falls asleep on his shoulder as he listens to her "drunken snores" (185).

The sleeping woman embodies the grotesque woman of naturalism in her intrusiveness and in the messy reality of enforced contact with her bodily fluids. With "a bleeding cut upon her lip," her snoring, and the weight of her physical body resting on his, she overwhelms Algarcife's senses, and the flowing of blood from her lip challenges Algarcife's dry, abstract conceptions of suffering humanity. Direct contact with the wet, messy problems of poor people in general and bleeding women in particular appalls Algarcife, the latest in a continuing line of idealistic men in women's naturalism who hesitate or shrink from the abject. Women, in contrast, do not hesitate to touch those who are suffering, as when Margret Howth picks up the African American child in *Margret Howth* and Akershem's lover Anna picks up the "unwashed baby" in *The Descendant*. Uncomfortable contact with unwashed poor constitutes too much realism for Algarcife, however, and he retreats into idealism and the comforts of organized charity, where poor people are kept at a comfortable distance. In the morning, he pawns his watch, the symbol of naturalistic and biological clock time, and shortly thereafter reencounters Father Speares. Speares represents the world of religion and permanent illusions, and, as the phallic implications of his name and his earlier advice not to marry suggest, he promotes an insular, artificial world of celibacy and homoeroticism within the Episcopal Church as an alternative to biological time. Speares takes Algarcife home and builds him into a popular and charismatic Episcopal priest whose magnetism attracts wealthy female parishioners despite the loss of faith that Algarcife keeps well hidden.[39]

But belief is irrelevant to Algarcife's new calling, for what matters is his ability to move multitudes through sex appeal. In his new role, Father Algarcife applies an "electric battery to the sluggish limbs of the Church" (193) and drives "all the women into a religious mania" (192). As John Driscoll, the truth-telling newspaperman who also appeared in *The Descendant*, explains, "Religion might be called the feminine element of modern society. It owes its persistence to the attraction of sex" (192). This is the same Darwinian sentiment voiced by the truth-telling evolutionist Dr. Ledsmar of Harold Frederic's *The Damnation of Theron Ware*. Society women such as Mrs. Bruce Ryder lean close to Algarcife and confess that they feel that they "would do anything—for love," and women enter his office "with a great deal of rustling and no evident object in view" (211, 243). Nor is his power confined to the hearts of unsatisfied women. When during an incense-filled mass Algarcife, now Father Algarcife, lifts his voice in prayer, in "a deep undertone of unwavering richness," even the cynic Driscoll is moved as though he "had been drinking" (194, 195). As the novel makes clear, performance of religious ritual, even when the priest no longer believes, is a socially sanctioned drug, and Algarcife has become its chief dispenser. In abandoning his watch and entering the church, Algarcife escapes from naturalistic time and Bohemian time into the eternal world of religious ritual.

The one remaining threat to Algarcife's escape from time occurs when Mariana returns to New York. Now the widow of a wealthy Englishman, Mariana meets Algarcife by accident on a warm December morning when she recalls her childhood and the "the little brown lizards" that sunned themselves on the gravestones, the reference to mortality (gravestones) and evolution (lizards) signaling her place in biological time. Algarcife at first resists Mariana. He responds to her confession of being tortured by memory and remorse by saying that he is not her confessor and that "[t]here are drugs for both" (274), suggesting that he recognizes the opiate-dispensing nature of his calling. But their biological attraction to each other remains. At the end of their meeting, he "stoop[s] for her muff, which had rolled to the ground, brushing it lightly with his hand," a gesture linking hair, fur, and touch to their renewed attraction to one another (274, 283). A few days later, Mariana, after "rearranging the coil of her hair," sees herself in the mirror "irradiated by the glimmering firelight" before "touch[ing] the clock" as she waits for him, annoyed in the meantime by the "broken tune" of an organ-grinder in the street. The firelight, a conventionally poetic metaphor of desire, signifies their rekindled attraction, as does the attention to her "coil" of hair, but the clock and the broken melody suggest both biological time and the disruption of their former harmony. Algarcife promises to leave the ministry and move south with Mariana, but when she walks through the rain to watch him preach, she recognizes his gift and realizes that "the past is the one thing irremediable" (316). She cannot drag him from the artificial haven of eternal religious time into biological time, least of all for a visit to a past that they shared but that nearly destroyed them.

Throughout the novel, the restless Mariana has been most vivid to Algarcife when she approaches the coloring and stillness of a statue, bloodless, pale, and the antithesis of the naturalistically grotesque woman on the park bench. During her trip in the rain to see Algarcife, Mariana catches pneumonia, and, when she is near death, Algarcife watches her lying "motionless, her heavy hair tangled in the lace on the pillow" (321) and recalls her "look of one in a trance or in death," with "bluish shadows on her cold breast" (132) after Isolde's birth. The silent and vulnerable Mariana becomes both the motionless woman of the naturalistic novel and Poe's embodiment of the topos of perfect art, the body of a beautiful woman. Like Sylvia Elven's body in *The King in Yellow*, the still body of Mariana inspires male attention and arrests time. Her death seems to prefigure Algarcife's own, for, returning to his office, Algarcife uncorks a "small blue phial" of cyanide with the "pungent and pervasive odor of bitter almonds" (324), the last of the naturalistic smells in the novel that, like the smell of cabbage that Mariana abhors, signify the material manifestation of repressed psychological states. A messenger calls on him at that moment, asking him to speak to the strikers at the mill, and, putting the bottle away, "Father Algarcife" follows him to save suffering humanity en masse, although he could not save the woman closest to him.

Concluding with a life in service as the solution to Algarcife's anguish may have seemed inadequate to Glasgow's original readers, for the book "sold miserably and reaped abuse from the critics," according to Julius Rowan Raper (118). Raper further speculates that "Akershem, as an agnostic scientist of whom circumstances make an extremely successful priest ... seemed incredible" to the American public (119), although the same plot, of a successful preacher who becomes an unbeliever, had appeared in Harold Frederic's *The Damnation of Theron Ware* two years before.[40] Paired with *The Descendant*, however, *Phases of an Inferior Planet* completes Glasgow's exploration of Darwinian courtship in Bohemian settings and the limitations of Bohemian time for women. Although *Phases* is more direct than its predecessor about the squalor and poverty that result when biological time breaches the boundaries of Bohemian time and space, neither work provides a satisfactory solution for the woman artist. The idealism and subsequent disillusionment of men damages the women with whom they are involved, and in neither case can the woman leave biological time behind to immerse herself in a career in art. The incursions of the world beyond Bohemia prove that, for women, Bohemian time ceases when the biological time associated with sexuality and childbearing begins.

Mary Austin's *No. 26 Jayne Street*

Set in Greenwich Village in the days before and during World War I, *No. 26 Jayne Street* (1920) is Mary Austin's portrait of Bohemian New York and what she saw as the misguided idealism of its political movements. Her biographers Susan Goodman and Carl Dawson suggest that the novel "did nothing to advance her reputation," yet Austin recalled it in her autobiography *Earth Horizon* as her "best novel to date," saying that it failed because "it aimed to uncover the sleazy quality of current radicalism, the ways in which the personal expression of radicals contradicted and reversed the political expression."[41] Crowded with strikes, lectures, marches, and characters holding forth on their particular radical causes, *No. 26 Jayne Street* explores the political ramifications of gender inequality in romantic relationships, revealing that neither radical ideologies nor statements of gender equality live up to the heady illusions of those who promote them. The heroine, Neith Schuyler, takes an apartment in Greenwich Village after several years spent abroad caring for her invalid father, and, like her real-life model, the New Woman novelist and playwright Neith Boyce, immerses herself in the heady political culture of the place.[42] She falls in love with Adam Frear, a character based on Lincoln Steffens, but their engagement ends when she learns of his relationship with Rose Matlock, an idealistic reformer. Abandoning his proclamations about free love, Adam sends Rose packing and tries to patch up his relationship with Neith. Unimpressed and disillusioned with his solution, Neith breaks the engagement, having concluded that men pontificate publically about high ideals but act privately only in traditionally selfish and cowardly ways in relationships between the sexes.

Neith's story illustrates Austin's basic thesis: that Bohemian time and modern conceptions of free love cannot trump the biological and social realities of women's bodies and gender inequality. Living in a community of women determined to break the bonds of convention through birth control, free love, and voluntary motherhood, Neith encounters domestic arrangements and ideas that would shock her aristocratic New York family, represented by her widowed aunt, Mrs. Doremus; her spinster aunt, Miss Emmaline Schuyler; and her well-meaning but ineffectual cousin, the society reformer Millicent Havens. To shelter Neith from the harsh world, they object to her taking an apartment in Greenwich Village at 26 Jayne Street and would prefer that she marry her cousin twice removed, Eustace Rittenhouse. But even these conventional women resist complete domesticity by adopting seemingly harmless eccentricities. Aunt Emmaline follows "New Thought... as an antidote to the persistently unhappy things that kept thrusting themselves on her world," a soft-minded escape from her trivial problems that leaves her vulnerable to exploitation.[43] Devoid of occupation, education, and common sense, Emmaline Schuyler is a ready victim for the old roué General Rittenhouse, Eustace's grandfather, a womanizer who cons Emmaline into forging his wife's name so that he can plunder his wife's inheritance.[44] The general's long-suffering wife, Frances Rittenhouse, endures his infidelities because she believes in a domestic ideal. Like Glasgow's Rachel of *The Descendant*, she has molded herself into her husband's professed ideal and is now "defeated by her own earlier yielding to what she had been taught to think her husband would value most in her" (246). With the customary hypocrisy of men in Bohemian novels by women, the general then despises the person he had demanded that she become. He differs generationally but not substantively from the poseurs and frauds among the minor male characters in the novel, such as Bertie Condin, a Bohemian journalist who, to appear more intellectual, wears glasses that he does not need.

Despite their commitment to social change, the Bohemian women Neith encounters reveal that, where gender relations are concerned, radical women are as trapped as Frances Rittenhouse or domestic women of earlier generations. Three of the women she befriends—her protégée Sadie Comyns, her mentor Madelon Sherrod, and her rival Rose Matlock—show Neith the limitations of idealistic belief when confronted with the reality of men's actions. Sadie, an Irish and Russian Jewish "Syndicalist" (79) whose "pale, expanding cat's eyes" (213) signal her "mixed race," refuses to marry her lover, the significantly named Hippolyte Leninsky, out of principle, even after she becomes pregnant. But when Leninsky is killed in police custody, Sadie is crazed with grief and regrets not being married for financial as well as social reasons. Except for the money that Neith gives her, she is destitute, without the support of Leninsky's family or her own. Madelon Sherrod, Neith's mentor, is a beautiful and accomplished actress, but she too must confront the contradictions of Bohemian time and biological time. Madelon is older than Neith, and, like Neith, has attained a cosmopolitan and European perspective. As Madelon observes at one point, "Happy women have no history, and it's history we are making" (174). Yet to have even a modicum of happiness Madelon must compromise by turning a blind eye to her husband's philandering, a failing that Neith observes but, feeling ashamed of Madelon's desperation, does not discuss with her. Despite her fame and accomplishments, Madelon faces the reality that biological time does not favor older women in the competition for men, and, confronted with the clash between her ideals and her marriage, she chooses the latter.

For all that she sees of other women's unhappiness, Neith falls in love almost immediately with Adam Frear, a radical editor who "hardly wrote so well as he talked" (169). Adam proposes to her on the eve of his trip to Russia to meet "Trotzky" (147), but she hesitates until he returns, dreaming of him and unaware of the narrator's wry observation that "[i]t is doubtful if any man ever means as much by his love-making as the woman gets out of it" (145). In the meantime she turns down a proposal from Eustace Rittenhouse, who before going off to Europe to fight in the World War warns her that Adam is "the best of the Radical lot" (199) but that he is not of her kind. When Adam returns, he and Neith become engaged, but upon learning of the engagement, Rose Matlock visits Neith to reveal her long-term relationship with Adam. His façade of radicalism, like the façade of gentility, drops away during a confrontation when Rose arrives to stake her prior claim to him.

When Rose reveals to Neith that she and Adam had been lovers, Adam enters Neith's apartment, and the "white flash of his teeth between drawn lips, the hot spark of his eye, the flamelike spurt of his voice" all reveal the animal beneath his civilized exterior. He reverts to a naturalistic primitive type, atavistically snarling, curling his lip, and showing his teeth as he moves into Darwinian survival mode to fight Rose. He further betrays his radical roots by relying on the language of class and sexual shaming, dismissing Rose as he might dismiss a prostitute or lower-class lover who had sought him out by threatening her, saying, "What did I tell you if you dared—" (278). When Rose claims to want justice, he bursts out that he is "not interested in what you may be feeling" (279), denying her right to lay claim to him or indeed to address him at all. Ignoring his earlier rebellion against the laws of an unjust society, Adam uses the law's technicalities against her. "I never promised her I would marry her," he protests, the universal cry of seducers through the ages who renege on implicit promises. In mutual disgust at the legalistic rationalization, the two women, former opponents, "stood . . . together against him" (281) in a moment of feminist solidarity.

Seeing his treatment of Rose, Neith decides that despite his socialist credentials, Adam—and, given his biblical name, all men—is in spirit a capitalist. He possesses and discards women according to his own scheme, she realizes, and he no more understands a woman's concerns than the capitalist "stockholders [who] were shocked by the strike at Marcy" (310). He is "a bounder" who "had done an exceedingly bourgeois thing under the very banners and shibboleths of the Social Revolution" (328). In short, he has failed on the radical level of his Marxist beliefs, the social level of being a gentleman, and the idealistic level of gender equality and free love. Having shown himself to be a liar as well, by denying that he had sent Rose a cease and desist letter to stop harassing him, Adam completes the picture by failing to understand the justice of any side but his own. With "extraordinary clarity," Neith recognizes that to Adam "[a]t all times and occasions a woman was a secondary thing" (328) and that what he had done to one discarded woman, he would do to another. Adam had earlier declared "a man can't help what he feels" (302) with the "same fatuousness" that motivates General Rittenhouse's "pride in his complete befuddlement at the hands of a popular dancer" (306). Masculinity demands that men never be considered wrong in matters belonging to the world, even when men prove themselves incompetent or fraudulent, as General Rittenhouse does. But as is the case with Adam and General Rittenhouse, masculinity also demands that real men become fools in the presence of young women, since the primitive sexuality that defines masculinity ratifies this as a legitimate pursuit. In evolutionary terms, Adam's reversion to masculine type is like the general's fiduciary chicanery and philandering, both forms of corruption based in the selfishness and acquisitive instincts that Neith assigns to capitalism and now, given her experiences, to the nature of men.

Yet radical women fare no better than radical men in Austin's critique of idealism. The brief moment of sisterhood with Rose over Adam's defection dissolves when Neith realizes that for Rose, Adam existed primarily as a straw man to whom she had pinned a mishmash of ideals. During a speech at Cooper Union on the "Trotzky-Lenine Revolution" [*sic*], Rose tells Neith that Adam is in Russia. Drawing one last conclusion about the relationship of personal to political, Rose declares that the breakup of the relationship with Adam was worse for her than Neith's breakup had been, because it "turned out to be the falsification of my most sacred convictions" (351). She implies that she, Rose, has suffered more from a broken relationship than Neith has suffered from her broken engagement. Taking refuge in her own self-righteous idealism, Rose wins the contest of suffering by denigrating Neith's feelings and deciding to follow Adam to Europe until he recognizes her rights as a wronged woman, a stalker-like behavior in which she feels fully justified. Neith reflects that, like the praying mantis devoured by the mate that tears it limb from limb, "Adam Frear was to suffer in effect such a dismemberment for the fructification of Rose's soul" (351). Like the eponymous heroine of W. D. Howells's "Editha," who sends her lover to the Civil War based on self-dramatizing notions of patriotism and feminine power, Rose loves the ideal rather than the real man, and her desire for a self-sacrificing and self-dramatizing possession of him is finally as ignoble as Adam's capitalistic acquisition of women.

Austin contrasts the ephemeral nature of radical idealism with the grounded realism of sexuality and passion through the traditional material symbol of engagement and wedding rings. When Neith fears that the pregnant Sadie, haunted by Leninsky's death and her "heritage of pogroms" (239), might miscarry, Neith buys and "slip[s] on [Sadie's] unheeding finger a plain gold band," which Sadie "cuddle[s] on her pillow" and which brings her back to a sense that she is part of "the common round of living" (240). Neith's instinctive gesture reflects her sense that even radical women wish for a solid, material symbol of commitment. After Neith and Adam become engaged, Neith worries that Adam might think a ring would be too "bourgeois," and she conceals her feelings in order to fall in line with his radical ideology. He does not object, however, and he buys her a ring of antique square emeralds rather than diamonds. The power of the ring is both soothing, as the wedding ring is to Sadie, and erotic. At 26 Jayne Street, Neith resists Adam's passionate kiss and sexual promise only by the "drowning effort" of laying "the cool emerald of her ring against his cheek" (254), barring his advances with a material reminder of the convention of marriage. After the confrontation between Adam and Rose, Neith visits Rose to ask her to let Adam resolve the matter on his own terms. Before she talks to Rose, she suspends her engagement, removing her ring as "an immediate and concrete way" to signify the fact and to establish her "clean Anglo-Saxon sporting instinct to throw away her sword in the presence of an unarmed adversary" (304). Her racially based "Anglo-Saxon" sense of fair play overcomes any gender-based tendency to rely on womanly weakness or claims of commitment as a weapon. The ring is the woman's sword, the text implies, for it is the only weapon that carries authority within the legal system that men use to keep women in subjugation. Based in ancient systems of property rights, the ring enforces the only legal and social form of contract that men will recognize as binding, that of engagement and marriage.

No. 26 Jayne Street fleshes out the social ferment and the heady atmosphere of Bohemian New York effectively, but the heart of its message is conservative, even cynical, in its presentation of relationships between men and women. The caricatured idealism of its secondary characters like Fleeta Spence, who take their ideas from the *Proletariat* (Austin's thinly disguised name for the *Masses*) and the powerful speakers of the day like Lanier Stevens, who, the narrator satirically remarks, "had been [in Russia] a fortnight, at least, and ... was going to tell them what to think about the Proletariat Revolution" (346), is as hidebound by ideological correctness as the conventional "Van Droom-Schuyler" tribe to whom Neith belongs by birth. Only Neith's young relative and sometime suitor Eustace Rittenhouse shows any courage, volunteering for war service and acting to save another pilot in an aerial dogfight, an effort that ends in Eustace's death. Faced with a lonely future on Jayne Street—or "Jane" Street, for the slang term for an unmarried woman, as she jokes early in the novel—Neith feels "the future at her heart like a small, gnawing worm" (351) as she anticipates Adam's eventual return and the compromised existence she can expect if she takes him back. Beginning as a treatise protesting the seduction of women's wills and the consequences they suffer as a result of believing in men's idealism, *No. 26 Jayne Street* concludes that, in a culture of gender inequality, the best women can do is to recognize the types of compromises that they will inevitably make.

Bohemian Time and the Cinematic Voyeur

First published as "Coming, Eden Bower!" in *The Smart Set*, Willa Cather's "Coming, Aphrodite!" was one of four stories of opera singers that Cather wrote between 1916 and 1920. According to Hermione Lee, all were leftovers from *The Song of the Lark* and focused on "American opera singers struggling against their 'natural enemies' in a philistine, envious, interfering world."[45] As Cather's friend and early critic Elizabeth Shepley Sergeant noted in 1925, "Coming, Aphrodite!" follows one of her two "great patterns," the "artist pattern, with its sparkling superhuman aims and ambitions, and its imperfect and fragile human ties."[46] "Coming, Aphrodite!" is "Cather's Manifesto" on the types of success possible in art, for after her bold portraits of Hedger and Eden, Cather would avoid drawing characters that revealed herself as an artist, preferring instead to portray "women struggling to escape the type and to emerge as themselves," according to Susan Rosowski.[47] Holly Messitt, Mary Ryder, and Michele Barale have noted the story's themes of voyeurism and sexuality,[48] but "Coming, Aphrodite!" also suggests women's naturalism in its evolutionary themes, including water and animal images; its veiled potential for violence; its catalogs of refuse; and its focus on the spectacle of the woman's body. More provocatively, it incorporates the technologies of artistic projection and early film as part of its exploration of scopophilia and visuality.

Set in Greenwich Village, "Coming, Aphrodite!" is the story of Don Hedger, a shaggy-haired, intense artist, and the aspiring opera singer Eden Bower, née Edna Bowers. Hedger lives with his bulldog, Caesar, who is more elaborately groomed than his master: "fresh and shining," with "pink skin show[ing] through his mottled coat which glistened as if it had just been rubbed with olive oil."[49] Caesar is an externalization of his owner's interior artistic persona, clean where Hedger is scruffy, and he is as disturbed as Hedger is when Eden Bower, a young opera singer, moves into a recently vacated room that adjoins Hedger's studio. Eden brings with her multiple sensory distractions, from the piano that Hedger hears being installed behind the flimsy double doors that separate his room from hers to the new smells that Caesar sniffs at suspiciously in the crack beneath the doors. Taking full advantage of the rooming house setting, Cather uses the convention of the shared-but-nominally-split room familiar to readers from the works of O. Henry and Frank Norris, whose Old Grannis and Miss Baker likewise occupy separate small rooms carved from a larger one. But unlike Norris's elderly and asexual couple, the young and vibrant Eden and Hedger will never live side by side without speaking.

Cather prepares her readers for this level of reading through Hedger's first encounter with Eden. Catching him in the hallway after he has washed Caesar in the communal bathtub, she says, "I've found his hair in the tub, and I've smelled a doggy smell... It's an outrage!" (364). The peculiar intimacy of finding hairs in the bathtub that one shares with another, hairs that have been displaced onto the sexual symbol Caesar but might equally refer to human hairs, embarrasses Hedger. He immediately substitutes Caesar for himself as the target of her indignation, taking refuge in his dim recollections of Diana and the hunt ("man who was turned into a dog... because he unwittingly intruded upon the bath of beauty") (364) and protesting that the dog is cleaner than he is. Like Diana, Eden is furious rather than ashamed, and she squelches Hedger by retorting, "That I don't doubt!" to his excuse making about Caesar's cleanliness.[50] Although Hedger is comically cowed by Eden's Amazonian presence when she confronts him about the dog hairs in the bathtub, Caesar exhibits Hedger's repressed savagery and aggressiveness by sinking his teeth into Eden's ankle when she later goes up to his and Hedger's male preserve, the roof.

Soon Hedger discovers another source of distraction. As he collects a pile of "forgotten laundry" from the back of his closet, a simultaneous sign of his indifference to appearance and a foreshadowing of the cleansing that is about to take place in his vision of women, "a long ray of yellow light shot across the dark enclosure,—a knot hole, evidently, in the high wainscoating of the west room" (366). The story has already established the tone palette for Hedger's life in the gray light he prefers for his painting, the "blue and still" view from the roof with only a "silver moon" in the sky, and a "yellow quadrangle" of gaslight coming up from the hall marring the darkness (363). The knothole's unexpected source of light signifies the change about to come into his monastic existence. When he peers through the knothole, he sees Eden, completely nude and performing mild calisthenics in front of her mirror. Like Jewett's Mrs. Todd standing in the center of a braided rug that makes her seem like "Antigone alone on the Theban plain,"[51] Eden stands upon an "enchanted rug of sleeping colours" in "a room full of sun." As the title suggests, Eden becomes to Hedger goddess-like in her nakedness, with "the soft flush of exercise and the gold of afternoon sun... envelop[ing] her in a luminous mist" that "dissolves in pure light" (366), a numinous effect emphasized by the repetition of the "golden shower" of sunlight that creates a "lake of gold" and an "enchanted spot" where she had stood. Clothed, Eden is an irritant, a contemporary woman and an Amazonian scold. Unclothed, Eden is a classical figure who exists clean, unadorned, and out of time, with a body he thinks of "as never having been clad, or as having worn the stuffs and dyes of all the centuries but his own" (369). Without clothing and the temporal constraints it signifies, she personifies for him the indefinite time of artistic Bohemia.

After experiencing his vision of the naked and preternaturally clean Eden, Hedger feels "a little sick" as he descends from this timeless vision to the temporal filth of his own surroundings, for, as Michele Aina Barale suggests, the story lingers on the contrast between "clean versus maculate bodies."[52] Hedger gazes with distaste at his living space—"his old shoes, ... the black calico curtains ... white with dust.... [and the] three greasy frying pans in the sink" (367). What he sees, however, is not merely the contrast between his own living space and Eden's but the naturalistic catalog of refuse that marks his surroundings as temporally and spatially constrained. As in similar naturalistic catalogs, it is the tactile sensation evoked by the adjective "greasy" that most vividly evokes the aesthetic of disgust. The parallel is immediately reinforced, as in Crane or Norris, by two women who embody the catalog of filth. Nothing could be further from Eden's clean nakedness than the two overly clad women to whom he expresses his wish to have the room cleaned: the "fat, dirty janitress," whose pillowy body was "soft as a feather bed" and whose "face and arms were permanently coated with dust, grained like wood where the sweat had trickled," and "old Lizzie," who "smell[s] strongly of spirits and wear[s] several jackets which she had put on one over the other, and a number of skirts, long and short, which made her resemble an animated dishclout" (367). Like the corrupt social conventions with which they are associated, such as Tammany Hall in Mrs. Foley's case, the clothing they wear carries the taint of society with it, encasing them in grubbily tactile garments that ground them in the urban present. The cleaning scene within the realm of filthy poverty, which recurs in other naturalistic works, such as *Vandover and the Brute*, here makes the same point as in earlier works.

In contrast to Lizzie and the dirty water that she "swishe[s] about the place," spreading the dirt to different places rather than eliminating it, Eden is consistently associated with clear and moving water, from the bathtub contretemps to Hedger's first vision of Eden dressed in a lavender suit and carrying lilacs while she stands beside the fountain that is "throwing up a mist of rainbow water" (359). Water and its presence or absence, movement or stillness, frame Hedger's perspective, just as water and images of flight and looking upward, from the balloon adventure to the pigeons she watches, characterize Eden's. For example, as Eden looks up and watches flying pigeons from her window, Hedger, on the other side of the door, looks down "into a pool of dark turpentine, at his idle brushes" (375). The idea of vision and performance pervades their four excursions, each mixing the overtones of visuality and scopophilia central to the story with the imagery of water, clothing, and animality: a trip to Coney Island, during which Hedger tells Eden an ancient Aztec legend; Eden's trip to the rooftop, previously the all-male domain of Hedger and Caesar; Hedger's trip to Long Island to flee from Eden after a quarrel; and Eden's return to Washington Square eighteen years later.

Hedger seeks barriers even as Eden breaks them. As Susan Rosowski observes, "Reveal, perform, exhibit, and disclose—these are the key verbs in this story about partitions, locks, barriers, and fortresses," and in each case, Hedger avoids too much disclosure.[53] Valuing privacy and solitude, he warily accedes to opening the double doors between their rooms, whereas Eden cheerfully uses a "bronze Buddha" not for contemplation but as a physical tool to break open the bolt of the door that separates them and unleash the explosive power of female sexuality to break down the barriers between them.[54] As Marilee Lindemann contends, Eden is one of Cather's "Elastigirls" whose "penchants for exercise and ... liberated sense of fashion" match their physical flexibility and signal their "New Woman feminism."[55] With her Elastigirl power, Eden frees herself from constraining conventions by challenging the power of Hedger's male gaze through her actions: invading his roof, forgiving Hedger for observing her, instigating their affair, and destroying the barrier of the double doors that lie between them.

Taken together, water and vision signal two other naturalistic features of the story: its overtones of Darwinian evolution and its focus on vision and performance. When choosing a subject for his painting, Hedger settles on "a study of paradise fish at the Aquarium, staring out at people through the glass and green water of their tank. It was a highly gratifying idea; the incommunicability of one stratum of animal life with another—though Hedger pretended it was only an experiment in unusual lighting" (358). Framed as a technical challenge of painting glass and "unusual lighting," Hedger's choice of subject masks the evolutionary appeal of "one stratum of animal life" existing in a wholly different element and failing to communicate with animal life in other strata. His observations suggest his initial objectification of Eden Bower, whom he peers at as if she is a different species, and he views others with the same initial detachment. To Hedger, the wife of the "fish-man" "look[s] exactly like a fish, even to her eyes, on which cataracts were forming" (391), the cataracts linking her to the limited and faulty vision of Hedger's perspective.

Although Hedger justifies his choice of paradise fish as subject matter based on the technical complexities of painting glass, his choice suggests Darwinian evolution and courtship behaviors. Paradise fish are highly colored and somewhat aggressive gouramis, a class of fish with rudimentary lung structures called "labyrinths" that allow them to take oxygen from the air, hence evoking the idea of human evolutionary ancestors. Moreover, gouramis, like many labyrinth fish, hatch their eggs in bubble nests that the males are responsible for building. Male fish control the bubble nests; but in fish as in human beings, as Darwin showed in *The Descent of Man*, the principle of female sexual selection gives women the choice in courtship. When Eden leaves Hedger after their final quarrel, he sits by himself in his studio, an action described as "sitting in his tank with his dog" (393) as if his room were his fish tank, but unlike the fish he studies, he has been unable to attract Eden permanently to his bubble nest. The clear distinctions between species that Hedger had asserted so confidently when he set out to paint the paradise fish, casting this as a mere problem in aesthetics, instead demonstrates just how thoroughly aesthetics is unconsciously subordinated to sexual power. Hedger and the fish act as they do because they are drawn to act by evolutionary forces beyond their control.

Equally significant are the ways in which "Coming, Aphrodite!" explores the possibilities of film as a medium, an approach signaled by the famous closet scene. James Woodress and Susan Rosowski have analyzed the sexual overtones of Hedger's voyeuristic encounter, notably in the sexual pun in the story's title and the masturbatory imagery of Hedger's grasp of the charcoal that "seemed to explode in his hand" (366).[56] But Hedger's peeping through a knothole and being transfixed by the vision that he sees also recalls the stream of light in the darkness emitted by a movie projector, which delivered the moving picture to the person sitting in the darkened theater, and the story is filled with images that mimic the visual technologies of early cinema and concerns about its effect on the spectator. Moreover, Hedger is in the right place for an artist aware of his surroundings to be aware of the developing film industry. Following 1902, when the primary incidents of the story take place, struggling artists and Bohemians were not the only residents of the area that Cather describes. In 1903 D. W. Griffith's American Mutoscope and Biograph Company moved from its rooftop studios to a brownstone at 11 East Fourteenth Street at Fifth Avenue, a few blocks from Washington Square Park and its arch that provides such important visual cues in the story, and from the apartment at 5 Bank Street that Cather occupied with Edith Lewis beginning in January 1913. For ten years, until the company moved north to the Bronx, the Fourteenth Street location and its surroundings served as the location for Griffith's significant early movies.

Another connection between the knothole sequence and early film lies in the technology of film that it evokes. "Coming, Aphrodite!" visualizes contemporary debates over the effect of cinema on the human psyche, since its undeniable appeal to repeated visual sensations as a primary mode of engagement rendered it potentially addictive. In the mid-1890s, Edison's vision had been that the individual kinetoscope or "peep show," as he called it, would provide more profit than projected images. He resisted the projection methods being introduced by the Lumière brothers in Paris for this reason. Hedger's action in pressing his eye to the knothole mimics the action of thousands of men looking through kinetoscopic viewers in the parlors that sprang up in New York beginning in the mid-1890s, a viewing process that remained at once personal, since the film was seen individually rather than as a shared experience, and public, in that the kinetoscope parlors held rows of machines with separate films. Early cinema critics worried about the addictive properties of watching a moving picture rather than a live performance. They speculated that watching repetitive images on a screen could lead to indoctrination or passivity on the part of the spectator, with a consequent loss of selectivity of vision since the images were being processed for the viewer's eyes rather than being selected by the viewer.

Hedger's actions exemplify the critics' fears about the addictive properties of cinema. He watches the spectacle of Eden exercising not once, but daily, and when he violates his own rule by "peer[ing] through that fatal aperture" (370) at night, he behaves like an alcoholic breaking his self-imposed rule about controlling his drinking. Indeed, his response to the "fatal aperture," a term that in itself evokes a vital component of the movie camera, controls his life and enforces passivity as a movie does, by replacing his ideas with the overpowering spectacle that banishes them: "This thing, whatever it was, drank him up as ideas had sometimes done, and he sank into a stupor of idleness as deep and dark as the stupor of work" (368). In Hedger's voyeuristic and literally closeted adventures of looking at Eden, this faculty of vision has degenerated into a scopophilia that has not enhanced but has instead replaced his dedication to art. At first Hedger warrants this characterization, for he retains power initially by deliberately avoiding her, trying to preserve rather than breach the distance between the object of his gaze and any recognition of her as a fellow human being. The image of Eden that "vibrated, burned" within him was "a heathenish feeling; without friendliness, almost without tenderness" (368). Moreover, Hedger's voyeuristic sessions at the keyhole leave him feeling depleted, and his brushes and paints stand idle after his periods of watching her.

Not only Hedger's actions but also the setting and activities of the story suggest a cinematic frame. The color scheme evokes early silents, which were frequently hand-tinted frame by frame, as in the Lumière brothers' *The Golden Beetle* (1907), in which a woman is transformed by a magician into a golden-winged creature that glows in the darkness of her background. Like a shift in film from black-and-white to a tinted image, Hedger's subdued color palate, his shades of blue and gray, and even his shabby black suit contrast sharply with the magical world of "yellow light," the "golden shower" of sunshine, and Eden's skin tinged by "the gold of afternoon sun" (366) that he sees through the "fatal aperture." When the picture ends with Eden's leaving the room, Hedger looks about him and sees a black-and-white world once more: the "gray prison light," "the black calico curtains," and the windows "white with dust" (367). The two color schemes merge in the trip to Coney Island when Eden changes places with Hedger's friend Molly, an acrobat who ascends above the crowd in a tethered balloon and swings on a trapeze. The silver of the moon that Hedger had previously observed from his window is mirrored in the black tights and silver slippers that Eden wears in her performance and in the "fleet and silvery" pigeons (394) that rise above the "dirt and noise and squalor" as Eden does. The excursion to Coney Island itself reflects the culture of popular amusements that surrounded early film, for the place was a favorite subject of early filmmakers. As Leo Charney and Vanessa R. Schwartz explain, Coney Island was a refuge from the city, feeding "the increased appetite for mobile, kinetic sensation while packaging that appeal in the guise of a break from that sensation."[57] It is a backdrop not only for amusement but also for the disintegration and resumption of identity, an idea that Cather floats in the twinning episode in which Eden changes places with Molly.

The subject matter of Eden's naked form also ties the story to early film. Chief among the "cinema of attractions" that Tom Gunning identifies as a principal form of early film is the figure of the scantily clad human being whose rhythmic movements exhibit the human body as a means of pure spectacle. An obvious example of this is Sandow, who ripples his muscles in a two-minute Edison short of 1894, and the boxing films that were among the first movies to be made (and banned), but Carmencita and other "skirt dancers" had an equally sustained claim on audience attention in the preprojection era. During his last viewing session, in which he "violate[s] her privacy" (370) and watches Eden at night, Hedger watches her through the "fatal aperture" evocative of both movie camera and projector, expecting a repetition of the same film that he has seen each time: a naked woman exercising in front of a mirror, a consistent image in early cinema. But the vision has changed. Instead of an erotic spectacle that has varied so little that it resembled a cinematic spectacle—a cinema of attraction— Eden presents herself "sitting, fully dressed, in the window, smoking a cigarette and looking out over the housetops" (370). Her gaze is no longer directed to her own body but outward to the city, and as she rises, she "looked about her with a disdainful, crafty smile, and turned out the light" (370). The "disdainful, crafty smile," like her action in turning out the light, suggest that she has seen Hedger or at least intuited his presence, possibly because of the quality of artificial light rather than sunlight flooding the room.

Eden's ready forgiveness when Hedger finally confesses his voyeuristic actions suggests the possibility of her foreknowledge of his actions and also her pleasure in being the object of his gaze. In the context of film, the "crafty smile" suggests that she has placed herself on display consciously and ironically, as a self-conscious object for the male gaze, in order to call attention to, hence reverse, the power implicit in the gaze. Eden's smile recalls the action of gazing directly into the camera, shunned in most classical cinema but common in the "cinema of attractions" period prior to 1907 as a means of calling attention to the exhibitionistic medium itself, just as the story's numerous openings—knotholes, doors, arches—serve as framing devices that evoke the silent films of the day. Judith Mayne's analysis of this aspect of film grammar, its use of the keyhole to indicate point of view and frequently salacious content, provides another perspective through which to understand Cather's use of point of view in the story. As Mayne comments in *The Woman at the Keyhole*, "In early films a character (usually male) might look through a keyhole at another character (usually female), whereas this voyeuristic relationship would later be incorporated into camera movement, editing, and so on."[58] Mayne points out that many of the films made by women in this era either reverse the process or call attention to film's fictive and aesthetic properties through a conscious use of camera angles and shots. For example, *The Bride Retires* (1904) features a woman undressing while her new husband "peers at her from behind a screen," but her wink at the camera and the audience reveals her complicity in this transaction and returns the power to her rather than to the voyeuristic husband.[59] In cinematic terms, Eden's smile, like the bride's wink, confirms her control over the situation and also over her life. At the story's conclusion, Hedger and Eden are both successful, but only Eden has moved beyond the confines of Bohemia into the world of biological time.

At the end of the nineteenth century and the beginning of the twentieth, Bohemian spaces promised freedom from bourgeois constraints and a gender equality that could not be realized in conventional culture. The idealism with which Bohemians pursued a life in art posited a future in which bodies could be unconfined by social rules and the dictates of time. But despite their Bohemian characters' commitment to idealism, women writers of naturalism showed its consequences when their female characters took literally the rhetoric of gender equality and artistic purpose that existed in Bohemia. For Glasgow, Austin, and Cather, it was not enough to satirize the sort of popular depictions of Bohemia that appeared in *The Yellow Girl*, *A Philistine in Bohemia*, or *The Devil's Needle*, since the stakes for women in Bohemia could prove to be so high. For Glasgow's Rachel, the evolutionary imperative to commit to and shield one's mate leads her to abandon her career as a painter in favor of a self-sacrificing role as nurse to the dying man she loves; for Mariana, time spent in biological time within Bohemian spaces destroys her idealistic illusions and reveals those spaces to be naturalistic in their squalor, poverty, and death.

Austin's Neith Schuyler is caught up in the ferment of Bohemian ideas and those who promote them, yet she sees firsthand the failure of idealism when applied to gender relations. Cather's Eden Bowers fares best of all, for, in keeping artistic popularity with the masses rather than pure art as her aim, she learns how best to control her own life, including the affair she begins with Hedger and leaves, without regret, when she departs from Bohemia. She achieves her artistic goals not only because of her New Woman sensibilities, which insulate her from a too-serious relationship with Hedger, but also because in understanding the ephemeral quality of Bohemia and the need to promote her way out of it through influential friends, she is in tune with the fleeting nature of fame and popular taste. Her popular success, in contrast to Hedger's esteem by the art world, suggests that she embodies a fickle but enduring medium that would dominate the next century: the movies.

CHAPTER 4

Red Kimonos and White Slavery
The Fallen Woman in Film and Print

By the early years of the Progressive Era, the "girl of the painted cohorts" trailing down city streets, such as Crane's Maggie Johnson, had been supplanted by another figure: the "white slave," who, lured from her home in the country and forced into prostitution, implores passersby to free her from behind the barred windows of a brothel where she has been imprisoned.[1] The white slave panic revealed the fears of the nation, from xenophobia driven by the rising tide of immigrants from eastern Europe to fears about the New Woman's travel to urban centers outside the social control of the domestic sphere. With the advent of the white slave narrative, which depicted the enslavement of middle-class and rural young women in prostitution, the 1890s "girl who goes wrong" narrative that had presented the regrettable but understandable fall of a working-class girl became the Progressive Era's alarm over the abduction of middle-class American women.

The period of the white slavery panic was relatively brief, with the greatest popular and governmental interest occurring during the latter part of the Progressive Era from 1910 to 1914, yet it coincided with, and was indeed fed by, social and media forces including publicity culture, the advent of the story film, sensationalism in print culture, rising immigration, and growing sociological concerns over the fate of independent young women moving to the cities. Examining the visual and textual rhetoric surrounding the cultural moment of white slavery, with its naturalistic focus on the woman's body in public spaces, is central to recovering contemporary contexts for reading women characters and for understanding women writers' responses to the subject.

In addition, print and film productions of the white slave era provide a testing ground for unruly naturalism. Like classic or formulaic naturalism, they comprise a complicated mix of sordid realism, claims of accuracy and truth, pressures of heredity and environment, the fallen woman as subject matter, and often the plot of decline. Yet few are classic examples of naturalistic fiction, due in part to the variety of document forms that comprise the white slave narrative—memoirs, sociological case histories, reform tracts, journalistic exposés, novels, brothel dramas, and white slave films. With the sexualized bodies of young women at the center of the piece and the basic pattern of seduction and a downward trajectory as a common pattern, white slave literature and films retain the outlines and basic formula of classic naturalistic fiction such as *Maggie: A Girl of the Streets*. But these unruly narratives deviate from classic naturalism through their variations on the plot of decline; their inclusion of multiple themes and deviations from classic structure; their excesses of rhetoric and situation, sometimes sensationalized; and their unabashed use of melodrama, reform strategies, and sentimental touches across a wide range of nonfiction as well as fiction.

Evelyn Nesbit and Grace Brown

On the evening of June 25, 1906, the play *Mam'zelle Champagne* opened at the Roof Garden Theater atop the second Madison Square Garden, built in 1890. On this particular evening, its architect, Stanford White, sat in the audience enjoying the musical comedy, seemingly unaware of the intense stares of a young man who, unusually for the warm evening, was wearing an overcoat. As the tenor swung into "I Could Love a Million Girls," the young man left his seat and walked directly in front of White. "You have ruined my life!" the young man shouted, pulling a revolver from his coat and shooting White three times in the head and chest. White slumped to the floor, already dead and disfigured with powder burns, and the young man walked in a leisurely fashion toward the exit where, stopped by a uniformed fireman, he handed over his gun. The beautiful young woman who had accompanied him to the theater cried out, "Oh, Harry, what have you done? You're in a terrible fix now." "It's all right, dear," the young man replied calmly. "I have probably saved your life." He kept moving toward the elevators, later surrendering himself to police at the nearest precinct house and posing with supreme confidence for the waiting crowd of photographers.[2]

The young man was Harry K. Thaw, a millionaire from Pittsburgh, and the beautiful young woman with him was his unhappy wife, Evelyn Nesbit, who even before the murder was as famous in her own sphere as White was in his. Supporting her mother and brother through her work as a child model, Nesbit had moved to New York as a teenager and became a well-known artists' model widely sought out for her soulful looks and masses of dark hair. Nesbit posed for such noted figures as Charles Dana Gibson, who used her as the model for his iconic "Gibson Girl" portrait *The Eternal Question*, and by her late teens she had appeared in the Ziegfeld Follies before marrying millionaire Thaw. What her testimony at Thaw's trial revealed was another life lived between the stage and her marriage: her years as White's teenage protégée and mistress. When she told the story to Thaw before their marriage in 1905, he became obsessed with the idea of innocence destroyed by White's debauchery and forced her to recite the story repeatedly, brooding about it until he murdered White. On April 11, 1907, Thaw's first trial ended in a hung jury. The second concluded in February 1908 with a verdict of not guilty by reason of insanity. In a pattern that would become familiar in years to come, Nesbit's story, first reproduced in the newspapers and later appearing in her two autobiographies, was reenacted by Nesbit herself in a series of a dozen movies beginning with *The Unwritten Law: A Thrilling Drama Based on the Thaw-White Case* (1907) and *The Great Thaw Trial* (1907) and concluding with a Hollywood version on which Nesbit served as technical advisor, *The Girl in the Red Velvet Swing* (1955).[3]

The Thaw case vied for attention with a trial that dominated the New York press in late 1906 when Chester Gillette declared his innocence in the murder of Grace (Billy) Brown in upstate New York. The Thaw and Gillette trials contained the same irresistible elements, a combination of sex and violence in the unspooling narrative, breathlessly reported, of a young woman ruined by a man of higher social class. Chester Gillette's victim, Grace Brown, had moved a few years earlier from her family's small farm in upstate New York to the nearby city of Cortland. She found work in the Gillette Skirt Factory and later began a relationship with the owner's nephew, Chester Gillette. When Grace discovered that she was pregnant in the spring of 1906, Chester urged her to return to her family's farm, promising to rescue her at a later date. By early July, when he had not done so, Grace threatened to return to Cortland and hold him accountable. Chester then took her on a trip to the nearby Adirondack Mountains from which she never returned. A few years later, Theodore Dreiser used the Gillette case as the basis for *An American Tragedy* (1925), and it had a second life as media fodder in its two film adaptations, Josef von Sternberg's *An American Tragedy* (1931), a production that caused both Dreiser and Grace Brown's family to sue Paramount Pictures, and George Stevens's *A Place in the Sun* (1951), which starred Montgomery Clift, Elizabeth Taylor, and Shelley Winters in a contemporary adaptation of the story.

Coached by the traditions of melodrama, readers well understood the narrative of the innocent country girl who comes to the city looking for work to support her family. Falling into the hands of a man more wealthy or powerful than herself, she is seduced and driven to some lengths to conceal their affair, since exposure means the ruin of her reputation and, given the premium on female chastity, the commodity value of the innocence that is her stock in trade. But the press fed on the public's appetite for a dual unmasking and violation of the woman's body, not only through the familiar narrative of innocence seduced and betrayed but also through reportage that revealed the woman's secrets against her will. The stories of Grace Brown and Evelyn Nesbit exposed the public's uneasiness with bodies that could not be labeled according to the usual binaries of "respectable woman" and "prostitute," making readers work harder to interpret the puzzle that these women represented.

The visual spectacle of the woman's body was in each case paramount, whether as a witness, as in Nesbit's case, or as a victim, as in Brown's. Issues of surveillance, concealment, performance, and nationalism inform the narrative surrounding these spectacles of the woman's body. In the Thaw case, the focus remained on Nesbit. Clad in a plain suit with only a spray of violets for adornment, her hair simply dressed, Nesbit projected an innocent appearance at odds with the sordid tale she told, even as the appearance of innocence lent the details of her story credibility. The married White had showered her with money and attention, including lavish suppers at his flat, where the sixteen-year-old Nesbit entertained White by swinging in a red velvet chair that he had suspended from the ceiling. As a demurely dressed and tearful Nesbit testified on the witness stand, her career as his mistress began one night when White plied her with drugged champagne until she passed out, awakening to find White hovering above her, telling her "It's all over." Nesbit's account echoes the tableau of triumphant seducer and unconscious victim that forms the core of many naturalistic and white slave narratives, including naturalism's repeated tableau-like spectacle of a woman lying unconscious under male scrutiny.

Writing in 1914 about her affair with White, Nesbit reflects, "it is hard to tell the story without melodrama," and the theatrical metaphors she employs recall not only her background as an actress but also her recognition that all in the affair were players whose roles were well established. White "had a formula that apparently never varied" of befriending and seducing young girls, and, with an eye toward her readers, Nesbit disparaged the affair as a "miserable friendship." Twenty years later, Nesbit described White as the love of her life, a claim as extravagant and theatrical, in its way, as her earlier characterization of White as "a great man" but "vicious" in his moral character.[4] Her conflicting assessment of White on these two occasions played to the audience response she anticipated each time. As Nesbit understood, concealment was of the essence and the only sin was "being found out." The performance of *Mam'zelle Champagne*, by Nesbit's account a "putrid" show, was overshadowed by what she accurately termed a real-life melodrama. When Thaw shot White, his "finger upon the trigger ... had released the curtain, which hid us all from the gaze of the world," Nesbit writes, recognizing that the public's appetite would raise the curtain on the private show that White had stage-managed so effectively with Nesbit and others. "[A]ll the intimate things of life," she concludes, were now "in the million mouths of New

York," as words to spread the exposure of her past and as tasty morsels of gossip to be consumed by the city-beast.[5]

Nesbit's testimony and autobiography also underscore the connections between performance, surveillance, and nationalism. In addition to his whispered-about reputation as a connoisseur of young women, White was officially the aesthetic arm of McKim, Mead, and White, the partner whose acknowledged expertise in the visual arts, decorative arts, and design had helped to propel the firm's reputation to stratospheric heights. Nesbit describes White's studio on West Twenty-Fourth Street as an exotic fairyland, decorated with an "Orientalism... refined and delicate," with "Oriental" tables and "Oriental" designs, and she notes that White imported Japanese kimonos especially for her.[6] The connection between aestheticism and "Oriental" furnishings renders White more foreign than American. Thaw, by contrast, was portrayed as overcome by "dementia Americana," a term invented by the defense to describe a red-blooded American male's need to avenge any outrage committed against his beloved's innocence.[7] The net effect was to encode Thaw's actions as chivalrous and to naturalize his behavior as both masculine and patriotic in contrast to White's aesthetic "foreign" decadence.

But Nesbit's story, the story of the body of the woman at the heart of the trial, reveals a different narrative, that of the woman who first makes her living by being a spectacle for men as an artists' model or an actress and ends by becoming an object of private surveillance and manic rage. After she confessed her affair with White, Thaw became obsessed with her story rather more than with Nesbit as a person, having her followed and cross-examining her whenever she moved out of his sight. His desire for control over her body extended to extremes, including having dental work paid for by White removed from her mouth, as if any remaining trace of White were a continued violation and invasion of Nesbit's body. The two models of masculinity were exaggerated in the press: White was portrayed as the womanizer who with his foreign aesthetic judgments treated young girls as disposable art objects to be enjoyed, and Thaw became the self-proclaimed protector of innocent American girls. Nesbit's sensational story revealed both models as equally spectatorial and abusive, however. Nesbit's stories of White watching her as she swung in the red velvet chair, urging her to go so high that she kicked through the paper Japanese umbrella hung from the ceiling, another "Oriental" touch, echo those she tells of Thaw's cross-examination of her whereabouts whenever she might be visible to other men. Thaw and White were united in their desire to keep her visibility concealed and her body enshrined for their own purposes, purposes that Nesbit, as a woman whose attractiveness lies in her pliability and whose face is her fortune, understands but presents herself as powerless to resist.

The spectacle of the woman's body in the city plays out differently in the story of Grace Brown. Having moved from her family's farm to Cortland, there she met Chester Gillette, an ambitious nephew of the owner of the Gillette Shirtwaist Factory. Although those at the factory were aware of the blossoming relationship, Chester took care to keep Grace out of sight on social occasions, squiring the well-to-do daughters of Cortland's merchant class to dances and visiting Grace at her rooming house after hours. When she became pregnant in the spring of 1906, the wall of invisibility and class exclusion that Chester had sought to maintain broke down. Associates noticed Grace's tears and her extended visit back to the family farm, and they recalled a telephone call from Grace to Chester at the factory, an unusual enough event that several remarked on it at his trial. Put simply, Grace's body, with its advancing pregnancy, and her use of technology to communicate with Chester made visibility inevitable. Faced with Grace's ultimatum that he take her away from the farm, Chester proposed a trip to the nearby Adirondacks but sought to cover his tracks by giving false names at the hotels where they stayed. On July 11, Chester rented a boat and rowed Grace around Big Moose Lake, knowing that she could not swim. Her body and the overturned boat were found in an isolated inlet the next day. When the authorities caught up with Chester at another resort hotel a few days later, he disclaimed all knowledge of her death, and he continued to maintain his innocence throughout the trial and appeal that followed, although he was eventually convicted.[8]

Like the Thaw case, the Gillette trial attracted wide attention in the press. The strategic invisibility on which Chester had prided himself and which he had sought to visit upon Grace had unraveled with lightning speed as witnesses emerged from every stage of their journey to testify to his lies, Grace's tears and general distress, and the relationship that the two had shared. Grace's body, so carefully hidden in Chester's seduction and murder scheme, provided mute testimony of his actions in its predeath cuts and bruises. The prosecution even brought in the fetus of the child she was carrying, preserved in formaldehyde in a jar wrapped with brown paper, and threatened to show it to the jury if Chester refused to acknowledge his seduction of Grace. Most eloquent of all were the letters, pleading and desperate, that Grace sent to Chester. Read aloud in a dramatic fashion by the prosecutor and transmitted word for word by telegraph to be printed in the New York papers, they were also published as a booklet and sold for ten cents apiece, a hot-selling souvenir for the crowds that flocked to the trial. The letters were even adapted as sheet music, with a cover that reproduced a photograph of Grace superimposed over a picture of the bay where she had picked water lilies on the day of her death. Abandoning his disastrous attempts at concealment, Chester tried to turn its opposite—publicity—to his own advantage. Sitting at the defendant's table, he alternately projected an insouciant jauntiness, cracking his gum and joking on the witness stand, and boredom, even when Grace's letters were read aloud in court to a weeping jury. His answer to the booklets of Grace's letters was to sell pictures of himself at a dollar apiece, which kept him in pocket money but seems not to have convinced anyone of his innocence.

Convicted based on the circumstantial evidence, Chester went to prison while a judicial appeal made its way through the courts. After the appeal failed and New York governor Charles Evans Hughes turned down a request for clemency by Chester's mother, Gillette was executed. Gillette's assumptions about the class protections he enjoyed as a nephew of the owner proved to be merely potent illusions, like those about the invisibility of the lower-class woman's body. The publicity of the news reports, Grace's letters, and the sheet music derived from them gave her a visibility beyond her death, permitting her posthumous voice to speak as a woman whose body and trust were violated. In *An American Tragedy*, however, Dreiser shifts sympathy from the woman's violated body to his Chester Gillette surrogate, Clyde Griffiths. Instead of Chester Gillette, the calculating murderer who, the jury decided, struck Grace Brown with a tennis racket, Dreiser's Griffiths is driven by a class-conscious consumerist ethos and is bewildered at the exposure of actions that he had been at such pains to hide. Drawn from trial testimony, Dreiser's account of the visibility of Griffiths as a man whose social standing did not guarantee him the privacy he had assumed makes him the victim of a class-bound consumer culture, with Roberta Alden, the Grace Brown figure, as collateral damage in a system rigged against both of them.

In 1906 and the following two years, the widely publicized Gillette and Thaw trials brought national attention to issues that would ignite during the white slave years: the migration of women to the cities and the potential for sexual exploitation to be found there; the desire for an elusive class mobility that drove poor girls like Nesbit and Brown to seek their fortunes with higher-status men; the seduction plot made easier by the availability of alcohol and, if Nesbit is to be believed, knockout drops; and the efficient transportation systems that facilitated the women's travel to the city and hence isolation from family and social supports. In addition, the seduction that each woman underwent owed much to the impersonality of private urban spaces, with an expectation of privacy for White and Griffiths that rested squarely on their level of class and gender privilege. The narratives that Nesbit and Brown were forced to reveal became legible only through an invasive scrutiny of their bodies that the publicity machine, around Nesbit especially, sought to reconcile with existing narratives of seduction and betrayal. The two cases prefigure the elements of the white slave panic that was shortly to grip the nation, including xenophobic fears of men associated with cosmopolitan elites, like White with his "Oriental" furnishings and the well-traveled Chester Gillette, who had attended Oberlin Academy and lived in cities throughout the

West and Hawaii. Above all, they demonstrated a populist suspicion about the governmental institutions that would shield men from the consequences of their actions while the women involved suffered a loss of innocence, humiliation, and even death.

The Nesbit and Brown stories help to recover the cultural context for reading narratives of women in the intersection of debates over publicity, privacy, and sexuality. For one thing, fallen-woman narratives by women writers complicate the dividing line between respectability and ostracism that remained a staple in melodrama, as prostitution memoirs, journalistic and sociological accounts, white slave novels, and films all show. Prostitution memoirs by Madeleine Blair and Nell Kimball offer an alternative to the redemption narrative by redefining success as becoming a madam rather than being saved. Novels by Elizabeth Robins, Virginia Brooks, Estelle Baker, and Miriam Michelson, and films such as *Traffic in Souls* and *The Red Kimona* present not only victims but also heroic women, including some who brave physical danger and leverage their abilities with visual and sound technologies to rescue other women. The consistent element is an exploration of the invasion of the woman's memory and consciousness and what it means to expose her secrets in film and print, as with Evelyn Nesbit and Grace Brown, since the public exposure of the violation constitutes a reviolation of the woman's body. The scenes of exposure, spying, and other forms of surveillance on the part of women reporters and undercover agents are attempts to wrest this level of control back from the power of men to the power of women. Looking through the keyhole at the unknowing or unconscious woman and the scopophilic or voyeuristic pleasure to be gained from it had been the province of men, cloaked under the guise of amusement (the kinetoscopic peep show and its analogous scenes in early film) or of scientific observation, in literature through naturalism with its doctrine of objectivity. Prostitution narratives, white slave novels, and films redirected scrutiny from the "girl of the streets" and the white slave to the social institutions that facilitated her exploitation.

The White Slave Panic

One of the many reforms launched during the Progressive Era was an attempt to eradicate "the social evil," or prostitution, as a threat to the American home and the social fabric of the nation. From roughly 1910 through 1913, these efforts focused on the abduction and forced prostitution of young white women in what came to be known as "white slavery," and the national outrage and hysteria over these practices as "the white slave panic." As Ruth Rosen explains in *The Lost Sisterhood*, the term "white slavery" originally referred to the exploitation of British workers as wage slaves, but by the late nineteenth century it had acquired its Progressive Era meaning of "the traffic in women."[9] The white slave story involves an innocent country girl who abandons her home when lured to the city, often with false promises of employment or marriage. Arriving in the city disoriented, bewildered, and clinging to the man who had abducted her, the white slave was stripped of her street clothes and her identity, locked in a room, raped, sometimes beaten or injected with drugs, and supplied with inadequate clothing and a house name, a pseudonym or nickname that indicated her new status. Thus confined and suffering physical, sexual, and emotional abuse, the white slave had little choice but to capitulate to her new circumstances.

The processing and subsequent distribution of women nationally and internationally raised alarm over immigration and the security of national borders. In "The Daughters of the Poor" (*McClure's*, November 1909), George Kibbe Turner focused on the international connections in the "New York System" backed by the organization of Tammany Hall, with each immigrant group establishing a different method of preying on women: "Polish and Slovak servant-girls," who "arrive here more like tagged baggage than human beings," are picked up in public dance halls; "little Italian peasant girls" are promised marriage, brought to the United States, and "closely confined," unable to escape because they cannot speak English; and "Jewish-American" girls "[sacrifice] themselves uselessly to give the boys of the family an education," a practice that reformers contended gave rise to pampered men who became procurers instead of working for a living.[10] White slavery was further thrust into national attention by reports like Clifford G. Roe's *The Great War on White Slavery* (1911), T. P. Curtis's *Traffic in Women* (1912), and Paul Elliot's *White Slavery and What It Is* (1910). Men who seduced or abducted the white slaves were almost always characterized as urban and foreign, ethnically Other and not American at a time when the fragmentation of whiteness into discrete and lesser subclasses by national origin meant that the epitome of whiteness—the Anglo-Saxon—defined the true American.[11] In *The Great War on White Slavery*, for example, Roe confidently asserts, "While the cadets, as these procurers are known in the east, are men of all kinds and colors, the French cadets and the negro cadets are without doubt by far the cruelest."[12]

Statistics did not bear out some of the worst fears of the white slave campaigns. The fear of foreigners was especially overblown, according to Ruth Rosen: "Of men convicted under the Mann Act, 72.5 percent were native-born Americans, 11.5 percent were Italians, and 3.5 percent were Russians."[13] Some interstate and international trade did develop, which the Mann Act prohibition of the transportation of women across state lines for immoral purposes was designed to curb. Yet as Barbara Meil Hobson writes, "The majority of prostitutes in the United States had not been trapped unknowingly in houses of bondage.... Vice commission statistics on prostitutes revealed that the majority of prostitutes were native-born daughters of immigrants," making them second-generation citizens with aspirations toward greater wealth and social mobility but a limited means of achieving it, a consistent theme in films of the period.[14] The memoirs of prostitutes and madams confirm the statistics. In an afterword to the anonymously published *Madeleine: An Autobiography*, "Madeleine Blair" declares, "I do not know anything about the so-called white-slave trade, for the simple reason that no such thing exists"; on the contrary, she claims, some young women have been driven to insanity by the false threats and mistrust promoted by "white slave" tracts.[15] Arguing that "[a] good whore has to *want* to be a whore, or she's no credit to the place," Nell Kimball downplays white slavery, although she alludes to an "underground railroad" of girls tricked into prostitution by "Italians and Eastern Europeans" and fears being drugged and imprisoned when she lives in New York City, where white slavery "did exist."[16] Writing much later than the rest, the San Francisco madam Sally Stanford said that she "never met a white slave in my life" and that the problem was rather too many unsuitable girls knocking at her door.[17]

Despite the conflicting evidence on the traffic in women, the white slave panic reflected deeper national concerns. Fears of governmental corruption, of immigrants and racial "contamination," of industrial systems and urbanization, and of women's sexuality and shifting roles in the urban marketplace all contributed to the urgency of the campaign against white slavery. Like the crusading journalism of Progressive Era muckrakers such as Lincoln Steffens, Upton Sinclair, Ida B. Wells-Barnett, and David Graham Phillips, the campaign against white slavery exposed governmental corruption and the rise of parallel systems of criminality. White slave novels, films, documentary reports, and memoirs vary in their accounts of the procurement methods and treatment of women, but every one of the accounts agrees that without a corrupt police force and government, neither prostitution nor white slavery could function. (The sole exception is the Royal Canadian Mounted Police or "Mounties" in Alberta, who in *Madeleine* are portrayed as incorruptible, unlike the provincial police.)

The framework of prostitution and the Progressive Era study of it revealed the ways in which its use of technology, media, transportation, and centralized organizational systems mirrored those of more legally sanctioned industries. Advances in pharmaceuticals meant that knockout drops could render girls immobile, as happens in David Graham Phillips's *Susan Lenox* and in the film *The Inside of the White Slave Traffic*, and readily available opiates could keep them sedated and eventually addicted. Cheap magazines and films encouraged false hopes about the possibilities of wealth in urban life and, increasingly, a career as an actress on the stage or in the movies. Mass distribution and lowered printing costs made it easier for procurers to recruit girls through ads for fictitious job openings, playbills for nonexistent theater companies seeking girls, and even false marriage licenses. Dubious employment agencies sprang up beside legitimate ones to divert the influx of immigrants and women from the country seeking jobs, a plot point in the film *Traffic in Souls* when Swedish girls are guided to a brothel with a temporary sign out front that reads "Swedish Employment Agency."

Like other businesses in the Progressive Era, prostitution became more ruthless as it became more impersonal and organized. When bewildered immigrants or country girls arrived at the docks or train stations, madams or procurers were on hand to meet them, gaining their trust and promising them safe passage to a respectable boardinghouse before imprisoning them in a brothel, as happens in Elizabeth Robins's *My Little Sister* and *Traffic in Souls*. New levels of intermediaries, as Brian Donovan argues, bred more violence, as "informal consortiums of brothel proprietors, ward politicians, saloon owners, and real estate agents" demanded their share.[18] Among those who needed to be paid were the "cadets" responsible for finding and selling young and varied "live stock"—to use the term from *Little Lost Sister*—and pimps, who, according to reformers such as George Kneeland and Maude Miner, gained new powers as managers of prostitutes during this time.[19] "Have you a girl to spare?," an illustration from *The Great War on White Slavery*, shows an assembly line of girls entering a brothel that resembles a factory building, with black-clad women exiting another door and falling into the grave as though they are a by-product or waste from the production line. A girl in the lower right-hand corner looks on at the spectacle.

Fears of immigrants, their moral and physical contagion, and the threats that they posed to citizenship and the body of the republic coalesced under the banner of fears about white women being contaminated, officially by disease but more damagingly through contact with "foreign" men. Women who sought work in urban centers raised the specter of increasing economic autonomy and sexual freedom for themselves and a decrease in the nation's control over its primary resource, young women as the future producers of the nation's citizens. Moreover, anxieties over white slavery gave Progressive Era reformers an arena in which to indulge their passion for applying scientific methods to effect a social good. As Katie N. Johnson concludes, "Prostitution thus became a framework to analyze mass production, modern technology, and the entry of women into the urban workforce—the prostitute becoming the personification of these changes."[20]

In sociological studies, sensational novels, and film, the white slave was portrayed both as victim, stolen from rural innocence by foreign procurers and imprisoned in a brothel, and as vampire, a *prostitute fatale* spreading contagion as part of a more general scene of urban chaos and decay.[21] In her position as victim, she embodied national anxieties about racial purity and the supposed contamination of American womanhood, just as her position as a vampire spreading

HAVE YOU A GIRL TO SPARE?
Sixty Thousand White Slaves die every year. The Vice Resorts cannot run without this number is replaced annually. Are you willing to give your daughter to keep up this terrible business?

"Have you a girl to spare?" from Clifford G. Roe's *The Great War on White Slavery* (1911). The sign reads "Wanted: sixty thousand girls to take the place of 60,000 white slaves who will die this year."

contagion rendered her a threat to American manhood. According to Amanda Anderson, the "rhetoric of fallenness" carries with it fears of contamination and the transformation of victim into perpetrator: "The pervasive trope of metalepsis [in which an effect is transformed into a cause] reflects just how contaminating fallenness was perceived to be: any distanced view of the fallen woman as victim could easily transmute itself into an anxious apprehension that she would communicate her condition to others."[22] Moral and physical contamination became a staple plot of popular dramas such as Eugène Brieux's *Damaged Goods* (1913), which, like Ibsen's *Ghosts* (first produced in New York in 1894), explored the human cost that syphilis brought home by men inflicts on innocent women and children. For example, Charlotte Perkins Gilman's novel *The Crux* (1911) deals frankly with the choice that its heroine, Vivian Lane, must make when her friend, a female doctor, explains that her weak-willed lover Morton has contracted syphilis from a promiscuous widow. Seeing her housekeeper's son, who was born with mental deficiencies due to the syphilis that his father had transmitted to his mother, Vivian determines not to marry Morton. Redeeming her lover from worldly dissipations and temptations was the duty of the heroine in domestic fiction, but Gilman makes clear that where physical disease rather than moral corruption constitutes the problem, the modern heroine must give up her lover for the good of her future children.

With its overtones of contamination, the fallen-woman narrative further concentrates attention on the economic issues of waste and production. Like the surplus bodies of immigrants and poor people, prostitutes became the visible waste products of modernity. The trajectory of the prostitute's career made her unusually visible as the waste of the city. Young women who started out as one man's mistress or in a brothel, sheltered behind walls and with police protection, gradually worked their way down the ladder until they became unprotected street girls. As street girls, they were a visual rebuke to all who passed them, for if they were not physically rendered unappealing through age, disease, disability, or behavior, they still were living reminders that, as William Gray's 1894 song "She Is More to Be Pitied than Censured" put it, "A man was the cause of it all." The "public woman," another synonym for the prostitute, visually embodied the distinction between publicity and privacy that had troubled the readers of Evelyn Nesbit's and Grace Brown's reluctantly revealed private narratives.

A popular theory of the day regarded prostitutes as a safety valve for men's desires, and their presence testified to the hypocrisy of men who preferred not to acknowledge their existence during daylight hours and to the sexual brutality that existed beneath men's public personae. As the madam Nell Kimball explained the safety-valve theory, "The city needed whores, whores needed houses, houses kept nice young men and brutes from raping their daughters, sisters, wives," although another madam, Josephine Washburn, cynically claimed that "[w]hen you hear a man say that the social evil [prostitution] is a necessary evil for the protection of good women, just put it down that the man is one of those who wants the public house in his city for other reasons than the safety of good women."[23] In addition to being a safety valve for men's desires, the prostitute was discarded as waste once her working life, commonly estimated at about five years, was over. In this she mimicked the labor cycle of the unskilled industrial worker, for her physical attributes, like those of other workers, are a time-limited commodity. Unlike the skilled worker, however, whose value increases along with his skills, the prostitute grows less valuable with every act that increases her experience and skills. Prostitution, with its associated graft and the purchasing power of its workers, was essential to the economic function of the nation, yet, after being discarded, the individual worker becomes a visible form of surplus population, a worker for whom there is no place. As Zygmunt Bauman argues in *Wasted Lives: Modernity and Its Outcasts*, "'[O]verpopulation' is a fiction of actuaries.... 'Surplus population' is one more variety of human waste."[24]

White slave and prostitution narratives differed in tone and genre depending on the audience, the era, and the degree to which they adopted a reform purpose. All claimed to tell the truth about the events they described, a purpose that they shared with naturalism, and all used varying degrees of sensationalism to do so. Their adaptation of other forms and genres, including the slave or liberation narrative, the documentary case history, the success novel, and Gothic naturalism, allow the authors to adjust the level of rhetorical excess either to downplay, hence normalize, the events they describe, which contributes to the effect of realism, or to ramp up the sense of outrage that the reader feels and thus drive home the necessity for reform.

The White Slave Narrative as Liberation Narrative

The white slave narrative borrows the rhetoric and aims of the slave narrative, also known as the freedom or liberation narrative, such as Frederick Douglass's *Narrative of the Life of an American Slave* (1845) and Harriet Jacobs's *Incidents in the Life of a Slave Girl* (1861). Like those works, white slave narratives involve a redemption and rescue plot. Moreover, as in the liberation narrative, the white slave narrative directed its outrage not only toward those immediately perpetrating the rape and captivity of young women but also toward the institutions and individuals that profited from it. The white slave narrative demands expressions of shame, remorse, and repentance. Repentance becomes the uplifting conclusion for the white slave narrative that the redemption and deliverance to the north becomes in the liberation narrative.

As in the liberation narrative, the victim in the white slave narrative is brought from a state of innocence into a recognition of her degradation, not through the awareness of slavery's bondage, as in the case of Douglass, but through a sexual encounter at a young age that, like Douglass's recognition of race, changes forever the way that she views herself. Often this occurs in a time of family dissolution, with the death or abandonment of a parent depriving the girl of social supports and plunging the family into poverty. Her youth and the social chaos and poverty that surround the girl combine to make her easy prey for white slavers, and those protesting white slavery emphasized the extreme youth of its victims. For example, Jane Addams writes that many "little inmates in the [rescue] home wanted to play with dolls and several of them brought dolls of their own."[25] In *Autobiography of a Magdalen* (1911), Louise C. Wooster recalls that, having trusted the friendship of a Major Robert Harlow, she "soon yielded to his seductive powers. . . . At this time I was barely eleven years old." "In passing judgment consider my circumstances and my age," Wooster pleads, judging, probably correctly, that she and not Harlow would be blamed for her fall.[26]

Like the African American child in the liberation narrative who becomes aware of the social implications of her race, the young woman abducted into white slavery looks anew at her body and learns that it has become irrevocably devalued. Her response is defamiliarization and dissociation from her own body. Her developing sense of a unified self becomes divided as she recognizes the categories into which she now falls: impure (as opposed to pure), black (as opposed to white), and owned (as opposed to owning). She begins to see herself as little more than a commodity. Like the enslaved African American too, the white slave has her spirit broken and her hopes of eventual escape systematically destroyed by those who own her. As part of the process of her education and of educating the reader about the system's abuses, she hears stories of others' experiences, often of those who have suffered even worse fates. In the liberation narrative, the representation of violence and of sexual abuse is rendered in vivid terms, as when Douglass describes his aunt's being whipped until her blood ran, for resisting the overseer's advances. The counterpart in the white slave narrative is the first sexual encounter or first customer, usually rendered allusively rather than graphically but unmistakably conveying the victim's rape by a stranger or, worse, by someone she has heretofore trusted. These sensational descriptions provoked moral outrage but also titillated audiences with raw sex and violence that they might otherwise have been ashamed to contemplate.

Specialized clothing marks the woman's new status as a brothel inmate and prevents her from escaping by its inadequacy for street wear. She quickly and involuntarily falls into debt to the madam for the clothing, room, and board charged to her account, including the iconic red kimono, which compounds the problem of escape. In describing white slave and prostitution films, *Variety* uses the term "patchouli and kimona" pictures, for like the heavy scent of patchouli, the kimono, functionally a dressing gown in most turn-of-the-century fiction, becomes shorthand for the woman's status, especially in red, the color of sexuality and passion.[27] In one of the accounts in Roe's *The Great War on White Slavery*, for example, Mildred, a white slave, weeps as the madam, "a large blond woman wearing a bright red kimona," threatens to whip her.[28] As Josephine Washburn comments in her advice to wives wishing to keep their husbands at home, "Red is a favorite shade with men and has some such an effect upon them as it has upon some kinds of animals."[29] Eventually, as in Reginald Wright Kauffman's *The House of Bondage*, the girl caught in the white slavery trap may be rescued and rehabilitated, but her reintegration into society is never complete.

In addition to its plot trajectory of fall, imprisonment, and hoped-for deliverance, the white slave narrative shares two stylistic features with the slave or liberation narrative: a heightened rhetorical language that mingles sensational description with calls to reform, and authenticating documents that reassure the reading public about the veracity of the writer's claims. Like the liberation narrative, the white slave narrative is framed by authenticating documents provided by political or religious authorities such as ministers and abolitionists, who model engagement with rescuing victims from the trade but are distanced from it by their institutional reputation. *The Autobiography of a Magdalen*, for example, includes a foreword stating that "[t]his book is founded on fact.... It is not a work of fiction" and an introduction signed simply "MINISTER," a dubious authentication that would nonetheless reassure readers that its aims are instructional rather than prurient.[30] The 1913 film *The Inside of the White Slave Traffic* includes a long list of endorsers, including Charlotte Perkins Gilman, Inez Haynes Gilmore, and Carrie Chapman Catt, and its publicity claimed documentary location shots in New York and Chicago.[31] Works such as *The Great War on White Slavery* rely instead on heightened rhetoric. Each chapter is structured as case study combined with a sermon, mixing hortatory and judgmental language as a means of creating a sense of urgency about reform and often concluding with a Bible verse. In "Whose Daughter Art Thou?," for example, the narrative directly addresses the reader, abjuring fathers to remember that "every girl sold into a den of vice is somebody's daughter" and concluding with a Bible verse.[32] Taking a different rhetorical stance, the scientific language of social work and economics, Jane Addams's *A New Conscience and an Ancient Evil* uses the metaphor of abolition to attribute the social evil to economics and the capitalist ethos that refuses to pay a shop girl a living wage. According to Addams, the causes for chattel slavery and white slavery, primarily economic in origin, cannot be overcome without a shift in the nation's vision of those whom the system oppresses, and the same moral obligation exists to eradicate white slavery as to abolish chattel slavery.

As in the failure of half measures or gradual accommodation in the liberation of slavery, the white slave narrative demolishes weak arguments and the halfhearted reforms that had made little difference in the condition of women working as prostitutes. Like Douglass with his bitter jabs at slave-abusing pious Christians, the white slave narratives indict corrupt police, landlords, and politicians as well as the men who frequent prostitutes, making it plain that a deeply entrenched bureaucracy and a smooth-running cadre of interlocking institutions serve their own interests by keeping the current systems of oppression in place. Hypocritical, stony-hearted respectable women who refuse to hire reformed prostitutes, employers who fail to pay women a living wage, and reformers who offer tracts instead of real assistance are responsible for the systemic problems that enable prostitution to thrive. A common criticism of the reformers is that they had no plan for reintegrating rescued women into the fabric of society, or rather they had no plan for doing so that would be palatable to the women they rescued. For example, in a letter to the *World* that Maimie Pinzer copied and sent to her correspondent Mrs. Howe, the "working girls' home" is described as a place "where they always put you to sleep with four or sometimes eight others in a room, so that rest is impossible, giving you the poorest of food, making you feel like a pauper generally, and rounding out all material deficiencies with very long prayers and useless restrictions."[33] Reformed prostitutes were advised to educate themselves or return to the honest toil of factory work, yet reformers recommending the rescued women's return to the inadequate pay and poor conditions of factory work failed to realize that they were merely substituting wage slavery for white slavery.

Documentary Realism and the Success Narrative

Alfred Kreymborg's *Edna: The Girl of the Street* exemplifies the problems that occur when, as with some slave narratives, a sincere interlocutor who has not lived his subject's life tries to shape her narrative to fit a pattern legible in his reform framework. It is the short tale of a single encounter between Kreymborg, under the name "Amos Lane," and a young prostitute, Edna, whose story includes almost more authenticating documents than text: the 1919 edition features George Bernard Shaw's letter to the publisher, Guido Bruno, and his "Advice to the New York Vice Society"; Bruno's account of his arrest and imprisonment in 1916 for selling the book; and Kreymborg's description of the circumstances of his encounter. Like Crane's *Maggie: A Girl of the Streets*, which its title echoes, *Edna: The Girl of the Street* treats the life of the young prostitute with realism rather than sensationalism, yet Lane, the narrator, is shocked at every turn by Edna's refusal to fit into his framework of the seduced and abandoned street girl.

Seeing a flirtatious Edna and her friend Irene near the Metropolitan Opera House one evening, Lane begins to wonder whether Edna is a "street woman" or an "every day girl," opposing categories in his mind.[34] He assesses her as a "street woman" based on her use of the slang term "kid"—"of all appellations, kid!" (16). Seeing a chance to study her as a specimen, he invites the two out to dinner, where he detects "[d]istinct traits of a lust for pleasure" (20), with "lust" and "pleasure" betraying his judgment even before he hears her story. Hiring her for the evening so that she can tell her story, he listens as she explains that hard work without respite had driven her to the streets. A Boston department store was "Hell" not because she could meet unscrupulous men outside the home, as reformers feared, but because the pay was so low. Failing as an actress, she sees no future in marriage, for "It'd be Hell to sleep with the same fellow every night" (26). Lane realizes that he "meant nothing to her... except business." He decides that she has "grown repulsive" (26), after which the sadder but wiser "sentimental sociologist" (27) finds his way home. Trying to construct a narrative of victimhood, Kreymborg instead finds a businesswoman, and this, combined with her frank statement of sexual desire, makes her repellant to him.

What Kreymborg uncovers but rejects is the truth rigorously suppressed in the reformers' accounts of why young women enter prostitution: because it pays well, better than inadequate department store wages. In twice using the word "Hell," a shocking departure from modest behavior at the time, Edna redefines it from signifying the confinement of the brothel to that of monogamy and asserts her ability to control her time and her life. Yet although he had paid to hear Edna's story, Lane was prepared to hear only the tale that men like to hear, as Madeleine Blair and Nell Kimball describe it, of innocence violated, a secret that the woman shares with him alone—until, as Kimball and Blair confirm, they repeat the story for the next customer who asks. Unlike Kimball and Blair, and unlike Evelyn Nesbit, who was forced to repeat the tale of her seduction by White not only to Harry Thaw during their marriage but also to an insatiable public for decades thereafter, Edna refuses to indulge Lane's fantasies of lost innocence. Lane is doubly shaken by Edna's admission, since in his mind paying for a story differs from paying for sex, but for Edna, who keeps hinting that his time is up, they are the same thing. Her time is worth money, just as it is for the successful businessmen of the era, and in reminding him of it, she also reasserts her control over their business meeting. Her exercise of power causes Lane to retreat to his class privilege as he asserts that "she, like the whole of her class, was mercenary" (27), as if an innate trait of her class and not extreme poverty were responsible for her actions. In resisting her role in the white slave narrative, Edna, like Madeleine Blair and Nell Kimball, refuses the role of the victim and asserts autonomy often absent from the victim-rescuer paradigm of the prostitution narrative.

The narratives of Madeleine Blair and Nell Kimball exemplify the success novel of prostitution, revealing a business-oriented account of their lives as prostitutes and as madams in several cities. Unlike *The Maimie Papers*, these accounts were written as complete texts intended for publication, with *Madeleine: An Autobiography* appearing in 1919 and *Nell Kimball: Her Life as an American Madam* being offered to journalist Stephen Longstreet (1907–2002) by Kimball in 1932 and published in 1970. In contrast to an intensified rhetoric of shame and a plea for social change, the mode of Lydia Taylor's *From under the Lid: An Appeal to True Womanhood* (1913), Louise Wooster's *Autobiography of a Magdalen* (1911), and Josephine Washburn's *The Underworld Sewer: A Prostitute Reflects on Life in the Trade, 1871–1909* (1909), Kimball's and Blair's accounts include sensational reports of their experiences but downplay the rhetoric of outrage. Instead they emphasize the ordinary domestic details of running a house and their business methods for doing so. By including details about the kinds of foods, wines, furnishings, and domestic routines (such as keeping track of linens) common in their houses, Kimball and Blair describe the process of housekeeping in the one kind of house that their middle-class women readers would probably never enter, catering to a curiosity less prurient but no less devouring than that which women readers may have had about the house's sexual routines. (In the film *The Red Kimona*, for example, a society woman badgers Gabrielle, the heroine, with salacious questions about her sexual experiences in a house.) Both narratives read more like the business success stories that appeared in Progressive Era magazines such as *Success* than accounts of victimhood. The outrage in these accounts is directed toward church and civic institutions for their hypocritical periodic efforts to suppress brothels and reform their inmates without providing any realistic means for the women to reenter society and earn a living wage.

Nell Kimball: Her Life as an American Madam covers Kimball's life from her birth in 1854 up through the closing of her house in New Orleans when Storyville, the legal prostitution district, was shut down in 1917. In recounting the major events of her life, Kimball reverses the narrative of white slavery. Instead of a time of innocence and healthful country living, Kimball, then known as Goldie Brown, recalls her childhood on a poverty-stricken farm as a time of hunger, cold, poverty, cruelty, and indifference. The only kind person she knew was her Aunt Lettie, who left Goldie the gold watch she had been given by Zig Flegel, who ran one of the best houses of prostitution in St. Louis. In many prostitution narratives, the young woman faces a time of being alone and abandoned in a city, which drives her to sell herself to survive, as in David Graham Phillips's novel *Susan Lenox*. When a fifteen-year-old Goldie follows her lover to St. Louis and he deserts her, however, she recalls her aunt's good life at Flegel's, finds the house, and is immediately hired there. In conventional white slave novels and narratives, the moment when the trapped woman is forced to see her first client is a nightmare. For Goldie, perfumed, bathed, and with enough to eat for the first time in her life, lying in the "big soft bed" (70) is dreamlike and pleasurable rather than terrifying. She prospers at Flegel's and later as a kept woman in St. Louis, learning how to run her own home as well as a house of prostitution after she determines that of the three options available to a retired "house girl"—suicide, marriage, or becoming a madam—she has the brains and ambition to set up her own establishment. As in a business autobiography or novel such as Abraham Cahan's *The Rise of David Levinsky* (1917) and Dreiser's *The Financier* (1912), the tension in the book and its main plot derives from the success narrative of seeing Kimball achieve her ambitions.

Much of the book follows this success narrative, with sequences devoted to Kimball's life as a madam in New Orleans and San Francisco. Kimball illustrates the tale of her success with extended descriptions of her business methods, incidents that she handled effectively, and her acquaintance with those who became famous in her profession, such as Madam Ah Toy in San Francisco and the Everleigh sisters in Chicago. In contrast to her business life, Kimball's domestic life of being a good woman leads to misery. She marries a gambler, moves to New York, has a child who dies of diphtheria, and, in a "purity trance" (191), faces starvation and homelessness rather than returning to prostitution. In this interlude as a wife, mother, and widow, Kimball confronts the reality behind the vague, optimistic promises of the white slave redemption narrative, which avoid the fact that there are few places in society for the reformed prostitute. "It's the Good People who exploit poor girls who make a lot of whores," she writes, explaining that returning to prostitution was "better than going blind in a sweat shop sewing, or twenty hours [of daily] work as a kitchen drudge, or housemaid" (250).

When she becomes a madam, Kimball learns to manage all the details of a successful business, including selecting the best wines and furnishings, establishing the prices she will charge and the clientele she will encourage, choosing employees, and developing relationships with the politicians and police whom she pays off to remain open. "In my way I was an American success like Mr. Frick, Mr. Carnegie, Teddy Roosevelt or Mrs. Astor," she recalls (224), reinforcing an earlier comment by Zig Flegel that "it took as much brains to run a good whorehouse... as it does to run a railroad system" (104). Earlier narratives published during the white slave era, such as those by Wooster and Washburn, subordinate their success narratives to the rhetoric of shame that conveys the reform message. By placing herself among titans of industry like Frick and Carnegie, whose pragmatic and flexible moral code resembled her own, Kimball highlights the trajectory of her success in business as the real moral imperative in American capitalist culture.

Madeleine: An Autobiography, published pseudonymously in 1919, describes the career of "Madeleine Blair" as an expensive prostitute and madam in St. Louis, Kansas City, Chicago, Butte, Spokane, Winnipeg, and Calgary. As Marcia Carlisle notes in her introduction to the modern Persea Books edition, the narrative contains two thematic strands: the rise of Madeleine from streetwalker to madam, and a plea for understanding about her plight, with "the woman as legitimate social actor, not the woman as victim" as its overarching message.[35] Already pregnant when she leaves home to support her family by working in St. Louis, Madeleine meets an older man who infects her with a "disease" (52). After her cure, she works for "Miss Laura," who runs a high-class house and advises her to marry Paul Martin, a man from Winnipeg who has proposed to her. Instead, after the birth and death of her child, Madeleine goes to Chicago to work for "Miss Allen" at the most luxurious brothel on Dearborn Street, where the women must wear expensive evening gowns.

Unlike Nell Kimball, who describes herself with pride as a "marvelous whore" (94), Madeleine despises the life, sullenly refusing to entice any customers and reciting poetry, including Elizabeth Stuart Phelps's "Galatea" from *Songs of the Silent World*, to endure their attentions. Knowing that she must support her improvident family and that this is her only choice, however, she stays for five years with Miss Allen. After working in several cities, bearing another child, inducing a second-trimester abortion that nearly kills her, and reuniting with Paul many times while refusing to marry him because of their incompatible temperaments, Madeleine, now twenty-eight years old, establishes a successful brothel in a Canadian town "which I shall call Malta, because it is not the name" (255). At first determined to train the young women who work in her house for better lives by teaching them to sew, over the course of six years Madeleine deteriorates into an alcoholic and disgusts every person who comes into contact with her, driving Paul away for the last time by mailing him an obscene letter, and corrupting a young, idealistic doctor who tries to save her. She has become an outcast scorned even by society's outcasts, and as she looks at herself in a mirror, she decides to change.

At the book's conclusion, Madeleine turns her brothel over to a housekeeper and takes the pledge of sobriety. She is thirty-four years old and a "valued employee" (328) in a respectable business, despite having been driven out of previous positions, for if "a woman is again made whole and seeks to use her dearly bought knowledge for the benefit of others, these same good Christians will have none of her" (325). Her skepticism about the hypocrisy of "good Christians" in permitting women to reenter society is consistent with that of Josephine Washburn, Maimie Pinzer, and every other woman writing from the point of view of the redeemed prostitute. As she says to a critic who wonders whether reintegration will spoil the "social fabric," "If the present social fabric is only a moth-eaten piece of cloth . . . then it is high time we began weaving a clean, strong, new fabric" without the pretense that prostitution does not harm women (329). Madeleine's choice to alienate those who would help her, her drinking, and her reckless gambling indicate self-destructive patterns and a lack of self-awareness, yet her astute observations about the cities and establishments she visits, her evident pride in running the best brothel in Malta, and her glee at evading the Mounties and outwitting her rivals demonstrate an intelligent assessment of her situation. Like Kimball's autobiography, *Madeleine* mixes historical context, travel description, and a plethora of how-to details about running a brothel. The business success narrative in *Madeleine* runs in tandem with a story of moral regeneration in which the price of regeneration is the deliberate loss of the successful business. Although her lover Paul, like many men, regards prostitution as a necessary evil, subscribing to the moral safety valve theory, Madeleine prefers the contagion theory, that "every fallen woman who is restored to decency... means the healing of a contagious ulcer on the social body" (230). The sexually transmitted disease that she had suffered early in her career literalizes the moral "contagious ulcer" of prostitution, and only by addressing the problem can the nation be healed.

The Victim as Vampire

In addition to documentary realism, the liberation narrative, and the success narrative, white slave fiction incorporates genre features of naturalism and the Gothic, including the dramatic elements and rhetorical excesses common to both. Like the Gothic, naturalism explores the dark underside of the human psyche, and its interest in the thin membrane between civilized behavior and desire mirrors the Gothic's exploration of the divide between rationality and madness. Invested, like the Gothic, in exploring the space between life and death, naturalism focuses on the excesses of the flesh, including desire and decay, much as excesses of the spirit and violent emotion pervade the Gothic text. The result is that the containment of excess creates a distortion or lack of balance in ordinary reality, a reality elusive both in naturalism, with its extreme states of being, and in the Gothic, with its tenuous grasp of a reality touched by the supernatural. Part of this containment of excess, in both naturalism and the Gothic, resides in the realistic detail that masks the perceptual and cognitive distortions of time, of space, and of states of being. As one key to understanding these distortions, Eve Kosofsky Sedgwick usefully identifies the spatializing of the self as central to the Gothic, with the self being "massively blocked off from something to which it ought normally to have access," such as "its own past, the details of its family history." Forced apart, the self and its missing counterpart "continue separately, becoming counterparts rather than partners" in lives that run in parallel rather than in tandem.[36]

In addition to the spatialized self that results in a divided consciousness, naturalist Gothic in the form of the white slave narrative distorts time and space. The distortion of time applies to the woman behind the barred windows of the brothel, watching the ordinary life of the streets move by at a tempo unavailable to her as she endures her slow imprisonment. Naturalism's distortions of vast exterior space, as in Jack London's "To Build a Fire," match the Gothic's distortions of interior space, the labyrinthine buildings in which rooms, doors, halls, windows, and locked compartments thwart the physical and metaphoric reunion of the divided self. The brothel intensifies the claustrophobic effect of the Gothic because it confirms that the constructions of human beings—governmental systems, institutions, houses—designed for human protection are actually capable of inflicting the most potent harm. As in the Gothic convent tale, the elegant house that seems a place of sanctuary becomes instead a brothel and a prison. Guarding these spaces are authority figures who should come to the victim's aid but are complicit with the forces keeping her imprisoned. In Elizabeth Robins's *My Little Sister* and Frank Norris's "The Third Circle," distortions of time and space combine with the failure of institutional guardians to prevent the violation of the white slave's body, a failing that leaves her, and by extension the nation, helpless in the hands of foreign corruption. As victim and as vampire, another form of the divided self, the white slave threatened citizenship and the republic, signifying larger corruption in the body politic through her transgression of national boundaries through sexual contact with a foreign Other.[37]

MY LITTLE SISTER

First published in two parts in *McClure's Magazine* from December 1912 through January 1913, a few months after the publication of Jane Addams's white slave exposé *A New Conscience and an Ancient Evil*, Elizabeth Robins's *My Little Sister* "'startled a continent,' arousing more discussion and stirring more consciences to action 'than any similar document of the last decade,'" according to the publicity in *McClure's*.[38] An American actress and women's rights advocate, Elizabeth Robins (1862–1952) starred on the London stage in the plays of Shaw, Pinero, and her friend Henry James, becoming famous for her interpretation of Ibsen's heroines in *A Doll's House* and *Hedda Gabler* before turning to writing social problem fiction. Begun as a collaborative project with the poet John Masefield, *Where Are You Going To . . . ?*, titled *My Little Sister* in the United States, was based on an incident told to her in 1907 by a fellow feminist, Maud Pember Reeves, about "two innocent young Englishwomen enticed to a brothel." It sold more than one thousand copies a day at the height of its popularity.[39] *My Little Sister* was adapted into a film released on June 15, 1919. Produced by Fox Film Corporation, the film gave Evelyn Nesbit a cinematic regeneration of sorts, for she starred as the unnamed elder sister, a piece of casting that transposed her from her real-life notoriety as the sexual victim of Stanford White to the more resourceful of the two young women in the novel.

As in many white slave tales, the genesis of *My Little Sister* has the flavor of an urban legend, but the documentary evidence of sociological reports, case studies, trial transcripts, and statistical surveys supports the novel's report of its most agonizing sequence, which entails the indifference of government bureaucracy and police to the abduction and rape of a young woman. *My Little Sister* (1913) exemplifies the overlap between the Gothic and naturalism, including doubling of the victim and vampire figure, distorted narrative time and space, the characters' imprisonment or entombment, and the symbolic use of interpretive symbols—totemic emblems, unreadable spaces, and symbolic songs—as illustrative of a lost order signifying rationality. *My Little Sister* and its focus on the body of the violated woman represents a larger corruption of the social order, one blamed on contact with racial others but ultimately the work of corrupt, arrogant white individuals and institutions.

Like Jane Austen's *Sense and Sensibility*, *My Little Sister* employs the device of two sisters: the older and wiser unnamed narrator and her younger sister, the innocent and impetuous Bettina. Referred to in the film credits as "Elder Sister," the narrator's lack of a name suggests that she is an everywoman and a stand-in for the reader, someone who must fight against the white slave trade and rescue its victims. The pair live simply with their widowed mother in a country house and despite their lack of means become involved with their well-to-do neighbors, the Helmstones. The early chapters unfold as in an Austen novel, but beneath the surface of their placid country life lie hints of a troubled past tinged with racial and sexual overtones. Growing up in India, the mother tells the narrator, she "had seen a great deal of evil."[40] This conflation of colonial oppression and sexual exploitation culminates in the mother's story of her grandfather, who had brought a young girl to live with him, a "sort of cousin" (114) who "ministered to his whims and perversities" (115).[41]

The clear signs of trauma that the mother had endured affect every facet of the girls' lives. Until she falls ill and is forced to accept help, the mother turns away visitors, refuses to let the girls visit their neighbors, and is happiest when locking the doors against any possible intruders. Shutting out the world means ignorance of its ways for the two girls and also an indifference to its sufferings. The mother shuts the window in the face of a starving, haggard hop-picker (43) who begs for money one day, saying that "infection" could contaminate the household, and she shows no mercy to a servant who becomes pregnant. She refuses to allow the narrator to study medicine and makes no plans for her daughters' future. The sisters cannot use the village public telephone, the technology that enables contact with the external world, because their mother declares it to be "full of germs" (51), a fear that conflates social contagion and modern germ theory. Artificially compressing, hence distorting, the time and space that the girls inhabit by forbidding them to use modern technology and to mingle in the public sphere, the mother unwittingly sets the conditions for their downfall.

Even life in a country village cannot prevent sexual threat and foreign contagion, a point that Robins emphasizes through repeated references to the backdrop of imperial England and its colonies. The events of the novel are bookended with two specific references to colonial time and space: the mother's past in India, a colonized space that the mother casts as a site of racial otherness and sexual perversity, and the upcoming coronation of King George V on June 22, 1911, signifying modernity and civilized order. The family reveres "the Army and the Royal Family" (24), and they even mark time by saying that Bettina was born in the same year (1894) as "the little Prince" who would be king (25). But the mother's colonial past and her fear of modernity and the outside world taint all possibilities of her daughters' acquisition of the modern knowledge they need to survive, since the elder, at least, wholeheartedly adopts her mother's suspicions. So committed is the narrator to the hermetic existence in their country home that when her mother's suitor, Colonel Dover, appears at their door in the midst of a driving rainstorm, she refuses to let him in. As he brandishes his metal-tipped umbrella, a phallic substitute for his sexual intrusion into their house and into their lives, lightning strikes the tip and electrocutes him, a supernatural death that destroys the threat of masculine power and empire. Imperial and colonial references signify corruption again when the worldly Lady Helmstone, who wishes to skip "the Coronation fuss" (153), invites Bettina on a six-month cruise on her yacht, the *Nautch Girl*, a name referring to Indian dancing girls with overtones of sexuality. The mother rejects the invitation, saying that old families like the Helmstones display "a kind of treason" in refusing to attend the coronation (153), a misplaced faith in an empire and in institutions that are not worthy of her trust.

Knowledge of the abuses of empire confers only a generalized suspicion of foreigners, however, not the knowledge of contemporary urban life necessary to protect the girls. Relying on domestic ideology and rejecting Lady Helmstone's advice that girls have their best chances in the marriage marketplace before the age of twenty (157), the mother weakly says that the girls' husbands will take them traveling once they are equipped with social graces like playing music. Because their mother's naïve general suspiciousness ill equips them to recognize danger, they fail to see it in the form of a French dressmaker, Madame Aurore, who not only has "scars on her neck and dead-looking yellow hair" (224) but also reeks of patchouli, the scent traditionally worn by prostitutes. Despite their mother's distrust of foreigners, neither Aurore's French nationality, her appearance, her theft of a picture of the wealthy aunt, Josephine Harborough, whom they are to visit, nor her pointed questions about their family's jewels alarm the sisters. Aurore is a procuress who alerts the madam of a brothel about the sisters' plans to visit their Aunt Josephine in London and sends the aunt's picture ahead of her. The sisters, never having been warned explicitly of sexual danger, fail to read the danger signs.

In the last third of the novel, when the sisters travel to London to visit an aunt they have never seen before, they experience the dissociation characteristic of the Gothic. Beginning with the train journey, nothing is what it appears to be, from the people they meet to the social life of London. The "aunt" who greets them at Victoria Station resembles her portrait only to Bettina's careless eyes. The woman who greets them, as the narrator notes, has an aquiline nose unlike the portrait of their Aunt Josephine, rapidly darting eyes, strong perfume, and a satanic "full yellow eye, the iris almost black" (257). At the house, the narrator misinterprets all she sees as evidence of her aunt's wealth, such as the house's thick carpets and barred windows, "immense mirrors separated by gilded columns" (256), a large bed "like an Oriental throne with rose-silk hangings" (257), and "pictures of women ... in different stages of the bath" or "asleep in a strange position with nothing on" (261). To a more experienced observer, and to the readers of the novel, the "Oriental" trappings, pictures of nude women, mirrors, barred windows, and red hangings establish it as a brothel, but the narrator represses her sense of uneasiness and describes her surroundings without interpreting them.

Of more concern to the narrator is that she and Bettina, accustomed to sleeping in the same room, have been given separate rooms with large beds. The two sisters have always operated as a pair, with the elder narrator curbing Bettina's superficial judgments and passionate nature. On the trip to London, for example, Bettina had encouraged the stares of strange men and accused the narrator of wanting to be an old maid: "You are a sort of nun. *You* never feel as if all your blood had been whipped to a syllabub" (249). Now physically separated from the sister who acts as her wiser self, Bettina sees only the admiration she attracts and not the danger she courts. The separation of the sisters suggests Sedgwick's conception of the Gothic separation of the self from something to which it normally has access. Denied access to the narrator's restraining influence, Bettina can express the desire for attention and the sexual impulsiveness that lead to her downfall.

Determined to read events through the frame of family and proper social protocols, the narrator dangerously misinterprets the people she meets as well as her surroundings. In one room, the narrator sees a woman, clad in a "kimono of scarlet silk embroidered in silver" (262), the red kimono signifying prostitution. The woman addresses her in a non-European foreign language through Lamia-like "lips so brightly red, they looked bloody" (261) as if feasting on a victim's blood, a vampire in all but name, with makeup that confirms her status at a time when respectable women wore little or none. Her "aunt" hurries down the hall dressed in "a gown all covered with little shining scales, like a snake's skin" (262), a sign of her role as the satanic serpent in this place. The narrator then sees a silent man ascending the stairs and wearing a hat in the house, like the physician in Edgar Allan Poe's "The Fall of the House of Usher," whom Poe's narrator sees on the stairs with a "countenance [wearing] a mingled expression of low cunning and perplexity."[42] Robins's narrator is told that the man is the doctor, but this answer, like all those she receives at the house, obscures the issue. If he is the doctor and not merely one of the woman's clients, his presence suggests the vampire's capacity for contagion, for the woman who is "ill" but "not very" (265), as the narrator is told, may have sought treatment for a sexually transmitted disease or possibly an abortion. Physicians or scientists in naturalism, like Dr. Mandelet of *The Awakening* or Dr. Ledsmar of *The Damnation of Theron Ware*, serve as truth-tellers against whom reality may be tested. In romances like Nathaniel Hawthorne's "The Birthmark" or "Rappaccini's Daughter," their devotion to science warps their humanity. But in the Gothic setting of Poe's story, as in the brothel of Robins's *My Little Sister*, they confirm the corruption of the place by their complicity with the institutional structures that it contains, signifying knowledge of evil that they both possess and suppress.

The deceptions culminate in a supposed society dinner party in which the sisters are introduced to a number of men. Clad in their new dresses, the narrator in white and Bettina in green, both colors of innocence, they descend the staircase on their way to dinner and see themselves "going by in mirrors between the golden columns. The whole place was full of tall girls in white, and little girls in apple-green, wearing forget-me-not wreaths in their hair" (265). In addition to its allusion to the traditional mirrors of the brothel, the scene epitomizes the reflection and refraction of their previous selves, momentarily together yet fractured by the repeated images in the mirrors that ironically multiply the many "little sisters" who will "fill" the place that they currently hold in the immediate confines of the brothel and the larger world of white slavery. Like the narrator of "The Yellow Wallpaper," the narrator misinterprets the barred windows of the house, reading them first as protection against burglars and then as evidence of a private madhouse. At the table, the conversation ostensibly centers on racehorses, but the men speak in *double entendres* about the women of the house, including the "foreign lady" upstairs (270). A crack in the façade appears when a man comes in and introduces himself as "Williams" (272) when, as Bettina artlessly blurts out to the table, he is actually Guy Whitby-Dawson, a friend of the Helmstone family. He blandly denies his identity, knowing that in this place his false name will protect him and that he can easily shed it when he leaves the house. The girls, by contrast, will be forced into new names and identities that they can never shed and may never leave the house under their own power.

Robins emphasizes the violation of the girls' innocence through the narrator's misreading of the attention that the men shower on Bettina. Her visual pleasure at seeing Bettina the center of attention contrasts ironically with the erotic, near-pedophilic charge that an old roué, "The Colonel," receives by encouraging Bettina to perform as a little girl, another instance of the corruption of British institutions and individuals. At their urging, Bettina, already trained to please men, sings songs of childhood, including "Where Are You Going to, My Pretty Maid?," the song that gives the English edition of the novel its title, and she holds "her green skirt with both hands, like a child about to curtsey.... Such a baby she looked!" (301). The narrator's fond musings are soon shattered, however, when the lone decent man in the group takes her aside and tells her that she is "in one of the most infamous houses in Europe" (286). He will help her to escape, the informant explains, but she can pass unnoticed only if she leaves Bettina behind to distract the male customers. The narrator escapes, takes a cab to her real aunt's house, and demands immediate rescue for Bettina, but she is conscious that her only hope of rescue forced her to leave her sister behind, the sister who represents the most vulnerable part of herself.

Throughout the novel, social pressures have conspired to keep the narrator ignorant. Her mother's ominous hints about her Indian childhood notwithstanding, the narrator has been thwarted in her attempts to gain knowledge of the world, not only her abortive medical education but also that of sexual desire. As Molly Hite suggests, the "overriding theme" of the novel "is that feminine innocence is sustained by a calculated withholding of exactly the information that might allow women to protect themselves."[43] Now the narrator learns from her informant the dangers of male sexual desire and its connection with empire: the British fleet anchors off the Irish coast, he tells her, because more women, and, implicitly, women under colonial domination, are available there. Men and their institutions—"the Army and the Royal Family" that the narrator had once revered—rationalize the exploitation of women in much the same way that their imperialist ideology justifies the subjugation of nonwhite sovereign nations.

Naturalism and the Gothic depend on a revelation of a hidden, horrifying reality beneath a placid surface and the revelation of brutal truths without the individual's ability to rectify them. The sense of inevitable events closing in sustains itself both psychologically and spatially, with characters trapped by walls, prisons, or institutions that thwart their attempts to escape a set of tragic consequences. In *My Little Sister*, the walls that surround Bettina are literal, as in the barred windows of the brothel, and figurative, in the institutional indifference with which established institutions greet the news of her disappearance. The real Aunt Josephine has been too entangled with the false values of society and the equally false values of theosophy to pay attention to her brother's family. Faced with the narrator's information yet still invested in a sense of national superiority, she refuses to believe the narrator's account because "It isn't possible.... This is England" (305). The police, who to the narrator's surprise keep a list of brothels, are mildly interested to learn that Bettina is an upper-class girl but are indifferent to her abduction. The procurers "meet the trains," a policeman tells her, but are "not allowed" to be arrested (325), protected by governmental institutions that proclaim a defense of women but refuse to enforce it. Only the narrator feels a sense of urgency to rescue Bettina before she is sexually abused and spirited overseas, but since she cannot remember the house number or street of the brothel, and the cabman, when found, does not recall the house, she is helpless to act. Ranny, Bettina's suitor turned detective, traces Bettina to Paris but loses the trail. Awakening from a long, unspecified illness like the brain fever of domestic fiction to "a feeling quite safe and sure, at last, that Betty was free" (342), the narrator has a vision of "Betty leaning out of heaven" (344) and concludes with relief that she is dead.

My Little Sister indicts prostitution as just one form of corruption in institutional structures built by and for men but upheld with the complicity of women. As signified by the endless mirrors of the brothel, the marriage market and prostitution market mirror each other in the selling of girls prized for their youth and innocence. The same code that protects the men in the brothels with false identities endorses the exploitation of young women eroticized as victim or vampire: the near-pedophilia of Bettina's forced performance and the patchouli-and-red-kimono brazen sexuality of the painted woman. The disreputable Madame Aurore, who scouts for the white slavers, and the madam who emphasizes Bettina's forced performance of innocence to increase anticipation in "the jaded" (296) are the mirror of women like the mercenary Lady Helmstone, who measures female flesh and marriage prospects in much the same way. Equally at fault are women like the girls' aunt, Mrs. Harborough, who refuses to believe that prostitution can touch middle- and upper-class women, and the girls' mother, whose refusal to educate her daughters leaves them vulnerable to exploitation. Domestic ideology and the overprotected life that they had lived in the country, where windows had been shut abruptly against male intruders like "The Colonel," are mimicked and doubled in the brothel's closed and barred windows. But in the false domestic space of the brothel, which is, like the sisters' home, ruled by a dominant woman, male intruders are welcomed, not excluded or providentially struck by lightning. The damage done by male institutions, including those that promote such harmful domestic ideologies as female ignorance of sex and desire, distrust of technology, culturally sanctioned narratives of female weakness, and a lack of geographical awareness of her surroundings, has rendered both Bettina's fate and the narrator's response to it a preventable tragedy.

"THE THIRD CIRCLE"

Frank Norris's "The Third Circle" was first published in *The Wave*, a weekly San Francisco magazine, on August 28, 1897. Like Robins with her references to the coronation, Norris authenticates Gothic elements through references to specific places and sensational contemporary events in San Francisco's Chinatown. These include the murder of "Little Pete" (Fung Jing Toy), a Chinese leader killed on January 23, 1897, whose funeral Norris had covered for *The Wave*, and the See Yups, one of the Chinese associations or tongs. The title refers to the "three parts of Chinatown—the part the guides show you, the part the guides don't show you, and the part that no one ever hears of" where a "strange, dreadful life ... wallows ... in the lowest ooze of the place."[44] Joanna Levin reads "The Third Circle" as demonstrating "the arrogance of slumming" in its punishment of the white woman, although as Karen Keely points out, Norris spares little concern for "yellow slavery," the well-documented traffic in Chinese women that arose with the Chinese Exclusion Act.[45] Told by a narrator who hears the tale from others, the same retrospective narration as in *My Little Sister*, it tells of a young engaged couple who wander into "a See Yup restaurant on Waverly Place" (103) and find themselves enmeshed in the "third circle" of Chinatown, a Gothic plot that parallels that of *My Little Sister* in expressing anxieties about white women held in sexual slavery by racial Others.

The story is told in two episodes set twenty years apart. In the first, Miss Harriett "Harry" Ten Eyck and Tom Hillegas, her fiancé, are touring San Francisco. They are "from the east" and, like tourists everywhere, go out of their way to find unique spots unfrequented by other tourists like themselves. Charmed by the exotic nature of their surroundings, Hillegas pauses a moment to reflect on Harry as a beauty of "unmixed American stock" (103), with her Dutch name signifying her as the stock of the first settlers of New York. His reflection emphasizes the story's obsession with racial purity, now heightened by the contrast of her appearance in unfamiliar Chinese surroundings. Aroused by the unbroken expanse of her white skin and its connotations of sexual and racial purity, he kisses the "little crumpled round of flesh that showed where her glove buttoned" (104–5), a circle of whiteness that mirrors the circle of Harriett's engagement ring and later her tattoo. His act seals his possessorship of Harriett, the erotic promise of her flesh, and the whiteness that her heritage and her skin both signify to him.

As they enter a deserted restaurant, which "might just as well be in China itself" (104), Hariett and Tom wonder why the guides have never shown them this spot and ask the Kanaka-Chinese "fortune-teller" to tell their fortunes. Instead he offers to tattoo Harriett's little finger with the figure of a small butterfly, a gesture that will pierce Harriett's unbroken white skin, penetrating the surface and impregnating it with a foreign dye, a foreshadowing of the sexual violation she later endures. More daring than Hillegas in her quest for the exotic, Harriett declares that a tattoo would be "awfully queer and original." Her "marquise" (diamond engagement ring) will hide it, she tells Hillegas, who worries that marring her skin with a tattoo will make it so that she "never could wear evening dress" (105), a statement that shows his concern for her skin as a trophy of her whiteness. The permanent tattoo of the butterfly symbolically displaces Hillegas's kiss and his engagement ring on Harriett's hand, and it foreshadows another displacement by marking her as the permanent property of the space she now inhabits.

As in other Gothic tales like *My Little Sister*, nothing is what it seems, and seemingly harmless buildings reveal themselves to be prisons, disorienting the characters in time and space. As Robins does in *My Little Sister*, Norris creates a disturbing sense of tension through the characters' inability to interpret their surroundings, including the oddly empty spaces in a crowded neighborhood, and the Chinese fortuneteller who is neither entirely Chinese nor a fortuneteller. To an alert San Franciscan, the situation would have set off alarm bells because of its distortions of time and space: The restaurant is within sight of "Aunt Harriett's rooms" (104) yet it is "in China" and deserted. The fortune-telling tattoo artist is racially marked right down to his "brown teeth" (105) and offers only one form of tattoo, which is less a butterfly than "a grotesque little insect, as much dragonfly as anything else" (106). After he leaves Harriett at the table and goes in search of a waiter, Hillegas finds a Chinese man adding up accounts and assumes the imperial authority of the white man by trying to order him about in pidgin: "I say, John.... Get plenty much move on. Hey?" But in another reversal of expectations, the Chinese merchant speaks in a more educated manner than Hillegas: "You will, no doubt, be attended to presently. You are a stranger in Chinatown?" (106). The merchant is a stranger too, having leased the shop from the See Yups who own it. In this dreamlike atmosphere, time lengthens as Hillegas "stay[s] for some little while talking to this man" (107). When he returns to the table, Harriett has vanished, and "no white man" ever sees her again (107).

Twenty years later, the narrator seeks out information on Harriett by enlisting the aid of a "Plaza bum," Manning, who takes him to a "slave-girl joint under Ah Yee's tan room" (108), a fan-tan gambling place. Three white slave women live there with Ah Yee and "a policeman named Yank," all races made equal in corruption by addiction to *yen shee*—"the cleanings of the opium pipe" (108). The men find the women "four floors underneath the tan room ... in a room about as big as a big trunk" (108), which suggests not only imprisonment but also entombment, a death in life akin to that suffered by Madeline Usher in Poe's story. One of the women, Sadie, is "a dreadful-looking beast of a woman, wrinkled like a shriveled apple, her teeth quite black from nicotine" (109) as she smokes a cigar. Sadie cannot speak unless drunk, and even after they give her gin and ask her about "Harriett Ten Eyck," she claims not to remember her. She then thrusts out her left hand, with a butterfly tattooed on the little finger: "Say, how did I get that on me?" (110). It is ironically true that "no white man" ever sees Harriett again, for Sadie is no longer Harriett, after she was purchased "from a sailor on a junk in the Pei Ho river" (110). Her teeth are now as black as those of the tattoo artist were brown, a suggestion not only of her new race but also of her vampiric preying upon outsiders as an opium peddler and a prostitute. Living a form of death in life in her grave-like hole, Sadie sells opium to the prisoners at San Quentin, and the contamination that she sought by inviting the tattoo has spread until its color, and its contamination, pervades her teeth and body.

Both *My Little Sister* and "The Third Circle" preach the dangers of the victim becoming a vampire, since the body of the white woman, once violated, cannot be redeemed, and no trace of whiteness remains. The woman herself disappears, as Bettina does in *My Little Sister*, or assumes another racial identity, as Harriett does in "The Third Circle." Harriett's smooth skin becomes wrinkled, her white skin and teeth turn dark, and only the tattoo, the mark that once "married" her to Chinatown and rendered her identity permanent, unlike the temporary marquise, remains intact from the woman she had been twenty years before. "The Third Circle" anticipates the white slavery panic in its warnings about the safety of the white woman who ventures a little too far in looking for an adventure in the unknown parts of a city, its censure of the overcivilized and overconfident man who carelessly refuses to see the ominous signs around him and fails to protect the woman in his care, the malevolent racial Other who presses white women into prostitution, and the inevitable downfall of the white woman who, crossing the racial barrier, becomes as addicted to degradation as she is to opium.

Like the curse of a granted prayer, Harriett/Sadie's desire for the "queer" and exotic, like Bettina's wish to please and attract men, has ironically taken both women to places they could have dreamed of only in their nightmares, and having once crossed this line, neither can ever return to the white world. In the Gothic and naturalistic environments of the white slave narrative, the only means of transcending the living victim–contagious vampire dichotomy is to die, as Bettina does. In their anxiety over whiteness, both works offer a critique of entrenched institutional indifference, male complicity in endangering women, and carelessly arrogant misreadings of ethnic Others through the lens of empire and white superiority. As revealed through the sensational Gothic and naturalistic elements of each work, the real horror lies not only in the forced prostitution of a nation's women but also in the indifference that governmental institutions display where women's lives and women's bodies are concerned.

Undercover Narratives

A YELLOW JOURNALIST

Like her contemporary Frank Norris, Miriam Michelson (1870–1942) used San Francisco as a backdrop for her fiction, including her first and most famous novel, *In the Bishop's Carriage* (1904). A feature writer and eventually dramatic editor for the *San Francisco Call*, Michelson covered everything from the Berkeley women's sports teams to current fiction, but her feature articles of the late 1890s reveal a leaning toward social justice issues. Reporting from Hawaii, she made "stirring appeals" on behalf of Hawaiian sovereignty, such as her September 30, 1897, article, "Strangling Hands upon a Nation's Throat."[46] Even on a local level, her stories demonstrated racial sensitivity, as in 1897's "The Woes of Mr. and Mrs. Ngong Fong," which sympathetically chronicles the racism experienced by an interracial couple, the Stanford-educated Ngong Fong and his Caucasian wife. In the early twentieth century, Michelson assumed roles of public prominence in organizations such as the Citizens' League of Justice, lecturing on reform and women's issues, but she continued publishing novels, short stories, and plays until her death in 1942.

First published serially in the *Saturday Evening Post*, *A Yellow Journalist* shares with *In the Bishop's Carriage* a charming but ethically dubious heroine who learns the error of her ways. The "yellow journalist" is Rhoda Massey, an aspiring and ultimately successful newspaperwoman—or, as the *San Francisco Call* described her, a "reporterette"—whose cases are "vividly imaginative buildings upon the true stories of our city's romances, crimes, and scandals."[47] Working her way from freelance reporter to city editor, Rhoda pursues each scoop with an intensity that brushes aside any hint of danger or moral scruples. As one character remarks to another, the difference between Miss Massey going after a scoop and a bulldog is that a bulldog will eventually let go. She sometimes puts herself in physical danger to get the story, in one episode by riding with the sheriff to protect a condemned man from a lynch mob and in another crawling onto a high ledge to eavesdrop on a meeting of corrupt officials. More frequently, she uses her wits and her ability to impersonate whomever the object of the story needs her to be: a sympathetic listener who fabricates a confession, a nurse, or a Chinese slave woman in Chinatown.

Rhoda Massey's adventures in Chinatown comprise two chapters of *A Yellow*

Journalist, "The Fascination of Fan-Tan" and "In Chy Fong's Restaurant," the second a memorable undercover adventure that challenges the plot of Norris's "The Third Circle." Against her editor's wishes, Rhoda dons a "sleek, black" wig and, with the help of Gum Tai, "the duenna of the slave girls," and of Ah Oy, "the most expensive slave girl in Chinatown, worth $3,000 in white man's money" (101), slips into the gambling establishment of Yet Kim Gai and is accepted along with the other girls.[48] To her managing editor, and implicitly to the reader, Rhoda optimistically answers the question of whether a small, blonde white woman could pass for Chinese by emphasizing not the visual presentation of her face but the primacy of other cues for identification, among them behavior and voice. She tells him that she has learned the rules of behavior from her preceptors—"No talk. No look see. No bite lips"—and has learned to sing in Chinese, so by wearing a wig, she will surely pass (101).

By insisting upon overall presentation rather concerning herself with her phenotypically Caucasian high-bridged nose and other features, Rhoda, and by extension Michelson, reveals the truth that, in going undercover, half the battle is won by seeming to be what an unsuspecting and preoccupied populace expects to see. Her theory is borne out when she comes face to face with Sergeant Wyss, whose graft she had exposed in a front-page scoop only the day before. Unlike the gambling den proprietor Yet Kim Gai, who is a perfect gentleman where Rhoda is concerned, Sergeant Wyss makes physical contact with the women at the gambling house. Entering the place, he had "patronizingly hugged a slave girl—not as a man might a woman, but as though she were a child, a doll, or any pretty, non-human, soulless thing that couldn't speak or feel" (113). Her gender and her supposed race render her only a "slave girl" and not a full human being to him. He then looks into Rhoda's eyes without recognizing her, despite having been her guide on a Chinatown raid a few nights before. In a reversal of Norris's racial schema, in Michelson's novel the Chinese Yet Kim Gai is Rhoda's protector and the white Sergeant Wyss is the source of sexual danger.

In yet another satiric take on the white slave fears of Norris's story, Rhoda, waiting on the steps of the place to see whether Wyss will accept a bribe, suddenly has a blanket thrown over her head and is tossed into a wagon. The moment of suspense initially suggests the presumed capture of the white woman in "The Third Circle." But in a comic turn, Rhoda has not been shanghaied but "rescued ... by the good, stupid, angelic Mission, that helps Chinese girls to escape from slavery" (117). The mission, run by a "Miss McIntosh," has mistaken her for Ah Oy and captured her. Rhoda's undercover adventure has failed on all fronts: Sergeant Wyss is not punished but promoted. Miss McIntosh is denied publicity for the rescue, since she could not claim to have rescued Ah Oy. McCabe, the editor, is denied a story because Rhoda dares not tell him about this undercover adventure. And Rhoda is denied another scoop. Yet her adventure has succeeded in one essential respect. Despite the improbability of this act of undercover passing, Rhoda, it seems, has successfully impersonated a woman of another race, an act that stretches the reader's credulity nearly past the breaking point, thus poking gentle fun at the other suspensions of disbelief required to take seriously the undercover narrative.

In this tale of San Francisco, Michelson mixes documentary specificity variously with action, sensational melodrama, and humor in ways that challenge the undercover narrative through their very improbability. Norris's melodramatic "The Third Circle" provides in its character of Harriett/Sadie Ten Eyck a cautionary tale about the dangers for women in seeking undercover knowledge. In contrast, Michelson deploys the same Chinatown tropes as Norris and even sets her story in some of the same specific places, but she uses humor to deflect the serious nature of the undercover narrative. The "death's head" (107) figure who is the head of the See Yups makes Rhoda shiver, for example, but she also sees the Chinese as individuals, nearly breaking her cover by stifling a laugh when Yet Kim Gai proposes to sing a song for Sergeant Wyss and breaks into the popular hit "There'll Be a Hot Time in the Old Town Tonight." The absurdities of her forays into Chinatown, her fearlessness despite the warnings of white men like her editor, and the comic conclusion of her adventures and general intrepidity provide a popular corrective to the seriousness with which undercover narratives were supposed to be read.

THE ROSE DOOR

Estelle Baker's *The Rose Door* (1911) incorporates the victim-as-vampire concept through its themes of contamination and enclosure, but it also includes an undercover narrative and a conclusion that includes rescue, exposure of women's imprisonment in the system, and a treatise on the root causes of the social evil. The novel combines the stories of three women whose lives intersect at the brothel that gives the novel its title, and each of the stories treats a woman from a different social class. Rebecca, an immigrant garment worker in San Francisco, believes she cannot earn enough to bring her fiancé, Benjamin, from the old country unless she prostitutes herself. Anna, an abused orphan, has her romance with a wealthy youth broken up by his father. Grace Howells, a college student, is seduced by a married man. Through networks of communication and of contamination, their lives intersect with those of "respectable" characters as the consequences of poverty, child abuse, and a refusal to take the problems of fallen women seriously merge in the concluding chapters. Yet instead of concentrating on young, lower-class women as other narratives tend to do, *The Rose Door* demonstrates that intelligent, educated, middle-class women can fall into a life of prostitution and exhorts both classes of women to stop white slavery by standing together.

The first half of the novel introduces the three women and their stories, suspending the reader's knowledge of their fates until the three meet again at the Rose Door. Rebecca's story, the first section, follows the classic pattern of the Jewish immigrant that Turner described in "The Daughters of the Poor." While living with her brother and his wife in San Francisco, Rebecca tries to save enough money to bring Benjamin from the old country. In her spare time she learns English and studies to better herself. Even by following this American success script, Rebecca cannot get ahead, since she pays most of her salary for housing. When her brother asks her to move, she listens to Max, a family friend, who tells her he knows of better-paying work. Desperate to earn passage money, Rebecca lets Max set her up in a room and accepts all customers except him. When Max refuses to give her the money she has earned and tells her that Benjamin has married, Rebecca escapes with only the clothes on her back.

Anna's story, the second section, is of a girl born to an impoverished, consumptive mother. Anna and her brother John are still children when a male boarder crawls into bed with them and sexually abuses them, "bind[ing] to secrecy two children who had no one to tell."[49] Though mentioned obliquely by Addams and Robins, child sexual abuse as a precursor to other forms of the abuse of women is rarely so directly stated. In Anna's case, her suffering is compounded when a reformer, Mrs. Miller, refuses to take her in lest her own daughter be contaminated, an echo of Josie's plight in Wyman's "The Child of the State." Anna works and finds happiness after falling in love with a University of California student from Hawaii, Ralph Young, with whom she shares long conversations about William Burckhardt's thesis that "extinction always follows" (100) white settlers' attempts to live in tropical zones. Promising to come back to marry her after his father consents, Ralph returns to Hawaii but fails to write to her due to his father's machinations, leaving Anna destitute.

In contrast to the other two women, Grace Howells, the subject of the third story, is a high-minded University of Minnesota student obsessed with the poems of Elizabeth Barrett Browning. She meets and falls in love with Merritt Jordan, a man "handsome as a Greek god" (116), with whom she reads poetry. When he confesses to being married and says she should leave him for her own good, she whispers, "Stay, Merritt" (133), thus understanding and accepting her fall. Although all three women technically acquiesce in these sexual encounters, hard economic and social realities lead them ultimately to the Rose Door.

The public, social world of middle-class respectability and the private world of the three ruined women intersect some years later, publicly at an engagement party and privately at the Rose Door. Some years after the earlier events, a well-to-do group of friends gather to celebrate the engagement of Lieutenant Herbert Kenyon to Mary Miller, the daughter of the same Mrs. Miller who had declined to rescue Anna. Shortly thereafter, Lieutenant Kenyon and Robert Miller visit the Rose Door, pairing off with Rebecca and Anna. Their choice signals the men's cross-contamination of the respectable middle-class women in their home life with the diseased women of the Rose Door. Worried about a sore on her arm, Anna learns from a doctor that her old lover Ralph has died of leprosy (Hansen's disease) and that she has caught the disease from him. Mrs. Miller had refused to take Anna into her home because she feared moral contamination. Now the contagion, this time physical and sexual rather than simply moral, has been brought into her home and has infected her son. Anna, now a prostitute and, in the terminology of the time, a leper, writes to Mrs. Miller and explains that her son "Robert has been my friend for two years and has visited me often" (160). Transposing a sexual disease into a contagious disease of empire, Baker suggests the ease of its spread from those whom the culture does not value—colonized subjects and sexually abused children—to those that it does.

Similar revelations about their men await the middle-class women in the other two stories. Rebecca writes to tell Mrs. Lillian Kenyon that her husband, Mr. Kenyon, is keeping a mistress in a nearby building. Rather than ignoring his infidelity for the sake of her social standing, Lillian decides to investigate. She goes undercover and disguises herself as a hairdresser in the building where his mistress, "a lady in a pink kimono" (166), lives. When she knocks on the mistress's door one day and discovers Mr. Kenyon there, Lillian confronts him. Pleading for his social standing, he asks Lillian to continue with their marriage for the sake of appearances, but driven by the anger of "a near savage ancestry" (169), she declares that she will divorce him. In the denouement of the third story, Grace Howells, now dying, tells her story to Mrs. Merritt J. Thompson, who has taken her into her home to care for her. Grace has borne a child by the man she knew as Merritt Jordan, and, forced out of legitimate employment by "good women," she has supported her child by being the mistress of one man. As the two women talk, Mr. Thompson looks in on the two, Grace calls him "Merritt," and Mrs. Thompson realizes that her husband, Merritt Jordan Thompson, is the father of Grace's daughter. She resolves to bring the child to live with her, to live separately from Mr. Thompson, and to learn all she can by reading a book about prostitution that Grace has given her, *The Social Evil* (1909) by Joseph H. Greer. In a parable that Grace tells Mrs. Thompson, the social evil operates as if men and women were in a boat that had capsized but could save themselves by clinging to a bridge above them. Passersby lift the men to safety, but women tread upon the hands of the other women clinging to the bridge, sending them back into the water: "[W]hile both fall into the water, the woman likes it so well that she always remains with the mermaids" (181), "mermaids" being the fable's analogy for a life of prostitution. The book's socialism caused critic Walter Rideout to describe *The Rose Door*'s message as "the wages of capitalistic sin is death," yet the cooperation that the novel promotes is less about organized labor than the collaboration of women to expose the social evil that inevitably touches their lives.[50]

All the stories intertwine at the Rose Door, but instead of being an end point for women's shattered lives, the place becomes a clearinghouse for women to meet and expose the secrecy and hypocrisy of men's lives. Like other white slave novels, *The Rose Door* exposes an underground system. Yet this network is composed not of women snatched and drugged against their will but of the secrecy and hypocrisy of men's networks. The double lives that men lead contaminate the home front with physical and moral disease, but their hidden networks of power and privilege can be exposed if women work together with the devices available to them, including the technology of writing and the assumption of undercover identities. Although its strong reform message precludes a designation of classic naturalism, *The Rose Door* combines familiar elements of unruly naturalism, including abjection and the treatment of women as waste, sexual abuse, and physical and moral contamination, with a strong Progressive reform message that recommends the development of women's networks through the power of communications technologies and the written word.

LITTLE LOST SISTER

In *My Battles with Vice* (1915) and *Little Lost Sister* (1914), Virginia Brooks (1886–1929) turns personal experiences into a nonfiction narrative and a white slave novel. *My Battles with Vice* is an undercover narrative in which Brooks adopts a series of disguises to infiltrate a working-class restaurant, department store, mail-order house, sweatshop, and vaudeville theater to observe firsthand the girls lured into prostitution, even posing as a madam to establish how easy it would be to procure girls for a brothel. At the Cafe Sinister, a place with an allegorical name that plays a prominent role in *Little Lost Sister*, she sees a gray-haired man buying drinks for a young girl, and Lil, her companion explains that he is "a trailer for a gang. . . . It's a red kimono for hers, and not much else. Do you get me?"[51] The iconic red kimono as the uniform of prostitution recurs throughout the book. Hearing that the girl has committed suicide, Brooks reflects that the man "no doubt has found another tenant for the red kimono Lil spoke of" (93). She later meets a "little girl of fifteen" (94) dressed in "red slippers and a red kimono" who is so "delirious with drugs" that she can barely remember her own name (96). In her undercover disguise, Brooks receives advice on how best to get money from men, and she sees and hears beatings, thefts, and horrifying stories told in coarse language. When she emerges to tell her story, Brooks concludes that society is at fault for the poverty, the overcrowding, and especially the ignorance of "the essentials of sex knowledge" (244) that would have prevented some of the girls from falling into the trap.

Little Lost Sister trims the multiple vignettes of white slavery and disguises in *My Battles with Vice* to a single undercover narrative and rescue plot. As with other white slave novels such as *The House of Bondage*, *Little Lost Sister* underwent several adaptations in drama and film. It sparked what would today be called musical tie-ins such as sheet music showing a weeping young woman banished from her parents' humble country home, an image that has everything to do with generic white slave images and nothing to do with "Virginia Brooks's Great White Slave Play," as the cover proclaims. Yet its publication history contains a mystery, one that aligns changing literary fashions with the reception of women's writing. The first edition of the novel, published in 1914 by Gazzolo and Ricksen, appears with a title page that states "By Virginia Brooks, author of 'My Battles with Vice.'" A frontispiece portrait of Brooks bears her signature, and Laura Hapke credits Brooks as the author in *Girls Who Went Wrong*. Yet retrospective accounts by Westbrook Pegler and Charles Washburn published in the 1930s attribute authorship to a host of men—Arthur Pegler, Charles Michelson, Edward Rose, and Robert E. Ricksen—everyone whose name was associated with the project, in fact, except Brooks herself. Their recollections not only deny Brooks's authorship but also ignore the undercover narrative of the crusading reformist heroine in favor of ridiculing the old-fashioned sentimentality of the white slave plot.

Little Lost Sister began life as a play "by Virginia Brooks; dramatized by Arthur James Pegler and Edward E. Rose" from a series of newspaper articles.[52] In 1938, the conservative columnist Westbrook Pegler recalled his father, Arthur James Pegler, as writing three acts in a week for $100 an act—"I know he wrote it because I saw him write it"—and credited his father with the original muckraking articles on which the novel was based. He downplays Brooks's involvement by calling her "just a local vice crusader" whose "name was hot" and consequently got paid more for the use of her name than Pegler did.[53] When the play was revived in 1939 under the title *She Gave Him All She Had*, the former *Chicago Tribune* reporter Charles Washburn identified himself as the coauthor of the play and provided a slightly different version of the novel's genesis. It "started innocently enough as a serial expose of Chicago's underworld and was cooked up by one Charles Michelson, then editor of *The Chicago American* and later rather prominent in Democratic national circles."[54] According to Washburn, Pegler wrote the articles and was, with Washburn, commissioned by A. P. Gazzolo to write a play based on the articles. Gazzolo wanted to use Brooks's name and, through Washburn, she as-

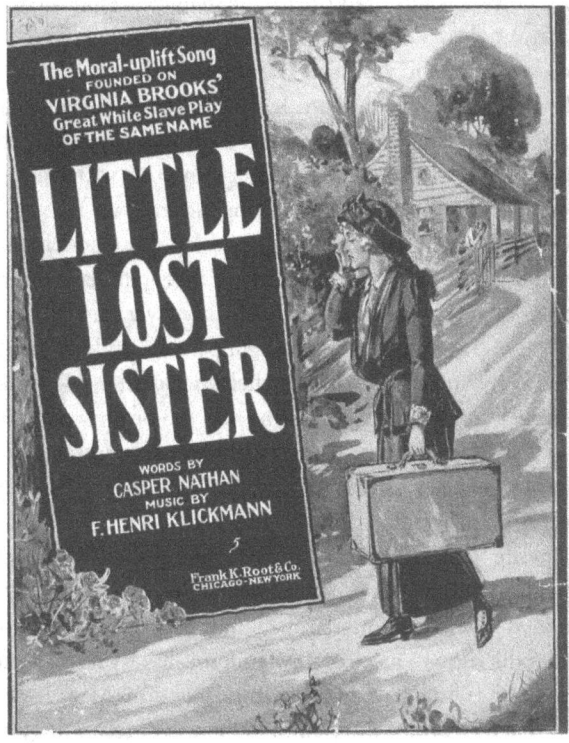

Sheet music cover for "Little Lost Sister" by Caspar Nathan and F. Henri Klickman, "The Moral-uplift Song Founded on Virginia Brooks' Great White Slave Play of the Same Name," 1914.

sented, since Washburn was then "managing" her affairs as a sideline, as he coyly puts it. Married at the time, Brooks and Washburn were divorced in 1917.[55]

In 1934, however, Washburn gave a different version of the book's genesis in *Come into My Parlor: A Biography of the Aristocratic Everleigh Sisters of Chicago*. Brooks "was in the news, but she couldn't write," he recalls.[56] Pegler's version "was dumped after the spring try-out" (242), leaving the "play doctor" "Edward E. [*sic*] Rose" to rescue it, which he did. "It sold out at every performance. It was the first of the 'white slave' plays, timely, open-faced, and popular-priced—one dollar for the best seats" (242), Washburn reports. He adds that it has "the greatest third act opening of all the 'white slave' dramas': two men sit in a cabaret with red lamps on the tables, while offstage a whip cracks, a girl screams, and one man on stage announces to another that the man with the whip is "goin' to keep beatin' her till she gives in to him" (243). "How could the play fail? . . . It was all show, all 1913, all chambermaid," adds Washburn, amused at the shameless emotional appeal to unsophisticated lower-class audiences, especially women, who liked their morality liberally sauced with sex and violence. Washburn credits Charles Michelson and indirectly Elizabeth Robins with the title: "Mr. Michelson, while seeking a title for the newspaper series, picked up a copy of the book, 'My Little Sister,' lying on his desk, remarking: 'If we can get Little Sister into a title we have something.' He added the Lost, a stroke of genius and befitting the era" (242).

In *Little Lost Sister*, with its title a masterstroke of public relations reworked from the simplicity of Robins's, the sincerity of the white slave reform novel becomes purely an object of ridicule. A scornful reviewer for the *New York Times* called the revival of the play an "overwrought parable" and faulted it for not being as hilarious as it should be.[57] And Michelson had an inside track on a satirical view of the white slave narrative, for he was the brother of Miriam Michelson, author of *A Yellow Journalist* (1905). Although accounts apportion varying levels of credit to Pegler, Washburn, Rose, and Michelson, the men surrounding Brooks, each is consistent in downplaying Brooks's involvement and abilities ("she couldn't write"), making her an old-fashioned and slightly ridiculous figure. Each also ridicules a form of drama and a plot that seemed hopelessly sentimental and old-fashioned in an age of modernism. In their eagerness to sweep the play and novel under the rug as a piece of silly feminine literary history and to ridicule the melodrama of the white slave hysteria, none mentions Mary Randall, the novel's dauntless female reformer who, through the use of technology and disguise, engineers the exposure of the white slave trade and rescues the young girl caught in its trap.

Little Lost Sister combines two stories, the first a traditional white slave tale with two sisters, and the second an undercover narrative of the woman reformer determined to break up the vice ring. When Elsie Welcome, a mill worker, asks for but does not receive a raise to support her alcoholic father and sickly mother, she declares that she will go to Chicago. Her small-town beau, Harvey Spencer, proposes to her, but instead she leaves for Chicago with the smooth-talking Martin Druce, who promises Elsie a career as a singer, tricks her with a mock marriage, and forces her into prostitution. In the meantime, Elsie's older and more level-headed sister Patience goes to Chicago to find her. Glimpses of the old white slave plot appear in this strand of the novel: Elsie, pathetically clinging to Druce, whom she still believes is her husband, is finally rescued and returns to Millville with her mother, where she reconciles with the faithful Harvey on her deathbed before breathing her last.

In a nod to the moral lessons of other white slave narratives, *Little Lost Sister* employs allegorical language and symbolic naming to emphasize its points. When Elsie flees, Lou calls her "a little lost lamb turned loose in a den of you human hyenas" (228). A reformer is "Wyat Carp," reflecting the tough stance of lawman Wyatt Earp and the fact that the character "carps" about reform but takes no action. Elsie's surname is "Welcome," for her trusting nature; her sister is "Patience," for that virtue and her fortitude; and her employer is the capitalist John Price. The chief of police is Captain Shammer (123), who does not arrest brothel keepers but sends a henchman to "tell the girls to go slow on the piano playing," thus keeping up appearances without altering the status quo (124). A Reverend Stillwell is "cautious in all things" (126), including refusing to stir up muddy waters by leading a crusade against corruption. The "Cafe Sinister," the center of the action, is a place of "men shrunk to the moral stature of animals," including Boland the tiger and Druce "the wolf; cunning, ruthless, prowling" (204). Early in the novel, Druce announces himself as "a dealer in live stock" (56), and to drive the point home, Kentucky Lou, a hardened prostitute, explains to Elsie that Druce is "a dealer in human live stock, a trafficker in women, one of the oldest professions in the world—and the dirtiest" (224). She herself was "prime stock" (226) and, when she escaped to "one of these institutions that advertise to help friendless girls" (227), they gave her only "tracts, and sermons and advice" (227) in place of help, a familiar complaint. The novel employs other stereotypes as well, providing a clueless detective in the form of Elsie's faithful Millville suitor, Harvey Spencer, and making Martin Druce an over-the-top drug addict who immediately after getting out of prison shoots himself up with morphine, drinks absinthe, and sends Elsie out for laudanum (298) before his well-deserved death.

In contrast to the traditionally allegorical white slave plot, the reform plot features Mary Randall, the resourceful heroine who goes undercover to expose the white slavery ring and to rescue the young women. Impatient with the slow pace of reform, Mary announces that "the time for theory is over" and that "[s]omeone has got to go into action against the wolves" (113), by which she means not simply brothel keepers but the system of corrupt businesses and government officials that allows them to function. In keeping with the novel's scheme of allegorical naming, the alias Mary takes for herself is "Miss Masters," indicating her intent to dominate her enemies. She goes undercover and gets a job as secretary to John Boland, the head of the Electric Trust. From here she gathers evidence for what she calls her "bombs," anonymous blue envelopes containing incriminating messages that, left at the offices of the businessmen, cause them to change course in their support for corruption. When the system itself is corrupt, Mary, like an anarchist of the era, believes the best solution is to take matters into her own hands to effect violent change.

From her place behind the typewriter, Mary wields real power, refusing entrance to Boland's office for those wishing to renew their leases on the brothels. From here she goes further undercover to trap the malefactors, staying at the Cafe

Sinister and posing as a madam to purchase girls as part of her exposé. Mary's most ingenious plan is to use multiple recording technologies to gather evidence. With the help of her maid, Anna, she installs a "complete dictagraph apparatus" with a transmitter hidden beneath the carpet,[58] a camera in the window that takes a picture when the curtain is raised, and, in a closet, a "small table, a pocket electric light and her stenographer's notebook" (243) so that Anna, also a trained stenographer, can record the conversations. Her plan to trap the white slavers includes the strategic deployment of recording technologies and the collaboration of another woman whose expertise in stenography matches her own. With this system in place, Mary assumes an undercover identity that, like Rhoda's Chinese woman in *A Yellow Journalist* and Mrs. Kenyon's disguise as a hairdresser, allows her to hide in plain sight and collect evidence to expose the networks that protect the traffic in women.

As in *The Rose Door* (and as in a later section of *A Yellow Journalist*), recording technologies level the playing field. Dictograph, camera, and knowledge of stenography all give women the means to form networks through writing and to record to counter men's secret strategies for continuing white slavery. In their early positions as mediators of transcription technologies such as typewriters and dictographs, women were considered as virtually parts of the machine, necessary human mediators or transmitters through which men's thoughts would pass without alteration. *The Rose Door*, *A Yellow Journalist*, and other novels by women challenge this assumption by showing women who seize control of recording technologies for their own purposes, using technological means to rectify the imbalance of power and privilege that allows male corruption to thrive.

White Slavery in Film

Women's use of technology to thwart networks of corruption appears in white slave films as well, most notably *The Inside of the White Slave Traffic*, *Traffic in Souls*, and *The Red Kimona*. *The Inside of the White Slave Traffic* follows Annie, a hardworking young woman who meets George, a procurer, who drugs her drink and keeps her out all night. Her stern father, living in "The Home of Yesterday," throws her out, a parental mistake that occurs elsewhere in white slave texts as well as in Crane's *Maggie: A Girl of the Streets* and Theodore Dreiser's "Old Rogaum and His Theresa" (1901). Tricked into a mock marriage with George and left by him in a brothel, she escapes to other cities, but, as an intertitle puts it, "The system is everywhere." Much telegraphing occurs between Annie's captors, and as part of its documentary evidence the film devotes one intertitle to the telegraphic "[c]ode used by Traffickers in the United States." After being arrested and put through a program of rehabilitation, Annie works in a department store, but she "grows weary of being poor" and goes back to her old life. Thinking of home, she eventually dies and is "laid away, an outcast, in the Potter's Field." In addition to the classic white slave tropes (drugged drinks, mock marriage, parental misunderstanding), *The Inside of the White Slave Traffic* suggests the dangers of leisure spaces such as drugstores and restaurants for young women. More significantly, it indicts the national vice networks that make Annie's imprisonment possible through communications technologies like the telegraph.

Traffic in Souls employs many of the same significant tropes as white slave fiction, including the two-sister plot with a frivolous younger sister rescued by her sensible older sister, and its popularity ensured that these would reach an audience beyond that of white slave narratives in print. According to Christopher Diffee, on the "opening night of *Traffic in Souls* on November 24, 1913, a thousand people were turned away from Joe Weber's Theater in New York City.... More than thirty thousand people saw the film in its opening week," although by February 1914 the wave of white slave films had passed, with "both *Variety* and *Moving Picture World* refus[ing] to accept further advertisements for vice films."[59] As Diffee, Shelley Stamp, and Tom Gunning have shown in their comprehensive analyses of the film, intersecting plots in *Traffic in Souls* indict the social class that profits from white slavery and herald the resourcefulness not only of the middle-class heroine but also of the policeman who, contrary to the usual negative depictions of indifferent law enforcement in these films, acts courageously to expose the traffickers.[60] In the middle-class family at the center of the plot, Mary Barton and her younger sister, Lorna, work in a candy store and live with their disabled and homebound father, an inventor, until Lorna is enticed away from the candy shop where both sisters work. In the upper-class family, wealthy businessman William Trubus heads the International Purity and Reform League and encourages his daughter's engagement to the scion of a prominent family, the "greatest society 'catch' that season." But Trubus also heads the vice ring that runs the traffic in women, and when Mary goes undercover as his secretary, she and Officer Burke record evidence of his crimes. In a race-to-the-rescue chase, police find and release Lorna from the confines of the brothel before it is too late. Confronted with the evidence, which has also been turned over to the police, Trubus crumbles with grief, and his daughter's fiancé spurns the now-disgraced family.

In addition to the traditional features of the white slave narrative, women's use of technology drives the plot of *Traffic in Souls*. The film calls attention to the importance of writing and recording devices early in the film by having one character ask another about the wax cylinder recording device on the desk. Trubus replies, "It's a dictagraph," but he does not explain the other ingenious technological device, a writing tablet and electric stylus that causes the words he writes

Mary Barton and Officer Burke hide the dictograph in a wastebasket to catch Mr. Trubus, who runs the city's white slave operations, from *Traffic in Souls* (1913).

to appear on a remote tablet in his henchman's office. The counterpoint to Trubus's device is Mary's father's invention of an amplification device. When Mary becomes Trubus's secretary and discovers his control over the city's prostitution racket by listening to his dictograph, she borrows her father's invention to amplify and record the sound from Trubus's private office. An extended sequence shows Mary and Officer Burke, who is in love with her, wiring Trubus's office and hiding the device in the wastebasket. Armed with the wax cylinders that have recorded Trubus's guilt, Mary and Burke reveal all to the police captain, whose men raid the brothel and rescue her sister. In *Traffic in Souls* as in *Little Lost Sister*, women's undercover identities and their ingenious use of technology allow them to expose and to destroy the networks that men have arranged to keep the white slave trade hidden.

Less overtly concerned with technology, *The Red Kimona* focuses instead on the forms of publicity that make reintegration into society difficult. Produced by Dorothy Davenport, billed as "Mrs. Wallace Reid," who appears at the beginning and end of the film in an authenticating sequence, *The Red Kimona* was written by the journalist Adela Rogers St. Johns and edited by Dorothy Arzner, who would become one of Hollywood's few female directors in the 1930s and 1940s. It is based on the true story of a woman, Gabrielle, forced into prostitution by her lover, whom she kills when he announces that he will marry someone else. The film's primary message is that of false and true redemption: the false reintegration into society promised by a fickle society woman, Mrs. Fontaine, who shows off Gabrielle as this year's pet project, and the true redemption that occurs when Gabrielle joins the Red Cross to do war work. After the authenticating prologue, the film opens as Gabrielle tells her story in flashback from the witness box where she is on trial for murder. She recalls her adolescence in a small town and the indifference of her parents: her father is too distant and irritable, and her mother too caught up in reading a magazine, to notice when she leaves the house to meet Howard Blaine, the man who promises to marry her when they reach New Orleans. Instead of marrying her, he sets her up in a house of prostitution, where she labors for ten years in a run-down row house. The entrance to the dark, shabby neighborhood has a large stone portal, an arch with a red light affixed to it, that announces a clear demarcation between its inhabitants and the daylight life of the city.

As suggested by the arch, the movie's symbolism is largely rendered visually rather than through intertitles, a more sophisticated technique characteristic of films made during the last years of the silent era, 1925–27. For example, when a group of gossipy society women press Gabrielle to tell of her experiences, a maid's perspective reveals them dissolving into a circle of cats watching a helpless mouse. As in Austin's *No. 26 Jayne Street*, rings signify the heroine's legal status and carry enormous emotional weight. As a badge of her profession, Gabrielle wears an elaborate, expensive ring that Blaine has given her, which she looks at sadly from time to time as she contemplates her life. Her discovery of Blaine's faithlessness occurs when, in looking wistfully at a display of wedding rings in a jeweler's window, she sees him buying a wedding ring for another woman. Distraught at his actions, she kills him, and her elaborate ring goes to pay for the lawyer who defends her. When Gabrielle, released from jail and working as a maid, sees her ring again, it is on the hand of her lawyer's wife, reinforcing the idea that respectable women may condemn women living in prostitution but are not too proud to profit from the money and goods stripped from them.

The contrasting rings reinforce another visual cue, the use of the color red in the otherwise black-and-white movie. At one point, Gabrielle looks into a mirror and imagines herself in a bridal veil, only to have the image dissolve into the reality of herself dressed in a red kimono, the garment hand-tinted red in those frames to dramatically emphasize the color, a feature that visually links red with prostitution throughout the film. When Gabrielle seeks work in a hospital, the administrator asks her, "Aren't you that Gabrielle woman?" and, as Gabrielle nods her assent, he sees a scarlet A glowing on her white dress. Most overtly, the red of Gabrielle's kimona and of the light that illuminates the archway to the red-light district where she lives visually echoes the red of the Red Cross posters that she sees throughout the movie. Because red connotes shame in the film's visual iconography, the red of the posters is not tinted, since it represents salvation through service.

Repeatedly asking for useful work to do, Gabrielle believes that hard physical

Gabrielle imagines the bride she might have been,
from *The Red Kimona* (1925).

A few moments after envisioning herself as a bride,
Gabrielle turns away from the image of what she has become,
from *The Red Kimona* (1925). In the original prints,
the kimono (or "kimona") was hand-tinted in red.

labor, such as nursing or working as a cleaning woman, will effect her redemption. Despite the idleness she is forced to endure at Mrs. Fontaine's, she finds a champion in Freddy, Mrs. Fontaine's chauffeur. Freddy, whose real name is Terrance O'Day, brings an Irish working-class irreverence and humor to the film that contrasts with the snobbery and hypocrisy of his employer. When the housekeeper chastises Gabrielle for borrowing a book from Mrs. Fontaine's library, he quips, "No, Buttercup—you know that's the bunk—the Duchess don't even know she has a book." Later, before quitting, he tells Mrs. Fontaine, "You just happened to be lucky—you got a wedding ring," linking the wealthy woman's respectability to chance and a ring rather than to innate morality. He takes Gabrielle to an amusement park, sympathetically dismisses her past as a tough break, and asks her to marry him. He understands her need to earn "the right to happiness" by scrubbing floors and serving in the hospital during the flu epidemic and agrees to wait until the war is over.

By agreeing to wait, Freddy credits Gabrielle with having the same code of honor about paying one's moral debts that a man might have, and his acceptance both of her past and of waiting suggests that theirs will be an equal partnership. When Freddy finds her at last after a series of missed chances, Gabrielle is scrubbing the floor of the hospital under a Red Cross poster on the wall. Gabrielle's literal cleansing of the floors renders a figurative transformation of the blot represented by her past—not her killing of Blaine, but the life of prostitution. The film ends on this message of forgiveness in the concluding authenticating frame, when Mrs. Wallace Reid (Dorothy Davenport) reappears to urge the audience to "[r]emember the deathless words of the Carpenter of Nazareth, 'Ye that is without sin among you, let him cast the first stone.'" In making a case for a sympathetic treatment of the fallen woman, even one who murders the man who betrayed her, Davenport, St. Johns, and Arzner make a case for practical regeneration through service and the promise of a happy marriage of equals to follow.

With their reform messages, journalistic roots, and overt evocation of sympathy, women's fallen-woman narratives rarely fall under the category of classic naturalism but instead suggest unruly naturalism. Indeed, with the exception of Edith Wharton's fragment "One Day," straightforward naturalistic treatments of the street girl are much more scarce in women's fiction than in the fiction of Norris, Crane, Dreiser, and London, although they appear repeatedly in case studies, journalism, memoirs, and film. Nor is the fallen woman a single, easily defined entity. For example, as the cases of Evelyn Nesbit and Grace Brown reveal, the simple pattern of evil seducer and innocent victim becomes complicated when triangulated with the biological fact of women's sexual desire and the need for social mobility, factors further blurred by the demands of a sensationalized publicity culture that requires the exposure of their secrets.

The structural and rhetorical choices of women's fallen-woman narratives also require a balancing act, since each provides the possibility of rhetorical excesses. Too much religious or reform rhetoric would render the narratives dull or unreadably vague, as with parts of Mrs. Lydia Taylor's *From under the Lid: An Appeal to True Womanhood* (1913). Too much sensationalism would discourage middle-class readers who might see the tale as suitable only for pulp outlets, yet too much sentimentalism could dilute the reform message in a shared pool of ineffectual tears. The problem that the writers faced was to make compelling a single situation of seduction, rape, and forced prostitution or abandonment when hundreds of such cases could be amassed in a single documentary volume. For example, the case studies in *The Great War on White Slavery* or *A New Conscience and an Ancient Evil* give the effect of narrative sameness despite the details of their documentary evidence. To combat this sameness, writers adapted other forms, such as the liberation narrative and the Gothic, to transmit the horrors of their stories at an affective and visceral level as well as an intellectual one. Writers such as Robins and Norris intensify rhetorical strategies such as the distortion of time and space common to the Gothic, whereas Kimball and Blair distort the white slave plotline of innocence, recognition, trials, and redemption borrowed from the liberation narrative. The straightforward narration in Kimball's and Blair's accounts of their lives as businesswomen whose profession happened to be prostitution lends credence to their success narratives and confirms the business novel as one part of the model that they adopted.

In their undercover narratives, Baker, Michelson, and Brooks demonstrate that transcription technologies of writing and recording, especially the dictograph and typewriter, amplify the power of women's words. To the narrative tension of rescuing the young victim before she is ruined, they add other naturally occurring forms of suspense, such as the woman's daring undercover journey to find evidence, her solving the mystery of untangling the web of corrupt institutions that permit white slavery to flourish, or her thwarting the forces aligned against her so that she can reveal the corruption to the world. Although they cannot compete with men's physical strength in keeping women imprisoned, as both white slave novels and films such as *The Inside of the White Slave Traffic* and *Traffic in Souls* make clear, the elder sister, undercover reporter, vice crusader, or a combination of the three can, through ingenious uses of technology, make men convict themselves by using their own words against them.

CHAPTER 5

Where Are My Children?
Race, Citizenship, and the Stolen Child

In Edith Wharton's *Summer* (1917), as part of a day's excursion that the protagonist, Charity Royall, takes with her lover, Lucius Harney, the two of them go to the movies. The film has an almost hypnotic effect on Charity and "the crowd around her, the hundreds of hot sallow candy-munching faces, young, old, middle-aged, but all kindled with the same contagious excitement" who "became part of the spectacle, and danced on the screen with the rest."[1] During the early years of the twentieth century, the experience of watching a moviegoing crowd, usually construed as working-class or immigrant spectators, fascinated contemporary middle-class writers as well as modern film historians and theorists. In her classic *Babel and Babylon: Spectatorship in Silent Film*, Miriam Hansen posits the viewing space of cinema as a "time-place," a "heterotopia" that both in the "theater's physical space" and the "phantasmagoric space on the screen" held particular promise for women, who could "experience forms of collectivity different from those centering on the family."[2] In the Progressive Era, when the medium of film and the dynamics of film spectatorship were as much the subject of discussion as the films themselves, Wharton was not alone in commenting on the ability of a film, however ludicrous in plot, to merge the audience momentarily into a single whole as they identified with the characters on the screen and became "part of the spectacle."

In its early years film was seen as a medium for national assimilation, a form that could unite disparate, polyglot, and often illiterate immigrant populations and educate them in American values. In "Some Picture Show Audiences" for the *Outlook* in 1911, Mary Heaton Vorse noted that "[t]he American-born sat next to the emigrant who had arrived but a week before" and "for the moment they were permitted to drink deep of oblivion of all the trouble in the world." To these audiences, Vorse continues, the movies are "[o]pportunity—a chance to glimpse the beautiful and strange things in the world that you haven't in your life," a sentiment that prefigures Wharton's "all the world has to show." Like Wharton, Vorse sees a class dimension to immersion in this spectacle, for "the keener your intellectual ability... the more difficult it is to find this total forgetfulness."[3] Unlike the bored operagoers of Wharton's *The Custom of the Country* and *The Age of Innocence*, who, except for Newland Archer, ignore the spectacle on stage in favor of the social spectacle in the audience, the working-class audience of Vorse's piece, like the audience at Nettleton, becomes immersed in the life they see on the screen. Only Harney stands apart, since he shares Wharton's upper-class lack of ease at such an outpouring of manufactured emotion and a class-based sense of himself as an observer of the film experience rather than a participant in it.

Although progressives such as Jane Addams were initially reluctant to acknowledge the teaching function that films could provide, by the end of the decade they understood the medium as an important tool for disseminating information about the goals and practices of citizenship.[4] Yet to avoid what reviewers increasingly derided as "preachment," filmmakers like Alice Guy-Blaché, Reginald Barker, Oscar Micheaux, and Lois Weber relied increasingly on signifiers within a film that would question the country's definitions of citizenship as well as teaching its boundaries. By freighting the ordinary object with extraordinary meaning and encoding it with multiple significances, they were able to suggest not only the qualifications for citizenship but also its problematic nature. In fiction, women writers and writers of color challenged exclusionary definitions of citizenship and the dominant culture's pressure to assimilate through a theme that appears in women's writing during the early twentieth century: the "stolen child." The stolen child is an assault on racial and class lines, an attempt to wrest control of what ought to be a basic human right—the bearing of children—and make it conform to the dictates of the state. Fiction by Sui Sin Far, Alice Dunbar-Nelson, and Ann Petry reaffirms the grim realists' conviction that no institutional home can compete with an actual home. Taking their argument a step further, Mary E. Wilkins Freeman's *The Portion of Labor* and Wharton's *Summer* link definitions of citizenship with the woman's body, in Freeman's case the appropriation of children by a ruling class, and in Wharton's case the ability of a woman to rise above her origins to claim citizenship and make her own reproductive choices. The unruly naturalism of these narratives exists in the women's use of technology, the prominence of children, the treatment of race, and the progressive social vision that overrides naturalism's clinical objectivity in favor of ambiguous affective appeals.

Making American Citizens

Immigration films of the early silent era relied on a series of familiar tropes. Among these were the departure from the old country, often depicted as a site of desolation and poverty; an emotional parting from family and community; shipboard scenes and the first sight of the Statue of Liberty; the documentation process at Ellis Island; and an adjustment to American customs. As Kevin Brownlow explains, because most film companies of this era were located in New York or New Jersey, many films such as *Gateway to America* (1912) included scenes shot on Ellis Island or footage of immigrants disembarking from the ferries that carried them from the island to the Battery at the tip of Manhattan.[5] Despite the general premise that immigration to the United States would result in prosperity, a conclusion generally established by shots of the protagonists adapting to American ways, the films did attempt to address the anxieties of those leaving their homeland for an unknown future. For example, *Adrift in a Great City* (1914) dramatized fears of failing to meet one's family members at the pier, and *One More American* (1918) features a corrupt physician turning back an immigrant family after falsely declaring a child diseased. In a more positive vein, *An American in the Making* (1913), a film produced by U.S. Steel, emphasized the industrial safety features in its plants and such amenities as its reading rooms, all with signs in multiple languages, to encourage laborers to work in its mills. Leaving aside those such as *Emigranten* (1910), produced in Sweden specifically to discourage emigration to America, these films extolled the virtues of the American way of life and advertised its need for immigrant labor. Their role in educating "greenhorns," the slang term used for immigrants unaccustomed to American ways, often took the form of comedies in which the greenhorn learned to assimilate by making a series of humorous mistakes until his education was complete. Yet later immigrant films also expressed anxieties over the dissolution of families as the new generation rejected the ways of the old country.

The immigrant film transferred the ethnic stereotyping and nostalgia found in vaudeville to a new medium. As in fiction, nostalgia took two forms: the immigrant or ethnic humor stereotypes held up for both recognition and mockery, and the search for a mythic location of stable American values. Irish, German, Swedish, and other forms of ethnic and race-based humor provided forms of instant identification that operated across all media. As Henry B. Wonham argues in *Playing the Races*, the caricature that constitutes ethnic stereotyping "performs a defensive function, stabilizing the realist's social vision against threats of upheaval from outside" but may also "disturb an excessively complacent social vision by entertaining the possibility that identity may be entirely a performative affair."[6] In serious literature, such as that of Howells, Wharton, and James, among those whom Wonham cites, the contrast exists contextually on the page, either within the illustration of the ethnic character or the text itself. The contrast between ethnic exaggeration in dialect and the narrator's realist prose relies on the reader's ability to read both registers.

Ivan Orloff drives as his wife is hitched to the cart,
from Alice Guy-Blaché's *Making an American Citizen* (1912).

In early film and vaudeville, on the other hand, identity had to be "entirely a performative affair." Exaggerated costumes and gestures make the ethnic persona impossible to read seriously as realism since it exists apart from a realist narrative frame in a moment that cannot be compared or repeated. On the stage, outsize gestures, exaggerated dialects, and costumes with signature ethnic features required belief in the artifice, at least for unsophisticated working-class viewers such as those in Crane's *Maggie* or Norris's *McTeague*. Silent film removed the affective dimension of sound, forcing the performers to render their effects through key material signifiers such as a monocle for an Englishman or a moustache, hoop earrings, and slouch hat for Italian men. Stereotypical gestures completed the picture, since the representation of dialect in intertitles was clumsy at best and a barrier to understanding for those in the audience who spoke or read little English.[7] The effect was to create a shared understanding of a distant and mythical homeland, one composed of the stereotypical signs of ethnicity that evoked the sentiments of patriotism for a distant fatherland.

Alice Guy-Blaché's one-reel comedy *Making an American Citizen* (1912) treats the issues of immigration with a feminist touch, making the respectful treatment of women a prime requirement for citizenship.[8] The film opens with Ivan Orloff and his wife on a road where some happy emigrants are about to leave for the United States. Unremarked by anyone in the group is the fact that Ivan's wife is hitched to the cart beside the donkey while Ivan, seated in the cart, brandishes a whip over both of them. Guy-Blaché's choice of visual comedy shifts the focus from the narrower problematic form of anti-immigrant sentiment to the comedy of relationships between the sexes, a gesture that displaces xenophobic anxiety onto the more universal agreement about the proper treatment of women in America.

Through a series of four lessons, Ivan becomes a U.S. citizen, which the film construes as learning to treat his wife as a person rather than as a work beast. Lesson one occurs in New York when Ivan's wife, staggering under the weight of all their possessions, stumbles to her knees despite Ivan's forceful proddings with a walking stick. A well-dressed American man intervenes, forcing Ivan to shoulder the bundle and teaching the wife to give Ivan a few prods with the stick in return.[9] From this encounter, Ivan concludes not that treating his wife as a beast of burden is wrong but that doing so in public brings consequences. When the two move into a tenement flat, Ivan again begins to abuse her, and another American bursts in to stop Ivan from beating her, apparently not bound by conventional expectations of privacy because of his class and nationality. Class is not the only key to Americanism: Ivan's every action is corrected by American men of every class, all of whom threaten violence against him whenever he abuses his wife. Like all the lessons that Ivan receives, the message is reinforced by legal as well as extralegal means. The Orloffs move to a house in the country, where Ivan sits on the porch and supervises his wife's hard labor in the garden. When she complains and nearly faints, Ivan begins to beat her. This time, men passing by rush into their cottage to rescue her and take her into the house, seeing to it that Ivan is sent to jail for assault.

The final scenes show Ivan after being released from jail. He now works willingly in the garden and brings a choice melon to his wife, who has assumed her proper American place in the domestic sphere inside the house. Prosperity and better manners are now theirs, and both cross their arms in prayer before eating dinner. Even before this ritual prayer before the meal, a holdover from the old country, Ivan participates in a ritual that signals his American rather than Russian citizenship: despite the heat of the day, Ivan carefully takes off his gardening smock and puts on a suit coat in preparation for dining. Providing a visual distinction not only between exterior and interior but also between work and leisure, the old ways and the new, the suit coat and the ceremonial pride with which Ivan dons it recalls the well-dressed man of the first lesson. He is putting on Americanism, and with it prosperity, at last.

Making an American Citizen presents a dual perspective on the nature of citizenship and privacy. The distinction between public and private seemingly does not exist for new immigrants like Ivan, for he is subjected to surveillance not only on the public space of the pier but also within his tenement flat, and later on his own front porch. Both city and country constitute the space of a panopticon, it seems, when one is designated as immigrant rather than citizen. Only when Ivan learns his fourth lesson about respect for women is his right to privacy within his own home guaranteed. The invasion of Ivan's privacy recalls a narrative device common to slum fiction and Progressive Era problem dramas, the much-hated intrusion of reformers into the homes of the poor and the state-ordered breakup

Ivan and his wife say grace before dinner,
from *Making an American Citizen* (1912).

of families supposedly for their own good, as in D. W. Griffith's *The Mother and the Law* (1914). Yet the behavioral policing to which Ivan is subjected occurs at the hands of his fellow citizens and not under the orders of the authorities, and the film ultimately appears to endorse, rather than condemn, lessons in citizenship roughly enforced as long as they include the equally important rights of women. Despite its xenophobic construction of Ivan's, and by extension his countrymen's, ignorance of respectful communications between the sexes, *Making an American Citizen* not only teaches American cultural mores but, through comedy, also promotes solidarity in the audience and a shared sense of community, even if that takes the uncomfortable form of ridiculing greenhorns.

Less comic and more realistically conceived is Reginald Barker's *The Italian* (1915), which presents a sympathetic portrait of an Italian immigrant, Beppo Donnetti, quite unlike that of earlier films such as *The Black Hand* (1906), which associated Italians with organized crime. The film begins as an Italian romance with the happy, singing gondolier Beppo falling in love with the beautiful Annette. To win her father's approval and stave off the advances of a rich, older suitor (whom the film establishes visually as an "old goat"), Beppo must leave Venice and go to the United States to seek his fortune. Seeking one's fortune is a plot staple of immigration films, and Barker includes the familiar scenes of the Statue of Liberty and a scene of anxiety when Beppo fears that he has missed Annette after she gets off the ferry. But if Beppo's story is conventional, its presentation is not. Instead of the usual scenario of leaving a grimly impoverished homeland for a golden America, the film depicts Italy as a fertile land of romance, whereas the urban slums of New York are presented in full naturalistic squalor.[10]

In New York, Beppo's shoeshine stand prospers, so he sends for Annette, marries her, and rejoices at the birth of their son, Tony. The action soon shifts to Beppo's fight to save his family against the indifference and criminality of native-born Americans and their institutions. Regulations enacted for the benefit of poor people fail repeatedly. The "pure milk" campaigns of the Progressive Era, which resulted in legislation to require that milk be pasteurized, mean little to Beppo, given the greater expense of the pasteurized milk needed to save his son. When Tony falls ill, an intertitle explaining the oppressive summer heat of New York tenements and a vivid shot of a crusted, fly-covered pan of milk that Annette must use to feed him reveal the source of his illness and subsequent death. Little Tony's illness destabilizes Beppo's precarious hold on citizenship, and his subsequent actions are cued to contemporary concerns about uncontrolled immigrant bodies and the ideological as well as physical diseases they might spread. In writing of this dual sense of contagion, Priscilla Wald notes that stories featuring "[t]he symbolic fluidity of diseases and their microbes ... helped to recast public health as national security, enlist[ing] bacteriologists and public-health officials ... in the project of representing the importance of social measures that reinforced national borders and documented individuals."[11]

The benefits of U.S. citizenship, so desirable in theory, are in practice bought and sold by Corrigan, for whom Beppo has faithfully turned out the Italian vote. Yet when two Americans steal the money he has saved to buy milk and Beppo asks for help, Corrigan refuses to aid him. Instead Beppo, because of his Italian ethnicity, is mistaken for the thief and imprisoned. When Beppo is released and learns of Tony's death, he decides to seek revenge by killing Corrigan's child. Once again the film resists stereotyping: in Corrigan's child's room, Beppo hesitates because the child's gesture of putting her hand under her chin while sleeping reminds him of little Tony. The gesture reins in the stereotypical gesture of an unrestrained immigrant seeking violent revenge, restoring Tony to his sense of humanity and to the self-control that marks his growth in citizenship.

Like *Making an American Citizen*, *The Italian* preaches self-control as a requirement for gaining citizenship. George Beban's much-praised restraint in acting the part of Beppo and the realism of the film's photography help him to sidestep the stereotype of the passionate, volatile Italian and to become what reviewers called the real figure of the Italian. But audiences had already been primed to see Beban as a restrained figure, since he appears as himself in the prologue and epilogue to the film. As the film begins, a pair of stage curtains draws back to reveal a cultured man, Beban, surrounded by the accoutrements of intellectual luxury, reading the story of *The Italian* just before the audience sees him acting in the title role. According to Charlie Keil, framing the story through the legitimate medium of print certifies the importance of the work for a middle-class audience.[12] Yet the copy of *The Italian* that Beban holds is itself a fiction generated for the screen rather than a demonstration of literacy. Credited to C. Gardner Sullivan and Thomas Ince, the illustrated book that Beban holds did not exist except as a prop. Moreover, Beban, a well-known stage actor, was actually an immigrant from Northern Ireland who had previously made a specialty of playing Frenchmen. As Sabine Haenni contends, the middle-class theatergoers would have recognized these shifts in identity, and all audiences, including those composed of immigrants, would have been forcefully reminded of the artifice by the framing sections.[13] The device of seeing Beban as himself in the framing sections, like the constant reminder of his real name in illustrated intertitle frames that announce Beban as the star, suggest that multiple identities, successfully negotiated, are one key to successful citizenship.

A more graphic indictment of bad citizenship than *The Italian* is Oscar Micheaux's *Within Our Gates* (1919), the earliest surviving feature film by an African American filmmaker, which like the earlier film portrays native-born white Americans betraying the ideals of the nation. The film is Micheaux's response to *The Birth of a Nation* (1915) and to the Chicago riots of 1919, and the climax of its complex plot is the lynching of an innocent black family and the attempted rape of the film's heroine. The film follows the efforts of its African American heroine, Sylvia Landry, to pursue a mission of racial uplift first by teaching in a church-run southern school for poor sharecroppers and then by raising funds for the school from white northerners. The thematic journey Sylvia undertakes is the struggle for education, equal rights, and a life unencumbered by the racist, patronizing manner of some whites and the racially motivated violence of others. Sylvia endures a number of tribulations, including suffering the duplicity of her friend Alma, being jilted by her fiancé, having her purse stolen, being struck by a car, and being threatened with blackmail by her friend's criminal brother, but the most serious, told in flashback, is the simultaneous lynching of Sylvia's adoptive family and the attempted rape of Sylvia by her (white) father.

Set in the South, the flashback sequence unfolds as Sylvia's friend Alma tries to explain Sylvia's background to Dr. V. Vivian, a man who had rescued Sylvia from a purse snatcher and had fallen in love with her. Film viewers who had read Henry Sydnor Harrison's *V. V.'s Eyes* (1913) would recognize at once that Dr. V. Vivian was the hero of *Within Our Gates*, for a character of the same name, also a physician, is the idealistic hero of that novel. Focusing at first on the theme of literacy, the early scenes of the flashback show Sylvia calculating the accounts of Jasper, her adoptive father, so that Mr. Philip Gridlestone will not be able to cheat him on his cotton crop. When Jasper tries to settle accounts with Mr. Gridlestone, Gridlestone knocks Jasper down and threatens him with a gun. A poor white sharecropper watches the scene through one window, and Efrem, Gridlestone's servile black butler, watches through another. When the white sharecropper shoots Gridlestone, Efrem spreads the word that Jasper is to blame. This staging of surveillance from two points of view, one from a white character and one from an African American, continues in the dual perspective of white and black informants. Micheaux reprises the scenes as they appear in the false accounts of the white-dominated newspaper, which features headlines about the "kindly white man" and the "crazed negro" who shoots him. In addition to his focus on surveillance and spectacle, Micheaux emphasizes the indiscriminate nature of violence against African Americans. When Sylvia's parents and younger brother Emil are dragged from their home in broad daylight by a crowd of white people, including women and children, the perpetrators are ordinary members of the crowd usually hidden behind Klan robes, deflating the grandeur with which Griffith invests the Klan and hammering home the concept that all white citizens are equally invested in, and responsible for, the senseless horror of lynching.

The scene of attempted rape connects the public violence of white lynching of innocent African Americans with the private violation of African American women. Seizing the opportunity while the town is distracted by preparations for the lynching, Gridlestone's brother Armand tracks down Sylvia during the lynching and assaults her. The two engage in an extended fight, and when Sylvia is cornered, Armand, in tearing her gown in preparation for raping her, uncovers a scar on her chest that forces him to recognize her as his daughter. The rapid crosscutting of scenes between scenes of the lynching and Gridlestone's attack on Sylvia echoes Griffith's crosscutting between the attempted rape of Flora by the "renegade" Gus and the ride to the rescue of the KKK in *The Birth of a Nation*. Although it contributes to a certain level of narrative confusion, at least in the extensively modified version of the film now extant, the scene of attempted rape supplies an important missing context for the erroneous history of black male aggression against white women that Griffith makes the centerpiece of *Birth of a Nation*: the real history of sexual abuse of black women by white men. As Jane Gaines contends, the "attack on Sylvia stands in as protest against all the master's sexual encounters with his own slave women, representing these encounters as acts of symbolic incest."[14]

Micheaux's use of the lynching plot is not new in cinema. In *A Spectacular Secret*, her study of the visual grammar of lynching photographs, Jacqueline Goldsby writes, "In early cinema—prior to either *Birth of a Nation* or *Within Our Gates*—lynching was a recurrent, organizing sight-event in the American movies," appearing in *Avenging Crime; or, Burned at the Stake* (1903) and Edwin S. Porter's *The Whitecaps* (1905) as well as in actual footage of an 1893 lynching, with later added sound, that played in Bowery theaters as late as 1908.[15] But the flashback to the lynching scene in *Within Our Gates* makes legible Sylvia's actions and the temporally disconnected shots of a pensive Sylvia staring into the middle distance. As David Gerstner suggests, Micheaux's use of flashback "penetrates the filmic present with the weight of a traumatic past" and contributes to the film's spatial and temporal ambiguity since "the spectator...is never given a precise correlation of time between cinematic spaces."[16] The constant surveillance, invasion of the private sphere, and comically delivered beatings that Ivan Orloff had to endure in *Making an American Citizen* intensify in *Within Our Gates* into the violent surveillance delivered in the name of citizenship, the invasion of the Landry family home during the lynching scene, and the fatal, indiscriminate nature of the policing effort—Efrem is also lynched, just because he is available—that indict officially promoted concepts of citizenship.

Even within such a horrific vision of America, however, Micheaux uses visual iconography to promote a different vision of citizenship. In a dialogue-heavy series of intertitles near the end of the film, Dr. Vivian reassures Sylvia about the future of the United States, urging her to recall the bravery of African Americans who served in Cuba with Theodore Roosevelt, in Mexico, and in France during World War I. As Koritha Mitchell writes, "[T]he black soldier personified African Americans' admirable character and valid claim to full citizenship.... Accordingly, periodicals brimmed with discussions of black soldiers," an observation confirmed by the May 1919 cover of *The Crisis*, the magazine of the NAACP.[17] Dr. Vivian has throughout been identified with Roosevelt: he is introduced as a "progressive," and in establishing his intellectual credentials the film lingers over shots of the doctor reading a copy of *Literary Digest* with Roosevelt on the cover.[18] Like Roosevelt, Dr. Vivian is a man of action as well as intellect and conscience: he and Sylvia first meet when he hears Sylvia's cries after her purse is stolen, and he catches the thief. Of the long list of battles Dr. Vivian cites in chronicling the bravery of African American troops and thus convincing Sylvia to stay in America, he mentions only one leader—Roosevelt—by name. Moreover, Dr. Vivian concludes his reasons for staying in the United States by saying, "We were never immigrants." According to Amy Kaplan, he asks Sylvia "to forget that domestic violence by another kind of displacement, by remembering military ventures abroad and marrying into imperial citizenship."[19]

But the appeal "We were never immigrants" is also a claim for authenticity of citizenship. Although it elides any mention of the horrors of slavery, Dr. Vivian's statement situates African Americans as primarily "Americans" and differentiates them from the "hyphenated Americans" that Roosevelt had attacked in a 1915 speech. By appealing to African Americans' superior sense of patriotism and citizenship tested in battle, Dr. Vivian does not ask Sylvia to forget all that she has suffered and look to imperial ventures, although Roosevelt signifies these as well. Instead he appeals to the image of Roosevelt as a progressive reformer, implying she must become a progressive and reform the nation instead of abandoning it.

Dr. V. Vivian looks at a picture of Theodore Roosevelt on the October 18, 1919, cover of the *Literary Digest*, from *Within Our Gates* (1919).

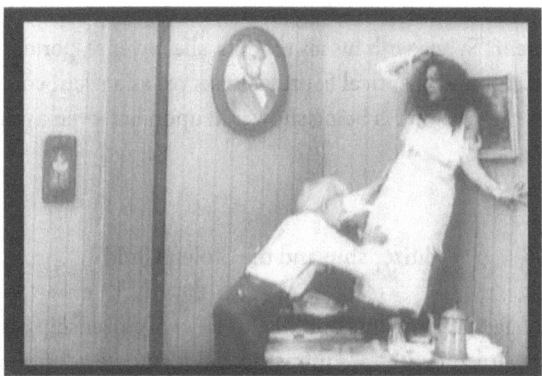

Sylvia fights off her attacker as a portrait of Lincoln looks on, from *Within Our Gates* (1919).

To reinforce this message of progressive future versus impotent past, Micheaux introduces a curious visual artifact in the rape scene. As Gridlestone wrestles with Sylvia, she takes refuge by climbing on a table, close to where a large oval portrait of Lincoln decorates the wall. At one point, the portrait's sight lines and Sylvia's gaze intersect, but even the image of the president revered for the Emancipation Proclamation can do nothing for Sylvia in the present when she is faced with a white southerner intent on harming her. Linking citizenship with romance, patriotism with protection, Dr. Vivian ultimately assures Sylvia, "You will always be a patriot, and a tender wife. I love you!" Yet throughout the long scene in which

Telling Sylvia "We were never immigrants," Dr. Vivian tries to convince a dubious Sylvia to remain in the United States, from *Within Our Gates* (1919).

Dr. Vivian presents Sylvia with his arguments, she never responds in words. Her obviously reluctant and skeptical expression serves as a silent counterargument to the patriotic rhetoric that is being showered upon her, even as she later agrees to marry Dr. Vivian.

Citizenship and the Stolen Child

Another challenge to the nation's optimistic vision of citizenship occurs in stories that feature the stolen child. In contrast to the fortunate adoptions of orphans in sentimental slum tales, the child in women's unruly naturalism is removed or threatened with removal from its parents by reformers or governmental forces, a plot used in films such as D. W. Griffith's *The Mother and the Law* (1914), Charlie Chaplin's *The Kid* (1921), and as late as 1927 in Clarence G. Badger's *It*, starring Clara Bow. Stolen child stories express the mother's, and by extension the oppressed culture's, anxieties about abuses of governmental power that put the lie to the nation's celebration of democracy. Unlike the short stories of grim realism and naturalism, in which the child is waste discarded by an uncaring society due to the sexual mores of parents or the child's presence as an indicator of poverty and social indifference, children in the Progressive Era come into their own as a national resource and potential workers. The struggle over the stolen child pits national citizenship and individual freedoms against the need for obedient masses of labor in an industrial marketplace.

The stolen child becomes the contested ground for competing ideological discourses of race, class, immigration, and citizenship. In the colonized terrain of urban tenements, where immigrants and people of color work for a dominant and isolated ruling class, stolen child stories are told from the point of view of the colonized instead of the colonizers. The emotionally charged incident of the theft of a child allows a voice of resistance—sometimes through the narrator, and sometimes through the characters themselves—to pierce the mantle of benevolence, uncover the structures of power and control that lie beneath, and resist the imperatives of class or cultural co-option that the stories reveal. Among the works in which the figure of the stolen child appears are Alice Dunbar-Nelson's unpublished 'Steenth Street stories "Miss Tillman's Protégé" and "Witness for the Defense," Sui Sin Far's "In the Land of the Free," Ann Petry's *The Street*, and Mary E. Wilkins Freeman's *The Portion of Labor*.

ALICE DUNBAR-NELSON, *THE ANNALS OF 'STEENTH STREET*

Less well known than her stories of Louisiana, Alice Dunbar-Nelson's (1875–1935) *The Annals of 'Steenth Street* is a collection of five stories of New York street life written from 1901 to 1910, only two of which were published during her lifetime. Drawn from Dunbar-Nelson's experiences as a settlement worker and teacher in 1897–98, the 'Steenth Street stories describe the impoverished Irish neighborhoods of the East Side of New York, specifically those bounded by Eighty-Seventh Street and Third Avenue.[20] They constitute Dunbar-Nelson's rewriting of the slum tale in its two principal forms. The first type, the sentimental tale of urban local color fiction celebrating the rough manners but good hearts of the poor, appears in "The Revenge of James Brown" and "The Ball Dress," and the second, the sensationalistic slice-of-life drama, in "Witness for the Defense." In stories such as "Witness for the Defense" and "Miss Tillman's Protégé," Dunbar-Nelson uses Irish immigrants in the tenements of 'Steenth Street to signify the African American community that she does not name. In these stories, children are the voice of resistance to the paternalistic or pseudomaternal ministrations of a dominant culture. The 'Steenth Street stories uncover the structures of power and control that lie beneath the impulses of white benevolence and reveal the ways in which communities resist these imperatives of class and cultural co-option.

In choosing to write about Irish Americans rather than African Americans in these stories, Dunbar-Nelson follows her usual practice of using class to signify issues of race, but she also uses a number of other "diversionary tactics," as Thomas Strychacz has called them, to raise issues of race and citizenship.[21] For example, in the surprisingly grim story "Tony's Wife" from *The Goodness of St. Rocque*, all the characters have their ethnicity loudly announced on their entrance into the story:

Antonio "Tony" Maletesta is a "great, black-bearded, hoarse-voiced, six-foot specimen of Italian humanity"; Mary is the meek German woman who lives with him and puts up with his physical abuse; and his "fair and blond" brother John is from Northern Italy.[22] When Tony lies dying and in so much pain that he can no longer beat Mary, she begs him to make her a respectable woman by marrying her, but fearing that she is after his money, Tony gives the money instead to John, who ignores her and leaves her destitute.

Dunbar-Nelson signals the symbolic nature of the two brothers by stretching the biological extremes of their appearance: they are not only physical opposites but despite being in the same family hail from two distinct parts of Italy. The darker Tony evokes the threatening stereotypes of the dark immigrant and the naturalistic brute, whereas his lighter brother John suggests the northern European who has assimilated into the nation's rules of citizenship. Both are equally brutal to women, however. Neither Tony, who inflicts pain upon Mary, nor John, who refuses to give her money and leaves her to starve, spares any thought for Mary, a suffering Madonna figure. Despite their differences of race and region, they unite in masculine indifference to Mary's plight. Dunbar-Nelson's feminist critique operates as an allegory of national indifference on the part of men of both races.

The first of the 'Steenth Street stories, "Miss Tillman's Protégé," reveals racial complexities in its decidedly unsympathetic portrait of its title character, a wealthy do-gooder who decides to adopt Hattie Gurton, the disabled child of a poor family. Miss Tillman tells Mrs. Morton, a settlement house matron, that she would like to adopt Hattie because "[s]he'd look lovely in a dear white apron with her hair smooth sitting at my feet in my study."[23] Miss Tillman is clearly interested in possibilities the adoption offers for patronage on her part and servitude on Hattie's, a desire made manifest in Miss Tillman's wish to see Hattie seated below her, her hair and demeanor controlled by Miss Tillman's touch. Moreover, unlike the Anglo-named Miss Tillman, Hattie and her family are Irish, a choice that makes them an ideal signifier for absent racial and ethnic Others, given the historically low position of the Irish, their status as a colonized people, and their positioning as ambiguously white.

Given the racial schemata of the times, it is not surprising that Miss Tillman treats Irish Americans as untouchable subaltern subjects whose unruly bodies must be tamed through their adoption of dominant modes of decorum. Like Melicent in Chopin's *At Fault*, who threatens to snip off Mandy's pigtail, Miss Tillman, who wishes to smooth out Hattie's presumably wild and untamed hair, enacts the colonizing gestures that lend extra force to class distinctions. Moreover, Miss Tillman's seeming benevolence cannot be separated from her excitement at slumming. As the narrator comments, "She was fond of taking her out of town friends 'slumming' and if perchance someone to whom she had been kind at one time met her with recognition, she would point out the incident rapturously and expatiate on the gratitude of the lowly" (103). Miss Tillman experiences a "thrill of pity" when she looks at Hattie and a "thrill of horror" when visiting Hattie's family's dark, smelly apartment building, visceral emotions that define the slumming experience in which middle- or upper-class cultural tourists are stimulated by contact with the class-differentiated Other. In Miss Tillman's case, Hattie represents an exoticized body both through her ethnicity and through her disability.

Contrary to her expectations, Miss Tillman's visit to the Gurton family's apartment does not follow the conventions of the sentimental slum tale. She is disappointed to find that the Gurton family's apartment is neat and clean, albeit so colorfully decorated that it gives her a "nervous headache" (105). Moreover, Hattie refuses to confirm the stereotypes that Miss Tillman has about the slums. She discovers that Hattie is rarely, not frequently, left alone and has a "warm and pretty" coat and hat instead of rags to wear. When she asks Hattie, "Do your papa and mama whip you very much?" Hattie answers, "I never did have a beating." Despite the evidence of an intact family and a happy home, Miss Tillman takes Hattie away for the afternoon, and the two return to a hysterical Mrs. Gurton and a policeman who has been informed that the child has been stolen. Miss Tillman's explanation scarcely helps: "I wanted to take her home with me and keep her for my little playmate" (106).

But Hattie's mother, Mrs. Gurton, exposes the rich woman's false benevolence, angrily asking, "What do you want with my child? To make a servant or a monkey out of her? She don't want no 'doptin' of yours" (107). Recognizing that Miss Tillman wants a plaything and that Hattie will be further reduced to the status of an animal, Mrs. Gurton understands that the poor can never be anything but manipulated objects for the rich, even if, as in Hattie's case, they become momentarily objects of desire. Even the policeman, often in slum stories an enforcer of dominant structures of power rather than an agent of justice, decrees that Miss Tillman has done wrong by taking the child. Miss Tillman cannot understand his reasoning and drives away, shuddering at "the thoughtless ingratitude of the poor" (108). As Miss Tillman drives away, Mrs. Gurton performs a mocking imitation of her society airs, revealing that benevolence and the parody of benevolence are equally false performances. "Miss Tillman's Protégé" is Dunbar-Nelson's satiric attack on the blindness of middle-class do-gooders, an attack heightened by the irony of having Hattie, who physically cannot see clearly, be more aware of her circumstances than the ego-blinded Miss Tillman.

"Witness for the Defense," another naturalistic 'Steenth Street story, features a variant of child stealing: child imprisonment by the state. In this tale, Lizzie Williams witnesses the murder of her drunken, abusive stepfather, Randolph Williams, by her mother, Belle. Taken into custody as a witness, Lizzie learns that her mother's only hope of escaping the death penalty is her eyewitness testimony. Placed under oath, Lizzie confronts the moral choice of lying to save her mother or telling the truth and having her mother executed. She lies, and her mother goes free, but Lizzie's innocence is shattered: "[S]he would never meet her mother's eyes or suffer her caress without a shuddering memory of her face on that awful day" of the murder.[24] More than the other 'Steenth Street stories, "Witness for the Defense" echoes Stephen Crane's Bowery tales in its stylistic juxtaposition of elaborate, Latinate vocabulary with the dialect of the slums and its use of two poles of conduct—for Crane, the church and the saloon, and for Dunbar-Nelson, the Pure in Heart Settlement House and McEneny's saloon—to demarcate the characters' moral choices. The figure of the "monstrous mother" of the slums appears in Lizzie's recollection of her mother's "distorted features working in convulsive rage" (112), a description that recalls Crane's depiction of Mrs. Johnson, the mother in Crane's *Maggie: A Girl of the Streets*.

As in "Miss Tillman's Protégé," Dunbar-Nelson provides a voice of resistance to official regulation and interference that fails to account for the complex lives of those who live in poverty. "Witness for the Defense" pairs the ultimate violence of murder with the daily domestic violence that Lizzie has witnessed and Belle has endured. In Crane's *Maggie*, Mrs. Johnson beats her husband as frequently as he beats her, but neither ever does the other a permanent injury, a circumstance that, together with the incessant repetition of the fights between them, lends an almost cartoonlike quality to the pair's exaggerated episodes of violence. By contrast, the violence of Belle's murder of Randolph is shocking, for she attacks him with scissors, the tools of her trade. Her attack severs a vital artery, after which Randolph runs downstairs and falls dead on the sidewalk. Despite this incident, 'Steenth Street, through the voice of the narrator, renders a judgment sympathetic to Belle. Because "woman-kind . . . had quietly taken its beatings" while the Darwinian "primitive law of the jungle prevailed, which decrees that the female shall grow uncomely, weighted by the burden of rearing its young unaided, while the male, more youthful and beautiful, bounds away for fresher fields," Belle's initial passivity is biologically determined, but her reaction was not without motivation. The narrator distinguishes between the unofficial Darwinian "survival of the strongest" law of the double standard enshrined in custom and the equally unofficial "right" that Belle seizes "to live and kill too": "for so long had the survival of the strongest been the implacable law that now when one woman had broken the bonds of custom and established the right to live and to kill too, there was great rejoicing. . . . Emancipation was in the air" (112). Dunbar-Nelson not only highlights the plight of victims of domestic violence but also acknowledges the right of oppressed people to act violently against their oppressors and thereby gain "Emancipation," a term evocative of the Emancipation Proclamation as well as the emancipation of women.

SUI SIN FAR, "IN THE LAND OF THE FREE"

Sui Sin Far's "In the Land of the Free" addresses a similar anxiety about the stolen child in its tale of Hom Hing and his wife Lae Choo, whose young son, born after the official certificate of entry has been applied for, is taken away at U.S. Customs because an official decides that the boy has "no certificate entitling him to admission to this country."[25] Left dangling by an indifferent bureaucracy and swindled out of all their treasure by a series of corrupt lawyers, Hom Hing and Lae Choo do not see their son again for ten long months. When they are reunited with him at last, he fails to recognize Lae Choo and turns to the white "mission woman" (101) as his mother. Earlier in the volume, in the title story of *Mrs. Spring Fragrance*, Sui Sin Far had satirized the standard patriotic trope of the nation as a domestic shelter when Mrs. Spring Fragrance writes to Mr. Spring Fragrance that his brother is "detained under the roof-tree of this great Government instead of under your own humble roof."[26] "In the Land of the Free" protests such detention policies more directly. Its stolen child theme expresses anxieties about cultural assimilation, for the child, even if returned, cannot recognize his mother and symbolically his culture. Moreover, the figure of the stolen child comes to signify the plight of all children stolen by the state for its own purposes, whether those include indoctrinating Native American children in boarding schools, as in the writings of Zitkala-Ša, or removing children of immigrants or poor people based on cultural misunderstandings of what constitutes adequate parenting.

ANN PETRY, THE STREET

Although Ann Petry refused to be identified with any particular literary tradition, until recently her 1946 novel *The Street* has been considered a work of modern naturalism in the tradition of Richard Wright's *Native Son*, a novel Petry admired. When read against Dunbar-Nelson's variations on the naturalistic slum tale, *The Street* (1946) reveals the sophisticated ways in which Petry infuses a racialized and a gendered naturalism into the novel. As Clare Eby notes, *The Street* has often been compared with Richard Wright's *Native Son*, "a comparison that has not generally worked in Petry's favor" because the criteria are those of classic naturalism.[27] However, current critics such as Eby, Bill V. Mullen, and Meg Wesling see *The Street* as a critique of naturalistic determinism, with Wesling proposing that it lies within the tradition of writing by African American women who "take up the question of black motherhood as a site of contradiction ... to map the convergence of the material relations of power and exploitation that underpin the very meanings of public and private personhood."[28] Published forty years after most of the stolen child stories, *The Street* seems at first an anomaly. Stories of the stolen child feature anxieties about the assimilation and loss of immigrant cultures, but as immigrant groups came to control their participation in the nation, fewer such stories appeared. In contrast, the historic trauma encoded in African American experience and the racism that prevented participation in, let alone assimilation into, the national narrative of progress require a continuing interrogation of the social concerns that gave rise to them.

The Street's deviations from classic naturalism reflect the artistic choices of unruly naturalism, since its determinism, its narrowing of options for Lutie Johnson, the main character, and its setting all mark it as a naturalist text. As she moves into an apartment in Harlem and struggles to make a living for her young son, Lutie Johnson finds her attempts thwarted by a combined racism and sexism. Avoiding the easy option of prostitution offered by her neighbor, the madam Mrs. Hedges, and trying to keep her son safe from the poisoned charms of the street, Lutie tries to escape by pursuing a singing career at a club at the suggestion of Boots, a man to whom she is attracted. But Lutie can find no way out of these enclosed spaces. The club, like the street, is controlled by Junto, a white man who plans to seek her sexual favors, just as her drab apartment is controlled by Jones, the unhappy, spiteful African American superintendent whose desire for Lutie curdles into hatred once she rejects him.

Novels of classic naturalism in which the characters lack the power to reflect on their situation frequently incorporate a truth-telling authorial stand-in, often a doctor (like Dr. Mandelet in *The Awakening*) or a newspaperman (like Skaggs in Paul Laurence Dunbar's *The Sport of the Gods* or John Driscoll in Glasgow's *The Descendant*) to comment on their plight. Lutie, however, is a modern character in the self-aware mode of second-stage naturalism. As Donald Pizer writes, the mature phase of American naturalism allows for a "tragic irony inherent in the conflict between a character's felt belief in his autonomy and a social contingency that does indeed shape his destiny."[29] Lutie understands the full magnitude of the forces arrayed against her, which she personifies as a single enemy, the street. She reflects that her life has been spent within an "ever-narrowing space" and that the streets of Harlem are "the North's lynch mobs."[30] Marjorie Pryse and others have suggested that Lutie makes "wrong choices," yet every episode of the novel suggests that her actions are not of her choosing but determined by her environment.[31] Feeling desperate when her son, Bub, is framed by Jones for stealing the mail from the apartment building's mailboxes, Lutie turns to Boots for the money to set him free. When Boots first tries to seduce her and then slaps her, Lutie, overcome by a lifetime of rage, bludgeons him to death with a candlestick. The trajectory of the novel and its use of space confirm that Lutie's life is, metaphorically speaking, a series of closing doors. (In Angelina Weld Grimké's "The Closing Door," another stolen child story, Agnes Milton kills her infant son to spare him from growing up in a U.S. lynching culture too massive and omnipresent to fight.) By killing Boots, Lutie "was striking at the white world which thrust black people into a walled enclosure from which there was no escape" (430), but she closes a door to her own future, since Boots is only the agent and not the white prime mover of her oppression.

The "street" of Petry's novel is a colonized space or plantation where a white overlord, Junto, controls everything from sexuality to recreation. Although Petry goes out of her way to depict him as the least racist white man in the book, Junto, whose name suggests Benjamin Franklin's famous Junto Club and thus Franklin himself, meddles in his employees' relationships: for example, he prevents the natural development of the relationship between Boots and Lutie because he intends to save Lutie for himself. He also establishes the rate of exchange for Lutie's services singing at the club, advising Boots to buy her presents rather than give her money, a transaction more reminiscent of a slave economy than a modern one. As was the case with Miss Tillman, Junto's benevolence masks a desire for control and the ability to bend others to his will, something that on a larger scale aligns him with the dominant culture responsible for the oppression of Lutie and everyone else on the street.

Yet the one character who suffers actual physical rather than metaphorical imprisonment is Bub. Lutie's consistent fears that the street would steal Bub away from her are not realized, but the government steals him through its system of juvenile homes and prisons. All Lutie's legal maneuverings, like those of the family in Sui Sin Far's "In the Land of the Free," have not been able to pry Bub loose from a government determined to hold and to discipline him. So demoralized is Lutie by the street that as she flees town and leaves him behind forever, she rationalizes to herself that Bub will have a better chance in reform school. Her line of reasoning renders her situation all the more tragic since she is now complicit in the very logic of the nation and the false rhetoric of its benevolence that she had earlier critiqued.

The theme of the stolen child rewrites one of naturalism's key questions: since classic naturalism features so many female protagonists, the question of agency, of "who controls the body of the woman?," becomes a central preoccupation for the characters in the works. Alice Dunbar-Nelson, Sui Sin Far, and Ann Petry ask instead a question far more salient: who controls the body of the child and with it the transmission of cultural heritage? In naming the mother's, and by extension the culture's, anxiety over this issue, they indict the structures and representatives of power that range from egotists like Miss Tillman to the governmental institutions of the reform school and the penitentiary.

MARY E. WILKINS FREEMAN,
THE PORTION OF LABOR

In Mary E. Wilkins Freeman's *The Portion of Labor* (1901), the stolen child represents the future of labor in a New England mill town. Although W. D. Howells defended Freeman's portrayal, later critics took issue with her treatment of the subject, which was, according to Granville Hicks, a "strange mixture of insight into New England character and childish ignorance of industrial conditions."[32] Hicks's condescending assessment of Freeman's "childish ignorance" about industrialism and his eagerness to pigeonhole her achievement as "insight into New England character" strikes a familiar note of faint praise for women regionalists. His comment reveals the challenges that women writers of naturalism faced when shifting from writing about the domestic sphere to investigating the political and economic forces governing the world beyond the home. Freeman's novel tells the story of Ellen Brewster, a working-class girl whose beauty as a child leads Cynthia Lennox, an upper-class childless woman, to kidnap her for a few days before releasing her after experiencing a change of heart. As Ellen grows into a young woman, she is torn between accepting the education at Vassar that Cynthia Lennox offers and working in the shoe factory that is the town's major employer. Increasingly radical in her sentiments, Ellen incites the factory workers to strike but in the novel's climactic moment convinces them to back down. *The Portion of Labor* is structured around three major episodes in which the heroine, Ellen Brewster, tries to maintain a sense of autonomy despite being the center of class conflict. Each episode culminates in a decisive moment during which Ellen must choose between the town's aristocracy, the class that had stolen her, and its laboring class, the class into which she is born.

The first episode, Ellen's abduction, employs that most common trope of desire in naturalism, the plate-glass window of a store that separates the young woman from the goods that entice her. Like Dreiser's Carrie Meeber, Ellen escapes from her drab surroundings into the color and light of the downtown streets where she stands bewitched in front of the "great expanse of plate-glass" that frames a market's tableau of meats and vegetables. Although Leah Blatt Glasser traces Ellen's social consciousness and political activism to the "maternal thinking" she learns through repeated loving relationships with women, Ellen's empathic social conscience is born in this moment of desire.[33] The hypnotic effect of the "dazzling mosaic" recedes as Ellen, noticing the hanging bodies of dead rabbits and partridges, learns "the hard actualities of things," her heart swelling "to the size of a woman's... with the sight of helpless injury and death."[34] Her insight parallels that of Frank Cowperwood in Dreiser's *The Financier*, who sees that "things lived on each other" after watching a lobster kill a squid. Ellen learns a different lesson, for unlike Frank she pities the helpless rather than admiring the strong.[35]

To complete this lesson, Ellen is then literally carried away by the wealthy Cynthia Lennox, whose "unassuaged longing" (23) for a child causes her to hide Ellen in her house for two days despite the town's frantic search for her. The theft of Ellen by the gray-haired yet oddly youthful Cynthia illustrates the novel's theme of perverse maternity, an idea compounded by the failure of institutional and familial mothering. Ellen's family is filled with unfit mothers. Her grandmother, Andrew's harshly critical mother Mrs. Zelotes, is indeed a zealot, one of Freeman's old-family New Englanders who withholds affection and money unless her wishes are obeyed. Ellen's mother, the aptly named and highly emotional Fanny Loud, understands only a portion of the person her daughter is capable of becoming. The worst of the three, Fanny's sister Eva, first protests being a mother at all, since children drag working families into poverty, and then tries to cut her daughter Amabel's throat with a carving knife.

The theft of Ellen is an economic parable in which a child representing the strength, future, and capital of the working class is stolen to satisfy the needs, in this case the perverse maternal instincts, of a preternaturally youthful upper class whose vitality is sustained by the bodies and labor of others. Trapped in Cynthia's house against her will, Ellen is transformed into an object, a physical fetish, in an experience that simultaneously evokes a Cinderella-like transformation into a realm of wealth and the unspeakable act of child imprisonment and seduction. Never letting Ellen act for herself, Cynthia "washed her and dressed her, and curled her hair" (43) before subjecting her to the "tenderest violence." Her presence a "soft smother of violets," she presses Ellen "against the soft red silk over her bosom, and kiss[es] her little, blushing cheeks with the lightest and carefulest kisses" (42). Cynthia becomes an emotional seducer in the best sentimental tradition, a Lovelace in gray hair ignoring Ellen's cries of "I want my mother." She manipulates Ellen into self-betrayal by promising "treasures and pleasures which made her [Ellen's] mouth twitch into smiles in spite of herself" (44), in the eroticized language of physical possession and victim's helplessness that describes the encounter. Throughout this episode, Cynthia knows she is committing a crime, but like any naturalistic character, she is driven by physical and emotional impulses beyond her control. Significantly, she gives Ellen a doll that through "the sentiment of emulative motherhood in her childish breast console[s] her for her need of her own mother" (45), replacing a natural relation with an artificial one.

When Ellen escapes and is taken home, the doll serves as the token of her silence about the abduction, the artifact of the moneyed class's attempt to purchase the future and subvert by arrogating to itself the natural relationship between parent and child.

Ellen faces her second moment of choosing between class solidarity and upward mobility when Cynthia attends her graduation from high school. Her valedictory address, delivered in front of stiffly disapproving mill owners and enthusiastic mill workers, calls for "the laborer, and the laborer only, [to receive] the reward of labor" (192). Her sentiment seems "almost anarchistic" (193), causing Cynthia's friend and later husband Lyman Risley to joke, "She may have a bomb somewhere concealed among those ribbons and frills" (194). Although Cynthia has lost interest in Ellen, since she is no longer a child to be cuddled and kissed, she offers to send Ellen to Vassar to atone for her actions. Ellen rightly sees this as a threat as well as an opportunity, and as she looks at the doll Cynthia had given her, she feels a "vague sense of injury . . . as if in some way she were being robbed instead of being made the object of benefit" (244). At some level Ellen understands that her commitment to her class is being undermined and that she is still merely a doll to Cynthia. The narrative confirms this when, after accepting the offer, in a classic expression of transferring her allegiance from the true mother to the false one, from the class that nourishes her to the one that exploits her, she realizes that she loves Cynthia "with a fervor which was strange to her" (252).

Ellen is drawn back to her working-class family, however, after her aunt Eva tries to kill Amabel, her daughter. She decides against Vassar and gets a job at Lloyd's, the shoe factory, to pay for Eva's treatment in an asylum. Like Dreiser, in whose world "determinism rules . . . and there are no chance events," Freeman emphasizes a causal chain that governs her characters' fates, and in a mill town all actions spring from management's treatment of the workers.[36] Ellen's chance at an education is ruined because Eva's husband Jim, moved by management around from job to job "as if he was a piece on a checker-board," starts "to act as if he wasn't a man" (285). He asserts his masculinity by turning to drink and leaving Eva. Jim's absence, in turn, causes Eva to go mad and try to kill Amabel, a name suggesting the "good love" that the system has destroyed. In another blow to her aspirations, Ellen, like Dreiser's Carrie Meeber, experiences the aching muscles and emotional fatigue that accompany repetitive, boring physical work, and she also learns that the novel she attempts to write is "trash" because it fails to "see things and people the way they really" are (368).

The third class confrontation, the workers' strike against the Lloyd factory, pits Ellen against Robert Lloyd, Cynthia's nephew, who is in love with her. Early in the novel, the fight between capital and labor for Ellen's soul had been cast as a struggle between Cynthia and Fanny, her false and true mothers. Now she is torn between false and true suitors: factory owner Robert Lloyd and Granville Joy, a working-class man who has loved her since childhood. By rights Granville should be the romantic hero of the story. He is intelligent, he brings Ellen small tokens of his affection and defends her against harm, and he gives her her first kiss. Moreover, he is the boy whom an old folk charm predicts that Ellen will marry (163). But Ellen loves Robert, in part because he alone has guessed the secret behind her possession of the doll since it was his doll when he lived at Cynthia's house. As in Freeman's "The Reign of the Doll," the doll signifies the many faulty mother-child relationships in the story, and Ellen both mothers it and identifies with it, dressing it in poor clothing like her own. It experiences in miniature Ellen's treatment at Cynthia's hands and allows Robert to equate Ellen with Cynthia, for when he recognizes the doll, he asks Ellen jokingly, "Are you a child kidnapper?" (216). Its muteness echoes Ellen's silence on her abduction, and its never-explained presence in the Brewster home is a continual reminder of the power that Cynthia wields. The doll brings Robert and Ellen together as a tangible reminder of their lives as children who suffered from Cynthia's obsessive mothering. Yet in their treatment of the doll Robert and Ellen differ, for when he owned the doll Robert had "burned her head with the red-hot end of a poker to see if she would wake up" (216), leaving a scar that Ellen had often kissed. In loving Robert, Ellen chooses the man whose instrumental approach to the doll parallels his indifferent perspective on the working class that it represents, and, to an extent, Ellen herself.

Freeman reinforces the symbolism of the doll through another form of signification, the treatment of workers as animals, in a scene with echoes of Darwinian courtship and female sexual selection. The novel links the wearing of fur, already a symbol of capitalist power and luxury, to the helpless dead animals Ellen sees in the first few chapters by having Amabel ask Robert how the animal keeps warm if Robert has its fur. Robert explains that the animal was "shot for his fur," and Amabel asks, "To make you a coat?" (380). Amabel's distress at the injustice of stealing from the weak to cover the strong, a situation analogous to that of the factory hands, wavers momentarily when Robert wraps her in the coat. However, unlike similar images of women in furs, such as Bessy Westmore in *The Fruit of the Tree* or Mariana in *Phases of an Inferior Planet*, the scene casts a disturbing shadow. Being wrapped in furs often signals Darwinian courtship, but Amabel is a child, and Robert's action uncomfortably echoes the implicitly sexualized child abduction of Ellen by his aunt Cynthia. Another parallel between Amabel and Ellen is that Amabel asks the question that Ellen should have asked, indeed had felt through her sympathy for the dead animals in the shop window. Yet Ellen's conversion to the gospel of wealth is not absolute, for when Robert cuts wages because of an economic slump, declining to explain his reasons to the workers, Ellen rouses them to action by telling them that the "great capitalists" have made the workers' hard times "by shifting the wealth too much to one side." After calling the workers to unite so that none must suffer, she concludes, "If I were a man... I would beg, I would steal—before I would yield—I, a free man in a free country—to tyranny like this!" (478). The workers strike, and in retaliation Robert closes the factory.

Ellen learns that the strike for better wages leads to the reality of out-of-work girls like her workmates Mamie Bemis and Mamie Brady being driven to prostitution and suicide. "I did not count the cost," Ellen admits to a group of strikers. "[T]he cost is a part of principle in this world" (516). Reversing her earlier support of the strike, she leads a parade of workers back toward the factory through a crowd shouting "Scabs!" and throwing stones. Freeman wraps up every other plot line in a happy ending as well: Eva is cured and comes home; Andrew's worthless mining stock is revealed to be worth a fortune; Cynthia Lennox marries her longtime suitor, Lyman Risley, after he is shot and blinded by a striker; and Robert, showing his compassion by meeting the workers halfway on the wage issue, becomes engaged to Ellen. Given the last word, Ellen's father, Andrew, reflects that "the portion of labor" is the "growth in character of the laborer," an oddly philosophical view for one whom the system threw out to starve (563).

The unruliness of Freeman's naturalism in *The Portion of Labor* becomes most apparent in its concluding chapters, which defy the novel's previous logic of labor relations. Like the endings of *Margret Howth*, *Hedged In*, and *A Singular Life*, the consolatory ending strikes a false note that calls attention to its own artifice. More authentically disturbing are the novel's stolen or abused children and their substitutes: the abused doll; the dead animals; Ellen, snatched as a fetish to satisfy a rich woman's whims of motherhood; and Amabel, threatened with death at the hands of a monstrous mother driven mad and a father turned brute by the cruel causality of industrial capitalism. Disrupting idealized visions of the mother-child relationship by substituting a complicated, class-inflected relationship between women's bodies that labor and those that nurture, *The Portion of Labor* refuses the easy solution that the unrealistic ending appears to endorse.

What Charity Saw

Edith Wharton was emphatically not a movie fan. In fact, as she wrote to Edward Sheldon in 1924, "I believe the movie has killed imagination, and that the allusive, the elliptical and the metaphorical are going to be, to this young generation, as much of a 'dead language' as English is rapidly becoming to them."[37] Yet Wharton's fiction tells a different story. Her later novels such as *Twilight Sleep* and *Hudson River Bracketed* include numerous references to the movie industry and its upstart producers, perhaps as a sop to the movie-mad magazine readers upon whom Wharton's income increasingly depended.[38] From the mid-1890s until her final move to France after 1911, Wharton wrote stories of New York when the city was a capital of film production and its streets and slums a frequent setting for films. In her early novellas such as "Bunner Sisters" and *Summer*, the presence of contemporary film culture is reflected in her narrative choices and in overt references to films.

Wharton follows her naturalistic contemporaries in anticipating the conventions of early film, including parallel cutting and selective omniscience into characters' thoughts as revealed through camera angles, images of sound-producing objects, and visual representations of the screen to indicate point of view. In silent films, sounds were often visually conveyed by an inserted shot of the device creating the sound or a character's glance at a musical instrument, a barking dog, or a factory whistle. In Wharton's "Bunner Sisters," a ticking clock and other such repetitive clicking devices, such as the pinking machine, perform this function. Visual representations of the screen, such as windows and camera lenses, evoke the desiring gaze that constitutes the self and call attention to the scrutinizing gaze of the detached narrative observer, another feature that appears in "Bunner Sisters" and *Summer*. The view through a window or a movie screen suggests an important shift away from the interior reflections of realism, as when Isabel Archer stares into the fire and meditates over her marriage to Gilbert Osmond in chapter 42 of Henry James's *The Portrait of a Lady*. Unlike the realism of interior reflection associated with Isabel's fireside contemplation, naturalism features a more technologically mediated and visually constructed concept of the self. For example, in "Mrs. Manstey's View" the view from Mrs. Manstey's window, a technology of vision that functions as a screen to see the world, becomes so important to the elderly title character that she is willing to commit arson to preserve the view that authenticates her sense of herself in her surroundings.

Wharton, like other naturalistic writers, uses forms of spectacle and symbolic objects, especially those related to technology, to reflect and to amplify for the reader the character's state of mind. The stereopticon show in "Bunner Sisters" and the silent film in *Summer* reveal thoughts the character may not be able to articulate.[39] They reinforce the artificiality of artistic performance and introduce a substitute for the fictional form of the novel into the narrative, one that reflects the distanced, ironic, and self-referential narrator common to naturalism. In addition, Wharton uses contemporary movie culture to enrich the context of films within the novels. The crucial movie scene in *Summer* reflects the state of mind of the main character, Charity Royall, and calls the reader's attention to the multitude of contemporary films that form a context for Charity's decision, including the groundbreaking birth control drama *Where Are My Children?* "Bunner Sisters" and *Summer* demonstrate that film and naturalism are technologies of the real, both within the text and through allusions that suggest external contexts.

"BUNNER SISTERS"

Written in 1892 but not published until 1916, "Bunner Sisters" is the story of two sisters, Ann Eliza and Evelina, who own the fabric and notions shop that bears their name. The story tells of two sisters in love with the same man, Mr. Ramy, a clock repairman, and the extraordinary sacrifices Ann Eliza makes for Evelina. Despite the "well-washed" panes of the shop windows and Ann Eliza's efforts on her sister's behalf, the sisters live in an area of "cast-iron balconies and cat-haunted grass-patches behind twisted railings," the term "cat-haunted" evoking the same landscape of squalor that Mamie of Wharton's fragment "One Day" confronted when looking out the window of her basement flat. Behind the windows of their shop, the sisters are momentarily safe from exposure to the littered streets, but the possibility of women being discarded as waste hovers over the story. The naturalistic urban setting confirms this direction, from the "chronic cluster of refuse-barrels" recalling the classic slum photographic subject of children posed next to waste barrels to the carefully enumerated catalog of refuse: "[T]he fissured pavement formed a mosaic of coloured hand-bills, lids of tomato cans, old shoes, cigar-stumps and banana skins, cemented together by a layer of mud, or veiled in a powdering of dust, as the state of the weather determined."[40]

As in other Darwinian courtship narratives, the stability of the sisters' lives is shattered when they compete for the attentions of Ramy. When Ramy proposes to Ann Eliza, she sacrifices her own happiness and turns him down. When Evelina accepts him and complains that they cannot marry and move away because they have no funds, Ann Eliza sacrifices herself again and turns over the sisters' savings to the couple. The plot devolves into naturalism in its second half when Ann Eliza, searching for her absent sister, learns that Ramy is a drug addict. Abandoned by Ramy, Evelina turns up on the doorstep of Bunner Sisters with a story to tell: she has borne a child and seen it die, has contracted a fatal illness, and equally shocking for Ann Eliza, has become a Roman Catholic. After Evelina's death and the demise of their shop, Ann Eliza goes forth into the littered streets in search of a job, only to learn that the shops are looking for stylish girls, "not over thirty" years old, and that she is not wanted (436).

"Bunner Sisters" evokes the atmosphere of early film in its setting and the characters' visual fixation on spectacle and on mechanical objects.[41] Like the wares in their shop, which "had the undefinable grayish tinge of objects long preserved in the show-case of a museum," the sisters exist in a setting of stasis amid "orderly counters and white-washed walls." Only the comings and goings of their customers as seen through the "well-washed panes" of the shop window provide variety in their daily routines. The "screen" of the window is their visual technology for fantasizing about lives that they will never live, just as the stories that their neighbor Miss Mellins tells suggest the melodrama of theater and early film. The narrative also references the sisters' auditory as well as visual focus on the mechanical ticking of the clock, the sound of the sewing machine, and the clicking of the pinking machine, descriptions that recall the film technique of camera inserts of mechanical devices used to indicate sound in visual terms. Like the camera operators of early film, who cranked the cameras by hand, the sisters must operate these devices by hand, becoming in effect part of the machine, an elision of the mechanical and biological that is a standard trope of naturalism.

What disrupts this repetitive process for Evelina is the stereopticon show with slides of Berlin to which Ramy takes her after Ann Eliza declines to go. The visual spectacle causes time to stand still for Ann Eliza when awaiting their return, and to fly by for Evelina at the stereopticon show, suggesting the power of spectacle to disrupt normal sensations of time for the sisters. This disjuncture of perception through spectacle also indicates the distortion of natural time and the rupture of their increasingly unnatural and one-sided relationship. Its primary purpose, however, may be to call attention to the performances within the story: Ann Eliza pretending not to love Ramy, Evelina condescending to her sister from her superior position as a woman being courted, and Ramy concealing his addiction while casting camera-like glances at the "well-fixed" shop that the sisters maintain. Wharton's story does not derive from film sources, but in these and other ways it participates in the film grammars of its time.

SUMMER

At the end of its chapter 9, the exact structural midpoint of Edith Wharton's *Summer* and the exact midpoint in the novel's summertime chronology, Charity Royall, the protagonist, and her lover, Lucius Harney, travel from sleepy North Dormer to the larger town of Nettleton for a Fourth of July celebration. Amid the rest of the day's events, Charity and Harney go to the movies, after which Charity sees a brick house "with a conspicuous black and gold sign across its front. 'Dr. Merkle; Private Consultations at all hours. Lady Attendants'" (229). Read in isolation, the scene of moviegoing followed by Charity's seeing Dr. Merkle's sign is one of the smaller incidents of the day, which includes a meal at a questionably "French" restaurant and Lawyer Royall's memorable drunken denunciation of his ward, Charity, as a "damn bare-headed whore" (235). Read in the context of social problem dramas of the Progressive Era, such as Lois Weber's birth control drama

Where Are My Children?, however, this seemingly minor trip to the movies provides a useful framework for reading two of the novel's more shocking scenes to a 1917 readership, Charity's two visits to an abortionist, Dr. Merkle. Charity does not literally see Weber's film, of course, as Wharton's readers would have had the chance to do. Yet for Charity, not a reader herself but a rapt consumer of the movies, the context of the social problem film provides a way of understanding her decisions in light of the era's fears about uncontrolled female sexuality and reproduction, including stealing the nation's children and future citizens through birth control and abortion.

Summer is a novel filled with anxieties about class, race, and nationalism as signified by the characters' movements among several symbolic locations: Springfield, defined as the cosmopolitan metropolis where Charity's lover Lucius Harney lives; Nettleton, the region's big city; North Dormer, the village where Charity and Lawyer Royall live; and "the Mountain," a place where the law is afraid to venture. Born on "the Mountain" but brought to North Dormer as a child by Royall, her guardian, Charity belongs in neither place. She is visually different, with a "small swarthy face" (159), dark eyes, and curly, unruly brownish-red hair that make her quite unlike the thin, pale figures of Ally Hawes and other New England girls. Wharton further emphasizes the sense of Charity's liminal status by providing a series of houses within these communities where she attempts to fit in. In addition to Royall's "red house," these include the "grey house," a deserted house in a ruined Eden of an apple orchard, where Charity and Harney become lovers; the "brown house" owned by Charity's relatives, the Hyatts; the brick house of Dr. Merkle; and the house that presents a national and international perspective, the movie palace at Nettleton. In her travels with and without Harney, Charity visits each of these houses, some multiple times, like a New England Goldilocks trying to find a space she can inhabit successfully.

Taking shelter from a storm within the walls of the Hyatts' "brown house," Lucius and Charity experience the first of the novel's two discovery-of-squalor sequences. As their eyes adjust, they see the dirt and disorder of the interior, with a drunken, hairy, half-dressed man sleeping on a barrel in a corner, a pair of "cowed children," and a "weak-minded old woman" grabbing at a sick kitten that tries to run from her (200). As in similar scenes in Davis's *Margret Howth* and Phelps's *Hedged In*, the nauseating odors of the place reinforce the sense of decay, with "air heavy with the smell of dirt and stale tobacco" (199). "Every instinct and habit made her a stranger among these poor swamp-people living like vermin in their lair," Charity thinks. The comparison of human beings to "vermin" such as rats or other nuisance animals rather than to other forms of animal life intensifies the sense of degradation of the brown house's inhabitants, but the Darwinian language shows that by nature ("instinct") as well as by training ("habit"), Charity is from the Mountain but not part of it.

In contrast, the "red house" of Lawyer Royall, once the scene of a sexual threat for her, seems a haven. Surveying the squalor of the brown house or the even more chaotic conditions of the Mountain, Charity thinks with gratitude about the red house, where she grew up, seeing it as "the very symbol of household order" with its "engraving of 'The Surrender of Burgoyne' over the stove" (201). Meant to hang next to his painting *Declaration of Independence* in the Capitol, John Trumbull's painting of Burgoyne's surrender to the American general Horatio Gates in 1777 evokes the national spirit of the Revolution that Miss Hatchard, the town's elderly owner of the library, tries to keep alive with patriotic pageants. In the gentlemanly actions of Gates, who refused to humiliate Burgoyne even after the surrender, there is an echo of Royall, who refuses to humiliate Charity when he discovers her pregnancy and marries her anyway. Royall sheds his previous distasteful attributes when he stands up for Charity, revealing latent nobility and justifying his name. As Wharton wrote to Bernard Berenson, "I'm so particularly glad you like old man Royall. Of course, *he's* the book!"[42] Royall gains new stature in Charity's eyes during his Old Home Days speech urging residents to come back "for good... and not for bad... or just for indifference" (258). In so doing, he solidifies his position as American native in the sense that the novel endorses: of Anglo-American heritage and a native descended from settlers in the early days of the republic, Royall is, like the dying rural hamlet of North Dormer, an American in decline but ripe for rescue.

Of these structures, the motion picture theater provides Charity with a different way to understand the varieties of nationhood and the past she has previously encountered, which include Harney's cosmopolitan fetishization of antiquities, Royall's links to the early days of the republic, and her Hyatt relatives' atavistic lapses into degenerate behavior. When Harney reluctantly agrees to accompany Charity to the movies, the two enter a "glittering place" with a "velvet-curtained auditorium packed with spectators" (228). This space in itself signifies modernity, for the concept of the "moving picture palace" was less than a decade old in 1916.[43] Previously, motion pictures had been shown in empty stores or other buildings after hours, with sheets hung up at the end of the long, narrow rooms to serve as screens. Indeed, prior to this excursion, Charity has seen only the pictures that Mr. Miles has taken her to, which were shown "in an austere Y.M.C.A. hall, with white walls and an organ" (228). Mr. Miles, the "new Episcopal clergyman from Hepburn" serves as a religious and cultural emissary from the larger mill town of Hepburn, and even this first glimpse of a new visual technology had given her a broader perspective. When Mr. Miles takes "the young people down to Nettleton to hear an illustrated lecture on the Holy Land... Charity Royall had, for the first and only time, experienced railway-travel, looked into shops with plate-glass fronts, tasted cocoanut pie, sat in a theatre, and listened to a gentleman saying unintelligible things before pictures that she would have enjoyed looking at if his explanations had not prevented her from understanding them" (160). Mentioned on the second page of the novel, the railroad, plate-glass shop windows, and theater, along with the tropical overtones of tasting "cocoanut pie," suggest from the outset the modern urban culture to which Charity compares her life in North Dormer, and the images of the magic lantern show seal the connection between visual culture and modernity.

Charity's trip to the movie palace with Harney situates Charity at the historical transition from one form of film modernity into another that occurred at the end of the 1910s. The Holy Land lecture and other "church shows," common across Massachusetts but not the rest of New England, were on their way out by 1920 in favor of urban picture palaces, which the "glittering place" of the Nettleton movie theater tries to emulate.[44] At this, her second Nettleton show, Charity sees more directly the imaginings of empire: "All the world has to show seemed to pass before her in a chaos of palms and minarets, charging cavalry regiments, roaring lions, comic policemen and scowling murderers" (229). This hyperbolic and satiric description of the film's contents suggests the kind of escapist fare that Wharton understood movies to contain. The statement "all the world has to show" presents the spectacle from Charity's perspective and alerts the reader to her limitations.

The context of film and its association with spectacle adds depth to the scenes dealing with Charity's pregnancy, including her trip to the Mountain and her two visits to Dr. Merkle. After Merkle confirms her pregnancy, Charity sets out for the Mountain, believing that her family of origin will not judge her for having a child when she is not married. As she begins her ascent, Mr. Miles overtakes her in his buggy, telling her, "My child, your mother is dying. Liff Hyatt came down to fetch me" (285). When they reach the house, Charity "sat staring straight ahead of her at the darkening scene while Mr. Miles and Liff Hyatt went up to the house." She is a passive spectator, dissociated from the scene as she might be in a movie audience, until Mr. Miles, "his smooth pink face" differentiating him from the "brown" Mountain folk, tells Charity her mother is dead (288). Mr. Miles had taken Charity to see her first movies, in the Y.M.C.A. hall, the effect of which had been effaced by her trip to the movies at Nettleton with Lucius Harney, where her imagination, filled with fantastical visions of empire, "danced on the screen with the rest." For this third instance of a man leading her to see an unfamiliar spectacle, Mr. Miles reenters the picture, leading her to the place that has "become a reality" to her as she approaches the threshold, a liminal space signaling a significant transition from one realm to the next (288). Charity is about to enter a scene of momentous spectacle, just as she had with Harney, but as a horrified participant rather than as a gratified spectator.

What follows is the classic discovery-of-squalor sequence of grim realism and naturalism, intensified by the naturalistic tableau of the body of an unmoving woman on display. As Charity and Mr. Miles enter "what appeared to be the only room in the house... [i]t was so dark that she could just discern a group of a dozen people sitting or sprawling about a table made of boards laid across two barrels" (288). The interior gradually becomes visible only when the outsiders' eyes adjust to the darkness, and the inhabitants blend into the squalor of their surroundings as in a tableau in which "no one moved" even though "a woman's thick voice" announced their presence. When someone produces a candle, there is no way to light it, since there is no fire in the stove, until Mr. Miles "drew out a matchbox" and does so, suggesting his more general role as a bringer of what light and civilization the Mountain inhabitants experience. "[A] faint circle of light fell on the pale aguish heads that started out of the shadow like the heads of nocturnal animals" (288), the naturalistic combination of perennial illness (ague) and humans as animals recalling the similar scene in *Margret Howth* when Dr. Knowles shows Margret "a bit of hell: outskirt."

In a scene that echoes Selden's discovery of Lily Bart's body in *The House of Mirth*, Charity sees her mother's body: "[T]hey stood before a mattress on the floor in a corner of the room. A woman lay on it, but she did not look like a dead woman; she seemed to have fallen across her squalid bed in a drunken sleep, and to have been left lying where she fell, in her ragged disordered clothes. One arm was flung above her head, one leg drawn up under a torn skirt that left the other bare to the knee: a swollen glistening leg with a ragged stocking rolled down about the ankle. The woman lay on her back, her eyes staring unblinkingly at the candle that trembled in Mr. Miles's hand" (288–89). Both Lily's body and that of Mary Hyatt, Charity's mother, seem to be asleep rather than dead, but there the parallels end. In a room flooded with sunlight, Lily's body, lying on "a narrow bed along the wall," has "motionless hands and a calm, unrecognizing face."[45] Mary lies sprawled on a mattress, her "squalid bed," as if "in a drunken sleep," and none of the survivors has performed the customary rites of decency, such as covering her, straightening out her limbs, or closing her staring eyes. Mary's posture is the more naturalistically horrifying for the way in which it opens the body to scrutiny. Lying on her back with an arm above her head, she embodies a grotesque spectacle and a caricature of a pose familiar from nude paintings like Giorgione's *Sleeping Venus* (1508–10), Goya's *La Maja Desnuda* (1797–1800), or Alexandre Cabenal's *The Birth of Venus* (1863). Her legs are apart, with "one leg drawn up" and another "bare to the knee" save for "a ragged stocking rolled about the ankle," another revelation of partially clothed naked flesh that evokes a grotesque variation of erotic painting or the rigors of childbirth.

Charity "trie[s] to compose her mother's body" by "pulling the skirt down to the battered upturned boots" and drawing "the stocking over the dreadful glistening leg," the repetition of "glistening" evoking the shine of putrescence. Charity performs the rites of decency for her drunken mother that Margret Howth had performed for Hetty, the Irish girl who had drunk herself to death. Only then does Charity look at "her mother's face, thin yet swollen, with lips parted in a frozen gasp above the broken teeth," a rictus of death that, like the staring eyes, communicates nothing except the material reality of itself, unlike the "word which made all clear" that Selden fancies passes from Lily's closed lips to his ears. Mr. Miles completes Charity's task, crossing Mary's arms, putting a handkerchief over her face, and covering her with his coat as he says the offices for the dead amid the family's loud squabbling over Mary's possessions. The words of the service compound the ironic overtones of the scene as Mr. Miles utters the words of the service. He intones "Who shall change our vile body that it may be like unto His glorious body" as the earth is shoveled over "the vile body of Mary Hyatt" (292), a repetition of "vile" that, given the death scene Charity has witnessed, emphasizes its literal truth. After the burial, when Mr. Miles has left, Charity lies "on the floor on a mattress, as her dead mother's body had lain," looking out through a window at a desolate "deep funnel of sky" (294). She has taken her mother's place, unmarried, pregnant, and living on the Mountain, and, like other protagonists in women's naturalism, looks out the window only to see a future as bleak as the present. Harney has led her to the first scene of squalor and to the motion picture palace. Mr. Miles has taken her to the Y.M.C.A. films on the Holy Land and to the second and more disturbing sequence of squalor. In their separate ways, they have framed Charity's experiences with life as experiences of the movies.

In addition to its evocations of nationalism, empire, Americanization, and modernity, moviegoing in *Summer* may have suggested to the novel's first readers an allusion to contemporary birth control dramas. As Kevin Brownlow explains in *Behind the Mask of Innocence*, the Progressive Era was an extraordinarily rich period for social problem dramas, from white slave films such as *Traffic in Souls* (1913) and *The Inside of the White Slave Traffic* (1913) to birth control dramas such as *The Miracle of Life* (1915), *The Question* (1916), and Lois Weber's *Where Are My Children?* (1916). *Where Are My Children?*, the only one of the birth control films still extant, endorses birth control but condemns abortion, both of which were illegal at the time of its release, and, more significantly, it also promotes eugenics. As Shelley Stamp notes in *Movie-Struck Girls*, *Where Are My Children?* "makes the case that poverty-stricken women ought to practice birth control... whereas women of wealth and 'good breeding' were selfish if they chose to remain childless."[46] A similar plot about the dangers of well-educated women choosing abortion occurs in the film *The Valley of Decision* (1916), in which Rhoda, a socially prominent woman, wants her candidate Arnold to become governor.[47] The two convince his pregnant wife, Jane, not to have the child she carries, after which she dies. All ends happily when Arnold realizes that the loss of Jane and his child has been only a dream. Both films suggest the problem of socially and politically ambitious women who control their reproductive health at the expense of the family and the nation.

WHERE ARE MY CHILDREN?

Where Are My Children? is the story of crusading district attorney Richard Walton, whose home life would be happy, the audience is informed, if only he and his wife had children. Played by Tyrone Power Sr., Walton conveys his longing for children by his wistful looks at the children of the family next door in their well-to-do Los Angeles suburb. The film also emphasizes Walton's admiration for his sister's "eugenically born" healthy baby, with crosscutting between lingering shots of the baby and Walton's heavy sighs about having no child of his own. The eugenics and birth control message of *Where Are My Children?* lands forcefully when Walton must prosecute Dr. Homer, a crusader accused of prescribing birth control to poor people. In scenes that visually evoke Margaret Sanger's stories of poor women living in cramped slum housing, women who are desperate not to become pregnant again, Weber inserted vignettes of poverty-stricken homes overburdened with children, some with desperate parents and some with drunken and abusive ones. Walton does not know the reasons for his own family's childlessness, however: that his wife has had repeated abortions so that her social life will not be disturbed. When Mrs. Walton, arriving early for a bridge party, sees that her hostess is distressed, she asks about the problem. Learning that pregnancy is the issue, she accompanies her friend on a trip to her abortionist, Dr. Malfit. Weber conveys what has happened through an imaginative device used throughout, a special effect of winged children, shown in gauzy soft focus, being wafted back up from earth to the heavenly gates.

In the film's subplot, the housekeeper's daughter, Lillian, is not as fortunate as Mrs. Walton's fashionable friends. Having been seduced by Mrs. Walton's brother in a plot that recalls the upper-class man and lower-class woman plot of *Summer*, Lillian despairs of her pregnancy and is taken by Mrs. Walton for an abortion. Unfortunately, as a title card informs us, this time Dr. Malfit bungles the operation and Lillian dies. Knowing he will be prosecuted, Dr. Malfit blackmails Mrs. Walton into trying to make Mr. Walton drop the case, but to no avail. After his conviction, Malfit dashes from the witness box toward Walton, asking Walton, "Are you sure your own house is in order?" Upon looking in Dr. Malfit's account books, Walton discovers multiple payments from his wife and her society friends for services rendered. Crushed, he returns home, throws the society women out of his house, and asks his wife accusingly, "Where are my children?" Turned away from her husband, Mrs. Walton looks toward the camera with a shocked expres-

Dr. Homer, on trial for promoting birth control, recalls a
poverty-stricken home, from *Where Are My Children?* (1916).

sion on her face, a departure from the film's previous shots and one that challenges the audience by nearly breaking the fourth wall. Mrs. Walton repents of her selfishness but now cannot bear "the diadem of motherhood" because she has "perverted nature's ways" too many times through abortion. In a scene at the end, a double-exposed shot shows the Waltons sitting alone by their empty fireplace as the imagined children they will never have frolic around them. In another such shot, they appear as an old couple imagining the handsome grown children they would have had but for Mrs. Walton's actions.

Where Are My Children? was an extraordinarily successful film for its time. Despite efforts by the National Board of Review to ban the film and complaints by critics over its confusing message (was it a pro-birth-control film or an anti-abortion film?), it was shown across the country, even in Boston, where two thousand patrons were turned away on its opening night there in July 1916.[48] As writer Henry MacMahon reported in 1920, it was said to have "earned one million dollars," a huge sum for the time and one that MacMahon used to declare that, even if this sum were "discounted by half," this "famed woman-made story still represents a sum equal to the life-time earnings of the unusually successful man."[49] But the film was threatening for more than its controversial subject matter. First, as MacMahon's comment suggests, female producers and directors like Lois Weber were relatively plentiful in the early days of film and had the opportunity to be successful, a gender balance in film production that would disappear almost entirely by the late 1920s. Moreover, the prominent British birth control advocate Marie Stopes publicly protested the film on the grounds that it demonized women when "[t]here is much evidence of the dislike of men" to assume the

District Attorney Richard Walton asks his wife
"Where are my children?" in a climactic scene from
Where Are My Children? (1916).

burdens of fatherhood. It was too educational, Stopes continues, but in the wrong way, for she heard a woman in the audience saying "I did not know before that if you were in trouble you could get out of it in this way," missing the film's ethical point opposing abortion and picking up on the practical point that it works.[50] Given that young women represented both the subject matter and the target audience for white slave films and other Progressive Era social problem dramas, Wharton's readership, or the younger female portion of it, might well have seen *Where Are My Children?* before reading *Summer*.

Where Are My Children? and its promotion of eugenics also sheds a different light on Wharton's more complex treatment of the same issue. Dale Bauer contends that Wharton does not so much endorse as critique the eugenics movement in *Summer*.[51] Yet in its approval of Charity's decision to keep her child and in its unsympathetic depiction of the abortionist, the novel echoes Theodore Roosevelt's concerns over race suicide, the failure of white women to have enough children. According to Roosevelt, "A race that ... practiced race suicide—would thereby conclusively show that it was unfit to exist," a judgment that the *New York Dramatic Mirror* said was exactly the message of *Where Are My Children?*: "a strong preachment against race suicide."[52] Bearing children, according to Roosevelt, was the woman's equivalent of risking her life in battle, and refusing to do so was un-American. By insisting that their bodies belonged to themselves and not to the state for the purposes of childrearing, the society women in Weber's film are as unpatriotic as they are selfish. In their lack of patriotism, they are in league with doctors like Dr. Malfit, whose name suggests not only his evil intentions in helping the women to practice race suicide but also is coded as foreign, probably

Confronted with his crimes, Dr. Malfit lunges toward Richard
Walton (lower right) in *Where Are My Children?* (1916).

French, by virtue of his name ("Evil-doer"), his clothing (wearing spats and being better dressed than any American man in the film), his pointed, satanic beard, and his wild gesticulations on the witness stand.

Charity's encounters with the abortionist Dr. Merkle directly suggest the context of the movies. Dr. Merkle is "a plump woman with small bright eyes, an immense mass of black hair coming down low on her forehead, and unnaturally white and even teeth.... Her hands were large and smooth, and quick in all their movements; and she smelt of musk and carbolic acid" (275). The "musk and carbolic acid," the "large gold-framed photographs of showy young women" that adorn her office, and the mulatto maid who answers the door are all film conventions that mark Dr. Merkle as a procurer of young women for prostitution. Carbolic acid, at that time a key ingredient in Lysol, was a disinfectant used in doctor's offices, but it was also used diluted in brothels for contraceptive purposes.[53] Dr. Merkle confirms this impression of her dual profession. She tells Charity that after the abortion she can visit a "lady friend in Boston who's looking for a companion." As viewers of white slave films like *Traffic in Souls* would know well, promising a job as a companion and befriending a girl new to a city were two of the chief methods by which madams gained new girls for their brothels. If Charity, like many of her peers in this era, had seen white slave films as part of her moviegoing experiences, the signs would be unmistakable to her and would have contributed to her uneasiness with Dr. Merkle. Charity's discomfort reveals not only a natural response to Dr. Merkle's unnatural "false hair ... false teeth, [and a] false murderous smile" but also a learned response, the application of the lessons she has learned from the films that teach "what every girl should know," as the tag line for one white slave film proclaimed.

Moviegoers would also recognize Dr. Merkle, with her false hair and dark complexion, as a character type both foreign and malevolent, a classification scheme that Wharton follows in the book. Given her lower-class dialect, Dr. Merkle may not be a doctor at all, and, as Dale Bauer suggests, her name is German, a touch that would be consistent with Wharton's passionately anti-German propaganda during the war. Annoyed that Charity cannot pay and disappointed that she plans neither to have an abortion nor to become a prostitute, Dr. Merkle takes as a pledge of payment the blue pin that Harney had given Charity. When Charity, immediately after her marriage to Royall, tries to pay Dr. Merkle the five dollars she owes for the visit, Dr. Merkle demands all that Charity has, the forty dollars Royall has given her for new clothes. She then resorts to blackmail: "It seems you got married yesterday, up to the 'Piscopal church.... It would be a pity, wouldn't it, to let Mr. Royall know you had an account running here?" (309). Like the other foreign abortionist, Dr. Malfit, Dr. Merkle has no professional ethics or personal conscience to bother her when making threats against American women.

At the end of the novel, Charity, now married to her foster father Royall, returns to his "red house," not the "gray house" she shared with Harney, signifying not only her inevitable participation in, and domination by, cultural and biological forces, but also her commitment, however reluctant, to the preservation of the nationalistic American family rather than to its cosmopolitan (Harney) or savage (Mountain people) alternatives. Critics have typically viewed this ending as problematic, with some celebrating Charity's marriage to Royall as a fitting conclusion—Rhonda Skillern suggests that "Marilyn French, Cynthia Griffin Wolff, Barbara A. White, and Candace Waid all but throw rice on this marriage"—but others condemning it as an emotionally incestuous pairing.[54] What is clear is that Wharton, with an anthropological level of interest, devised classificatory mechanisms centered on the novel's places and tribal customs. Viewed from an anthropological perspective, the novel seems to suggest that, as Jennie Kassanoff contends, emotional incest is less significant than the biological exogamy that ensures the survival of the group.[55] In having Harney's child and ignoring the young men of North Dormer as well as Liff Hyatt, her cousin from the Mountain, Charity has moved two steps, rather than one, outside her kinship group. By taking Charity as his wife, Royall too practices exogamy of the sort needed to ensure vigor in the clearly vitiated strain of "native" American that his connections with the American past suggest.

The question of citizenship, its qualifications, and its exclusionary tactics, formed a vital theme in the American narrative of progress during the early years of the twentieth century. In immigrant films such as *Making an American Citizen* and *The Italian*, regulation of the body and emotions constitutes an education in citizenship for immigrants such as Ivan and Beppo, with Beppo learning self-control even in the face of unjustified racial assaults when he is mistaken for a thief and lied to by the political boss. Micheaux's *Within Our Gates* promotes the strong Progressive Era message of education through Sylvia's story and Dr. Vivian's pleading near the end of the film, yet the horrific injustices that the nation has inflicted in the form of racism, rape, and lynching leave Sylvia dubious not only about whether citizenship is possible in such a country but also whether it is even desirable, given the white citizens who populate it. The wariness that Sylvia feels toward the nation expresses itself in the stolen child stories as the righteous indignation of immigrants when its representatives—customs officials in "In the Land of the Free," wealthy do-gooders in the 'Steenth Street stories—exercise regulatory powers that have little to do with benefiting would-be citizens and everything to do with consolidating national control over immigrant bodies. The stolen child in Freeman's and Petry's novels raises equally serious questions, for in the case of Ellen, in *The Portion of Labor*, and Bub, in *The Street*, the co-option of class and racial affinities is permanent. Ellen is imprisoned for a short time, but the unsettling consequences cause her to waver in her class-based loyalties. In Bub's case, imprisonment in an industrial home hauntingly suggests permanent incarceration, the theft of a child by the state.

Summer and *Where Are My Children?* take the stolen child concept a step further by implicating the body of the mother. As each work makes clear, society and government share a vested interest in controlling reproduction from before the birth of the child, an interest supported by Progressive Era ideologies of eugenics and public health that conferred citizenship not by assimilation and self-control, as in the citizenship films, but through the pseudosciences governing bloodlines and class. Bred on the Mountain, an ungovernable colony that does not acknowledge the rule of the mother country, Charity brings to her marriage not only the defiance and bloodlines of the unruly colonial subject but also the civilized quality of the assimilated immigrant. Her "swarthy" blood brings vitality to the enervated New Englander Royall. Given the era's racial politics, in strengthening him she strengthens the nation as well, a goal that echoes the Rooseveltian politics of Weber's film. Both the film and Wharton's book suggest that ethnic Others are in the business of preventing eugenically desirable—or, in the Progressive Era context, white, Anglo, and American—babies from being born. Charity establishes citizenship through maternity, demonstrating that she has learned the lessons of Rooseveltian citizenship, and she refuses to let her child be stolen by Dr. Merkle. By refusing to submit to a foreign abortionist, Charity not only fulfills her love for Harney but in Rooseveltian terms performs a patriotic act, a sentiment that Lois Weber, in *Where Are My Children?*, had already preached to the moviegoing millions.

CHAPTER 6

"Manure Widows" and Middlebrow Fiction
Rural Naturalism in the 1920s

In the January 28, 1928, issue of the *New Yorker*, Dorothy Parker began her Constant Reader column by apologizing for what she called a bad case of "the rams," which are "much like the heebie-jeebies, except that they last longer, strike deeper, and are, in general, fancier." In addition to their other features, which otherwise suggest the symptoms of a hangover, the rams leave their victims unable to "like anything much," including current books by the popular middlebrow authors Fannie Hurst and Booth Tarkington. Among her objections to Fannie Hurst's *A President Is Born* is that it features "one of those big, wise, calm, broad-hipped, level-eyed women who puts the farm on a paying basis by her efforts—why do our lady authors so love to write of those?"[1] The "lady authors" had been in Parker's critical sights the previous month as well, when she opened a review of current short story collections by giving five examples of stories she could not stand to read. Three of them were recognizable satires of women's magazine fiction, including the cheerful tale of a "twinkling" old Granny Wilkins sitting on a quaint front porch, a dialect sketch of a "right peart gal," and the story of a young, resolute schoolmistress standing on a station platform as the train chugs away across the prairie: "She looked very small indeed, standing there, and really ridiculously young.... "Oh, Daddy-Daddy, I miss you so!"[2] Sentimental stories of female fortitude, especially in dialect, were just too much for Parker to bear, with or without a case of the rams.

Nor were her examples wholly imaginary. "Granny Wilkins" is a sentimentalized version of a regionalist story, as is the dialect sketch, while the allusion to "farm women" suggests Edna Ferber, whose Pulitzer Prize–winning *So Big* (1924) features a young schoolmistress alone in a prairie town mourning the loss of her beloved father. Hurst and Ferber, constant targets of Parker's satiric jabs at their subject matter and style, were two of the most popular authors of their day. Hurst specialized in the lives of urban working women, from downtrodden immigrant servants like Bertha of *Lummox* (1923) and entrepreneurial widows like B. Pullman in *Imitation of Life* (1933) to self-sacrificing mistresses like Ray Schmidt of *Back Street* (1931). Ferber too was known for her working women: her energetic middle-aged traveling saleswoman Emma McChesney gained a following that included Theodore Roosevelt, who took time from his presidential run in 1912 to admire Emma's "spunk."[3] But Parker charged the serious "magazines with quieter covers" like the *American Mercury* with running to formulas too, providing "[s]edulous agony ... as monotonous as sedulous sunshine."[4] Both popular and serious magazines provided no relief from rural fiction, for while there are "no golden-hearted cow-punchers ... there are the inevitable Midwestern farm families." Like its popular counterpart the sentimental story, the "stark" rural story had become a cliché in Parker's eyes, and the only remedy was stories like Ernest Hemingway's "superb 'The Killers.'"[5] Swift, taut, understated, and most of all unsentimental—in a word, modernist—"The Killers" represented for Parker what was right with contemporary fiction, just as farm fiction written by and about women represented much of what was wrong with it.

Parker was not alone in complaining that "lady authors" and farm novels were threatening to overrun current fiction. In May 1925, F. Scott Fitzgerald mildly protested to his editor, Maxwell Perkins, that writers of rural fiction, including Willa Cather and Ruth Suckow, were writing about a nonexistent "peasantry," but he diplomatically concludes that "maybe its [sic] good; a lot of people seem to think so."[6] By June 1, Fitzgerald was less circumspect. Railing against the reign of rural fiction, he argues that "the American peasant as 'real' material scarcely exists." He outlines a "History of the Simple Inarticulate Farmer and His Hired Man Christy" that includes Sherwood Anderson, Ruth Suckow, and Willa Cather, who "turns [Christy] Swede" (119). Anderson excluded, all the rest are "good second raters" (118) but better than the "Cheapskates," including Edna Ferber, who "turns from her flip jewish [sic] saleswoman" to "a strong silent earthy carrot grower" (119), and Margaret Wilson, whose *The Able McLaughlins* "wins $10,000 prize & is forgotten the following wk." (119). His comic exasperation about the rural novel, or "the Great Beautiful Life of the Manure Widder," as he puts it, arises from critics' equation of soil-bound plots, inarticulate peasants, and plodding style with weighty and significant fiction, consigning elegant stylists like Fitzgerald and Wharton to the position of "mere superficial 'craftsmen'" (119). Fitzgerald attributes this turn toward the rural to "a stubborn seeking for the static in a world that for almost a hundred years has simply not been static" (119), a turn to the kind of regionalist nostalgia in the face of urbanization that characterized the late nineteenth century.

Parker and Fitzgerald were not wrong, however, about the rising tide of rural fiction. In 1921, the same year that Edith Wharton became the first woman to win the Pulitzer Prize for fiction for *The Age of Innocence*, Zona Gale became the first woman to win the Pulitzer for drama with *Miss Lulu Bett*, an adaptation of her novel about a small-town woman oppressed by her overbearing family. In 1923 Willa Cather's war novel *One of Ours* won the Pulitzer for fiction, but as Fitzgerald's letter suggests, her métier had long been rural novels such as *O Pioneers!* and *My Ántonia*. Wilson's *The Able McLaughlins*, a pioneer-themed novel set in Iowa, received the fiction prize in 1924, and, as Fitzgerald predicted, dropped from sight shortly thereafter. In 1925, the year when *The Great Gatsby* was published to modest sales, Edna Ferber won the Pulitzer for *So Big*, a best-selling novel that combined both of the trends that Parker had ridiculed, the "young schoolmarm left alone in the world" and the "broad-hipped, level-eyed woman" who puts the farm on a paying basis. With rural fiction flooding the market in the 1920s, Parker and Fitzgerald could readily believe that modernist work was not outclassed but was definitely being outsold by Ferber and other authors celebrating what Fitzgerald called "the Great Beautiful Life of the Manure Widder."

The "Manure Widder" farm novels suggest their middlebrow roots in their positioning within Andreas Huyssen's "great divide" between mass culture and high modernism.[7] Put more simply, the middlebrow aspires to convey something of worth to its readers but refuses both the mind-candy style and overt didacticism of sensationalist literature and the stylistic and structural alienation of readers demanded by highbrow aesthetic principles. As Meredith Goldsmith and Lisa Botshon write in their introduction to *Middlebrow Moderns*, the term "middlebrow" is defined "by what it is not: lacking the cachet and edginess of high culture ... [and] the authenticity of the low" while still being linked to "other slightly soiled middles, including the middle class and middle life."[8] Because its prose is deliberately unchallenging, and because it prizes readers' affective responses rather than strenuous intellectual engagement, the middlebrow faces automatic suspicion of its content, often seen as sentimental or, after the fact, as critically subpar. As such, it presents a challenge to high-culture readers, for, as Nicola Humble maintains, "[m]iddlebrow texts carry within their physical form a threat to this status: they are not serious, they are not properly cultured, anyone can read them, and so our unique reading skills may not be so unique after all."[9]

Another challenge of the middlebrow is the tendency of works to slip in status after their initial classification as critically celebrated or praiseworthy. Middlebrow novels tend to be so perfectly in tune with the cultural assumptions of their times that the assumptions are rendered invisible, making them all the more subject to seeming dated when read in later decades. Few critics today would classify Pearl S. Buck's *The Good Earth* and its sequels, Margaret Mitchell's *Gone with the Wind*, or, to use Fitzgerald's example, *The Able McLaughlins* as other than middlebrow despite the critical praise lavished on each when it appeared. Because they were aspirational texts, appealing in their own time to the "audience of moderately educated readers who seek to become cultured," according to Janet Galligani Casey, "many Pulitzer Prize winners ... were middlebrow successes and are now largely unknown."[10] Literary prizes were not the key to middlebrow success, however; reader engagement was. In recovering the "oft-scorned terrain" of the middlebrow as a level playing field for comparing Willa Cather's *My Ántonia* and Bess Streeter Aldrich, Melissa Homestead shows that, although Cather has achieved a canonicity denied to Aldrich, readers wrote to both in similar ways, "claim[ing] Cather, Aldrich and their characters as friends, and even as 'family.'"[11] The immediacy of reader engagement and the transmission of affect were central to the middlebrow reading experience, just as the erasure of aesthetic distance promoted by stylistically challenging modernist texts contributed to the denigration of the middlebrow.

A common feature of the middlebrow is its national perspective. In the pioneer saga, the family chronicle, and the multigenerational novel, the middlebrow defies the insularity and ahistoricity of modernist writing by celebrating the historical quotidian of American life with insertions of political critique. The middlebrow shares naturalism's interest in Taine's "race, moment, milieu," but its positivistic approach toward the evolution of human progress separates it from such naturalistic chronicles such as Zola's Rougon-Macquart series. Using the family saga, Ferber, Aldrich, and Cather shaped plots that would account for the rise of U.S. power on the world stage, promoted and critiqued its myths of American exceptionalism, and explained the country to itself through its incorporation of varying ethnicities, its historical narratives of settlement, and its espousal of common values. As such, it has a political agenda and a specificity of time and place abhorrent to the universalizing tendencies of modernism. Rather than moving disjointedly through time and space, through classical myth and contemporary popular culture, the middlebrow writer attributes a sense of alienation and loss to the material lives of individuals living in a particular historical moment rather than to modernity and its effect on the human condition. Nor is this tendency confined to American middlebrow novels, for the agrarian myth that informs middlebrow American novels appears in British literature as the chronicle of upward mobility seen through historical events, including overtones of empire, as in Arnold Bennett's Clayhanger series and the three trilogies comprising John Galsworthy's Forsyte chronicles (*The Forsyte Saga, A Modern Comedy, End of the Chapter*). In Canada, Mazo de la Roche's sixteen-volume Jalna series followed an Anglo-Canadian family through four generations, headed by an ancient and irascible matriarch, Adeline Whiteoak, in place of Galsworthy's family of patriarchs. But precisely because it is doubly dated, written about a particular time and place distant from the present moment and national concerns, the middlebrow novel makes fewer claims to universality and immortality than other literary forms, rendering it potentially forgettable when literary fashions change.

Read in the context of middlebrow culture and a readership shaped by film, the "Manure Widder" farm novels of all types—the multigenerational pioneer chronicle, the survival narrative, the fable of production, and the naturalistic tale of isolation and despair—proved a more varied and durable form of fiction than Parker's and Fitzgerald's dismissive remarks would suggest. Beneath the triumphal intergenerational tale of endurance and positive, even lyrical, style and tone of these novels exists a hard spine of naturalistic elements in both classic and unruly form. These include the themes of women's courtship choices, sexuality and desire, and environmental determinism of classic naturalism coexisting with unruly naturalism's focus on the grotesque body of the naturalistic woman, the depiction of children as waste, scenes of childbirth, and men's violence toward women, for which women themselves must shoulder the blame, as in Cather's *O Pioneers!* The sharp-edged sentiment of Ferber's *So Big* rewrites itself as tragedy in Cather's *O Pioneers!* despite both novels' triumphal conclusions about the relationships between women and the land.

"Rube Comedies" and Rural Fiction

In the 1920s, the public's appetite for the Manure Widder and her wise-eyed, broad-hipped sisters had been whetted not only by fiction but also by film. The boom in popular rural fiction paralleled a late-blooming nostalgia for a preindustrial and agricultural world rapidly vanishing under urbanization. Automobiles and movie projectors, along with improved roads and primitive film exchanges for movie rentals, encouraged the moviegoing habit among small-town residents and farmers. The rural dream was sold to those who knew better than anyone else the hardships of farm life, yet they happily consumed cinematically enhanced versions of themselves filmed by companies based in New York, New Jersey (Fort Lee), or, later, Hollywood. In Sinclair Lewis's *Main Street*, the immigrant maid Bea Sorenson, who provides a counterpoint to his sophisticated heroine Carol Kennicott, is astonished to find a "regular theater, just for movies" when she comes to Gopher Prairie circa 1910, instead of a movie "once every two weeks" shown in a store or church hall against a portable screen, an experience that parallels that of Wharton's Charity Royall.[12] Going to the movies signifies urban sophistication for Bea, but for Carol Kennicott the movies are a cultural marker of the low tastes of her husband, Will, and his friends. Trying to win him away from the movies by reading Yeats aloud, Carol admits defeat, suggesting that they go to see the enormously popular comedies that Lewis parodied as "Mack Schnarken and the Bathing Suit Babes" (198), his alias for Mack Sennett's comedies featuring his corps of Bathing Beauties and the Keystone Kops. By the mid-teens, film had elevated its social status somewhat from the lower-class amusement of the early nickelodeon parlors, but for intellectuals like Carol Kennicott and her creator, it was not yet an art form.

In the 1910s, "rube" or rural comedies and, later, melodramas presented the countryside as the escape from modernity that Fitzgerald had predicted.[13] Rube comedies exaggerated stereotypical characteristics of farmers and their families, finding broad comedy in everything from classic slapstick routines involving rural situations (squirting milk directly from a cow at an unsuspecting bystander, landing in a pile of mud or manure) to the city slicker's ignorance of country ways. Rural films could be enjoyed precisely because they bore a recognizable relationship to a place and time safely distanced from contemporary reality, with D. W. Griffith's *True Heart Susie* (1919), *A Romance of Happy Valley* (1920), and *Way Down East* (1920) promoting rural values as those of a vanishing America. Like the "greenhorn" films of the 1910s that promoted American customs and citizenship by ridiculing the ignorance of those fresh off the boat, rural films allowed the recently urbanized audience to laugh in recognition at the bewilderment of rural types in the city and city slickers in the country. Instead of winning over the greenhorn to American ways, however, the rube comedy endorses rural rather than urban values. The most popular plots for rube comedy involved country folk hoodwinking the city slickers who try to cheat them. By 1920, the types and plots were so familiar that Mack Sennett's *Down on the Farm* (1920) bills its stock characters as the Farmer's Daughter, the Rustic Sweetheart, the Farmer, the Sportive Banker with the Mortgage, the Gossipy Villager, and so on.

By the 1920s, the rube comedies had to compete with more sophisticated fare. Audiences clamored for glossy romantic comedy-dramas such as Cecil B. DeMille's *Why Change Your Wife?* (1920), which featured glamorous stars like Gloria Swanson in an array of expensive gowns and catered to the consumers' aspirations by showcasing elaborate interiors. More sophisticated still were the films of Erich von Stroheim, such as *The Wedding March* (1928) and *Blind Husbands* (1918), which encoded references to sadomasochism and other forbidden practices in their tales of adultery and seduction. To keep up, rural films showed a greater sophistication and variety. For example, Mary Pickford starred in vehicles such as *Pollyanna* (1920) and *Rebecca of Sunnybrook Farm* (1917) set in a mythically innocent past, yet her *Stella Maris* (1918) and *Sparrows* (1926) were darker, the latter featuring Pickford's character leading her charges through a swamp and away from their cruel masters at a baby farm. According to Eileen Whitfield, "discussion of Pickford's portrayal of children often omits her significant roles as girls who live harsh lives beyond the margins of society," such as Mavis in *The Heart o' the Hills*, who stops her mother from beating her by carrying a shotgun.[14] Elements of rube comedy appeared as late as the 1930s in the films that Will Rogers made for 20th-Century Fox, including *David Harum* (1934) and *Judge Priest* (1934). What rarely occurred in film, however, was the critique of the rural as a site of oppression, poverty, and family violence, although glimpses of this occur in *Stark Love* (1927), *Tol'able David* (1921, 1930), and the early Bette Davis feature *Way Back Home* (1931).[15] The latter opens with a comic scene of a farmer bamboozling a city tax man but includes a plot of an abusive father who beats his son. In both their rural subject matter and in their critique of rural life, the novels of Edna Ferber and her middlebrow contemporaries Ruth Suckow and Bess Streeter Aldrich fit solidly into a context of farm films and current nostalgia for the vanished past of pioneer days.

In complaining about the critical credibility automatically granted to rural fiction, Fitzgerald echoed larger debates about the "realism" of films. In "To Here from Modernity," Charlie Keil notes that the definitions of realism that film exhibitors and reviewers used at the time differ from those critical categories as commonly understood. The "realism" celebrated by trade-press writers defined films as "close to life" if they represented emotional truths but disdained stunts included for the sake of sensation or thrills on the part of the audience.[16] To put this in literary terms, the desirable "realism" of films is the same form that W. D. Howells had promoted as part of his campaign for realism from the 1880s until his death in 1920: "the light of common day" rather than the sensational and sordid, code words that, then as now, connoted naturalism instead of realism.[17] In this, Howells anticipates realism as defined by early film critics. Erich von Stroheim, the director of the quintessentially naturalistic *Greed* (1923), an adaptation of Frank Norris's *McTeague*, named rural dramas and comedies rather than urban dramas as exemplifying realism on the screen: "Little realism has been seen on the screen. There are 'Miss Lulu Bett,' some of Will Rogers's pictures, 'Grandma's Boy' and 'The Kid' in comedies."[18] What stands out in Stroheim's equation of realism with comedy is that none of these were straight-out slapstick films of the Mack Sennett variety. Rather, the realism is connected to both comedy and pathos as rendered through small, true-to-life comic touches and gestures.

Scenario writers thus received contradictory advice from the literary and film worlds. Scenarists or scenario writers were told that pathos, or "heart interest ... an appeal to the sympathies, the sentimental emotions of the audience," as Charles Donald Fox defines it in *The Fox Plan of Photoplay Writing*, is essential.[19] But modernists like Parker, Fitzgerald, and H. L. Mencken fought sentiment in favor of a higher literary culture based in its absence. To incorporate "heart interest" was to abandon any pretense of modernist literary merit. Yet since films demanded "heart interest," scenarists had to supply it and content themselves with the solace of money instead of literary fame. Indeed, modernists and proletarian writers of the twentieth century may have disagreed about the nature and function of art, but both despised what they saw as sentimentalism. As Jennifer Williamson sums up their perspectives, "The term *sentimental* becomes Marxist shorthand for feminized and maudlin attempts to influence readers into an emotional state."[20] The affective elements that modernism sought to evoke through understatement were transformed into the "heart interest" of the movies, yet in neither modernist nor popular forms were the excesses of sentimentality permitted.

Banishing sentimentality but retaining the "heart interest" necessary to a film was a problem fit for Solomon, or, in the 1910s and 1920s, the legion of female scriptwriters or "scenario writers," who were represented in numbers far exceeding those of today. According to Lizzie Francke in *Script Girls*, women wrote half of the twenty-five thousand scenarios deposited for copyright at the Library of Congress between 1911 and 1929. In comparison, in 2013, women wrote 15 percent of film scripts and 28 percent of television scripts.[21] There was no shortage of advice for aspiring scenario writers in movie magazines like *Photoplay*, and, given the magazine's readership, there was every expectation that women could follow this career. For example, "Mail Order Genius," in the June 1916 issue, warned against correspondence schools for learning the art of scenario writing but included "A 'Model' Scenario" for readers who wanted to try their hand at writing one, encouragement that the magazine had already reinforced with scenario-writing contests.[22] Anita Loos and John Emerson explain the importance of the scenario writer in *Breaking into the Movies*: "It is the scenarioist or continuity writer who really gives to the story its screen value—hence the very large prices paid for this work when it is well done," because "no story can survive a badly constructed scenario."[23] Even at the young age of thirty-three Loos was an acknowledged authority on scenario writing. Beginning with *The New York Hat* (1912), which she claimed to have sold to D. W. Griffith at the age of thirteen, she and her husband John Emerson successfully wrote scenarios and intertitles and published *How to Write Photoplays* (1920) as a practical guide to aspiring newcomers.[24] In contrast to "heart interest," Loos and Emerson advise creating "star sympathy," or adapting themes to the strengths of the star: "Don't write a story for [boyish rural actor] Charles Ray which deals with the soulless villain. Don't send Charley [sic] Chaplin the great heart interest story."[25]

In following such fictional formulas, middlebrow women writers, who knew what their audiences liked, met with the success the how-to advice had promised to women scenario writers, who had learned the same lesson. Women fiction writers who worked as Hollywood screenwriters on the side, including Winnifred Eaton (Onoto Watanna), Anita Loos, and, later, Dorothy Parker, or whose popular fiction was destined for the movies, like Fannie Hurst and Edna Ferber, needed to retain "heart interest" while avoiding sentimentality. The result was a sharp-edged sentiment that manifested itself in tart, witty dialogue, in Loos's and Parker's case, and in the bitterness of environmental adversity, family tragedy, and social critique, in the case of Ferber, Aldrich, Haldeman-Julius, Suckow, Cannon, Cather, Kelley, and Scarborough.

Sharp-Edged Sentiment and Middlebrow Naturalism

Popular middlebrow farm novels such as Edna Ferber's *So Big* (1924) and Bess Streeter Aldrich's *A Lantern in Her Hand* (1928) establish the history of a region. These multigenerational family sagas or pioneer novels typically move from the recent past of the 1880s up through the 1920s present. Despite their optimistic appeals to the idea of self-reliance, they acknowledge the hazards of settling a new place, usually a harsh landscape barren of comforts and trees, a place that promised much but delivered little. Characters battle disease, face crop failure and financial ruin, suffer through childbirth and the death of children, and endure drought, hail, fire, and blizzards. Because of the multigenerational element, the pioneer farm novel is evolutionary in scope, since the individual suffers and experiences disillusionment, yet the collective genetic pool of the family advances and thrives. Framed by real history, middlebrow farm novels create an origin story that confirms ownership through endurance and confers citizenship by right of possession.

SO BIG

As Edna Ferber described it in her 1939 autobiography *A Peculiar Treasure*, *So Big* "was a story of the triumph of failure. There was in it practically no action. The book's high dramatic point came when Selina drove to town with a load of cabbages, turnips, and beets."[26] Its protagonist, Selina Peake, embodies two of Parker's bêtes noires: the schoolteacher whose adored father dies and the woman who puts the farm on a paying basis. Selina adores her gambler father Simeon, who can barely support her financially but gives her an appreciation of beauty and a clearheaded response to reading character, dividing worthwhile people into "wheat" and "emeralds," or utilitarian and artistic senses of beauty. When Simeon dies, Selina rejects the help of her wealthy friend Julie Hempel and instead accepts a position teaching school in High Prairie, a community of Dutch truck farmers south of Chicago. Her chance remark that a field of cabbages is beautiful strikes her host, Klaas Pool, as hilarious, but Klaas's son Roelf, a budding artist, agrees with her.

After her marriage and the early death of her husband, Pervus DeJong, Selina and her son, Dirk, drive their vegetables to market, scandalizing the town, which believes that only men can engage in commerce. Chided by Reverend Dekker to stay at home and remember that God provides—"Remember the two sparrows. 'One of them shall not fall to the ground without'"—Selina pragmatically replies, "I don't see what good that does the sparrow, once it's fallen," a succinct statement of the consistent Ferber theme of the divide between men's idealism and women's realism.[27] Selina puts Dirk through the state university, hoping he will live out her vision of creating beauty by becoming an architect. Instead, seduced by money and by Julie's married daughter, Paula, he becomes a bond salesman, an empty profession compared to Selina's farming, Roelf's painting, or, as Dallas O'Mara, a young female artist tells him, any other profession that means something to him. When Roelf returns as an internationally famous artist, he declares that even in her battered hat and weathered skin, Selina is beautiful because she has character. They recognize the artist's worth in one another: "You're wheat, Selina." "And you're emerald" (357). Dirk realizes that, in contrast, he is nothing but a "rubber stamp." Bereft of any chance with Dallas, he realizes that his wealth is meaningless and that his mother's life, which seemed so narrow, has actually been lived to the fullest extent.

As in many of Ferber's novels, the family saga serves as a popularizing framework to contain her real subject matter, the transformation of a nineteenth-century rural America into a twentieth-century urban one. Janet Galligani Casey concludes that *So Big* is "less a rural novel than a novel about the effects of modernity *and* urbanity" that "evades the simplistic nostalgia for the farm that some other works with substantial rural elements exploited."[28] Ferber doubled theme and critique in her other novels as well. The most obvious example is *Show Boat*, which shares with novels such as *Great Son* the device of American theatrical history as a reflecting mirror for the racial injustices that American mythology too often conceals. In its melodramatic plot of interracial love and its historical one of appropriation of African American music by white performers, *Show Boat* condemns racism despite its participation in racial stereotyping. *Come and Get It* and *Saratoga Trunk* protest the rapacity of timber barons and railroad tycoons, while *Cimarron* and *Giant* reveal the Oklahoma land rush of 1889 and the settlement of Texas as two versions of the great American land grab. But like the "triumph of failure" idea for *So Big*, few of Ferber's readers recognized her critique. As Ferber wrote in *A Peculiar Treasure*, "*Cimarron* had been written with a hard and ruthless purpose. It was, and is, a malevolent picture of what is known as American womanhood and American sentimentality. . . . I doubt that more than a dozen people ever knew this."[29] Several years later, she counted *So Big* as another misunderstood work: "In *Cimarron* I wrote a story whose purpose was to show the triumph of materialism over the spirit in America, and I did show it, but perhaps I was too reticent about it.... In *So Big* I used the same theme.... Same result. Terrific sales; about nine people knew what I was driving at."[30]

So Big establishes the prototype for two of Ferber's most familiar plots. The first is derived from nineteenth-century domestic fiction but with a twist: an adolescent girl, orphaned or with only one surviving and feckless parent, is left to fend for herself in the world when the parent dies. Instead of learning self-denial and the control of natural impulses, she learns to channel her inventiveness into making a living. *So Big* also includes a second major plot trajectory in Ferber's work, roughly as follows: a young woman marries, loses her husband when he dies or disappears, and not only adopts the man's profession but excels at it. In *So Big*, Selina Peake DeJong makes her farm prosper "[o]ut of a book" (125) despite the scorn of her husband, Pervus, but after his death she develops a thriving business in specialty vegetables, including asparagus, which Pervus had refused to plant because he shortsightedly believed it took too long to grow. During her improvident husband Yancey's many absences, *Cimarron*'s Sabra Cravat takes over the newspaper he founded, the *Oklahoma Wigwam*, and makes it a respected organ of public opinion. Magnolia Ravenal, in *Show Boat*, carries on her stage career as a singer long after her husband, Gaylord Ravenal, deserts her. Despite their initial hands-on domestic tasks, all achieve a success that allows them to delegate their domestic duties to servants and other employees, leaving them free to pursue a career and express their aesthetic principles, even if the heroine's aesthetic sense is, as in Sabra Cravat's case, woefully lacking.

Despite Parker's and Fitzgerald's low opinion of Ferber, *So Big* follows modernist principles in articulating an aesthetic of authenticity that critiques modern forms of mass production in favor of handcrafted art forms informed by material utility, an aesthetic represented through the novel's use of architecture and interior design. When Dirk abandons his career in architecture, a profession that requires the ability to create intrinsic beauty through utility, for a career as a bonds salesman, a profession in which the value of the product depends entirely on extrinsic systems of value, he transgresses the system of values that Selina has tried to instill in him. Dirk's pursuit of the invisible value created by the bond market marks him as empty. In contrast, the hand-carved chest that Roelf carves for Selina upon her marriage, and the items that she keeps in it—Roelf's first drawing, a pair of mud-stained boots—have beauty because of their meaning for her. Furnished by Selina with well-worn old furniture, Dirk's first flat is a thing of beauty, but his second one, decorated by Paula and her legion of interior designers, is "as cosy as a cathedral" (311). The division between authentic and inauthentic values pervades education as well, for the state university draws two kinds of students, the "classified" traditional-age students, for whom fraternities and social life are paramount, and the "unclassifieds" or nontraditional students. To the latter, serious, shabby, and hungry for knowledge and asking for "the bread of knowledge..., the University gave...a stone" (231). Scorned by other students and professors alike, the authentic student who wants to learn has no place in a modern university system that "turned [students] out by the hundreds—almost by the link" like "fine plump sausages" (229), because in an extrinsic system of values, the semblance of education is more valuable than the education itself.

Tied to the novel's critique of mass production is its celebration of artistic individualism and the authentic material object. When Dirk commissions an advertising poster from the young artist Dallas O'Mara, he asks its price:

> "Fifteen hundred dollars," said Miss O'Mara.
> "Nonsense.... You mean fifteen hundred dollars for a single drawing?"
> "For that sort of thing, yes."
> "I'm afraid we can't pay that, Miss O'Mara."
> Miss O'Mara stood up. "That is my price." She was not at all embarrassed. (323)

Dallas later admits that it seems a lot of money to her too, after a career spent drawing hats for twenty-five cents apiece, but she is "not at all embarrassed" because she recognizes and accepts the arbitrary nature of the valuation. In other words, she knows what her name is worth on a drawing, the value of her brand in the marketplace. Selina too recognizes the value of branding. Her long-term thinking pays off in the production of asparagus from her "asparagus plantation," the clay soil that Pervus had refused to help her reclaim for planting because seeing a profit would mean a wait of ten years. In the novel's present, the asparagus is sought after by Chicago restaurants and proudly advertised on menus as "DeJong asparagus" (312). In linking beauty with utility, and in inveighing against 1920s tastes for imitation antiques and imitation careers in bond sales, Ferber articulates a modernist aesthetic based in material practice. The farm is merely the means through which Selina expresses her sense of beauty through utility.

So Big's approach to authenticity and art extends to the production of food on the farm, a work of art that cannot be produced without hard work and the raw material of dirt. Food, always lovingly detailed in Ferber's novels, signifies the approach to sensual experiences necessary for artistic creation, just as the novel's attention to hands represents the necessity of hard work to create beautiful objects. When Selina's artistically arranged shoebox lunch is held up to ridicule at the schoolhouse raffle early in the book, Pervus bids ten dollars for it and spurns Widow Paarlenburg's heavy hamper full of food, securing Selina's gratitude as well as her affection. After Pervus's death, Selina's artistic eye causes her to group and scrub her vegetables for market, the first step toward making them a specialty item with the commission agents. Selina's approach to beauty through utility and her recognition that dirt is essential to creativity links her to Dallas O'Mara. Dallas is an artist with carelessly arranged hair, occasionally dirty hands due to her work, and a hearty appetite. She orders "a steak and some potatoes au gratin" (333) when dining with Dirk, who recalls that Paula only "nibble[s] fragile curls of Melba toast, a lettuce leaf, or half a sugarless grapefruit" (334) when they eat together. Restraining her hunger for food has made Paula "a little haggard" (334), and her hands are "brown, and awfully thin and sort of—grabby" (245). Hands that do no useful work, like Paula's, are grasping and restless, or, like Dirk's, "fine strong unscarred" (348) hands. Dallas would prefer "a horny-handed son of toil, and if I do [marry] it'll be the horny hands that will win me" (347). Having fallen in love with Dallas, Dirk offers to go back to architecture if it would give him a chance, to which Dallas says, simply, "Don't" (348). Her hands remind Dirk of Selina's because of the scars from life that hers have and his lack. Shortly after this, Roelf Poole, returning from France as an internationally celebrated artist, kisses Selina's "rough, work-worn hand" (358).

Through these contrasts, Ferber drives home one of her themes: the aesthetic value of materiality, authentic expression, and artistic idealism rather than ephemerality, mass production, and cynicism. The novel resets readers' expectations of beauty through the dirt- and work-infused realism of Selina DeJong and her spiritual children, Roelf Poole and Dallas O'Mara.[31] As if to confirm the novel's critique of mass-produced modernism, Paula views her babies as merely "lumps of flesh," living but uninteresting waste by-products of her unhappy marriage, whom she looks at but does not touch. In contrast, Selina rejects the artificial in favor of the real when she prefers live theater to the movies. "Like fooling with paper dolls when you could be playing with a real live baby," she tells Dirk. She prefers to live in the body and in real life rather than in the artificial version represented by the "motion pictures" (265). As a means to an end rather than the end itself, Selina's farm and the food associated with it testify to a work-centered aesthetics of material reality that trumps the evanescent value rendered by the bond market and the movies. A true twentieth-century aesthetic, Ferber argues, must celebrate modern, though not necessarily modernist, conceptions of beauty through utility. Echoing the Chicago architect Louis Sullivan's creed of "form follows function," *So Big* rejects both the late nineteenth-century Decadents' celebration of uselessness and the Lost Generation's embrace of cynicism and despair.

A LANTERN IN HER HAND

Bess Streeter Aldrich's *A Lantern in Her Hand* (1928) pits beauty against utility in the pioneer saga. Narrated in part as an extended flashback from the viewpoint of a dying elderly woman—in itself an ignored modernist feature of the text—the novel touches on social and political history from 1854 through the 1920s. Yet its narrative focus remains firmly planted in the domestic and economic affairs of a family and community as seen through the eyes of Abbie Mackenzie Deal. Traveling west from Chicago to Iowa by covered wagon, a standard part of the pioneer narrative, the eight-year-old Abbie asks her older sister Isabelle to recount once again the story of their parents' meeting and courtship. After Scottish aristocrat Basil Mackenzie sees the beautiful Irish peasant girl Margaret O'Conner standing by a rose bush, he falls instantly in love, marries her, and forces his proud family to accept her. The story is a democratized version of the American family romance of noble origins and a fantasy version of the seduction plot. The hidden aristocratic roots of the couple's children are confirmed by the possession of talismanic objects—a portrait, a shawl, and a string of pearls that belonged to Basil's mother, Isabelle Anders-Mackenzie—and of evolutionary outcroppings such as Abbie's tapering aristocratic fingers. Despite her ambitions to be a singer, an artist, and a writer, ambitions fostered by her half-hearted engagement to a young doctor who promises to take her to New York, Abbie abandons the promise of wealth to marry the farmer Will Deal when he returns from the Civil War.

The Deals and their children move to a new land, Nebraska, where with the German Reinmuellers and Lutzes they form a new town. Drought, grasshoppers, and economic hard times beset the family, yet as Abbie's children become adults, each expresses, in the genetic sense, what she had transmitted to them through her example as well as through her blood: Mack becomes a banker and a patron of the arts through his training in Shakespeare; Margaret marries but is also a painter; John becomes a lawyer; Isabelle becomes a professional singer; and Grace, who adamantly refuses to marry, teaches at Wesleyan University. The novel comes full circle when Abbie gives to her granddaughter Katherine, on her wedding day, Isabelle Anders-Mackenzie's pearls, the talisman that she had preserved carefully through hard times, and Abbie's son Mack presents Abbie with the long-lost portrait of Isabelle Anders-Mackenzie wearing the pearls that he had traced and purchased after hearing his mother's stories. The giving of these heirlooms demonstrates the different significance of the past for the younger generation and their elders. Abbie, seeing the portrait, is overcome by tears at all that it signifies, but Katherine casually accepts the pearls, which carry a heavy symbolic weight for Abbie. Indifferent to the significance of Abbie's sacrifices and those of previous generations, she simply says, "Thanks, Granny, dear. They're darling."[32]

After the struggle for simple survival in a hostile environment, the primary message of the pioneer novel is that the frontier dehumanizes its inhabitants by stripping life of all but its elemental meanings of birth, death, and survival. Aldrich contrasts the idealism and Irish romanticism of Abbie's view, as shown by her signature song "The Lady of the Lea," with the materialism and pragmatism of her German neighbors Sarah Lutz and Christine Reinmueller. Always fashionably dressed and restless for travel, Sarah cares for her family but does not make her children her life, as Abbie does. Christine values material goods above spiritual ones, seeing in the acquisition of land the only pursuit that matters and deriding Christmas festivities as a foolish waste of time. All three are necessary in the new land: Abbie's imagination and artistic vision, Sarah's interest in the world beyond the home, and Christine's frugality. Thrown together by their chance arrival in the same place on the frontier at the same time, the three forge a bond based less in similarity of interests than in similarities of adversity. Sarah loses a child to snakebite shortly after they arrive and Abbie consoles her, as others console Abbie after her husband, Will, dies suddenly at a relatively young age, and a child, a son, is stillborn.

Aldrich's pioneer story claims the making of history and community as its subject by grounding history in domestic matters, including maternity, the literal birth of new citizens, and childbirth, a terrifying process that pits woman alone against a natural force that can easily kill her just as surely as men are tested against animals and the environment in classic naturalism. During one of her deliveries, Abbie "knew the greatest fear for all prairie women,—to be alone on the desert of grass with the pangs of childbirth upon her" (56–57), before Christine comes to help with the delivery. Aldrich repeats the scene with a further variation later in the novel when Abbie, now forty, goes into labor with another child and struggles to get home in the midst of a blizzard. Christine again intervenes, helping Abbie to walk and navigating in the blinding snow by counting the nine cedars that the Deals have planted. The trees, a testament to Abbie's love of beauty and Will's devotion to her, break up the bleak prairie landscape, confirming that small actions as well as great ones comprise the history of a place. As Abbie explains to her brisk, efficient daughter Grace, who has just commented that her mother's life has been "narrow," "I've seen history in the making... three ugly wars flare up and die down.... I've seen the feeble beginnings of a raw state" (164). Abbie and her cohort not only settle the town but also name it (Cedartown). They plant flowers, establish schools and women's literary societies, and participate in the Old Pioneer Days that the town eventually celebrates. What the novel recuperates into memory is the idea that women forge the history and culture of a place by bridging their knowledge from the old world "back east" and shaping the common narrative of the new one "out here."

The triumphant ending of *A Lantern in Her Hand* does not warrant the charges of sentimentality that it has received. Rather, as in other novels of unruly naturalism, it caps a narrative that, if not for the overall tone, would reflect classic naturalism in its grim details of poverty, loss, and death. In defending the novel, Denise D. Knight compares it to the stories of Hamlin Garland, which frequently include a sentimental denouement, and contends that "there is a strong naturalistic strain in her writing" consisting of "the utter randomness of nature."[33] Melissa Homestead confirms Knight's assessment by calling the novel "far grimmer and less optimistic than *My Ántonia*."[34] That Aldrich consciously situates *A Lantern in Her Hand* in a middlebrow rather than modernist tradition becomes evident near the end of the book when Abbie's granddaughter, Katherine, comes to visit. Enthralled with Michael Arlen's popular modernist bestseller *The Green Hat*, Katherine reads aloud to Abbie a passage in which "love is like a hammer.... It beats and beats inside him and presently ... it doesn't beat at all" (259). Unimpressed, Abbie replies, "The words are very clever. But not all clever words are true" (259), an answer to the stylistic gymnastics of modernism from the point of view of the previous generation. Self-aware and grounded in the history of her family and the history of her nation, Abbie is not the traditional naturalistic heroine buffeted by forces that she does not understand. Rather, her understanding of those forces and the bitter memories that she retains of their power in her life aligns her with other naturalistic protagonists who, as Donald Pizer describes them, recognize "that we live in a contingent universe ... but also that we continue to share in the myth of the autonomous self that is capable of realizing and choosing its own fate."[35]

Survival Narratives and Fables of Production

Survival narratives such as Emanuel and Marcet Haldeman-Julius's *Dust* (1921), Ruth Suckow's *Country People* (1924), and Cornelia James Cannon's *Red Rust* (1928) have a strong Darwinian and naturalistic bent, given their emphasis on inherited traits and on environmental factors, including brutal marriages, that threaten their women characters. Survival narratives emphasize the grinding poverty of farm life that renders female inhabitants little better than beasts of burden with a consequent destruction of the spirit. The animals on the farm experience violence both planned and accidental: the cyclical butchery of animals necessary to ensure a food supply parallels accidents and illnesses that beset the human beings, who are crushed by animals, succumb to fever or overwork, or die in childbirth. In addition to this violence by natural means, the farm setting exacerbates Darwinian tensions in the competition for scarce economic and sexual resources. Subplots in *Dust* and *Red Rust* include the threat of quasi-incestuous relationships or the replacement of wives with their younger female relatives. Fables of production such as Cather's *O Pioneers!* (1913) and Edith Summers Kelley's *Weeds* (1923) show women able to wrest a living from the land. They grant women more agency than do the farm-wife plots of Peattie and Cleary but at a cost greater than that of the big-picture optimists of the family saga. Together with Dorothy Scarborough's *The Wind*, these novels focus on a woman's battle with the land, often at the cost of her personal life (in Cather), her health (in Kelley), or her sanity (in Scarborough).

DUST

Dust (1921), by social reformers Emanuel Haldeman-Julius (1889–1951) and Anna Marcet Haldeman-Julius (1887–1941), recalls Dreiser's *The Financier* and Glasgow's *The Descendant* in its naturalistic portrait of a boy hardened by his environment into a flinty egotist whose love of money crowds out his capacity for love.[36] On a hardscrabble farm in rural Kansas, Martin Wade watches his baby brother die of starvation when the layers of dust cloaking the ground prevent the family cow, and the family itself, from receiving sufficient nourishment to survive. Noticing that hard work cures his emotional pain, he labors on the farm after the deaths of his parents and the marriage of his sister. At age thirty-five, after paying off the mortgage and selling his coal rights for the relative fortune of $16,000, Martin decides that a wife would add to his comfort and travels to town in search of a woman to marry. His choice is Rose Conroy, an old schoolmate now running her late father's newspaper, and, after he promises to build her a two-story house with running water and a fireplace, she agrees to marry him. But after the two are married, Martin reverts to the moneymaking machine he had been before marrying Rose. In an echo of Mary E. Wilkins Freeman's "The Revolt of 'Mother,'" he reneges on the promise of amenities in the new house, buying equipment for the barn instead of installing the promised running water and fireplace. From their marriage until Martin's death, Rose struggles in a naturalistic universe in which the environmental forces that have shaped Martin's grimly utilitarian perspective ultimately wring all joy from her life.

As in other naturalistic farm novels, the heroine's romantic idealism, rather than sustaining her imaginatively, provides her with repeated frustration as she tries to interest her indifferent husband. Raised with dust and starvation as constants in his life, Martin controls the utilitarian cycle of consumption and production on the farm to an extreme degree. Fearing that a child would consume resources instead of producing them, Martin stops sleeping with Rose early in their relationship. When Rose does become pregnant and a cow kicks her in the abdomen, causing her to give birth to a stillborn son, Martin has no sympathy for her loss but instead rails at her clumsiness in upsetting the cow, one of his best milkers. In his mind, the cow produces something of value, but Rose merely produces a child, a waste product of their sexual relationship that cannot produce but can only consume resources. When Rose eventually has a child, Billy, Martin proves as hostile to him as he is to Rose, refusing even to give the boy a room of his own. In a naturalistic epiphany like that of Frank Cowperwood of Dreiser's *The Financier* or Judith Pippinger in Kelley's *Weeds*, Billy receives a horrifying education when he sees an old sow devour one of her piglets. Though couched in animal form, the lessons of the sow's cannibalism and filicide are hammered home shortly thereafter when Rose charges Martin with "eating the heart out of your own boy" (130). The farmer too must participate in this cruel consumption: Billy hears the mournful moos of old Molly crying for her calf and learns that her calf has already been butchered for veal. As he grows, Billy must inflict "inhuman torture... upon animals that had learned to trust him" (130). The farm is a naturalistic universe, filled with betrayal and killing for the sake of survival.

The cycle of eating and unnatural nourishment, carnage and waste, which had begun with the dust consumed by Martin's baby brother, manifests itself differently in Rose. On an economic level, Martin sustains himself and his farm on the food Rose cooks as well as on her unstinting work and devotion, yet he refuses to participate in any reciprocal exchange of affection or goods with her. His parsimony has consequences. As in other naturalistic farm novels such as Suckow's *Country People*, the woman's body transforms itself into socially grotesque forms in response to the challenges of its environment. Starved for affection, Rose, in her younger days a Junoesque figure, substitutes food for the emptiness within. Her body balloons to 240 pounds, with the result that Martin finds her sexually unappealing and avoids her even more strenuously than before. Having rejected his wife, Martin falls in love with her namesake and niece, young Rose. In a subplot often repeated in the farm novel, one with Darwinian and incestuous overtones, when young Rose, now grown and looking for work as a stenographer, returns to live with the family, Martin falls in love with her and buys expensive furniture and a Victrola for her, even building her the room that he had denied to his son. To no one's surprise, he confesses to his wife that he is in love with her niece. Rose decides that she will give him a divorce, should he ask for it, and will ask for half the fortune that he would not have amassed but for her efforts.

The shower of love and gifts that Martin withholds from his family but heaps on young Rose demonstrates the fundamental flaw in his utilitarian dream of a strict accounting of the exchange of material objects for services rendered. He is crushed when young Rose deserts him for a life in town, which in the exchange economy he has established should not have happened. But the elder Rose's economy based on self-sacrificing love fares little better. She decides to stand by Martin despite his passion for her niece and even after their son dies in a mine explosion. Her life has been spent in loving, and being abused by, a brutal man who has not loved her. Yet when Martin lies dying some years after Billy's death, Rose reflects that "she had salvaged so much more out of living than he" and that the things he had worked for and loved all his life—the farm and the money it provided—are now hers.[37] The term "salvage" suggests recycling or remaking the elements of life into an item of value, and what transmutes it is Rose's belief in a sense of love or beauty beyond the material one. It is "dust in [her] hands," she thinks, just as Martin's life was "like a handful of dust thrown into God's face and blown back again by the wind to the ground" (251).

After Martin's death, Rose now is free to enjoy her life in town, which includes going to the movies. With her women friends, she discovers that "the movies... would tide her over.... She who had been married for years and had borne two children without ever having had the joy of one overwhelming kiss, would find romance at last, for an hour, as she identified herself with the charming heroines of the films" (249). Rose has survived and has retained her capacity for love despite the absence of it in her own life, and her means of engaging in it is the movies, the product of the 1920s dream factory. The movies become the antithesis of Rose's naturalistic life of hardship, scarcity, and loss, and she clings to the illusion of the movies as Martin had clung to the illusion of the love he felt for young Rose. Rose's dream of escape through the movies is no more destructive than Martin's conviction that he can control his fate through withholding affection and material goods from those around him. In the freedom she finds in town, with her women friends, she has escaped the worst parts of a life lived solely in pursuit of wealth—or, as this novel has it, dust.

COUNTRY PEOPLE

Country People (1924), by Ruth Suckow (1892–1960), recalls Cather's *O Pioneers!* in its focus on the land and the immigrants who have farmed it, the Kaetterhenry family, whose lives Suckow reports with the clinical, occasionally ironic detachment of naturalistic narration. The novel begins with a panorama of the land, culminating in the sign "August Kaetterhenry, 1907" and flashing back to August's hard work in establishing the farm to the point at which such a proud sign would be warranted.[38] August courts and marries Emma Stille, and although he shares none of his wealth with her, he eventually builds Emma a house and does not insist that Emma work in the fields. Like Martin, his counterpart in *Dust*, August's abiding passion is his farm, and he hoards money so that he will not be a failure when he retires. His greatest fear is to "go back on" or having his children "go back on"—that is, rely for support on—someone else, rendering them dependents.

When "Grandpa and Grandma" Stille, Emma's sensitive, religious father and her domineering, crafty mother, come to live with the family, August refuses to let the mother's "sullenness" and "tantrums" rule the house, although Emma tends her devotedly during the five years she lies in bed after suffering a stroke. Like Willa Cather, Suckow seems to relish creating unpleasant characters: the grasping, bullying Mrs. Stille recalls Cather's grasping, bullying Mrs. Shimerda of *My Ántonia*, both of them domineering women married to sensitive husbands who shrink under their behavior. Mrs. Stille, a stout woman, is a dead weight when Emma must tend to her after her stroke, for she and her husband have outlived their usefulness as well as their money. Although humanistic and religious ideals require that relatives selflessly care for the elderly, the naturalistic and biological economy of the farm silently argues that age and the resources that it consumes constitute an inordinate waste of energy and lives.

Country People confirms the message of *Dust* in representing a purely material existence without spiritual or intellectual interests as a limited life. In the relentlessly material world of the farm, characters with any kind of intellectual life, such as Grandpa, their daughter Mary, and their son Johnnie, are dismissed and discounted. Mary's love of reading makes her "have queer spells" (87), and August refuses to indulge her wish for more schooling, just as he refuses to pay for any lessons for family members to learn to play the organ that Grandpa and Grandma bring with them or to understand why Johnnie's service in World War I has made him "restless ... nervous, [and] jumpy" (111) and unwilling to work unceasingly on the farm. The greatest events in Emma and August's life are the extended trips they take to the Mayo Clinic in Rochester, Minnesota. After a lifetime of being ignored by everyone, Emma becomes the center of attention when she needs her gall-bladder removed, and years later they return when August begins to have "spells" due to high blood pressure resulting from years of overwork and overeating. After turning the farm over to their son Carl and his wife, retiring to town, and building a house, neither Emma nor August have much to do. Work has been their life, and they are lost without it. Emma tries to help with the children, and August helps with the farm, but when he suffers a stroke, his children fervently hope that he will die and not live on as Grandma Stille did. Emma and August's goal has been to do well and have the leisure not to work, but with no intellectual or emotional resources, when they achieve leisure they have no purpose for living.

After years spent in denying the body and any form of pleasure, except for August's overeating, Emma and August experience the trips to the Mayo Clinic as energizing, even exciting, variations from their routine. They have lived a relentlessly material existence, and unlike Rose in *Dust*, they have no capacity for forethought or imagining a change that does not involve the farm. Yet each stage of evolutionary change, each death of a domineering character, brings a welcome "loosening up"—the title of one segment—that makes life better for those left behind. In town, after August's death, Emma bakes cookies, sews, and cares for

Johnnie's baby, finding "mystery and contentment" in slowly and thoroughly doing the housework, which she had had no time for when the children were growing up. Reflecting that "many things had not turned out as they had thought they would" (213), Emma and her friend agree that at least they have "good homes, and children to look after us if we need it" (213) rather than being sent to the poorhouse. In short, Emma's leisure in retirement is merely an intensification of the work she did all her life, but since she fears the future and all technology, including the automobile, the "mystery and contentment" constitute her happiness. Despite the superficial prosperity narrative common to the multigenerational saga, *Country People* and its relentless materialism suggests unruly naturalism in its portrait of elemental characters with limited self-awareness existing in a challenging environment that circumscribes their choices.

O PIONEERS!

Willa Cather's *O Pioneers!* (1913) depicts a woman, Alexandra Bergson, who wrests a living from the unforgiving earth through her farsighted adoption of better farming methods, a topic that the novel shares with Ferber's *So Big* (1924), Jack London's *Valley of the Moon* (1913), and Ellen Glasgow's *Barren Ground* (1925).[39] Although less specific than these novels about the details of farm management, *O Pioneers!* celebrates Alexandra's acquisition of land and her scientific approach to farming, concluding with a scene that brings Alexandra together with her longtime lover, Carl, and their mutual recognition of the importance of the land. *O Pioneers!* suggests unruly naturalism in the lyrical surface that masks its naturalistic content of theories of race and evolution, violence, and sexual desire, just as the triumphal tone of Ferber's *So Big* obscures the hardships of farm life. The discord between subject matter and tone, between naturalism and lyricism, reveals itself most strongly in the novel's happy ending, which features Alexandra's forgiveness of the man who killed her beloved friend Marie and Alexandra's brother Emil. Stripped to its essence, Alexandra's contentment relies on her ability to justify violence against women who, like Grace Brown or Evelyn Nesbit, are too visible and inspire too much heterosexual desire in men.

On the surface, *O Pioneers!* resembles *So Big* or the other novels that Dorothy Parker had criticized in which a "big, wise, calm, broad-hipped, level-eyed woman ... puts the farm on a paying basis by her efforts." Like Ferber's Selina Peake DeJong, who creates a successful farm by "farming out of a book," Alexandra successfully plants alfalfa based on advice she gets "from a young man who had been to the University" against the wishes of the tradition-minded men who believe they have authority over her: Oscar and Lou, her brothers.[40] Unlike Oscar and Lou, who want to sell the farm after their father's death and later try to bully her into sharing the profits of the thriving farm she creates after buying them out, Alexandra anticipates the crops and management strategies that the family will need to survive. She nurtures and educates a younger man, her brother Emil, as Selina does with her son, Dirk, in *So Big*, and like Selina she hopes for a brighter future for him. Both women see these young men fail to achieve their dreams because they each fall in love with the wrong woman, who deflects each from his path. Like Selina, Alexandra is interested in other cultures, such as the eccentric Ivar's fear of bathtubs, and she delights in ethnic celebrations, such as the festivals and ball games at the French settlement. Alexandra too thrives through a bifurcated vision of past and future, embracing the future in economic matters but rejecting contemporary social standards she regards as superficial and pretentious in favor of the old ways. Able to defer her relationship with Carl and committed to her love of the land, Alexandra has a mind like a "white book, with clear writing about weather and beasts and growing things" (86). Although "[s]he had never been in love" (86), when she is tired, she has a persistent "sensation of being lifted and carried by a strong being" (87), the arms of a lover or of a higher power who could erase the weariness she feels.

In contrast to Alexandra, Marie Shabata, Alexandra's closest friend, is naturalistically described in Darwinian terms of animals, atavism, and passion. When Emil teases his friend Amédée's new bride by embracing her, he sees "Marie Shabata's tiger eyes flashing from the gloom of the basement doorway" until he "hand[s] the disheveled bride over to her husband" (71). Marie's "tiger eyes" and "Bohemian" blood contrast with the "good deal of the cow" that Alexandra tells her is in "most Swedish girls" (95). Marie's religious primitivism reveals itself in the first scene with Emil in the grove when she tells him that despite her Catholicism, "[t]he Bohemians, you know, were tree worshippers before the missionaries came" (67). The close and easy homosocial bond existing between Alexandra and Marie is part of what C. Susan Wiesenthal calls the novel's challenge "to dominant contemporary theories of sexuality," in which "heterosexuality... is presented as the direct cause" of violence, jealousy, and tragedy.[41] Even the "strong arms" of the figure Alexandra fantasizes about are less important to her than Marie's companionship, and when Marie betrays her by sleeping with Emil, it marks the only instance in the book in which Alexandra harshly condemns anyone. Alexandra's position resembles the premise of James M. Cain's much later novel *Serenade*, in which the protagonist, John Howard Sharpe, is in love with his same-sex mentor and can only move forward with his life when the man is murdered. So too with Alexandra: only when her brother and her closest female friend are dead can she form a straightforward heterosexual relationship with Carl that does not rely on the physical distance between them. After Emil and Marie are dead, Alexandra reaches out to Carl by writing "a single page of note-paper" (116), an act that brings them together for the final time.

The incident in which Frank Shabata discovers Emil and Marie and kills them is at once the most naturalistic and the most lyrical in the book. It is described twice, once from Frank's and once from the narrator's perspective. Armed with his sense of perpetual "injury and outrage" (107), for which he blames everyone but himself, Frank takes "his murderous 405 Winchester" to the orchard, where he sees Emil's horse and a woman lying in the shadows. Raising his gun "he sight[s] mechanically and fire[s] three times without stopping" (108), hiding "like a rabbit" as he peers through the hedge at the woman, who moans as she drags herself through the "stained, slippery grass" (111). Cather uses contrasting diction in the passage to intensify its brutality. The poetic repetition of "white mulberries" stained with "dark blood" is juxtaposed with medical diction in the clinical assessment of the wounds: "One ball had torn through her right lung, another had shattered the carotid artery. She must have started up and gone toward the hedge, leaving a trail of blood" (110–11). Frank's perspective represents his disjointed thoughts, for although he "knew he had murdered somebody... he had not realized before that it was his wife" (109). However, since he would have had no other reason to shoot the figures in the orchard unless he believed the woman to be Marie, this manifestly false statement confirms Frank's self-delusion. "Why had Marie made him do this thing; why had she brought this upon him?" he asks himself (110). The sense of self-importance that had initially attracted Marie and caused him to think that "he was wasting his best years among these stupid and unappreciative people" (109) places this statement in context. As he has always done, and as the narrator has commented earlier in the chapter, Frank assigns blame to everyone but himself, which should indicate that his perspective should be read skeptically. Knowing Frank's inflated sense of self-importance, Alexandra should recognize this, but she chooses to take his statements at face value.

Alexandra's response would fit neatly into a sentimental novel but rests uneasily in a naturalistic one. She soon forgives Frank, since she "could understand his behavior more easily than she could understand Marie's" (116), perhaps identifying with his passionate jealousy more than with Marie's heterosexual desire. When she visits Frank in prison, Alexandra participates in his self-delusion by encouraging his idea that Marie is the cause of the crime rather than himself. "If she been in dat house, where she ought-a been.... Honest to God, but I hate her!" Frank tells Alexandra (120), blaming Marie for daring to go beyond the domestic sphere into the natural one of the grove. Alexandra agrees, for "[s]he blamed Marie bitterly" (120). "They were more to blame than you," Alexandra repeats twice, adding, "I know you never meant to hurt Marie" (119, 120). The idea that he did not mean to hurt Marie is logical and defensible only if Alexandra subscribes to the theory of racial types by holding Frank's passionate, primitive Bohemian nature rather than Frank as an individual responsible for the murders. "I am never going to stop trying until I get you pardoned," she adds. In Alexandra's eyes, Marie had first ruined Frank Shabata by choosing him and, regretting her choice, had then ruined Emil by turning to him. Without questioning her indictment of Marie, Alexandra pauses to wonder how a woman with a "happy, affectionate nature" could bring "destruction and sorrow to all who had loved her" (120).

Alexandra also condemns Marie for the change that has come over Frank. She has transformed Frank from "a gay young fellow" to a prisoner with a shaved head, who seems to Alexandra nearly a naturalistic brute, pitiable and "somehow, not altogether human" (120), as she explains to Carl after her visit. Carl agrees, explaining that some women "spread ruin around them through no fault of theirs, just by being too beautiful, too full of life and love" (123). In classic naturalistic fashion, heredity, in the form of Marie's and Frank's Bohemian blood, plus the natural environment and chance have conspired to cause Marie's death. As Emil had earlier reflected when thinking about his own life and Amédée's, "It was like that when Alexandra tested her seed-corn in the spring, he mused. From two ears that had grown side by side, the grains of one shot up joyfully into the light, projecting themselves into the future, and the grains from the other lay still in the earth and rotted; and nobody knew why" (71). Alexandra and Carl do not know why Marie sowed destruction or why her happiness would cause such grief, but they are certain that the responsibility lies with her.

The last paragraphs of the novel bring Carl back to Alexandra's side after the tragedy. Previous chapters in *O Pioneers!* open by picturing an isolated single figure against a landscape before the action of the chapter begins, as when Emil sharpens his scythe at the beginning of part 2, chapter 1. The last chapter repeats this pattern with a variation as Alexandra and Carl "[pause] on the last ridge of the pasture" to contemplate their future together (124). Alexandra reflects, "We come and go, but the land is always here," adding, "We don't suffer like—those young ones" (125). Their movement seems to be toward a form of eternal time that is rooted in the land, beyond the deadly consequences of heterosexual passion. Read through the novel's lyrical prose, Alexandra seems an admirable figure of intelligence and tolerance, educating Emil and the Swedish girls who work for her, caring for Ivar and other poorly assimilated immigrants, and putting aside her own happiness to contribute to the growth of her farm and region until Carl returns at last. But their shared community of understanding implicitly rests on their agreement about another basic point: that Marie is responsible for her own murder, and that the punishment of death for women's expression of passionate heterosexual desire is fundamentally just and inevitable.

WEEDS

In Edith Summers Kelley's *Weeds*, Judith Pippinger Blackford, a Kentucky girl, has a talent for drawing that her poverty and narrowly circumscribed life on a tobacco farm leave her little time to pursue. According to Charlotte Margolis Goodman, "*Weeds* is a quintessential example of female literary naturalism."[42] Like Mary E. Wilkins Freeman's Ellen Brewster and Theodore Dreiser's Frank Cowperwood, Judith experiences the classic naturalistic epiphany about the brutal nature of the world. After she rescues a kitten being tortured by some boys, she is horrified a few days later to see the kitten "fish[ing] up a live minnow with its paw and crunch[ing] it mercilessly between its small, strong jaws."[43] Her recognition that "the big fishes eat the little ones" and the strong devour the weak prepares her for the cycle of birth and death she experiences on the farm.

Kelley focuses on Darwinian and deterministic themes. Judith's father, an indifferent farmer, would have made a fine blacksmith if circumstances had been different, and the preacher who speaks at her mother's funeral had "been elbowed into this remote corner by the law of the survival of the fittest" (51). A Darwinian anomaly in her family and community, Judith is ill-suited to the life she must lead, for in addition to having intelligence and imagination, she loves the outdoors and has little use for the domestic arts. Neither a human beast nor a character of mature naturalism who can view her situation with ironic detachment, Judith yearns after beauty but finds that only old Jabez Moorhouse, another sensitive soul equally trapped in this uncongenial place, can understand her. She finds beauty in nature and in realism, preferring "something that was real, vital and fluid" in the barnyard to the "deadening negation of life" (57) implied by domesticity. But petty domesticity inevitably rules her actions, for each time she acts in accordance with her nature, she is hemmed in by domestic and social constraints. For example, although she and Jerry Blackford consummate their relationship before their wedding, she does not immediately get pregnant as the logic of the sentimental or conventional romance would demand. Yet when Jerry mistakenly "publish[es] abroad his sexual achievements" (184), she is ashamed before his friends because of the social prohibition on premarital sex.

Weeds undercuts optimistic visions of triumphant "manure widows" and the pleasures of farm life through its emphasis on the boredom, poverty, hard work, and filth of country life. Like Hamlin Garland, Kelley acknowledges the beauty of nature on a farm but debunks the romantic view of rural life that appears in the magazine her friend Hat swears by, the *Farm Wife's Friend*. When Hat takes her husband's overalls, "stiffly encrusted with mud and axle grease and many other varieties of filth and soused them up and down in the dirty, stinking, mouse-gray water," she thinks about the poems she has read about the nobility of washing clothes, like "Be a Beam of Sunshine" and "And the Wind Is Right to Dry" (132). Also punctured are visions of the honesty of country people, for Hat's husband steals Jerry's tobacco plants, and the most admired man in the county, the symbolically named Uncle Sam, takes great delight in cheating Jerry and others through his horse trading, an action seen as smart rather than larcenous by the farmers.

The authorial voice reinforces this disparity between sentimental illusions about rural people and the reality: "There is an idea existing in many minds that country folk are mostly simple, natural and spontaneous, living in the light of day and carrying their hearts on their sleeves. There is no more misleading fallacy. No decadent court riddled with lust of power, greed, vice, and intrigue ... ever moved under a thicker atmosphere than that which brooded over the little shanty where these four fresh-faced young country people stood stripping tobacco" (152). The novel refuses to sentimentalize desire as well, treating sexual expression as natural physical right that Judith can enjoy without guilt. Late in the book, Judith attends a revival meeting and is drawn to the young preacher, who some nights later comes "up to her where the alfalfa field spilled its subtle fragrance into the warm night air" (272) and kisses her, which she returns "with an ecstasy transcending anything that she had ever felt in her life" (272). The two meet in various spots in a lushly described, fecund landscape that symbolically reinforces the theme of Judith's awakening of the senses and becoming "intensely conscious of her body" (272).

But reality intrudes when an uneasy sense of time passing and a subsequent revulsion toward the preacher begin to "awaken her from her dream" (276). Finding herself pregnant, she tries to self-abort by stabbing herself with a knitting needle, brewing "nasty smelling decoctions" of pennyroyal (286), and riding her mule wildly across the field, finally miscarrying after wading into a pond and accidentally cutting her foot. Like Chopin's Edna Pontellier, Judith tries to drown herself, but her instinct for life is strong and manifests itself in her almost-lost ability to swim to shore. Although the community understands what she has done and disapproves of it—Aunt Maggie Slatten, who comes to care for her during her illness, comments that Judith was "kinder lookin' fer it [the miscarriage] right along" (289)—the narrative voice here and elsewhere holds no sentimental brief for children and their place in Judith's life. Indeed, when pregnant with her second child, Judith feels the baby kick and reflects that "she hated them both, the born and the unborn, two greedy vampires working on her incessantly, the one from without, the other from within ... bent upon drinking her last drop of blood" (208).

The idea of the child as parasite or vampire, and of nature working its will on the woman's body without her consent, combine the "children consume resources" and children-as-waste themes of unruly naturalism. It is most strikingly portrayed in "Billy's Birth," a chapter deleted before publication. Kelley had intended this graphic description of pain-wracked childbirth to be the twelfth of the novel's twenty-six chapters and thus literally central to the text, but it was omitted as being "too typical to be of real interest." The chapter disrupts the seemingly simple relation between Judith's rediscovery of her sexuality and her renewed connection to the earth during her affair with the preacher, for according to Janet Galligani Casey it "disallow[s] the potential role of communal earth mother that Judith's closeness to the land might encourage in a more culturally orthodox text" and "suggests that motherhood is but *pure* labor."[44] In fact, the description of Judith during labor strikingly recalls the monstrous and out-of-control Mary Johnson of Crane's *Maggie*: "Her eyes were closed now, her face a dark purple with dreadfully swollen veins and salient muscles; her body driving, driving, driving with the force and regularity of some great steel and iron monster" (345). *Weeds* suggests that childbirth renders mothers as laboring machines, a stripping away of humanity that implicitly marks women with the vestiges of a primal force not entirely covered by the pious fiction of maternal instinct. Judith and Jerry come together over the sickbed of their daughter after a long estrangement, yet the novel presents a world of Darwinian profligacy in which reproduction and labor of all sorts yields only more organisms to struggle and die, a combination of unrealistic ending and Darwinian content suggestive of unruly naturalism.

RED RUST

Red Rust (1928), by Cornelia James Cannon (1876–1969), is an evolutionary success narrative that places improving the land and careful breeding of better crops firmly at the center of the characters' lives. According to her biographer Maria I. Diedrich, Cannon shared with "Edith Wharton, Theodore Dreiser, Willa Cather, [and] Jack London... a profound eugenic commitment, but [their] naturalistic determinism... conflicted with her optimistic progressivism."[45] Although reviews at the time described *Red Rust* as the story of a farmer whose environment frustrated his scientific genius, a theme that informs Edith Wharton's *Ethan Frome*, *Red Rust* is the story of three individuals whose lives are thwarted by circumstance: Matts Swenson, the protagonist; Lena Jensen, the victim of an abusive husband, whom Matts rescues and marries; and Olga Swenson, Matts's disabled sister, whose brush with a casual seducer changes the course of her life. The ending promises solace for Lena, religious consolation for Olga, and belated recognition for Matts, but they fail to achieve what they had hoped. On another level, *Red Rust* comprises three stories of Darwinian evolution, with hereditary traits explored at individual, familial, racial, and national levels. Deliberate intervention in the environment shapes the genetic expression of those traits, and although the novel contains the traditional scenes of American pastoral—the churchgoing, haying, and other rituals that form the cycle of social life in a farming community—it emphasizes the evolutionary themes of heredity and variation.

Matts is an evolutionary anomaly, a man who dislikes the routine cruelty meted out to children, wives, and farm animals, and he supports ideas that break with the old order of Swedes' understanding of gender roles. He teaches one of Lena's sons to milk the family cow, although that is considered women's work, and stimulates the children's imagination with stories of nature. In his intense study of nature, Matts combines elements of transcendentalism and Darwinism. His habits of learning other languages, reading, and studying the behavior of ants and bees make him an outlier in his community. His intellectual awakening occurs when, in the *American Farmer's Paper*, he reads selections from Darwin. He realizes that variation in plants is not random but the result of environment and that "the selection for survival or destruction was dependent on the capacity for adaptation that lay within the seed itself."[46] Intervention into the "increasingly inflexible world about him" by even so small an act as "increasing the size of a kernel of wheat" (30) provides a sense of purpose for him. Born in a series of moments of intellectual discovery, his development of a superior strain of wheat through the principles of applied evolutionary principles runs in tandem with his interventions in other portions of his life. Indifferent to conventional religion, Matts "doesn't believe in hell" (101), yet when he later looks at the wheat he has bred, he "lives intensely in the presence of a single absorbing idea" (181).

Matts's love affair with the idea of breeding the perfect specimen of wheat parallels the growth of his relationship with Lena Jensen, who embodies the attitudes toward race and hybridity fostered by Darwinian theory. Like Marie Shabata, whose Bohemian blood marks her difference from the community, Lena is small and dark in a community of light-complexioned, blond Swedes. She is not entirely trusted, because many, like Matts's mother Brigitta, had "never quite trusted a dark-haired Swede" with possible "alien blood" (77). As if to confirm her membership in a darker, more passionate race, Lena is an alien in other ways as well. Spontaneous rather than methodical, imaginative rather than stolid, affectionate instead of undemonstrative, she captures Matts's attention when she is abused, first verbally and then physically, by her drunken husband Olaf, a situation that parallels the relationship between Emil and Marie in *O Pioneers!* Sensing Matts's sympathy, Lena refuses to be silent about the abuse that she suffers at the hands of her drunken husband, telling Matts, "I have been that man's slave and dog, to kick and abuse, for fifteen years" (57). She shares with Matts the status of being an evolutionary anomaly due to her intelligence and her uncommon skills. Trained as a nurse, she encourages Matts's interest in science, although her greater interest lies in their emotional openness and mutual sympathy. He is attracted by her "expressions of affection... as natural as breathing" (178) and she by a fierce passion for him. As in Darwin's theory of female sexual choice in courtship, it is Lena's love that awakens Matts's love for her after Olaf's death in a threshing accident. When the two stand together to pollinate Matts's experimental wheat, she holds the "paper covered with the little yellow anthers, like tiny berries" (194), as a fertility goddess might, and confesses her love as tears roll down her cheeks. Their courtship is sealed not only with Matts's kiss but also with the culmination of his experiment with the wheat. Their bonding over the wheat is the defining experience of their lives, and it becomes their only child.

The remainder of the novel unfolds with a combination of evolutionary logic and chance events. When she realizes that her young daughter Christina has fallen in love with Matts and that Matts is attracted to her, Lena realizes that "there could be no peace in life for her or for them until that look was wiped from their faces forever" (247) and sends Christina away to work, ridding her family of her rival, in this case her daughter, to preserve the rest of the family unit. Axel, the mentally disabled child born during Lena's marriage to the drunken Olaf, shoots Matts without realizing what he has done, and although Matts recovers for a time, the wound weakens him. He dies at a young age without ever having seen his work with the wheat recognized. His scientific discoveries about the rust-proof wheat live on, however, for Lena sends samples of his crop to the state agronomist, where his contribution is celebrated at last.

As in *A Lantern in Her Hand*, the parallel between the perfection of the wheat adapted to the new land and the success of the assimilated second generation of immigrants in *Red Rust* provides a triumphant conclusion that overshadows the poverty, abuse, and deaths that the first generation had to suffer. But there is no second generation for Matts, since he and Lena never have a child together. In writing of Cannon's eugenic views, Diedrich explains that, having borne a mentally disabled child, Lena "no longer qualifies for American motherhood" and that, because of her five children, "Lena and Matts's childlessness... represents them as the deserving poor" who recognize their responsibility to limit the number of children they bring into the world.[47] Although Cannon "rejected [naturalism] as bleak and unpleasant," according to Diedrich, the novel's representation of poverty, abuse, and Darwinian principles suggests its evolutionary roots despite the optimistic progressivism of its conclusion.[48]

The Wind: Women's Naturalism in Fiction and Film

Dorothy Scarborough's (1878–1935) *The Wind* employs the themes and techniques of naturalism to challenge romantic myths of western spaces and what Sherrie Inness has called the "heroic frontier woman."[49] First published anonymously in 1925, the book raised the ire of Texas readers for its unsparing portrait of the West Texas landscape during the drought of 1886–87 and its dismantling of popular western myths of the frontier.[50] Letty Mason, a delicately nurtured woman of eighteen, travels from Virginia to Texas after the death of her parents to take up residence with her closest relative, an older male cousin named Beverly. On the train, she meets an older man, Wirt Roddy, to whom she is attracted. Upon seeing the desolation of the misleadingly named town of Sweetwater, she is fleetingly tempted by his offer to run away with him to a more civilized place but realizes that she has no choice but to make her home with her cousin. The confrontation of eastern sensibilities with western nature does not, as in the romantic frontier narrative, result in an infusion of fresh vigor into an attenuated stock, nor does it change Letty into a stalwart frontier wife or "manure widow" of mythical resourcefulness and strength. Instead Letty is treated as an unwelcome guest by her cousin's wife, Cora, and pressured into marrying a kindly but uncouth rancher, Lige Hightower, whom she does not love. The rest of the novel follows Letty's increasingly frantic attempts to shield her body and some portion of her sanity from the relentless winds, a battle that she ultimately loses on both counts. Debilitated mentally and physically by the ceaseless assault of the elements, she comes to see herself increasingly as an animal trapped by circumstances that offer her no avenue of escape. When Roddy seduces her during one of Lige's absences, she kills him and wanders out the door to certain death on the wind-driven plains, acknowledging her defeat at the hands of interior and exterior natural forces.

The opening chapter sets the scene for the rest of the novel by introducing the parameters of Letty's world: the unfamiliar Texas landscape, the wind, and Wirt Roddy, a "rather handsome man" (7) who responds to her obvious curiosity by explaining the landscape as they ride by. Seen through Letty's eyes, the landscape is filled with trees and what she tritely refers to as "cunning" small animals. But as Roddy informs her, the trees are mesquite, a nuisance species, not peach trees, as she had thought, and the animals are prairie dogs. When Letty asks him whether she will like Sweetwater, he replies, "This country's not like what you've been used to. Take my advice and vamoose—while the going's good" (19). Wirt tells the truth, refusing to lie to Letty in his account of the isolation of the ranches, the loneliness of the women, and the wind that ruins complexions and eyes, including Texas "northers" and cyclones. The train, always a symbol of modernity as it speeds toward the city, in Letty's case goes in the opposite direction from city to country and slows as it strikes objects on the tracks. As Letty discovers, the objects are the mangled and dying cattle that the train has mowed down. The scene recalls the opening chapter of Norris's *The Octopus*, in which Presley watches as a speeding train slaughters a herd of innocent sheep, announcing the conflict between technological modernity and the bodies it destroys. In *The Wind*, this scene anticipates the novel's scenes of animals starving, dying of thirst, or wounded by the train and left to die, all suggesting Letty's ultimate fate.

As Letty contemplates the Texas landscape, she feels "a strange depression" but also "a strange, fluid fear ... a dreamy unrest that was by turns ice and flame" (36). Throughout the novel, Letty alternates between the "dreamy unrest" that signals her underlying fear of the harsh environment and her brief outbursts of hysterical reaction against it. Her attraction to Wirt Roddy is composed of the same fascinated repulsion. The power of her repressed sexuality reveals itself in the object she unconsciously chooses, a man whose brutal and phallic name indicates his attraction for her, "Wirt" suggesting "Quirt," a type of whip, and "Roddy" the nature of his appeal. As if to emphasize the connection, Roddy's gift to her later in the novel is a gun. Letty reveals her discomfort first through nervous laughter at his "mustache-like" eyebrows but soon finds herself drawn to him. As predicted in Darwinian theories of women's sexual selection, his facial hair (mustache and eyebrows) attracts her at a primitive level even as her sense of propriety makes her declare that he repels her.

The evolutionary themes of cruelty, brutality, courtship, and survival within a harsh environment reinforce the novel's primary as well as its psychosexual naturalism. Psychological or psychosexual naturalism approaches the primal drives that characterize naturalism through a psychological or Freudian lens, giving a prominent role to sexual drives that the naturalistic text signals through animal and machine imagery. But Scarborough takes the traditional animal and machine symbolism a step further by linking them to Letty's immature and ultimately self-centered anthropomorphizing. When she gets off the train, she sees it as "the last link between her and her old life" and reflects, "Trains [are] heartless things!" (41). When she exits the train and Roddy "caught her to him for an instant to steady her," "[s]he shiver[s] at his touch" (37). Roddy, like the wind, signifies a natural force that neither her well-bred Virginia background nor her position as a genteel young woman has prepared her to control. The sentimentalizing of nature in which Letty engages reflects her limited perspective and the problems to come. She does not see that adaptation leads to evolutionary success for the various creatures that Lige describes to her, from the horned toad that squirts blood from its eyes to foil its enemies to the coyotes and vultures that prey upon the remains of those unfit to survive.

At the home of her cousin Bev, where his jealous wife Cora makes Letty feel out of place, Letty tells stories to Bev and Cora's children to avoid contact with her surroundings, but her tastes run to stories of romance and rescue, featuring "an imagined figure, a dark-eyed, dark-haired knight of modern days" (111) whom she imagines as a protector and into whose armor she casts Wirt Roddy. The memory of Virginia and of her "mammy's" stories provides an anchoring counternarrative, almost a schizophrenic other voice for Letty, sometimes soothing and sometimes warning her of danger.

Of all the stories that Letty hears, the only one pinned to historical fact and most analogous to her own situation is the captivity narrative of Cynthia Ann Parker. During the course of a long drive, Lige tells her "the tragic story of Cynthia Ann Parker, into whose life despair came twice" (58), first when she was captured by the Comanches and "all but died of homesickness" (58) before marrying the chief's son, and a second time when Texas Rangers killed her husband and recaptured her along with her infant daughter, in the process separating her from her sons, including Quanah, later a great Comanche leader. Lige continues his tale by describing Parker's heartbreak at her failure to escape when she "set and mourned, with a look on her face fit to make a stone cry" (60). For the rest of her life, Parker mourned the loss of her Comanche life and family, never readapting to the white world she had left at age nine. Like Parker, Letty refuses to adapt when stranded in the West, yet she fails to see the connection between Parker's story and her own life. Instead she derives just one racist and trivial lesson from this story of heartbreak, longing, and assimilation: "Indians are terrible creatures, aren't they?" (60). Her habit of generalizing and stereotyping about uncouth cowboys, quaint natives, and people of color reveals a lack of empathy and an inability to apply the knowledge of others' hardships to her own life, as if she, like the women of Virginia, will never know the forms of loss and hardship that others have endured. Later in the novel, she does not recall Cynthia Ann Parker despite feeling like "a prisoner eager for the visioned end of his captivity" (201).

Letty's dissociative sense of the separation between mind and body intensifies after she marries Lige and goes to live on his isolated ranch. During the ceremony itself, as she stands "mechanically saying her 'I do,' she saw, as on a stage before her eyes, the wedding she had always visioned for herself" (180). She experiences "a queer remoteness from reality, as if only her body were there, and she herself were far away" (181). The positioning of Letty's body, as a thing separate from herself that she watches from a distance, signals a break in her consciousness that becomes more marked as the book progresses, as the Virginia of her past life floats before her sight and seems at times more real to her than the sand and wind that torment her. Letty characterizes this feeling through a reference to an early visual technology that predated film, the lantern-slide show: "It was like a picture on a lantern-slide, with all the appearance of reality, but soon it would vanish and its place be taken by another" (181–82). As the wind takes on shape, form, and purpose in a steady process of embodiment, Letty becomes increasingly detached from her body and sense of self, as if watching herself in a film or lantern slide show: "[H]er body ate and slept and walked around in the performance of household tasks, but it was not she herself" (201). Like the narrator of Charlotte Perkins Gilman's "The Yellow Wallpaper," Letty slowly goes mad in an environment bereft of mental stimulation.

The Wind thematizes Letty's fear of and attraction toward sexual intimacy through its depictions of her sense of touch. Her primary relationship in the novel is with the wind, with human beings serving as embodiments of its force (Wirt Roddy) or shields against its power (Lige Hightower). The wind and sand creep through to Letty's skin until she feels it "crawling inside her clothing like vermin" (197), a sexualized image of intimacy more specifically described than any encounter that she has with another human being. When the sand touches her, she is terrified and miserable, suggesting a displaced reaction to her married state. Letty is "appalled" by "the intrusions, the intimacies of married life" (187), but she construes "intimacies" as a lack of privacy. That she has sold herself to Lige to escape Cora and is paying for her escape with sexual favors passes unremarked in the novel as part of Letty's refusal to acknowledge reality. Although Letty professes delicacy in the face of vulgarity, such as her revulsion at having to eat "son-of-a-gun ... stew" and her distress at Lige's and Sourdough's table manners, she is silent on the question of her sexual acquiescence. Both domestic ideology and the narrative conventions of naturalism would dictate that Letty express some reaction at the prospect of sleeping with Lige, but her acceptance undercuts her claims of delicacy. Even Lige, pained as he is to learn that Letty does not love him, is horrified and disgusted to realize that she would sleep with him without love: "You lived with me—not lovin' me? ... *Christ!* What sort of a woman are you?" (286).

When Wirt Roddy suddenly reappears after months of absence, he reestablishes his power over Letty by telling her "your cheeks aren't quite so pink as they used to be ... your eyes aren't so blue and clear" (212). By stating the truth, he denigrates her appearance, a common abuser's trick to undercut the victim's self-confidence and throw her off balance. Roused from her somnolent state by Roddy's presence, Letty feels "her old, throbbing fear of him" (213), the "throbbing" suggesting desire despite her overt attempts to suppress it. In an instance of foreshadowing, he has also brought with him two other elements of destruction, one psychological and one material. Roddy repeats his performance of the "mournful tune" he had sung to her on the train, "Bury Me Not on the Lone Prairie," which she asks him to stop singing. As in the sequence on the train, Roddy confronts her with a truth that she does not want to acknowledge—death on the prairie—and he follows it up with the gift of a rifle. When Letty declares that she "couldn't bear to kill anything," Roddy mockingly points out her inconsistency: "It's likely you eat game that other folks shoot" (215). Until she can look at life with the same clear-eyed directness that Roddy shows her, Letty can never awaken, either to reality or to her own sexuality, and both retain their power over her by her resolute attempts to shut them out. For Letty, fear and dominance comprise a goodly portion of the romantic myth of the white knight, which she contrasts in her fantasies with the myth of the white and black horses that signify terrifying weather. The wind and Roddy are powerful forces of nature that cannot be contained or controlled, and only they have the power to cancel each other out.

The final chapters of *The Wind* culminate in the convergence of Letty, Wirt, and the wind. Letty asks Lige to send her back east, although he has no money to do so. Desperate to escape, she confesses that she has never loved him. He slams out of the house, and for the third time Wirt Roddy appears as if in answer to an unspoken call. As the wind pounds at the house, Letty throws herself into Roddy's arms as a refuge from the wind, and the two consummate their affair. The next morning, she awakens to self-loathing, regret, and a newfound love for Lige. When Roddy tries to force her to leave with him, she shoots him with the gun he had given her, thus ironically fulfilling both his prediction that she would use it some day and the promise of his song, "Bury Me Not on the Lone Prairie." She hears the song in her mind as she drags him to a sand pile and buries him. As she stands at the window and surveys the sand pile, the wind scours the sand from the spot, revealing Roddy's dead face with its "black mustache" (334). Believing that her struggle against the wind, "a force that [is] a devil, and all-powerful," is useless, Letty rushes out into the storm and into certain death, "borne along in the force of the wind that was at last to have its way with her," the sexual overtones of "have its way with her" completing the double seduction by Roddy and the wind that she had feared throughout the novel.

The 1928 MGM film adaptation of *The Wind* retains many of the naturalistic plot elements of the novel with one significant difference: the ending. Written by Frances Marion, it features Lars Hanson as Lige and Lillian Gish as Letty, a significant choice given that Gish's portrayal of sensitive innocence had made her a major star beginning with her work in D. W. Griffith's Biograph shorts like *The Musketeers of Pig Alley* and moving on to *Intolerance*, *The Scarlet Letter*, and *Way Down East*. By 1928, Gish had played a number of iconic roles, Elsie Stoneman in *Birth of a Nation* among them, and she excelled at playing frail young women in peril. A highlight of her performance as the child Lucie Burrows in *Broken Blossoms* is a harrowing scene in which she is trapped in a closet and turns around and around as her father, Battling Burrows (Donald Crisp), pounds on the door prior to beating her to death. Filmed in the Mojave Desert with giant wind machines in 120-degree heat, *The Wind* was a difficult shoot for all involved. Gish and Marion insisted that the happy ending with Lige and Letty together again had been added after previews showed that audiences rejected the original tragic ending. However, as Charles Affron writes in his biography of Gish, "All the early drafts of the script ... conclude with the reconciliation of Letty and Lige." Despite the happy ending, *The Wind*, released in 1928 with a hastily added soundtrack after *The Jazz Singer* (1927) proved the viability of sound pictures, lost $87,000 for MGM and was Gish's last film for the studio.[51]

The naturalistic vision of the farm-wife plot in both Dorothy Scarborough's novel and Frances Marion's script for the film retains its force despite the compromises made between novel and film. Lige, a kind-looking man who is Sourdough's companion in the novel, notably becomes a handsome hero type in the film, with Sourdough relegated to the position of sidekick. The novel's scenes of storytelling and the cowboy legends that Letty collected (Scarborough was a folklorist as well as a novelist) become the film's lighter comedy scenes, often with gestures and jokes reminiscent of early rube comedies. The film visualizes the novel's contrasts in both obvious ways, as when Letty irons ruffles while Cora guts a steer, and in less obvious ones, such as staging all its comic scenes in shots of crowds and all the tense dramatic confrontations in close shots of two people. The most sophisticated addition on the part of the film may be its translation of Letty's desire for Roddy into visual form. The novel demonstrates repeatedly that Letty is blind to her own desires, repressing them in favor of externalizing them as naturalistic forces that overwhelm her, like the wind that forces sand into her clothing and touches her skin. In its simplest form in the film, this becomes the sand in Letty's hair and the dust that creeps through the door despite her best efforts to shut it out. Letty's interior projection of the overwhelming power of the wind, and with it Roddy, is externalized through the special effect of a double-exposed image of a galloping horse, which exists purely as a projection of Letty's disordered mind.

The two scenes of sexual violation, Letty's wedding night and her brief affair with Wirt Roddy, are rendered differently, the first emphasizing Letty's agency and the second her helplessness. On their wedding night, when Letty and Lige return to the ranch, he kisses her twice and she reaches up to kiss him. She retreats to the bedroom and lets down her waist-length hair, usually in a Gish film a sign of sexual or personal freedom, as it is in the forest scene of *The Scarlet Letter*. The tension builds as Lige (and the audience) anticipate the next step, which the film indicates symbolically: Lige brings her the gift of a cup of coffee, a metaphor for her communion in his way of life and her acceptance of their relationship. Letty, after taking a small sip, rejects the gift, dumping the coffee in the water pitcher and hiding the cup. She will accept nothing physical that Lige can give her. The film heightens the picture of her vulnerability as the point of view alternates between shots of Letty, alone in their bedroom, and Lige, pacing the floor outside. Soon the film focuses exclusively on their feet, his mud-stained boots and her maidenly slippers, as both sets of feet pace and stop before the door. He kicks aside the cup, the vessel of his tender gesture, breaks into the room, and kisses her violently, but she rejects him before he forces himself on her. In the aftermath, she says, "Lige, you've made me hate you," and, seeing the rejected coffee in the pitcher, he assures her that he will never touch her again.

Featuring both Wirt and the wind as unstoppable forces, Letty's encounter

Letty draws a gun on Wirt Roddy, from *The Wind* (1928).

Letty watches the wind uncover Wirt's body as her eyes betray her madness, from *The Wind* (1928).

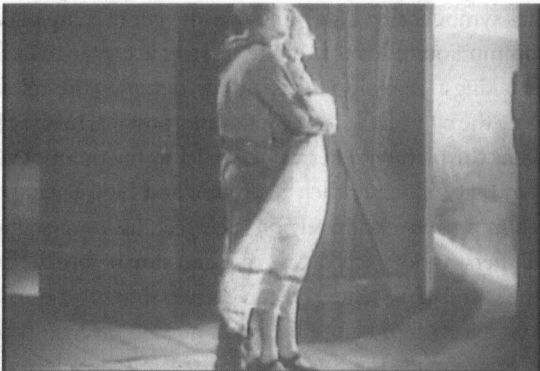

Reconciled and fearing the wind no longer, Letty and Lige face the future together, in the happy ending of *The Wind* (1928).

with Wirt Roddy removes even this limited amount of agency. The wind breaks the cabin's window, starting a fire, and as Letty smothers the fire with a blanket, Wirt Roddy enters. The white horse of cowboy legend, which appears in the book as emblematic of an overwhelming force of nature, has appeared throughout the film in double exposure. Now, as the wind blows her about the room, she sees the white horse again and faints into Roddy's arms. The next morning, as Roddy commands her to pack and go with him, she pulls a gun on him, and, when he will not let go of the barrel, she fires. She buries him in a sand drift, watching from the window as the wind exposes her crime. Once again her hair is undone, this time reinforcing the disorder and madness that her eyes reveal. Lige returns, and she confesses to killing Wirt Roddy—but from Lige's perspective, the audience sees that there is no body to be uncovered. Lige tells her that the wind has its own form of justice, thus transforming it from a malevolent natural force to a beneficial one. Letty proclaims her love for Lige, and the film concludes with the two fearlessly facing into the wind and implicitly envisioning their future together. Whether her killing of Roddy was an illusion or whether his entire visit was an illusion, as the shot of the intact sand pile might suggest, or whether her secret will be kept by the wind as an agent of justice is left undetermined.

Dorothy Parker's and F. Scott Fitzgerald's anxieties over a monolithic "manure widow" farm novel taking over fiction in the 1920s proved to be overblown. The triumphal vision of the woman who "puts the farm on a paying basis" occurs in some novels of the decade, *O Pioneers!* and *So Big* among them, but they are outnumbered by those showing women as beasts of burden at the mercy of poverty, the hard conditions of farm life, or the indifference or cruelty of their husbands. The "stubborn seeking for the static in a world that for almost a hundred years has not been static," as Fitzgerald put it, had propelled rural comedies with their "realism" and "heart interest" to popularity, and by the 1920s these had become somewhat clichéd. When D. W. Griffith revived the play *Way Down East* for his 1920 film starring Lillian Gish and Richard Barthelmess, he paid $175,000 for a play considered to be old-fashioned even at the time. As Gish wrote later, the Griffith stock company thought "that Mr. Griffith had lost his mind" to remake a play that featured as its great set piece an erring heroine being ordered out of the house and being rescued by the son of the house from the ice floes where she has fallen when crossing a river.[52] What Griffith understood, however, was that "heart interest" would sell tickets not merely because audiences were so close to the rural events, including the rube comedy scenes he inserted, but because they were not. The ironic distance that high-culture modernism had opened up between Americans and their rural roots paralleled the physical distance that the Model T, the telephone, and the movies themselves had bridged to reach a rural space that could no longer be defined as existing in the past. Regionalism as it had existed in the late nineteenth century in the work of Charles W. Chesnutt or Sarah Orne Jewett was no longer an operative category. Instead, the regional novel would be part of the national scene, as in the work of Willa Cather.

The figure of the "manure widow" in middlebrow fiction that so threatened Fitzgerald and Parker was precisely designed to bridge that space between modernity and nostalgia. In her "calm, broad-hipped, level-eyed" guise of Selina Peake of Ferber's *So Big* or Aldrich's Abbie Deal of *A Lantern in Her Hand*, she demonstrates how the pioneer spirit can triumph over the poverty and problems on the farm, at least for the generations that succeed her. But if her environment tips toward extreme naturalistic forces, she will not be able to locate that balance. In Emanuel and Anna Marcet Haldeman-Julius's *Dust*, Rose exists in a cycle of bitter competition for affection and resources, forced to suppress her affection and creativity because poverty has stunted Martin's emotional growth since childhood. Emma of Ruth Suckow's *Country People* never experiences a life beyond work. The "manure widow" archetype also involves a significant level of self-denial for the sake of the land. Alexandra Bergson of Cather's *O Pioneers!* sets aside her mild feeling for Carl to care for the land, and only when the land proves her vision to be correct does she call him back. Lena of Cannon's *Red Rust* endures beatings in her first marriage and, like Rose, sees her second husband fall in love with a younger version of herself, but she takes the expansive view that for the good of the family unit and the survival of her ethnic kin, one of its members, her daughter, must be sent away, another form of sacrifice. Judith Pippinger Blackford is kept perpetually off balance by poverty, farm life, her children and excessive fertility, and ultimately the desire she feels for the preacher. Letty in Scarborough's *The Wind* considers herself too sheltered and finely bred to adopt the "manure widow" ways of her sister-in-law Cora, and her failure to adapt and to acknowledge her own desires keep her perpetually off balance as well. Those who, like Letty, take refuge in fanciful stories and refuse to learn the correct lessons from true stories such as the captivity of Cynthia Ann Parker demonstrate their inability to stand up to the environmental forces that confront them and align them not with successful adaptation but with failure.

CHAPTER 7

Waste, Hoarding, and Secrets
Modernist Naturalism and the Servant's Body

In *The Autobiography of Alice B. Toklas*, Gertrude Stein wrote that her purchase of a Cézanne painting of a woman was "an important purchase because in looking and looking at this picture Gertrude Stein wrote Three Lives."[1] Stein was at this time posing for her own portrait, spending nearly "every afternoon" in Picasso's studio before walking back: "During these long poses and these long walks Gertrude Stein meditated and made sentences. She was then in the middle of her negro story Melanctha Herbert, the second story of Three Lives and the poignant incidents that she wove into the life of Melanctha were often those she noticed in walking down the hill from the rue Ravignan."[2] By engaging in these activities—"looking and looking" at the portrait of a woman, posing for her own portrait, observing "poignant incidents," and above all "meditat[ing] and [making] sentences"—Stein found that she could concentrate on the subject matter of ordinary women's lives while she worked on the experimental language that she would use for *Three Lives*. As Marianne DeKoven explains, *Three Lives* "represents [Stein's] first concerted break with conventional modes of writing" and the "stylization of the prose surface in order to render the essence of a character's identity."[3] But if her "long poses" spent "looking and looking" gave Stein the experimental form of her sentences, the claim that walks about Paris gave her the "poignant incidents" tells only part of the story. "Melanctha" originates in *Q.E.D.*, but the other two sections owe more to Flaubert's "Un coeur simple," the classic tale of a servant woman and her uneventful life.[4] First translating this story into English and then incorporating it into "The Good Anna," the first section of *Three Lives*, Stein had found in Flaubert's tale "both a subject and a structural model."[5] In looking back to the ironic realism of Flaubert, Stein sets a pattern for treating the servant's body as subject matter and anticipates other portraits of the servant woman in naturalistic modernism.

The servant woman, or the self-sacrificing domestic drudge, emerges as a prototype for naturalistic treatments of the woman's body in modernist texts, anticipated in Wharton's *The House of Mirth* (1905) and developed in Stein's "The Good Anna" and "The Gentle Lena" from *Three Lives* (1909), Nella Larsen's *Quicksand* (1928), Evelyn Scott's *The Narrow House* (1921), Fannie Hurst's *Lummox* (1923), and Zona Gale's *Miss Lulu Bett* (1920). The character takes various forms: the woman forced by economic circumstances or domestic ideology into servitude, like Hurst's Bertha and Scott's Mrs. Farley; the woman trapped by pregnancy and biology, such as Larsen's Helga Crane; and the "old maid," the relic of regionalist fiction brought into a Freud-inflected modernist era, such as Alice in *The Narrow House* or Lulu Bett in Gale's *Miss Lulu Bett*. The woman's body is problematic in modernism because the modernist dichotomy between high culture and low positions "inferior mass culture as feminine," in Andreas Huyssen's classic formulation. In this, the modernists, like the Romantic poets, saw women as "providers of inspiration for the artist" but not artists themselves. To add to their problematic quality, servant women represent "the identification of woman with the masses as a political threat."[6]

With theories of primitivism and the association of free sexuality with lower-class bodies, modernist authors situated the woman's body, especially the raced woman's body, as a site of competing discourses about the effects of civilization and maternity. In Jean Toomer's *Cane*, for example, the main character of "Karintha" is a woman who "carries beauty," as if beauty is a property bestowed upon but separate from herself. Karintha entices men through her nature rather than her words. Unable herself to create art, or indeed to carry a child to term, the traditional analog for it, Karintha becomes the medium through which men can connect with their own essential selves, but her own soul, "a growing thing [that] ripened too soon," receives as little nurturing from the male gaze as her child has received from Karintha.[7] She is sentimentalized in men's eyes as mythic earth goddess, an unspeaking primitive subject whose idealization and fragmentation at the hands of men can only cause her harm.

Novels by Wharton, Larsen, Scott, Hurst, and Gale refute this type of sexualized, earth-mother idealization through their depictions of the servant woman's body. They depart from the subject of the young, sexual woman to include the aged and infirm women common to local color fiction and the worn-out or abusive mothers of classic naturalism. Their portraits of servant women show bodies gnarled and deformed by the work they do and the children they bear, reflecting the blows of a dominant culture that denigrates their labor while refusing to acknowledge its necessity. Servant women as protagonists challenge the norms of domesticity, emphasizing not its emotional satisfactions but its thankless, repetitive drudgery. Their bodies are racialized and objectified by ethnicity and class, revealing a class structure nominally democratic but rigidly hierarchical. In the figure of the servant woman, women's unruly naturalism reveals its fascination not only with the sexual body, the traditional subject matter for naturalism and those modernist texts that deal with women, but also with the other features of a woman's body, ones that characterize women who are elderly, disabled, ungainly with pregnancy, or unmarriageable because of their looks and body types. To call additional attention to the transformation of women's bodies, Hurst, Larsen, Scott, and Gale use melodrama or the movies to sharpen the contrast between the situation in which servant women find themselves and the idealized vision of womanhood that film and melodrama represent. In situating the body as a natural site not just for desire but also for age, maternity, and the waste both from and of human lives, the servant woman's body foregrounds the unruly naturalistic subject of the unseen and unmentionable body made visible.

Bodies, Waste, and Race

Naturalism's focus on bodies, economic injustice, and class has long signified the complicity of social and economic systems of valuation within a culture. As Mary E. Papke contends, naturalism privileges commodity fetishism and posits "the phantasmagoric value of things" in "the ways we continue to pay for America's emergence in the nineteenth century as the leading capitalist, industrial power in the world."[8] Classic naturalism frequently interests itself more in the acquisition and consumption of goods than in other parts of the commodity cycle. It emphasizes the desire that goes into conceptualizing and acquiring them, as in *Sister Carrie*, and the obsessive, fetishistic hoarding and sense of loss that attends their possession and occasional theft, as in *McTeague*. The missing piece is unruly naturalism's equal attention to the detritus left behind when acquiring, possessing, hoarding, and losing are finished, a detritus that exists as the catalog of refuse or squalor that pervades naturalistic texts. Catalogs of refuse appear in works ranging from Zola's *L'Assommoir* to Ann Petry's *The Street* and Sinclair Lewis's *Main Street* as a signpost of the work's genre, its engagement with the real. For the most part, however, the catalog is a signpost rather than a sustained metaphor. It appears as a descriptive passage to signal the atmosphere of waste that the character notices in passing rather than as something that affects his or her life.

A notable exception to this peripheral use of the catalog of waste occurs in the last chapter of Frank Norris's *Vandover and the Brute* as Vandover, reduced to penury, cleans out the cubbyhole under a sink:

> Prone in the filth under the sink, in the sour water, the grease, the refuse, he groped about with his hand searching for the something gray that the burnisher's wife had seen. He found it and drew it out. It was an old hambone covered with a greenish fuzz.... Vandover crawled back, half the way under the sink again, this

time bringing out a rusty pan half full of some kind of congealed gravy that exhaled a choking, acrid odour; next it was an old stocking, and then an ink bottle, a broken rat-trap, a battered teapot lacking a nozzle, a piece of rubber hose, an old comb choked with a great handful of hair, a torn overshoe, newspapers, and a great quantity of other debris that had accumulated there under the occupancy of the previous tenant.[9]

Norris's catalog of refuse piles detail upon repellant detail with clinical thoroughness to create naturalism's trademark aesthetic of disgust. Each item is not only decayed or broken in itself but repels in visual, tactile, and olfactory ways: "greenish fuzz," "great handful of hair," "choking, acrid odour." The passage obsessively catalogs objects, a standard feature of naturalism, but it shows the character's engagement with the filth it describes, rather than merely his observation of it. Reaching into dark, wet, murky spaces to retrieve the discarded waste turns Vandover into a handler of objects rather than merely an observer of them. Overtly positioned as a servant, he is transformed perversely into a collector again, a parodic version of his former self as an aesthete and connoisseur of objects. His position as a servant feminizes him by virtue of his abject position in a damp, wet hole under a sink, his economic need to take orders from a woman, and his contact with waste.

For female servants, however, contact with waste does not signal an end point of degradation but a daily event. In describing the principle of abjection, Julia Kristeva claims that "filth is not a quality in itself, but it applies only to what relates to a *boundary*, and, more particularly represents the object jettisoned out of that boundary, its other side, a margin." Bodily excretions are a form of the disruption that "disturbs identity, system, order," a rupture at its most literal level of the boundary between the interior of the body contained by its skin and the outside world, and an extension of naturalism's anxieties over other boundaries, such as those existing between human beings and animals or madness and sanity. Kristeva's insight explains the horrors of Vandover's diving for refuse under the sink and of Zola's Gervaise Coupeau, of *L'Assommoir*, having sex with her lover amid the dirty laundry that contains the wastes of others. Through contact with filth, the characters breach a boundary that threatens what Kristeva calls an "own and clean self."[10] Vandover's obsession with order can find no greater dissolution of self than this descent into a boundaryless mess of servitude, just as Gervaise gives up all pretenses to self-respect as she trades thrift and planning for the future for gluttony and desire in the present. Yet for servant women in Stein, Scott, Larsen, Hurst, and Gale, this contact with the dissolution of boundaries that waste provides constitutes the primary portion of their everyday lives.

In addition to the catalog of waste, naturalistic narratives often focus on discarded things and the ways in which characters collect, curate, and hoard them, as exemplified by Zerkow's obsessive hoarding of tin dishes or Maria Macapa's theft under the guise of collecting waste in *McTeague*. Women's servant narratives zero in on additional forms of waste, those less durable and more subject to decay, to conclude that waste is the necessary product of living and that, rightly or wrongly, women must clean it up. This idea of women's responsibility for sanitation gained momentum in the late nineteenth and early twentieth centuries. In analyzing George E. Waring's *How to Drain a House* (1885), for example, William Gleason argues that what had begun as a movement to increase women's health by making the processes of elimination both more private and more sanitary became a "surveillant regime" under which the housewife must "watch her servants as scrupulously as she watches her house, her family, and herself for signs of filth." Waring preached that abandoning the "remote and inhospitable privy" in favor of a hygienic earth closet would bring sanitation into the home and under the woman's control.[11] But references to the benefits to women's health were dropped in subsequent editions because the references to waste were too threatening to the delicacy of public sentiments. Instead, emphatic warnings about women's responsibilities for keeping the family's health intact replaced them.

With sanitation an obsession, the general acceptance of germs rather than "miasmas" as disease vectors, and the rise of Progressive Era professional housekeeping in the form of home economics, a family's health became more than ever the woman's responsibility. In addition, books such as *The New Housekeeping: Efficiency Studies in Home Management* (1912) by Christine Frederick, the household editor for the *Ladies' Home Journal*, proposed that practical solutions for household management and cleanliness were well within the competency as well as the responsibility of middle-class women. Yet for all her emphasis on efficiency, home economics, and labor-saving tips, Frederick focuses more on the waste of time than on the household wastes that Catharine Beecher, her acknowledged predecessor, had addressed half a century earlier. It is this gap in service between the ideal of household cleanliness and the reality of its wastes that the servant woman is expected to fill.

Dirt, Secrets, and the Raced Body

The figure of the servant woman, with its attendant associations of dealing with dirt and filth, crosses psychological boundaries as well, those dealing with emotions, sexuality, and family secrets. She acts as the repository for the modern family's excess emotion and is expected to listen to and solve its problems. Because the servant possesses a woman's body but is not defined as married or attached to a single man, she functions as the same sort of loose signifier as the prostitute in becoming the end point of a culture's desires, not merely its bodily waste but its messy excess of emotion. She must contain the culture's effluvia, clean up after it, and absorb it without having any means of ridding herself of what she contains. Her reward for this is to become the abject and the scapegoat, driven out to preserve the intact boundaries of a family. The classic example of regulating the servant's body in relation to sexuality is the case of the maidservant dismissed because she has attracted the attention of a son of the family: the desire and fault rest with the son, but the penalty must be paid by the woman of lesser cultural rank. The issues of waste, sexuality, and maternity are imbricated in the figure of the servant woman in ways that emphasize the occult culture of secrecy that surrounds her work duties, an intensification of the secrecy surrounding women's bodily functions more generally.

In addition to mediating the products of the body and medicating its ailments, the servant woman represents an emotional connection, both to comfort and to disgust or horror. Citing Lacan, Susan Stewart describes the relation of bodily wastes to culture as the result of the position they occupy: "Those products which cross such boundaries thereby become products of great cultural attention. What is both inside and outside the body (feces, spittle, urine, menstrual blood, etc.) tends to become taboo because of its ambiguous and anomalous status. A great deal of cultural regulation is required to privatize the erotogenic zones and to prohibit the projection of their pleasure within the domain of public space, and such regulation simultaneously aids in the development not only of the individual subject but also of the 'private space' occupied by that subject."[12] Stewart's observation illuminates the position that servant women occupied in relation to the wastes produced by households and by the culture at large. As those who organized and separated the products of the body from its cleanliness and integrity to create an "own and clean self," they were primary guardians of culture. Yet as figures not paired biologically or sexually with members of the household, they occupied an unstable position on the threshold of an intact family. Stallybrass and White expand on this idea in Freudian terms in *The Politics and Poetics of Transgression* by positing that the maidservant doubles the mother and provides a necessary outlet for erotic attraction, one linked to her functions of cleaning up after the child, as in Freud's memory of an "'old and ugly' nurse" who attacks his "standard of cleanliness" and becomes his standard for "the rational bourgeois subject's sense of shame and anxiety."[13] Employers rid themselves of servants as they rid themselves of the effluvia with which servants are associated. When a servant has been forced to transgress the family's boundaries, as in the scenario of the son propositioning a chambermaid, the family banishes the physical reminder of its shame by firing the servant. Judged by their levels of expertise, servants should have been considered professionals, but since the professionalization niche was already occupied by middle- and upper-class women filled with zeal for their role as domestic managers, servants necessarily existed on a lower rung.

Servants' bodies are insistently classed and raced. Less obviously, they are frequently figured as grotesque, either by their plain features or by their size. In *Three Lives*, Anna and Lena are German (or "german" in Stein's spelling) and plain.[14] Hurst's Bertha, Scandinavian by birth, is five foot nine and a huge and ungainly woman for her day, cruelly called a "lummox" by her employers. Lulu Bett, plain by virtue of being an "old maid," though "once handsome," has "flat, bluish shadows under her wistful eyes."[15] In their ethnic Otherness women like Hurst's Bertha and Stein's Anna exist in an uneasy relation to the house and family they serve, external to the family but essential for its internal operations. Reading the United States as that family, servant women reflect anxieties over immigration and the rise of the working class. With each wave of nineteenth-century immigrants landing in the United States and seeking work, the ethnicity of the previous generation of the servant classes changed. As Christine Stansell explains, in the early nineteenth century "New York [female] servants were a heterogeneous group" of rural women and immigrants, but "[b]y 1855, 74 percent of New York's domestics were Irish; only 4 percent were native-born whites."[16] The advent of textile mills in New England brought an alternative to domestic service for young rural women, whose places were soon filled by immigrant labor in successive waves, often the Irish in large cities and throughout the East, although the women of some immigrant groups, such as Italians, preferred piecework or other forms of manufacturing to domestic service. In the Midwest, Swedish and later eastern European women were the servants that Cather describes in *My Ántonia* and Lewis in *Main Street*, and in the South, African American women filled the majority of domestic service positions.

The class and racial barriers that helped to maintain the positions of servant women were bolstered by the social ideologies of a democratic culture uneasy with the overt distinctions of class difference. In middle-class U.S. households, the status of the hired girl was not designated as a long-term form of employment, as in the rigid class structures of European countries. Rather, the position was a training ground for the day when the servant would have her own home to manage. Catharine Beecher's *The American Woman's Home* and other household manuals emphasized the mistress's duties to inform and educate her servants toward the hired girl's graduation day, the point at which she would assume responsibility for a home of her own. According to Laurie Ousley, Beecher's readers had to keep appropriate class distinctions while realizing that "[w]ages, accompanied by marriage and perhaps a move westward, can allow for a servant to become a mistress."[17] Too often, managing servants took the form of intrusive demands on their time and privacy, demands that elevated the mistress's sense of status and ownership as they reduced the servant's. As Stansell notes, "One could not really *be* a lady if one did not have a problem with servants," and complaints about servants established the mistress's authority as a knowledgeable housekeeper with suitably high standards.[18]

In addition to these issues of class, the racial discourse surrounding servants conflated the wastes that they had to clean and the potential for contamination that this contact generated. According to Kathleen Brown, "Articulations of the boundary-defining functions of cleanliness appear in middle-class women's comments about the Irish, African Americans, the poor, and even other middle-class people. These judgments were often passed against the same groups of people whose domestic labor made them witnesses to genteel people's filth—the backstage grooming, dressing, eating, and cleaning that allowed for public presentations of refined, disciplined bodies."[19] Witnesses to the production of a family's waste, both the physical waste generated by daily life and the secrets that accrue within families, servants suffered contamination by association and could not be trusted to keep secrets. Fearing the transmission of diseases and vermin—the smaller annoyances like lice and bedbugs as well as deadly contagions such as typhoid—mistresses rationalized their regulation of the servant's body as necessary to health as well as to moral status.

Thus the quandary of the middle-class matron: the ethnically defined servant had to be clean, moral, and well-regulated to demonstrate her mistress's superior housekeeping abilities; she had to deal with wastes without being contaminated by them; yet she could not be "white" in the class and racial sense of her mistress, since to be too well dressed could break down class barriers and confuse the identities of servant and mistress. Susan Strasser reports that in the South women gave their old clothing to their servants, a "practice... not widespread in the North, where mistresses worried that well-dressed domestics might be mistaken for women of their own class and where maids who wore nice clothes were faulted for putting on airs."[20] Indeed, shopgirl romances and popular magazine articles promised that a beautiful lower-class young woman could attract the attention, and the marriage proposal, of a higher-status man with little more than a fetching smile and a becoming dress, a Cinderella scenario that Dreiser shows the sensational newspapers exploiting when they discover Jennie's relationship with Lester Kane in *Jennie Gerhardt* (1911).

Along with its material care, servant women had to manage the family's psychological dirt and flow of private information, since their position within a family made them the inadvertent keepers of some of the family's intimate secrets. This knowledge helped to balance the power relationships between servant and employer, for although the employer could threaten to fire a servant or give her a bad reference, the servant as keeper of secrets could threaten the family with exposure to social ridicule. The figuratively occult nature of the knowledge that servants held took on a more literal form too, as Brian McCuskey points out in "Not at Home: Servants, Scholars, and the Uncanny." At private séances, servants often took their place with the family, epitomizing the "ideological confusion and subjective turbulence heightened by the mixing of classes."[21] The spiritualism that supplemented emotional communication was thought to flow more freely through servants, since their more emotional and "primitive" nature enhanced their ability to cross the boundaries between the living and the dead. Servants sometimes discovered a gift for becoming mediums in their own right, which, as McCuskey notes, could have social and economic advantages. The sort of psychic turbulence that might include messages from spirit guides or warnings for the future merely extended the range of unruly desires, spent feelings, and family secrets to which the servant was already privy. How fitting, therefore, that the same psychological turmoil witnessed as part of the servant's unwritten job description be transmuted into psychic information and doled out in mystic language to the employers requesting it. Moreover, only in the darkness and clasped hands of the séance could the servant's body be unremarked and unmentioned. Mapped onto modernist and naturalist concerns, then, the idea of the servant as medium coincides nicely with her other functions. If in physical terms she represents a cleansing machine for excess waste in the economy of the home as body, in psychological terms she serves the same function as an affective repository for feelings too messy and excessive to handle.

In writing of waste culture, women writers of naturalism transform traditional servant narratives and stereotypes, either in characters' encounters with servants or through the perspectives of the servants themselves, to argue that women not only produce waste but also come to embody it. The desperate sex-for-money exchanges of Crane's Maggie Johnson, Dreiser's Carrie Meeber, Phillips's Susan Lenox, and Norris's Minna Hooven of *The Octopus* focus attention on women's sexuality as an economic commodity, but the domestic servitude narratives of Stein, Larsen, Hurst, Scott, and Gale concentrate on those whom society has designated either as waste or the tenders of waste. These include the unmarried "surplus women" existing at the edges of nuclear families in Gale and Scott; the sickly women, enervated by incessant childbearing, in Scott, Stein, and Larsen; the tenders and hoarders of waste in Wharton and Scott; and the children and babies, by-products of desire, that exist as hungry, demanding animals in Larsen and Scott. Viewed through the eyes of the servant woman, waste is not peripheral but central to a society and to the naturalistic narratives that depict the most realistic and least savory parts of women's lives. If waste is the trace, in effect the writing, of what a society values, then understanding the servant woman's relationship to waste, and its portrayal in naturalistic novels by women writers, is central to understanding unruly naturalism in the era of modernism.

The Case of Lily Bart, Hoarder

In a 1904 letter, Edith Wharton confessed to being "discouraged by criticism ... & the assumption that the people I write about are not 'real' because they are not navvies & char-women."[22] As if to prove her critics wrong, her next novel, *The House of Mirth*, prominently features a charwoman and other working-class characters not merely as set dressing but as parts of the plot, antagonists and would-be helpers of the heroine, Lily Bart. Much critical discussion has focused on Lily's gambling and the novel's use of the stock market as signifying the marriage market, with fluctuating exchange values that bear on Lily's marketability as a marriageable woman. But the novel focuses as much on the issues of waste, expenditure, and destruction as it does on the corrupt and corrupting values of exchange that power the plot.

For Lily's social set, wasting time and goods is a prized form of social display, as Thorstein Veblen had outlined it in *The Theory of the Leisure Class* (1899). Echoing what Veblen had said about the necessary uselessness of conspicuous consumption as a marker of social status, Georges Bataille explains in "The Notion of Expenditure" that not just inutility but actual waste is essential, both in the form of pointless commodity destruction, like the potlatch, and of evanescent social display, for "social rank is linked to the possession of a fortune, but only on the condition that the fortune be partially sacrificed in unproductive social expenditures such as festivals, spectacles, and games." Upper-class women become the moving potlatch, draped in the jewelry and expensive gowns that, as Bataille says, fit the contradictory needs of "acquisition" and "the need to destroy and lose."[23] Bataille's idea of expenditure, like Veblen's theory of conspicuous consumption, is expressed in the gambling, operagoing, and *tableaux vivants* of *The House of Mirth*. As Wharton claimed about *The House of Mirth* in her autobiography, *A Backward Glance*, "A frivolous society can acquire dramatic significance only through what its frivolity destroys. Its tragic implication lies in its power of debasing people and ideals."[24] Wharton's idea of destruction, like Bataille's, confers significance through the process of creating waste.

The working-class characters in *The House of Mirth* bear witness to this culture of pointless waste but do not profit from it. They represent the literal but hidden waste that a society leaves behind in its cycle of constant consumption and destruction to create social capital. Early in the novel, Laurence Selden thinks of

Lily: "He had a confused sense that she must have cost a great deal to make, that a great many dull and ugly people must, in some mysterious way, have been sacrificed to produce her" (7), and much later, Lily assesses herself as a "rare flower grown for exhibition, a flower from which every bud had been nipped except the crowning blossom of her beauty" (512). Both Selden's mechanical metaphor and Lily's natural one express the same sentiment, one reflecting Bataille's argument that "[t]he rich man consumes the poor man's losses, creating for him a category of degradation and abjection that leads to slavery" (125). In the late nineteenth century and early twentieth century, the devaluation process of "degradation and abjection" operates most strongly in the realm of seduction, of virginity and reputation as negotiable commodities. A common argument in favor of prostitution was that it provided a safety valve for men's sexual urges so that middle- and upper-class women would not be subjected to rape. Poor women, deprived of chastity and driven into prostitution, are in this equation the waste products necessary to ensure the rarefied atmosphere that produces a Lily Bart.

In *The House of Mirth*, narratives of expenditure and waste, the contamination implied by the servant woman's narrative and the cautionary tale of Lily Bart's being jettisoned from society, occur in a series of encounters between Lily and two working-class women: Mrs. Haffen, the charwoman who sells Bertha Dorset's letters to Laurence Selden, believing that Lily is the writer, and Nettie Struther, a young working woman whom Lily had helped through Gerty Farish's working girl's club. Both sets of encounters oppose the social mercantilism of New York society, for they present Lily with alternative ways to see the circulation of the by-products of desire: discarded letters and the depreciated value of the fallen woman.

Lily encounters the charwoman Mrs. Haffen twice, in meetings where she erroneously believes she has the upper hand. The first occurs when Lily, after her first visit to Selden's apartment, descends the stairs where Mrs. Haffen is scrubbing. A "stout" woman with "a broad sallow face, slightly pitted with small-pox, and thin strawberry-colored hair through which her scalp shone unpleasantly" (20), Mrs. Haffen has defects in precisely those areas in which Lily excels and foreshadows Lily's downfall in the deficiencies that she displays. Like Mrs. Haffen's reddish-blonde hair, Lily's luxuriant blonde hair will grow thinner over the course of the book, and her perfect complexion will show traces of wrinkles by the time of her death. Even Lily's hand—relaxed, graceful, and, as Selden notes, "polished as a bit of old ivory, with its slender pink nails" (10)—contrasts with Mrs. Haffen's "clenched red fists" (20), which hint at a class-based belligerence. Lily misreads Mrs. Haffen's silence and grudging acquiescence as yet another tribute to her beauty: "The poor thing was probably dazzled by such an unwonted apparition" (20). In addition to witnessing Lily's indiscretion with Selden, Mrs. Haffen, of the skimpy hair, red hands, and stout body, is the figure of the naturalistic grotesque woman, and the presence of her servant's body, juxtaposed with Lily's on the stairs as she makes her literal and symbolic descent, should warn Lily of the same possibility for her own body. But Lily, imperceptive and self-deluding as always after an encounter with Selden, feels no kinship and fails to recognize her naturalistic double.

Mrs. Haffen appears for the second and final time when she visits Lily to sell Selden's torn letters from Bertha Dorset. Having incorrectly concluded that Lily is the writer and can be blackmailed accordingly, Mrs. Haffen launches into a "diffuse narrative" (165) that a more sophisticated or more guilty woman would immediately recognize as a threat disguised beneath an overt bid for sympathy. Mrs. Haffen explains that her husband, Haffen, is out of work, and that they must sell the letters to survive. Because Lily does not understand, Mrs. Haffen pulls out Bertha's letters, fastened together with pasted strips from a dirty newspaper. The juxtaposition of newspaper and intimate letters constitutes a material threat of publication if Lily refuses to pay and, given the oily smudges of the newspaper, a tactile reminder of the repugnance with which Lily handles the whole affair. (Wharton's own practice of pasting together sheets of manuscript with strips of paper heightens the contrast with Mrs. Haffen's repurposing of the only paper readily available to her: the words of others.) Quite apart from the threat imposed by the situation, the forms of paper with which Mrs. Haffen confronts Lily should serve as a warning to her, for words on paper, from love letters to telegrams, figure as disruptive or dangerous objects in Wharton's works. The inanimate objects of a love affair, even if collected as souvenirs, remain waste and should be discarded lest they poison current relationships, as in Wharton's stories "The Letters" and "The Day of Her Funeral."

But Lily is a hoarder, refusing to discard the letters or to put them back into circulation. They represent a treasure to her, a physical talisman of power that she has yet to exercise, much as her beauty is a potential asset that she can exercise by agreeing to the right marriage proposal. Yet Lily does not own the letters, despite her purchase of them. They are another's letters purchased with borrowed money, and their value depends on factors other than Lily's willingness to trade them. Rescued from their status as waste and transformed once more into property, they must be placed back into circulation if they are not to poison their environment. Lily handles this treasure, as she handles all investments, badly. She does not understand that there is no safe possession of a volatile commodity: as waste, it must be discarded expeditiously, and as treasure, it must be recirculated and invested promptly. To hoard waste, as Lily does with the letters, encourages a false accumulation of worthless goods and the equally false sense of security that accompanies them. Lily dies because her fastidiousness will not allow her to recirculate the tarnished objects of her reputation and to part with what she has hoarded. Her stubbornness about holding onto what her society does not value—her principles, her love for Selden, and her scruples about a little judicious blackmail—has caused her friends Judy Trenor, Carry Fisher, and Simon Rosedale to intervene, yet Lily refuses to let her treasures go. She crumbles under the weight of social expectations and memories, exemplified by the objects she hoards, chief among them the dresses that she spreads out on the bed and the letters that, like all her other investments, she holds too long without recouping their value.

Lily's meeting with Nettie Struther is her second opportunity to learn from a working-class naturalistic double. Nettie is a character straight out of melodrama and naturalistic fiction: the working-class girl seduced and abandoned by a man of a higher class. The seduction plot charts the course of this devaluation, with the loss of virginity, for working-class women, and the loss of its discourse substitute, reputation, in upper-class women, foretelling the ways in which each may be discarded. From Lily's perspective, Nettie is a fallen woman to be rescued, yet if Nettie is the prototypical fallen woman, Lily is the woman fallen and likewise needs help. The situation is reversed when Nettie instead rescues Lily from the littered New York streets and provides her with a cup of tea and a baby to hold. Both plots of devaluation conclude with the image of discarded human beings. For Nettie, the waste product of desire, her grandly named daughter "Marry Anto'nette" (508), is an object of value, but for Lily the waste product is her body, now discarded and as out of circulation as the fantasy of the baby that she holds in her last moments.

Both women need to jettison a hoarded commodity, Nettie the shameful secret of her seduction and Lily the secret of Bertha's letters. In contrast to Lily, Nettie rejects false pride: she places herself back into circulation, as Lily refuses to do, and recycles herself as a wife and mother. By telling her husband of her affair, Nettie gives up her hoarded secret and dispels its toxicity. But Lily cannot take the lesson of circulation, of recycling and reinventing herself as Nettie has done. By preserving society's emotional secrets through hoarding Bertha's letters for too long, Lily becomes the servant contaminated with the unshed waste of her society. The servant narratives in *The House of Mirth*, of which Lily Bart has only a dim glimpse in her encounters with Mrs. Haffen and Nettie Struther, reveal a relationship between women's bodies and waste, and women's bodies *as* waste, that Lily recognizes only during her last visit to Selden: "One must get back to it or be thrown out into the rubbish heap—and you don't know what it's like in the rubbish heap" (498).

Dirt and the Female Subject

Stein's *Three Lives* takes the woman servant as its subject in two of its three sections, "The Good Anna" and "The Gentle Lena." Written in 1906 before Stein adapted "Melanctha" from a previous novel, *Q.E.D.*, these portions of *Three Lives* reflect the "naturalist novels" that Stein had read and, as Linda Wagner-Martin notes, mark a radical choice of "inarticulate, lower-class characters as protagonists" and a "harshly objective style."[25] In recent decades, "Melanctha" has attracted the bulk of critical attention for its treatment of race, sexuality, and female autonomy as well as its stylistic innovations, with "The Good Anna" and "The Gentle Lena" receiving less critical focus. Considered separately from "Melanctha," however, and in light of the themes of the servant woman's body in naturalism, "The Good Anna" and "The Gentle Lena" provide differing portraits of the figure: one of dominance and one of submission, one of sterility and economic control and the other of fecundity and economic powerlessness. Yet both reflect a transition to modernist women's naturalism through their treatment of the woman servant's body amid waste and disorder and the treatment of childbirth and female biology beyond the parameters of sexual expression.

"The Good Anna" is the story of Anna Ferderner, a thin, angular, bossy woman of about forty, of "solid lower middle-class south german stock."[26] As Fannie Hurst does in *Lummox*, Stein structures narrative time through Anna's employers, most of whom are "large, abundant women, for such were always lazy, careless or all helpless" (16) and willing to let Anna dominate them. The story is told in three parts. Part 1, beginning in medias res, describes Anna's life with Miss Mathilda. Part 2 backtracks to Anna's earlier life, her dislike for her half-brother's family, and her romance, falling out, and eventual reconciliation with Mrs. Lehntman. Part 3 returns Anna to the present, including her final illness and death. "The Good Anna" is a meditation on power and its inversion in domestic relationships, with the key dynamic being the variable positions occupied by mistress and servant depending on the exchange of love or money. Anna is the servant, yet she rules over all her households and dominates her relationships, a cliché of servant tales that Stein parodies even as she reinforces it. Anna's power over her employers derives from their weakness and laziness. Her power over her friends, including Mrs. Drehten and Mrs. Lehntman, derives from the money she gives them. As Linda Wagner-Martin observes, "Anna [is] happy only when she control[s] the people for whom she work[s]" (236), and her inability to control people, like her absurd attempt to control the sexual behavior of her beloved pet dogs, sets up a classic naturalistic losing competition between social rules and biological behavior.

Lena Mainz of "The Gentle Lena" is as submissive as Anna is controlling.

The two share an ethnic background as "german" immigrants and a life in service, but Stein uses them for different purposes. If "The Good Anna" is Flaubert's "Un coeur simple" turned inside out, with Anna rejecting the parrot that her prototype, Félicité, had believed to be the incarnation of the Holy Ghost, then the template for "The Gentle Lena" is an inverted Cinderella tale, with Lena as the downtrodden slavey oppressed by her class-conscious aunt, Mrs. Haydon, and her cousins, two "unkneaded, unformed mounds of flesh" (152), as Cinderella's wicked stepmother and stepsisters. At Mrs. Haydon's insistence, Lena becomes engaged to the reluctant Herman Kreder, who is repeatedly described as interested only in men. After first leaving her at the altar on the day they are to be wed, he later does marry her and takes her to live with his parents, "stingy dirty people" (168) who bully Lena and Herman. Only her friend the "good german cook" realizes Lena's situation, but there is no remedy for it.

Both "The Gentle Lena" and "The Good Anna" depict children as surplus or waste, a drain on the mother. After her marriage, Lena, now called "poor Lena" instead of "the gentle Lena," becomes "more and more lifeless" (174) through repeated childbearing. Stein uses the term "lifeless" first figuratively, in describing Lena's mental and physical debilitation, and then literally, in showing her death in childbirth. In "The Good Anna," Julia Lehntman, a widow and "the only romance Anna ever knew... loved best in her work to deliver young girls who were in trouble" (33), which she could afford to do only with Anna's financial help. She even adopts a child in addition to her own two, an action that makes Anna "every minute paler with indignation and heat" (28) because of Mrs. Lehntman's "careless" ways. After she and Anna part ways, Mrs. Lehntman, a midwife by profession, goes to work assisting an abortionist, a "mysterious and evil man" who "got into trouble doing things that were not right to do" (41).

The moralistic reference to abortion, elided in the narrative's free indirect discourse as filtered through Anna's simple, judgmental, almost childlike voice, obscures the fact that the opposite is true. In helping to provide abortions, Mrs. Lehntman is participating in an underground economy that disposes of the waste products of desire, much as she had done before when helping "young girls... in trouble" to deliver their babies. Anna disapproves of Mrs. Lehntman's new work, but she had equally disapproved of Mrs. Lehntman's adoption of a child when she plucked it from the round of waste children sent to orphanages or to the still-existing horror of baby farms. In offering abortion services or helping the doctor to administer abortions, Mrs. Lehntman plies her trade in a way consistent with other midwives at the time. *The Social Evil in Chicago* reports that of twenty midwives asked to perform abortions, six refused absolutely, two refused but referred clients to another midwife, and "the remaining twelve agreed to perform the supposed abortion for different sums of money."[27] Given the text's, and Anna's, negative perspective on surplus children, the narrative observation that Mrs. Lehntman and the doctor were "doing things it was not right to do" reflects Anna's self-contradictory attitudes, for Mrs. Lehntman's disposal of waste children actually parallels Anna's war on dirt.

As consumers rather than producers, children present problems even when they are loved. In "The Good Anna," Anna's friend Mrs. Drehten, sickly and afflicted with a tumor that is presumably the result of childbearing, lives in the country with a drunken husband and seven children. Anna idealizes them at first as a Rooseveltian ideal of "four stalwart, cheery, filial sons, and three hard working obedient simple daughters" (29) before hearing that they were unworthy of the money that she showered on them: "the four big sons carrying on and always lazy, the awkward, ugly daughters dressing up with Anna's help" (32). The process of childbearing likewise wears out Lena Mainz of "The Gentle Lena." She becomes "always careless, and dirty, and a little dazed, and lifeless" (173) until, by the time her last child is born, "Lena had died, too, and nobody knew just how it had happened to her" (174). As in "Melanctha," the idea of care and carelessness forms a repeated linguistic pattern: the carelessness that enables Mrs. Lehntman to shrug off Anna's scoldings and ignore her children is protective rather than reprehensible, because those who care too much, like Mrs. Drehten, or who grow careless about self-preservation because of repeated childbearing, like Lena, lack the capacity to survive. If the women do not treat the children as waste—by ridding themselves of children, or by being "careless" about them—they themselves become waste.

In addition to the treatment of children, the presence of dirt in "The Good Anna" and "The Gentle Lena" reveals their connection with women's naturalism. As a Cinderella figure before her marriage to Herman Kreder, Lena was accustomed to cleaning and serving, but her marriage plunges her into the ashes rather than removing her from them. She discovers that she has married a family rather than simply a man, and a family for whom dirt was a way of life. In keeping with the novella's gradations of ethnicity, in which Lena, as a recent immigrant, is to her American-born cousins "earth rough ... ugly and dirty, and as far below them as were italian or negro workmen" (158), each ethnicity possesses its own form of stereotypically defined dirt. As her friend Irish Mary tells Lena, the old couple had not the sort of "free-hearted, thoughtless, fighting, mudbespattered, ragged, peat-smoked cabin dirt that irish Mary could forgive and love" but "the german dirt of saving, of being dowdy and loose and foul in your clothes" to save the effort of washing. Irish dirt derives from expenditure of emotion and of effort, representing a kind of joy. German dirt, on the other hand, derives from a miserly saving of emotion and effort by an old couple living cheaply for no other object than that "from their nature they just had to and because it made them money but also that they could never be put in any way to make them spend their money" (167). The product not of exertion but of hoarding, the Kreders' dirt becomes emblematic of their money: they will not part with money, and they will not part with their wastes, a conflation of money and dirt that, as in *The House of Mirth*, proves poisonous in the long run.[28] Lena succumbs to the dirt and her undifferentiated role as part of a family when repeated childbearing erodes both her cleanliness and her individuality.

The issue of dirt in "The Good Anna" culminates in Anna's visit to a spiritualist. Feeling uncertain about taking a new job, Anna is persuaded to see a fortuneteller. When she and Mrs. Lehntman arrive, the medium embodies all that Anna abhors: a "dusty, dowdy woman ... [with] very greasy hair," with a house that is "full of dirty things all made by hand" (37). "Dusty" and "greasy" intensify "dirty" as descriptors, but "dowdy" belongs to a different level of signification, one that looks ahead to "The Gentle Lena" and its phrasing of "being dowdy and loose and foul in your clothes," as if a lack of style is as serious as a lack of cleanliness. The medium's house reflects less the trappings of the spirit world than the grubby materialism of this one: "It has a round table in the centre covered with a decorated woolen cloth, that has soaked in the grease of many dinners, for though it should always be taken off, it is easier to spread the cloth upon it than change it for the blanket deadener that one owns. The upholstered chairs are dark and worn, and dirty. The carpet has grown dingy with the food that's fallen from the table, the dirt that's scraped from off the shoes and the dust that settles with the ages. The somber greenish colored papers on the walls has been smoked a dismal dirty grey, and all pervading is the smell of soup made out of onions and fat chunks of meat" (38). Grease-soaked cloth, the stains of many meals, the street dirt from shoes, the dust, the smoked greenish-grey walls, and the poverty-evoking smells of cooking onions: like the waste-filled catalog of refuse from *Vandover and the Brute*, the description overwhelms every sense except hearing. The dirt results from the same hoarding of energy that occurs in the Kreders' home, for as the suddenly censorious narrator informs the reader, leaving the cloth on instead of exchanging it for "the blanket deadener" is the act of a person too lazy to remove the cover. The medium's house, like her profession, operates in the waste corners of a modern economy, much as Mrs. Lehntman's and the doctor's abortion business does.

By evoking the cramped room of other naturalistic texts, the spiritualist's home suggests the category confusion between work and domestic spaces that occurs in *L'Assommoir* and prostitution narratives. Indeed, fortunetellers sometimes operated as fronts for houses of prostitution. In Mary Stambury Watts's *The Rise of Jennie Cushing* (1914), for example, the authorities grow suspicious over a woman who "called herself Countess Paolini, a clairvoyant or medium or something—the one that kept a joint up on Cass Street, and the police ran her out of town ... after two of her women got into a scrap over some fellow and one of 'em knifed the other."[29] Like the lower-class cribs of the prostitution narratives, where the women worked and slept in beds with an oilcloth strip across the bottom to protect the sheets from customers' boots, the medium's house draws no boundaries between her public and private lives. Operating on the fringes of legality, the fortuneteller caters to women's illicit needs for spiritual reassurance as prostitutes cater to men's physical ones. Surrounded by squalor, the medium places herself in a trance through a series of sexualized bodily movements—choking, deep breaths, swallowing—that evoke scenes of prostitution, another profession in which money changes hands for a woman's embodied performance of being out of control.

In linking fortunetelling to prostitution and abortion, Stein expects her readers to make a connection that was already common knowledge. In *A New Conscience and an Ancient Evil*, Jane Addams singles out "dealers in futurity" who "are sometimes in collusion with disreputable houses," seeing as "pathetic" the young couples "who come out on the street from a dingy doorway which bears the palmist's sign of the spread-out hand" and act upon fantasies of riches: "One hardworking girl of my acquaintance, told by a palmist that 'diamonds were coming to her soon,' afterwards accepted without a moment's hesitation a so-called diamond ring from a man whose improper attentions she had hitherto withstood."[30] The "dingy doorway" and the vague, optimistic promises turn one young girl toward "the easiest way" of prostitution. The visit to the medium's dingy home is out of keeping for Anna, not only because it enables Mrs. Lehntman to manipulate her through the words of the medium, but also because despite her career as a carping moralist she is blind to the false assurances that it provides and to the squalor of its associations. In their connection to dirt and waste, Stein's servant women Anna and Lena reveal the costs to the woman's body of engaging with wastes, both the limitations of avoiding them, as Anna does, and the fatal consequences of falling too deeply into contact with them as the price of establishing the usual heterosexual trajectory of marriage and childbirth, as Lena does.

Quicksand and the Melodramatic Imagination

Nella Larsen's first novel, *Quicksand*, is a restless odyssey of self-discovery for its mixed-race heroine, Helga Crane, as she shuttles between black and white communities, tied to both but feeling a full member of neither. Helga discards several situations in turn. As a teacher at the Naxos Institute she protests the colorless and conventional existence she is forced to lead there. As the employee of a racial uplift society, which she at first embraces, she feels "as if she were shut up, boxed up, with hundreds of her race," a feeling that her visit to a jazz club does nothing to counteract.[31] Yet when Helga travels to Copenhagen and her mother's relatives, she finds herself typed as exotic, with "the warm impulsive nature of the women of Africa" (87), according to Axel Olsen, the artist who hopes to make her his mistress. Critical commentary on *Quicksand* has focused on Helga's search for racial identity and her failure to find it in any of the worlds that she inhabits. For example, Amelia DeFalco reads Helga's response to the nightclub scene as flight from a primitivism she wants to embrace, and Cherene Sherrard-Johnson finds the many tableaux-like scenes of the mulatta body to be Larsen's resistant response to the "race woman" as seen in Archibald J. Motley's paintings. As Laura Doyle explains, "With no 'people,' Helga has no ready point of entrée into the freedom story. She cannot do 'uplift' into freedom if she is not fully identified with or accepted by any race.... Helga displays for us how transnational travel has structured the terms of race identity."[32]

Quicksand also participates in the tradition of women's unruly naturalism, through the traditions of film melodrama that guide Helga's actions in the first twenty chapters, and through the descent into a naturalistic space in the last five. In the first or cosmopolitan section of the novel, Helga treats her body less as the site of feeling, which she tries to reason away, than as a canvas on which to try out her search for "color," a word that signifies literally her wish to adorn herself in colorful clothing and symbolically her quest for a proper relation to her mixed-race heritage.[33] The second part occupies less than a fifth of the total, the concluding five chapters out of twenty-five, but it resolves the psychological indecision and modernist doubt of the heroine by imprisoning her in a destiny, including marriage, motherhood, and racial certainty, that had been no part of her earlier plan. In the freedom story of her transnational travel, Helga enacts the narrative of a New Woman in film melodrama, but in the naturalistic story she falls prey to an existence rooted in religious fervor, Darwinian desire, ceaseless childbearing, and servitude, all signified by literal and symbolic waste. Her life is in two parts and two genres, the first a film in which she is scenarist, audience, lead actor, and director, and the second a naturalistic novel in which she is an object helplessly overwhelmed by biology.

Melodrama, like naturalism and film, relies on excess emotion, power, and sexuality. As Peter Brooks defines the term, it includes "the indulgence of strong emotionalism; moral polarization and schematization; extreme states of being, situation, actions; overt villainy, persecution of the good, and final reward of virtue; inflated and extravagant expression; dark plottings, suspense, breathtaking peripety."[34] The key to each of these is the idea of excess as applied to the twist on a common situation—a middle-class family thrown into debt to a villainous banker, for example—in ways that call into question the concept of a moral universe. Melodrama, for Brooks, is "a response to the loss of the tragic vision" that occurs in "a world where the traditional imperatives of truth and ethics have been violently thrown into question, yet where the promulgation of truth and ethics, their instauration as a way of life, is of immediate, daily, political concern" (15). The idea of traditional values "violently thrown into question" recalls Frank Norris's view of naturalism as a literature of lives "twisted from the ordinary."[35] Keith Newlin defines the link between naturalism and melodrama as "a tendency to see the world in terms of a polarized conflict between representatives of some simplified set of ideas" but identifies an "aesthetics of excess" as key to both, something that Ben Singer defines as central to early film as well.[36] According to Singer, "cinematic melodrama obviously showcases emotional excess" and evokes a consequent "mode of visceral excess in the spectator."[37] The evocation of feeling in the spectator suggests the transmission of affect that runs throughout grim realism and naturalism. Rather than limiting cinematic melodrama to these characteristics, however, Singer proposes a "cluster concept" that combines traditional elements of melodrama (pathos, excessive emotion, sensationalism) with the specific structural and technical demands of filmmaking (episodic construction, scenic spectacle).

Brooks's, Newlin's, and Singer's definitions of melodrama come especially close to the principles of naturalism in their discussions of excess in subject matter and treatment. In naturalism, the idea of excess applies equally to behavior and to the traditional cascade of calamities, a causal chain of coincidences that undermine the character's best efforts to extricate himself or herself from a seemingly inevitable fate. Naturalistic characters, often laconic and uncommunicative on the surface, have their thoughts rendered by the narrator in stylistically excessive ways that elevate narrator and reader above the characters. In *McTeague*, for example, at the variety show at the Orpheum, Owgooste's wetting his pants is described hyperbolically—"What a misery! It was a veritable catastrophe, deplorable, lamentable, a thing beyond words!"—yet McTeague steps out of the kindergarten after murdering Trina and observes only "I'll bet it'll rain tomorrow," an understatement of emotion as excessive in its way as Owgooste's outburst (63, 207). Applied to two such disparate situations, the hyperbolic dialogue applied to the first and the laconic tone of the second obscure both scenes' roots in melodrama, and, as if to emphasize the idea of excess, both scenes feature bodily fluids (the second involving Trina's blood) spilled in an excess of emotion.

Quicksand follows the path of melodramatic excess in both its plots: the early novel of manners centered on race and cosmopolitanism and the last five chapters centered on naturalistic squalor. In the first twenty chapters, Helga acts as the heroine of a screen melodrama. She is sensitive and reactive, or, as Sianne Ngai suggests, excessively irritated, in responding to others' perceptions of her, traits that Larsen emphasizes through Helga's self-dramatizing poses in crucial moments.[38] Like Winnie in Scott's *The Narrow House*, Helga glides through the novel in a series of Delsartian gestures, arranging herself in chairs and posing in doorways, a feature emphasized through her modeling sessions for Axel Olsen. Like Irene Redfield and Claire Kendry in Larsen's *Passing*, Helga is consistently aware of the racial frame within which, and through which, she is viewed, and the frame for Helga includes the proscenium arch, the cinematic and melodramatic worldview that she brings to bear on her actions. Helga's flamboyant, chic clothing contributes to the sense of the theatrical and cinematic manner in which she approaches reality. As Meredith Goldsmith writes in "Shopping to Pass, Passing to Shop," "The aesthetic of the shop window dominates *Quicksand* from its first scene," and, given the association between windows as movie camera and film screen, Helga's actions in the first twenty chapters illustrate her adoption of a cinematic aesthetic.[39]

The cinematic aesthetic dominates the novel in two ways: through the image of the shop window as cinema screen, and through the commodity culture shaped by the movies. By the mid-1920s, screen fashions in clothing and home décor had permeated every town large enough to support a movie theater. The glamour shots and makeup tips published in fan magazines such as *Photoplay* led fans to imitate Mae Murray's bee-stung lips, Clara Bow's tousled bobbed hair, Colleen Moore's and Louise Brooks's "black helmet hair," or Gloria Swanson's beauty mark, a trend of imitation that dated back to the 1910s fashion of girls wearing long Mary Pickford curls. Clothing fashions and interiors in film were also influential. Because of elaborate bathing scenes in Cecil B. DeMille's *Male and Female* and other films, matching bathroom fixtures began to be advertised in popular magazines as a means of dressing up this once-humble room. Even courtship rituals were imitated from scenes in the movies: how to deliver an F. Scott Fitzgerald–type wisecrack, learned from the intertitles of an Anita Loos–written picture, how to move in for a kiss, and how to deflect one. Although African American filmmakers faced more challenging funding and distribution conditions than their white counterparts, Noble Johnson, with his Lincoln Motion Picture Company, and Oscar Micheaux produced films in several genres, from Micheaux's true-crime mystery *The Gunsaulus Mystery* to melodramas like *Deceit*, *The Dungeon*, and *The Brute*.[40] Many of Micheaux's productions, like most other silent films, are now lost, but the extant *Within Our Gates* and *Veiled Aristocrats* show that the conventions of melodrama and the modified Delsartian movements of silent film (back of hand to head to indicate distress, bowed head to indicate shame, and so on) comprised part of the melodramatic effect in these as well.[41] A modern woman of the 1920s, Helga internalizes these responses and would have them ready to hand when a crisis arose in her life.

As the heroine of a film melodrama, Helga attempts to seize power within its generic conventions during her last meeting with the man she loves, Robert Anderson. Even her gestures are keyed to melodrama, as in one scene in which she adopts a telling prop for her actions. While she waits at her apartment to have a showdown with him after a night of "riotous and colorful dreams," she "[catches] up a filmy scarf" as she "pace[s] back and forth across the narrow room" (105). The action has no overt physical purpose, either in the text or for Helga's state of mind, yet for audiences accustomed to the conventions of silent film melodramas, it would register as an expression of inner turmoil in the sensitive, upper-class woman. Like Helga's other gestures, the restless pacing with the filmy scarf signifies her degree of self-dramatization. The entire chapter, in fact, plays out as a scene from a melodrama. "[T]he very terms of melodrama," Peter Brooks writes, consist in "the effort to articulate the moral universe" (52) and "the struggle for the assertion of selfhood that coincides with the movement toward enunciation of ethical truth" (52). Caught between two races and feeling securely connected to neither, Helga suffers a restlessness that stems from a "struggle for the assertion of selfhood" that projects her toward an "enunciation of ethical truth." Her gestures betray an attempt to reconcile the two—the scarf, the outward sign of soignée composure that now signifies her distress, and the pacing, which reveals not only her inner turmoil but also her outward sense of a dramatic gesture.

Yet assuming the role of the heroine of a melodramatic film can only succeed if the other actors understand that they too are playing a role, and Robert does not. As he stands "looking at some examples of African carving" (106), she holds out her hand, her knees tremble, and she "[g]ratefully slid[es] into the chair which he hastily placed for her" (106). She has compelled some portion of his attention by being overcome by emotion, but only momentarily, since he drones on with his "long dissertation on African sculpture." Before meeting him the next day, Helga prepares by "spending hours before the mirror" to rehearse, much as an actress would do (107). When the confrontation occurs, it too comes straight from the conventions of melodrama. Anderson apologizes for kissing her rather than taking her in his arms, which humiliates her. She "suddenly savagely slap[s] Robert Anderson with all her might, in the face" and, without another word, leaves the room and goes upstairs. All these actions derive from melodrama and the movies. In silent melodrama, if the heroine slaps her beloved and runs up the stairs, the audience expects that he will follow her, apologize, and take her in his arms. Helga signals that this is the genre in which she wishes to be read through her restless pacing with the filmy scarf, posing in the chair, rehearsing for Robert's visit by staring in the mirror, and slapping him in the face. But Robert is both colossally self-absorbed and interested only in racial uplift. He fails to pick up his cue and leaves without another word. Misreading her audience, as Robert misreads her cues, Helga has exhausted the limits of what this self-composed melodrama can offer through the ineffectual nature of its props and cues.

The last five chapters establish Helga's movement from melodrama to naturalism through an emphasis on the body, dirt, Darwinian desire, repeated childbirths, and the environmental constraints that lead to the diminution of self and consciousness. After her failure to find an identity as heroine of a drawing-room melodrama in the scene with Robert, Helga tries to "make herself very drunk" but manages only to "make herself very sick" (108), a reference to bodily fluids that is a characteristic feature of naturalistic texts. Tightly controlled despite her restlessness and impulsiveness, Helga has only allowed herself to unbend, to move with "grace and abandon, gravely, yet with obvious pleasure" (62) when she visits a jazz club. Here, however, she tries through drink to break the tight bonds of control that she has imposed on herself. Humiliated because "[d]esire had burned in her flesh with uncontrollable violence" (109), she lacerates herself with self-doubt until she can no longer stand being inside her room and, metaphorically, her body.

Throughout the novel Helga has exhibited dry self-composure. Now she walks the deserted streets, buffeted by wind and drenched by rain, a symbolic representation of her interior state, until "a whirl of wind... tosse[s] her into the swollen gutter" (110). While "lying soaked and soiled in the flooded gutter" (110) she decides against committing suicide "in such a messy wet manner" (110). The contrast between her customary dry fastidiousness and the "messy wet" situation in which she now finds herself indicates the depth of her moral quandary. The scene evokes the novel's title, *Quicksand*, through its combination of earth and water and does so through the element (mud) and place (the gutter) that signal naturalism. Having already admitted to what she felt were the excesses of physical desire that she felt for Robert, she has turned her body over to the "messy wet" universe. Her mind is about to follow.

From the controlled performance of her private film melodrama, Helga dissolves into a conspicuously public and uncontrolled spectacle when she stumbles into a church service and sits on the floor, "a dripping heap" who laughs at the peculiarly appropriate hymn lyrics about "showers of blessings" (111). She then begins to weep, adding her tears to the water of the rain and the words of the hymn. She melts into her surroundings through the production of excess sentiment that, in the form of tears as well as laughter, demonstrates the reluctant loss of control common to naturalism. Separated from the crowd at first by what she perceives as the grotesque excess of feeling that they display, she "observ[es] rites of a remote obscure origin" as "faces of the men and women took on the aspect of a dim vision" (113). Helga is back watching a movie, the "dim vision" of a melodrama, the form designed to evoke emotion from its spectators.

Helga, once again "afraid that she [is] going to be sick" (113), pauses before being swept along with the crowd's emotion. Her nausea, different in kind but striking because it occurs so closely after her solitary drinking episode, suggests not the modernist nausea of the innocent encountering modernity but the reverse. From witnessing primitive rites, she travels further back down the evolutionary trail by seeing women "crawl[ing] over the floor like reptiles" (114), a powerful statement of the ability of sentiment to erase civilized behavior and reunite human beings with their evolutionary forbears. In naturalistic terms, Helga has broken through the veneer of civilization or post-Enlightenment rationality that comprised her cool detachment and has now entered the world of religious emotion.

The naturalistic section of Helga's life repeats the tragedy of her relationship with Robert as farce with the Reverend Pleasant Green. Green is, like Robert, a pompous, self-absorbed man who revels in "his own sense of superiority" (120), and he listens to Helga as little as Robert did. Initially recoiling from him when she suffers an attack of vertigo, instead of accepting his help as she had Robert's, Helga instantly thinks that a relationship with him would be "too awful," but this soon gives way to "voluptuous visions" and sexual desire (109). In each relationship, Helga in her more rational moments sees the object of her desire as unsuitable, Robert because of his marriage and because of his insulting rejection of her, which marks him as unworthy, and Pleasant Green because of his physical presence, his unquestioned religious beliefs, and his clichéd forms of speech. Seeing Helga's marriage as one more protest against the uplift narrative, Keguro Macharia writes, "In choosing to marry Reverend Green, Helga makes a dysgenic choice that refuses to fulfill nativism's eugenic demand."[42] But Helga makes no decisive choice, for her desire is not rational: she "did not reason about this feeling, as she did not at that time reason about anything. It was enough that it was there, coloring all her thoughts and acts" (121). If her conversion had not "blunt[ed] her sense of humor," she could have "amused herself by tracing the relation of this constant ogling and flattering on the proverbially large families of preachers" (120). For much of the narrative, Helga's voice has replicated or mimicked that of the narrator: bemused, ironic, distanced even in her distress. Now her interior voice is blunted. The ironic distance granted to the cosmopolitan Helga is not permitted to the naturalistic Helga.

Darwinian themes predominate as Larsen surrounds Helga with natural images that contrast with the props of modernity and melodrama, such as the colorful clothing and the filmy scarf that had marked her earlier life. Now she is multiply trapped by biology, with its dirt and waste. Her house is an "ugly brown," and about the church and social center "the odor of manure still clung" (121) from its former life as a stable. The muck of the gutter into which she had temporarily fallen in the rain now becomes a permanent condition of her existence, not least in the person of her husband, who has dirt under his fingernails, "fail[s] to wash his fat body, or to shift his clothing, as often as Helga herself," and smells of "sweat and stale garments" (121). Green's dirt and rank smell perversely signal desire to Helga, as does his powerful attraction for the women of the congregation, which in Darwinian terms suggests the competition for a mate common to female courtship rituals. Moreover, a body that evokes disgust and exudes smells, as Green's does, necessarily succeeds in making its presence known through pheromones, and Helga's body responds with sexual desire: "Emotional, palpitating, amorous, all that was living in her sprang like rank weeds at the tingly thought of night, with a vitality so strong that it devoured all shoots of reason" (122). The garden that Helga now keeps in her work as a lower-class housewife exists outside her "ugly brown" house and also within her, where desire springs up like "rank weeds" and kills the "shoots of reason" that had governed her actions. The classic opposition between desire and rationality becomes a Darwinian contest, with desire an animal that devours reason.

Helga's solution, less a conscious one than a response to fatigue and constant work, is to let her house go "unswept and undusted" and her children "unwashed" (124), yielding, as she has in the matter of religious belief, to the stronger forces surrounding her. In keeping with the overwhelming presence of the dirt outside and the kindred garden within her, she does not discriminate between types of dirt, which becomes a naturalistic force in itself when combined with the exhaustion of her life and the other extremes that she suffers. She immerses herself in religion for "a kind of protective coloring, shielding her from the cruel light of an unbearable reality" (126), another feature that marks her successful Darwinian adaptation, like that of a snowy owl or a field mouse, to the Reverend Green's world. Darwinian sexual selection reasserts itself after her child is born, when Green puts his "moist hand" in hers, a relic of the male's grasping claw in Darwin's *The Descent of Man*, and glances with obvious sexual interest at her breasts, "covered only by a nightgown of filmy crepe." In response, she grimaces and "her petulant lip curl[s]" because this reminder was "like the flick of a whip to him" (129). Grimaces and lip curls are among the features that Darwin describes as primal, instinctive, and unmistakable to read. They negate the promise of sexual desire or acquiescence, as evidenced in this case when Green "flinche[s]" at the sight as if it is "the flick of a whip," yet the possibility of her sexual dominance excites even as it disturbs him.

The culmination of her adaptation and sexual desire is the primal scene of women's naturalism: childbirth. Helga bears her fourth child in "that appalling blackness of pain" (128), the demonstrative pronoun "that" articulating the specific parameters of her suffering and suggesting through deixis the reader's complicit vision, even as the contradictions of whiteness and blackness in the language ("pall" in "appalling" and "blackness") mirror her lifelong torment of being trapped between races. In the defining moment of a near-death experience at the hands of nature, the naturalistic protagonist emerges with a greater respect for the power of nature and a renewed interest in living life at a more intense level. Childbirth is just such a defining moment for Helga, but instead it shakes loose the "ballast of her brain" and causes her to "[hover] for a long time on the edge of consciousness, an enchanted and blissful place" unlike "the tumult, the heat, and the smell" that crowd her senses in the sickroom where she lies recovering. She awakens to a new form of consciousness, one that rejects her current life and brings clarity of vision of her past.

Helga experiences this vision while lying in darkness, "that serene haven, that effortless calm where nothing was expected of her. There she could watch the figures of the past drift by" (128). Her experience, in short, is that of sitting in a movie theater, rewinding and reviewing the insubstantial figures of her past: Robert, who affected her life in a "remarkably cruel degree" because of her love for him; "lovely, secure, wise, selfish" Anne; and others who float through the rooms "[f]lashingly, fragmentarily" as on a movie screen. Helga thinks in colors throughout the novel, as often noted by critics, yet in this scene the only colors she recalls are the "formal black and white" of the men's evening wear, the vivid chiaroscuro contrasts that marked the silent screen lighting of the 1920s as well as her racial choices. Viewing this internal movie, this "immersion in the past" (129) with its sharply delineated flashes of black and white, clears her clouded perspective, and she realizes that she feels only revulsion for Green. Helga's only recourse is to find "refuge in sleep" (131), which further distances her from Green, whom she bitterly hates, and from her children, from whom she is so detached that she feels relief at the death of her newborn. Thinking only "One less," she again falls asleep.

By the end of the novel, the temporary nature of Helga's life and attachments has settled into a certainty as time and the "bog into which she had strayed" (134) determine her life. She tries to recapture her sense of irony by hearing the nurse read Anatole France's "The Procurator of Judea," but she falls asleep before the "superbly ironic ending" (132). Even her restlessness provides no relief, for she means to leave Green but cannot leave her children. Settled into her body and into a racial determinacy that she has previously resisted, she notes that at least her children will be spared her torment of being caught between black and white, for they are "all black together" (135). Revisiting in memory the "freedom and cities" that she had once enjoyed (135), she "doze[s] and dream[s] in snatches of sleeping and waking, letting time run on" (135). Like Kate Chopin's Edna Pontellier in *The Awakening*, who dozes off when she reads the philosophizing of Emerson, Helga sleeps because she lives now only in the body, not in intellectual abstractions. As in other women's naturalistic writings, biological time outpaces the distortions of time that human illusions encourage. "Time run[s] on" faster than Helga can plan, and she is barely out of bed when "she [begins] to have her fifth child" (135). Like the "reptilian" women crawling on the floor at the church service, Helga has been reduced to a few simple physical actions, bearing children and sleeping being chief among them. The cosmopolitan world that was the whole of her life now occupies only a tiny, intangible portion of it, and the biological demands that she had suppressed and analyzed as a modern woman now consume the rest of it.

Beastly Meals in *The Narrow House*

The Narrow House (1921) by Evelyn Scott (1893–1963) casts a modernist and darkly psychological cold eye on the small town satirized by Sinclair Lewis and the oppressive family relationships of *Miss Lulu Bett*. Less well known today than Stein, Scott was celebrated as a serious modernist in the 1920s and 1930s for her experimental style and frank subject matter. Scott followed *The Narrow House* with two others making up a trilogy, *Narcissus* (1922) and *The Golden Door* (1925); a memoir, *Escapade* (1923); and three historical novels of the period from before the Civil War through World War I: *Migrations* (1927), *The Wave* (1929), and *A Calendar of Sin* (1931). Censorship problems arising from Scott's subject matter and personal entanglements caused her publishing difficulties after 1941, but her waning reputation had more to do with the gender politics of literary criticism, according to Dorothy Scura: "[I]n the beginning of Scott's career she was compared to a large field of writers, male and female, American and international, including Dostoevsky, Mann, Gorki, Joyce, Eliot, Lawrence.... But by the 1930s ... she was mentioned primarily along with American women writers—Willa Cather, Ellen Glasgow, and Elizabeth Madox Roberts."[43]

When *The Narrow House* was published, Scott was hailed for the novel's psychological acuity and for its frank, naturalistic presentation of desire and small-town lives. In the *New York Times Book Review*, Sinclair Lewis declared, "Salute to Evelyn Scott!... *The Narrow House* is an event, it is one of those recognitions of life by which life itself becomes the greater."[44] H. L. Mencken and Ludwig Lewisohn praised her, the latter stating that "by her cold acuteness of psychological observation, by her peering exactness of physical vision, she succeeds in giving 'The Narrow House' and 'Narcissus' and above all 'Escapade' a hardness of surface that seems to protect these books from decay. They have an intellectual lucidity and a powerful and bitter moral vision that keeps them fresh and memorable."[45] Intellect, power, lucidity and "hardness of surface"—all are terms of praise that reassured any modernist readers worried about sentimentality in the subject matter of a small-town, multigenerational, middle-class family. Writing to Scott on the publication of *The Narrow House*, D. H. Lawrence understood the psychological devastation that Scott had recorded beneath the veneer of middle-class manners, calling it "all vile, but true, and therefore valuable." "I feel it is white America's last word," he continues, "before a cataclysm sets in, or a new start. Two more words, and the life-centre of all the people, and even the authoress, will have broken, and unresisted putrescence set in." But she could have done more, he adds: "Kick the posterior of creeping love, and laugh when it whimpers. Pah, it is a disease, love, and apparently you love dying of it." Playfully telling her that it was "incomplete—*A Narrow House* without a watercloset!" Lawrence anticipated the censorship issues that Scott would face in publishing her memoir *Escapade*.[46] The memoir included plenty of waterclosets and latrines, along with descriptions of sex, pregnancy, and childbirth that were censored before publication.[47]

Scott's naturalism was purposeful, as contemporary critics realized. In *Contemporary American Novelists* (1922), his study of "the drift of naturalism" in the first two decades of the twentieth century, Carl Van Doren heralds Evelyn Scott's *The Narrow House*, Waldo Frank's *The Dark Mother*, and Ben Hecht's *Erik Dorn* as a "new style" of those who "followed naturalism into the 'exposure' of small towns or cramped lives" yet achieved "a more elastic, a more impressionistic technique, breaking up the 'gray paragraph' and quickening the tempo of their narratives."[48] According to her biographer D. A. Callard, Scott saw the novel not only "as a deliberate excursion into a sordid world, but also as an exercise in naturalism," a judgment borne out in *The Narrow House*.[49] Scott confirms her debt to naturalist authors in her memoir *Background in Tennessee*: "While I was at school in New Orleans, the works of Stephen Crane, Frank Norris and Theodore Dreiser influenced me far more significantly than did my half-creole milieu, discussed idyllically in the stories of George Washington Cable."[50] Discarding the idea of place and region, Scott imagines a national community of letters through the unifying and universalizing literature of childhood and adolescence. Her dividing lines are not spatial and regional but literary: realism and naturalism versus "idyllic" romance.

Like Crane in *Maggie: A Girl of the Streets*, Scott understands that caging a family within four walls creates not domesticity but reverberating trauma as acts of violence are observed, imitated, and intensified in an endlessly repeating cycle. After two chapters of unremitting violent conflict in *Maggie*, for example, an old woman asks the child, "Eh, Gawd, child, what is it dis time? Is yer fadder beatin' yer mudder, or yer mudder beatin' yer fadder?" (35), as if violence is a given and its perpetrators are interchangeable. Like Crane, and like Henry James in *What Maisie Knew*, Scott uses the character and point of view of a child who acts as sounding board, scapegoat, and ineffective mediator in the family drama to demonstrate the damage, in increased wariness, detachment, and premature adulthood, that the family dynamic has caused.

To this recognition of trauma and violence within the family dynamic, Scott adds modernist technique and the psychological acuity of a post-Freudian writer. She distinguishes herself as a woman naturalist writer not only through the suffocating family dynamics of the novel but also through her exploration of the objectification of women's bodies. Scott presents a toxic portrait of the servant woman as drudge and the conflicted impulse toward self-sacrifice that propels her to subordinate her wishes to those of others. *The Narrow House* addresses the topic not through a single character but through a chain of interfamilial servitude based in perverse conceptions of self-sacrifice and psychological bondage. It intensifies earlier women's naturalistic novels in its presentation of sexual desire and sexual choice; the conflation of waste, filth, appetite, and childbirth with the sense of contamination and gender-based fear that they bring to the naturalist novel; the thematic use of mirrors, windows, and self-dramatizing points of view that evoke the visual qualities of film melodrama; and naturalistic scenes of feeding on carcasses, emotional cannibalism, and a violent competition for food.

Told through multiple points of view and an omniscient narrator, *The Narrow House* describes a year in the lives of a dysfunctional midwestern family, the Farleys, whose prosaic, seemingly monotonous existence is disrupted by two events: the revelation of the father's long-ago affair with a woman in Chicago, and the daughter-in-law's present-day death in childbirth. The monotony is only external, however, for the novel is tense with the drama of interactions between the characters, each an abyss of neediness and self-love demanding from the others what they cannot, or will not, give in return. Mrs. Farley, the mother, prides herself on self-abnegation and being the family drudge; and her husband has sunk into domestic lethargy after the end of his affair, halfheartedly envisioning a life with his mistress and their son far from the misery of his current home. The Farleys' daughter Alice, a self-loathing and self-described "old maid" of thirty-six, nurses an unrequited love for her employer, and their son, Laurence, a scientist, balances disappointment with his career and the care of his narcissistic wife, Winnie, who has been told that another pregnancy will kill her. All believe that they feel love and want to be loved in return, but what passes for love is instead composed of a variety of unhealthy substitutes. Winnie defines love as sexual desire mingled with a death wish and a desire for dominance, successfully enslaving her husband Laurence to her monstrous level of need. Mr. and Mrs. Farley compete to be the greater martyr in the family, each defining love as self-sacrifice. Alice channels sexual aggression from her unrequited love affair into self-mutilation and cruelty toward May, Laurence and Winnie's daughter.

Like a traditional drama, *The Narrow House* is divided into five parts, each with an incident or revelation of character that propels the action and each with some form of grotesque eating, with bloody roasts, fly-bitten feasts, or ravenous babies taking center stage. Part 1 is staged primarily in the poisonous, gloomy atmosphere of the Farleys' home or in the butcher shop, where human flesh and animal flesh seem interchangeable. The opening chapter describes Mrs. Farley's stop at the butcher shop with repellant naturalistic detail. The shop, "white as death," smells of "blood and sawdust" and is filled with dead animals: "The feet of the hens were a sickly bluish yellow, and the toes, cramped together yet flaccid, still suggested the fatigue which follows agony."[51] In the naturalistic vision of *The Narrow House*, all food, like all human beings, is reducible to flesh, and the vision of knives cutting flesh pervades the book. At dinner, Mrs. Farley "grasped the hilt of a long horn-handled knife and the thin flashing blade sunk into the brown crusted beefsteak, so that the beautiful wine-colored blood spurted from the soft pink inner flesh and mingled with the grease that was cooling and coating the bottom of the dish" (26). The violence of the "flashing" blade sinks into the "brown crusted" exterior, releasing not oozing but "spurt[ing]" blood from "soft pink inner flesh," anticipating the release of passive-aggressive violence that Mrs. Farley is about to precipitate because she has just intercepted a telegram from Mr. Farley's mistress. The dinner scene evokes memories of violence for other family members as well. Alice and her brother Laurence both recall the time when Alice "hurled" a paper knife at him, cutting his hand (32), and Alice tries to cut her wrist against her teeth but does not break the skin (35). Her silent love for her employer, Horace Ridge, leads her to stab herself with nail scissors when he leaves for South America. Even innocent fruits and vegetables appear in terms of blood and violence: Mrs. Farley carries "a bloody peach and a dull bright knife" (67) as a snack for the ailing Winnie. At each meal, the Farleys gather to tear at each other emotionally as predators before a bloody haunch of beef or a "huge flayed bone of the dead beast" (185). The repeated skin-over-bloody-flesh metaphor of holding life or passion in by an easily breached integument raises to a new intensity the traditional naturalistic symbol of the thin veneer of civilization covering the beast within.

Scott reinforces this connection between violent appetites and death in the relationship that drives the events of the book, the emotional cannibalism of the marriage between Winnie and Laurence Farley. Winnie, whose frail health leads her to spend most of her time in bed, is a monster of need who has only one topic of conversation for everyone throughout the book: "Love me. Do you love me?" She hoards affection as much as she craves it, demanding protestations of love from all but rarely reciprocating the emotion, since doing so means "a terrible sense that she was losing some unknown thing which was precious and belonged to her but of which she was afraid" (70). In the Farley household, withholding love constitutes power and expressing it constitutes weakness. Calling on the sentimental language of motherhood, Winnie forces a declaration of love from May, her daughter, as she demands reassurance about her beauty. Her principal struggle, however, is with her husband, Laurence. After bearing two children, May and Bobby, Winnie has been told that she can have no more unless she first undergoes an operation, advice that she and Laurence interpret as meaning that they must abstain from sex. Like all prohibitions, this one immediately engenders their mutual desire to break it. The intensity of their sexual desire expresses their desire for dominance: Winnie entices Laurence into sexual activity to put him in her power, and Laurence resists for the same reason. When he finally succumbs, he becomes "the death-giver, glad, in spite of himself, of the drunkenness of moving with the unseen. Through the banality of sex, which oppressed him, there pushed the will of an exalted and passionate horror. He took her. They were dead" (98). Winnie is "dead" because of her inevitable pregnancy, which feeds her death wish, but triumphantly alive because she now has power over Laurence. Laurence, the "death-giver," has lost his D. H. Lawrence–style struggle with Winnie and any dreams of escape.

Alice's struggle with desire, the primary plotline of part 2, parallels Winnie's. Her status as an unmarried daughter makes her a natural fit for the position of a domestic drudge, as in *Miss Lulu Bett*, but Alice vehemently rejects the part. More self-aware and less self-absorbed than Winnie, Alice tries to diagnose her own motives and problems while recognizing, as Winnie does not, the place of the outside world in creating them, a trait that Scott renders through Alice's greater variation of language and point of view. Throughout the novel, Scott uses opposing images to reveal the characters' contrasting states: the hot and cold skin temperatures that characters experience in contrast to their surroundings; mirrors and windows; the light outdoors and dark interiors of rooms, with shadows as interstitial spaces; and sunshine and rain, the latter, like scenes in shadow, signaling times of truth telling, as when Alice confesses to loathing her mother and tells her father to leave her (76). Pat Tyrer argues that "Scott creates the tension of sexuality quite effectively by continually pairing Winnie with mirrors and Alice with windows," yet both characters actually rely on mirrors, with Alice reading a grim assessment of her body and Winnie a self-deluded tribute to her beauty.[52] Alice looks at herself in the mirror, the primary realist trope of self-assessment, standing "before the glass, hating herself" and seeing "the swell of her big firm breast. Her face was heavy and ugly with rebellion, sallow, the eyes inflamed" (34). A few minutes later, she reflects that "[c]lothes made her virgin when she was a mother" (37). Alice believes that the material fact of her large breast confirms her true maternal nature, but as happens consistently in *The Narrow House*, any physical confirmation of maternity is a delusion that masks an absence of maternal feeling. Trying to get at a recognizable truth, she misreads the physical facts of her body as a spiritual fact, a reading of Emerson's "[e]very natural fact is a symbol of some spiritual fact" gone badly awry. But Alice gets another portion of her search for truth right. The imagery of clothing and nakedness, of the clothing of civilization covering the nakedness of the beast, always prominent in the naturalist text, reinforces the idea of the skin as a thin covering for a body that is basically meat. In trying to cut herself, in effect to slice herself like meat, Alice shows that she lives in a naturalistic, deterministic universe, and she knows it.

In contrast, Winnie's mirror-gazing signifies her investment in film melodrama. Like a fairy-tale wicked stepmother, she seeks constant confirmation of her youth and beauty at the expense even of her own children. When she asks her mother-in-law for reassurance, Mrs. Farley tells her, "Look in the mirror. They'll love you" (69). The sight of other people serves as a mirror for Winnie's narcissism. As Mrs. Farley tends to her, "Winnie, lying back, gloated over the thin white hair, the lined flaccid cheeks" (69), seeing in the older woman a mirror of age that contrasts unfavorably with her own youth. She returns from weeks in the country and begins "keenly dramatizing herself": "She glanced stealthily sideways at the mirror and the Madonna look came into her face" (160). Like an actress in a movie, she relies on the image in the film camera, the mirror, to arrange her face in the prescribed sentimental mode of motherhood. But unlike a movie camera, which can be moved to display one's best angles, and unlike a film image, which can be cut to reveal a subjective point of view, the mirrors in Winnie's world reveal truths that she would prefer not to see. Put on bed rest because of her dangerous pregnancy, she becomes "so bored when she was alone that she sometimes put on a fancy house gown, powdered her nose, and went downstairs," as if to enact the role of an invalid. Moving from the bedroom, where she controls everything, to the rest of the house, where she is instead controlled because of her illness, means that she must face a reality that destroys the illusion that she has so carefully nurtured: "When she passed the long mirror in the little-used parlor, and saw herself hideous and inflated, she burst into tears" (166). The romance of pregnancy, with its overtones of courting death in the service of desire, attracts her, but its reality, the swollen body of the grotesque naturalistic woman, reveals her as a monstrous mother in the way that no psychological self-reflection ever does.

Like the childbirth scenes in *Weeds*, *The Awakening*, and *Quicksand*, the birth of Winnie's child emphasizes the woman's dissociative state. Experiencing the intensity of physical pain as a battle with the child struggling to be born, Winnie becomes hyperaware of the darkness surrounding her. Time is distorted, extending itself and standing still, a point emphasized by the novel's many references to clocks and to "bottles that seemed never to have moved since the world began" (172). Winnie perceives the room as a study in contrasts and chiaroscuro: the "shaded lamp" that casts shadows in the darkness; the "cold hand" on Winnie's "warm flesh"; the "gray becalmed glass," not of a mirror this time, but of a "print of the German gamekeeper" (172), evoking the blood sport of the brutal scene being enacted when the child "wrestle[s]" (171) with her. Given chloroform—but "[n]ot enough"—she feels "[h]er head danc[ing] like a golden thistle on a pool of blood" while viewing her body on the bed, a gruesomely incongruous image that reflects her dissociative state. With similar detachment she observes a gust of wind that "bellied the shade before the window and swung it slowly inward," an evocation of Winnie's pregnant body when she was dismayed by her reflection in the mirror. The discrete, random images of nature and technology coalesce in a final, vivid vision of the "long claws of steel," the forceps for removing the baby (174), that links the natural violence of childbirth with the technological violence necessary to save the child's and mother's life. The child "emerge[s] from the blackness" but Winnie remains in "the torture that went on without it" (174). As she hears that her child has been born, "an ugly and living shudder [runs] through her," and she dies. The primal quality of her suffering, and the violent pain that she endures, suggest the gruesome forms of death in a Jack London story, all within the walls of a middle-class home.

Winnie's death renders the rest of the family newly voracious for life, an attitude expressed through scenes of eating and of nursing the child. Gathered for a ritual meal after Winnie's death, no one eats, but a "young fly [clings] to the huge flayed bone of the dead beast. It crawled on moist, quivering legs along the dry and fleshless parts, only to slip back uncertainly when it clutched at the fat" (185). The fly's clinging to the "dead beast" is juxtaposed with the hunger of Winnie's baby, who, squalling and full of vitality, clings tenaciously to the breast of the wet nurse. The naturalistic order of things demands that even dead bodies nourish the living, whether as meat, as in the fly's crawling over it, or as confirmation of a psychological freedom. After Winnie's death, Laurence, recognizing that "[h]e had drained himself dry that her agony might be rich" (191), in effect nourishing her while he starved, hovers over Winnie's corpse like a vampire to confirm her death, a grotesque reprise of the last moment of *The House of Mirth*, when Laurence Selden hovers over Lily Bart's body to seek "the word which made all clear" (369).

In contrast to the vampire-victim dyad of Winnie and Laurence, a parody of romantic need and desire, is the equally parodic dyad of maternal-child love represented by Alice and May. Alice, disconcerted by her fierce and conflicted feelings, tries to commit suicide but returns home to "grow mean and hard and withered in her unbelief" (205). Like Alice Hindman of Sherwood Anderson's

Winesburg, Ohio, who runs naked into the rain to "find some other lonely human and embrace him" but finds only an elderly deaf man who cannot understand her message, Alice Farley wants to share her knowledge with another human being and alleviate her crushing sense of loneliness.[53] Her desire is sincere, but her approach is violent: after slapping May and calling her a crybaby, Alice enfolds May in "a fierce, unkind, smothering hug," placing "May's loose fingers ... [a]gainst her breast" to make "the child's nakedness ... cut her heavy flesh into feeling" (195), an action that mimics the wet nurse suckling the newborn baby. An example of the grotesque mother of naturalism, Alice gives abuse rather than sustenance, inarticulate rage rather than knowledge, to the struggling May. But May will not yield to victimhood and retaliates by announcing to the family that "Aunt Alice talks to herself" (217). May's struggles continue in the next two books of the trilogy. In *Narcissus*, the first sequel to *The Narrow House*, an adolescent May is ignored by her father, despised by her stepmother, and seduced by her lover Paul. In *The Golden Door*, the second sequel, she is married to Paul and trapped by poverty, pregnancy, and his Bohemian insistence that she accept his mistress as part of the family. But the vicious dinner politics of her youth have taught May that since reciprocated love is impossible, the power to hold on and fight back is the best substitute.

The last word of the novel falls to Mrs. Farley, who has resolutely refused to acknowledge her own or her family's misery despite Alice's demands that her parents divorce. Mrs. Farley's defense is always that of domesticity, and she retains power by martyring herself as a servant to the family. When Laurence returns from visiting Winnie's grave to announce that he will not move away, saying "I've given up the struggle" (218), she answers with a non sequitur that reinforces the status quo: "Do your father and Alice know that dinner is nearly ready?" (219). This most fraught of family rituals has for her the appearance of family harmony, always more important to her than its reality. As Alice's assaults and her husband's indifference wear upon her, Mrs. Farley responds by turning herself more decisively into a servant, a representation of how they treat her as waste: "The gray dust settled on her uncovered hair, but she did not seem to know it. Stiff locks, sticky with dirt, hung about her grimed face. Her flannel waist was half out of the band of her draggled skirt. Her hands, crimson at the knuckles, and grained with the filth of labor, clutched the ash can stiffly" (167). Clutching an "ash can" as a physical defense against her world, Mrs. Farley is "grained with the filth of labor" as an outward sign of the emotional detritus that she refuses to acknowledge. Mr. Farley attempts to mend fences with his wife by bringing her a new dress, but she rejects it "with weak patience, victoriously, ungiving" as she "[holds] out against life" (221). The echo of death in Mrs. Farley's position "against life" is reinforced by the sole sound audible as she scrubs "the sides of the porcelain bowl" of the sink: "A fly buzzed fiercely in the luminous dark against the windowpane, then was still, like a spring that had fiercely unwound" (221). The fly hearkens back to the striving fly representing the baby seeking a secure perch on the "dead beast" at the dinner table, yet it also echoes Emily Dickinson's "I heard a Fly buzz — when I died." "With Blue — uncertain — stumbling Buzz," the fly in Dickinson's poem bumps against the windowpane as the narrator details her last breaths until she "could not see to see." Less a moral symbol than a naturalistic one, the fly, irritating and associated with death, keeps the focus on the physical body, reminding readers that regardless of Mrs. Farley's efforts to eradicate dirt and nature in all its forms, death and the flies that feed on it have the last sound.

In addition to naturalistic elements such as the body as meat to be consumed, the connection between desire and death, the emotional violence of family dynamics, the use of melodrama and film, and the aesthetics of disgust in the servant woman's narrative, Scott's *The Narrow House* unsparingly figures children as waste. Positioned midway between the suffering adults, whose bodies trouble them with desire and cause them pain but who can rationalize and delude themselves about what they feel, and the animals that exist as unthinking, occasionally malign objects, children and babies are bodies with consciousness but no means of filtering their impulses. Because of their physical and psychological neediness, they cannot be ignored and must be nourished and tended. Scott is not the only naturalistic writer to depict children as the waste products of desire. The children of Larsen's Helga Crane Green are less individuals than a multiform torment that saps her strength. Rose in Stein's "Melanctha" is so careless about her child that it dies, and Judith Pippinger Blackford envisions her children as parasites. More chilling still is the episode in Scott's autobiographical *Escapade* in which the narrator's servant Petronilla, described as animalistic because of her "short, prehensile feet," starves her child to death because "it represents an added burden to her penury."[54] Scott's trilogy represents the most sustained attack on conventional presentations of children as beloved innocents, for they recognize that their survival depends not on an ability to appeal to adults through helplessness but to fight with equally Darwinian weapons. What links the novels of Scott's trilogy as naturalistic is the sense that the suffering of the human condition, brought on by forces beyond the characters' control, cannot be avoided. What marks the novels as modernist is the sense that the opposite of suffering is not relief but anomie and blankness, a position that makes suffering more attractive than the alternative.

Popular Naturalism: Fannie Hurst's *Lummox*

By the time Fannie Hurst (1889–1968) published *Lummox* in 1923, according to her biographer, Brooke Kroeger, she "had been the quintessence of the American success story for more than a decade. Since 1912, a magazine's inclusion of one of her short stories could almost guarantee the issue would sell out." Best known today for the movie adaptations of her novels *Back Street* (1931) and *Imitation of Life* (1933), the latter a subject of renewed critical interest because of its treatment of race, Hurst was known in her own time for her best-selling fictions of working women and stories of Jewish families, particularly those focusing on immigrant assimilation and cultural loss. Her serials ran in the *Saturday Evening Post* and *Cosmopolitan*, and her stories were treated as popular publishing events. For example, "Roulette," a story of "Russian twins separated at birth," ran in *Cosmopolitan* under the headline "We enlarged this magazine, at a cost of thousands of dollars, so we could publish this powerful story complete in one issue."[55]

Contemporary reactions to Hurst praised the realism of her subject matter and the power of her writing while expressing doubts about her unusual style and penchant for sentimentality. As early as 1914, Elliott Blake, writing in the "Harper's Bookshelf" for the *Harper's Magazine Advertiser*, praised Hurst's collection *Just around the Corner* in terms that would become standard in responses to her work, remarking on "the sort of realism that results from perfect familiarity rather than painful effort.... The profuse dialogue, strongly flavored with vivid colloquialisms and with those provincial or foreign peculiarities of speech that constitute neither 'dialect' nor 'broken English,' reveals the very turn of thought and prevailing sentiment of the types described."[56] Hurst's specialty, in other words, was writing comfortable realism in language that suggested dialect without striving for dialect's authenticity. But as reviewers at the time recognized, *Lummox* was a more serious "sort of realism" than her earlier work. Writing in the *New York Tribune*, John Farrar compared Hurst to Sherwood Anderson for her "naturalistic" style and celebration of "the mother instinct."[57] The *Bookman* noted a "new style of Miss Hurst's.... Occasionally awkward, occasionally poetic, occasionally downright funny."[58] Heywood Broun even found Gertrude Stein a strong influence on Hurst, although he thought that "someone ought to speak to her severely about adverbs."[59] But the critic for the *New York Times* was unimpressed: "Miss Hurst's style of writing wears its heart upon its sleeve, so eager is she to unburden all her mind and emotion. First person, second person, third person: It matters not at all; subjective writing covers a multitude of grammatical sins. But the verbless sentences of one or two words make for brain fatigue when read through many pages."[60]

Like her fellow Algonquin Round Table member Broun, Dorothy Parker had a mixed reaction to Hurst. Admitting to a "deep admiration for Miss Hurst's work" in the same shamed tones as she would admit to "a fondness for comic strips [and] chocolate-almond bars," Parker writes, "There have been times when her sedulously torturous style, her one-word sentences and her curiously compounded adjectives, drive me into an irritation that is only to be relieved by kicking and screaming."[61] Of course, stylistic experimentation was also the hallmark of modernism, and one-word sentences, compounded adjectives, repetition, and "verbless sentences" were not unknown in other modernist writers, including Jean Toomer and Evelyn Scott. The sweet "chocolate almond-bars" sentimentality that Parker saw in Hurst, when combined with Hurst's "brain-fatigu[ing]" style, barred Hurst from consideration as a serious novelist in Parker's eyes, yet *Lummox* bears little resemblance to Parker's characterization of Hurst's usual novels.

Lummox is the story of Bertha, whose identity is shaped wholly by her position as a servant. Born of an unknown father and a mother who dies two minutes before her birth, Bertha has no living relatives and a vaguely defined ethnic identity composed of "a good smattering of Scandinavian and even a wide streak of western Teutonic. Slav, too."[62] Five foot nine, large-framed, and inarticulate, Bertha seems to her employers "a great serene peasant girl with that slow kind of strength that makes an invaluable servant" (205), right down to her stereotypically Swedish accent ("I bane going," "yah"). The accent is the first of Hurst's deviations from realism, for Bertha has had no opportunity to acquire or even hear a Swedish accent. An orphan, she is raised in a sailors' rooming house whose slatternly proprietor speaks the dialect of the New York slums. Despite these departures, *Lummox*, as Lori Harrison-Kahan writes, exemplifies Hurst's "ability to meld the reformist sensibility of naturalism with modernist experimentation."[63] In strength and seeming impassivity Bertha is the female counterpart of the primitive male naturalistic brute. The naturalistic aesthetic of disgust abounds in the gray, slimy water used to scrub floors, the fish scales that stick to her arms, and the running sores of another servant with whom Bertha is told to share a bed. Evolutionary traces appear in the odd agglomeration of ethnic strains that Bertha is supposed to embody. Her accent and the unconscious race memories that stir in her when she hears the music of eastern Europe reflect contemporary theories of the racial inheritance of cultural traits. As a primitive peasant with deep feelings, Bertha embodies the diverse motherlands of urban dwellers who have lost touch with the true source of their artistic and emotional power. As a servant woman, she acts not only as a repository of family secrets but also as a voice of the Jungian collective unconscious.

The story of Bertha's life unfolds in two parallel layers, the temporal strand of her life in service defined by a successive series of employers, and the spatial strand of her personal life, which takes place in a series of slum dwellings and cramped rooms. Of her several employers, three represent contrasting forms of family dysfunction: the Farleys, where the artistic son of an exacting mother seduces Bertha; the Musliners, where a childlike young wife with another lover avoids sex with her older husband; and the Oessetrichs, where an energetic widow works tirelessly to bend her daughters to her will.

At Mrs. Farley's, Bertha becomes an unlikely muse to her son Rollo Farley, who admires both what he sees as her primitive peasant strength and her whiteness. He praises her as "white... [d]eeply white, like the flesh of a magnolia" (15) and wants to "write [her] into great oxen words" (16), a simultaneous tribute and insult to her strength that contrasts with his effete aestheticism. Hurst reverses the modernist convention of black primitivism in Rollo's response to Bertha, for her whiteness, coded as strong and primitive, with "the beat of her pulse setting him on fire" (12), functions as ethnic blackness. When he comes to her room late one night, she hesitates but feels that part of herself "had gone over to him ... The jeweled sands were pouring" (16). Bertha moves "down into his arms," the act helping her to pour herself, the jeweled sands of her thawed emotion, into an inarticulate language that she transfers to Rollo.[64] The result is his one masterpiece, a book of poetry called *The Cathedral Under the Sea*. But when Bertha hears him read the book to another woman, she has no more words for him:

> It was late when Bertha went upstairs.
> She had polished and twisted twenty-four crystal wine goblets into nothingness. It was so with her pain. She wanted sullenly to twist it for twisting her. But it curved away. Nothingness.
> It was good to set out the milk bottles. Six in a row. They were so there. Quarts. Bulge. Dimension. (21)

The inarticulate Bertha expresses her pain through physical objects, through things. Her feelings, the "jeweled sands" that she cannot articulate, have been transmuted into words by Rollo and exploited for his artistic reputation and his marriage to another woman. Hurst's modernist compression of language analogizes the sands of Bertha's words, fired into poetic glass by Rollo, with the empty crystal of the wine glasses that she can never drink from but only touch in her capacity as a servant. The glasses contrast with the solidity of the emptied glass of the milk bottles with their "[b]ulge" and "[d]imension," descriptors often used for Bertha herself. She is emptied of emotion, as they are emptied of milk, and she now lacks the milky "whiteness" that Rollo had valued as "primitive" blackness. Bereft of the child that she inevitably bears as a result of their encounter (the baby is adopted by a married couple), she owns neither her race-based poetic primitivism nor the child who signified its transmission to a new generation.

Bertha's second major position casts her as an intermediary within an unhappy marriage. Working for a newly married couple, Erna and Ben Musliner, she notices that the childlike bride Erna finds ways to avoid sleeping with Ben, "evading his wetted lips and their background of brown face" (63). The descriptions of Ben Musliner's "wetted lips" suggest sexual revulsion, since the same descriptor, "a wet mouth" (186), is used later to characterize a man in a brothel. The "brown face" hints at another form of revulsion, Erna's anti-Semitic prejudice against her kindly Jewish husband. As Bertha's presence had earlier given life force to the pallid verse of Rollo Farley, so now her presence precipitates a crisis in the Musliners' relationship when, during a picnic, she hears a Ukrainian folk song, takes off her shoes, and begins to dance, stirred by race memories of her Slavic past. Castigated by a fellow servant for dancing ethnically "like a dago's monkey" (75) instead of behaving like a proper American, Bertha feels drained and emptied of joy, as she had when Rollo rejected her. Bertha's primitivism injects peasant vitality into an enervated urban elite, and, like a fertility rite that exhausts the dancer and energizes the audience, her dance ignites the tensions between the Musliners. Later that night, Erna goes to Bertha's room and refuses to sleep with Ben, sobbing that he is "so terribly, terribly brown." Leading Erna back to his room, Bertha replies, "Yoost so the heart is not brown" (83), a sentiment that cuts through the novel's complicated racial politics to reveal Bertha's primitive yet enlightened approach toward ethnic prejudice. But as happens with many domestic servants, Bertha now knows too many of the Musliners' secrets and is the repository of their shame. Ben fires Bertha, embarrassed by her presence after what she has witnessed of their discord, a pattern of being punished for good deeds that she shares with other servant women.

Bertha's position with a family of women led by an energetic matriarch, the Oessetrichs, exposes her to a more toxic form of family dysfunction. The mother, Mathilde, is a New Woman steeped in psychological jargon and Progressive Era pragmatism, and she runs her daughters' lives according to the latest notions of domestic efficiency. She respects no boundaries except her own, hounding Bertha to work at a dozen tasks at once, invading her room on her days off, and rendering the house as a machine for living in which rest is absent. A monstrous mother of the sort that psychoanalysis was beginning to blame for neurosis, Mathilde is a naturalistic, grotesque mother who uses psychological rather than physical weapons. As Hurst's grimly humorous pun on the sound of her name suggests—Oessetrich or "ostrich"—Mathilde buries her head in the sand and refuses to see anything but material causes for her daughters' ailments, with calamitous results. The eldest, Paula, goes mad, becoming a recluse who spends her days sewing filmy negligees and baby clothes for a life and family that she will never have. The second daughter, Ermengarde, falls in love with a sensitive writer with few prospects. After Mathilde drives him away, Ermengarde requires morphine and the calming presence of Bertha to recover, eventually eloping with a much older married man. With her short hair, lack of interest in men, plain, mannish clothing, and independent trip to France to do war work, Olga, the third daughter, may be not only a New Woman but also a lesbian, which Mathilde pathologizes as a "sex complex" (226), ignoring the fact that Olga is the strongest and most well-adjusted of her daughters. When the daughters depart, Mathilde turns her fierce attention on Bertha, unjustly accuses her of a theft committed by Bertha's protégée, Helga, and fires her.

Lummox intercuts the stories of grotesque motherhood in these dysfunctional middle-class families with tales of Bertha's substitute children. Bertha had earlier mothered the family members of her employers. At the Wallensteins', she took care of Mrs. Wallenstein, an elderly immigrant Jewish woman despised by her abrasive Gentile daughter-in-law, and even performed a dubiously merciful act of euthanasia by withholding medication when Mrs. Wallenstein, who has been abandoned by her son at his wife's command, has a heart attack. The substitute children that she nurtures outside her employers' homes include Chita (a child rescued from an abusive home) and Willy, a childish manservant who is Bertha's conduit to the son she bore with Rollo Farley and gave up for adoption. In keeping with the naturalistic practice of reading human beings as animals, the child-substitutes she cares for in her tenement environment are grotesque characters given the traits of animals. For example, Bertha, herself often compared to an ox, sees the streetwise Chita as chittering and talking like Jocko, the pet monkey at the sailors' boarding house. Willy is monkeylike with his strange sounds ("Slk-k-k-k!") and childish love of candy. He is impotent and "had never been a man" (164) in his sexless relationship with Bertha, because he prefers the pornographic films seen "through the lenses in the Fourteenth Street nickelodeons" (182). What he lacks in heterosexual drive he takes out of Bertha in monkeyish behavior, "hanging over her couch with his face all drooly... and his hands drooping loosely from the wrists so that they swept her face." Like Norris's McTeague, who bites Trina's fingers to force money from her, Willy tortures Bertha by smashing her fingers and scratching her palms (165).

That the less-evolved members of the urban populace resemble monkeys may be Hurst's nod to the evolutionary principles of naturalism and the views of Darwinian evolution in the popular press, a view confirmed in Bertha's view of them from her window. Like Dreiser's Carrie Meeber, who stands in her sister's doorway as the life of the city stirs her desire to be part of it, Bertha spends hours looking through the window of her cramped room, but what she sees confirms the city's sordid reality rather than its promise of a more exciting life. She sees not individual human beings but humans en masse, an excess of human flesh treated as waste in the hot summer streets: "It was horrible. Babies cried and died in that welter. The bare, tossing little limbs were sprawled on the stoops and fire escapes. She could rest her chin upon the sill and look out at the litter of them and on the mothers whose arms were filled with the hot, sick droop of prostrated children. The tired senile infants in the thick of their battle with the tenements" (187). The vision of a mass of sick and dying infants, prematurely old ("senile") without ever living a full life, as they and their mothers battle the indifferent, deadly tenements, recalls the opening of Crane's *Maggie: A Girl of the Streets*, with its "careening building" that "gave up loads of babies to the street and the gutter" (11). In looking through the window, naturalism's equivalent of the screen and film camera, Bertha experiences the view cinematically.[65] The visual equivalent of the street scene appears in the establishing shots of "slum streets" in films of the day such as *The Italian* (1915) and *Kindling* (1915). The latter illustrates its dramatic intertitle "Victims of the City" by showing a mother holding an obviously ailing child and a toddler left alone on a fire escape, the bars making him appear to be in prison.

Lummox's happy ending undercuts the surface of the heroine's temporary happiness by implying new problems to come. Bertha loses several jobs as a charwoman due to her age, and her decline into a naturalistic pattern of degradation seems inevitable, since her body, already seen as grotesque in size, gradually loses the strength that had made her employers value her. A chance encounter arrests her descent when she stumbles into employment with a widower, Mr. Meyerbogen, who owns a bakery and ice cream shop. She makes herself indispensable to both father and children, and she finds a permanent place at last where the family accepts her as one of them rather than as the combination of peasant, servant, mother, and artistic inspiration that her earlier employers had demanded. Bertha's transition from object of desire to object of a marriage of convenience elides the issue of her sexuality as an older woman. As Dale M. Bauer points out, the sexuality of an older female character poses a threat in a post-Freudian modernist age: "[M]iddle-age sexuality was represented either as symbolic incest, as when an older woman took up with a younger man, or as child endangerment."[66] Defusing the threat, Bauer continues, involved both Freud's insistence that an older woman could not possibly be desirable to a younger man and sociologist E. A. Ross's declaration that women's attractiveness and sexual energy vanished at age forty. Unlike her contemporaries Gertrude Atherton, Mary E. Wilkins Freeman, and Edith Wharton, who defended older women's identities as sexual beings, Hurst followed the course of Edna Ferber, whose novels render detailed scenes of eating and food as substitutes for romance, much as Evelyn Scott's scenes of eating substitute for a barely contained physical violence.[67] In her new position as servant-mother in a bakery, Bertha revels in the love of the Meyerbogen children and the material affection signified by the baked goods that surround her, content to be a mother figure without the sexual identity that might threaten the ménage of her final years.

Like other unruly naturalistic novels with an ambivalently happy ending, *Lummox* underscores the disparity between the ideal and the real through a cinematic experience. As a charwoman in a movie theater during one interlude between positions, Bertha had watched movies with the rapt attention of other naturalistic heroines: "To Bertha and the rows and rows like her sitting there in the darkness, it was as if they had been kissed on a bunched-up mouth by love in a brown velveteen smoking jacket and prettified eyes. Stinging vicarious sweetness." (170). The sexual love promised by even an effete movie star with "prettified eyes" will never be hers, however. At the Meyerbogen bakery Bertha is surrounded by the sweetness of candy, cakes, and ice cream, and she has found a haven at last where she can sit in the garden and squish her toes in the dirt, an act of primitive connection to the earth that other employers have prohibited. But contact with the earth has two sides, and Bertha is still a servant woman associated with waste who must clean out the grease clog of the "sink drain pipe" (328), a task she can never escape. Like Wharton's *Summer*, *Lummox* offers its protagonist a relationship with a widower rather than a grand passion, a future of daily toil and compromise rather than the romance of the movies, and an ironic rejoinder to the desires that the movies raise but never satisfy.

Miss Lulu Bett:
Play into Novel into Film

In his October 17, 1920, review of Edith Wharton's *Age of Innocence* for the *New York Times Book Review*, William Lyon Phelps noted, "In the present year of emancipation it is pleasant to record that in the front rank of American living novelists we find four women. . . . The big four are Dorothy Canfield, Zona Gale, Anne Sedgwick, [and] Edith Wharton."[68] In *Miss Lulu Bett*, her sixth novel, Gale later explained, she attempted to "[h]eighten [the modern American novel's] compactness, take from it certain affectations such as deliberate sordidness" and pour the "interpenetrating beauty of common life" into "the clear crystal of a form as honest as a milk bottle."[69] Gale received the Pulitzer Prize for drama for adapting *Miss Lulu Bett* from her 1920 novel, but she outraged supporters and critics by changing the book's ending twice. At the ending of the novel, Lulu runs away with her suitor, Neil Cornish, but the first version of the play has her deciding to be alone, and the revised play reunites her at the end with her bigamous husband, Ninian Deacon. William deMille's silent film adaptation reverts to the book's ending and pairs Lulu with Neil Cornish.[70] Released in December 1921, slightly less than a year after the play opened, the film was universally praised, with *Variety* calling it "a well-wrought, closely-knit, straight-away, cumulative domestic drama of rural life," with Lois Wilson as Lulu Bett being "as nearly perfection as one could imagine."[71] Since no films were made of *Three Lives*, *The Narrow House*, or *Quicksand*, and since the filmed version of *Lummox* (1930) is inaccessible, an examination of all four versions of *Miss Lulu Bett* provides a unique opportunity to show how the "domestic drudge" narrative that Gale shares with Scott, Stein, Hurst, and Larsen had to be adapted for 1920s audiences.[72]

Miss Lulu Bett is the story of a thirty-four-year-old unmarried woman who toils as a household drudge in the home of her married sister, Ina, in the small town of Warbleton. Besides Ina, the household consists of Ina's husband, Dwight Deacon, a domineering dentist and justice of the peace; Di, a moody and love-struck teenage daughter; Monona, a younger daughter who as her name suggests manages to be unvaryingly shrill and annoying; and Mrs. Bett, Lulu and Ina's mother, who tries unsuccessfully to rule the house by refusing to eat. Like Sinclair Lewis's *Main Street*, published in the same year, *Miss Lulu Bett* renders the American vernacular humorously in two registers. In addition to the satiric thrusts in her own authorial voice, Gale shows how American humor has degenerated into a means of social control by which powerful characters like Dwight abuse the powerless through cruel, relentless teasing and witless puns. Confined by a combination of a deadly dull domestic routine, Ina's patronizing manner, Dwight's jocular bullying, and her own sense of obligation and poverty, Lulu accepts her lot until a potential means of escape arrives in the form of Dwight's brother, Ninian.

At Ninian's insistence, Lulu joins in family gatherings rather than remaining in the kitchen like a servant, and, during a dinner out with Ina and Dwight, Ninian and Lulu jokingly say wedding vows to liven up the party. When Dwight says that because he is a justice of the peace, the vows may be binding, the two take him at his word and consider themselves married. Lulu Bett's marriage to Ninian Deacon seems at first an outlandish plot contrivance, and so it would be in the realm of realist fiction. However, the "accidental wedding" or "wedding stunt" motif pervades early film comedies such as Buster Keaton's *Seven Chances* (1925) and the Billy Bevan comedy *His Unlucky Night* (1928), in which a couple at a dance hall win the prize of a spontaneous wedding simply because they are standing on a lucky number. The accidental marriage proves a turning point in Lulu's awakening sense of freedom. She returns alone from her wedding trip a little more than a month later, saying that Ninian had confessed to having another wife, an explanation that the family rejects in favor of believing that Ninian had deserted her. Despite its temporary nature, Lulu has gained self-confidence through her marriage. She wears a new red dress, defies Dwight, and lies to protect Di during the latter's failed elopement. Having declared her independence once previously by leaving the house with Ninian, she decides to leave again. When the piano salesman Neil Cornish asks her to marry him, she accepts, and the novel ends with the two of them hurrying toward the train station and away from the oppressive atmosphere of Warbleton.

Gale's dramatic adaptations of her novel, the second and third versions of the story, preserve its signature exchanges on gender and power relationships while heightening the comic elements and verbal repetition. The Lulu of the play has more of a social conscience. Instead of saying "I hope I can do something nice before I quit" as in the book,[73] she tells Ninian that she wants to "take care of folks that needed me."[74] Yet in the play she still meets Ninian with an exchange that shows both spirit and wit:

> NINIAN: Well now—is it Mrs.? Or Miss Lulu Bett?
> LULU: It's Miss. . . . From choice.
> NINIAN: You bet! Oh, you bet! Never doubted that.
> LULU: What kind of a Mr. are you?
> NINIAN: Never give myself away. Say, by George, I never thought of that before.
> There's no telling whether a man's married or not, by his name. (102)

As Deborah Lindsay Williams notes in *Not in Sisterhood*, by listening to Lulu, Ninian helps her to find an "alien tongue" that allows her to "free herself from enslavement . . . as if she literally needs a new language in order to redefine herself."[75] To compensate for the loss of the ironic authorial voice, Gale's play increases the amount of verbal humor, giving Mrs. Bett some stereotypically rural comedy malapropisms, such as calling Ninian a "whited centipede" instead of "whited sepulcher" and multiplying Dwight's mispronunciations, as when Ina tells him, "That's randevoo, Dwightie. Not rendezvous."[76] Although Dwight's abusive joking is emphasized, as he continually refers sarcastically to "Lulu, the charmer," his mispronunciations make him the butt of humor. Another linguistic feature, the play's repetition of individual words, enhances the play's interest in oral performance, as when Lulu hears southern dialect for the first time during her honeymoon trip with Ninian.[77] In the context of Gale's ideas about the compression of language necessary in "the novel of tomorrow," the malapropisms and repeated dialogue demonstrate her commitment to making the ordinary events of *Miss Lulu Bett* a vehicle for "reflect[ing] the familiar as permeated by the unfamiliar," a modernist purpose disguised by the domestic setting and realist plot.[78]

The most significant changes between the book, the play as originally performed, and the play as finally published occur in Gale's revision of the ending. In the novel, the original version of the plot, Lulu Bett marries Neil Cornish and the two are last seen "hurrying toward the railway station" (264), away from Warbleton and the jocular bullying of the Deacon family. In the play that Gale adapted from the novel, Lulu declines rather than accepts the proposal from Neil Cornish so that she can leave town by herself and "see out of [her] own eyes" (161), a feminist ending that emphasizes Lulu's courage. It was this version that premiered first at Sing Sing Correctional Facility in Ossining, New York, on December 26, 1920, opening the following night at the Belmont Theater in New York City to widespread critical acclaim. After the play ran for less than a week with the ending of

Lulu venturing into the world alone, Gale rewrote Act III so that Ninian, having learned that his first wife had died, returns to resume his life with Lulu. By making this change, Gale couldn't win, except at the box office, for, as Deborah Williams explains, "her radical ending had led some critics to label the play as nothing more than feminist propaganda, while the revised ending led other critics to accuse her of pandering."[79]

Despite the reservations of critics such as Heywood Broun, who thought the happy ending "about as sensible as demanding feathers on a mountain lion," the new ending was a hit with audiences.[80] Gale defended her choice on technical grounds in a statement to the New York papers, saying that "Lulu could not marry two men in the space of an evening, no matter how vehemently the programme announced that time had elapsed."[81] She then asked, more philosophically, "Why... is the unmarried ending the artistic ending?... Why is marriage inartistic?"[82] She promised to keep the "open ending" in the published version of the play and did, although the play is usually printed with both endings. The controversy apparently did not hurt Gale's chances for the Pulitzer Prize.[83] Hamlin Garland, the chair of the drama and fiction prize committees, expressed disappointment and did not think it "a great play," but he recommended that "as the award has not gone to a woman before perhaps it would be a graceful concession to give [Zona Gale] this years [sic] prize."[84] Of the three endings—marrying Neil Cornish, in the novel; leaving Warbleton but staying single, in the first version of the play; and marrying Ninian, in the second version of the play—the first and third are therefore, as Marilyn Atlas suggests, "modern without being overtly threatening to the institution of marriage."[85]

The one version usually ignored in discussions of *Miss Lulu Bett* is the fourth version, William deMille's film adaptation written by Clara Beranger and starring Lois Wilson as Lulu.[86] The film adaptation appeared at the cultural intersection of two important factors that would influence its reception: an audience and body of critics for whom aesthetic criteria for judging the relatively new medium of film were still emerging, and an artistic and economic climate that treated women's stories seriously and granted women opportunities in filmmaking that would gradually disappear as the studio system became entrenched in later decades. In addition to Frances Marion and Clara Beranger, a few of these powerful women included Jeannie Macpherson, scenarist for Cecil B. DeMille; Anita Loos, who worked with D. W. Griffith and other directors; June Mathis; and Bess Meredyth.[87] In the early twenties, strong stories for female characters were the province of female scenarists and directors such as Frances Marion and Lois Weber, and they were credited with shaping the films they adapted as well as those they wrote. In trying to decide whether a cinematic adaptation could indeed be called an independent work of art, the reviewer for the *New York Times* distinguished between a simple adaptation and one that used the unique features of the medium: "To achieve any degree of individual distinction, a photoplay must be pictorially dynamic.... [C]ompared with other photoplays as they come and go, it [*Miss Lulu Bett*] may be counted exceptionally cinematographic, and in a number of its scenes it is completely expressive by means of motion pictures alone. Thus it takes rank as an entertaining and significant screen work."[88] The *New York Times* was quick to credit director William deMille for making the film "exceptionally cinematographic" with such naturalistic details as a shot of ants in the sink when Lulu is not there to wash the dishes and adds that deMille was "aided, presumably" by scenarist Clara Beranger. "Presumably" understates Beranger's role considerably, for she had already written fifty-six features, mostly for William deMille, before she adapted both book and play versions of *Miss Lulu Bett* into a 144-page script. For the *New York Times* to heap praise on deMille's direction with only a short nod to Beranger, by whom he was "aided, presumably" hints at other credits denied to women scenarists. For example, as Frances Marion recalled later, she, Meredyth, and Loos were "asked our advice on virtually every script MGM produced in the thirties" but had to "carry the scripts in 'unmarked plain covers' because they were painfully aware of the whispers about 'the tyranny of the woman writer.'"[89]

DeMille and Beranger's adaptation follows the novel and preserves the most stirring of Lulu's defiant speeches, but it is indeed "exceptionally cinematographic." For example, the film extends one of the book's and play's central symbolic patterns: the cooking and eating of food, here as in *The Narrow House* a source of conflict rather than a medium for emotional nourishment. In the novel version of *Miss Lulu Bett*, characters are marked by what they do or do not eat. Monona, a fussy eater, prefers milk toast and making extra work for Lulu to whatever else is on the table. Her counterpart at the other end of the age spectrum, Mrs. Bett, similarly expresses her rage at her powerlessness through "tantrims" (tantrums) that involve the refusal of food to gain attention. The whole family is, of course, nourished by the food that Lulu cooks, and she feeds them as she starves for attention amid their selfishness. Only Ninian Deacon feeds Lulu Bett, first by showing her attention by taking her on a picnic and then by taking her out to dinner. The film reinforces the food symbolism spatially as well. An opening title informs the audience, "If you want to know a family, look at the dining room," followed by a shot of Victorian furniture and glassware that to a 1920s audience would have looked hideously outdated.[90] As the family's domain is the dining room, Lulu's is the orderly kitchen with an ever-present double boiler of oatmeal steaming away.

Given the publicity surrounding *Miss Lulu Bett*'s multiple endings, William deMille uses visual contrast to reinforce the tension surrounding Lulu's ultimate choice by ensuring that the two suitors, Ninian and Neil Cornish, consistently share screen space. Neil Cornish, a schoolteacher in the film rather than a hapless law student and piano salesman, is introduced much earlier, on the same day that Ninian returns, and both men are seen at different times lingering by the gate before going up to the house. At one point, deMille cuts from a medium shot of an expansive Ninian lying about his travels—"I got this off a lion I fought in South America," he tells a group of neighbors—to a closer shot of a glowering Neil. In another contrast, Neil merely wonders where Lulu is, while Ninian acts at once, going out to the kitchen to bring her into the gathering. Later, deMille contrasts Lulu's responses to each. When Neil comes to the door one morning, he tells Lulu, "I came to see you." As her face brightens, he asks her if she will cook for a local fund-raising event, but then, seeing her disappointment, tells her not to do it. He has just begun to sense something in her beyond the tight, unflattering hairstyle and shapeless housedresses she wears. Ninian, on the other hand, literally sees a different Lulu, for he visits at night when figuratively and literally her hair is down.

To increase the suspense, deMille introduces visual elements that misleadingly suggest Ninian as the object for Lulu's fantasies of escape and wish fulfillment. Lynn Rhoades mentions in passing the Cinderella elements in the story, but the Cinderella motif plays a far more important role in the film than in the other versions.[91] At their first meeting, Ninian picks up Lulu's shapeless knitted wool slipper and hands it to her, a gesture of gallantry that suggests he may be the Prince Charming she unconsciously seeks. An added scene in the movie shows that the allusion is deliberate. When Ninian and Lulu are alone in their hotel, after Ninian tells her about his first wife, from whom he has never been divorced, the camera cuts to a shot of Lulu's beautiful white satin high-heeled pump, which dissolves into an image of the shapeless slipper as she realizes she must leave him and return home. He is no longer a prince, and she can stay no longer at the ball.

Neil's heroism is, by contrast, domestic as well as romantic. Standing in Lulu's kitchen, he learns to dry dishes and thus share rather than add to her labor, and he gallantly rescues Lulu when she falls from a chair she is standing on, showing his hero credentials, in the time-honored way, not by dazzling her with travel and objects but by rescuing her from danger. The same visual system reveals Lulu's thoughts through other objects. The suitcase, the subject of so many questions in the book and play versions, is settled when Lulu, packing her new silk clothes in Ninian's suitcase, is surprised when Ninian presents her with one of her own marked "Mrs. Ninian Deacon." In a well-rendered piece of visual symbolism, the film reinforces the book's implicit claim that by awakening her sexuality Ninian gives Lulu the key to leave the oppressive home she has at the Deacons'. Later, when Di borrows the suitcase, she figuratively borrows Lulu's transgressive ap-

Lulu Bett explodes at Dwight and knocks the oatmeal from the stove before breaking a number of dishes, angrily telling him, "My work's paid for these," from *Miss Lulu Bett* (1921).

proach to sexuality as signified by Lulu's silk undergarments. Other parallels in the film link Di and Lulu in their sexual adventures. After her marriage to Ninian, a pensive Lulu sits in the same arbor where Di meets her boyfriend, suggesting that she, like Di, now exists in the sexualized realm of romance.

The ending of the film provides one of the most inventive adaptations of Gale's ideas. Whereas the book focuses on Lulu's seeming submission and secret flight from the house, the play version emphasizes her lengthy feminist speech about her plight. For the film version, however, Beranger and deMille have Lulu speak through objects rather than words. In one of the opening scenes, when Dwight hounds her about the cost of a flower she has bought, Lulu throws away the plant she has purchased but says nothing to Dwight himself, a mute form of protest. In the penultimate scene of the film, Dwight asks her to stay with them, and, presumably, in the kitchen, for good. This time, Lulu finds her voice, speaking not of self-sacrifice but of money: "My work's paid for these." She explodes, knocking the steaming oatmeal to the floor, hurling pots and pans, and, after throwing a bucket of water at the wall, telling Ina and Mrs. Deacon, "Do your own dishes." Declaring "I hate you! I hate your house! I wouldn't stay in it! I'm through!" she storms out of the kitchen and out of the visual space of her symbolic enslavement, leaving her tormenters in the kitchen she has abandoned.

After this scene, she leaves the house and a month later drops by Neil's schoolhouse. The multiple intertitles of the previous scene are almost entirely absent in this final scene, which uses handwriting on the blackboard and in a letter to dispense with their artificial interruptions of the action. As Neil greets Lulu, a child writes on the board, "Teacher loves L——." Neil dismisses the students, who watch

Neil proposes to Lulu by writing on the board and inviting her to write her response there, from *Miss Lulu Bett* (1921).

from the doorway as Lulu shows him a letter from Ninian. An inset shot of the letter reveals that because Ninian's wife is still alive, Lulu is not married to him, and she is now free. Elated, Neil continues to write, adding "Does Lulu love me?" She takes the chalk from him, confirming her agency in this relationship, and writes a "Y," after which he folds her in his arms while the children watch and giggle from the doorway. Their act of shared writing emphasizes, without the imposition of intertitles, the mutual and egalitarian nature of their relationship, the life script that they will write together as equals. Despite its absence of the feminist vision of a newly liberated Lulu Bett declining all proposals so that she can "see through her own eyes" for a change, deMille and Beranger's version provides an ending that promises a companionate marriage rather than the oppressive domesticity of the Deacon household.

In their treatments of the servant woman's body, Wharton, Stein, Larsen, Scott, Hurst, and Gale transform a nineteenth-century naturalistic subject matter through modernist techniques. Surrounded by and associated with the dirt, secrets, and other detritus of civilization, the servant woman is an evolutionary throwback, an embarrassing reminder of bodies and the waste that even a technologically advanced, streamlined modernism cannot banish. Capturing excesses of emotion expressed through melodrama and treated as waste, both elements mapped onto the bodies of women servants, the works of these writers vary from the strict precepts of naturalism. Recasting Lily Bart as the servant of the society she intends to dominate, Wharton demonstrates the problems inherent in hoarding and in ignoring the invisible message of the grotesque naturalistic body of the socially undesirable woman. Typically overshadowed by "Melanctha," Stein's paired portraits of the servant woman in "The Good Anna" and "The Gentle Lena" reveal as centrally naturalistic the treatment of children as waste, the links between spiritualism and prostitution, and the connections between dirt and hoarding. Larsen's Helga Crane moves from a melodramatic universe into a naturalistic one replete with themes of evolution, sexual desire, children as waste products, and the violence of childbirth, naturalistic themes addressed with added psychological intensity as the emotional cannibalism of monstrous mothers in Scott's *The Narrow House*.

Hurst's *Lummox* combines the familial dysfunction of Scott with evolutionary primitivism of Jungian race memories, the self-sacrificing woman of domestic fiction, and the grotesque female body of women's naturalism. Gale's Lulu Bett resists the emotional violence common to all the family dynamics in these novels. Like Lena, Helga, Winnie, and Bertha, she expresses her sexuality, but unlike them this act liberates rather than entraps her in an inescapable biological recursion of childbearing and the carrying of waste that marks naturalistic bodies. Burdened with secrets and potential sentiment, sometimes primitive or violent in her desires and actions, and covered in the messy detritus of a culture that refuses to include her grotesque, sometimes lumbering, female body as part of its aesthetic of a fast-paced technological modernity, the servant woman of these novels reminds modernism of what it leaves behind and the naturalistic elements that it can never entirely erase.

CONCLUSION

American women's literary naturalism, in either its classic or unruly forms, raises a host of issues not only for reading works within this tradition but also for applying to the work of classic male naturalists. The problems of determinism, heredity and environment, desire, and elemental behavioral traits masked by a thin veneer of civilization occur in the works of women writers as well as their male contemporaries, and indeed their fiction has been treated in these terms. Why, then, beyond reasons of simple parity, should we treat women writers as naturalists? What is to be gained by this additional classification?

The most comprehensive reason is that reading writers such as Wharton, Glasgow, Cather, and Chopin and their contemporaries in this fashion restores missing contexts and repairs, in a sense, the fragmentation of the literary analytical categories that might have divorced them from this context in the first place. The process of establishing a canon is necessarily one of selection and judgment, of establishing criteria and holding individual authors and works up to scrutiny as exemplifying—or, conversely, failing to meet—the standards. In the ex post facto differentiation of naturalism from realism, from regionalism, from sentimentalism, from reform literature, and from romance, some alliances, such as Norris's famous pronouncement that naturalism was essentially romantic rather than realistic, were retained while others fell by the wayside, most obviously sentimentalism. But even novels generally acknowledged as classics of naturalism, such as *McTeague* or *Maggie: A Girl of the Streets* did not appear in a vacuum but participated broadly in the popular culture and literature of their time, as evidenced by the vaudeville shows in each and the novels' debt to melodrama and tracts. Opening up the context for naturalism reveals that, rather than a few isolated islands of naturalistic purity in a stream of popular literature, naturalistic novels by both men and women were instead part of this larger stream, which included documentary reports, newspaper stories, performance cultures of vaudeville, early cinema and its rhetoric of participation, and the visual culture of film itself.

The context of documentary evidence is important, for women writers of naturalism functioned as fully as recorders of events as did their male counterparts. They investigated the transmission of affect and sought to locate emotion and sexual desire in evolutionary biology and Darwinian theories of courtship rather than in the so-called sentimental responses of a previous generation. The emphasis placed on women as recorders of experience who use technological means to further their own ends—the exposure of men's networks in white slave novels and films, for example—highlights their positioning as agents and subjects rather than muses and objects, as in the Bohemian art novel. While not shying away from the sordid and sensational events such as murders, seductions, and other forms of violence that gave naturalism its reputation as a genre of excess, women writers look past the sensational foreground of the naturalistic plot to illuminate the elements of the background. Much as the discovery-of-squalor sequence in grim realism and naturalism only gradually illuminates the scene and allows the human figures to be distinguished from the cluttered background, women writers look past the sensational events to see the additional features of the naturalistic landscape, including the catalog of refuse, the children and women treated as waste, and the additional burdens that age, disability, and childbirth confer upon female characters. The reform purposes and occasional didacticism used to disqualify women's novels as naturalism are merely part, not the entirety, of the works in which they appear, and their presence is no more jarring than the pleas for reform in Norris's *The Octopus* or Upton Sinclair's *The Jungle*. In characterizing women as waste and as abject, and in focusing on waste and hoarding, women's novels claim a portion of naturalism seemingly incidental but highly consequential for reading naturalism beyond its classic dimensions.

Reading women writers of naturalism in the context of evolutionary theory and Darwin's theories of female sexual selection also restores a missing context, for, from the 1980s on, some schools of criticism theorized that women were naturally cooperative, helpful, and self-sacrificing as well as acting in innate solidarity with one another. The examples of self-sacrifice to be found in, for example, Wharton's "Bunner Sisters" or Hurst's *Lummox* suggest what current biological theory hypothesizes as an unselfishness gene, and women's cooperation is often read as a feminist resistance to the strictures of patriarchy. But to read characters such as Ann Eliza Bunner or Helga in terms of self-sacrifice misses the essentially ruthless biological competition that women's naturalism establishes and that these writers' immersion in Darwinian theories of evolution would predict. In effect, for one woman to succeed at survival or, in what most novels is the same thing, at finding a man to marry her, in true Darwinian fashion another woman must fail. In *At Fault*, Thérèse can have no happy ending unless Fanny, her rival, dies. Justine Brent cannot have Amherst in *The Fruit of the Tree* unless she kills

Bessy Westmore. In "Bunner Sisters," Evelina's ruthless self-absorption, a trait she shares with Scott's Winnie of *The Narrow House*, makes her supremely able to manipulate her sister into giving up Mr. Ramy. Even Alexandra Bergson in *O Pioneers!* cannot find happiness with Carl until Marie Shabata is not only dead but has been thoroughly denounced by Alexandra and Carl. Sensing competition for her husband, Lena of *Red Rust* sends her young daughter-turned-rival away from the farm, thereby avoiding the fate of Rose in *Dust*, who sees her husband fall in love with a younger version of herself. Standing in feminist solidarity with Rose Matlock, Neith Schuyler prepares to abandon her relationship with Adam Frear only to have Rose pursue him with increased determination. Finally and most famously, among the many contributing factors to Lily Bart's death in *The House of Mirth* is her refusal to accept that her women friends are actually her enemies and that they will never back her when the stakes are as high as keeping one's husband. Women are victims not merely of patriarchy or men's idealism but also of the primitive and ruthless competition of other women, a naturalistic scenario repeated throughout several novels.

Women's naturalism achieves different perspectives than those of classic naturalism. In pursuit of those perspectives, women writers represent women as documentary recorders and technology users, and their investigations, like those of their characters, reveal the ways in which the culture discards children, disabled individuals, and women as waste. They challenge Bohemia's so-called freedoms and the progressive national narrative surrounding race and citizenship. They use Darwinian courtship principles to counter assumptions about female sexuality and to ground the trajectory of desire and its aftermath, childbirth, in biology rather than in sentiment. Stripping away the overlay of common assumptions about women's writing—that it celebrates women's cooperation and resistance to patriarchy, or that its domestic settings reflect sentimental or inconsequential concerns—reveals naturalism's elemental landscape of desire, violence, atavism, and trauma. Like their male counterparts, women writers write naturalism using its familiar elements of determinism, the interplay of heredity and environment, and the biological factors governing characters' lives. Yet by placing women's bodies and women's lives in the foreground, and by exploring the dusty and less-than-clear-cut corners of naturalism, women writers restore to the movement some of the vitality that may have been lost in more clinical debates over heredity versus environment. The unruly elements that women writers bring to the mix provide new ways of reading not only their own books through a cinematic lens but also those of their naturalistic contemporaries.

NOTES

Introduction

1. Wharton, "One Day."
2. James, "Letter to Edith Wharton, 20 August 1902," 34.
3. Wharton, "Great American Novel," 648.
4. Glazener, *Reading for Realism*, 6.
5. Howard, *Form and History in American Literary Naturalism*, 30, 36, 40.
6. Link, *The Vast and Terrible Drama*, 12.
7. Pizer, "*Maggie* and the Naturalistic Aesthetic."
8. Brooks, *Realist Vision*, 123.
9. For a brief overview of naturalism's recent critical history, see Christophe Den Tandt, "Refashioning American Literary Naturalism"; Donna Campbell, "American Literary Naturalism: Critical Perspectives."
10. Link, *The Vast and Terrible Drama*, 20.
11. Howard, "Sand in Your Mouth," 99.
12. Fleissner, *Women, Compulsion, Modernity*, 163.
13. Sawaya, *Modern Women, Modern Work*, 56.
14. Norris, *The Octopus*, 1087, 1097.
15. Bill Brown, *Material Unconscious*, 67, 77.
16. Fleissner, *Women, Compulsion, Modernity*, 11.
17. Elbert, "The Displacement of Desire," 198, 199.
18. Joslin, "Turning Zola inside Out," 278, 280.
19. Pizer, "Late Nineteenth-Century American Literary Naturalism," 191, 201.
20. Ammons, "Expanding the Canon of American Realism," 443.
21. Boyd, *Writing for Immortality*, 249.
22. Dimock, *Through Other Continents*, 74.
23. Long, "Genre Matters: Embodying American Literary Naturalism," 171. Kenneth Warren argues for the importance of considering race in realism in *Black and White Strangers*. In addition to Long and Warren, see Dudley, *A Man's Game*; Von Rosk, "Coon Shows, Rag-

time, and the Blues"; Jarrett, "Second-Generation Realist"; Dudley, "Special Issue: Naturalism and African American Culture"; and Papke, "Necessary Interventions in the Face of Very Curious Compulsions: Octavia Butler's Naturalist Science Fiction."

24. I am indebted to Mary Papke for the expression of this idea.

25. The idea that the human being is a type of machine has a long history in naturalism. For an extended discussion, see Mark Seltzer, *Bodies and Machines*.

26. For a discussion of the "monstrous mother" character, see Seltzer, *Bodies and Machines*, 98. For the "fallen woman" in naturalism, see Laura Hapke, *Girls Who Went Wrong*.

27. Crane, *Maggie: A Girl of the Streets*, 41, 70. Subsequent references are cited in the text.

28. Bender, *The Descent of Love*.

29. Quoted in Stanley Corkin, *Realism and the Birth of the Modern United States*, 51.

30. Frederic, "Stephen Crane's Triumph," 22.

31. Quoted in Bill Brown, *The Material Unconscious*, 109.

32. Howells, "Editor's Easy Chair," 635, 637.

33. For a reading of Norris's text and Griffith's film, see Katherine Fusco, "Taking Naturalism to the Moving Picture Show."

34. Howells, "The Future of Motion Pictures," 193.

35. Gunning, "An Aesthetic of Astonishment: Early Film and the (in)Credulous Spectator," 114.

36. Mayne, *The Woman at the Keyhole*, 31.

37. Bill Brown, *The Material Unconscious*, 47.

38. Gitelman, *Scripts, Grooves, and Writing Machines*, 25.

39. Belletti, *Adventures of a Hollywood Secretary*, 205.

40. Hallett, *Go West, Young Women!*, 14.

41. Corkin, *Realism and the Birth of the Modern United States*, 110.

42. Claudy, "The Degradation of the Motion Picture," 163, 164.

43. Auerbach, *Body Shots*, 35.

44. Cartwright, *Screening the Body*, 18.

45. For "cinema of attractions" and "story films," see Tom Gunning, "The Cinema of Attraction," 56–62.

46. Cohen, *Silent Film and the Triumph of the American Myth*, 10, 11.

47. Norris, *McTeague*, 60. Subsequent references are cited in the text.

48. Peucker, *The Material Image*, 5.

49. Peter Brooks, *Realist Vision*, 183.

50. Friedberg, "Les Flaneurs Du Mal(l)," 422. See also Friedberg's *The Virtual Window*.

51. Thrailkill, *Affecting Fictions*, 7.

52. Although the preferred terms now are "sex work" and "sex worker," I use the terms "prostitution" and "prostitute" throughout this book since they are the terms that were current when the texts under discussion were published.

53. London uses the term "work beasts" to describe the dehumanizing effect of the soulless drudgery that his character Martin performs when working in a laundry in chapter 9 of *Martin Eden*: "All that was god-like in him was blotted out. The spur of ambition was

blunted; he had no vitality with which to feel the prod of it. He was dead. His soul seemed dead. He was a beast, a work-beast" (694).

Chapter 1. Grim Realism and the Culture of Feeling

1. Elizabeth Stuart Phelps, "Stories That Stay," 118. Subsequent references are cited in the text.
2. Burrows, *A Familiar Strangeness*, 27.
3. Howells, "Editor's Study," 483.
4. Howells, *London Films*, 1. Subsequent references are cited in the text.
5. Clayton, "London Eyes," 384.
6. A memorable instance of the term "grim realism" applied to Jack London's *The Children of the Frost* occurs in critic Elinor M. Hoyt's "In Lighter Vein": "From Jack London one knows what to expect—and one expects much.... Grim realism and wild romance consort oddly in the tales" (445). Hoyt would become an important poet under the name Elinor Wylie.
7. "Review," *Bookman* 1, no. 5 (1895): 353. In addition to its futuristic opening tale "The Repairer of Reputations" and its linked horror stories about an eponymous play, *The King in Yellow*, which drives mad all who read it, many of the stories are set in Bohemian Paris.
8. Bergman and Bernardi, *Our Sisters' Keepers*, 11.
9. Morgan, *Questionable Charity*, 9, 15.
10. See Jane P. Tompkins, *Sensational Designs*.
11. Halpern, *Sentimental Readers*, 107.
12. Brennan, *The Transmission of Affect*, 5, 6.
13. Jameson, *The Antinomies of Realism*, 35.
14. June Howard, *Publishing the Family*, 223, 245.
15. Jameson, *The Antinomies of Realism*, 36.
16. Howard, *Form and History in American Literary Naturalism*, 101.
17. Giles, *The Naturalistic Inner-City Novel in America*, 16.
18. Kristeva, *Powers of Horror*, 3, 4.
19. For a debate that considers the evidence for Maggie's suicide, see Robert M. Dowling and Donald Pizer, "A Cold Case File Reopened."
20. Stallybrass and White, *The Politics and Poetics of Transgression*, 135, 139.
21. Elizabeth Stuart Phelps, *Hedged In*, 6. Subsequent references are cited in the text.
22. Fisher, *Hard Facts*, 118, 119.
23. Warhol, "As You Stand, So You Feel and Are," 118.
24. Edwards, *Discourse and Cognition*, 115.
25. Davis, "Life in the Iron-Mills," 3. Subsequent references are cited in the text.
26. Bill Brown, *A Sense of Things*, 54, 56.
27. Dreiser, *Sister Carrie*, 1.
28. Crane, "The Open Boat," 885, 902.
29. Mary Eleanor Wilkins Freeman, "A Church Mouse," 100.

30. Tracey, "Stories of the Poorhouse," 26.

31. Peter Brooks, *Realist Vision*, 17.

32. Bill Brown, *A Sense of Things*, 18.

33. Clifford Odets's *Street Scene* uses much the same dynamic between teeming street and crowded tenement rooms.

34. Wharton, *The House of Mirth*, 142, 427. Subsequent references are cited in the text.

35. Matthews, "In Search of Local Color," 38.

36. Armstrong, *Fiction in the Age of Photography*, 92–93.

37. Jameson, *The Antinomies of Realism*, 148. Jameson debates whether naturalism should be considered a part of realism, concluding that its "trajectory of decline and failure" (149) and "the fear of déclassement," or what June Howard terms the fear of proletarianization, render it a "specialized" (150) form.

38. Thomson, "Benevolent Maternalism and Physically Disabled Figures," 563–64.

39. Harris, *Rebecca Harding Davis and American Realism*, 29.

40. Ibid., 3, 5.

41. Harris, "A New Era in Female History," 613.

42. Goodling, "The Silent Partnership," 4.

43. Pfaelzer, *Parlor Radical*, 35.

44. Davis, *Margret Howth*, 10. Subsequent references are cited in the text.

45. James, "Preface," 12.

46. Yellin, "Afterword," 281. Subsequent references are cited in the text.

47. Lisa Long notes in passing that Dr. Knowles, with his monomania for prison reform, reflects the subject of Hollingsworth's obsession ("Imprisoned in/at Home," 72).

48. See chapter 4 for a discussion of patchouli as signifying prostitution. Early twentieth-century films featuring prostitutes were categorized as "kimona and patchouli" films. See the December 12, 1913, "Review: *The Inside of the White Slave Traffic*."

49. Pfaelzer, *Parlor Radical*, 69–70.

50. According to Yellin, "Afterword," Davis's original manuscript, "The Deaf and the Dumb," broke the pattern "in which a 'good woman' saves a flawed hero" by "killing off [the hero] in the fire and leaving [the heroine]" to continue her social work among the poor instead of concluding with their marriage (291).

51. Knadler, "Dis-Abled Citizenship," 101.

52. See the discussion of *At Fault* in chapter 2 for another example of this plot element.

53. Elizabeth Stuart Phelps, "The Tenth of January," 70. Subsequent references are cited in the text.

54. See, for example, book 2, chapter 20, "Surprises," in Alcott, *Little Women*, when Jo talks to Laurie about his marriage: "She is the sun and I the wind, in the fable, and the sun managed the man best, you remember" (348). "The fable" suggests that everyone will recognize the allusion.

55. *An Authentic History of the Lawrence Calamity*, 26. Subsequent references are cited in the text.

56. Elizabeth Stuart Phelps, "One of the Elect," 185. Subsequent references are cited in the text.

57. Quoted in Paul Sorrentino, *Stephen Crane*, 110.

58. The mention of pink ribbons suggests Hawthorne's use of them in "Young Goodman Brown" to represent the superficial faith of Brown's wife Faith. Since Margaret's self-examination in this chapter involves whether she, unlike Mrs. Myrtle, has true faith rather than false religion, the allusion strengthens the point.

59. Bergman, "Oh the Poor Women!," 199.

60. The final image of Eunice clinging to the cross anticipates by a few years Johannes Adam Simon Oertel's hugely popular painting *Rock of Ages* (1876), which depicts a woman clad in white and clinging to a cross while a storm rages about her. The original painting is at the Fogg Museum, Harvard University, but it was widely reproduced as a popular print throughout the late nineteenth century. In Laura Ingalls Wilder's *These Happy Golden Years*, for example, as Laura and Almanzo stand before Reverend Brown to be married, Laura notices the painting: "On the wall was a large colored picture of a woman clinging to a white cross planted on a rock, with lightning streaking the sky above her and huge waves dashing high about her" (280).

61. Harde, "His Spirituality or His Manliness," 145.

62. Phelps's *A Singular Life* anticipates another famous portrait of ministry of the time, Harold Frederic's *The Damnation of Theron Ware*. As in Phelps's novel, Frederic's minister learns of evolutionary theory, falls in love with a woman after she plays him songs on a piano (an echo of Darwin's theories of music in *The Descent of Man*), and has his doctrine questioned and his faith tested by the dogmatic elders of his congregation, and like Phelps's minister, Frederic's is sensitive to the point of tears. But where Theron Ware fails—at separating Christian dogma from Christian action, in assimilating Darwinian thought without losing his faith, and in being a true masculine leader to his congregation—Bayard succeeds at all three. His death and apotheosis, which, like Nixy's, is attended by an unusual sunset that stains a white dress red and a subsequent storm, confirms his status as a Christ figure.

63. Elizabeth Stuart Phelps, *A Singular Life*, 238. Subsequent references are cited in the text.

64. Donaldson, "Elizabeth Stuart Phelps, Realism, and Literary Debates on Changing Gender Roles."

65. Sterne, *The Audible Past*, 191, 192.

66. Elizabeth Stuart Phelps, *Chapters from a Life*, 292.

67. For an account of Garfield's assassination and its aftermath, see Candice Millard, *The Destiny of the Republic*.

68. Wyman, "Black and White."

69. Grimké, "Review of *Gertrude of Denmark*," 420.

70. According to Rose in "Recovering Lillie Buffum Chace Wyman and 'The Child of the State,'" "Wyman demonstrates a naturalist's awareness of environmental determinism and a reformer's concern for the social responsibility implicit in that awareness" (40).

71. Wyman, "The Child of the State," 118. Subsequent references are cited in the text.

72. Wyman, "And Joe," 217. Subsequent references are cited in the text.

73. In *Elizabeth Buffum Chace*, Lillie Buffum Chace Wyman and Arthur Crawford Wyman write, "She [Sophia Foord] was a dark-skinned, pudgy-featured woman who always

remained a spinster. Can it do any harm now to say that she believed in the twin-soul theory, and confided to Mrs. Chace her conviction that Thoreau's soul was twin to hers, and that in 'the Other World' her spirit and his would be united?" (I: 131). Foord reportedly proposed to Thoreau by letter, according to Richard Bridgman (*Dark Thoreau*, 58). Foord was governess to Wyman and to Louisa May Alcott at different times. Bronson Alcott hired Foord to teach at his proposed school at Hillside, in Concord, and "Louisa [May Alcott], hoping to add a touch of grandeur, called Foord her governess," according to John Matteson (*Eden's Outcasts*, 173).

74. Wyman, "Luke Gardiner's Love," 92. Subsequent references are cited in the text.
75. Wyman, "Valentine's Chance," 303. Subsequent references are cited in the text.

Chapter 2. The Darwinists

1. Pryse, "Sex, Class, and 'Category Crisis.'"
2. Jack London satirizes this "man who knows natives" figure in his story "The Inevitable White Man."
3. Peattie, *Impertinences*, 9.
4. Peattie, "After the Storm," 393. Subsequent references are cited in the text.
5. Kimball, *Nell Kimball*, 99. Another example of the "fast" reputation of milliners occurs in the character of Mrs. Swiftwaite, the town milliner in Sinclair Lewis's *Main Street*, who has a reputation for dating married men.
6. Cather, *The Selected Letters of Willa Cather*, 52.
7. Cather, "When I Knew Stephen Crane," 933.
8. Roosevelt, *The Strenuous Life*, 2–3, 4.
9. Peattie, "The Man at the Edge of Things," 321. Subsequent references are cited in the text.
10. For an examination of Roosevelt's use of these opposing terms, see Kevin P. Murphy, *Political Manhood*.
11. For a discussion of American masculinity and empire, see Kaplan, *The Anarchy of Empire in the Making of U.S. Culture*.
12. Bill Brown, "Thing Theory," 4.
13. Jewett, *Deephaven*, 18–19. Subsequent references are cited in the text.
14. Cleary, "The Rebellion of Mrs. McLelland," 186. Subsequent references are cited in the text.
15. Cleary, "Feet of Clay," 144. Subsequent references are cited in the text.
16. Floyd, "A Sympathetic Misunderstanding?," 152.
17. Foote, "The Trumpeter: Part I" and "The Trumpeter: Part II." References are cited in the text.
18. Miller, *Mary Hallock Foote*, 170.
19. Pratt, *Imperial Eyes*, 95, 97. Although Pratt uses the term "transracial" as a more politically charged version of "interracial," Stephanie Hawkins uses it to mean biracial but transcending the idea of race (Hawkins, "Building the 'Blue' Race").

20. *United States Federal Census*, 1870.

21. Lindsay, "The Lone Star's Bonanza," 257.

22. Ibid.

23. Bashford, "The Literary Development of the Far Northwest," 317.

24. A Present Scribe, "California Talent Finds a Gratifying Reception among Eastern Literati," *San Francisco Call*, October 25, 1896, 21.

25. "Writers of Books," *San Francisco Call*, February 24, 1901, 4.

26. Higginson, "Cover Leaves," 7.

27. Lindsay, "The Old Law," 35. Subsequent references are cited in the text.

28. Lindsay, "Squaw Charley," 72.

29. Lindsay, "The Half-Breed's Story," 248.

30. The name is probably taken from Quo-doultz-spu-den, the name of the Black River near Renton, Washington. The Duwamish are the tribe of Chief Si'ahl' or Seattle.

31. *Dictionary of Chinook Jargon with Examples of Use in Conversation*.

32. Lindsay, "Kwelth-Elite, the Proud Slave," 534. Subsequent references are cited in the text.

33. Raibmon, *Authentic Indians*, 75.

34. Grasso, "Inventive Desperation," 18.

35. Mary Eleanor Wilkins Freeman, "Old Woman Magoun," 361. Subsequent references are cited in the text.

36. "Where Are You Going to, My Pretty Maid?" furnished the title for the British edition of *My Little Sister*, which was called *Where Are You Going To . . . ?* when published in London by Heinemann (John, *Elizabeth Robins*, 185). The theme of the stranger seducing the girl using these words is echoed in Joyce Carol Oates's much-anthologized story "Where Are You Going, Where Have You Been?"

37. The clinical details recall the lengthy death scene when Emma takes arsenic in Flaubert's *Madame Bovary*.

38. "Natural settings that are wild and entangled": Bender, *The Descent of Love*, 18.

39. Quoted in Emily Toth, *Unveiling Kate Chopin*, 89.

40. Chopin, "Confidences," 700.

41. Chopin, "In the Confidence of a Story-Writer," 704.

42. Chopin, "Émile Zola's 'Lourdes,'" 697, 698.

43. Several critics have argued that *The Awakening* is naturalistic, among them Seyersted, *Kate Chopin: A Critical Biography*; N. Walker, "Women Writers and Literary Naturalism; Skaggs, *Kate Chopin*; Bender, *The Descent of Love*; Pizer, "A Note on Kate Chopin's *The Awakening* as Naturalistic Fiction"; Margraf, "Kate Chopin's *The Awakening* as a Naturalistic Novel"; Witherow, "Flaubert's Vision and Chopin's Naturalistic Revision"; Fleissner, *Women, Compulsion, Modernity*. Bender focuses on the novel's echoes of Darwin, whereas Pizer and Seyersted emphasize the elements of biological determinism in Edna's position as mother. Walker finds the novel's naturalism incompatible with its feminism, but Margraf argues for "naturalism as feminism" (93). Pizer reads Edna's recognition that she cannot overcome the processes of the natural world as proof of the novel's naturalism, and Fleissner

reads the characters' repetitive actions within the novel as a set of natural rhythms that Edna tries to, but ultimately cannot, resist.

44. Fluck, "Kate Chopin's *At Fault*."
45. Koloski, "The Structure of Kate Chopin's *At Fault*," 90.
46. Ringe, "Cane River World," 158, 160.
47. "Latter-day Arcadia": Arner, "Landscape Symbolism in Kate Chopin's 'At Fault,'" 146. Maureen Anderson argues that *At Fault* is an inversion of southern pastoral and its gender roles since "the female protagonist assumes the traditionally male pastoral role" ("Unraveling the Southern Pastoral Tradition," 2).
48. Chopin, *At Fault*, 744. Subsequent references are cited in the text.
49. See chapter 4 of Fleissner's *Women, Compulsion, Modernity*.
50. For a further discussion of Chopin's use of Darwin in *At Fault*, see Bender, *The Descent of Love*, 199–203.
51. Ewell, *Kate Chopin*, 33; Menke, "Chopin's Sensual Sea and Cable's Ravished Land," 92.
52. Beer, *Kate Chopin, Edith Wharton and Charlotte Perkins Gilman*, 27, 30.
53. The site has its roots in Chopin's life. The grave they visit is that of Robert McAlpin, said to be the prototype for Simon Legree. Chopin's father-in-law, Dr. Victor Jean Baptiste Chopin, bought the plantation after McAlpin's death and, since he was notoriously cruel to his wife and slaves, was sometimes confused with McAlpin. See Emily Toth, *Kate Chopin*, 122.
54. Stoler, "Intimidations of Empire," 4.
55. Birnbaum, "Alien Hands," 303.
56. "Review of *At Fault*," 165.
57. Papke, *Verging on the Abyss*, 51.
58. Lee, *Edith Wharton*, 70–71, 330.
59. Wharton, *The Letters of Edith Wharton*, 136.
60. On Wharton and sexual selection, see Bender, *The Descent of Love*; Kornasky, "On 'Listen[ing] to Spectres Too'"; Farwell, *Love and Death in Edith Wharton's Fiction*. On Wharton and evolution, see Kassanoff, *Edith Wharton and the Politics of Race*; Saunders, *Reading Edith Wharton through a Darwinian Lens*; Ohler, *Edith Wharton's Evolutionary Conception*; Saltz, "The Vision-Building Faculty."
61. Wharton, *The Letters of Edith Wharton*, 91.
62. Wharton, "The Great American Novel," 648.
63. Wharton, "Tendencies in Modern Fiction," 172, 171.
64. Bentley, *The Ethnography of Manners*, 50.
65. *A Moment's Ornament* was one of Wharton's original titles for *The House of Mirth*.
66. Dimock, "Debasing Exchange," 787.
67. Wharton, *The House of Mirth*, 515; Kassanoff, *Edith Wharton and the Politics of Race*, 56. Subsequent references to *The House of Mirth* are cited in the text.
68. Wharton, *Ethan Frome*, 150.
69. Wharton, *The Age of Innocence*, 52. Subsequent references are cited in the text.
70. "With a purpose": Wharton uses this phrase about *The House of Mirth* in a letter to Dr.

Morgan Dix, December 5, 1905: "*No* novel worth anything can be anything but a novel 'with a purpose,' & if anyone who cared for the moral issue did not see in my work that *I* care for it, I should have no one to blame but myself—or at least my inadequate means of rendering my effects" (*The Letters of Edith Wharton*, 99).

71. Louis Auchincloss identifies this as a significant Wharton theme in *Edith Wharton, a Woman in Her Time*.

72. Wharton, *The Fruit of the Tree*, 15. Subsequent references are cited in the text.

73. For an extended discussion of Miltonic echoes in the novel, see Deborah Carlin, "To Form a More Imperfect Union." Carlin suggests that "Wharton delineates the limitations of *Paradise Lost*'s quiescent and subordinate Eve of Book Four in Bessy Westmore" but "scripts the novel's 'New Woman' [Justine] as the transgressive and self-willed Eve of Book Nine" (63).

74. "That forbidden tree": John Milton, *Paradise Lost*, book 1, page 2; book 12, 646.

75. "[B]roken-backed novel": Tuttleton, "Justine," 161. Ellen Dupree, in "The New Woman, Progressivism, and the Woman Writer in Edith Wharton's *The Fruit of the Tree*," places Justine in the context of the "New Woman" novels of the Progressive Era, reading what others have seen as a lack of unity as Wharton's consciously ironic rewriting of a traditional form. Thus the "problem novel's negative or transitional New Woman" who is "typically a shrewd social climber" is embodied in Bessy, a strategy that redefines the problem from "the modern woman's uncontrolled ambition" to "the traditional woman's incompetence" (52). In "The Fall of the Knowledgeable Woman," Ann Jurecic finds the novel's lack of unity a natural consequence of its exploration of its competing sentimental and realist modes, a division that Justine both represents and may potentially reconcile in her capacity as a nurse who signifies both. Ultimately, however, Jurecic contends that "Nurse Brent becomes a defeated interpreter, and she must also be recognized as a silenced writer" because of the failed romance she wrote in her youth" (47). Katherine Joslin sees the clash of genres as central to the novel's structure in "Architectonic or Episodic?" She takes as her key text a quotation from Wharton's often-quoted November 19, 1907, letter to Robert Grant about the novel: "The fact is that I am beginning to see exactly where my weakest point is.—I conceive my subjects like a man—that is, rather more architectonically & dramatically than most women—& then execute them like a woman; or rather, I sacrifice, to my desire for construction & breadth, the small incidental effects that women have always excelled in, the episodical characterization, I mean" (Wharton, *The Letters of Edith Wharton*, 124). According to Joslin, "Architectonic or Episodic?," the plots and subplots "cohere perhaps too well. The *hand* of labor is mangled and therefore helpless to effect social change; the *back* of the mill owner is crushed and therefore incapable of supporting the responsibilities of management in its relationship to labor; the *head* of the mill, the manager, then weds the *heart* of the novel, the nurse" (70).

76. R. W. B. Lewis, *Edith Wharton*, 181; Totten, "The Machine in the Home," 262.

77. Wolff, *A Feast of Words*, 135.

78. According to Frederick Wegener, Pierre Loti was the pseudonym of Louis-Marie-Julien Viaud (1850–1923), a French novelist of whom Henry James had said to Wharton:

"Oh, well, you see, I love Loti's books so, even when I don't like them." Quoted in "Henry James in His Letters," a review of *The Letters of Henry James*, ed. Percy Lubbock, in *Quarterly Review* (July 1920); reprinted in Wegener, *Edith Wharton*, 149.

79. Wharton, *A Backward Glance*, 856.
80. Rebecca Garden, "Sympathy, Disability, and the Nurse," 239.

Chapter 3. Bohemian Time

1. Curtis, "Editor's Easy Chair," 705.
2. Levin, *Bohemia in America, 1858–1920*, 135.
3. Gluck, *Popular Bohemia*, 18, 19.
4. Mizruchi, *The Rise of Multicultural America*, 5–6.
5. Levin, *Bohemia in America, 1858–1920*, 307.
6. Borus, "The Strange Career of American Bohemia," 377.
7. Christine Stansell, *City of Women*, 34, 169.
8. Elizabeth Freeman, *Time Binds*, xii.
9. Dimock, *Through Other Continents*, 127, 129.
10. Levin, *Bohemia in America, 1858–1920*, 165.
11. "A Girl in Bohemia," *Motion Picture News*, November 15, 1919, 3640.
12. "A Girl in Bohemia," *Variety*, November 7, 1919, in *Variety Film Reviews 1907–1920*, n.p.
13. "A Girl in Bohemia," *Motion Picture News*, November 15, 1919, 3640.
14. "The Girl from Bohemia," *Variety*, August 23, 1918.
15. Janvier's sketches use the names of paints, such as "Rose Madder," for the characters.
16. *The Yellow Girl*, directed by Edgar Keller (1916). Quotation transcribed from the print at George Eastman House, Rochester, New York.
17. Chauncey, *Gay New York*, 229.
18. Lewis, *Main Street*, 420.
19. Chauncey, *Gay New York*, 228; Jewell, "Willa Cather's Greenwich Village," 64.
20. *The Devil's Needle*, directed by Chester Withey (Kino Lorber, 2012). This print is of the 1923 version, the only one extant. Subsequent quotations are transcribed from this version and appear in the text.
21. *A Philistine in Bohemia*, directed by Edward H. Griffith (1920). Quotations appear in the print at George Eastman House, Rochester, New York.
22. "The Devil's Needle," *Motion Picture News*, August 16, 1916, 788.
23. "The Devil's Needle," in *Variety Film Reviews 1907–1920*, n.p.
24. Brownlow, *Behind the Mask of Innocence*, 98.
25. Ibid., 102.
26. Ibid., 100.
27. Zieger, *Inventing the Addict*, 136.
28. In *The Social Secretary*, Norma Talmadge plays Mayme, an attractive young woman who dresses as a frump to avoid sexual harassment and get a job as a social secretary with a wealthy family. After various plot complications, including some with a young Erich von Stroheim as "Adam Buzzard," a gossip reporter, Mayme reveals her true looks and marries

the son of the house. The existing print of the film is at George Eastman House, Rochester, New York.

29. Raper, *Without Shelter*, 51.

30. Glasgow, *The Woman Within*, 124, 197–98. Subsequent references are cited in the text.

31. For a discussion of Gertrude Christian Fosdick's Bohemian novel, see Donna Campbell, "A Forgotten Daughter of Bohemia."

32. Glasgow, *The Descendant*, 50. Subsequent references are cited in the text.

33. Raper, *Without Shelter*, 74.

34. Scheick, "Chambered Intimations," 8.

35. Chambers, *The King in Yellow*, 126.

36. Ibid., 142.

37. Glasgow, *Phases of an Inferior Planet*, 35, 51. Subsequent references are cited in the text.

38. Given the Aesthetic movement and Decadent movement overtones of the novel, the name "Bodley" may refer to John Lane and Elkin Matthews's Bodley Head Press, of which the most famous early product was *The Yellow Book*.

39. A similar dynamic occurs in *The Damnation of Theron Ware*, in which Theron Ware preaches his most powerful and persuasive sermons after he has lost his faith.

40. Glasgow had been indirectly compared with Frederic earlier in her career. In *The Woman Within*, Glasgow reports, "While I was [in Paris] a cabled message, from home, told me that Harper had eagerly accepted *The Descendant*, and were enthusiastic about it.... My name was not on the title page, and none of the firm had suspected that it was the work of a girl who had spent only two weeks in New York. One of their critics had insisted that it was an anonymous work by Harold Frederic" (121).

41. Goodman and Dawson, *Mary Austin and the American West*, 164; Mary Hunter Austin, *Earth Horizon*, 337.

42. In addition to her appropriation of Boyce's unusual first name, Austin was doubtless aware of the troubled marriage of Neith Boyce and Hutchins Hapgood. Hapgood sought to justify his professed belief in gender equality with his multiple infidelities by encouraging his wife to follow suit, something that brought her deep unhappiness, as evidenced in their coauthored play *Enemies* (1916). See Boyce, *The Modern World of Neith Boyce*.

43. Austin, *No. 26 Jayne Street*, 177. Subsequent references are cited in the text.

44. According to Goodman and Dawson, *Mary Austin and the American West*, Rittenhouse is based on General Dan Sickles, who before his Civil War career had been acquitted for shooting his wife's lover in 1859 and who lived in the flat below Mary Austin in 1912 (131).

45. Lee, *Willa Cather*, 161.

46. Sergeant, "Willa Cather," 77.

47. Rosowski, "Cather's Manifesto for 'Coming, Aphrodite,'" 54, 55.

48. See Michele Aina Barale, "Violations and Fatal Apertures"; Mary R. Ryder, "Looking for Love in All the Wrong Places"; Holly Messitt, "The Internal Gaze."

49. Willa Cather, "Coming, Aphrodite!," 357. Subsequent references are cited in the text.

50. Alice Hall Petry in "Caesar and the Artist in Willa Cather's 'Coming, Aphrodite!'" notes that Caesar shares both the name and the symbolic function of the bulldog in Mary Wilkins Freeman's "A New England Nun."

51. Jewett, *The Country of the Pointed Firs*, 417.
52. Barale, "Violations and Fatal Apertures," 262.
53. Rosowski, "Cather's Manifesto for 'Coming, Aphrodite,'" 54.
54. For an examination of the story's *Smart Set* publication, sexuality, and the issue of privacy, see Hamilton, "Breaking the Lock."
55. Lindemann, "Cather's 'Elastigirls,'" 195.
56. Rosowski, "Cather's Manifesto for 'Coming, Aphrodite'"; James Woodress, *Willa Cather*.
57. Charney and Schwartz, *Cinema and the Invention of Modern Life*, 5; Rabinovitz, *Electric Dreamland*.
58. Mayne, *The Woman at the Keyhole*, 158.
59. Ibid., 166.

Chapter 4. Red Kimonos and White Slavery

1. "Girl of the painted cohorts": Crane, *Maggie: A Girl of the Streets*, 70.
2. Account of the killing: Broderick, *Triumvirate*, 495; Uruburu, *American Eve*.
3. Thaw, too, would go on to have Hollywood connections after his release from Matteawan State Hospital. He sponsored Anita Page, a popular film star of the 1920s, during her first trip to Hollywood.
4. Nesbit, *Tragic Beauty*, 32, 50.
5. Ibid., 47, 70.
6. Ibid., 34.
7. Uruburu, *American Eve*, chapter 15.
8. A thorough account of the crime and trial can be found in Brandon, *Murder in the Adirondacks*. The trial transcripts from which some information was drawn for this section of the chapter are no longer available online.
9. Rosen, *The Lost Sisterhood*, 116.
10. Turner, "The Daughters of the Poor," 54, 56, 58.
11. Theodore Roosevelt's famous speech decrying "hyphenated Americans" is but one example of this definition. "America for Americans: Afternoon Speech of Theodore Roosevelt at St. Louis, May 31, 1916," Almanac of Theodore Roosevelt, http://www.theodore-roosevelt.com/images/research/txtspeeches/672.pdf.
12. Roe, *The Great War on White Slavery*, 248.
13. Rosen, *The Lost Sisterhood*, 119.
14. Hobson, *Uneasy Virtue*, 142–43.
15. *Madeleine: An Autobiography*, 320.
16. Kimball, *Nell Kimball*, 192, 250.
17. Stanford, *The Lady of the House*, 95.
18. Donovan, *White Slave Crusades*, 20.
19. Hobson, *Uneasy Virtue*, 144.
20. Johnson, *Sisters in Sin*, 11.
21. According to Katie N. Johnson, "[T]he *prostitute fatale* represents the deadly part of

pleasure, the evil side of the flower . . . the dangerous potential of unchecked female sexuality" (168).

22. Amanda Anderson, *Tainted Souls and Painted Faces*, 16.
23. Kimball, *Nell Kimball*, 205; Josie Washburn, *The Underworld Sewer*, 25.
24. Bauman, *Wasted Lives*, 39.
25. Addams, *A New Conscience and an Ancient Evil*, 136.
26. Wooster, *The Autobiography of a Magdalen*, 34.
27. "Review: *The Inside of the White Slave Traffic*."
28. Roe, *The Great War on White Slavery*, 29.
29. Josie Washburn, *The Underworld Sewer*, 213.
30. Wooster, *The Autobiography of a Magdalen*, n.p.
31. For accounts of the film and its reception, see Stamp, *Movie-Struck Girls*; Kevin Brownlow, *Behind the Mask of Innocence*.
32. Roe, *The Great War on White Slavery*, 96.
33. Pinzer, *The Maimie Papers*, 174–75.
34. Kreymborg, *Edna*, 10, 15. Subsequent references are cited in the text.
35. Carlisle, "Introduction," in *Madeleine: An Autobiography*, vi–vii.
36. Sedgwick, *The Coherence of Gothic Conventions*, 12, 13. For a comprehensive overview of theories of the Gothic, see Elbert and Marshall's introduction to *Transnational Gothic*.
37. In tracing the connection between the figure of the vampire and governmental corruption, Marilyn Michaud links "the consumptive and oppressive habits of the vampire" to "the eighteenth-century fear of corruption, tyranny, and degeneration" (*Republicanism and the American Gothic*, 61). Later in the Progressive Era, as a result of the popularity of the destructive temptress played by Theda Bara in the film *A Fool There Was* (1915), based on Rudyard Kipling's poem "The Vampire" and Edward Burne-Jones's painting of the same name, the term would acquire its secondary meaning of a sexually active and predatory female who lures men to their doom.
38. Quoted in John, *Elizabeth Robins*, 185.
39. John, *Elizabeth Robins*, 185.
40. Robins, *My Little Sister*, 115. Subsequent references are cited in the text.
41. Robins's biographer Angela V. John speculates that this hints at incestuous sexual abuse, which Robins had learned was a primary factor in many young women's descent into prostitution (John, *Elizabeth Robins*, 188).
42. Poe, "The Fall of the House of Usher," 317.
43. Hite, "The Public Woman and the Modernist Turn," 528.
44. Norris, "The Third Circle," 103. Subsequent references are cited in the text.
45. Levin, *Bohemia in America, 1858–1920*, 311; Keely, "Sexual Slavery in San Francisco's Chinatown."
46. Miriam Michelson, "Strangling Hands upon a Nation's Throat," *San Francisco Call*, September 30, 1897, 1.
47. "Story of a Reporterette and Some Others," *San Francisco Call*, October 29, 1905.
48. Michelson, *A Yellow Journalist*, 101. Subsequent references are cited in the text.
49. Baker, *The Rose Door*, 25. Subsequent references are cited in the text.

50. Rideout, *The Radical Novel in the United States, 1900–1954*, 68.

51. Virginia Brooks, *My Battles with Vice*, 83, 85.

52. *Little Lost Sister* is a "drama in 4 acts," according to the Library of Congress Catalog of Copyright entries. The authors are listed as Arthur James Pegler and Edward A. Rose, but it was copyrighted on September 12, 1913, by Virginia Brooks Washburne and Robert E. Ricksen, Chicago, suggesting that Pegler and Rose's version came first.

53. Pegler, "Fair Enough," 4.

54. Charles Washburn, "On *Little Lost Sister*," *New York Times*, November 19, 1939, x2.

55. "News from the Dailies," *Variety*, October 5, 1917, 16. The notice in its entirety reads as follows: "Virginia Brooks Washburn, author of 'Little Lost Sister,' is defendant in a divorce suit brought by her husband, Charles M. Washburne, formerly connected with a vaudeville booking office. Mr. Washburne charges desertion." To add to the confusion, Washburn is spelled variously with an "e" and without one.

56. Washburn, *Come into My Parlor*, 241. Subsequent references are cited in the text.

57. "The Play," *New York Times*, December 2, 1939, 23.

58. Although "dictograph" is the preferred generic term, the novel uses "dictagraph," as do other contemporary sources.

59. Diffee, "Sex and the City," 414.

60. Gunning, "From the Kaleidoscope to the X-Ray"; Stamp, *Movie-Struck Girls*.

Chapter 5. Where Are My Children?

1. Wharton, *Summer*, 229. Subsequent references are cited in the text.

2. Hansen, *Babel and Babylon*, 108, 118. Recent challenges to Hansen's thesis include Maltby, Stokes, and Allen, *Going to the Movies*.

3. Vorse, "Some Picture Show Audiences," 71, 72, 74.

4. For an account of women audiences and their responses to film and of Jane Addams's Hull House nickelodeon, see Rabinovitz, *For the Love of Pleasure*.

5. Brownlow, *Behind the Mask of Innocence*, 303.

6. Wonham, *Playing the Races*, 36.

7. In Mark Twain's "Jim Smiley and His Jumping Frog," for example, Simon Wheeler describes the buckshot-filled frog as "Dan'l give a heave, and hysted up his shoulders—so—like a Frenchman" (*Collected Tales, Sketches, Speeches and Essays, 1852–1890*, 176).

8. For an analysis of Guy-Blaché's feminist perspective, see Alison McMahan, *Alice Guy Blaché*; Karen Ward Mahar, *Women Filmmakers in Early Hollywood*.

9. Although Ivan and the others shown in these films were Americans as well, of course, I use the term "American" as it was used in the films to designate a U.S.-born person of European ancestry.

10. Both segments were shot in the United States: the Venice, Italy, segment in Venice, California, and the New York City sequences in San Francisco or Los Angeles (accounts vary on this point). Brownlow asserts that film was "used to guide Francis Ford Coppola in re-creating turn-of-the-century New York for *The Godfather, Part II*" (Brownlow, *Behind the Mask of Innocence*, 319).

11. Wald, *Contagious*, 83.

12. C. Gardner Sullivan's scenario was originally titled *The Dago*. Beban, who was starring in *The Sign of the Rose* on Broadway and, like most stage actors, considered film an inferior medium, insisted that the title be changed, in part so that it could be "a special and not a cheap program picture" (Brownlow, *Behind the Mask of Innocence*, 319).

13. Haenni, *The Immigrant Scene*, 198.

14. Gaines, *Fire and Desire*, 177.

15. Goldsby, *A Spectacular Secret*, 221, 224, 228.

16. Gerstner, *Manly Arts*, 108.

17. Mitchell, *Living with Lynching*, 82.

18. The January 18, 1919, issue, with cover photo and cover story "Theodore Roosevelt—American," is the probable source for this image.

19. Kaplan, *The Anarchy of Empire in the Making of U.S. Culture*, 163.

20. Hull, introduction to *The Works of Alice Dunbar-Nelson*, xxxviii.

21. Strychacz, "You ... Could Never Be Mistaken," 79.

22. Dunbar-Nelson, "Tony's Wife," 22, 29.

23. Dunbar-Nelson, "Miss Tillman's Protégé," 101. Subsequent references are cited in the text.

24. Dunbar-Nelson, "Witness for the Defense," 119. Subsequent references are cited in the text.

25. Sui Sin Far, "In the Land of the Free," 95. Subsequent references are cited in the text.

26. Sui Sin Far, "Mrs. Spring Fragrance," 21.

27. Eby, "Beyond Protest," 33.

28. Wesling, "The Opacity of Everyday Life," 118; Mullen, "Object Lessons."

29. Pizer, "American Naturalism in Its 'Perfected' State," 165.

30. Ann Petry, *The Street*, 323. Subsequent references are cited in the text.

31. Pryse, "Pattern against the Sky"; Eby, "Beyond Protest," 34.

32. Howells replied to a reader's assertion that Gerhart Hauptmann's industrial play *The Weavers* was superior by noting that "[m]isery for misery, the average mind prefers that which is foreign" (Howells, *Criticism and Fiction, and Other Essays*, 343); Hicks, *The Great Tradition*, 64.

33. Glasser, *In a Closet Hidden*, 185.

34. Mary Eleanor Wilkins Freeman, *The Portion of Labor*, 19. Subsequent references are cited in the text.

35. Dreiser, *The Financier*, 8.

36. "Determinism rules": Lehan, *Realism and Naturalism*, 138.

37. Quoted in Dale M. Bauer, *Edith Wharton's Brave New Politics*, 69.

38. For information on film adaptations of Wharton's works, see Boswell, *Edith Wharton on Film*; Cahir, "Wharton and the Age of Film."

39. For readings of the visual in *Bunner Sisters*, see Solan, "Striking Stereopticon Views"; Totten, "Objects Long Preserved."

40. Wharton, *Bunner Sisters*, 310, 311. Subsequent references are cited in the text.

41. For readings of *Bunner Sisters* as naturalism, see Fleissner, "The Biological Clock"; Kornasky, "On 'Listen[ing] to Spectres Too'"; Campbell, *Resisting Regionalism*.

42. Wharton, "Letter to Bernard Berenson, 4 September 1917," 398.

43. In her discussion of birth control in *Summer*, Jennifer Haytock states that *Summer* is "set in the late nineteenth century," but the picture palace references, possibly a deliberate anachronism on Wharton's part, place the date as early in the twentieth (Haytock, *Edith Wharton and the Conversations of Literary Modernism*, 57).

44. According to Kathryn H. Fuller-Seeley, "Massachusetts was reported to have a number of church shows, but they were rarely found across the rest of New England" (Fuller-Seeley, *At the Picture Show*, 88). For more on the transition in movie venues and audiences, see Stamp, *Movie-Struck Girls*; Maltby, Stokes, and Allen, *Going to the Movies*; Keil and Stamp, *American Cinema's Transitional Era*; Stokes and Maltby, *American Movie Audiences*.

45. Wharton, *The House of Mirth*, 526. Subsequent references are cited in the text.

46. Stamp, *Movie-Struck Girls*, 275.

47. The film shares the title but bears no other resemblance to Wharton's novel *The Valley of Decision* (1902).

48. Stamp, *Movie-Struck Girls*, 283.

49. Quoted in Lant and Periz, *Red Velvet Seat*, 549.

50. Stopes, "Where Are My Children?," 317.

51. Bauer, *Edith Wharton's Brave New Politics*, 43.

52. Simmons, "Where Are My Children?," 79.

53. Tone, *Devices and Desires*, 170–71.

54. Skillern, "Becoming a 'Good Girl,'" 118.

55. Kassanoff, *Edith Wharton and the Politics of Race*, 149.

Chapter 6. "Manure Widows" and Middlebrow Fiction

1. Parker, "Re-Enter Miss Hurst, Followed by Mr. Tarkington," 483, 485, 486.

2. Parker, "The Short Story, through a Couple of the Ages," 472.

3. Decker, *Made in America*, 28.

4. Parker, "The Short Story, through a Couple of the Ages," 474.

5. Ibid.

6. Fitzgerald, *A Life in Letters*, 113. Subsequent references are cited in the text.

7. Huyssen, *After the Great Divide*.

8. Botshon and Goldsmith, Introduction to *Middlebrow Moderns*, 3.

9. Humble, "Sitting Forward or Sitting Back," 46.

10. Casey, "Middlebrow Reading and Undergraduate Teaching," 29.

11. Homestead, "Middlebrow Readers and Pioneer Heroines," 76, 83.

12. Lewis, *Main Street*, 40. Subsequent references are cited in the text.

13. An example from the theater would be *Rube and His Ma: A Merry Rural Comedy in Three Acts*, by William and Josephine Giles (1908).

14. Whitfield, "An Evaluation of Mary Pickford's Youngest Characters," 31.

15. Karl Brown's *Stark Love* (Paramount, 1927) was shot on location in Appalachia using local people as actors. For discussions of the film, see J. W. Williamson, *Hillbillyland: What the Movies Did to the Mountains and What the Mountains Did to the Movies*; Kenaga, "America Is Developing a Distinct Type of Man."

16. Keil, "To Here from Modernity," 57. Keil argues against the "modernity thesis," which suggests that modernity itself becomes the subject matter of films. Instead, "films may not have contributed to the formation of a modern subject by bombarding her or him with sensorial overload as much as they revisited the ephiphenomena of modernity and duplicated them on the screen. Trains, telegraphs, and a host of other modern inventions populate films of the period so extensively that watching them plunges the viewer into the imagery of modernity in an intensified fashion" (59). What modernity theorists see as an aesthetic choice for representing modernity through technology, speed, and sensory overload, in other words, Keil views as an artifact of the viewing practices of occasional moviegoers such as "cultural commentators ... responding to the novelty of cinema" rather than to the "weekly deluge of repetitive narratives reviewers had to contend with" (58).

17. Howells, *Heroines of Fiction*, 227.

18. Quoted in Jacobs, *The Decline of Sentiment*, 49.

19. Fox, *The Fox Plan of Photoplay Writing*, 151.

20. Jennifer A. Williamson, *Twentieth-Century Sentimentalism*, 9.

21. Francke, *Script Girls*, 6. In contrast, the Writers Guild of America reports that in 2013 women wrote 15 percent of films and 28 percent of television shows—and that figure represents an increase over that of previous years. "Turning Missed Opportunities into Realized Ones: The 2014 Hollywood Writers Report," Writers Guild of America, West, http://www.wga.org/uploadedFiles/who_we_are/hwr14execsum.pdf.

22. According to Joanne Bernardi, "By 1915 there were sixty-one screenwriting schools throughout the United States" (*Writing in Light*, 102).

23. Emerson and Loos, *Breaking into the Movies*, 6.

24. Loos reports in "Working with D. W. Griffith," a three-part essay published in the 1931 pressbook of Griffith's *The Struggle*: "When I was a child of thirteen I had written my very first motion picture, and it had been directed by Mr. Griffith" (n.p.). Born in 1888, Loos was actually twenty-two at the time.

25. Emerson and Loos, *How to Write for the Movies*, 25.

26. Ferber, *A Peculiar Treasure*, 276.

27. Ferber, *So Big*, 161. Subsequent references are cited in the text.

28. Casey, *A New Heartland*, 101.

29. Ferber, *A Peculiar Treasure*, 339.

30. Gilbert, *Ferber*, 312. For an examination of Ferber's sharp sentiment and racial politics in *Show Boat* and *Cimarron*, see Harrison-Kahan, *The White Negress*; Campbell, "Written with a Hard and Ruthless Purpose"; Kenaga, "Edna Ferber's *Cimarron*, Cultural Authority, and 1920s Western Historical Narratives"; Zink, "Peyote in the Kitchen"; McGraw, *Edna Ferber's America*; Berlant, "Pax Americana."

31. Dallas O'Mara is probably based on the well-known commercial artist Neysa McMein (1888–1949), who, like Ferber, was a member of the Algonquin Roundtable.

32. Aldrich, *A Lantern in Her Hand*, 289. Subsequent references are cited in the text.

33. Knight, "I Try to Make the Reader Feel," 288.

34. Homestead, "Middlebrow Readers and Pioneer Heroines," 85.

35. Pizer, "American Naturalism in Its 'Perfected' State," 165.

36. Anna Marcet Haldeman-Julius was the niece of Jane Addams. For more about the relationship, see Joslin, *Jane Addams, a Writer's Life*.

37. Haldeman-Julius and Haldeman-Julius, *Dust*, 227. Subsequent references are cited in the text.

38. Ruth Suckow, *Country People*, 13. Subsequent references are cited in the text.

39. For brief discussions of *Barren Ground* and naturalism, see Campbell, "Where are the ladies?"; Brennan, "American Literary Naturalism and Psychology."

40. Cather, *O Pioneers!*, 73. Subsequent references are cited in the text.

41. Wiesenthal, "Female Sexuality in Willa Cather's *O Pioneers!*," 408, 409.

42. Charlotte Margolis Goodman, afterword to *Weeds*, 365.

43. Kelley, *Weeds*, 21. Subsequent references are cited in the text.

44. Casey, "Agrarian Landscapes, the Depression, and Women's Progressive Fiction," 107, 108, 109.

45. Diedrich, *Cornelia James Cannon and the Future American Race*, 5.

46. Cannon, *Red Rust*, 27. Subsequent references are cited in the text.

47. Diedrich, *Cornelia James Cannon and the Future American Race*, 173, 174.

48. Ibid., 165.

49. Inness, "Good Enough for a Man or a Dog."

50. Kollin, "Race, Labor, and the Gothic Western."

51. Affron, *Lillian Gish*, 229.

52. Ibid., 139.

Chapter 7. Waste, Hoarding, and Secrets

1. Stein, *The Autobiography of Alice B. Toklas*, 40.

2. Ibid., 60.

3. DeKoven, *A Different Language*, 27.

4. On *Q.E.D.* and "Melanctha," see DeKoven, *A Different Language*.

5. Walker, "Three Lives," 339.

6. Huyssen, *After the Great Divide*, 50.

7. Toomer, *Cane*, 4.

8. Papke, "Naturalism and Commodity Culture," 292.

9. Norris, *Vandover and the Brute*, 258. Subsequent references are cited in the text.

10. Kristeva, *Powers of Horror*, 53, 64, 69.

11. Gleason, "The Most Radical View of the Whole Subject," 60, 64.

12. Stewart, *On Longing*, 105.

13. Stallybrass and White, *The Politics and Poetics of Transgression*, 161.

14. According to Marianne DeKoven, "Stein frequently uses the lower case for nationality and ethnicity, signifying that it has no more weight or significance than other personal characteristics" (Stein, *Three Lives* and *Q.E.D.*, 8n8).

15. Gale, *Miss Lulu Bett*, 13. Subsequent references are cited in the text.

16. Stansell, *City of Women*, 156.

17. Ousley, "The Business of Housekeeping," 143.

18. Stansell, *City of Women*, 161.
19. Kathleen Brown, *Foul Bodies*, 283.
20. Strasser, *Waste and Want*, 49.
21. McCuskey, "Not at Home," 423.
22. Wharton, "Letter to William Crary Brownell," 91.
23. Bataille, *The Accursed Share*, 123, 121.
24. Wharton, *A Backward Glance*, 207.
25. Wagner-Martin, "Writing the Early Novels," 235.
26. Stein, *Three Lives and Q.E.D.*, 15. Subsequent references are cited in the text.
27. Chicago Vice Commission and American Vigilance Association, *The Social Evil in Chicago*, 225.
28. Gus and Christine Reinmueller in Aldrich's *A Lantern in Her Hand* share this characteristic of tolerating dirt (Christine's hair is always greasy, for example) and valuing money only for the sake of the land that it will buy rather than the experiences it will bring. See chapter 6.
29. Watts, *The Rise of Jennie Cushing*, 15.
30. Addams, *A New Conscience and an Ancient Evil*, 121.
31. Larsen, *Quicksand*, 54. Subsequent references are cited in the text.
32. Doyle, *Freedom's Empire*, 551; Sherrard-Johnson, "A Plea for Color"; DeFalco, "Jungle Creatures and Dancing Apes."
33. On Larsen's use of color and commodities to signify Helga's plight, see Goldsmith, "Shopping to Pass, Passing to Shop"; Simone Weil Davis, *Living up to the Ads*; Lutes, "Making up Race."
34. Brooks, *The Melodramatic Imagination*, 11. Subsequent references are cited in the text.
35. Norris, "Zola as a Romantic Writer," 1107.
36. Newlin, "The Naturalistic Imagination and the Aesthetics of Excess," 15.
37. Singer, *Melodrama and Modernity*, 39, 40.
38. Ngai, *Ugly Feelings*.
39. Goldsmith, "Shopping to Pass, Passing to Shop," 268.
40. For more information on Micheaux, see Bowser, Gaines, and Musser, *Oscar Micheaux and His Circle*.
41. For more on Delsartian gestures in early film, see Jacobs, *The Decline of Sentiment*.
42. Macharia, "Queering Helga Crane," 268.
43. Scura and Jones, *Evelyn Scott*, xiv, xv, xvii.
44. Quoted in D. A. Callard, *Pretty Good for a Woman*, 60.
45. Quoted in Scott, *Background in Tennessee*, x.
46. Lawrence, *The Letters of D. H. Lawrence*, 733, 734.
47. See Scura, afterword to *Escapade*, for a discussion of the censored items.
48. Van Doren, *Contemporary American Novelists, 1900–1920*, 176.
49. Callard, *Pretty Good for a Woman*, 61.
50. Scott, *Background in Tennessee*, 285–86.
51. Scott, *The Narrow House*, 9. Subsequent references are cited in the text.
52. Tyrer, "A Bird Alive in a Snake's Body," 52.

53. Anderson, *Winesburg, Ohio*, 119.
54. Scott, *Escapade*, 91, 93.
55. Kroeger, *Fannie*, xiii, 77.
56. Blake, "Harper's Bookshelf," n.p.
57. Farrar, "Lummox," 24.
58. "Lummox," *Bookman*, 320.
59. Quoted in Kroeger, *Fannie*, 92.
60. "[Review of *Lummox*]," *New York Times*, 14 October 1923, BR5.
61. Parker, "Re-Enter Miss Hurst, Followed by Mr. Tarkington," 485.
62. Hurst, *Lummox*, 1. Subsequent references are cited in the text.
63. Harrison-Kahan, *The White Negress*, 102.
64. Phyllis Palmer (*Domesticity and Dirt*, 36) writes that Bertha is "essentially raped" by Rollo. Although the power differential between master and servant woman lends credence to this view, Bertha's position above Rollo, her moving down into his arms, and her love for him before and during their relationship suggest that the act may be consensual.
65. Bertha's perspective anticipates Elmer Rice's 1929 play *Street Scene*, in which the action takes place in front of an impoverished New York apartment house.
66. Bauer, *Sex Expression and American Women Writers, 1860–1940*, 75.
67. Atherton's *Black Oxen* presents an older woman who, rejuvenated through surgery in Europe, fascinates a horde of younger beaux. See Prebel, "Engineering Womanhood"; Atherton, *Black Oxen*. For an account of how Mary Wilkins Freeman derailed the composite novel *The Whole Family* by portraying a flirtatious "old maid aunt," see Howard, *Publishing the Family*; Campbell, "Howells' Untrustworthy Realist." On Wharton's older women, see Horner and Beer, *Edith Wharton*.
68. William Lyon Phelps, "As Mrs. Wharton Sees Us," 1.
69. Gale, "The Novel of Tomorrow," 72.
70. Although his more famous brother Cecil capitalized his surname ("DeMille"), William used "deMille." See Eyman, *Empire of Dreams*, 15.
71. "Review: *Miss Lulu Bett*," *Variety*, December 23, 1921, 35.
72. *Lummox* exists in a single nitrate print in the archives of the British Film Institute. See Collections Search, British Film Institute, http://collections-search.bfi.org.uk/web/Details/ChoiceFilmWorks/150037092.
73. Gale, *Miss Lulu Bett*, 50.
74. Gale, "Miss Lulu Bett," in Barlow, *Plays by American Women, 1900–1930*, 104.
75. Williams, *Not in Sisterhood*, 112.
76. Gale, "Miss Lulu Bett," in Barlow, *Plays by American Women, 1900–1930*, 147, 149.
77. Ackerman, "Infelicities of Form in Zona Gale's *Miss Lulu Bett*," 65.
78. Gale, "The Novel of Tomorrow," 61.
79. Williams, *Not in Sisterhood*, 117.
80. Quoted in Simonson, *Zona Gale*, 85.
81. Derleth, *Still Small Voice*, 146.
82. Quoted in Williams, *Not in Sisterhood*, 117.
83. *Miss Lulu Bett* was being considered for the Pulitzer Prize for the novel, which eventu-

ally went to Edith Wharton's *Age of Innocence* despite strong sentiment for Sinclair Lewis's *Main Street*. Hamlin Garland, chair of the prize committee and a friend of Gale's, did not feel it sufficient for the prize, calling it "very slight hardly more than a short story" but for all that "amazingly deft," with "a kind of *short-handing* of diction.... Its content is not large but is juicy." This was a considerable compliment given that he found Wharton's prizewinning work, in contrast, "well done of course but . . . rather arid" (Garland, *Selected Letters of Hamlin Garland*, 284, 285).

84. Ibid., 291.

85. Atlas, "From Novel to Play," 38.

86. Wilson, twenty-seven years old when she appeared in *Miss Lulu Bett*, had already made fifty-four movies and often portrayed complex, intelligent characters with an inner beauty. She would go on to star as Daisy Buchanan in the now-lost 1926 version of *The Great Gatsby*. Even the *New York Times*, which called the work of the other actors "satisfactory," praised Wilson's avoidance of "the easy way of sentimental appeal" for the more difficult task of putting "a true character on the screen" and "becoming Lulu Bett" ("Screen: Two Current Pictures").

87. June Mathis helped to turn a young extra into the heartthrob Rudolph Valentino, and Bess Meredyth's influence extended well into the sound era through nightly story conferences with her husband, Michael Curtiz, director of *Casablanca* (1942) and a host of Warner Brothers hits throughout the 1940s.

88. "Screen: Two Current Pictures," 65.

89. Beauchamp, *Without Lying Down*, 355.

90. Quotations are transcribed from deMille, *Miss Lulu Bett*.

91. Rhoades, "Maid or Writer?"

WORKS CITED

Ackerman, Alan. "Infelicities of Form in Zona Gale's *Miss Lulu Bett*." *Journal of American Drama and Theatre* 16, no. 1 (2004): 50–68.
Addams, Jane. *A New Conscience and an Ancient Evil*. New York: Macmillan, 1912.
Affron, Charles. *Lillian Gish: Her Legend, Her Life*. New York: Scribner, 2001.
Alcott, Louisa May. *Little Women or Meg, Jo, Beth, and Amy*. Edited by Anne K. Phillips and Gregory Eiselein. New York: W. W. Norton, 2004.
Aldrich, Bess Streeter. *A Lantern in Her Hand*. New York: Grosset and Dunlap, 1928.
Ammons, Elizabeth. "Expanding the Canon of American Realism." In *Documents of American Realism and Naturalism*, edited by Donald Pizer, 435–52. Carbondale: Southern Illinois University Press, 1998.
Anderson, Amanda. *Tainted Souls and Painted Faces: The Rhetoric of Fallenness in Victorian Culture*. Ithaca: Cornell University Press, 1993.
Anderson, Maureen. "Unraveling the Southern Pastoral Tradition: A New Look at Kate Chopin's *At Fault*." *Southern Literary Journal* 34, no. 1 (2001): 1–13.
Anderson, Sherwood. *Winesburg, Ohio*. Edited by John H. Ferres. New York: Viking Press, 1966.
Armstrong, Nancy. *Fiction in the Age of Photography: The Legacy of British Realism*. Cambridge, Mass.: Harvard University Press, 2002.
Arner, Robert D. "Landscape Symbolism in Kate Chopin's *At Fault*." *Louisiana Studies* 9 (1970): 142–53.
Atherton, Gertrude Franklin Horn. *Black Oxen*. Edited and introduced by Melanie Dawson. Peterborough, Ont.: Broadview Press, 2012.
Atlas, Marilyn Judith. "From Novel to Play: Zona Gale and the Marriage Plot in Three Versions of *Miss Lulu Bett*." *Midwestern Miscellany* 30 (2002): 35–43.
Auchincloss, Louis. *Edith Wharton, a Woman in Her Time*. New York: Viking Press, 1971.
Auerbach, Jonathan. *Body Shots: Early Cinema's Incarnations*. Berkeley: University of California Press, 2007.
Austin, Mary Hunter. *Earth Horizon: An Autobiography*. Albuquerque: University of New Mexico Press, 1991.

———. *No. 26 Jayne Street*. Boston: Houghton Mifflin, 1920.
An Authentic History of the Lawrence Calamity. Boston: John J. Dyer, 1860.
Baker, Estelle. *The Rose Door*. Chicago: C. H. Kerr, 1911.
Barale, Michele Aina. "Violations and Fatal Apertures: Cather's 'Heathenish' Aesthetics." In *Violence, the Arts, and Willa Cather*, edited by Joseph R. Urgo and Merrill Maguire Skaggs, 261–72. Madison, N.J.: Fairleigh Dickinson University Press, 2007.
Barker, Reginald, dir. *The Italian* (1915). DVD. In *Perils of the New Land: Films of the Immigrant Experience (1910–1915)*. Kino Lorber, 2008.
Bashford, Herbert. "The Literary Development of the Far Northwest." *Overland Monthly* 196, no. 33 (April 1899): 316–20.
Bataille, Georges. *The Accursed Share: An Essay on General Economy*. New York: Zone Books, 1988.
Bauer, Dale M. *Edith Wharton's Brave New Politics*. Madison: University of Wisconsin Press, 1994.
———. *Sex Expression and American Women Writers, 1860–1940*. Chapel Hill: University of North Carolina Press, 2009.
Bauman, Zygmunt. *Wasted Lives: Modernity and Its Outcasts*. N.p.: Polity, 2003.
Beal, Frank, dir. *The Inside of the White Slave Traffic* (1913). DVD. In *The Devil's Needle and Other Tales of Vice and Redemption*. Kino Lorber, 2012.
Beauchamp, Cari. *Without Lying Down: Frances Marion and the Powerful Women of Early Hollywood*. New York: Scribner, 1997.
Beer, Janet. *Kate Chopin, Edith Wharton and Charlotte Perkins Gilman: Studies in Short Fiction*. New York: St. Martin's, 1997.
Belletti, Valeria. *Adventures of a Hollywood Secretary: Her Private Letters from inside the Studios of the 1920s*. Edited by Cari Beauchamp. Berkeley: University of California Press, 2006.
Bender, Bert. *The Descent of Love: Darwin and the Theory of Sexual Selection in American Fiction, 1871–1926*. Philadelphia: University of Pennsylvania Press, 1996.
———. *Evolution and "the Sex Problem": American Narratives during the Eclipse of Darwinism*. Kent, Ohio: Kent State University Press, 2004.
Bentley, Nancy. *The Ethnography of Manners: Hawthorne, James, Wharton*. Cambridge: Cambridge University Press, 1995.
Bergman, Jill. "'Oh the Poor Women!' Elizabeth Stuart Phelps's Motherly Benevolence." In *Our Sisters' Keepers: Nineteeth-Century Benevolence Literature by American Women*, edited by Jill Bergman and Debra Bernardi, 190–212. Tuscaloosa: University of Alabama Press, 2005.
Bergman, Jill, and Debra Bernardi, eds. *Our Sisters' Keepers: Nineteenth-Century Benevolence Literature by American Women*. Tuscaloosa: University of Alabama Press, 2005.
Berlant, Lauren. "Pax Americana: The Case of *Show Boat*." In *Cultural Institutions of the Novel*, edited by Deidre Lynch and William B. Warner, 399–422. Durham: Duke University Press, 1996.
Bernardi, Joanne. *Writing in Light: The Silent Scenario and the Japanese Pure Film Movement*. Detroit: Wayne State University Press, 2001.

Birnbaum, Michele A. "'Alien Hands': Kate Chopin and the Colonization of Race." *American Literature: A Journal of Literary History, Criticism, and Bibliography* 66, no. 2 (1994): 301–23.

Blake, Elliott. "Harper's Bookshelf." *Harper's Magazine (Advertiser)*, November 1914, n.p.

Borus, Daniel H. "The Strange Career of American Bohemia." *American Literary History* 14, no. 2 (2002): 376–88.

Boswell, Parley Ann. *Edith Wharton on Film*. Carbondale: Southern Illinois University Press, 2007.

Botshon, Lisa, and Meredith Goldsmith. Introduction to *Middlebrow Moderns: Popular American Women Writers of the 1920s*, edited by Lisa Botshon and Meredith Goldsmith, 3–21. Boston: Northeastern University Press, 2003.

Bowser, Pearl, Jane Gaines, and Charles Musser, eds. *Oscar Micheaux and His Circle: African-American Filmmaking and Race Cinema of the Silent Era*. Bloomington: Indiana University Press, 2001.

Boyce, Neith. *The Modern World of Neith Boyce: Autobiography and Diaries*. Edited by Carol DeBoer-Langworthy. Albuquerque: University of New Mexico Press, 2003.

Boyd, Anne E. *Writing for Immortality: Women and the Emergence of High Literary Culture in America*. Baltimore: Johns Hopkins University Press, 2004.

Brandon, Craig. *Murder in the Adirondacks: "An American Tragedy" Revisited*. Utica, N.Y.: North Country Books, 1986.

Brennan, Stephen. "American Literary Naturalism and Psychology." In *The Oxford Handbook of American Literary Naturalism*, edited by Keith Newlin, 183–202. Oxford: Oxford University Press, 2011.

Brennan, Teresa. *The Transmission of Affect*. Ithaca: Cornell University Press, 2004.

Bridgman, Richard. *Dark Thoreau*. Lincoln: University of Nebraska Press, 1982.

Broderick, Mosette Glaser. *Triumvirate: McKim, Mead and White: Art, Architecture, Scandal and Class in America's Gilded Age*. New York: Alfred A. Knopf, 2010.

Brooks, Peter. *The Melodramatic Imagination: Balzac, Henry James, Melodrama, and the Mode of Excess*. New Haven: Yale University Press, 1995.

———. *Realist Vision*. New Haven: Yale University Press, 2005.

Brooks, Virginia. *Little Lost Sister*. Chicago: Gazzolo and Ricksen, 1914.

———. *My Battles with Vice*. New York: Macaulay, 1915.

Brown, Bill. *The Material Unconscious: American Amusement, Stephen Crane, and the Economies of Play*. Cambridge, Mass.: Harvard University Press, 1996.

———. *A Sense of Things: The Object Matter of American Literature*. Chicago: University of Chicago Press, 2003.

———. "Thing Theory." *Critical Inquiry* 28, no. 1 (2001): 1–21.

Brown, Kathleen M. *Foul Bodies: Cleanliness in Early America*. New Haven: Yale University Press, 2009.

Brownlow, Kevin. *Behind the Mask of Innocence*. Berkeley: University of California Press, 1992.

Burrows, Stuart. *A Familiar Strangeness: American Fiction and the Language of Photography, 1839–1945*. Athens: University of Georgia Press, 2008.

Cahir, Linda Costanzo. "Wharton and the Age of Film." In *A Historical Guide to Edith Wharton*, edited by Carol J. Singley, 211–28. Oxford: Oxford University Press, 2003.

Callard, D. A. *"Pretty Good for a Woman": The Enigmas of Evelyn Scott*. New York: W. W. Norton, 1985.

Campbell, Donna. "American Literary Naturalism: Critical Perspectives." *Literature Compass* 8, no. 8 (2011): 499–513.

———. "A Forgotten Daughter of Bohemia: Gertrude Christian Fosdick's *Out of Bohemia* and the Artists' Novel of the 1890s." *Legacy: A Journal of American Women Writers* 25, no. 2 (2008): 275–85.

———. "Howells's Untrustworthy Realist: Mary E. Wilkins Freeman." *American Literary Realism* 38, no. 2 (Winter 2006): 115–31.

———. *Resisting Regionalism: Gender and Naturalism in American Fiction, 1885–1915*. Athens: Ohio University Press, 1997.

———. "'Where are the ladies?' Wharton, Glasgow, and American Women Naturalists." *Studies in American Naturalism* 1, no. 1–2 (2006): 152–69.

———. "Women Writers and Naturalism." In *The Oxford Handbook of American Literary Naturalism*, edited by Keith Newlin, 223–40. Oxford: Oxford University Press, 2011.

———. "'Written with a Hard and Ruthless Purpose': Rose Wilder Lane, Edna Ferber, and Middlebrow Regional Fiction." In *Middlebrow Moderns: Popular American Women Writers of the 1920s*, edited by Lisa Botshon and Meredith Goldsmith, 25–44. Boston: Northeastern University Press, 2003.

Cannon, Cornelia James. *Red Rust*. Boston: Little, Brown, 1928.

Carlin, Deborah. "To Form a More Imperfect Union: Gender, Tradition, and the Text in Wharton's *The Fruit of the Tree*." In *Edith Wharton: New Critical Essays*, edited by Alfred Bendixen and Annette Zilversmit, 57–77. New York: Garland, 1992.

Carlisle, Marcia. Introduction to *Madeleine: An Autobiography*, v–xxxii. New York: Persea Books, 1986.

Cartwright, Lisa. *Screening the Body: Tracing Medicine's Visual Culture*. Minneapolis: University of Minnesota Press, 1997.

Casey, Janet Galligani. "Agrarian Landscapes, the Depression, and Women's Progressive Fiction." In *The Novel and the American Left: Critical Essays on Depression-Era Fiction*, edited by Janet Galligani Casey, 96–117. Iowa City: University of Iowa Press, 2004.

———. "Middlebrow Reading and Undergraduate Teaching: The Place of the Middlebrow in the Academy." In *Middlebrow Literary Cultures: The Battle of the Brows, 1920–1960*, edited by Erica Brown, Mary Grover and Faye Hammill, 25–36. New York: Palgrave Macmillan, 2012.

———. *A New Heartland: Women, Modernity, and the Agrarian Ideal in America*. Oxford: Oxford University Press, 2009.

Cather, Willa. "Coming, Aphrodite!" In *Willa Cather: Stories, Poems, and Other Writings*, edited by Sharon O'Brien, 357–96. New York: Literary Classics of the United States, 1992.

———. *O Pioneers!* Edited by Sharon O'Brien. New York: W. W. Norton, 2008.

———. *The Selected Letters of Willa Cather*. Edited by Andrew Jewell and Janis P. Stout. New York: Alfred A. Knopf, 2013.

———. "When I Knew Stephen Crane." In *Willa Cather: Stories, Poems, and Other Writings*, edited by Sharon O'Brien, 932–38. New York: Literary Classics of the United States, 1992.

Chambers, Robert W. *The King in Yellow*. New York: F. T. Neely, 1895.

Charney, Leo, and Vanessa R. Schwartz. *Cinema and the Invention of Modern Life*. Berkeley: University of California Press, 1995.

Chauncey, George. *Gay New York: Gender, Urban Culture, and the Makings of the Gay Male World, 1890–1940*. New York: Basic Books, 1994.

Chicago Vice Commission and American Vigilance Association. *The Social Evil in Chicago: A Study of Existing Conditions with Recommendations by the Vice Commission of Chicago*. 4th ed. Chicago, 1912.

Chopin, Kate. *At Fault*. In *The Complete Works of Kate Chopin*, edited by Per Seyersted, 741–877. Baton Rouge: Louisiana State University Press, 1997.

———. "Confidences." In Chopin, *Complete Works of Kate Chopin*, 700–702.

———. "Émile Zola's 'Lourdes.'" In Chopin, *Complete Works of Kate Chopin*, 697–99.

———. "In the Confidence of a Story-Writer." In Chopin, *The Complete Works of Kate Chopin*, 703–5.

Claudy, C. H. "The Degradation of the Motion Picture." *Photo-Era: The American Journal of Photography* 21, no. 4 (October 1908): 161–65.

Clayton, Owen. "London Eyes: William Dean Howells and the Shift to Instant Photography." *Nineteenth-Century Literature* 65, no. 3 (2010): 374–94.

Cleary, Kate. "Feet of Clay." In *Kate M. Cleary: A Literary Biography with Selected Works*, edited by Susanne George, 141–51. Lincoln: University of Nebraska Press, 1997.

———. "The Rebellion of Mrs. McLelland." In *Kate M. Cleary: A Literary Biography with Selected Works*, edited by Susanne George, 173–86. Lincoln: University of Nebraska Press, 1997.

Cohen, Paula Marantz. *Silent Film and the Triumph of the American Myth*. Oxford: Oxford University Press, 2001.

Corkin, Stanley. *Realism and the Birth of the Modern United States*. Athens: University of Georgia Press, 1996.

Crane, Stephen. *Maggie, a Girl of the Streets*. In *Stephen Crane: Prose and Poetry*, edited by J. C. Levenson, 5–78. New York: Literary Classics of the United States, 1984.

———. "The Open Boat." In *Stephen Crane: Prose and Poetry*, edited by J. C. Levenson, 885–909. New York: Literary Classics of the United States, 1984.

Curtis, George William. "Editor's Easy Chair." *Harper's New Monthly Magazine* 19 (1859): 702–7.

Davis, Rebecca Harding. "Life in the Iron-Mills." In *A Rebecca Harding Davis Reader: "Life in the Iron-Mills," Selected Fiction and Essays*, edited by Jean Pfaelzer, 3–34. Pittsburgh: University of Pittsburgh Press, 1995.

———. *Margret Howth: A Story of To-Day*. New York: Feminist Press at the City University of New York, 1990.

Davis, Simone Weil. *Living up to the Ads: Gender Fictions of the 1920s*. Durham: Duke University Press, 2000.

Decker, Jeffrey Louis. *Made in America: Self-Styled Success from Horatio Alger to Oprah Winfrey*. Minneapolis: University of Minnesota Press, 1997.

DeFalco, Amelia. "Jungle Creatures and Dancing Apes: Modern Primitivism and Nella Larsen's *Quicksand*." *Mosaic: A Journal for the Interdisciplinary Study of Literature* 38, no. 2 (2005): 19–35.

DeKoven, Marianne. *A Different Language: Gertrude Stein's Experimental Writing*. Madison: University of Wisconsin Press, 1983.

DeMille, William, dir. *Miss Lulu Bett* (1921). DVD. *The Cecil B. DeMille Classics Collection*. Passport Video, 2007.

Den Tandt, Christophe. "Refashioning American Literary Naturalism: Critical Trends at the Turn of the Twenty-First Century." In *The Oxford Handbook of American Literary Naturalism*, edited by Keith Newlin, 427–44. Oxford: Oxford University Press, 2011.

Derleth, August. *Still Small Voice: The Biography of Zona Gale*. New York: D. Appleton-Century, 1940.

"The Devil's Needle" [Review]. In *Variety Film Reviews 1907–1920*. New York: Garland, 1983, n.p.

"The Devil's Needle" [Review]. *Motion Picture News*, August 16, 1916, 788–89.

Dictionary of Chinook Jargon with Examples of Use in Conversation. Portland, Ore.: J. K. Gill, 1887.

Diedrich, Maria. *Cornelia James Cannon and the Future American Race*. Amherst: University of Massachusetts Press, 2011.

Diffee, Christopher. "Sex and the City: The White Slavery Scare and Social Governance in the Progressive Era." *American Quarterly* 57, no. 2 (2005): 411–37.

Dimock, Wai-chee. "Debasing Exchange: Edith Wharton's *The House of Mirth*." *PMLA: Publications of the Modern Language Association of America* 100, no. 5 (1985): 783–92.

———. *Through Other Continents: American Literature across Deep Time*. Princeton: Princeton University Press, 2006.

Donaldson, Susan V. "Elizabeth Stuart Phelps, Realism, and Literary Debates on Changing Gender Roles." In *Realism and Its Discontents*, edited by Danuta Fjellestad and Elizabeth Kella, 87–111. Karlskrona, Sweden: Blekinge Institute of Technology, 2003.

Donovan, Brian. *White Slave Crusades: Race, Gender, and Anti-Vice Activism, 1887–1917*. Urbana: University of Illinois Press, 2006.

Dowling, Robert M., and Donald Pizer. "A Cold Case File Reopened: Was Crane's Maggie Murdered or a Suicide?" *American Literary Realism* 42, no. 1 (2009): 36–53.

Doyle, Laura. *Freedom's Empire: Race and the Rise of the Novel in Atlantic Modernity, 1640–1940*. Durham: Duke University Press, 2008.

Dreiser, Theodore. *The Financier*. New York: New American Library, 1967.

———. *Sister Carrie*. Edited by Donald Pizer. 3rd ed. New York: W. W. Norton, 2006.

Dudley, John. *A Man's Game: Masculinity and the Anti-Aesthetics of American Literary Naturalism*. Tuscaloosa: University of Alabama Press, 2004.

———. "Special Issue: Naturalism and African American Culture." *Studies in American Naturalism* 7, no. 1 (2012): 1–134.

Dunbar-Nelson, Alice. "Miss Tillman's Protégé." In *The Works of Alice Dunbar-Nelson*, edited by Gloria T. Hull, 3:101–8. New York: Oxford University Press, 1988.

———. "Tony's Wife." In *The Works of Alice Dunbar-Nelson*, edited by Gloria T. Hull, 1:19–33. New York: Oxford University Press, 1988.

———. "Witness for the Defense." In *The Works of Alice Dunbar-Nelson*, edited by Gloria T. Hull, 3:108–19. New York: Oxford University Press, 1988.

Dupree, Ellen. "The New Woman, Progressivism, and the Woman Writer in Edith Wharton's *The Fruit of the Tree*." *American Literary Realism* 31, no. 2 (1999): 44–62.

Eby, Clare Virginia. "Beyond Protest: *The Street* as Humanitarian Narrative." *MELUS: The Journal of the Society for the Study of the Multi-Ethnic Literature of the United States* 33, no. 1 (2008): 33–53.

Edwards, Derek. *Discourse and Cognition*. Thousand Oaks, Calif.: SAGE Publications, 1997.

Elbert, Monika M. "The Displacement of Desire: Consumerism and Fetishism in Mary Wilkins Freeman's Fiction." *Legacy: A Journal of American Women Writers* 19, no. 2 (2002): 192–215.

Elbert, Monika, and Bridget M. Marshall. Introduction to *Transnational Gothic: Literary and Social Exchanges in the Long Nineteenth Century*, edited by Monika Elbert and Bridget M. Marshall, 1–16. Farnham, England: Ashgate, 2013.

Emerson, John, and Anita Loos. *Breaking into the Movies*. New York: James A. McCann, 1921.

———. *How to Write for the Movies*. New York: James A. McCann, 1920.

Ewell, Barbara C. *Kate Chopin*. New York: Ungar, 1986.

Eyman, Scott. *Empire of Dreams: The Epic Life of Cecil B. DeMille*. New York: Simon & Schuster, 2011.

Farrar, John. "Lummox." *New York Tribune*, October 14, 1923.

Farwell, Tricia M. *Love and Death in Edith Wharton's Fiction*. New York: Peter Lang, 2006.

Ferber, Edna. *A Peculiar Treasure*. New York: Doubleday, Doran, 1939.

———. *So Big*. Garden City, N.Y.: Doubleday, 1924.

Fisher, Philip. *Hard Facts: Setting and Form in the American Novel*. Oxford: Oxford University Press, 1985.

Fitzgerald, F. Scott. *A Life in Letters*. Edited by Matthew J. Bruccoli and Judith Baughman. New York: Simon & Schuster, 1995.

Fleissner, Jennifer L. "The Biological Clock: Edith Wharton, Naturalism, and the Temporality of Womanhood." *American Literature: A Journal of Literary History, Criticism, and Bibliography* 78, no. 3 (2006): 519–48.

———. *Women, Compulsion, Modernity: The Moment of American Naturalism*. Chicago: University of Chicago Press, 2004.

Floyd, Janet. "A Sympathetic Misunderstanding? Mary Hallock Foote's Mining West." *Frontiers: A Journal of Women Studies* 22, no. 3 (2001): 148–67.

Fluck, Winfried. "Kate Chopin's *At Fault*: The Usefulness of Louisiana French for the Imagination." In *Transatlantic Encounters: Studies in European-American Relations*, edited by Udo J. Hebel and Karl Ortseifen, 218–31. Trier, Germany: Wissenschaftlicher, 1995.

Foote, Mary Hallock. "The Trumpeter: Part I." *Atlantic Monthly*, November 1894, 577–97.
———. "The Trumpeter: Part II." *Atlantic Monthly*, December 1894, 721–29.
Fox, Charles D. *The Fox Plan of Photoplay Writing*. N.p., 1922.
Francke, Lizzie. *Script Girls: Women Screenwriters in Hollywood*. London: British Film Institute, 1994.
Frederic, Harold. "Stephen Crane's Triumph." *New York Times*, January 26, 1896, 22.
Freeman, Elizabeth. *Time Binds: Queer Temporalities, Queer Histories*. Durham: Duke University Press, 2010.
Freeman, Mary Eleanor Wilkins. "A Church Mouse." In *A Mary Wilkins Freeman Reader*, edited by Mary R. Reichardt, 93–106. Lincoln: University of Nebraska Press, 1997.
———. "Old Woman Magoun." In *A Mary Wilkins Freeman Reader*, edited by Mary R. Reichardt, 361–77. Lincoln, Nebraska: University of Nebraska Press, 1997.
———. *The Portion of Labor*. New York, London: Harper & Brothers, 1901.
Friedberg, Anne. "Les Flaneurs Du Mal(l): Cinema and the Postmodern Condition." *PMLA: Publications of the Modern Language Association of America* 106, no. 3 (1991): 419–31.
———. *The Virtual Window: From Alberti to Microsoft*. Cambridge, Mass.: MIT Press, 2006.
Fuller-Seeley, Kathryn. *At the Picture Show: Small-Town Audiences and the Creation of Movie Fan Culture*. Washington, D.C.: Smithsonian Institution Press, 1996.
Fusco, Katherine. "Taking Naturalism to the Moving Picture Show: Frank Norris, D. W. Griffith, and Naturalist Editing." *Adaptation: The Journal of Literature on Screen Studies* 3, no. 2 (2010): 155–78.
Gaines, Jane. *Fire and Desire: Mixed-Race Movies in the Silent Era*. Chicago: University of Chicago Press, 2001.
Gale, Zona. "Miss Lulu Bett." In *Plays by American Women, 1900–1930*, edited by Judith E. Barlow, 87–163. New York: Applause Theatre Book, 1985.
———. *Miss Lulu Bett, Illustrated with Scenes from the Play Produced by Brock Pemberton*. New York: Grosset and Dunlap, 1920.
———. "The Novel of Tomorrow." In *The Novel of Tomorrow and the Scope of Fiction*, edited by Mary Hunter Austin and Joseph Hergesheimer, 65–74. Indianapolis: Bobbs-Merrill, 1922.
Garden, Rebecca. "Sympathy, Disability, and the Nurse: Female Power in Edith Wharton's *The Fruit of the Tree*." *Journal of Medical Humanities* 31, no. 3 (2010): 223–42.
Garland, Hamlin. *Selected Letters of Hamlin Garland*. Edited by Keith Newlin and Joseph B. McCullough. Lincoln: University of Nebraska Press, 1998.
Gerstner, David A. *Manly Arts: Masculinity and Nation in Early American Cinema*. Durham: Duke University Press, 2006.
Gilbert, Julie Goldsmith. *Ferber: A Biography*. Garden City, N.Y.: Doubleday, 1978.
Giles, James Richard. *The Naturalistic Inner-City Novel in America: Encounters with the Fat Man*. Columbia: University of South Carolina Press, 1995.
"The Girl from Bohemia" [Review]. *Variety*, August 23, 1918. In *Variety Film Reviews 1907–1920* (New York: Garland, 1983), n.p.

"A Girl in Bohemia" [Review]. *Motion Picture News*, November 15, 1919, 3640.
"A Girl in Bohemia" [Review]. *Variety*, November 7, 1919. In *Variety Film Reviews 1907–1920* (New York: Garland, 1983), n.p.
Gitelman, Lisa. *Scripts, Grooves, and Writing Machines: Representing Technology in the Edison Era*. Stanford: Stanford University Press, 1999.
Glasgow, Ellen Anderson Gholson. *The Descendant, a Novel*. New York: Harper, 1897.
———. *Phases of an Inferior Planet*. New York: Harper & Brothers, 1898.
———. *The Woman Within*. New York: Hill and Wang, 1980.
Glasser, Leah Blatt. *In a Closet Hidden: The Life and Work of Mary E. Wilkins Freeman*. Amherst: University of Massachusetts Press, 1996.
Glazener, Nancy. *Reading for Realism: The History of a U.S. Literary Institution, 1850–1910*. Durham: Duke University Press, 1997.
Gleason, William. "'The Most Radical View of the Whole Subject': George E. Waring Jr., Domestic Waste, and Women's Rights." In *Histories of the Dustheap: Waste, Material Cultures, Social Justice*, edited by Elizabeth Mazzolini and Stephanie Foote, 49–72. Cambridge, Mass.: MIT Press, 2012.
Gluck, Mary. *Popular Bohemia: Modernism and Urban Culture in Nineteenth-Century Paris*. Cambridge, Mass.: Harvard University Press, 2008.
Goldsby, Jacqueline. *A Spectacular Secret: Lynching in American Life and Literature*. Chicago: University of Chicago Press, 2006.
Goldsmith, Meredith. "Shopping to Pass, Passing to Shop: Consumer Self-Fashioning in the Fiction of Nella Larsen." In *Middlebrow Moderns: Popular American Women Writers of the 1920s*, edited by Lisa Botshon and Meredith Goldsmith, 263–90. Boston: Northeastern University Press, 2003.
Goodling, Sara Britton. "The Silent Partnership: Naturalism and Sentimentalism in the Novels of Rebecca Harding Davis and Elizabeth Stuart Phelps." In *Twisted from the Ordinary: Essays on American Literary Naturalism*, edited by Mary E. Papke, 1–22. Knoxville: University of Tennessee Press, 2003.
Goodman, Charlotte Margolis. Afterword to *Weeds*, by Edith Summers Kelley, 365–81. New York: Feminist Press, 1996.
Goodman, Susan, and Carl Dawson. *Mary Austin and the American West*. Berkeley: University of California Press, 2008.
Grasso, Linda M. "Inventive Desperation: Anger, Violence, and Belonging in Mary Wilkins Freeman's and Sui Sin Far's Murderous Mother Stories." *American Literary Realism* 38, no. 1 (2005): 18–31.
Griffith, Edward H., dir. *A Philistine in Bohemia*. 1920. Print at George Eastman House, Rochester, New York.
Grimké, Angelina Weld. "Review of *Gertrude of Denmark*." In *Selected Works of Angelina Weld Grimké*, edited by Carolivia Herron, 419–24. New York: Oxford University Press, 1991.
Gunning, Tom. "An Aesthetic of Astonishment: Early Film and the (in)Credulous Spectator." In *Film Theory and Criticism: Introductory Readings*, edited by Leo Braudy and Marshall Cohen, 114–33. New York: Oxford University Press, 1999.
———. "The Cinema of Attraction: Early Film, Its Spectator and the Avant-Garde." In

Early Cinema: Space, Frame, Narrative, edited by Thomas Elsaesser and Adam Barker, 56–62. London: British Film Institute, 1990.

———. "From the Kaleidoscope to the X-Ray: Urban Spectatorship, Poe, Benjamin, and Traffic in Souls (1913)." *Wide Angle: A Film Quarterly of Theory, Criticism, and Practice* 19, no. 4 (October 1997): 25–61.

Guy, Alice, dir. *Making an American Citizen*. DVD. In *The Movies Begin*, vol. 5. Kino Lorber, 2002.

Haenni, Sabine. *The Immigrant Scene: Ethnic Amusements in New York, 1880–1920*. Minneapolis: University of Minnesota Press, 2008.

Haldeman-Julius, E., and Marcet Haldeman-Julius. *Dust*. New York: Brentano's, 1921.

Hallett, Hilary A. *Go West, Young Women! The Rise of Early Hollywood*. Berkeley: University of California Press, 2013.

Halpern, Faye. *Sentimental Readers: The Rise, Fall, and Revival of a Disparaged Rhetoric*. Iowa City: University of Iowa Press, 2013.

Hamilton, Sharon. "Breaking the Lock: Willa Cather's Manifesto for Sexual Equality in 'Coming, Aphrodite!'" *Women's Studies: An Interdisciplinary Journal* 42, no. 8 (2013): 857–85.

Hansen, Miriam. *Babel and Babylon: Spectatorship in American Silent Film*. Cambridge, Mass.: Harvard University Press, 1991.

Hapke, Laura. *Girls Who Went Wrong: Prostitutes in American Fiction, 1885–1917*. Bowling Green: Bowling Green State University Popular Press, 1989.

Harde, Roxanne. "'His Spirituality or His Manliness': Elizabeth Stuart Phelps's (Re)Constructions of Christian Masculinity." In *Women Constructing Men: Female Novelists and Their Male Characters, 1750–2000*, edited by Sarah S. G. Frantz and Katharina Rennhak, 137–53. Plymouth, England: Lexington, 2010.

Harris, Sharon M. "'A New Era in Female History': Nineteenth-Century U.S. Women Writers." *American Literature: A Journal of Literary History, Criticism, and Bibliography* 74, no. 3 (2002): 603–18.

———. *Rebecca Harding Davis and American Realism*. Philadelphia: University of Pennsylvania Press, 1991.

Harrison-Kahan, Lori. *The White Negress: Literature, Minstrelsy, and the Black-Jewish Imaginary*. New Brunswick, N.J.: Rutgers University Press, 2011.

Hawkins, Stephanie L. "Building the 'Blue' Race: Miscegenation, Mysticism, and the Language of Cognitive Evolution in Jean Toomer's 'The Blue Meridian.'" *Texas Studies in Literature and Language* 46, no. 2 (2004): 149–80.

Haytock, Jennifer. *Edith Wharton and the Conversations of Literary Modernism*. New York: Palgrave Macmillan, 2008.

Hicks, Granville. *The Great Tradition: An Interpretation of American Literature since the Civil War*. Rev. ed. New York: Biblo and Tannen, 1967.

Higginson, Ella. "Cover Leaves." *Seattle Times*, May 22, 1901, 7.

Hite, Molly. "The Public Woman and the Modernist Turn: Virginia Woolf's *The Voyage Out* and Elizabeth Robins's *My Little Sister*." *Modernism/Modernity* 17, no. 3 (2010): 523–48.

Hobson, Barbara Meil. *Uneasy Virtue: The Politics of Prostitution and the American Reform Tradition*. New York: Basic Books, 1987.

Homestead, Melissa. "Middlebrow Readers and Pioneer Heroines: Willa Cather's *My Ántonia*, Bess Streeter Aldrich's *A Lantern in Her Hand*, and the Popular Fiction Market." In *Crisscrossing Borders in Literature of the American West*, edited by Reginald Dyck and Cheli Reutter, 75–94. New York: Palgrave Macmillan, 2009.

Horner, Avril, and Janet Beer. *Edith Wharton: Sex, Satire, and the Older Woman*. Houndmills, England: Palgrave Macmillan, 2011.

Howard, June. *Form and History in American Literary Naturalism*. Chapel Hill: University of North Carolina Press, 1985.

———. *Publishing the Family*. Durham: Duke University Press, 2001.

———. "Sand in Your Mouth: Naturalism and Other Genres." In *The Oxford Handbook of American Literary Naturalism*, edited by Keith Newlin, 92–103. Oxford: Oxford University Press, 2011.

Howells, William Dean. *Criticism and Fiction, and Other Essays*. New York: New York University Press, 1959.

———. "Editor's Easy Chair." *Harper's Monthly*, September 1912, 634–37.

———. "Editor's Study." *Harper's* 74 (1887): 482–86.

———. "The Future of Motion Pictures." In *A Realist in the American Theatre: Selected Drama Criticism of William Dean Howells*, edited by Brenda Murphy, 190–95. Athens: Ohio University Press, 1992.

———. *Heroines of Fiction*, vol. 1. New York: Harper & Brothers, 1901.

———. *London Films*. New York: Harper & Brothers, 1905.

Hoyt, Elinor. "In Lighter Vein." *Book Buyer* 25, no. 5 (December 1902): 445.

Hull, Gloria T. "Introduction." In *The Works of Alice Dunbar-Nelson*, edited by Gloria T. Hull, 1:xxix–lvi. 3 vols. New York: Oxford University Press, 1988.

Humble, Nicola. "Sitting Forward or Sitting Back: Highbrow v. Middlebrow Reading." *Modernist Cultures* 6, no. 1 (2011): 41–59.

Hurst, Fannie. *Lummox*. New York: Harper, 1923.

Huyssen, Andreas. *After the Great Divide: Modernism, Mass Culture, Postmodernism*. Bloomington: Indiana University Press, 1986.

Inness, Sherrie. "'Good Enough for a Man or a Dog, but No Place for a Woman or a Cat': The Myth of the Heroic Frontier Woman in Dorothy Scarborough's *The Wind*." *American Literary Realism* 28, no. 2 (1996): 25–40.

Jacobs, Lea. *The Decline of Sentiment: American Film in the 1920s*. Berkeley: University of California Press, 2008.

James, Henry. "Letter to Edith Wharton, 20 August 1902." In *Henry James and Edith Wharton: Letters: 1900–1915*, edited by Lyall Harris Powers, 33–35. New York: Charles Scribner's Sons, 1990.

———. "Preface." In *The Portrait of a Lady*, edited by Robert D. Bamberg, 1–15. New York: W. W. Norton, 1995.

Jameson, Fredric. *The Antinomies of Realism*. London: Verso, 2013.

Jarrett, Gene Andrew. "Second-Generation Realist; or, Dunbar the Naturalist." *African American Review* 41, no. 2 (2007): 289–94.

Jewell, Andrew. "Willa Cather's Greenwich Village: New Contexts for 'Coming, Aphrodite!'" *Studies in American Fiction* 32, no. 1 (2004): 59–80.

Jewett, Sarah Orne. *The Country of the Pointed Firs*. In *Novels and Stories: Deephaven; A Country Doctor; The Country of the Pointed Firs; Dunnet Landing Stories; Selected Stories and Sketches*, edited by Michael Davitt Bell, 371–492. New York: Library of America, 1994.

———. *Deephaven*. In *Novels and Stories: Deephaven; A Country Doctor; The Country of the Pointed Firs; Dunnet Landing Stories; Selected Stories and Sketches*, edited by Michael Davitt Bell, 7–141. New York: Library of America, 1994.

John, Angela V. *Elizabeth Robins: Staging a Life, 1862–1952*. London: Routledge, 1995.

Johnson, Katie N. *Sisters in Sin: Brothel Drama in America, 1900–1920*. Cambridge: Cambridge University Press, 2006.

Joslin, Katherine. "Architectonic or Episodic? Gender and *The Fruit of the Tree*." In *A Forward Glance: New Essays on Edith Wharton*, edited by Clare Colquitt, Susan Goodman and Candace Waid, 62–75. Newark: University of Delaware Press, 1999.

———. *Jane Addams, a Writer's Life*. Urbana: University of Illinois Press, 2004.

———. "Turning Zola inside Out: Jane Addams and Literary Naturalism." In *Twisted from the Ordinary: Essays on American Literary Naturalism*, edited by Mary E. Papke, 276–88. Knoxville: University of Tennessee Press, 2003.

Jurecic, Ann. "The Fall of the Knowledgeable Woman: The Diminished Female Healer in Edith Wharton's *The Fruit of the Tree*." *American Literary Realism* 29, no. 1 (1996): 29–53.

Kaplan, Amy. *The Anarchy of Empire in the Making of U.S. Culture*. Cambridge, Mass.: Harvard University Press, 2002.

Kassanoff, Jennie A. *Edith Wharton and the Politics of Race*. Cambridge: Cambridge University Press, 2004.

Keely, Karen A. "Sexual Slavery in San Francisco's Chinatown: 'Yellow Peril' and 'White Slavery' in Frank Norris's Early Fiction." *Studies in American Naturalism* 2, no. 2 (2007): 129–49.

Keil, Charlie. "Reframing *The Italian*: Questions of Audience Address in Early Cinema." *Journal of Film and Video* 42, no. 1 (1990): 36–48.

———. "'To Here from Modernity': Style, Historiography, and Transitional Cinema." In *American Cinema's Transitional Era: Audiences, Institutions, Practices*, edited by Charlie Keil and Shelley Stamp, 51–65. Berkeley: University of California Press, 2004.

Keil, Charlie, and Shelley Stamp, eds. *American Cinema's Transitional Era: Audiences, Institutions, Practices*. Berkeley: University of California Press, 2004.

Keller, Edgar, dir. *The Yellow Girl*. 1916. Print at George Eastman House, Rochester, New York.

Kelley, Edith Summers. *Weeds*. New York: Feminist Press, 1996.

Kenaga, Heidi. "'America Is Developing a Distinct Type of Man': *Stark Love*, Eugenics, and Nativist Discourses of the 1920s." In *Race and the Production of Modern American Nationalism*, edited by Reynolds J. Scott-Childress, 221–46. New York: Garland, 1999.

———. "Edna Ferber's *Cimarron*, Cultural Authority, and 1920s Western Historical Narratives." In *Middlebrow Moderns: Popular American Women Writers of the 1920s*, edited by Lisa Botshon and Meredith Goldsmith, 167–202. Boston: Northeastern University Press, 2003.

Kimball, Nell. *Nell Kimball: Her Life as an American Madam*. Edited by Stephen Longstreet. New York: Macmillan, 1971.

Knadler, Stephen P. "Dis-Abled Citizenship: Narrating the Extraordinary Body in Racial Uplift." *Arizona Quarterly: A Journal of American Literature, Culture, and Theory* 69, no. 3 (2013): 99–128.

Knight, Denise D. "'I Try to Make the Reader Feel': The Resurrection of Bess Streeter Aldrich's *A Lantern in Her Hand* and the Politics of the Literary Canon." In *Separate Spheres No More: Gender Convergence in American Literature, 1830–1930*, edited by Monika M. Elbert, 282–96. Tuscaloosa: University of Alabama Press, 2000.

Kollin, Susan. "Race, Labor, and the Gothic Western: Dispelling Frontier Myths in Dorothy Scarborough's *The Wind*." *MFS: Modern Fiction Studies* 46, no. 3 (2000): 675–94.

Koloski, Bernard J. "The Structure of Kate Chopin's *At Fault*." *Studies in American Fiction* 3 (1975): 89–95.

Kornasky, Linda. "American Literary Naturalism and Sexuality." In *Oxford Handbook of American Literary Naturalism*, edited by Keith Newlin, 241–56. Oxford: Oxford University Press, 2011.

———. "On 'Listen[ing] to Spectres Too': Wharton's *Bunner Sisters* and Ideologies of Sexual Selection." *American Literary Realism* 30, no. 1 (1997): 47–58.

Kreymborg, Alfred. *Edna: The Girl of the Street*. New York: G. Bruno, 1919.

Kristeva, Julia. *Powers of Horror: An Essay on Abjection*. New York: Columbia University Press, 1982.

Kroeger, Brooke. *Fannie: The Talent for Success of Writer Fannie Hurst*. New York: Times Books, 1999.

Lang, Walter, and Dorothy Davenport [Mrs. Wallace Reid], dir. *The Red Kimona* (1925). Kino Lorber, 2000.

Lant, Antonia, and Ingrid Periz. *Red Velvet Seat: Women's Writings on the First Fifty Years of Cinema*. London: Verso, 2006.

Larsen, Nella. *Quicksand*. In *Quicksand and Passing*. Edited by Deborah E. McDowell. 1–135. New Brunswick, N.J.: Rutgers University Press, 1986.

Lawrence, D. H. *The Letters of D.H. Lawrence*, vol. 3, *October 1916–June 1921*. Edited by James T. Boulton and Andrew Robertson Cambridge: Cambridge University Press, 2002.

Lee, Hermione. *Edith Wharton*. New York: Knopf, 2007.

———. *Willa Cather: Double Lives*. New York: Vintage Books, 1991.

Lehan, Richard Daniel. *Realism and Naturalism: The Novel in an Age of Transition*. Madison: University of Wisconsin Press, 2005.

Levin, Joanna. *Bohemia in America, 1858–1920*. Stanford: Stanford University Press, 2010.

Lewis, R. W. B. *Edith Wharton: A Biography*. New York: Fromm International, 1985.

Lewis, Sinclair. *Main Street*. New York: Harcourt Brace, 1920.

Lindemann, Marilee. "Cather's 'Elastigirls': Reckoning with Sex/Gender Violence in the Woman Artist Stories." In *Violence, the Arts, and Willa Cather*, edited by Joseph R. Urgo and Merrill Maguire Skaggs, 190–203. Madison, N.J.: Fairleigh Dickinson University Press, 2007.

Lindsay, Batterman. "The Half-Breed's Story." *Land of Sunshine and Out West Magazine* (May 1897): 248–50.

———. "Kwelth-Elite, the Proud Slave." *Overland Monthly* 33, no. 198 (June 1899): 534–39.

———. "The Lone Star's Bonanza." *Land of Sunshine* 10, no. 5 (April 1899): 257–339.

---. "The Old Law." *Black Cat* 16, no. 7 (April 1911): 34–38.
---. "Squaw Charley." In *Derelicts of Destiny*. New York: Neely, 1900. 71–76.
Link, Eric Carl. *The Vast and Terrible Drama: American Literary Naturalism in the Late Nineteenth Century*. Tuscaloosa: University of Alabama Press, 2004.
London, Jack. "The Inevitable White Man." In *South Sea Tales*. New York: Regent Press, 1911. 235–55.
---. *Martin Eden*. In *Novels and Social Writings*, 555–932. New York: Literary Classics of the United States, 1982.
Long, Lisa A. "Genre Matters: Embodying American Literary Naturalism." *American Literary History* 19, no. 1 (2007): 160–73.
---. "Imprisoned in/at Home: Criminal Culture in Rebecca Harding Davis' *Margret Howth: A Story of To-Day*." *Arizona Quarterly: A Journal of American Literature, Culture, and Theory* 54, no. 2 (1998): 65–98.
Loos, Anita. "Working with D. W. Griffith." In *Pressbook for D. W. Griffith's 'The Struggle'*. N.p.: United Artists, 1931.
"Lummox." *Bookman*, November 1923, 320.
Lutes, Jean Marie. "Making up Race: Jessie Fauset, Nella Larsen, and the African American Cosmetics Industry." *Arizona Quarterly: A Journal of American Literature, Culture, and Theory* 58, no. 1 (2002): 77–108.
Macharia, Keguro. "Queering Helga Crane: Black Nativism in Nella Larsen's *Quicksand*." *MFS: Modern Fiction Studies* 57, no. 2 (2011): 254–75.
Madeleine: An Autobiography. 1919; repr., New York: Persea Books, 1986.
Mahar, Karen Ward. *Women Filmmakers in Early Hollywood*. Baltimore: Johns Hopkins University Press, 2008.
Maltby, Richard, Melvyn Stokes, and Robert Clyde Allen, eds. *Going to the Movies: Hollywood and the Social Experience of Cinema*. Exeter, England: University of Exeter Press, 2007.
Margraf, Erik. "Kate Chopin's *The Awakening* as a Naturalistic Novel." *American Literary Realism* 37, no. 2 (2005): 93–116.
Matteson, John. *Eden's Outcasts: The Story of Louisa May Alcott and Her Father*. New York: W. W. Norton, 2007.
Matthews, Brander. "In Search of Local Color." *Harper's Monthly* 89 (1894): 33–40.
Mayne, Judith. *The Woman at the Keyhole: Feminism and Women's Cinema*. Bloomington: Indiana University Press, 1990.
McCuskey, Brian. "Not at Home: Servants, Scholars, and the Uncanny." *PMLA: Publications of the Modern Language Association of America* 121, no. 2 (2006): 421–36.
McGraw, Eliza R. L. *Edna Ferber's America*. Baton Rouge: Louisiana State University Press, 2014.
McMahan, Alison. *Alice Guy Blaché: Lost Visionary of the Cinema*. New York: Continuum, 2002.
Menke, Pamela Glenn. "Chopin's Sensual Sea and Cable's Ravished Land: Sexts, Signs, and Gender Narrative." *CrossRoads: A Journal of Southern Culture* 3, no. 1 (1994): 78–102.
Messitt, Holly. "The Internal Gaze: 'Coming, Aphrodite!' and the Panopticon." *Willa Cather Pioneer Memorial Newsletter* 36, no. 3 (1992): 34–37.

Michaud, Marilyn. *Republicanism and the American Gothic*. Cardiff: University of Wales Press, 2009.

Micheaux, Oscar, dir. *Within Our Gates* (1919). DVD. In *The Origins of Film*. Washington, D.C.: Library of Congress, 1993.

Michelson, Miriam. "Strangling Hands upon a Nation's Throat." *San Francisco Call*, September 30, 1897, 1.

———. *A Yellow Journalist*. New York: D. Appleton, 1905.

Millard, Candice. *The Destiny of the Republic: A Tale of Madness, Medicine and the Murder of a President*. New York: Doubleday, 2011.

Miller, Darlis A. *Mary Hallock Foote: Author-Illustrator of the American West*. Norman: University of Oklahoma Press, 2002.

Mitchell, Koritha. *Living with Lynching: African American Lynching Plays, Performance, and Citizenship, 1890–1930*. Urbana: University of Illinois Press, 2011.

Mizruchi, Susan L. *The Rise of Multicultural America: Economy and Print Culture, 1865–1915*. Chapel Hill: University of North Carolina Press, 2008.

Morgan, William M. *Questionable Charity: Gender, Humanitarianism, and Complicity in U.S. Literary Realism*. Hanover, N.H.: University Press of New England, 2004.

Mullen, Bill V. "Object Lessons: Fetishization and Class Consciousness in Ann Petry's 'The Street.'" In *Revising the Blueprint: Ann Petry and the Literary Left*, edited by Alex Lubin, 35–48. Jackson, Miss.: University Press of Mississippi, 2007.

Murphy, Kevin P. *Political Manhood: Red Bloods, Mollycoddles, and the Politics of Progressive Era Reform*. New York: Columbia University Press, 2008.

Nesbit, Evelyn. *Tragic Beauty: The Lost 1914 Memoirs of Evelyn Nesbit*. Edited by Deborah Dorian Paul. Morrisville, N.C.: Lulu, 2006.

Newlin, Keith. "The Naturalistic Imagination and the Aesthetics of Excess." In *Oxford Handbook of American Literary Naturalism*, edited by Keith Newlin, 3–17. Oxford: Oxford University Press, 2011.

"News from the Dailies." *Variety*, October 5, 1917, 16.

Ngai, Sianne. *Ugly Feelings*. Cambridge, Mass.: Harvard University Press, 2004.

Norris, Frank. *McTeague*. Ed. Donald Pizer. 2nd ed. New York: W. W. Norton, 1997.

———. *The Octopus*. In *Novels and Essays: Vandover and the Brute, McTeague, The Octopus, Essays*, edited by Donald Pizer, 573–1098. New York: Literary Classics of the United States, 1986.

———. "The Third Circle." In *The Apprenticeship Writings of Frank Norris*, edited by Joseph R. McElrath Jr. and Douglas K. Burgess, 103–10. Philadelphia: American Philosophical Society, 1996.

———. *Vandover and the Brute*. In *Novels and Essays: Vandover and the Brute, McTeague, The Octopus, Essays*, edited by Donald Pizer, 1–260. New York: Literary Classics of the United States, 1986.

———. "Zola as a Romantic Writer." In *Novels and Essays: Vandover and the Brute, McTeague, The Octopus, Essays*, edited by Donald Pizer, 1106–8. New York: Literary Classics of the United States, 1986.

Ohler, Paul. *Edith Wharton's Evolutionary Conception: Darwinian Allegory in Her Major Novels*. New York: Routledge, 2006.

Ousley, Laurie. "The Business of Housekeeping: The Mistress, the Domestic, and the Construction of Class." *Legacy: A Journal of American Women Writers* 23, no. 2 (2006): 132–47.

Palmer, Phyllis M. *Domesticity and Dirt: Housewives and Domestic Servants in the United States, 1920–1945*. Philadelphia: Temple University Press, 1989.

Papke, Mary E. "Naturalism and Commodity Culture." In *Oxford Handbook of American Literary Naturalism*, edited by Keith Newlin. Oxford: Oxford University Press, 2011, 291–306.

———. "Necessary Interventions in the Face of Very Curious Compulsions: Octavia Butler's Naturalist Science Fiction." *Studies in American Naturalism* 8, no. 1 (2013): 79–92.

———. *Verging on the Abyss: The Social Fiction of Kate Chopin and Edith Wharton*. New York: Greenwood, 1990.

Parker, Dorothy. "Re-Enter Miss Hurst, Followed by Mr. Tarkington." In *The Portable Dorothy Parker*, edited by Brendan Gill, 483–86. New York: Viking, 1973.

———. "The Short Story, through a Couple of the Ages." In *The Portable Dorothy Parker*, edited by Brendan Gill, 471–75. New York: Viking, 1973.

Peattie, Elia Wilkinson. "After the Storm: A Story of the Prairie." *Atlantic Monthly* 80, no. 479 (September 1897): 393–405.

———. *Impertinences: Selected Writings of Elia Peattie, a Journalist in the Gilded Age*. Edited by Susanne George-Bloomfield. Lincoln: University of Nebraska Press, 2005.

———. "The Man at the Edge of Things." *Atlantic Monthly* 84 (September 1899): 321–42.

Pegler, Westbrook. "Fair Enough." *El Paso Herald Post*, August 26, 1938, 4.

Petry, Alice Hall. "Caesar and the Artist in Willa Cather's 'Coming, Aphrodite!'" *Studies in Short Fiction* 23, no. 3 (1986): 307–14.

Petry, Ann. *The Street*. 1946; repr., Boston: Houghton Mifflin, 1991.

Peucker, Brigitte. *The Material Image: Art and the Real in Film*. Stanford: Stanford University Press, 2007.

Pfaelzer, Jean. *Parlor Radical: Rebecca Harding Davis and the Origins of American Social Realism*. Pittsburgh: University of Pittsburgh Press, 1996.

Phelps, Elizabeth Stuart. *Chapters from a Life*. Boston: Houghton, Mifflin, 1896.

———. *Hedged In*. Boston: Fields, Osgood, 1870.

———. "One of the Elect." In *Men, Women, and Ghosts*. Boston: Houghton Mifflin, 1869.

———. *The Silent Partner*. Boston: James R. Osgood, 1871.

———. *A Singular Life*. Boston: Houghton, Mifflin, 1895.

———. "Stories That Stay." *Century* 82, no. 1 (November 1910): 118–23.

———. "The Tenth of January." In *Men, Women, and Ghosts*, 43–89. Boston: Houghton, Mifflin, 1869.

Phelps, William Lyon. "As Mrs. Wharton Sees Us." *New York Times Book Review*, October 17, 1920, 1, 11.

Pinzer, Maimie. *The Maimie Papers*. Edited by Ruth Rosen, Sue Davidson, and Fanny Quincy Howe. Old Westbury, N.Y.: Feminist Press, 1977.

Pizer, Donald. "American Naturalism in Its 'Perfected' State: 'The Age of Innocence' and 'An American Tragedy.'" In *The Theory and Practice of American Literary Naturalism: Se-*

lected Essays and Reviews, edited by Donald Pizer, 153–66. Carbondale: Southern Illinois University Press, 1993.

———. "Late Nineteenth-Century American Literary Naturalism: A Re-Introduction." American Literary Realism 38, no. 3 (2006): 189–202.

———. "*Maggie* and the Naturalistic Aesthetic of Length." American Literary Realism 28, no. 1 (1995): 58–65.

———. "A Note on Kate Chopin's *The Awakening* as Naturalistic Fiction." Southern Literary Journal 33, no. 2 (2001): 5–13.

"The Play." New York Times, December 2, 1939, 23.

Poe, Edgar Allan. "The Fall of the House of Usher." In *Edgar Allan Poe: Poetry and Tales*, edited by Patrick F. Quinn, 317–36. New York: Literary Classics of the United States, 1984.

Pratt, Mary Louise. *Imperial Eyes: Travel Writing and Transculturation*. London: Routledge, 2008.

Prebel, Julie. "Engineering Womanhood: The Politics of Rejuvenation in Gertrude Atherton's *Black Oxen*." American Literature: A Journal of Literary History, Criticism, and Bibliography 76, no. 2 (2004): 307–37.

Present Scribe. "California Talent Finds a Gratifying Reception among Eastern Literati." San Francisco Call, October 25, 1896.

Pryse, Marjorie. "'Pattern against the Sky': Deism and Motherhood in Ann Petry's *The Street*." In *Conjuring: Black Women, Fiction, and Literary Tradition*, edited by Hortense J. Spillers, 116–31. Bloomington: Indiana University Press, 1985.

———. "Sex, Class, and 'Category Crisis': Reading Jewett's Transitivity." In *Jewett and Her Contemporaries: Reshaping the Canon*, edited by Karen L. Kilcup and Thomas S. Edwards, 31–62. Gainesville: University Press of Florida, 1999.

Rabinovitz, Lauren. *Electric Dreamland: Amusement Parks, Movies, and American Modernism*. New York: Columbia University Press, 2012.

———. *For the Love of Pleasure: Women, Movies, and Culture in Turn-of-the-Century Chicago*. New Brunswick, N.J.: Rutgers University Press, 1998.

Raibmon, Paige Sylvia. *Authentic Indians: Episodes of Encounter from the Late-Nineteenth-Century Northwest Coast*. Durham: Duke University Press, 2005.

Raper, Julius Rowan. *Without Shelter: The Early Career of Ellen Glasgow*. Baton Rouge: Louisiana State University Press, 1971.

"Review." Bookman 1, no. 5 (1895): 353.

"Review: *Miss Lulu Bett*." Variety, December 23, 1921, 35.

"Review of *At Fault*." St. Louis Post-Dispatch, October 5, 1890. In Kate Chopin, *At Fault*, edited by Suzanne Disheroon Green and David J. Caudle, 161–65. Knoxville: University of Tennessee Press, 2001.

"[Review of *Lummox*]." New York Times, October 14, 1923, BR5.

"Review: *The Inside of the White Slave Traffic*." [Review]. Variety, December 12, 1913. In *Variety Film Reviews 1907–1920*, n.p. New York: Garland, 1983.

Rhoades, Lynn. "Maid or Writer? The Rhetoric of Conformity and Rebellion in *Miss Lulu Bett*." Midamerica: The Yearbook of the Society for the Study of Midwestern Literature 23 (1996): 73–89.

Rideout, Walter B. *The Radical Novel in the United States, 1900–1954: Some Interrelations of Literature and Society*. Cambridge, Mass.: Harvard University Press, 1956.

Ringe, Donald A. "Cane River World: Kate Chopin's *At Fault* and Related Stories." *Studies in American Fiction* 3 (1975): 157–66.

Robins, Elizabeth. *My Little Sister*. New York: Dodd, Mead, 1913.

Roe, Clifford Griffith. *The Great War on White Slavery; or, Fighting for the Protection of Our Girls*. N.p., 1911.

Roosevelt, Theodore. *The Strenuous Life: Essays and Addresses*. New York: Century, 1903.

Rose, Jane Atteridge. "Recovering Lillie Buffum Chace Wyman and 'The Child of the State.'" *Legacy: A Journal of American Women Writers* 7, no. 1 (1990): 39–43.

Rosen, Ruth. *The Lost Sisterhood: Prostitution in America, 1900–1918*. Baltimore: Johns Hopkins University Press, 1982.

Rosowski, Susan J. "Cather's Manifesto for 'Coming, Aphrodite.'" *Willa Cather Pioneer Memorial Newsletter* 38, no. 3 (1994): 51–56.

Ryder, Mary R. "'Looking for Love in All the Wrong Places': Voyeurism in Cather's 1920s Fiction." *Willa Cather Newsletter and Review* 49, no. 1 (2005): 3–8.

Saltz, Laura. "'The Vision-Building Faculty': Naturalistic Vision in *The House of Mirth*." *MFS: Modern Fiction Studies* 57, no. 1 (2011): 17–46.

Saunders, Judith P. *Reading Edith Wharton through a Darwinian Lens: Evolutionary Biological Issues in Her Fiction*. Jefferson, N.C.: McFarland, 2009.

Sawaya, Francesca. *Modern Women, Modern Work: Domesticity, Professionalism, and American Writing, 1890–1950*. Philadelphia: University of Pennsylvania Press, 2004.

Scheick, William J. "Chambered Intimations: *The King in Yellow* and *The Descendant*." *Ellen Glasgow Newsletter* 34 (1995): 1, 4, 8–9.

Scott, Evelyn. *Background in Tennessee*. Edited by Robert L. Welker. Knoxville: University of Tennessee Press, 1980.

———. *Escapade: An Autobiography*. New York: Carroll and Graf, 1987.

———. *The Narrow House*. New York: Shoreline Books, 1986.

"Screen: Two Current Pictures." *New York Times*, December 25, 1921, 65.

Scura, Dorothy. Afterword to *Escapade*, by Evelyn Scott. Charlottesville: University Press of Virginia, 1995.

Scura, Dorothy M., and Paul C. Jones, eds. *Evelyn Scott: Recovering a Lost Modernist*. Knoxville: University of Tennessee Press, 2001.

Seastrom, Victor, dir. *The Wind*. MGM, 1928. Television broadcast, Turner Classic Movies.

Sedgwick, Eve Kosofsky. *The Coherence of Gothic Conventions*. New York: Methuen, 1986.

Seltzer, Mark. *Bodies and Machines*. New York: Routledge, 1992.

Sergeant, Elizabeth Shepley. "Willa Cather." In *Willa Cather Remembered*, edited by Sharon Hoover, 71–78. Lincoln: University of Nebraska Press, 2002.

Seyersted, Per. *Kate Chopin: A Critical Biography*. Baton Rouge: Louisiana State University Press, 1980.

Sherrard-Johnson, Cherene. "'A Plea for Color': Nella Larsen's Iconography of the Mulatta." *American Literature: A Journal of Literary History, Criticism, and Bibliography* 76, no. 4 (2004): 833–69.

Simmons, Scott. "Where Are My Children?" In *Program Notes: Treasures III: Social Issues in American Film, 1900–1934*, 76–81. San Francisco: National Film Preservation Foundation, 2007.

Simonson, Harold P. *Zona Gale*. New York: Twayne, 1962.

Singer, Ben. *Melodrama and Modernity: Early Sensational Cinema and Its Contexts*. New York: Columbia University Press, 2001.

Skaggs, Peggy. *Kate Chopin*. Boston: Twayne, 1985.

Skillern, Rhonda. "Becoming a 'Good Girl': Law, Language, and Ritual in Edith Wharton's *Summer*." In *Cambridge Companion to Edith Wharton*, edited by Millicent Bell, 117–36. New York: Cambridge University Press, 1995.

Solan, Yair. "'Striking Stereopticon Views': Edith Wharton's 'Bunner Sisters' and Nineteenth-Century Magic Lantern Entertainment." *Studies in American Naturalism* 7, no. 2 (2012): 135–50.

Sorrentino, Paul. *Stephen Crane: A Life of Fire*. Cambridge, Mass.: Belknap Press of Harvard University Press, 2014.

Stallybrass, Peter, and Allon White. *The Politics and Poetics of Transgression*. Ithaca: Cornell University Press, 1986.

Stamp, Shelley. *Movie-Struck Girls: Women and Motion Picture Culture after the Nickelodeon*. Princeton: Princeton University Press, 2000.

Stanford, Sally. *The Lady of the House: The Autobiography of Sally Stanford*. New York: Putnam, 1966.

Stansell, Christine. *City of Women: Sex and Class in New York, 1789–1860*. New York: Knopf, 1986.

Stein, Gertrude. *The Autobiography of Alice B. Toklas*. New York: Harcourt, Brace, 1933.

———. *Three Lives and Q.E.D.* Edited by Marianne DeKoven. New York: W. W. Norton, 2006.

Sterne, Jonathan. *The Audible Past: Cultural Origins of Sound Reproduction*. Durham: Duke University Press, 2003.

Stewart, Susan. *On Longing: Narratives of the Miniature, the Gigantic, the Souvenir, the Collection*. Durham: Duke University Press, 1996.

Stokes, Melvyn, and Richard Maltby. *American Movie Audiences: From the Turn of the Century to the Early Sound Era*. London: BFI, 1999.

Stoler, Ann Laura. "Intimidations of Empire: Predicaments of the Tactile and Unseen." In *Haunted by Empire: Geographies of Intimacy in North American History*, edited by Ann Laura Stoler and Nancy F. Cott, 1–22. Durham: Duke University Press, 2006.

Stopes, Marie. "Where Are My Children?" In *Red Velvet Seat: Women's Writing on the First Fifty Years of Cinema*, edited by Antonia Lant and Ingrid Periz, 291–95. London: Verso, 2006.

"Story of a Reporterette and Some Others." *San Francisco Call*, October 29, 1905, 28.

Strasser, Susan. *Never Done: A History of American Housework*. New York: Henry Holt, 2000.

———. *Waste and Want: A Social History of Trash*. New York: Henry Holt, 2000.

Strychacz, Thomas. "'You . . . Could Never Be Mistaken': Reading Alice Dunbar-Nelson's

Rhetorical Diversions in *The Goodness of St. Rocque and Other Stories*." *Studies in American Fiction* 36, no. 1 (2008): 77–94.

Suckow, Ruth. *Country People.* New York: Arno Press, 1977.

Sui Sin Far. "In the Land of the Free." In *Mrs. Spring Fragrance and Other Writings*, edited by Amy Ling and Annette White-Parks, 93–100. Urbana: University of Illinois Press, 1995.

———. "Mrs. Spring Fragrance." In *Mrs. Spring Fragrance and Other Writings*, edited by Amy Ling and Annette White-Parks, 17–28. Urbana: University of Illinois Press, 1995.

Thomson, Rosemarie. "Benevolent Maternalism and Physically Disabled Figures: Dilemmas of Female Embodiment in Stowe, Davis, and Phelps." *American Literature: A Journal of Literary History, Criticism, and Bibliography* 68, no. 3 (1996): 555–61.

Thrailkill, Jane F. *Affecting Fictions: Mind, Body, and Emotion in American Literary Realism.* Cambridge, Mass.: Harvard University Press, 2007.

Tompkins, Jane P. *Sensational Designs: The Cultural Work of American Fiction, 1790–1860.* New York: Oxford University Press, 1986.

Tone, Andrea. *Devices and Desires: A History of Contraceptives in America.* New York: Hill and Wang, 2001.

Toomer, Jean. *Cane.* Edited by Rudolph P. Byrd and Henry Louis Gates. 2nd ed. New York: W. W. Norton, 2011.

Toth, Emily. *Kate Chopin.* New York: Morrow, 1990.

———. *Unveiling Kate Chopin.* Jackson: University Press of Mississippi, 1999.

Totten, Gary. "The Machine in the Home: Women and Technology in *The Fruit of the Tree*." In *Memorial Boxes and Guarded Interiors: Edith Wharton and Material Culture*, 237–64. Tuscaloosa: University of Alabama Press, 2007.

———. "'Objects Long Preserved': Reading and Writing the Shop Window in Edith Wharton's 'Bunner Sisters.'" *Studies in American Naturalism* 6, no. 2 (2011): 134–60.

Tracey, Karen. "Stories of the Poorhouse." In *Our Sisters' Keepers: Nineteenth-Century Benevolence Literature by American Women*, edited by Jill Bergman and Debra Bernardi, 23–48. Tuscaloosa: University of Alabama Press, 2005.

Tucker, George Loane, dir. *Traffic in Souls* (1913). DVD. In *Perils of the New Land: Films of the Immigrant Experience (1910–1915).* Kino Lorber, 2008.

Turner, George Kibbe. "The Daughters of the Poor: A Plain Story of the Development of New York City as a Leading Center of the White Slave Trade of the World, under Tammany Hall." *McClure's Magazine*, November 1909, 45–61.

Turpin, Jeff. "American Naturalism and Modern Evolutionary Psychology." In *Oxford Handbook of American Literary Naturalism*, edited by Keith Newlin, 203–22. Oxford: Oxford University Press, 2011.

Tuttleton, James W. "Justine; or, The Perils of Abstract Idealism." In *The Cambridge Companion to Edith Wharton*, edited by Millicent Bell, 157–68. New York: Cambridge University Press, 1995.

Twain, Mark. *Collected Tales, Sketches, Speeches and Essays, 1852–1890.* New York: Literary Classics of the United States, 1992.

Tyrer, Pat. "'A Bird Alive in a Snake's Body': The New Woman of Evelyn Scott's *The Narrow House*." *Southern Literary Journal* 38, no. 1 (2005): 43–61.

United States Federal Census, 1870, Virginia City, Storey County, Nevada, roll M593_835, page 431A, image 241, Family History Library Film 552334, accessed via Ancestry.com.

Uruburu, Paula M. *American Eve: Evelyn Nesbit, Stanford White, the Birth of the "It" Girl, and the Crime of the Century*. New York: Riverhead Books, 2008.

Van Doren, Carl. *Contemporary American Novelists, 1900–1920*. New York: Macmillan, 1922.

Variety Film Reviews 1907–1920. New York: Garland, 1983.

Von Rosk, Nancy. "Coon Shows, Ragtime, and the Blues: Race, Urban Culture, and the Naturalist Vision in Paul Laurence Dunbar's *The Sport of the Gods*." In *Twisted from the Ordinary: Essays on American Literary Naturalism*, edited by Mary E. Papke, 144–68. Knoxville: University of Tennessee Press, 2003.

Vorse, Mary Heaton. "Some Picture Show Audiences." In *Red Velvet Seat: Women's Writings on the First Fifty Years of Cinema*, edited by Antonia Lant and Ingrid Periz, 68–75. London: Verso, 2006.

Wagner-Martin, Linda. "Writing the Early Novels." In *Three Lives and Q.E.D.*, edited by Marianne DeKoven, 231–39. New York: W. W. Norton, 2006.

Wald, Priscilla. *Contagious: Cultures, Carriers, and the Outbreak Narrative*. Durham: Duke University Press, 2008.

Walker, Jayne L. "*Three Lives*: The Realism of the Composition." In *Three Lives and Q.E.D.*, edited by Marianne DeKoven, 339–58. New York: W. W. Norton, 2006.

Walker, Nancy. "Women Writers and Literary Naturalism: The Case of Ellen Glasgow." *American Literary Realism* 18 (1985): 133–46.

Warhol, Robyn R. "As You Stand, So You Feel and Are: The Crying Body and the Nineteenth-Century Text." In *Tattoo, Torture, Mutilation, and Adornment: The Denaturalization of the Body*, edited by Frances E. Mascia-Lees and Patricia Sharpe, 100–125. Albany: State University of New York Press, 1992.

Warren, Kenneth W. *Black and White Strangers: Race and American Literary Realism*. Chicago: University of Chicago Press, 1993.

Washburn, Charles. *Come into My Parlor: A Biography of the Aristocratic Everleigh Sisters of Chicago*. New York: Arno Press, 1974.

———. "On 'Little Lost Sister.'" *New York Times*, November 19, 1939, x2.

Washburn, Josie. *The Underworld Sewer: A Prostitute Reflects on Life in the Trade, 1871–1909*. Lincoln: University of Nebraska Press, 1997.

Watts, Mary Stanbery. *The Rise of Jennie Cushing*. New York: Macmillan, 1914.

Weber, Lois, dir. *Where Are My Children?* (1916). DVD. In *Treasures III: Social Issues in American Film, 1900–1934*. National Film Preservation Foundation, 2007.

Wegener, Frederick. *Edith Wharton: The Uncollected Critical Writings*. Princeton: Princeton University Press, 1996.

Wesling, Meg. "The Opacity of Everyday Life: Segregation and the Iconicity of Uplift in *The Street*." *American Literature: A Journal of Literary History, Criticism, and Bibliography* 78, no. 1 (2006): 117–40.

Wharton, Edith. *The Age of Innocence*. Edited by Candace Waid. New York: W. W. Norton, 2003.

———. *A Backward Glance*. New York: D. Appleton-Century, 1934.

———. "Bunner Sisters." In *Xingu and Other Stories*, 309–436. New York: Charles Scribner's Sons, 1916.

———. *Ethan Frome*. In *Novellas and Other Writings: Madame De Treymes; Ethan Frome; Summer; Old New York; The Mother's Recompense; A Backward Glance*, edited by Cynthia Griffin Wolff, 63–156. New York: Library of America, 1990.

———. *The Fruit of the Tree*. Boston: Northeastern University Press, 2000.

———. "The Great American Novel." *Yale Review* 16 (July 1927): 646–56.

———. *The House of Mirth*. New York: Charles Scribner's Sons, 1905.

———. "Letter to Bernard Berenson, 4 September 1917." In *Letters of Edith Wharton*, edited by R. W. B. Lewis and Nancy Lewis, 398–99. New York: Macmillan, 1989.

———. "Letter to William Crary Brownell, 25 June [1904]." In *Letters of Edith Wharton*, edited by R. W. B. Lewis and Nancy Lewis, 91–92. New York: Macmillan, 1989.

———. *The Letters of Edith Wharton*. Edited by R. W. B. Lewis and Nancy Lewis. New York: Collier Books, 1989.

———. "One Day." Edith Wharton Collection, Beinecke Library, Yale University, New Haven, Connecticut.

———. *Summer*. In *Edith Wharton: Novellas and Other Writings*, edited by Cynthia Griffin Wolff, 159–311. New York: Literary Classics of the United States, 1990.

———. "Tendencies in Modern Fiction." In *Edith Wharton: The Uncollected Critical Writings*, edited by Frederick Wegener, 170–74. Princeton: Princeton University Press, 1996.

———. *Xingu, and Other Stories*. New York: Charles Scribner's Sons, 1916.

Whitfield, Eileen. "An Evaluation of Mary Pickford's Youngest Characters." In *Mary Pickford: Queen of the Movies*, edited by Christel Schmidt, 23–32. Lexington: University Press of Kentucky, 2012.

Wiesenthal, C. Susan. "Female Sexuality in Willa Cather's *O Pioneers!* and the Era of Scientific Sexology: A Dialogue between Frontiers." In *O Pioneers!*, edited by Sharon O'Brien, 396–414. New York: W. W. Norton, 2008.

Wilder, Laura Ingalls. *These Happy Golden Years*. New York: HarperTrophy, 1971.

Williams, Deborah Lindsay. *Not in Sisterhood: Edith Wharton, Willa Cather, Zona Gale, and the Politics of Female Authorship*. New York: Palgrave, 2001.

Williamson, J. W. *Hillbillyland: What the Movies Did to the Mountains and What the Mountains Did to the Movies*. Chapel Hill: University of North Carolina Press, 1995.

Williamson, Jennifer A. *Twentieth-Century Sentimentalism: Narrative Appropriation in American Literature*. New Brunswick, N.J.: Rutgers University Press, 2014.

Witherow, Jean. "Flaubert's Vision and Chopin's Naturalistic Revision: A Comparison of *Madame Bovary* and *The Awakening*." *Southern Studies: An Interdisciplinary Journal of the South* 8, no. 1–2 (1997): 27–36.

Withey, Chester, dir. *The Devil's Needle*. DVD. In *The Devil's Needle and Other Tales of Vice and Redemption*. Kino Lorber, 2012.

Wolff, Cynthia Griffin. *A Feast of Words: The Triumph of Edith Wharton*. 2nd ed. New York: Oxford University Press, 1995.

Wonham, Henry B. *Playing the Races: Ethnic Caricature and American Literary Realism*. Oxford: Oxford University Press, 2004.

Woodress, James. *Willa Cather: A Literary Life*. Lincoln: University of Nebraska Press, 1987.
Wooster, L. C. *The Autobiography of a Magdalen*. Birmingham, Ala.: Birmingham Publishing, 1911.
"Writers of Books." *San Francisco Call*, February 24, 1901, 4.
Wyman, Lillie B. Chace. "And Joe." In *Poverty Grass*, 204–56. Boston: Houghton Mifflin, 1886.
———. "Black and White." *New England Magazine* 11, no. 4 (1891): 476–82.
———. "The Child of the State." In *Poverty Grass*, 114–58. Boston: Houghton Mifflin, 1886.
———. "Luke Gardiner's Love." In *Poverty Grass*, 84–113. Boston: Houghton Mifflin, 1886.
———. "Valentine's Chance." In *Poverty Grass*, 278–320. Boston: Houghton Mifflin, 1886.
Wyman, Lillie Buffum Chace, and Arthur Crawford Wyman. *Elizabeth Buffum Chace*. 2 vols. Boston: W. B. Clarke, 1914.
Yellin, Jean Fagan. Afterword to *Margret Howth: A Story of Today*, by Rebecca Harding Davis, edited by Jean Fagan Yellin, 271–302. New York: Feminist Press, 1990.
Zieger, Susan Marjorie. *Inventing the Addict: Drugs, Race, and Sexuality in Nineteenth-Century British and American Literature*. Amherst: University of Massachusetts Press, 2008.
Zink, Amanda. "Peyote in the Kitchen: Gendered Identities and Imperial Domesticity in Edna Ferber's *Cimarron*." *Western American Literature* 47, no. 1 (2012): 66–89.

INDEX

Page numbers in *italic* refer to illustrations.

"Abandoned" (Lindsay), 64–65, 82, 86
Able McLaughlins, The (M. Wilson), 238, 239
abolitionists, 57, 61, 62, 165
abortion: fiction, 170, 176, 226, 236, 289–90, 291, 292; films, 14, 230–35, 236
Addams, Jane, 7, 164, 185, 200, 346n36; *A New Conscience and an Ancient Evil*, 19, 165, 172, 198, 292
Adrift in a Great City (film), 201
Affron, Charles, 270
African Americans, 8, 20, 46, 114; *At Fault* (Chopin), 93–100; films, 206–20, *209, 210*, 236, 295; liberation narratives, 163–66, 198; *Margret Howth* (Wharton), 42–44, 46, 133; *Quicksand* (Larsen), 292–301; as servants, 281; *The Sport of the Gods* (Dunbar), 65; *The Street* (Petry), 215–18, 236. See also abolitionists
"After the Storm" (Peattie), 67–70, 72, 74, 110
Age of Innocence, The (Wharton), 91–92, 102–3, 127, 128, 131, 316, 348–49n83; fair versus dark in, 107; grotesque body in, 11, 95; operagoers in, 200; Pulitzer Prize, 238–39
Alcott, Bronson, 334n73
Alcott, Louisa May, 46, 58, 334n73; *Diana and Persis*, 114
Aldrich, Bess Streeter, 240, 243; *A Lantern in Her Hand*, 245, 249–52, 265, 274, 347n28
Aldrich, Thomas Bailey, 73
Algie, the Miner (Guy-Blaché), 70
"Amber Gods, The" (Spofford), 22
American Indians. *See* Native Americans
American in the Making, An (film), 201
American Tragedy, An (Dreiser), 152, 156
American Tragedy, An (Sternberg), 152
Ammons, Elizabeth, 7–8
Anderson, Amanda, 161
Anderson, Maureen, 336n47
Anderson, Sherwood, 238, 310; *Winesburg, Ohio*, 307–8
"And Joe" (Wyman), 58, 59–61
Annie Kilburn (Howells), 59
Antinomies of Realism, The (Jameson), 26, 27, 35–36, 332n37
Armstrong, Nancy, 35
Arzner, Dorothy, 194
Assommoir, L' (Zola), 277, 278, 291
At Fault (Chopin), 4, 19, 66, 91–100, 109, 111, 212, 326, 336n47
Atherton, Gertrude, 315; *Black Oxen*, 348n67
Atlas, Marilyn, 319
"At the 'Cadian Ball" (Chopin), 62
Auerbach, Jonathan, 14
Austen, Jane, 173
Austin, Mary, 114; *Earth Horizon*, 136; *The Land of Little Rain*, 66; *No. 26 Jayne Street*, 19, 116, 136–41, 148, 195
Authentic History of the Lawrence Calamity, An, 47
Autobiography of Alice B. Toklas, The (Stein), 275
Autobiography of a Magdalen (Wooster), 164, 165, 168, 169
Autobiography of an Ex-Colored Man, The (J. W. Johnson), 114
Awakening, The (Chopin), 4, 91–92, 93, 95, 262, 300–301, 306, 335n43; African Americans in, 99; physicians in, 176, 216

Babel and Babylon (Hansen), 199
Background in Tennessee (Scott), 302

Back Street (Hurst), 238, 310
Backward Glance, A (Wharton), 284
Badger, Clarence G., 210
Baker, Estelle, 184–87, 192, 198
Barale, Michele Aina, 141, 143
Barker, Reginald, 200; *The Italian*, 204–6, 235–36
Barren Ground (Glasgow), 6, 124, 257
Bashford, Herbert, 82
Bataille, Georges, 5, 284, 285
Bauer, Dale, 235, 315
Bauman, Zygmunt, 163
Beauchamp, Cari, 14
Beban, George, 205–6, 343n12
Becker, George, 3
Beecher, Catharine, 279, 281
Behind the Mask of Innocence (Brownlow), 122, 230
Bender, Bert, 9–10, 92, 101; *The Descent of Love*, 92, 126, 335n43
Bender family, 68
Bentley, Nancy, 101–2
Beranger, Clara, 319, 320, 322
Bergman, Jill, 51; *Our Sisters' Keepers* (ed. with Bernardi), 24
Bernardi, Debra, 24
bildungsroman, 35, 36, 125
Birnbaum, Michele A., 99
birth control, 10, 225–26, 230–35, 344n43. *See also* abortion
Birth of a Nation, The (Griffith), 206, 207, 270
black Americans. *See* African Americans
blackmail, 108, 109, 206, 231, 235, 286, 287
Black Oxen (Atherton), 348n67
Blair, Madeleine, 157, 159, 167, 169–71, 198
Blake, Elliott, 310
Blindness of Virtue, The (C. Brooks), 89
Blithedale Romance, The (Hawthorne), 40
Blix (Norris), 113
"Blue Hotel, The" (Crane), 65
Bodies and Machines (Seltzer), 33
body, 9–11, 28, 33–34, 150, 154–55; in Cather, 143; in Davis, 38, 43–44; dismemberment, 46, 47; in Scarborough, 268; servant's, 275–324; in Suckow, 254, 255; in Wharton, 11, 95, 105, 107–8, 228–29; in Wyman, 57. *See also* disability
Bohemian fiction, 112–49
Borus, Daniel, 114
Botshon, Lisa, 239
Bow, Clara, 210, 295
Boyd, Anne, 8
Breaking into the Movies (J. Emerson and Loos), 244

Brennan, Stephen C., 6
Brennan, Teresa, 26, 27, 30
Brent, Justine, 105
Bride Retires, The (film), 148
Brieux, Eugène, 161–62
Broken Blossoms (Griffith), 270
Brontë, Charlotte, 129
Brooks, Cosmo, 89
Brooks, Peter, 32–33, 293–94, 296
Brooks, Virginia, 198, 342n55; *Little Lost Sister*, 160, 187–92, 194; *My Battles with Vice*, 187, 188
Broun, Heywood, 310, 319
Brown, Alice, 32
Brown, Bill, 30–31, 33, 71; *The Material Unconscious*, 13; *A Sense of Things*, 6–7
Brown, Grace (Billy), 152–53, 155–57, 162, 197, 257
Brown, Kathleen, 282
Brownlow, Kevin, 201; *Behind the Mask of Innocence*, 122, 230
Bruno, Guido, 166
"Brushwood Boy, The" (Kipling), 22
Buck, Pearl S., 239–40
"Bunner Sisters" (Wharton), 2, 87, 223, 224–25, 326, 327
Burrows, Stuart, 23
By the Light of the Soul (M. E. W. Freeman), 4

Cain, James M., 258
Callard, D. A., 302
Cane (Toomer), 276
Canfield, Dorothy, 70, 316
Cannon, Cornelia James, 21, 245; *Red Rust*, 252, 263–65, 274, 327
Carlisle, Marcia, 169
Cartwright, Lisa, 15
Casey, Janet Galligani, 240, 246, 263
Cather, Willa, 8, 114, 121, 240, 256, 274, 301; "Coming, Aphrodite!," 19, 116, 141–49; Diedrich's view of, 263; Fitzgerald's view of, 238; *My Ántonia*, 239, 240, 252, 256, 281; *One of Ours*, 239; *O Pioneers!*, 6, 21, 239, 241, 252, 255, 257–60, 264, 273, 274, 327; on Peattie, 70; *The Song of the Lark*, 141
censorship, 14, 147, 232, 301, 302
Chace, Elizabeth, 57
Chambers, Robert W., 24, 117, 130
Chaplin, Charlie, 244; *The Kid*, 210
Chapters from a Life (E. S. Phelps), 56
Charney, Leo, 147
Chauncey, George, 120
Chesnutt, Charles W., 274; "Dave's Neckliss," 83
Child, Lydia M., 46

childbirth, 5, 9, 229, 306, 326, 327; censorship and, 302; in farm novels, 241, 245, 251, 252, 262; in *The Narrow House* (Scott), 303, 306–7, 324; in *Phases of an Inferior Planet* (Glasgow), 132; in *Quicksand* (Larsen), 297, 299–300, 324; in Stein stories, 288, 289, 292; stillbirth, 251, 253
"Child of the State, The" (Wyman), 57, 58, 185
Children of the Frost, The (London), 331n6
Children of the Poor, The (Riis), 35
child-stealing stories, 20, 210–22, 236
Chinese Americans, 71, 72, 179–80, 182–84, 215
Chinook Jargon, 84, 86, 110
Chopin, Kate, 5, 6, 8, 9–10, 84; *At Fault*, 4, 19, 66, 91–100, 109, 111, 212, 326, 336n47; "At the 'Cadian Ball," 62; *The Awakening*, 4, 91–92, 93, 95, 99, 176, 216, 262, 300–301, 306, 335n43; "The Storm," 62; "The Story of an Hour," 16–17
Christianity, 51–56, 82–83, 99, 110, 133–34, 165, 170, 333n62
"Church Mouse, A" (M. E. W. Freeman), 32
Cimarron (Ferber), 246–47
Claudy, C. H., 14
Clayton, Owen, 23
Cleary, Kate, 66, 110, 253; "Feet of Clay," 66, 75–77; "Jim Lancy's Waterloo," 69; "The Rebellion of Mrs. McLelland," 75
"Closing Door, The" (Grimké), 217
Coast of Bohemia, The (Howells), 19, 113, 116, 125, 126
"coeur simple, Un" (Flaubert), 275, 289
Cohen, Paula Marantz, 15
color symbolism, 51, 56, 78, 117, 142, 146–47, 175, 176; red, 51–52, 55, 56, 164–65, 175, 195
comedy films, 119, 241–45, 317; Guy-Blaché, 202–4, 202, 204, 205, 208, 235–36
"Coming, Aphrodite!" (Cather), 19, 116, 141–49
Conflicting Stories (Ammons), 7–8
Contemporary American Novelists (Van Doren), 302
Corkin, Stanley, 14
Corner in Wheat, A (Griffith), 12
Country of the Pointed Firs (Jewett), 142
Country People (Suckow), 252, 254, 255–57, 274
Coxey's Army, 77, 80, 81
cramped spaces, 5, 27, 33, 34, 231, 291, 311, 314
Crane, Stephen, 2, 3, 7, 9, 37, 65, 197, 214; "The Blue Hotel," 65; influence on Scott, 302; *The Monster*, 10; "The Open Boat," 31–32; *The Red Badge of Courage*, 11; *The Third Violet*, 19, 113–14. See also *Maggie*
Crux, The (Gilman), 162
Cummins, Maria, 59
Curtiz, Michael, 349n87

Custom of the Country, The (Wharton), 10, 104, 200

Damaged Goods (Brieux), 161–62
Damnation of Theron Ware, The (Frederic), 114, 126, 134, 135, 176, 333n62, 339n39
Dark Mother, The (Frank), 302
Darwin, Charles, 2, 9, 18–19, 21, 64–111, 114, 115, 252; Cannon and, 252, 263–65; Cather and, 144–45, 258; Chopin and, 19, 91–100, 335n43; *The Descent of Man*, 9, 65, 106, 126, 128, 131, 144–45, 299, 333n62; Dunbar-Nelson and, 214; Glasgow and, 9, 124–29, 131, 134, 135; Kelley and, 263; Larsen and, 298, 299; *The Origin of Species*, 127; Scarborough and, 267; Scott and, 309; Suckow and, 252, 254; Wharton and, 19, 66, 103–11, 128
Daughter of the Tenements, A (Townsend), 2
Davenport, Dorothy, 122–23, 194, 197
"Dave's Neckliss" (Chesnutt), 83
David, Bette, 243
Davis, Rebecca Harding, 22, 24, 25, 33, 35, 36; Howells on, 23; "Life in the Iron Mills," 18, 22, 29, 30, 34, 36–38, 42, 49; *Margret Howth*, 29, 34, 37, 38–44, 46, 63, 129, 133, 222, 226, 229, 230
Dawson, Carl, 136
"Day of Her Funeral, The" (Wharton), 286
"Deal in Wheat, A" (Norris), 12
Deephaven (Jewett), 73
DeFalco, Amelia, 293
deixis, 30, 31, 32, 37
DeKoven, Marianne, 275, 346n14
Delsarte, François, 26, 295
DeMille, Cecil B., 319, 348n70; *Male and Female*, 295; *Why Change Your Wife?*, 242
DeMille, William, 316, 319–23
Derelicts of Destiny (Lindsay), 82, 86
Descendant, The (Glasgow), 19, 116, 124–30, 148, 216, 253, 339n40; compared with *No. 26 Jayne Street* (Austin), 137; compared with *Phases of an Interior Planet* (Glasgow), 131, 133, 134, 135
Descent of Love, The (Bender), 92, 126, 335n43
Descent of Man, The (Darwin), 9, 65, 106, 126, 128, 131, 144–45, 299, 333n62
Devil's Needle, The (film), 117, 121–24, 124, 148
Diana and Persis (L. M. Alcott), 114
Dickinson, Emily, 309
Diedrich, Maria I., 263
Diffee, Christopher, 193
Dimock, Wai Chee, 8, 115
dirt, 27–29, 278, 279–84, 288–92, 323–24; in "Coming, Aphrodite!" (Cather), 143, 147; in *A Lantern in Her Hand* (Aldrich), 347n28;

dirt (*continued*), in *Lummox* (Hurst), 316; in *The Narrow House* (Scott), 303, 308, 309; in Peattie stories, 69; in *Quicksand* (Larsen), 297, 298–99; in *So Big* (Ferber), 248–49; in *Summer* (Wharton), 226; in *Vandover and the Brute* (Norris), 27–28, 277–78; in *Weeds* (Kelley), 261

disability, 4, 5, 10, 24, 36, 64, 277, 326, 327; in *At Fault* (Glasgow), 93; in *The Descendant* (Glasgow), 129; in Dunbar-Nelson stories, 212, 213; in "Life in the Iron Mills" (Davis), 37, 38; in *Margret Howth* (Davis), 43–46; in *Red Rust* (Cannon), 263, 265; in Wyman stories, 58, 60, 61

discovery of squalor sequences, 34, 35, 37, 42, 49, 63, 226, 228–29, 326

distortion of time. *See* time, distortion of

Doctor Zay (E. S. Phelps), 53

Donaldson, Susan V., 53

Donovan, Brian, 160

Douglass, Frederick, 57, 163, 164, 165

Down on the Farm (Sennett), 242

Doyle, Laura, 293

Dreiser, Theodore, 2, 3, 9–10, 17, 19, 197, 220; *An American Tragedy*, 152, 156; Diedrich's view of, 263; *The Financier*, 169, 219, 253, 254, 261; *The Hand of the Potter*, 125; influence on Scott, 302; *Jennie Gerhardt*, 282; "Old Rogaum and His Theresa," 192. *See also Sister Carrie*

drug-themed films, 121–24, 124

Dudley, John, 8

Du Maurier, George, 113, 114

Dunbar, Paul Laurence, 5, 113; *The Sport of the Gods*, 4, 8, 65, 114, 216

Dunbar-Nelson, Alice, 84, 200, 217; *The Goodness of St. Rocque*, 211–12; 'Steenth Street stories, 211–15, 236

Dupree, Ellen, 105, 337n75

Dust (Haldeman-Julius), 252, 253–55, 256, 274, 327

Earth Horizon (Austin), 136

Eaton, Winnifred, 244

Eby, Clare, 215

Eden's Outcasts (Matteson), 334n73

Edison, Thomas, 13, 14, 23, 55, 145, 147

"Editha" (Howells), 139

Edna (Kreymborg), 166–67

Elbert, Monika, 7

Electrocuting an Elephant (film), 15

Eliot, George, 39–40

Emerson, John, 244

Emerson, Ralph Waldo, 40, 41, 301, 306

Erik Dorn (Hecht), 302

Escapade (Scott), 301–2, 309

"Ethan Brand" (Wharton), 87

Ethan Frome (Wharton), 87, 102, 103, 107, 263

eugenics, 20, 109, 230, 231, 233, 236, 263, 265, 298

Ewell, Barbara, 96

"Extracts from Mrs. Lofty's Diary" (Lindsay), 81

factory collapse and fire, Lawrence, Mass., January 10, 1860, 45–47

fallen-woman narratives, 9, 18, 19, 48–49, 50–52, 63, 150–98

"Fall of the House of Usher, The" (Poe), 176, 181

Familiar Strangeness, A (Burrows), 23

farm novels, 20–21, 237–74

farm-wife plots, 67–77, 110, 253, 271

Farrar, John, 310

Farwell, Tricia M., 101

"Feet of Clay" (Cleary), 66, 75–77

Ferber, Edna, 240, 243, 315; *Cimarron*, 246–47; Fitzgerald's view of, 238; *A Peculiar Treasure*, 245, 246; *Show Boat*, 246, 247; *So Big*, 237, 239, 241, 245–49, 257, 258, 273, 274

film comedies. *See* comedy films

films, drug-themed, 121–24, 124

films, immigration, 200–210, 242

filth. *See* dirt

Financier, The (Dreiser), 169, 219, 253, 254, 261

Fisher, Philip, 29

Fitzgerald, F. Scott, 238, 239, 242, 243, 247, 273, 274, 295; film adaptations, 349n86

Flaubert, Gustave, 125; "Un coeur simple," 275, 289

Flegel, Zig, 169

Fleissner, Jennifer, 6, 7, 96, 335–36n43

Floyd, Janet, 77

Fluck, Winfried, 93

Foord, Sophia, 61, 333–34n73

Foote, Mary Hallock, 66, 77–81, 110

For His Son (Griffith), 122

Fosdick, Gertrude Christian, 116, 125

"fourth wall," breaking of, 25, 118, 147–48, 231–32

Fox, Charles Donald, 243

Francke, Lizzie, 244

Frank, Waldo, 302

Frederic, Harold, 3, 9, 11; *The Damnation of Theron Ware*, 114, 126, 134, 135, 176, 333n62, 339n39; Glasgow compared, 339n40

Frederick, Christine, 279

Freeman, Elizabeth, 115

Freeman, Mary E. Wilkins, 5, 7, 66, 315; *By the Light of the Soul*, 4; "A Church Mouse," 32; "A

Mistaken Charity," 32; "A New England Nun," 128–29; "Old Woman Magoun," 66, 87–91, 110; *The Portion of Labor*, 200, 218–22, 236, 261; "The Reign of the Doll," 221; "The Revolt of 'Mother,'" 75, 253

Freud, Sigmund, 276, 280, 315

Friedberg, Anne, 17

From under the Lid (Taylor), 168

Fruit of the Tree, The (Wharton), 4, 91–92, 93, 103–10, 111, 221, 326–27; Darwinian influence, 19, 66, 106, 128

Fuller-Seeley, Kathryn H., 344n44

Gaines, Jane, 207

"Galatea" (E. S. Phelps), 170

Gale, Zona, 239, 276, 316–24

Garden, Rebecca, 106–7

Garfield, James A., 56

Garland, Hamlin, 7, 9, 50, 252, 261; "Mrs. Ripley's Trip," 75; Pulitzer Prize role, 319, 348–49n83

Garner, Margaret, 57

Gazzolo, A. P., 188

"Gentle Lena, The" (Stein), 276, 288–89, 290–91, 324

germs, 174, 279

Gerstner, David, 207–8

Gertrude of Denmark (Wyman), 57

Ghosts (Ibsen), 162

Giles, James R., 28, 39

Gillette, Chester, 152, 155–57

Gilman, Charlotte Perkins, 165; *The Crux*, 162; "The Yellow Wallpaper," 17, 76, 176, 268

Girl from Bohemia, The (McGill), 117

Girl in Bohemia, A (H. M. Mitchell), 116

Girl in the Red Velvet Swing, The (film), 152

Gish, Lillian, 270, 273

Gitelman, Lisa, 13

Glasgow, Ellen, 8, 9, 114, 124, 301; *Barren Ground*, 6, 124, 257; *Phases of an Inferior Planet*, 19, 73, 116, 124–25, 130–36, 221; *The Romantic Comedians*, 11; *The Woman Within*, 339n40. See also *Descendant, The*

Glasser, Leah Blatt, 218

Glazener, Nancy, 3

Gleason, William, 279

Gluck, Mary, 112

Golden Beetle, The (Lumière brothers), 146

Golden Door, The (Scott), 301, 308

Goldsby, Jacqueline, 207

Goldsmith, Meredith, 239, 295

Gone with the Wind (M. Mitchell), 239–40

"Good Anna, The" (Stein), 275, 276, 281, 288–91, 292, 324

Good Earth, The (Buck), 239–40

Goodling, Sara Britton, 37

Goodman, Charlotte Margolis, 261

Goodman, Susan, 136

Goodness of St. Rocque, The (Dunbar-Nelson), 211–12

Gothic, 171–73, 175–77, 179–81, 198

Grasso, Linda, 87

Great Gatsby (1926 film), 349n86

Great War on White Slavery, The (Roe), 89, 158, 160, 161, 164–65, 198

Griffith, D. W., 145, 242, 244, 270, 319; *The Birth of a Nation*, 206, 207, 270; *Broken Blossoms*, 270; *A Corner in Wheat*, 12; *For His Son*, 122; *The Mother and the Law*, 204, 210; *The Musketeers of Pig Alley*, 33, 270; *Way Down East*, 242, 270, 273

Grimké, Angelina Weld, 57, 63; "The Closing Door," 217

Gunning, Tom, 12, 147, 193

Guy-Blaché, Alice, 14, 200; *Algie, the Miner*, 70; *Making an American Citizen*, 202–4, 202, 204, 205, 208, 235–36

Haeckel, Ernst, 2, 100, 106

Haenni, Sabine, 206

Haldeman-Julius, Anna Marcet, 252, 253–55, 274

Haldeman-Julius, Emanuel, 252, 253–55, 274

Halpern, Faye, 26

Hand of the Potter, The (Dreiser), 125

Hansen, Miriam, 199

Hapgood, Hutchins, 339n42

Hapke, Laura, 188

Harris, Sharon, 36–37

Harrison, Henry Sydnor, 206

Harrison-Kahan, Lori, 311

Hawthorne, Nathaniel, 33, 176; *The Blithedale Romance*, 40; *Scarlet Letter* film adaptations, 270, 271; "Young Goodman Brown," 333n58

Haytock, Jennifer, 344n43

Heart o' the Hills, The (film), 242–43

Hecht, Ben, 302

Hedged In (E. S. Phelps), 18, 29, 33, 49–52, 58, 63, 129, 222; compared with *A Singular Life*, 53, 56; compared with *Summer* (Wharton), 226

Hemingway, Ernest, 238

Hicks, Granville, 218

Hidden Hand, The (Southworth), 59

Higginson, Ella, 82

Hite, Molly, 177

Hobson, Barbara Meil, 158–59

Homestead, Melissa, 252
homosexuality, 120, 133, 258, 313
Hopkins, Mellie A., 116
housekeeping and home economics, 168, 279, 281, 282
House of Bondage, The (Kauffman), 165, 188
House of Mirth, The (Wharton), 4, 42, 102, 104, 229, 276, 284–87, 323–24, 327; cramped space in, 33; fair versus dark in, 107; last moment in, 307; mate selection in, 10; unmoving woman in, 108
Howard, June, 3, 6, 26–27, 332n37
Howells, William Dean, 11–12, 15, 23–24, 26, 36, 58, 201; *Annie Kilburn*, 59; campaign for realism, 243; *The Coast of Bohemia*, 19, 113, 116, 125, 126; "Editha," 139; *London Films*, 23; view of *The Portion of Labor* (Freeman), 218
How the Other Half Lives (Riis), 34
How to Drain a House (Waring), 279
How to Write Photoplays (J. Emerson and Loos), 244
Hoyt, Elinor M., 331n6
Hudson River Bracketed (Wharton), 222–23
human body. *See* body
Human Wreckage (film), 122–23
Humble, Nicola, 239
Hurst, Fannie, 237–38; *Back Street*, 238, 310; *Imitation of Life*, 238, 310; *Just around the Corner*, 310; *Lummox*, 4, 237–38, 276, 281, 288, 309–16, 324, 326, 348nn64–65; *A President Is Born*, 237
Huxley, T. H., 53, 92, 100, 106, 125, 128
Huyssen, Andreas, 239, 276

Ibsen, Henrik, 172; *Ghosts*, 162
"I heard a Fly buzz" (Dickinson), 309
Imitation of Life (Hurst), 238, 310
immigration films, 200–210, 242
Indians. *See* Native Americans
Inside of the White Slave Traffic, The (film), 19–20, 159, 165, 192–93, 198, 230
interracial people. *See* mixed-race people
In the Bishop's Carriage (M. Michelson), 182
It (Badger), 210
Italian, The (Barker), 204–6, 235–36, 315
Italian Americans, 1–2, 158, 159, 211–12, 281; films, 119, 121, 202, 204–6, 235–36

James, Henry, 2, 15, 26, 104, 125, 172, 201; on Loti, 337–38n78; *Portrait of a Lady*, 39–40, 105, 223; *What Maisie Knew*, 303
Jameson, Fredric, 26, 27, 35–36, 332n37
Jane Eyre (Brontë), 129
Jennie Gerhardt (Dreiser), 282

Jewett, Sarah Orne, 274; *Country of the Pointed Firs*, 142; *Deephaven*, 73
"Jim Lancy's Waterloo" (Cleary), 69
Johnson, James Weldon, 113; *The Autobiography of an Ex-Colored Man*, 114
Johnson, Katie N., 160, 340–41n21
Johnson, Noble, 295
"Joint Owners in Spain" (A. Brown), 32
Joslin, Katherine, 7, 105, 337n75
Jungle, The (Sinclair), 326
Jurecic, Ann, 337n75
Just around the Corner (Hurst), 310

Kaplan, Amy, 208
Kassanoff, Jennie, 101, 105, 235
Kauffman, Reginald Wright, 165
Keely, Karen, 179
Keil, Charlie, 205, 243, 345n16
Keller, Edgar, 117–19
Kelley, Edith Summers, 5, 6; *Weeds*, 6, 10, 21, 252, 254, 260–63, 306
Kid, The (Chaplin), 210
"Killers, The" (Hemingway), 238
Kimball, Nell, 68, 157, 159, 162, 167–69, 170, 171, 198
kinetoscope, 11, 12, 16, 145–46, 157
King in Yellow, The (Chambers), 24, 117, 130, 135
Kipling, Rudyard: "The Brushwood Boy," 22; "The Vampire," 341n37
Knight, Denise D., 251–52
Kornasky, Linda, 6, 101
Kreymborg, Alfred, 166–67
Kristeva, Julia, 28, 115, 278
Kroeger, Brooke, 309–10
"Kwelth-Elite, the Proud Slave" (Lindsay), 83, 84–87

Lacan, Jacques, 280
Lamplighter, The (Cummins), 59
Land of Little Rain, The (Austin), 66
Lantern in Her Hand, A (Aldrich), 245, 249–52, 265, 274, 347n28
Larsen, Nella, 283; *Passing*, 295; *Quicksand*, 4, 10, 276, 292–301, 306, 316, 324
Lathrop, George Parsons, 11
"Law of Life, The" (London), 64
Lawrence, D. H., 301, 302, 305
Lecky, William, 100, 101, 102, 106
"Letters, The" (Wharton), 286
Levin, Joanna, 112, 113, 179
Lewis, R. W. B., 105
Lewis, Sinclair, 301; *Main Street*, 120, 241–42, 277, 281, 317, 334n5
Lewisohn, Ludwig, 301–2

liberation narratives, 163–66, 198
"Life in the Iron Mills" (Davis), 18, 22, 29, 30, 34, 36–38, 42, 49
Lindemann, Marilee, 144
Lindsay, Batterman (Annie), 66, 81–87, 110; "Abandoned," 64–65, 82, 86; *Derelicts of Destiny*, 82, 86; "Extracts from Mrs. Lofty's Diary," 81; "Kwelth-Elite, the Proud Slave," 83, 84–87; "My Great Aunt's Wedding," 83–84; "The Old Law," 82–83; "The Reapers," 81; "Under the Headin' of Truth," 81–82
Link, Eric Carl, 3; *The Vast and Terrible Drama*, 5–6
"Little Lost Sister" (song), 189
Little Lost Sister (V. Brooks), 160, 187–92, 194
London, Jack, 2, 3, 21, 24, 81, 82, 197, 307; *The Children of the Frost*, 331n6; Diedrich's view of, 263; "The Law of Life," 64; "Love of Life," 22; *Martin Eden*, 22, 330–32n53; "An Odyssey of the North," 74; *People of the Abyss*, 23, 34; Phelps's view of, 22, 24; *The Sea Wolf*, 125; "To Build a Fire," 64, 65, 172; "To the Man on the Trail," 74; *Valley of the Moon*, 257; "The White Silence," 72
London Films (Howells), 23
Long, Lisa, 8
Loos, Anita, 244–45, 319, 320; *How to Write Photoplays* (with J. Emerson), 244
Lost Sisterhood, The (Rosen), 157–58
Loti, Pierre, 337–38n78
"Love of Life" (London), 22
"Luke Gardiner's Love" (Wyman), 58, 60, 61
Lumière brothers, 145; *The Golden Beetle*, 146
Lummox (Hurst), 4, 237–38, 276, 281, 288, 309–16, 324, 326, 348nn64–65
lynching of African Americans, 206, 207, 208, 216, 217, 236

Macharia, Keguro, 298
Madeleine (Blair), 157, 159, 167, 169–71
Maggie (Crane), 4, 28, 48, 150, 202, 283, 325; "careening" tenement in, 29, 33–34, 315; childlessness in, 10; compared with *Edna* (Kreymborg), 166; Crane inscription to Garland, 50; domestic violence in, 214, 302–3; monstrous mother in, 9, 10, 102, 263; as outline for white slave narratives, 151, 192
Maimie Papers, The (Pinzer), 167
Main Street (S. Lewis), 120, 241–42, 277, 281, 317, 334n5
Making an American Citizen (Guy-Blaché), 202–4, 202, 204, 205, 208, 235–36
Male and Female (C. B. DeMille), 295
Mam'zelle Champagne, 151, 153

"Man at the Edge of Things, The" (Peattie), 67, 70–74
Mann Act, 158
"man who knows" figure, 65–66
Margraf, Erik, 335n43
Margret Howth (Davis), 34, 38–44, 129, 133, 222, 229, 230; compared with "The Tenth of January" (Phelps), 46; Goodling on, 37; smells in, 29, 63, 226
Marion, Frances, 270, 271, 319, 320
"Marjorie Daw" (T. B. Aldrich), 73
Martin Eden (London), 22, 330–32n53
Masefield, John, 172
Material Unconscious, The (B. Brown), 13
Mathis, June, 319, 349n87
Matteson, John, 334n73
Matthews, Brander, 34; *Vignettes of Manhattan*, 2
Maupassant, Guy de, 92, 125
Mayne, Judith, 12; *The Woman at the Keyhole*, 148
McAlpin, Robert, 336n53
McCuskey, Brian, 283
McGill, Lawrence B., 117
McMahon, Henry, 232
McTeague (Norris), 4, 314, 325; Brown views, 6–7, 30–31; canary in, 39; childlessness in, 10; "death in the wilderness" theme, 64; echolalia in, 30–31, 76; fetishization and hoarding in, 87, 277, 279; film adaptation, 243; melodramatic elements, 294; smell in, 26, 29; theatergoers in, 15–16, 202; Trina's hair in, 26, 106, 127; waste in, 28, 279
"Melanctha" (Stein), 275, 309
melodrama, 35, 59, 184, 277, 323, 325; "Bunner Sisters" (Wharton), 225; fallen-woman narratives, 151, 152, 157, 190; filmic, 14, 117, 119, 121, 242, 303, 306; *House of Mirth* (Wharton), 287; *The Narrow House* (Scott), 303, 306, 309; *Quicksand* (Larsen), 292–301, 324; real-life, 153; *Show Boat* (Ferber), 246
Melville, Herman, 33
Mena, María Cristina, 84
Mencken, H. L., 243, 301–2
Menke, Paula, 96
Meredyth, Bess, 319, 320, 349n87
Michaud, Marilyn, 341n37
Micheaux, Oscar, 200, 295–96; *Within Our Gates*, 20, 206–10, 209, 210, 236, 295
Michelson, Charles, 188, 190
Michelson, Miriam, 190, 198; *In the Bishop's Carriage*, 182; *A Yellow Journalist*, 20, 182–84, 192
"middlebrow" (term), 239
middlebrow fiction, 237–74
Middlemarch (Eliot), 39–40

Miller, Darlis A., 80
mill-girl romances, 45–47
Miss Lulu Bett (film), 316, 319–23, 322, 323, 349n86
Miss Lulu Bett (Gale), 239, 276, 281, 301, 316–24, 348n83
"Mistaken Charity, A" (M. E. W. Freeman), 32
Mitchell, Howard M., 116
Mitchell, Koritha, 208
Mitchell, Margaret, 239–40
mixed-race people, 40–44, 46, 77–81, 93–100, 292–301
Mizruchi, Susan L., 113
Monster, The (Crane), 10
monstrous mothers, 57, 102, 214, 218–22; in *Lummox* (Hurst), 313, 314; in *Maggie* (Crane), 9, 10, 102, 263; in *The Narrow House* (Scott), 306, 324; in "Old Woman Magoun" (Freeman), 87–91
Morgan, William, 24
Mother and the Law, The (Griffith), 204, 210
Movie-Struck Girls (Stamp), 230
"Mrs. Manstey's View" (Wharton), 2, 17, 223
"Mrs. Ripley's Trip" (Garland), 75
murder, 68, 93, 99–100, 179, 213–14, 258; films, 194, 195, 197, 273; infanticide, 52, 57, 217; in *Maggie* (Crane), 28; in *McTeague* (Norris), 31, 87, 294; in "Old Woman Magoun" (Freeman), 87, 97; in *O! Pioneers* (Cather), 257, 259, 260; of Stanford White, 151–57; in *The Wind* (Scarborough), 266, 273. *See also* lynching of African Americans
Murger, Henri, 112
Muscular Christianity, 52, 53
Musketeers of Pig Alley, The (Griffith), 33, 270
My Ántonia (Cather), 239, 240, 252, 256, 281
My Battles with Vice (V. Brooks), 187, 188
"My Great Aunt's Wedding" (Lindsay), 83–84
My Little Sister (Robins), 13, 19, 88, 89, 160, 172–79, 180, 181, 190

Narcissus (Scott), 301–2, 308
Narrow House, The (Scott), 10, 276, 295, 301–9, 316, 320, 324, 327
Native Americans, 40–41, 60, 64, 65, 77–81, 93–100, 215, 268
Native Son (Wright), 215
Nell Kimball (Kimball), 68, 157, 159, 162, 167–69, 170, 171, 198
Nesbitt, Evelyn, 151–54, 156–57, 162, 167, 172–73, 197, 257
New Conscience and an Ancient Evil, A (Addams), 19, 165, 172, 198, 292
"New England Nun, A" (M. E. W. Freeman), 128–29

Newlin, Keith, 6, 294
New Woman, 125, 150; in Austin, 136; in Cather, 144, 149; in Chopin, 92, 94, 96; films, 116, 120, 121, 293; in Glasgow, 125–26; in Hurst, 313; in Larsen, 293; in Phelps, 52–53, 55; in Wharton, 92, 337n75
Ngai, Sianne, 295
nickelodeons, 242, 314
Norris, Frank, 2, 3, 9–10, 37, 64, 141–42, 197, 198; *Blix*, 113; "A Deal in Wheat," 12; influence on Scott, 302; *McTeague* film adaptation, 243; *The Octopus*, 6, 12, 266, 283, 326; *The Pit*, 4; "The Third Circle," 20, 172, 179–82, 183, 184; *Vandover and the Brute*, 19, 27–28, 76, 112, 113, 114, 125, 277–78; view of naturalism, 294. *See also McTeague*
No. 26 Jayne Street (Austin), 19, 116, 136–41, 148, 195

Octopus, The (Norris), 6, 12, 266, 283, 326
odors and scents, 26, 28–29, 32, 226; in "After the Storm" (Peattie), 69; in "Coming, Aphrodite!" (Cather), 141, 142, 143; in Glasgow, 126, 132, 133, 135; in "The Good Anna" (Stein), 291; in *Hedged In* (Phelps), 49, 50, 226; in *Margret Howth* (Davis), 29, 39, 41, 63, 226; in *The Narrow House* (Scott), 304; in Norris, 26, 278; in "Old Mrs. Magoun" (Freeman), 90; in *Quicksand* (Larsen), 299, 300; synesthetic, 76. *See also* patchouli
"Odyssey of the North, An" (London), 74
Oertel, Johannes Adam Simon, 333n60
Oeuvre, L' (Zola), 112
O. Henry, 116, 117, 119, 121, 141
Ohler, Paul, 101
"Old Law, The" (Lindsay), 82–83
"Old Rogaum and His Theresa" (Dreiser), 192
"Old Woman Magoun" (M. E. W. Freeman), 66, 87–91, 110
"One Day" (Wharton), 1–2, 224
One More American (film), 201
One of Ours (Cather), 239
"One of the Elect" (E. S. Phelps), 47–49, 50, 53
"Open Boat, The" (Crane), 31–32
O Pioneers! (Cather), 6, 21, 239, 241, 252, 257–60, 273, 274, 327; compared with *Country People* (Suckow), 255; compared with *Red Rust* (Cannon), 264
Orientalism, 154, 156, 175
Origin of Species, The (Darwin), 127
Our Sisters' Keepers (Bergman and Bernardi, eds.), 24
Ousley, Laurie, 281
Out of Bohemia (Fosdick), 116, 125

Oxford Handbook of American Literary Naturalism, The, 6

Papke, Mary E., 100, 277; *Twisted from the Ordinary*, 5, 6
Parker, Cynthia Ann, 268, 274
Parker, Dorothy, 237, 243, 244–45, 247, 257, 273, 274; on Hurst, 310–11
Passing (Larsen), 295
patchouli, 41, 42, 164, 174
Peattie, Elia, 66, 67–74, 253; "After the Storm," 67–70, 72, 74, 110; "The Man at the Edge of Things," 67, 70–74
Peculiar Treasure, A (Ferber), 245, 246
peep shows: kinetoscope, 11, 12, 16, 145–46, 157; voyeurism, 141–48, 157
Pegler, Arthur James, 188, 189, 190, 342n52
Pegler, Westbrook, 188
Pember Reeves, Maud, 172
Pemberton Mill collapse and fire, Lawrence, Mass., January 10, 1860, 45–47
People of the Abyss (London), 23, 34
Petry, Ann, 5, 200; *The Street*, 11, 215–18, 236, 277
Peucker, Brigitte, 16
Pfaelzer, Jean, 37, 41
Phases of an Inferior Planet (Glasgow), 19, 73, 116, 124–25, 130–36, 221
Phelps, Elizabeth Stuart, 5, 18, 24, 25, 33, 35, 36; *Chapters from a Life*, 56; *Doctor Zay*, 53; "Galatea," 170; *Hedged In*, 8, 29, 33, 49–52, 53, 56, 58, 63, 129, 222, 226; Howells on, 23; "One of the Elect," 47–49, 50, 53; *The Silent Partner*, 37, 52, 56, 59; *A Singular Life*, 18, 45, 49, 52–57, 63, 222; "Stories That Stay," 22–23; *The Story of Avis*, 114; "The Tenth of January," 45–47
Phelps, William Lyon, 316
Philistine in Bohemia, A (film), 117, 119–21, 120, 148
Phillips, David Graham, 4, 159, 168, 283
photography and photographs, 23, 25, 34–35, 85–86
Pickford, Mary, 242–43, 295
Pinzer, Maimie, 166, 170; *The Maimie Papers*, 167
Pioneer Girl (Wilder), 68
Pit, The (Norris), 4
Pizer, Donald, 3, 7, 216, 252, 335n43
Place in the Sun, A (Stevens), 152
Playing the Races (Wonham), 201
plays, 116, 122, 151, 188–90, 273; Dreiser, 125; Gale, 316, 318–19, 320, 321, 322
Poe, Edgar Allan, 130, 135; "The Fall of the House of Usher," 176, 181

Politics and Poetics of Transgression, The (Stallybrass and White), 280
Portion of Labor, The (M. E. W. Freeman), 200, 218–22, 236, 261
Portrait of a Lady (James), 39–40, 105, 223
Poverty Grass (Wyman), 18, 57–63
Pratt, Mary Louise, 80–81
President Is Born, A (Hurst), 237
prostitutes and prostitution, 5, 6, 20, 53–54, 68, 113, 150–98, 222, 291–92; Katie Johnson on, 340–41n21; scents, 41; servants and, 279–80
Pulitzer Prize, 124, 237, 238–39, 240, 316, 318, 319, 348–49n83

Q.E.D. (Stein), 275, 288
Questionable Charity (Morgan), 24
Quicksand (Larsen), 4, 10, 276, 292–301, 306, 316, 324

racism, 65, 97–98, 99, 182, 206, 216, 217, 236; anti-Indian, 40–41, 268; *Show Boat* (Ferber), 246. *See also* lynching of African Americans
Raibmon, Paige Sylvia, 86
Raper, Julius Rowan, 125, 129, 135
"Reapers, The" (Lindsay), 81
"Rebellion of Mrs. McLelland, The" (Cleary), 75
Red Badge of Courage, The (Crane), 11
Red Kimona, The (film), 123, 168, 194–97, 196
Red Rust (Cannon), 252, 263–65, 274, 327
Reeves, Maud Pember, 172
refuse. *See* waste
regionalism, 18, 23, 113, 237, 238, 274, 276, 325; "Bunner Sisters" departures from, 87, 88; clutter in, 32; label for women authors, 2, 65, 218; untranslated words in, 84
Reid, Dorothy Davenport, 122–23, 194, 197
"Reign of the Doll, The" (M. E. W. Freeman), 221
"Revolt of 'Mother,' The" (M. E. W. Freeman), 75, 253
Rideout, Walter, 187
Riis, Jacob: *The Children of the Poor*, 35; *How the Other Half Lives*, 34
Ringe, Donald, 94
Rise of Jennie Cushing, The (Watts), 291–92
Rise of Susan, The (film), 122
Roberts, Elizabeth Madox, 301
Robins, Elizabeth, 185, 198; *My Little Sister*, 13, 19, 88, 89, 160, 172–79, 180, 181, 190
Rock of Ages (Oertel), 333n60
Roe, Clifford G., 158, 161, 164–65
Rogers, Will, 243
Romance of the Republic, A (Child), 46
Romantic Comedians, The (Glasgow), 11

Roosevelt, Theodore, 70–71, 72–73, 74, 169, 208, 209, 233, 238
Rose, Edward, 188, 189, 190, 342n52
Rose, Jane Atteridge, 58, 333n70
Rose Door, The (Baker), 184–87, 192, 198
Rosen, Ruth, 158; *The Lost Sisterhood*, 157–58
Rosowski, Susan, 141, 144, 145
Ross, E. A., 315
Rougon-Macquart novels (Zola), 3, 100, 240
"rube comedy" films, 241–45
rural fiction, 201–21, 237–74

Saltz, Laura, 101
San Francisco, 10, 159, 169, 179–85
Saunders, Judith, 101
Sawaya, Francesca, 6
Scarborough, Dorothy: *The Wind*, 21, 253, 265–70, 271, 274; *The Wind* (film adaptation), 270–73, 272
Scarlet Letter (1926 film), 270, 271
scents and odors. See odors and scents
Scheick, William J., 130
Schwartz, Vanessa R., 147
Scott, Evelyn, 5, 283, 311; *Background in Tennessee*, 302; *Escapade*, 301–2, 309; *The Golden Door*, 301, 308; *Narcissus*, 301–2, 308; *The Narrow House*, 10, 276, 295, 301–9, 316, 320, 324, 327
Script Girls (Francke), 244
scriptwriters ("scenario writers"), female, 244, 319, 320
Sea Wolf, The (London), 125
Secret Sin, The (film), 122
Sedgwick, Anne, 316
Sedgwick, Eve Kosofsky, 171
Segura, Dorothy, 301
Seltzer, Mark, 33
Sennett, Mack, 242, 243
sensationalism, 3, 50, 150, 151, 197, 243; Dreiser treatment, 282; in Dunbar-Nelson, 211; films, 14–15; in liberation narrative, 164; prostitution and, 19, 20, 160, 163–66, 168, 181, 184
Sense and Sensibility (Austen), 173
Sense of Things, A (B. Brown), 6–7
sentimentalism, 4–6, 8, 11, 25–27, 29, 30, 197, 244; Glasgow's view, 125; *A Lantern in Her Hand* (Aldrich), 251; naturalism and, 17, 25, 30, 35–36, 37, 325
Serenade (Cain), 258
servants, 21, 54, 71, 72, 158, 275–324
sexualization, 9, 19, 116, 151, 221, 269, 276, 292, 322
sex workers and sex work. See prostitutes and prostitution

Seyersted, Per, 335n43
Shaw, George Bernard, 166, 172
She Gave Him All She Had (play), 188
Sherrard-Johnson, Cherene, 293
Show Boat (Ferber), 246, 247
Silent Partner, The (E. S. Phelps), 37, 52, 56, 59
Sinclair, Upton, 326
Singer, Ben, 294
Singular Life, A (E. S. Phelps), 18, 45, 49, 52–57, 63, 222
Sister Carrie (Dreiser), 4, 7, 31, 277, 283; "begging man" in, 6; childlessness in, 10; compared with *At Fault* (Chopin), 96; compared with *Lummox* (Hurst), 314; compared with *The Portion of Labor* (Freeman), 218, 220
Skillern, Rhonda, 235
slave narratives, 163–66, 198
smells. See odors and scents
So Big (Ferber), 237, 239, 241, 245–49, 257, 258, 273, 274
Social Secretary, The (film), 338–39n28
Song of the Lark, The (Cather), 141
Southworth, E. D. E. N., 59
spaces, cramped. See cramped spaces
Spectacular Secret, A (Goldsby), 207
Spencer, Herbert, 2, 18, 53, 92, 100, 101, 106, 125
spiritualism, 283, 324
Spofford, Harriet Prescott, 22
Sport of the Gods, The (Dunbar), 4, 8, 65, 114, 216
squalor, discovery of. See discovery of squalor sequences
Stallybrass, Peter, 28–29; *The Politics and Poetics of Transgression* (with A. White), 280
Stamp, Shelley, 14, 193; *Movie-Struck Girls*, 230
Stanford, Sally, 159
Stansell, Christine, 115, 281, 282
'Steenth Street stories (Dunbar-Nelson), 211–15, 236
Stein, Gertrude, 283, 310, 346n14; *The Autobiography of Alice B. Toklas*, 275; "The Gentle Lena," 276, 288–89, 290–91, 324; "The Good Anna," 275, 276, 281, 288–91, 292, 324; "Melanctha," 275, 309; *Q.E.D.*, 275, 288; *Three Lives*, 275, 276, 281, 288–92, 316
stenography, 13, 192
stereopticon shows, 223, 225
Sternberg, Josef von, 152
Sterne, Jonathan, 55
Stevens, George, 152
Stewart, Susan, 280
stillbirth, 251, 253
St. Johns, Adela Rogers, 194, 197

stolen child stories, 20, 210–22, 236
Stoler, Ann Laura, 98
Stopes, Marie, 232–33
"Stories That Stay" (E. S. Phelps), 22–23
"Storm, The" (Chopin), 62
"Story of an Hour, The" (Chopin), 16–17
Story of Avis, The (E. S. Phelps), 114
Stowe, Harriet Beecher, 26, 61, 98
Street, The (Petry), 11, 215–18, 236, 277
Stroheim, Erich von, 242, 243, 338n28
Strychacz, Thomas, 211
Suckow, Ruth, 238, 243; *Country People*, 252, 254, 255–57, 274
Sui Sin Far, 20, 84, 200, 215, 217
Summer (Wharton), 20, 42, 200, 223, 225–30, 236, 344n43; compared with *Lummox* (Hurst), 316; theatergoers and moviegoers in, 15, 199, 225, 227, 228; *Where Are My Children?* (Weber) and, 231, 233
survival narratives, 252–65
Susan Lenox (Phillips), 4, 159, 168, 283
Swanson, Gloria, 242, 295

Taine, Hippolyte, 100–101, 240
Talmadge, Norma, 121, 123, 338n28
Taylor, Lydia, 168
technology, 13, 55–56, 145–46, 192, 193–94, 198, 345n16; "full of germs," 173–74; nickelodeons, 242, 314; stereopticon shows, 223, 225. *See also* kinetoscope
"Tendencies in Modern Fiction" (Wharton), 101
"Tenth of January, The" (E. S. Phelps), 45–47
Thaw, Harry K., 151–54, 156, 167, 340n3
Theory of the Leisure Class, The (Veblen), 284
These Happy Golden Years (Wilder), 333n60
"Third Circle, The" (Norris), 20, 172, 179–82, 183, 184
Third Violet, The (Crane), 19, 113–14
Thomson, Rosemarie Garland, 36
Thoreau, Henry David, 61, 71, 334n73
Thrailkill, Jane, 18
Three Lives (Stein), 275, 276, 281, 288–92, 316
time, distortion of, 115, 171–72, 173, 174, 180, 198, 301, 306–7
"To Build a Fire" (London), 64, 65, 172
Tolstoy, Leo, 24, 36, 125
Toomer, Jean, 311; *Cane*, 276
"To the Man on the Trail" (London), 74
Totten, Gary, 105
Townsend, Edward, 2
Tracey, Karen, 32

Traffic in Souls (film), 13, 19–20, 160, 192, 193–94, 198, 234
Trilby (Du Maurier), 113, 114
"Trumpeter, The" (Foote), 66, 77–81, 110
Turner, George Kibbe, 158, 185
Turpin, Jeff P., 6
Tuttleton, James W., 104
Twilight Sleep (Wharton), 222–23
Twisted from the Ordinary (Papke), 5, 6
Tyrer, Pat, 305

Uncle Josh at the Moving Picture Show (film), 12
Uncle Tom's Cabin (Stowe), 26, 29, 32, 42, 61, 98
"Under the Headin' of Truth" (Lindsay), 81–82
Underworld Sewer, The (J. Washburn), 168
"unruly naturalism," 4, 7, 17–18, 92–111, 116, 150–51, 200, 277, 327; children in, 210, 262; fallen-woman narratives, 197; farm novels, 241, 251, 257, 262, 263; in Glasgow, 125; "grim realism" and, 25; *Lummox* (Hurst), 316; *The Portion of Labor* (Freeman), 222; *Quicksand* (Larsen), 293; *Rose Door* (Baker), 187; servant women in, 276–77, 284, 315; *The Street* (Petry), 216

"Valentine's Chance" (Wyman), 58, 61, 62–63
Valley of Decision (film), 230–31
Valley of the Moon (London), 257
"Vampire, The" (Kipling), 341n37
vampires, 160–61, 171–82, 184, 307, 341n37; children as, 262
Van Doren, Carl, 302
Vandover and the Brute (Norris), 19, 27–28, 76, 112, 113, 114, 125, 277–78
Vast and Terrible Drama, The (Link), 5–6
Veblen, Thorstein, 105, 284
Vie de Bohème, La (Murger), 112
Vignettes of Manhattan (Matthews), 2
Virginian, The (Wister), 70
Vorse, Mary Heaton, 199–200
voyeurism, 141–48, 157
V. V.'s Eyes (Harrison), 206

Wagner-Martin, Linda, 288
Wald, Priscilla, 205
Walker, Nancy, 335n43
Warhol, Robyn R., 29–30
Waring, George E., 279
Warner, Susan, 26
Warren, Kenneth, 8
Washburn, Charles, 188–90, 342n55

Washburn, Josephine, 162, 165, 169, 170; *The Underworld Sewer*, 168
waste, 5, 21, 24, 27–28, 33–34, 37–38, 275–324; in "Bunner Sisters" (Wharton), 224; children as, 253; in *Hedged In* (Phelps), 49
Watts, Mary Stambury, 291–92
Way Back Home (film), 243
Way Down East (Griffith), 242, 270, 273
Weber, Lois, 14, 200, 319; *Where Are My Children?*, 20, 223–24, 225–26, 230–36, 232, 233, 234
Weeds (Kelley), 6, 10, 21, 252, 254, 260–63, 306
Weismann, August, 125, 129, 131
Wesling, Meg, 215–16
Wharton, Edith, 5, 6, 8, 201, 222–23, 315, 316, 337n75; *A Backward Glance*, 284; "Bunner Sisters," 2, 87, 223, 224–25, 326, 327; *The Custom of the Country*, 10, 104, 200; Darwin's influence on, 9, 56, 106; "The Day of Her Funeral," 286; Diedrich's view of, 263; "Ethan Brand," 87; *Ethan Frome*, 87, 102, 103, 107, 263; *The Fruit of the Tree*, 4, 19, 66, 91–92, 93, 103–10, 111, 128, 221, 326–27; *Hudson River Bracketed*, 222–23; James's comment to, 337–38n78; letters, 284, 337n75; "The Letters," 286; "Mrs. Manstey's View," 2, 17, 223; on novels "with a purpose," 336–37n70; "One Day," 1–2, 39, 197, 224; "Tendencies in Modern Fiction," 101; *Twilight Sleep*, 222–23. See also *Age of Innocence, The*; *House of Mirth, The*; *Summer*
What Maisie Knew (James), 303
Where Are My Children? (Weber), 20, 223–24, 225–26, 230–36, 232, 233, 234
"Where Are You Going to, My Pretty Maid?," 88, 177
White, Allon, 28–29; *The Politics and Poetics of Transgression* (with Stallybrass), 280
White, Stanford, 151–54, 156, 167, 173
"White Silence, The" (London), 72
white slave narratives, 4, 13, 19–20, 88, 89, 150–98, 234
"white slavery" (term), 157–58
Whitfield, Eileen, 242–43
Why Change Your Wife? (C. B. DeMille), 242
Wide, Wide World, The (Warner), 26

Wiesenthal, C. Susan, 258
Wilder, Laura Ingalls: Little House series, 69; *Pioneer Girl*, 68; *These Happy Golden Years*, 333n60
Williams, Deborah Lindsay, 318, 319
Williamson, Jennifer, 244
Wilson, Lois, 316, 319, 349n86
Wilson, Margaret, 238, 239
Wind, The (film), 270–73, 272
Wind, The (Scarborough), 21, 253, 265–70, 271, 274
Winesburg, Ohio (S. Anderson), 307–8
Wister, Owen, 70
Within Our Gates (Micheaux), 20, 206–10, 209, 210, 236, 295
Wolff, Cynthia Griffin, 105
Woman at the Keyhole, The (Mayne), 148
Woman Within, The (Glasgow), 339n40
women's bodies. *See* body
women scriptwriters, 244, 319, 320
"women writers" (label), 2
Wonham, Henry B., 201
Woodress, James, 145
Wooster, Louise, 164, 165, 168, 169
Wright, Richard, 215
Wylie, Elinor, 331n6
Wyman, Arthur Crawford, 333–34n73
Wyman, Lillie Chace, 25, 35, 36, 333n70; "And Joe," 58, 59–61; "The Child of the State," 57, 58, 185; on Foord, 333–34n73; *Gertrude of Denmark*, 57; Howells on, 23; "Luke Gardiner's Love," 58, 60, 61; *Poverty Grass*, 18, 57–63; "Valentine's Chance," 58, 61, 62–63

Yellin, Jean Fagin, 40, 42, 332n50
Yellow Girl, The (Keller), 117–19, 118, 148
Yellow Journalist, A (M. Michelson), 20, 182–84, 192
"Yellow Wallpaper, The" (Gilman), 17, 76, 176, 268
"Young Goodman Brown" (Hawthorne), 333n58

Zieger, Susan, 123
Zola, Émile, 3, 7, 17, 24, 29, 93, 100, 101; *L'Assommoir*, 277, 278, 291; *L'Oeuvre*, 112; Rougon-Macquart novels, 3, 100, 240

www.ingramcontent.com/pod-product-compliance
Lightning Source LLC
Chambersburg PA
CBHW011720220426
43664CB00023B/2892